Lecture Notes in Computer Science 12956

More information about this subseries at http://www.springer.com/series/7407

Osvaldo Gervasi · Beniamino Murgante ·
Sanjay Misra · Chiara Garau ·
Ivan Blečić · David Taniar ·
Bernady O. Apduhan · Ana Maria A. C. Rocha ·
Eufemia Tarantino · Carmelo Maria Torre (Eds.)

Computational Science and Its Applications – ICCSA 2021

21st International Conference
Cagliari, Italy, September 13–16, 2021
Proceedings, Part VIII

Springer

Editors
Osvaldo Gervasi ⓘ
University of Perugia
Perugia, Italy

Sanjay Misra ⓘ
Covenant University
Ota, Nigeria

Ivan Blečić ⓘ
University of Cagliari
Cagliari, Italy

Bernady O. Apduhan
Kyushu Sangyo University
Fukuoka, Japan

Eufemia Tarantino ⓘ
Polytechnic University of Bari
Bari, Italy

Beniamino Murgante ⓘ
University of Basilicata
Potenza, Potenza, Italy

Chiara Garau ⓘ
University of Cagliari
Cagliari, Italy

David Taniar ⓘ
Monash University
Clayton, VIC, Australia

Ana Maria A. C. Rocha ⓘ
University of Minho
Braga, Portugal

Carmelo Maria Torre ⓘ
Polytechnic University of Bari
Bari, Italy

ISSN 0302-9743   ISSN 1611-3349   (electronic)
Lecture Notes in Computer Science
ISBN 978-3-030-87009-6   ISBN 978-3-030-87010-2   (eBook)
https://doi.org/10.1007/978-3-030-87010-2

LNCS Sublibrary: SL1 – Theoretical Computer Science and General Issues

This Springer imprint is published by the registered company Springer Nature Switzerland AG
The registered company address is: Gewerbestrasse 11, 6330 Cham, Switzerland

Preface

These 10 volumes (LNCS volumes 12949–12958) consist of the peer-reviewed papers from the 21st International Conference on Computational Science and Its Applications (ICCSA 2021) which took place during September 13–16, 2021. By virtue of the vaccination campaign conducted in various countries around the world, we decided to try a hybrid conference, with some of the delegates attending in person at the University of Cagliari and others attending in virtual mode, reproducing the infrastructure established last year.

This year's edition was a successful continuation of the ICCSA conference series, which was also held as a virtual event in 2020, and previously held in Saint Petersburg, Russia (2019), Melbourne, Australia (2018), Trieste, Italy (2017), Beijing, China (2016), Banff, Canada (2015), Guimaraes, Portugal (2014), Ho Chi Minh City, Vietnam (2013), Salvador, Brazil (2012), Santander, Spain (2011), Fukuoka, Japan (2010), Suwon, South Korea (2009), Perugia, Italy (2008), Kuala Lumpur, Malaysia (2007), Glasgow, UK (2006), Singapore (2005), Assisi, Italy (2004), Montreal, Canada (2003), and (as ICCS) Amsterdam, The Netherlands (2002) and San Francisco, USA (2001).

Computational science is the main pillar of most of the present research on understanding and solving complex problems. It plays a unique role in exploiting innovative ICT technologies and in the development of industrial and commercial applications. The ICCSA conference series provides a venue for researchers and industry practitioners to discuss new ideas, to share complex problems and their solutions, and to shape new trends in computational science.

Apart from the six main conference tracks, ICCSA 2021 also included 52 workshops in various areas of computational sciences, ranging from computational science technologies to specific areas of computational sciences, such as software engineering, security, machine learning and artificial intelligence, blockchain technologies, and applications in many fields. In total, we accepted 494 papers, giving an acceptance rate of 30%, of which 18 papers were short papers and 6 were published open access. We would like to express our appreciation for the workshop chairs and co-chairs for their hard work and dedication.

The success of the ICCSA conference series in general, and of ICCSA 2021 in particular, vitally depends on the support of many people: authors, presenters, participants, keynote speakers, workshop chairs, session chairs, organizing committee members, student volunteers, Program Committee members, advisory committee members, international liaison chairs, reviewers, and others in various roles. We take this opportunity to wholehartedly thank them all.

We also wish to thank Springer for publishing the proceedings, for sponsoring some of the best paper awards, and for their kind assistance and cooperation during the editing process.

We cordially invite you to visit the ICCSA website https://iccsa.org where you can find all the relevant information about this interesting and exciting event.

September 2021

Osvaldo Gervasi
Beniamino Murgante
Sanjay Misra

Welcome Message from the Organizers

COVID-19 has continued to alter our plans for organizing the ICCSA 2021 conference, so although vaccination plans are progressing worldwide, the spread of virus variants still forces us into a period of profound uncertainty. Only a very limited number of participants were able to enjoy the beauty of Sardinia and Cagliari in particular, rediscovering the immense pleasure of meeting again, albeit safely spaced out. The social events, in which we rediscovered the ancient values that abound on this wonderful island and in this city, gave us even more strength and hope for the future. For the management of the virtual part of the conference, we consolidated the methods, organization, and infrastructure of ICCSA 2020.

The technological infrastructure was based on open source software, with the addition of the streaming channels on YouTube. In particular, we used Jitsi (jitsi.org) for videoconferencing, Riot (riot.im) together with Matrix (matrix.org) for chat and ansynchronous communication, and Jibri (github.com/jitsi/jibri) for streaming live sessions to YouTube.

Seven Jitsi servers were set up, one for each parallel session. The participants of the sessions were helped and assisted by eight student volunteers (from the universities of Cagliari, Florence, Perugia, and Bari), who provided technical support and ensured smooth running of the conference proceedings.

The implementation of the software infrastructure and the technical coordination of the volunteers were carried out by Damiano Perri and Marco Simonetti.

Our warmest thanks go to all the student volunteers, to the technical coordinators, and to the development communities of Jitsi, Jibri, Riot, and Matrix, who made their terrific platforms available as open source software.

A big thank you goes to all of the 450 speakers, many of whom showed an enormous collaborative spirit, sometimes participating and presenting at almost prohibitive times of the day, given that the participants of this year's conference came from 58 countries scattered over many time zones of the globe.

Finally, we would like to thank Google for letting us stream all the live events via YouTube. In addition to lightening the load of our Jitsi servers, this allowed us to record the event and to be able to review the most exciting moments of the conference.

Ivan Blečić
Chiara Garau

Organization

ICCSA 2021 was organized by the University of Cagliari (Italy), the University of Perugia (Italy), the University of Basilicata (Italy), Monash University (Australia), Kyushu Sangyo University (Japan), and the University of Minho (Portugal).

Honorary General Chairs

Norio Shiratori	Chuo University, Japan
Kenneth C. J. Tan	Sardina Systems, UK
Corrado Zoppi	University of Cagliari, Italy

General Chairs

Osvaldo Gervasi	University of Perugia, Italy
Ivan Blečić	University of Cagliari, Italy
David Taniar	Monash University, Australia

Program Committee Chairs

Beniamino Murgante	University of Basilicata, Italy
Bernady O. Apduhan	Kyushu Sangyo University, Japan
Chiara Garau	University of Cagliari, Italy
Ana Maria A. C. Rocha	University of Minho, Portugal

International Advisory Committee

Jemal Abawajy	Deakin University, Australia
Dharma P. Agarwal	University of Cincinnati, USA
Rajkumar Buyya	University of Melbourne, Australia
Claudia Bauzer Medeiros	University of Campinas, Brazil
Manfred M. Fisher	Vienna University of Economics and Business, Austria
Marina L. Gavrilova	University of Calgary, Canada
Yee Leung	Chinese University of Hong Kong, China

International Liaison Chairs

Giuseppe Borruso	University of Trieste, Italy
Elise De Donker	Western Michigan University, USA
Maria Irene Falcão	University of Minho, Portugal
Robert C. H. Hsu	Chung Hua University, Taiwan
Tai-Hoon Kim	Beijing Jaotong University, China

Vladimir Korkhov	St. Petersburg University, Russia
Sanjay Misra	Covenant University, Nigeria
Takashi Naka	Kyushu Sangyo University, Japan
Rafael D. C. Santos	National Institute for Space Research, Brazil
Maribel Yasmina Santos	University of Minho, Portugal
Elena Stankova	St. Petersburg University, Russia

Workshop and Session Chairs

Beniamino Murgante	University of Basilicata, Italy
Sanjay Misra	Covenant University, Nigeria
Jorge Gustavo Rocha	University of Minho, Portugal

Awards Chair

| Wenny Rahayu | La Trobe University, Australia |

Publicity Committee Chairs

Elmer Dadios	De La Salle University, Philippines
Nataliia Kulabukhova	St. Petersburg University, Russia
Daisuke Takahashi	Tsukuba University, Japan
Shangwang Wang	Beijing University of Posts and Telecommunications, China

Technology Chairs

| Damiano Perri | University of Florence, Italy |
| Marco Simonetti | University of Florence, Italy |

Local Arrangement Chairs

Ivan Blečić	University of Cagliari, Italy
Chiara Garau	University of Cagliari, Italy
Alfonso Annunziata	University of Cagliari, Italy
Ginevra Balletto	University of Cagliari, Italy
Giuseppe Borruso	University of Trieste, Italy
Alessandro Buccini	University of Cagliari, Italy
Michele Campagna	University of Cagliari, Italy
Mauro Coni	University of Cagliari, Italy
Anna Maria Colavitti	University of Cagliari, Italy
Giulia Desogus	University of Cagliari, Italy
Caterina Fenu	University of Cagliari, Italy
Sabrina Lai	University of Cagliari, Italy
Francesca Maltinti	University of Cagliari, Italy
Pasquale Mistretta	University of Cagliari, Italy

Augusto Montisci	University of Cagliari, Italy
Francesco Pinna	University of Cagliari, Italy
Davide Spano	University of Cagliari, Italy
Giuseppe A. Trunfio	University of Sassari, Italy
Corrado Zoppi	University of Cagliari, Italy

Program Committee

Vera Afreixo	University of Aveiro, Portugal
Filipe Alvelos	University of Minho, Portugal
Hartmut Asche	University of Potsdam, Germany
Ginevra Balletto	University of Cagliari, Italy
Michela Bertolotto	University College Dublin, Ireland
Sandro Bimonte	INRAE-TSCF, France
Rod Blais	University of Calgary, Canada
Ivan Blečić	University of Sassari, Italy
Giuseppe Borruso	University of Trieste, Italy
Ana Cristina Braga	University of Minho, Portugal
Massimo Cafaro	University of Salento, Italy
Yves Caniou	University of Lyon, France
José A. Cardoso e Cunha	Universidade Nova de Lisboa, Portugal
Rui Cardoso	University of Beira Interior, Portugal
Leocadio G. Casado	University of Almeria, Spain
Carlo Cattani	University of Salerno, Italy
Mete Celik	Erciyes University, Turkey
Maria Cerreta	University of Naples "Federico II", Italy
Hyunseung Choo	Sungkyunkwan University, South Korea
Chien-Sing Lee	Sunway University, Malaysia
Min Young Chung	Sungkyunkwan University, South Korea
Florbela Maria da Cruz Domingues Correia	Polytechnic Institute of Viana do Castelo, Portugal
Gilberto Corso Pereira	Federal University of Bahia, Brazil
Fernanda Costa	University of Minho, Portugal
Alessandro Costantini	INFN, Italy
Carla Dal Sasso Freitas	Universidade Federal do Rio Grande do Sul, Brazil
Pradesh Debba	The Council for Scientific and Industrial Research (CSIR), South Africa
Hendrik Decker	Instituto Tecnolčgico de Informática, Spain
Robertas Damaševičius	Kausan University of Technology, Lithuania
Frank Devai	London South Bank University, UK
Rodolphe Devillers	Memorial University of Newfoundland, Canada
Joana Matos Dias	University of Coimbra, Portugal
Paolino Di Felice	University of L'Aquila, Italy
Prabu Dorairaj	NetApp, India/USA
Noelia Faginas Lago	University of Perugia, Italy
M. Irene Falcao	University of Minho, Portugal

Cherry Liu Fang	Ames Laboratory, USA
Florbela P. Fernandes	Polytechnic Institute of Bragança, Portugal
Jose-Jesus Fernandez	National Centre for Biotechnology, Spain
Paula Odete Fernandes	Polytechnic Institute of Bragança, Portugal
Adelaide de Fátima Baptista Valente Freitas	University of Aveiro, Portugal
Manuel Carlos Figueiredo	University of Minho, Portugal
Maria Celia Furtado Rocha	Universidade Federal da Bahia, Brazil
Chiara Garau	University of Cagliari, Italy
Paulino Jose Garcia Nieto	University of Oviedo, Spain
Jerome Gensel	LSR-IMAG, France
Maria Giaoutzi	National Technical University of Athens, Greece
Arminda Manuela Andrade Pereira Gonçalves	University of Minho, Portugal
Andrzej M. Goscinski	Deakin University, Australia
Eduardo Guerra	Free University of Bozen-Bolzano, Italy
Sevin Gümgüm	Izmir University of Economics, Turkey
Alex Hagen-Zanker	University of Cambridge, UK
Shanmugasundaram Hariharan	B.S. Abdur Rahman University, India
Eligius M. T. Hendrix	University of Malaga, Spain/Wageningen University, The Netherlands
Hisamoto Hiyoshi	Gunma University, Japan
Mustafa Inceoglu	EGE University, Turkey
Peter Jimack	University of Leeds, UK
Qun Jin	Waseda University, Japan
Yeliz Karaca	University of Massachusetts Medical School, USA
Farid Karimipour	Vienna University of Technology, Austria
Baris Kazar	Oracle Corp., USA
Maulana Adhinugraha Kiki	Telkom University, Indonesia
DongSeong Kim	University of Canterbury, New Zealand
Taihoon Kim	Hannam University, South Korea
Ivana Kolingerova	University of West Bohemia, Czech Republic
Nataliia Kulabukhova	St. Petersburg University, Russia
Vladimir Korkhov	St. Petersburg University, Russia
Rosa Lasaponara	National Research Council, Italy
Maurizio Lazzari	National Research Council, Italy
Cheng Siong Lee	Monash University, Australia
Sangyoun Lee	Yonsei University, South Korea
Jongchan Lee	Kunsan National University, South Korea
Chendong Li	University of Connecticut, USA
Gang Li	Deakin University, Australia
Fang Liu	Ames Laboratory, USA
Xin Liu	University of Calgary, Canada
Andrea Lombardi	University of Perugia, Italy
Savino Longo	University of Bari, Italy

Ana Paula Teixeira	University of Trás-os-Montes and Alto Douro, Portugal
Senhorinha Teixeira	University of Minho, Portugal
M. Filomena Teodoro	Portuguese Naval Academy/University of Lisbon, Portugal
Parimala Thulasiraman	University of Manitoba, Canada
Carmelo Torre	Polytechnic University of Bari, Italy
Javier Martinez Torres	Centro Universitario de la Defensa Zaragoza, Spain
Giuseppe A. Trunfio	University of Sassari, Italy
Pablo Vanegas	University of Cuenca, Equador
Marco Vizzari	University of Perugia, Italy
Varun Vohra	Merck Inc., USA
Koichi Wada	University of Tsukuba, Japan
Krzysztof Walkowiak	Wroclaw University of Technology, Poland
Zequn Wang	Intelligent Automation Inc, USA
Robert Weibel	University of Zurich, Switzerland
Frank Westad	Norwegian University of Science and Technology, Norway
Roland Wismüller	Universität Siegen, Germany
Mudasser Wyne	National University, USA
Chung-Huang Yang	National Kaohsiung Normal University, Taiwan
Xin-She Yang	National Physical Laboratory, UK
Salim Zabir	National Institute of Technology, Tsuruoka, Japan
Haifeng Zhao	University of California, Davis, USA
Fabiana Zollo	University of Venice "Cà Foscari", Italy
Albert Y. Zomaya	University of Sydney, Australia

Workshop Organizers

Advanced Transport Tools and Methods (A2TM 2021)

Massimiliano Petri	University of Pisa, Italy
Antonio Pratelli	University of Pisa, Italy

Advances in Artificial Intelligence Learning Technologies: Blended Learning, STEM, Computational Thinking and Coding (AAILT 2021)

Alfredo Milani	University of Perugia, Italy
Giulio Biondi	University of Florence, Italy
Sergio Tasso	University of Perugia, Italy

Workshop on Advancements in Applied Machine Learning and Data Analytics (AAMDA 2021)

Alessandro Costantini	INFN, Italy
Davide Salomoni	INFN, Italy
Doina Cristina Duma	INFN, Italy
Daniele Cesini	INFN, Italy

Automatic Landform Classification: Spatial Methods and Applications (ALCSMA 2021)

Maria Danese   ISPC, National Research Council, Italy
Dario Gioia   ISPC, National Research Council, Italy

Application of Numerical Analysis to Imaging Science (ANAIS 2021)

Caterina Fenu   University of Cagliari, Italy
Alessandro Buccini   University of Cagliari, Italy

Advances in Information Systems and Technologies for Emergency Management, Risk Assessment and Mitigation Based on the Resilience Concepts (ASTER 2021)

Maurizio Pollino   ENEA, Italy
Marco Vona   University of Basilicata, Italy
Amedeo Flora   University of Basilicata, Italy
Chiara Iacovino   University of Basilicata, Italy
Beniamino Murgante   University of Basilicata, Italy

Advances in Web Based Learning (AWBL 2021)

Birol Ciloglugil   Ege University, Turkey
Mustafa Murat Inceoglu   Ege University, Turkey

Blockchain and Distributed Ledgers: Technologies and Applications (BDLTA 2021)

Vladimir Korkhov   St. Petersburg University, Russia
Elena Stankova   St. Petersburg University, Russia
Nataliia Kulabukhova   St. Petersburg University, Russia

Bio and Neuro Inspired Computing and Applications (BIONCA 2021)

Nadia Nedjah   State University of Rio de Janeiro, Brazil
Luiza De Macedo Mourelle State University of Rio de Janeiro, Brazil

Computational and Applied Mathematics (CAM 2021)

Maria Irene Falcão   University of Minho, Portugal
Fernando Miranda   University of Minho, Portugal

Computational and Applied Statistics (CAS 2021)

Ana Cristina Braga   University of Minho, Portugal

Computerized Evaluation of Economic Activities: Urban Spaces (CEEA 2021)

Diego Altafini   Università di Pisa, Italy
Valerio Cutini   Università di Pisa, Italy

Computational Geometry and Applications (CGA 2021)

Marina Gavrilova	University of Calgary, Canada

Collaborative Intelligence in Multimodal Applications (CIMA 2021)

Robertas Damasevicius	Kaunas University of Technology, Lithuania
Rytis Maskeliunas	Kaunas University of Technology, Lithuania

Computational Optimization and Applications (COA 2021)

Ana Rocha	University of Minho, Portugal
Humberto Rocha	University of Coimbra, Portugal

Computational Astrochemistry (CompAstro 2021)

Marzio Rosi	University of Perugia, Italy
Cecilia Ceccarelli	University of Grenoble, France
Stefano Falcinelli	University of Perugia, Italy
Dimitrios Skouteris	Master-Up, Italy

Computational Science and HPC (CSHPC 2021)

Elise de Doncker	Western Michigan University, USA
Fukuko Yuasa	High Energy Accelerator Research Organization (KEK), Japan
Hideo Matsufuru	High Energy Accelerator Research Organization (KEK), Japan

Cities, Technologies and Planning (CTP 2021)

Malgorzata Hanzl	University of Łódź, Poland
Beniamino Murgante	University of Basilicata, Italy
Ljiljana Zivkovic	Ministry of Construction, Transport and Infrastructure/Institute of Architecture and Urban and Spatial Planning of Serbia, Serbia
Anastasia Stratigea	National Technical University of Athens, Greece
Giuseppe Borruso	University of Trieste, Italy
Ginevra Balletto	University of Cagliari, Italy

Advanced Modeling E-Mobility in Urban Spaces (DEMOS 2021)

Tiziana Campisi	Kore University of Enna, Italy
Socrates Basbas	Aristotle University of Thessaloniki, Greece
Ioannis Politis	Aristotle University of Thessaloniki, Greece
Florin Nemtanu	Polytechnic University of Bucharest, Romania
Giovanna Acampa	Kore University of Enna, Italy
Wolfgang Schulz	Zeppelin University, Germany

Digital Transformation and Smart City (DIGISMART 2021)

Mauro Mazzei   National Research Council, Italy

Econometric and Multidimensional Evaluation in Urban Environment (EMEUE 2021)

Carmelo Maria Torre   Polytechnic University of Bari, Italy
Maria Cerreta   University "Federico II" of Naples, Italy
Pierluigi Morano   Polytechnic University of Bari, Italy
Simona Panaro   University of Portsmouth, UK
Francesco Tajani   Sapienza University of Rome, Italy
Marco Locurcio   Polytechnic University of Bari, Italy

The 11th International Workshop on Future Computing System Technologies and Applications (FiSTA 2021)

Bernady Apduhan   Kyushu Sangyo University, Japan
Rafael Santos   Brazilian National Institute for Space Research, Brazil

Transformational Urban Mobility: Challenges and Opportunities During and Post COVID Era (FURTHER 2021)

Tiziana Campisi   Kore University of Enna, Italy
Socrates Basbas   Aristotle University of Thessaloniki, Greece
Dilum Dissanayake   Newcastle University, UK
Kh Md Nahiduzzaman   University of British Columbia, Canada
Nurten Akgün Tanbay   Bursa Technical University, Turkey
Khaled J. Assi   King Fahd University of Petroleum and Minerals,
                                Saudi Arabia
Giovanni Tesoriere   Kore University of Enna, Italy
Motasem Darwish   Middle East University, Jordan

Geodesign in Decision Making: Meta Planning and Collaborative Design for Sustainable and Inclusive Development (GDM 2021)

Francesco Scorza   University of Basilicata, Italy
Michele Campagna   University of Cagliari, Italy
Ana Clara Mourao Moura   Federal University of Minas Gerais, Brazil

Geomatics in Forestry and Agriculture: New Advances and Perspectives (GeoForAgr 2021)

Maurizio Pollino   ENEA, Italy
Giuseppe Modica   University of Reggio Calabria, Italy
Marco Vizzari   University of Perugia, Italy

Geographical Analysis, Urban Modeling, Spatial Statistics (GEOG-AND-MOD 2021)

Beniamino Murgante	University of Basilicata, Italy
Giuseppe Borruso	University of Trieste, Italy
Hartmut Asche	University of Potsdam, Germany

Geomatics for Resource Monitoring and Management (GRMM 2021)

Eufemia Tarantino	Polytechnic University of Bari, Italy
Enrico Borgogno Mondino	University of Turin, Italy
Alessandra Capolupo	Polytechnic University of Bari, Italy
Mirko Saponaro	Polytechnic University of Bari, Italy

12th International Symposium on Software Quality (ISSQ 2021)

Sanjay Misra	Covenant University, Nigeria

10th International Workshop on Collective, Massive and Evolutionary Systems (IWCES 2021)

Alfredo Milani	University of Perugia, Italy
Rajdeep Niyogi	Indian Institute of Technology, Roorkee, India

Land Use Monitoring for Sustainability (LUMS 2021)

Carmelo Maria Torre	Polytechnic University of Bari, Italy
Maria Cerreta	University "Federico II" of Naples, Italy
Massimiliano Bencardino	University of Salerno, Italy
Alessandro Bonifazi	Polytechnic University of Bari, Italy
Pasquale Balena	Polytechnic University of Bari, Italy
Giuliano Poli	University "Federico II" of Naples, Italy

Machine Learning for Space and Earth Observation Data (MALSEOD 2021)

Rafael Santos	Instituto Nacional de Pesquisas Espaciais, Brazil
Karine Ferreira	Instituto Nacional de Pesquisas Espaciais, Brazil

Building Multi-dimensional Models for Assessing Complex Environmental Systems (MES 2021)

Marta Dell'Ovo	Polytechnic University of Milan, Italy
Vanessa Assumma	Polytechnic University of Turin, Italy
Caterina Caprioli	Polytechnic University of Turin, Italy
Giulia Datola	Polytechnic University of Turin, Italy
Federico dell'Anna	Polytechnic University of Turin, Italy

Ecosystem Services: Nature's Contribution to People in Practice. Assessment Frameworks, Models, Mapping, and Implications (NC2P 2021)

Francesco Scorza   University of Basilicata, Italy
Sabrina Lai   University of Cagliari, Italy
Ana Clara Mourao Moura   Federal University of Minas Gerais, Brazil
Corrado Zoppi   University of Cagliari, Italy
Dani Broitman   Technion, Israel Institute of Technology, Israel

Privacy in the Cloud/Edge/IoT World (PCEIoT 2021)

Michele Mastroianni   University of Campania Luigi Vanvitelli, Italy
Lelio Campanile   University of Campania Luigi Vanvitelli, Italy
Mauro Iacono   University of Campania Luigi Vanvitelli, Italy

Processes, Methods and Tools Towards RESilient Cities and Cultural Heritage Prone to SOD and ROD Disasters (RES 2021)

Elena Cantatore   Polytechnic University of Bari, Italy
Alberico Sonnessa   Polytechnic University of Bari, Italy
Dario Esposito   Polytechnic University of Bari, Italy

Risk, Resilience and Sustainability in the Efficient Management of Water Resources: Approaches, Tools, Methodologies and Multidisciplinary Integrated Applications (RRS 2021)

Maria Macchiaroli   University of Salerno, Italy
Chiara D'Alpaos   Università degli Studi di Padova, Italy
Mirka Mobilia   Università degli Studi di Salerno, Italy
Antonia Longobardi   Università degli Studi di Salerno, Italy
Grazia Fattoruso   ENEA Research Center, Italy
Vincenzo Pellecchia   Ente Idrico Campano, Italy

Scientific Computing Infrastructure (SCI 2021)

Elena Stankova   St. Petersburg University, Russia
Vladimir Korkhov   St. Petersburg University, Russia
Natalia Kulabukhova   St. Petersburg University, Russia

Smart Cities and User Data Management (SCIDAM 2021)

Chiara Garau   University of Cagliari, Italy
Luigi Mundula   University of Cagliari, Italy
Gianni Fenu   University of Cagliari, Italy
Paolo Nesi   University of Florence, Italy
Paola Zamperlin   University of Pisa, Italy

13th International Symposium on Software Engineering Processes and Applications (SEPA 2021)

Sanjay Misra   Covenant University, Nigeria

Ports of the Future - Smartness and Sustainability (SmartPorts 2021)

Patrizia Serra   University of Cagliari, Italy
Gianfranco Fancello   University of Cagliari, Italy
Ginevra Balletto   University of Cagliari, Italy
Luigi Mundula   University of Cagliari, Italy
Marco Mazzarino   University of Venice, Italy
Giuseppe Borruso   University of Trieste, Italy
Maria del Mar Munoz   Universidad de Cádiz, Spain
  Leonisio

Smart Tourism (SmartTourism 2021)

Giuseppe Borruso   University of Trieste, Italy
Silvia Battino   University of Sassari, Italy
Ginevra Balletto   University of Cagliari, Italy
Maria del Mar Munoz   Universidad de Cádiz, Spain
  Leonisio
Ainhoa Amaro Garcia   Universidad de Alcalà/Universidad de Las Palmas,
                                   Spain
Francesca Krasna   University of Trieste, Italy

Sustainability Performance Assessment: Models, Approaches and Applications toward Interdisciplinary and Integrated Solutions (SPA 2021)

Francesco Scorza   University of Basilicata, Italy
Sabrina Lai   University of Cagliari, Italy
Jolanta Dvarioniene   Kaunas University of Technology, Lithuania
Valentin Grecu   Lucian Blaga University, Romania
Corrado Zoppi   University of Cagliari, Italy
Iole Cerminara   University of Basilicata, Italy

Smart and Sustainable Island Communities (SSIC 2021)

Chiara Garau   University of Cagliari, Italy
Anastasia Stratigea   National Technical University of Athens, Greece
Paola Zamperlin   University of Pisa, Italy
Francesco Scorza   University of Basilicata, Italy

Science, Technologies and Policies to Innovate Spatial Planning (STP4P 2021)

Chiara Garau   University of Cagliari, Italy
Daniele La Rosa   University of Catania, Italy
Francesco Scorza   University of Basilicata, Italy

Anna Maria Colavitti   University of Cagliari, Italy
Beniamino Murgante   University of Basilicata, Italy
Paolo La Greca   University of Catania, Italy

Sustainable Urban Energy Systems (SURENSYS 2021)

Luigi Mundula   University of Cagliari, Italy
Emilio Ghiani   University of Cagliari, Italy

Space Syntax for Cities in Theory and Practice (Syntax_City 2021)

Claudia Yamu   University of Groningen, The Netherlands
Akkelies van Nes   Western Norway University of Applied Sciences,
        Norway
Chiara Garau   University of Cagliari, Italy

Theoretical and Computational Chemistry and Its Applications (TCCMA 2021)

Noelia Faginas-Lago   University of Perugia, Italy

13th International Workshop on Tools and Techniques in Software Development Process (TTSDP 2021)

Sanjay Misra   Covenant University, Nigeria

Urban Form Studies (UForm 2021)

Malgorzata Hanzl   Łódź University of Technology, Poland
Beniamino Murgante   University of Basilicata, Italy
Eufemia Tarantino   Polytechnic University of Bari, Italy
Irena Itova   University of Westminster, UK

Urban Space Accessibility and Safety (USAS 2021)

Chiara Garau   University of Cagliari, Italy
Francesco Pinna   University of Cagliari, Italy
Claudia Yamu   University of Groningen, The Netherlands
Vincenza Torrisi   University of Catania, Italy
Matteo Ignaccolo   University of Catania, Italy
Michela Tiboni   University of Brescia, Italy
Silvia Rossetti   University of Parma, Italy

Virtual and Augmented Reality and Applications (VRA 2021)

Osvaldo Gervasi   University of Perugia, Italy
Damiano Perri   University of Perugia, Italy
Marco Simonetti   University of Perugia, Italy
Sergio Tasso   University of Perugia, Italy

Workshop on Advanced and Computational Methods for Earth Science Applications (WACM4ES 2021)

Luca Piroddi	University of Cagliari, Italy
Laura Foddis	University of Cagliari, Italy
Augusto Montisci	University of Cagliari, Italy
Sergio Vincenzo Calcina	University of Cagliari, Italy
Sebastiano D'Amico	University of Malta, Malta
Giovanni Martinelli	Istituto Nazionale di Geofisica e Vulcanologia, Italy/Chinese Academy of Sciences, China

Sponsoring Organizations

ICCSA 2021 would not have been possible without the tremendous support of many organizations and institutions, for which all organizers and participants of ICCSA 2021 express their sincere gratitude:

Springer International Publishing AG, Germany (https://www.springer.com)

Computers Open Access Journal (https://www.mdpi.com/journal/computers)

IEEE Italy Section, Italy (https://italy.ieeer8.org/)

Centre-North Italy Chapter IEEE GRSS, Italy (https://cispio.diet.uniroma1.it/marzano/ieee-grs/index.html)

Italy Section of the Computer Society, Italy (https://site.ieee.org/italy-cs/)

University of Perugia, Italy (https://www.unipg.it)

University of Cagliari, Italy (https://unica.it/)

University of Basilicata, Italy
(http://www.unibas.it)

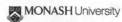

Monash University, Australia
(https://www.monash.edu/)

Kyushu Sangyo University, Japan
(https://www.kyusan-u.ac.jp/)

University of Minho, Portugal
(https://www.uminho.pt/)

Universidade do Minho
Escola de Engenharia

Scientific Association Transport Infrastructures,
Italy
(https://www.stradeeautostrade.it/associazioni-e-
organizzazioni/asit-associazione-scientifica-
infrastrutture-trasporto/)

Regione Sardegna, Italy
(https://regione.sardegna.it/)

Comune di Cagliari, Italy
(https://www.comune.cagliari.it/)

Città Metropolitana di Cagliari

Cagliari Accessibility Lab (CAL)
(https://www.unica.it/unica/it/cagliari_
accessibility_lab.page/)

Referees

Nicodemo Abate	IMAA, National Research Council, Italy
Andre Ricardo Abed Grégio	Federal University of Paraná State, Brazil
Nasser Abu Zeid	Università di Ferrara, Italy
Lidia Aceto	Università del Piemonte Orientale, Italy
Nurten Akgün Tanbay	Bursa Technical University, Turkey
Filipe Alvelos	Universidade do Minho, Portugal
Paula Amaral	Universidade Nova de Lisboa, Portugal
Federico Amato	University of Lausanne, Switzerland
Marina Alexandra Pedro Andrade	ISCTE-IUL, Portugal
Debora Anelli	Sapienza University of Rome, Italy
Alfonso Annunziata	University of Cagliari, Italy
Fahim Anzum	University of Calgary, Canada
Tatsumi Aoyama	High Energy Accelerator Research Organization, Japan
Bernady Apduhan	Kyushu Sangyo University, Japan
Jonathan Apeh	Covenant University, Nigeria
Vasilike Argyropoulos	University of West Attica, Greece
Giuseppe Aronica	Università di Messina, Italy
Daniela Ascenzi	Università degli Studi di Trento, Italy
Vanessa Assumma	Politecnico di Torino, Italy
Muhammad Attique Khan	HITEC University Taxila, Pakistan
Vecdi Aytaç	Ege University, Turkey
Alina Elena Baia	University of Perugia, Italy
Ginevra Balletto	University of Cagliari, Italy
Marialaura Bancheri	ISAFOM, National Research Council, Italy
Benedetto Barabino	University of Brescia, Italy
Simona Barbaro	Università degli Studi di Palermo, Italy
Enrico Barbierato	Università Cattolica del Sacro Cuore di Milano, Italy
Jeniffer Barreto	Istituto Superior Técnico, Lisboa, Portugal
Michele Bartalini	TAGES, Italy
Socrates Basbas	Aristotle University of Thessaloniki, Greece
Silvia Battino	University of Sassari, Italy
Marcelo Becerra Rozas	Pontificia Universidad Católica de Valparaíso, Chile
Ranjan Kumar Behera	National Institute of Technology, Rourkela, India
Emanuele Bellini	University of Campania Luigi Vanvitelli, Italy
Massimo Bilancia	University of Bari Aldo Moro, Italy
Giulio Biondi	University of Firenze, Italy
Adriano Bisello	Eurac Research, Italy
Ignacio Blanquer	Universitat Politècnica de València, Spain
Semen Bochkov	Ulyanovsk State Technical University, Russia
Alexander Bogdanov	St. Petersburg University, Russia
Silvia Bonettini	University of Modena and Reggio Emilia, Italy
Enrico Borgogno Mondino	Università di Torino, Italy
Giuseppe Borruso	University of Trieste, Italy

Michele Bottazzi	University of Trento, Italy
Rahma Bouaziz	Taibah University, Saudi Arabia
Ouafik Boulariah	University of Salerno, Italy
Tulin Boyar	Yildiz Technical University, Turkey
Ana Cristina Braga	University of Minho, Portugal
Paolo Bragolusi	University of Padova, Italy
Luca Braidotti	University of Trieste, Italy
Alessandro Buccini	University of Cagliari, Italy
Jorge Buele	Universidad Tecnológica Indoamérica, Ecuador
Andrea Buffoni	TAGES, Italy
Sergio Vincenzo Calcina	University of Cagliari, Italy
Michele Campagna	University of Cagliari, Italy
Lelio Campanile	Università degli Studi della Campania Luigi Vanvitelli, Italy
Tiziana Campisi	Kore University of Enna, Italy
Antonino Canale	Kore University of Enna, Italy
Elena Cantatore	DICATECh, Polytechnic University of Bari, Italy
Pasquale Cantiello	Istituto Nazionale di Geofisica e Vulcanologia, Italy
Alessandra Capolupo	Polytechnic University of Bari, Italy
David Michele Cappelletti	University of Perugia, Italy
Caterina Caprioli	Politecnico di Torino, Italy
Sara Carcangiu	University of Cagliari, Italy
Pedro Carrasqueira	INESC Coimbra, Portugal
Arcangelo Castiglione	University of Salerno, Italy
Giulio Cavana	Politecnico di Torino, Italy
Davide Cerati	Politecnico di Milano, Italy
Maria Cerreta	University of Naples Federico II, Italy
Daniele Cesini	INFN-CNAF, Italy
Jabed Chowdhury	La Trobe University, Australia
Gennaro Ciccarelli	Iuav University of Venice, Italy
Birol Ciloglugil	Ege University, Turkey
Elena Cocuzza	Univesity of Catania, Italy
Anna Maria Colavitt	University of Cagliari, Italy
Cecilia Coletti	Università "G. d'Annunzio" di Chieti-Pescara, Italy
Alberto Collu	Independent Researcher, Italy
Anna Concas	University of Basilicata, Italy
Mauro Coni	University of Cagliari, Italy
Melchiorre Contino	Università di Palermo, Italy
Antonella Cornelio	Università degli Studi di Brescia, Italy
Aldina Correia	Politécnico do Porto, Portugal
Elisete Correia	Universidade de Trás-os-Montes e Alto Douro, Portugal
Florbela Correia	Polytechnic Institute of Viana do Castelo, Portugal
Stefano Corsi	Università degli Studi di Milano, Italy
Alberto Cortez	Polytechnic of University Coimbra, Portugal
Lino Costa	Universidade do Minho, Portugal

Alessandro Costantini	INFN, Italy
Marilena Cozzolino	Università del Molise, Italy
Giulia Crespi	Politecnico di Torino, Italy
Maurizio Crispino	Politecnico di Milano, Italy
Chiara D'Alpaos	University of Padova, Italy
Roberta D'Ambrosio	Università di Salerno, Italy
Sebastiano D'Amico	University of Malta, Malta
Hiroshi Daisaka	Hitotsubashi University, Japan
Gaia Daldanise	Italian National Research Council, Italy
Robertas Damasevicius	Silesian University of Technology, Poland
Maria Danese	ISPC, National Research Council, Italy
Bartoli Daniele	University of Perugia, Italy
Motasem Darwish	Middle East University, Jordan
Giulia Datola	Politecnico di Torino, Italy
Regina de Almeida	UTAD, Portugal
Elise de Doncker	Western Michigan University, USA
Mariella De Fino	Politecnico di Bari, Italy
Giandomenico De Luca	Mediterranean University of Reggio Calabria, Italy
Luiza de Macedo Mourelle	State University of Rio de Janeiro, Brazil
Gianluigi De Mare	University of Salerno, Italy
Itamir de Morais Barroca Filho	Federal University of Rio Grande do Norte, Brazil
Samuele De Petris	Università di Torino, Italy
Marcilio de Souto	LIFO, University of Orléans, France
Alexander Degtyarev	St. Petersburg University, Russia
Federico Dell'Anna	Politecnico di Torino, Italy
Marta Dell'Ovo	Politecnico di Milano, Italy
Fernanda Della Mura	University of Naples "Federico II", Italy
Ahu Dereli Dursun	Istanbul Commerce University, Turkey
Bashir Derradji	University of Sfax, Tunisia
Giulia Desogus	Università degli Studi di Cagliari, Italy
Marco Dettori	Università degli Studi di Sassari, Italy
Frank Devai	London South Bank University, UK
Felicia Di Liddo	Polytechnic University of Bari, Italy
Valerio Di Pinto	University of Naples "Federico II", Italy
Joana Dias	University of Coimbra, Portugal
Luis Dias	University of Minho, Portugal
Patricia Diaz de Alba	Gran Sasso Science Institute, Italy
Isabel Dimas	University of Coimbra, Portugal
Aleksandra Djordjevic	University of Belgrade, Serbia
Luigi Dolores	Università degli Studi di Salerno, Italy
Marco Donatelli	University of Insubria, Italy
Doina Cristina Duma	INFN-CNAF, Italy
Fabio Durastante	University of Pisa, Italy
Aziz Dursun	Virginia Tech University, USA
Juan Enrique-Romero	Université Grenoble Alpes, France

Annunziata Esposito Amideo	University College Dublin, Ireland
Dario Esposito	Polytechnic University of Bari, Italy
Claudio Estatico	University of Genova, Italy
Noelia Faginas-Lago	Università di Perugia, Italy
Maria Irene Falcão	University of Minho, Portugal
Stefano Falcinelli	University of Perugia, Italy
Alessandro Farina	University of Pisa, Italy
Grazia Fattoruso	ENEA, Italy
Caterina Fenu	University of Cagliari, Italy
Luisa Fermo	University of Cagliari, Italy
Florbela Fernandes	Instituto Politecnico de Braganca, Portugal
Rosário Fernandes	University of Minho, Portugal
Luis Fernandez-Sanz	University of Alcala, Spain
Alessia Ferrari	Università di Parma, Italy
Luís Ferrás	University of Minho, Portugal
Ângela Ferreira	Instituto Politécnico de Bragança, Portugal
Flora Ferreira	University of Minho, Portugal
Manuel Carlos Figueiredo	University of Minho, Portugal
Ugo Fiore	University of Naples "Parthenope", Italy
Amedeo Flora	University of Basilicata, Italy
Hector Florez	Universidad Distrital Francisco Jose de Caldas, Colombia
Maria Laura Foddis	University of Cagliari, Italy
Valentina Franzoni	Perugia University, Italy
Adelaide Freitas	University of Aveiro, Portugal
Samuel Frimpong	Durban University of Technology, South Africa
Ioannis Fyrogenis	Aristotle University of Thessaloniki, Greece
Marika Gaballo	Politecnico di Torino, Italy
Laura Gabrielli	Iuav University of Venice, Italy
Ivan Gankevich	St. Petersburg University, Russia
Chiara Garau	University of Cagliari, Italy
Ernesto Garcia Para	Universidad del País Vasco, Spain,
Fernando Garrido	Universidad Técnica del Norte, Ecuador
Marina Gavrilova	University of Calgary, Canada
Silvia Gazzola	University of Bath, UK
Georgios Georgiadis	Aristotle University of Thessaloniki, Greece
Osvaldo Gervasi	University of Perugia, Italy
Andrea Gioia	Polytechnic University of Bari, Italy
Dario Gioia	ISPC-CNT, Italy
Raffaele Giordano	IRSS, National Research Council, Italy
Giacomo Giorgi	University of Perugia, Italy
Eleonora Giovene di Girasole	IRISS, National Research Council, Italy
Salvatore Giuffrida	Università di Catania, Italy
Marco Gola	Politecnico di Milano, Italy

A. Manuela Gonçalves	University of Minho, Portugal
Yuriy Gorbachev	Coddan Technologies LLC, Russia
Angela Gorgoglione	Universidad de la República, Uruguay
Yusuke Gotoh	Okayama University, Japan
Anestis Gourgiotis	University of Thessaly, Greece
Valery Grishkin	St. Petersburg University, Russia
Alessandro Grottesi	CINECA, Italy
Eduardo Guerra	Free University of Bozen-Bolzano, Italy
Ayse Giz Gulnerman	Ankara HBV University, Turkey
Sevin Gümgüm	Izmir University of Economics, Turkey
Himanshu Gupta	BITS Pilani, Hyderabad, India
Sandra Haddad	Arab Academy for Science, Egypt
Malgorzata Hanzl	Lodz University of Technology, Poland
Shoji Hashimoto	KEK, Japan
Peter Hegedus	University of Szeged, Hungary
Eligius M. T. Hendrix	Universidad de Málaga, Spain
Edmond Ho	Northumbria University, UK
Guan Yue Hong	Western Michigan University, USA
Vito Iacobellis	Polytechnic University of Bari, Italy
Mauro Iacono	Università degli Studi della Campania, Italy
Chiara Iacovino	University of Basilicata, Italy
Antonino Iannuzzo	ETH Zurich, Switzerland
Ali Idri	University Mohammed V, Morocco
Oana-Ramona Ilovan	Babeş-Bolyai University, Romania
Mustafa Inceoglu	Ege University, Turkey
Tadashi Ishikawa	KEK, Japan
Federica Isola	University of Cagliari, Italy
Irena Itova	University of Westminster, UK
Edgar David de Izeppi	VTTI, USA
Marija Jankovic	CERTH, Greece
Adrian Jaramillo	Universidad Tecnológica Metropolitana, Chile
Monalisa Jena	Fakir Mohan University, India
Dorota Kamrowska-Załuska	Gdansk University of Technology, Poland
Issaku Kanamori	RIKEN Center for Computational Science, Japan
Korhan Karabulut	Yasar University, Turkey
Yeliz Karaca	University of Massachusetts Medical School, USA
Vicky Katsoni	University of West Attica, Greece
Dimitris Kavroudakis	University of the Aegean, Greece
Shuhei Kimura	Okayama University, Japan
Joanna Kolozej	Cracow University of Technology, Poland
Vladimir Korkhov	St. Petersburg University, Russia
Thales Körting	INPE, Brazil
Tomonori Kouya	Shizuoka Institute of Science and Technology, Japan
Sylwia Krzysztofik	Lodz University of Technology, Poland
Nataliia Kulabukhova	St. Petersburg University, Russia
Shrinivas B. Kulkarni	SDM College of Engineering and Technology, India

Pavan Kumar	University of Calgary, Canada
Anisha Kumari	National Institute of Technology, Rourkela, India
Ludovica La Rocca	University of Naples "Federico II", Italy
Daniele La Rosa	University of Catania, Italy
Sabrina Lai	University of Cagliari, Italy
Giuseppe Francesco Cesare Lama	University of Naples "Federico II", Italy
Mariusz Lamprecht	University of Lodz, Poland
Vincenzo Laporta	National Research Council, Italy
Chien-Sing Lee	Sunway University, Malaysia
José Isaac Lemus Romani	Pontifical Catholic University of Valparaíso, Chile
Federica Leone	University of Cagliari, Italy
Alexander H. Levis	George Mason University, USA
Carola Lingua	Polytechnic University of Turin, Italy
Marco Locurcio	Polytechnic University of Bari, Italy
Andrea Lombardi	University of Perugia, Italy
Savino Longo	University of Bari, Italy
Fernando Lopez Gayarre	University of Oviedo, Spain
Yan Lu	Western Michigan University, USA
Maria Macchiaroli	University of Salerno, Italy
Helmuth Malonek	University of Aveiro, Portugal
Francesca Maltinti	University of Cagliari, Italy
Luca Mancini	University of Perugia, Italy
Marcos Mandado	University of Vigo, Spain
Ernesto Marcheggiani	Università Politecnica delle Marche, Italy
Krassimir Markov	University of Telecommunications and Post, Bulgaria
Giovanni Martinelli	INGV, Italy
Alessandro Marucci	University of L'Aquila, Italy
Fiammetta Marulli	University of Campania Luigi Vanvitelli, Italy
Gabriella Maselli	University of Salerno, Italy
Rytis Maskeliunas	Kaunas University of Technology, Lithuania
Michele Mastroianni	University of Campania Luigi Vanvitelli, Italy
Cristian Mateos	Universidad Nacional del Centro de la Provincia de Buenos Aires, Argentina
Hideo Matsufuru	High Energy Accelerator Research Organization (KEK), Japan
D'Apuzzo Mauro	University of Cassino and Southern Lazio, Italy
Chiara Mazzarella	University Federico II, Italy
Marco Mazzarino	University of Venice, Italy
Giovanni Mei	University of Cagliari, Italy
Mário Melo	Federal Institute of Rio Grande do Norte, Brazil
Francesco Mercaldo	University of Molise, Italy
Alfredo Milani	University of Perugia, Italy
Alessandra Milesi	University of Cagliari, Italy
Antonio Minervino	ISPC, National Research Council, Italy
Fernando Miranda	Universidade do Minho, Portugal

B. Mishra	University of Szeged, Hungary
Sanjay Misra	Covenant University, Nigeria
Mirka Mobilia	University of Salerno, Italy
Giuseppe Modica	Università degli Studi di Reggio Calabria, Italy
Mohammadsadegh Mohagheghi	Vali-e-Asr University of Rafsanjan, Iran
Mohamad Molaei Qelichi	University of Tehran, Iran
Mario Molinara	University of Cassino and Southern Lazio, Italy
Augusto Montisci	Università degli Studi di Cagliari, Italy
Pierluigi Morano	Polytechnic University of Bari, Italy
Ricardo Moura	Universidade Nova de Lisboa, Portugal
Ana Clara Mourao Moura	Federal University of Minas Gerais, Brazil
Maria Mourao	Polytechnic Institute of Viana do Castelo, Portugal
Daichi Mukunoki	RIKEN Center for Computational Science, Japan
Beniamino Murgante	University of Basilicata, Italy
Naohito Nakasato	University of Aizu, Japan
Grazia Napoli	Università degli Studi di Palermo, Italy
Isabel Cristina Natário	Universidade Nova de Lisboa, Portugal
Nadia Nedjah	State University of Rio de Janeiro, Brazil
Antonio Nesticò	University of Salerno, Italy
Andreas Nikiforiadis	Aristotle University of Thessaloniki, Greece
Keigo Nitadori	RIKEN Center for Computational Science, Japan
Silvio Nocera	Iuav University of Venice, Italy
Giuseppina Oliva	University of Salerno, Italy
Arogundade Oluwasefunmi	Academy of Mathematics and System Science, China
Ken-ichi Oohara	University of Tokyo, Japan
Tommaso Orusa	University of Turin, Italy
M. Fernanda P. Costa	University of Minho, Portugal
Roberta Padulano	Centro Euro-Mediterraneo sui Cambiamenti Climatici, Italy
Maria Panagiotopoulou	National Technical University of Athens, Greece
Jay Pancham	Durban University of Technology, South Africa
Gianni Pantaleo	University of Florence, Italy
Dimos Pantazis	University of West Attica, Greece
Michela Paolucci	University of Florence, Italy
Eric Pardede	La Trobe University, Australia
Olivier Parisot	Luxembourg Institute of Science and Technology, Luxembourg
Vincenzo Pellecchia	Ente Idrico Campano, Italy
Anna Pelosi	University of Salerno, Italy
Edit Pengő	University of Szeged, Hungary
Marco Pepe	University of Salerno, Italy
Paola Perchinunno	University of Cagliari, Italy
Ana Pereira	Polytechnic Institute of Bragança, Portugal
Mariano Pernetti	University of Campania, Italy
Damiano Perri	University of Perugia, Italy

Federica Pes	University of Cagliari, Italy
Marco Petrelli	Roma Tre University, Italy
Massimiliano Petri	University of Pisa, Italy
Khiem Phan	Duy Tan University, Vietnam
Alberto Ferruccio Piccinni	Polytechnic of Bari, Italy
Angela Pilogallo	University of Basilicata, Italy
Francesco Pinna	University of Cagliari, Italy
Telmo Pinto	University of Coimbra, Portugal
Luca Piroddi	University of Cagliari, Italy
Darius Plonis	Vilnius Gediminas Technical University, Lithuania
Giuliano Poli	University of Naples "Federico II", Italy
Maria João Polidoro	Polytecnic Institute of Porto, Portugal
Ioannis Politis	Aristotle University of Thessaloniki, Greece
Maurizio Pollino	ENEA, Italy
Antonio Pratelli	University of Pisa, Italy
Salvatore Praticò	Mediterranean University of Reggio Calabria, Italy
Marco Prato	University of Modena and Reggio Emilia, Italy
Carlotta Quagliolo	Polytechnic University of Turin, Italy
Emanuela Quaquero	Univesity of Cagliari, Italy
Garrisi Raffaele	Polizia postale e delle Comunicazioni, Italy
Nicoletta Rassu	University of Cagliari, Italy
Hafiz Tayyab Rauf	University of Bradford, UK
Michela Ravanelli	Sapienza University of Rome, Italy
Roberta Ravanelli	Sapienza University of Rome, Italy
Alfredo Reder	Centro Euro-Mediterraneo sui Cambiamenti Climatici, Italy
Stefania Regalbuto	University of Naples "Federico II", Italy
Rommel Regis	Saint Joseph's University, USA
Lothar Reichel	Kent State University, USA
Marco Reis	University of Coimbra, Portugal
Maria Reitano	University of Naples "Federico II", Italy
Jerzy Respondek	Silesian University of Technology, Poland
Elisa Riccietti	École Normale Supérieure de Lyon, France
Albert Rimola	Universitat Autònoma de Barcelona, Spain
Angela Rizzo	University of Bari, Italy
Ana Maria A. C. Rocha	University of Minho, Portugal
Fabio Rocha	Institute of Technology and Research, Brazil
Humberto Rocha	University of Coimbra, Portugal
Maria Clara Rocha	Polytechnic Institute of Coimbra, Portugal
Miguel Rocha	University of Minho, Portugal
Giuseppe Rodriguez	University of Cagliari, Italy
Guillermo Rodriguez	UNICEN, Argentina
Elisabetta Ronchieri	INFN, Italy
Marzio Rosi	University of Perugia, Italy
Silvia Rossetti	University of Parma, Italy
Marco Rossitti	Polytechnic University of Milan, Italy

Sergio Tasso	University of Perugia, Italy
Ana Paula Teixeira	Universidade de Trás-os-Montes e Alto Douro, Portugal
Senhorinha Teixeira	University of Minho, Portugal
Tengku Adil Tengku Izhar	Universiti Teknologi MARA, Malaysia
Maria Filomena Teodoro	University of Lisbon/Portuguese Naval Academy, Portugal
Giovanni Tesoriere	Kore University of Enna, Italy
Yiota Theodora	National Technical Univeristy of Athens, Greece
Graça Tomaz	Polytechnic Institute of Guarda, Portugal
Carmelo Maria Torre	Polytechnic University of Bari, Italy
Francesca Torrieri	University of Naples "Federico II", Italy
Vincenza Torrisi	University of Catania, Italy
Vincenzo Totaro	Polytechnic University of Bari, Italy
Pham Trung	Ho Chi Minh City University of Technology, Vietnam
Dimitrios Tsoukalas	Centre of Research and Technology Hellas (CERTH), Greece
Sanjida Tumpa	University of Calgary, Canada
Iñaki Tuñon	Universidad de Valencia, Spain
Takahiro Ueda	Seikei University, Japan
Piero Ugliengo	University of Turin, Italy
Abdi Usman	Haramaya University, Ethiopia
Ettore Valente	University of Naples "Federico II", Italy
Jordi Vallverdu	Universitat Autònoma de Barcelona, Spain
Cornelis Van Der Mee	University of Cagliari, Italy
José Varela-Aldás	Universidad Tecnológica Indoamérica, Ecuador
Fanny Vazart	University of Grenoble Alpes, France
Franco Vecchiocattivi	University of Perugia, Italy
Laura Verde	University of Campania Luigi Vanvitelli, Italy
Giulia Vergerio	Polytechnic University of Turin, Italy
Jos Vermaseren	Nikhef, The Netherlands
Giacomo Viccione	University of Salerno, Italy
Marco Vizzari	University of Perugia, Italy
Corrado Vizzarri	Polytechnic University of Bari, Italy
Alexander Vodyaho	St. Petersburg State Electrotechnical University "LETI", Russia
Nikolay N. Voit	Ulyanovsk State Technical University, Russia
Marco Vona	University of Basilicata, Italy
Agustinus Borgy Waluyo	Monash University, Australia
Fernando Wanderley	Catholic University of Pernambuco, Brazil
Chao Wang	University of Science and Technology of China, China
Marcin Wozniak	Silesian University of Technology, Poland
Tiang Xian	Nathong University, China
Rekha Yadav	KL University, India
Claudia Yamu	University of Groningen, The Netherlands
Fenghui Yao	Tennessee State University, USA

Fukuko Yuasa	KEK, Japan
Moayid Ali Zaidi	Ostfold University College Norway, Norway
Paola Zamperlin	University of Pisa, Italy
Peter Zeile	Karlsruhe Institute of Technology, Germany
Milliam Maxime Zekeng Ndadji	University of Dschang, Cameroon
Nataly Zhukova	ITMO University, Russia
Ljiljiana Zivkovic	Ministry of Construction, Transport and Infrastructure/Institute of Architecture and Urban and Spatial Planning of Serbia, Serbia

Contents – Part VIII

**International Workshop on Scientific Computing
Infrastructure (SCI 2021)**

**International Workshop on Smart Cities and User Data Management
(SCIDAM 2021)**

International Workshop on Privacy in the Cloud/Edge/IoT World (PCEIoT 2021)

Risk Analysis of a GDPR-Compliant Deletion Technique for Consortium Blockchains Based on Pseudonymization

Lelio Campanile[1], Pasquale Cantiello[2], Mauro Iacono[1],
Fiammetta Marulli[1], and Michele Mastroianni[1]($\boxtimes$)

[1] Dipartimento di Matematica e Fisica, Università degli Studi della Campania,
Caserta, Italy
{lelio.campanile,mauro.iacono,fiammetta.marulli,
michele.mastroianni}@unicampania.it
[2] Osservatorio Vesuviano, Istituto Nazionale di Geofisica e Vulcanologia, Napoli, Italy
pasquale.cantiello@ingv.it
http://www.unicampania.it, http://www.ingv.it

Abstract. Blockchains provide a valid and profitable support for the
implementation of trustable and secure distributed ledgers, in support
to groups of subjects that are potentially competitors in conflict of
interest but need to share progressive information recording processes.
Blockchains prevent data stored in blocks from being altered or deleted,
but there are situations in which stored information must be deleted
or made inaccessible on request or periodically, such as the ones in
which GDPR is applicable. In this paper we present literature solutions and design an implementation in the context of a traffic management system for the Internet of Vehicles based on the Pseudonymiza-
tion/Cryptography solution, evaluating its viability, its GDPR compliance and its level of risk.

Keywords: Blockchain · Privacy · GDPR · IoV · Risk analysis ·
Pseudonymization

1 Introduction

Blockchain technologies are now well established and appreciated for their intrinsic characteristics of security, reliability, transparency and inalterability of the
information stored. By virtue of these characteristics, in addition to the original applications relating to cryptocurrencies, their scope of use has expanded
to many other fields. Different areas of use are constantly being studied and
researched and in the literature there are now many scientific works that demonstrate their applicability, validity and the concrete advantages that can derive
from their adoptions. In particular, they can certainly be considered an excellent
alternative, also in terms of costs, to databases and registries managed centrally

O. Gervasi et al. (Eds.): ICCSA 2021, LNCS 12956, pp. 3–14, 2021.
https://doi.org/10.1007/978-3-030-87010-2_1

by recognized and regulated authorities. Even greater are the benefits that can be derived from using blockchains technologies in complex, federated and distributed ledgers that are participated by subjects that have potential conflicts of interests [4]. The design of GDPR-compliant Blockchain Systems is an emerging topic for researcher and practitioners, as documented in [17] and [10].

One of the fundamental properties of these technologies, the guarantee of the immutability of the stored information, can however, at first sight, place a constraint on particular areas of adoption where instead the possibility of modifying or deleting some information must be provided. In particular, in contexts in which data of natural persons must be processed, the European General Data Protection Regulation (GDPR) [6] guarantees a series of fundamental rights for the citizen. In detail, each natural person has the right, if there are no higher legal obligations that prohibit it, to request and obtain from the entity who processes the information (Data Processor) that his data be rectified (Article 16) or even erased (Article 17). In this case, the need to modify/delete personal data is in contrast with the immutability of the blocks making up the chain.

This problem has been addressed, among the others, by the French supervisory authority CNIL[1] [5] which has recognized, as a method to guarantee the right to erasure, the deletion, not of the data itself, but that of the means used to full decode it. In this way, although the information is still present, it will no longer be accessible.

In this paper one of these techniques, namely *Pseudonymization/Cryptography* [16] is analyzed and a possible implementation is proposed. This is contextualized in an Internet of Vehicle scenario with the necessity of management of all related information (traffic, safety, accounting, property) as described in [2]. Along with the implementation, a risk analysis is conducted in order to assess the good practice to pursue the GDPR compliance.

After this introduction, the paper continues in Sect. 2 with a brief introduction of the security advantages of blockchain systems in IoV contest. In Sect. 3 several approaches to data deletion in blockchain found in literature are presented, and one of them is detailed in Sect. 3.1. Two use cases with data requests and data update/deletion are shown in Sect. 4 with a risk analysis in Sect. 5. The paper ends in Sect. 6 with conclusions and future work directions.

2   Security Advantages of Blockchain Systems

A blockchain [7] can be seen as a distributed database of digital events and transactions shared between participating entities. The characteristics of immutability of data contained in blockchains [19] are guaranteed by the model, which is in fact an open and distributed ledger running on a peer-to-peer (P2P) network.

Transactions are intrinsically verifiable and traceable without involving parties external to the chains. In fact, each transaction is added to the public register and

---

[1] A recognition of a procedure by an EU based supervisory authority is legally valid and recognized by all Countries that adhere to the GDPR.

is verified by consensus by the majority of the parties. At all times, a blockchain contains a certain and verifiable record of every single transaction ever made. Precisely for this reason every single transaction, once inserted in the chain, cannot be altered or canceled in any way. The distributed consent thus allows to have the assurance that an event has occurred guaranteeing the irrefutable certainty of the associated information in what can be seen in all respects as a secure distributed public ledger. The partners involved in a chain obtain benefits both in terms of management costs and the reduction of associated risks to ensure data security. The improvement of cybersecurity and privacy protection using the blockchain was analyzed in [12], demonstrating how this technology can guarantee better performances than the cloud in terms of security and privacy, both as low susceptibility to manipulation and falsification by malicious entities and in terms of data breach containment.

The distributed nature of blockchain systems and the consensus mechanism acts as a protection against hacking, since it is necessary to hack more than 50% of the nodes in order to determine a real Data Breach. Moreover, these systems are obviously much less prone to DDoS attacks due to their distributed nature. Improvements on PKI can be also obtained, as publishing keys on a blockchain may eliminate the risk of false key propagation.

3   Methods for Deletion and Updating

The intrinsic nature of the blockchain (Read/Append only model) provides that no type of alteration to the information present is possible. Any attempt to perform modifications would invalidate the entire chain. Obviously, the impossibility of modifying data also prevents them from being deleted.

In order to allow the use of blockchains in the areas where this operations must be allowed, for example to comply with the guarantees provided for by the GDPR, some research lines have therefore headed towards the identification of alternative techniques to allow such cancellation being implemented, not in a direct form, but as an indirect effect.

The first approach is to avoid saving any personal data in blockchain blocks, rather storing them in a separate repository and/or periodically performing data pruning to erase older data. This can be adopted when only a small amount of the whole managed data consists of personal data and when not all of them are subject to the Regulation.

A remarkable example of this approach is the Delegated Content Erasure in IPFS [14], in order to address the off-chain erasure over the Interplanetary File System, upon which many chains are based. The authors propose an anonymous protocol for delegated content erasure requests to be integrated in the IPFS to distribute an erasure request among all the IPFS nodes and, ultimately, to fulfill the requirements foreseen in the Right to be Forgotten. In order to prevent censoring, erasure is only allowed to the original content provider or her delegates.

The *Hash Function Modification* approach has been presented in [1]. It is based on the so-called chameleon hash functions [11], that provide an undeniable commitment of the signer to the contents of the signed document (as regular digital signatures do) but, at the same time, do not allow the recipient of the signature to disclose the contents of the signed information to any third party without the signer's consent. In this way there is no possibility that personal data will be exposed to external entities, and this reduces the associated risk factor, but at the same time the technique does not fully guarantee the respect of the envisaged rights.

Another approach is the *Modification of Consensus Mechanism* presented in [15]. The authors introduce the concept of alternative versions of events and data (transaction set), and a shared consensus to determine the current (valid) version. In a transaction set, only one of the transactions is specified as active (typically the last one), while all the others are inactive alternatives. An update can be obtained by adding a new a transaction and specifying it the active one. Furthermore, every mutable transaction set includes the so-called nope transaction which is equivalent to "no operation" action. If selected as active, a nope transaction effectively hides the others and this removes a mutable transaction from the history.

Another way to address the problem is presented in [16] as *Pseudonymization/Cryptography Approach*. Personal data over the blockchains are subject to pseudonymization and so their status of "personal data" is valid only for those who are in possession of the additional information needed to associate those data to the natural person they belong. This method is used in our work, and it is described in detail below.

3.1 Pseudonymization/Cryptography

As already mentioned above, the characteristic of immutability of the information contained in the blockchains clashes with the right to modification and cancellation guaranteed by the regulation. The natural person, if there are no higher legal impediments that prohibit it, has the right to delete (or correct) his personal data. If those data are contained in a chain, that right cannot be guaranteed directly; but, if data in the chains are stored in such a way that they are not directly attributable to a specific natural person (pseudonymized), then they can no longer be considered as personal data. The only thing to ensure is that the information useful to permit the association between a natural person and his data is kept off-chains.

This pseudonymization can be achieved by encrypting the data with cryptographic hash functions applied over them, or by using pseudonymous identifiers. In this way only those participants who possess the additional information (encryption keys o person-pseudonym associations) required for attribution can act as controllers. In case of joint controllers, these key information must be shared among them with a specific agreement in order to establish clear responsibilities for compliance to the Regulation.

The right of erasure can be guaranteed by eliminating this additional key information. In this way the processor (or jointly with the other controllers as stated by agreements) will no longer have the ability to attribute that data to the person they belong to. This technical measure is reliable when based on a solution that ensures that the additional information required for the association can be shared securely and at the same time reliably deleted.

4   IoV Use Cases

The Internet of Vehicles represents a fairly new application context for blockchains. If we extend this scope to that of Smart Roads, we will find ourselves faced with an application scenario in which different actors are involved and exchange information mutually. In [2] a model is depicted in which a whole series of information relating to the world of both personal and commercial mobility is managed. In this sense, management includes data relating to movements, traffic, security, safety, accounting and the aspects relating to ownership of vehicles, most of them with privacy concerns [3].

As described in [4], in the IoV world some use cases with privacy implications can be identified. For this work we will describe more use cases: a vehicle data access request made by the owner or by a public authority, and a request to update vehicle data to fulfill the right to update guaranteed by the GDPR. A diagram is shown in Fig. 1. It can be easily seen that a request for deletion is a sub-case of update.

We know that, when a person buys (or rents) a new vehicle, his personal data begin to be associated with that vehicle. In case of buying, the transaction is registered in a public registry within a blockchain to assert the property, while in renting process the transaction is registered upon the renting company. In both cases the association is imposed by law, mainly for safety purposes, but also for taxes (and for commercial reasons in case of renting). In case of accident, injuries or violations of traffic rules the need arises for an authority to obtain, with no constraints, the full content of information records about the vehicle and who was in its possession at the time of the accident. The owner of the vehicle has the right to access all the personal data belonging to him too.

The public registry should be able to register pseudo identities, being the only entity that keeps the association between pseudo identities and user/vehicles.

In Fig. 2 the process is shown of accessing data that can be originated by a User or by an Authority. A request is made to the Public Registry and contains user and vehicle identification. The Public Registry performs a lookup on its private repository to find the corresponding pseudo-identity (if any). If found, a further lookup is executed to extract the ID that points to the block in the Blockchain containing data. After response, the block of data is decrypted using the key associated with the pseudo-identity to recover the original data that can be answered to the originating requester.

The sequence diagram of the other use case, related to the the updating of user data, is shown in Fig. 3. A request of update made by the User with updated

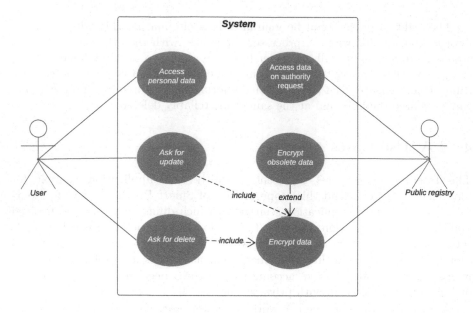

Fig. 1. Use case diagram

data (Art. 16 of GDPR - *Right to rectification*) causes the following operations to be performed: (i) a lookup of the pseudo-identity is performed on Public Registry private repository, (ii) a delete on that pseudo-identity is executed, in order to kill the associated private key, (iii) a new pseudo-identity is generated and stored for the User, (iv) data is encrypted with the new identity, (v) encrypted data is saved as a block in the Blockchain, (vi) the related block ID is stored in the private repository of the Public Registry and associated to the pseudo-identity. (vii) status code is sent to the User.

It is easy to notice that the previous block of data continues to be present in the chain but, since the key to decrypt it no longer exists, there is no way to access contained plain text data, therefore it is possible to consider them logically deleted.

Request to delete data (Art. 17 of GDPR - *Right to be forgotten*) starts as the previous one, but simply ends after deleting the pseudo-identity, so causing the impossibility to decryption the original data.

5 Risk Analysis

In the field of information security risk assessment, the most commonly used approach is the qualitative assessment approach. In the qualitative approach, classes and relative values are used to show the impact and probability of a particular scenario. This approach is widely used, due to the ease of understanding

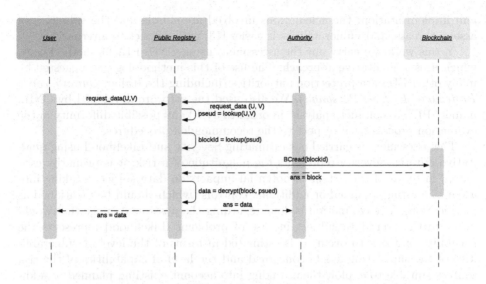

Fig. 2. Sequence diagram of user data access request

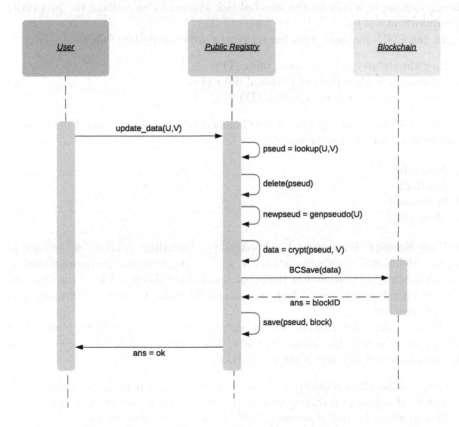

Fig. 3. Sequence diagram of user data update request

and implementation; the calculations involved are simple and the valuation of assets, threats, and vulnerabilities is easier [13] with respect to alternatives.

In this work, we carry out the assessment using CNIL-PIA [9] methodology, which uses a qualitative approach. The use of this methodology is suggested by many other EU data protection authorities (including the Italian *Garante per la Protezione dei Dati Personali*). We also used the software developed by CNIL, namely PIA, to conduct analysis, in order to avoid any possible difformity in the evaluation process with respect to the recommended procedures.

The assessment is carried out estimating Severity and Likelihood using qualitative criteria. Severity represents the magnitude of a risk: it is primarily estimated in terms of the extent of potential impacts on data subjects, taking into account existing, planned or additional controls (which should be mentioned as justification). The estimation is done regarding the possible damage that would occur to the user/data subject in case of problems. Likelihood represents the feasibility of a risk to occur: it is estimated in terms of the level of vulnerabilities of the supporting assets concerned and the level of capabilities of the risk sources suitable to exploit them, taking into account existing, planned or additional controls. The scale for classifying likelihood is related to the feasibility of the occurrence of a risk for the selected risk sources by exploiting the properties of supporting assets.

In the CNIL methodology, feared events are classified as follows:

- Illegitimate access to personal data **(I)**
- Unwanted modification of personal data **(U)**
- Disappearance of personal data **(D)**

Both Severity and Likelihood are classified in a 1–4 scale, while 1 is the lower level of risk and 4 is the higher level:

1. Negligible;
2. Limited;
3. Significant;
4. Maximum.

The Severity level may be lowered by including additional factors to oppose identification of personal data, such as encryption, pseudonymization, anonymization, and so on. On the other hand, the Likelihood level may be lowered by including additional factors, such as firewalls, logging, monitoring, and similar solutions [9].

At this point, determining the impact the users (Data Subjects) could face off in case of a data breach is necessary. The impacts taken into account, and the pertinent severity according to CNIL-PIA, are:

- Cost rise for Data Subjects (e.g. increased insurance prices) **(severity = 2)**;
- Targeted online advertising on a confidential aspect **(severity = 2)**;
- (Temporary) Denial of access to IoV services **(severity = 2)**;
- Fraud **(severity = 3)**.

The Risk Assessment procedure has been carried out by the authors. Each author is a computer security expert, and two of the authors are also Data Protection Officers (DPO). The working group is composed as follows: a IoT/IoV Expert (evaluation of threats and risks), a Software Expert (evaluation of threats and risks related to software modules), a Privacy Expert/DPO (review of the assessment), another Privacy Expert/DPO (assessment approval). What is here reported is the result of a panel discussion, after a separate analysis performed by each author in its own role, aiming at avoiding possible biases and ambiguity in the interpretation of partial reports and to synthesize the basis for the presented analysis.

Other impacts with higher severity, like "Loss of evidence in the context of litigation", have been excluded due to the distributed features of blockchain systems, which ensure virtually no permanent data loss.

Thereafter, a choice is necessary of which threats must be taken into account, to define the scope of this analysis and state the actual extent of its results. As this study aims to be general and is not related to a single practical case arose by a specific situation from the real world, in order to keep generality and to ensure realism in the process, our choice is based on data retrieved on Verizon 2019 Data breach Investigation report [18] and EY Global Information security Survey 2018–19 [8] about the most common and relevant threats that may be directed against a system based on the architecture proposed in [2]. The threats taken into account are:

- *Hacking*: it is the most frequent threat, circa 54%; due to the intrinsic robustness to hacking attacks [2], the likelihood is limited **Likelihood = 2**;
- *Use of stolen credential*: almost 30% of threats; in this case, the likelihood is significant, due to the possibility for a subject to access to important users' data **Likelihood = 3**);
- *Privilege abuse*: circa 10% of threats; for the same reason of the preceding point, the likelihood is significant **Likelihood = 3**);
- *Natural disasters*: although considered infrequent events, (circa 2% of total breaches), they are taken into account because they can lead to a severe data loss; the likelihood is negligible **(Likelihood = 1)**;
- *DDOS Attacks*: usually this kind of attack does not lead to a data modification or illegitimate access, but leads to loss of availability (data disappearing), which is considered a breach event in GDPR; due to the fact that Blockchain systems are virtually immune to DDOS attacks, the likelihood is negligible **(Likelihood = 1)**.

It is noticeable that the low Likelihood values for the last two threat categories are a direct consequence of the design choices behind the proposed architecture, in compliance with the purposes of our research. Interested readers may find further details and results about the risk analysis for the overall system, complementary for the analysis presented in this paper, in the Appendix of [4], together with a detailed description of the general technique applied here with relation to what required by the GDPR.

Figure 5 presents the results of the Risk Analysis conducted about the chosen deletion strategy. It may be noted that all three feared events, namely illegitimate access (I), unwanted modification (U), or disappearing (D) of personal data, are in the green zone (limited risk).

In order to evaluate the impact of the additional feature with respect to the overall architecture of the system, a comparison with the results of the overall risk analysis, available in [4], is needed. We report those results in Fig. 4, using the same format of Fig. 5 for an easier comparison. As evident, the new feature presents characteristics that do not lower the overall risk level of the system, as all evaluations for the new feature are in green zone and in a position on the grid that is equivalent or less severe with respect to the evaluations for the same events related to the system.

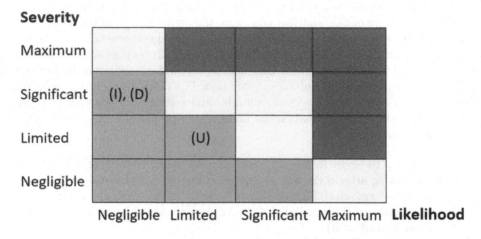

Fig. 4. Risk analysis results for the deletion feature

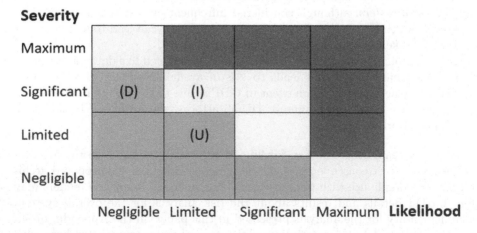

Fig. 5. Risk analysis results for the system [4] (Color figure online)

6   Conclusions and Future Work

In this article we focused on understanding the effects of one between all techniques literature offers to make blockchain compliant with the GDPR, namely the Pseudonymization/Cryptography Approach, on the risk exposure of an example blockchain-based complex data management architecture that involves data covered by GPDR. In particular, our interest focused on how to permit operations legally provided for by the Regulation, but which cannot be carried out directly on a blockchain by its immutable nature, in a system that is devoted to IoV management. Our study shows that this approach does not introduce into the system additional risk factors that are worsening the overall risk analysis results of the system.

Future work includes the analysis of other techniques and a comparison between the results, in order to evaluate the best alternative with respect to risk minimization, and a general evaluation of other dimensions of exploration of the advantages and disadvantages of the alternatives, in order to provide a global choice criterion.

References

1. Ateniese, G., Magri, B., Venturi, D., Andrade, E.: Redactable blockchain - or - rewriting history in Bitcoin and friends. In: 2017 IEEE European Symposium on Security and Privacy (EuroS&P), pp. 111–126 (2017). https://doi.org/10.1109/EuroSP.2017.37
2. Campanile, L., Iacono, M., Levis, A.H., Marulli, F., Mastroianni, M.: Privacy regulations, smart roads, blockchain, and liability insurance: putting technologies to work. IEEE Secur. Priv. **19**(1), 34–43 (2021). https://doi.org/10.1109/MSEC.2020.3012059
3. Campanile, L., Iacono, M., Marulli, F., Mastroianni, M.: Privacy regulations challenges on data-centric and IoT systems: a case study for smart vehicles. In: Proceedings of the 5th International Conference on Internet of Things, Big Data and Security, vol. 1, AI4EIoTs, pp. 507–518. INSTICC, SciTePress (2020). https://doi.org/10.5220/0009839305070518
4. Campanile, L., Iacono, M., Marulli, F., Mastroianni, M.: Designing a GDPR compliant blockchain-based IoV distributed information tracking system. Inf. Process. Manag. **58**(3), 102511 (2021). https://doi.org/10.1016/j.ipm.2021.102511
5. Commission Nationale de l'Informatique et des Libertés: Blockchain and the GDPR: solutions for a responsible use of the blockchain in the context of personal data. https://www.cnil.fr/en/blockchain-and-gdpr-solutions-responsible-use-blockchain-context-personal-data
6. Council of European Union: General Data Protection Regulation (2016). https://eur-lex.europa.eu/eli/reg/2016/679/oj
7. Crosby, M., Pattanayak, P., Verma, S., Kalyanaraman, V., et al.: Blockchain technology: beyond bitcoin. Appl. Innov. **2**(6–10), 71 (2016)
8. EY: EY Global Information security Survey 2018–19 (2019). https://assets.ey.com/content/dam/ey-sites/ey-com/en_ca/topics/advisory/ey-global-information-security-survey-2018-19.pdf

9. French Data Protection Authority (CNIL): Privacy Impact Assessment (PIA) - Knowledge Bases (2018). https://www.cnil.fr/sites/default/files/atoms/files/cnil-pia-3-en-knowledgebases.pdf
10. Haque, A.B., Islam, A.K.M.N., Hyrynsalmi, S., Naqvi, B., Smolander, K.: GDPR compliant blockchains-a systematic literature review. IEEE Access **9**, 50593–50606 (2021). https://doi.org/10.1109/ACCESS.2021.3069877
11. Krawczyk, H., Rabin, T.: Chameleon hashing and signatures. Cryptology ePrint Archive, Report 1998/010 (1998). https://eprint.iacr.org/1998/010
12. Kshetri, N.: Blockchain's roles in strengthening cybersecurity and protecting privacy. Telecommun. Policy **41**(10), 1027–1038 (2017)
13. Landoll, D.: The Security Risk Assessment Handbook: A Complete Guide for Performing Security Risk Assessments, 2nd edn. Second Edition. CRC Press Inc, Boca Raton (2011)
14. Politou, E., Alepis, E., Patsakis, C., Casino, F., Alazab, M.: Delegated content erasure in IPFs. Future Gener. Comput. Syst. **112**, 956–964 (2020)
15. Puddu, I., Dmitrienko, A., Capkun, S.: μchain: How to forget without hard forks. IACR Cryptology ePrint Archive (IACR), February 2017. https://eprint.iacr.org/2017/106
16. Rieger, A., Guggenmos, F., Lockl, J., Fridgen, G., Urbach, N.: Building a blockchain application that complies with the EU General Data Protection Regulation. MIS Q. Executive **18**(4), 263–279 (2019). https://doi.org/10.17705/2msqe.00020
17. Shi, S., He, D., Li, L., Kumar, N., Khan, M.K., Choo, K.K.R.: Applications of blockchain in ensuring the security and privacy of electronic health record systems: a survey. Comput. Secur. **97**, 101966 (2020)
18. Verizon Enterprise: 2019 data breach investigation report (2019). https://enterprise.verizon.com/resources/reports/2019-data-breach-investigations-report.pdf
19. Zheng, X., Zhu, Y., Si, X.: A survey on challenges and progresses in blockchain technologies: a performance and security perspective. Appl. Sci. **9**(22), 4731 (2019)

Vehicle-to-Everything (V2X) Communication Scenarios for Vehicular Ad-hoc Networking (VANET): An Overview

Eslam Farsimadan(✉)⬤, Francesco Palmieri⬤, Leila Moradi⬤, Dajana Conte⬤, and Beatrice Paternoster⬤

University of Salerno, Fisciano 84084, Italy
{efarsimadan,fpalmieri,lmoradi,dajconte,beapat}@unisa.it

Abstract. Nowadays both sciences and technology, including Intelligent Transportation Systems, are involved in improving current approaches. Overview studies give you fast, comprehensive, and easy access to all of the existing approaches in the field. With this inspiration, and the effect of traffic congestion as a challenging issue that affects the regular daily lives of millions of people around the world, in this work, we concentrate on communications paradigms which can be used to address traffic congestion problems. Vehicular Ad-hoc Networking (VANET), a modern networking technology, provides innovative techniques for vehicular traffic control and management. Virtual traffic light (VTL) methods for VANET seek to address traffic issues through using vehicular network communication models. These communication paradigms can be classified into four scenarios: Vehicle-to-Vehicle (V2V) and Vehicle-to-Infrastructure (V2I) and Vehicle-to-Network (V2N) and Vehicle-to-Pedestrian (V2P). In general, these four scenarios are included in the category of vehicle-to-everything (V2X). Therefore, in this paper, we provide an overview of the most important scenarios of V2X communications based on their characteristics, methodologies, and assessments. We also investigate the applications and challenges of V2X.

Keywords: Vehicular ad-hoc networking · Virtual traffic lights · V2X · V2V · V2I

1 Introduction

The use of normal traffic lights to control the flow of traffic on the road and at intersections is usually a challenging issue. By leveraging new technology in the area of communication, information science, and positioning, we will lead to more efficient, secure, safer, and thus more sustainable locomotion.

The advancement of vehicular communications systems, as well as the growing number of vehicles on the road, has created a requirement for the manufacturing and academic community to address the new challenges. The traditional

© Springer Nature Switzerland AG 2021
O. Gervasi et al. (Eds.): ICCSA 2021, LNCS 12956, pp. 15–30, 2021.
https://doi.org/10.1007/978-3-030-87010-2_2

traffic light scheme has a number of weaknesses. Vehicles encounter delays as a result of fixed time intervals, particularly when traffic is not heavy. It is difficult to manage traffic based on vehicle priority and road capacity when there is traffic congestion. In addition to the fast advancement of communication technologies, future cars are supposed to be intelligent enough to communicate with their environment in a variety of ways. Many car companies, including BMW, Tesla, Hyundai, and Google, are designing self-driving or autonomous vehicles. Accordingly, a new networking technique known as vehicular ad-hoc networking is receiving a lot of interest in vehicular communication systems study. Vehicle Ad-hoc Networking (VANET) is a new emerging field that is currently being studied extensively [1]. The information distributed for future vehicles is taken into account by car manufactures. Therefore, VANET is anticipated to incorporate various applications. Future vehicles applications will include traffic and parking data, weather situations, bus schedules, fuel costs, and entertainment applications [2]. Moreover, vehicles are supposed to communicating practical information same as location, speed, rout direction, and goods/passengers being transported to each other [3].

For VANET, a considerable number of algorithms have been suggested. The Virtual Traffic Light system (VTL) is one of the most famous traffic optimization methods for improving the movement of vehicles on the roads and intersections. Indeed, VTL and the smart traffic light system are alternatives that have been identified for the failings of the traditional traffic light system. Despite the advantages of having a smart traffic light system, there are still some issues to be considered, such as the cost of installing traffic lights on the roads and intersections and the high expenses of service, and preservation. Hence, researchers are currently focusing their efforts on designing traffic lights using VTL in the context of smart cities, Vehicle-to-Everything communications, and IoT. Ferreira et al. in [4] introduced the first VTL method for VANET. Many researchers have investigated and applied related experiments and performance monitoring since the first studies on VTL were published. In this paper a number of the most important researches in this area are investigated. Some of the advantages of VTL are as follows:

- Time is important in our life. VTL helps people to spend less time in traffic congestion.
- With spending less time in traffic congestion, VTL reduces air and environmental pollution.
- Traffic causes stress, pollution, and road rages. VTL helps us to reduce them and improve the health and life quality.
- VTL expedites large-scale deployment of autonomous vehicles.
- VTL increases safety at intersections, on highways, and other road segments.

As it was mentioned before, in 2010, VTL was presented for the first time. Its aim is to alleviate traffic congestion by utilizing communications paradigms known as Vehicle-to-everything technology (V2X) [5]. V2X is a new descendant of information and communication technology aimed at connecting vehicles to everything surrounding them. So many studies and researches have been conducted in this area since the first introduction.

The paper is organized as follows: Sect. 2 introduces V2X technology and describes some of its applications and challenges. Section 3 summarizes the main scenarios of V2X and gives a review of them. In Sect. 4 we discuss what we reviewed in the previous section. Finally, in Sect. 5 the conclusion is drawn.

2 V2X: Applications and Challenges

The transportation sector's accelerated growth is beset by major challenges, obstacles, and problems: how to reduce the number of road accidents, fossil energy dependency, the greenhouse impact induced by fossil fuel pollution, fossil fuel reliance, the greenhouse impacts induced by fossil fuels, ways of optimizing and making efficient use of automobiles, as well as enhancing the drivers' skills, and plenty of other significant and related issues.

One of the most serious challenges among those mentioned above is decreasing the number of deaths and injuries in road crashes, which is current throughout all countries around the world. Road deaths and accidents have far-reaching consequences not only for the victims but also for the whole of society and economic prosperity.

To overcome the aforementioned problems, a number of vehicle communication networks are being developed by both communications and automotive companies, and also scientific and government organizations around the world. Based on the participants that communicate information directly, various forms of vehicle communication networks exist. Vehicle-to-Vehicle (V2V) networks are made up of mobile nodes that are actually moving vehicles that directly communicate with each other. Vehicle-to-Pedestrian (V2P) or Vehicle-to-Infrastructure (V2I) networks are built when vehicles, which are moving on the roads, interact and communicate either with pedestrians or with roadside infrastructure. When the communication is between vehicle and data centers and/or IT networks, the structure of the network is vehicle-to-network (V2N). A widely known concept that incorporates all these modes of communication, that provide vehicle connections to different receivers, is called vehicle-to-everything (V2X) (Fig. 1).

V2X communications, together with the current capabilities of modern vehicles, can not only address the above-mentioned problems but will also provide better quality public transportation systems, more effective logistics strategies, better road quality, efficient utilization of transport facilities, especially accurate electronic maps and many other innovative and relevant services and solutions.

Dedicated Short Range Communication (DSRC) and Cellular Vehicle-to-Everything (C-V2X) communication systems are the two information exchange technologies generally used for V2X. The DSRC scheme consists of a number of IEEE and the Society of Automotive Engineers (SAE) standards [6]. C-V2X is a wireless networking system with a high data rate and monitored QoS [7,8], and is based on the 3rd Generation Partnership Project's concept of Long-Term Evolution mobile communication technology.

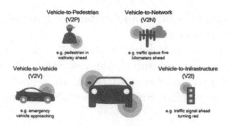

Fig. 1. V2X communications scenarios

2.1 Applications

V2X enables the existence of different applications as a result of technological advancements in the fields of wireless sensing and networking. Some of these applications are shown in Fig. 2. In general, applications of V2X communication can be classified into three categories: Safety, efficiency, and information services applications (Table 1) [5,9,10]:

- Safety applications reduce crashes and protect users from hazards by using wireless communications amongst entities in the vicinity. Every roadway entity sends a safety alert to all of its neighbors regularly to inform them of its current state. They will also be required to send out warning alerts if a local or global incident is observed. Personal safety applications, such as crashes, speeding alerts, and road hazard alerts, are included in this category.
- Green wave speed guidance and congestion alerts are examples of efficiency applications that help drivers to drive and enhance traffic efficiencies. To effectively control traffic and ensure seamless traffic flow, traffic-related applications are implemented. Their responsibility is aggregating traffic data and wirelessly sending it to a central server for processing. The results of the analysis are then delivered to vehicles for possible future use [11].
- Services such as eCall, traffic updates and route suggestions, automated parking, and entertainment are examples of information services applications. They provide drivers with these vehicle-related data to ameliorate the driving experience [7].

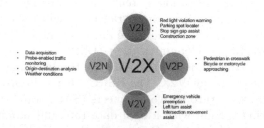

Fig. 2. Some applications of V2X communications

V2X will gently fulfill the criteria for autonomous automated driving and applications in intelligent traffic systems, in addition to the aforementioned applications. For these specialized strategies, the 3GPP distinguishes four categories of applications: Advanced Driving, Vehicle Platooning, Remote Driving, and Extended Sensors.

Table 1. Characteristics of V2X applications

Application	Channel models	Benefits	Latency	Packet loss rate
Road safety	Cellular network DSRC, Wi.Fi, Wave	Collision avoidance, Incident management, road sign notifications	Very low	Very low
Traffic management	Cellular network DSRC, ZigBee, Wave	Traffic management, road monitoring	Low	Low
Information, comfort, infotainment	Cellular network DSRC, WiMax, Wave	Route suggestion, entertainment, automated parking	Medium	Low

However, more conventional mobile applications, like entertainment providers, will gently join the V2X market and industry.

2.2 Challenges

Reliability and Latency Challenges: For applications involving low latency and high reliability, network performance is critical. To gain crash avoidance and multi-user accessibility, DSRC employs Carrier Sense Multiple Access with Collision Avoidance (CSMA/CA). DSRC has lower latency and better reliability when there are fewer cars, but it performs more poorly when there are more vehicles. The delay of C-V2X is fairly stable over time, and communication latency is less than 100 ms when it is based on the PC5 interface, which allows less interference and predictable and manageable delay [12]. Soon, 5G networks will be capable of supporting automatic-driving-oriented V2X systems with a transmission latency of less than 1 ms and 99.999% reliability and stability. V2X communication network encounters and is vulnerable to a variety of attacks that can cause it to perform poorly. Denial of service (DOS) and distributed DoS (DDoS) refers to intense attacks on target nodes by external or domestic attackers that cause network and service resources to be exhausted [13]. They can create negative effects, like high latency in communication, unavailability of the network, and node operation unavailability. DoS attacks include attacks like greedy behavior attacks and jamming attacks [14]. A greedy behavior attack occurs when a network node breaks channel access rules and takes up many other channel resources, which causes decreasing the efficiency of other nodes and creating network congestion problems [15]. A jamming attack is a kind of attack which is a threat to the physical layer. Via electromagnetic disturbance, the attacker blocks the wireless channel, causes reducing the reliability of the network and increasing the delay of V2X communication [5,16].

Challenges related to Security: As it is mentioned before, in vehicular communication context, V2X is frequently used in a variety of applications. These kinds of applications contain traffic safety, infotainment, and information applications that enforce different criteria to enable V2X implementation. These diversified needs lead to research challenges being developed. The main V2X security challenges are listed below [17,18].

- Scalability of the network: V2X communication technology contains a huge and large-scale worldwide network of vehicles. V2X standards, such as DSRC, do not require a universal authority to regulate and govern them. Controlling large networks while also dealing with security problems such as certificate exchange is a really difficult task to tackle. For such networks, security strategies that require prior information of participating vehicles/nodes are ineffective.
- Communication latency: Some specific issues, like which data to collect, which data to analyze, what data should be refined, and what must be transferred and received, can induce latency in V2X communication. Hence all factors relating to V2X communication latency must be investigated to manage security-critical and safety circumstances in real-time.
- Dynamic topology of the network: The dynamic and complex nature of the topology of the network in V2X (due to mobility) is a critical concern that is hard to manage, specifically when it comes to security features and frameworks. In general, vehicles move at high speed and therefore make connections for a short time. So it will be a tough challenge to adapt the security requirements to the quality of communication, which is affected by high-speed vehicles.
- Attack prevention: The vehicular communication network is expected to serve a wide range of applications and services. Vehicles would have to transfer important data, such as vehicle identity, to enable these operations, which demands maximum security for approval from the perspectives of the overall communication infrastructure. In V2X, attacks can be classified into two types: system-level attacks and user-level attacks. Creating a particular public key infrastructure framework for preserving the high mobility function of vehicular communication can be an effective strategy for minimizing the aforementioned threats [5].

There are some other challenges related to security same as data priority, heterogeneity, user's privacy and trust, and acceptance of future operating systems and platforms.

3   V2X Communications Scenarios

In previous sections, we mentioned that V2X incorporates all methods of vehicle communications, including V2V, V2I, V2N, and V2P. This section focuses on reviewing these paradigms. The first subsection investigates the V2V scenario, the most significant scenario of this series, addressing the principal services, systems, and applications that better satisfy the needs to attain effective collaboration between vehicles. In other subsections, we review some studies and features of V2I, V2N, and V2P.

3.1   Vehicle-to-Vehicle (V2V)

V2V communication technology includes wireless data transmissions among motorized vehicles. The main objective of such communication is to avoid possible crashes by enabling vehicles to exchange data on their location and speed using an ad-hoc mesh network [19]. Fully connected mesh topology improves the network structure's robustness. Whether a node fails or temporarily malfunctions, the paths are recomputed within the transmission tables in order to access all destinations.

Before, when mesh networks were still wired, fully connected topology was prohibitively costly and impossible to implement since each node needed to be physically connected to all of the others. Nowadays, with the emergence of Wireless Personal Area Networks (WPANs) and by using the benefits of wireless networking, these drawbacks have been solved. Each independent and moving node in these networks, connected to others, generates an arbitrary-sized graph (partially linked mesh network). In the network, instead of being dependent on a base station to organize the transmission of messages to each destination, Individual nodes send packets to each other independently. While wireless topology differs quickly and unpredictably, these nodes are able to move randomly and arrange themselves arbitrarily. Besides that, these networks may function independently or be in connection with the Internet to provide extra services.

Based on developments of new technologies, the vehicle driver will receive warnings when there is a crash risk, or the vehicle itself may take preventive strategies on its own, like emergency braking, if it is developed to perform safety strategies [20]. V2V communications are anticipated to be much more efficient than existing embedded systems developed by Original Equipment Manufacturers (OEMs) because vehicle safety depends on the performance of onboard radar systems, sensors, cameras, and so on [21]. Depending on the particular parameters observed by these instruments installed on the vehicle, the system responds to any potentially hazardous situations. Speed, location, traffic flow, distance from other vehicles or a hazard, and the existence of an automobile in the wrong or blind place are generally the most significant analyzed parameters Fig. 3. Nevertheless, while V2V communication technologies are becoming more accurate and reliable, calculation and measurement errors should not be overlooked. V2V communication strategies, on the other hand, can enhance safety performance by connecting all vehicles which are close together and enabling them to communicate with each other. They can help the vehicle to make appropriate decisions in dangerous situations (for example, a driver's nap, a component breakdown, and so on) and manage the arising problem. Thus, the main goal of each node in the mesh network will be aggregating data to ensure excellent safety and security for its own and its neighbors. This strategy is known as cooperative awareness [22]. However, as proposed in [23,24], it is highly beneficial to use appropriate coding techniques for real-time data access.

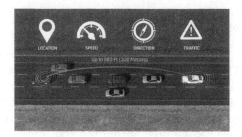

Fig. 3. V2V communications

V2V communication technology, in collaboration with already developed security frameworks, will result in effective handling of possible problems on the world's roadways. The modern Intelligent Transport Systems (ITSs) are going to utilize data provided by V2V communication to improve traffic management and enabling vehicles to have communications with roadside infrastructures like signs or traffic lights. In the future, V2V communication technologies can become compulsory by governments and leading to significant improvements in producing more reliable self-driving vehicles. However, the deployment of V2V communications and a smart transportation system faces some major challenges: the preservation of privacy and secrecy of data transmitted in broadcast and multicast, the requirement for making vehicle manufacturers accept operation and security laws, and the funding required for the production and distribution of all technologies. It is currently uncertain if public or private companies and individuals will fund and support the construction and preservation of communication infrastructure. Nonetheless, Audi, BMW, General Motors, Volvo, and Tesla are amongst the top vehicle manufacturers that focus on ITS and V2V communication networks. In the last years, the assessment of prototypes for V2V communication applications has become a type of research and advancement for several vehicles company all around the world, particularly in the United States. As a consequence of these efforts, through a series of analytical techniques, some experimental models have been performed in order to predict the possible future effects due to the large hypothetical incorporation of applications in the sector of vehicular communications, and also the potential environmental effects, which are difficult to analyze now due to the absence of a norm.

Many researchers have focused on V2V communication technologies to improve traffic flow on the roads and intersections, where the findings of the studies confirmed the effectiveness of implemented strategies. Ferreira et al. in [4] proposed switching from traditional traffic lights to virtual traffic lights inside of the vehicles since V2V communication networks support it. They presumed that each vehicle has a DSRC system. They also assumed a similar digital route map is shared by all of the vehicles, and they have a global positioning system (GPS). Eventually, it was supposed that the wireless service is reliable and secure, and its performance is acceptable for VTL's requirements.

Every vehicle is equipped with a specialized Application Unit (AU) that stores intersections and road information in advance to specify the locations of roads and intersections where a VTL is needed. When the vehicle arrives at these crossings, the AU looks for a VTL wireless signal followed by, if none is detected, a new VTL is made. If a VTL is required, the vehicles that are close to the intersection will select a vehicle to be the leader (which is the closest vehicle to the intersection). The leader will establish and operate the VTL, and temporarily facilitates the movement of vehicles by sending the traffic directions. Then, the leader transfers the intersection control to the next vehicle to complete the task of controlling the intersection and preserving the VTL. When the last car leaves the intersection, the VTL will terminate. This model was executed using DIVERT simulation, and the results indicated more than 60 improvement in intersections traffic flow.

Azimi et al. in [25] discussed, by simulations, the utilization of V2V communication technology among autonomous vehicles to maximize throughput and reduce accident risks at roads and intersections. Their findings demonstrated significant increases in secure throughput across a variety of traffic scenarios. The Red Light and Stop Sign Violation Warning system are some other prominent safety contributions of connected vehicles (CV).

Sepulcre and Gozalvez in [26] carried out several field experiments to assess three V2V collaborative safety applications in real circumstances: overtaking assistance, lane change assistance, and forward-collision warning. The experiments demonstrated the effect of vehicular blockages and communication power rate on the reliability of applications in various propagation conditions. The research findings experimentally demonstrated the strong relationship between the requirements of application and reliability, driving circumstances, and communications efficiency. Furthermore, considering the higher criteria imposed by collaborative active safety applications, the findings revealed some limitations created at high vehicular speeds.

Boban and D'Orey in [27] did several field experiments to analyze the effectiveness of V2V collaborative awareness systems in terms of delivered packet ratio, neighbor beyond range ratio, and neighborhood awareness ratio. They realized that collaborative awareness is highly dependent on connection quality and conditions of propagation. As a result, awareness ratios are lower for metropolitan scenarios, moderate for suburban scenarios, and highest for highway and freeway scenarios. In terms of connection type, the findings indicate that beneficial situations of Road Side Units (RSUs) increase awareness ratios for V2V communications.

Bazzi et al. in [28] presented a decentralized VTL method which is based on V2V communication technology, intending to identify priorities of intersections in a controlled and decentralized form in IEEE 802.11p V2V communications. The protocol operates in two phases: defining the first priority, as CVs reach a vacant intersection, defining the subsequent priorities. The next step (priorities when the first CV crosses) is dependent on a priority grant process from the CV whit priority to the next CV. Experiments implemented in both standardized laboratory settings and field trials confirmed the effectiveness of the method.

3.2   Vehicle-to-Infrastructure (V2I)

V2I communication technology is defined as the wireless exchanging of operational and safety information amongst vehicles and roadside infrastructure (through the use of roadside equipment or RSE) utilizing DSRC methods. The purpose of V2I communication is to avoid and minimize the intensity of vehicle accidents. Besides that, it can also improve mobility systems and environmental advantages by helping applications like speed standardization and traffic flow optimization. Roadside infrastructure aggregates real-time data on traffic arrangements and rules (e.g., variable speed restrictions and signal state) and dangers (e.g., crashes and violations) and transmits this data to relevant vehicles in the form of alerts or guidelines. The greatest benefit of the DSRC V2I framework is that it can customize messages to specific vehicles rather than propagating identical warning signals to all users. A wide range of communication technologies and algorithms can be used to implement V2I communication.

Sepulcre et al. in [29] proposed a heterogeneous context-aware V2I method in which vehicles choose the best radio access system with the help of roadside infrastructure to enhance both personal and system efficiency. Every vehicle makes the decision on its own, with infrastructure assistance. The obtained results indicate the advantages of the suggested approach as well as its reliability to the variability and precision of the context information.

In [30] Wuthishuwong et al. developed an autonomous system for smart transportation. The main purpose of this work is to develop a mechanism that guarantees a crash-free movement of an intersection while still reducing traffic congestion, as the second goal. Via the use of V2I communication technology, they tried to implement the technique for autonomous intersection control. The intersection challenge is modeled using discrete mathematics, and the direction of a vehicle is determined through dynamic programming. The results of the simulation indicate a crossing of the intersection without any accident. Also, vehicles move continuously.

Mohammed et al. in [31] introduced a V2I framework to increase the awareness of car drivers at signalized intersections. The primary goals are: (1) to perform a proof-of-concept field test by using the V2I communication framework at a signalized intersection and (2) to analyze the effect of the V2I communication framework on enhancing the performance of drivers when they are crossing the intersection. The application of the suggested V2I communication framework transmits an auditory advisory notification to inform the driver about traffic signal status. The driver's behavior and attitude are expected to change due to audible communication. Their study results indicated that maximum and average speeds were decreased as a result of crossing the intersection as well as the drop in deceleration values before arriving at the intersection, especially during the red phase.

Gheorghiu et al. in [32] presented a research work and focused on the possibilities of using ZigBee communication technology for V2I communication. In comparison with other technologies, these communications consume less energy and are suggested for crowded urban environments where infrastructure instrument density exceeds higher levels and requires significant energy consumption. As a method to evaluate V2I communications in the laboratory, a prototype for vehicle recognition using the Zigbee technology is introduced.

Al-qutwani and Wang in [33] proposed that rather than using traffic lights at each intersection, we can use a Roadside Unit (RSU) to function as the intersection manager. The RSU receives the signals of vehicles that have entered or will come to the intersection. Just after analyzing the orders in accordance with the priority rules and policy, RSU sends an instant message to each vehicle to move through the intersection or stop for a while. This method is appropriate for autonomous vehicles since instead of processing a large number of images, they just receive digital signals from RSU.

3.3 Vehicle-to-Network (V2N)

V2N communication technology illustrates the communications between the vehicle and a network provider that offers access and connectivity to the vehicle, maybe on several frequencies. This communication will include non-critical yet valuable information (like road blockage and congestion) and also some services based on the cloud, which amplify the experience of the passengers, while also acting as a hotspot for internet access. Furthermore, vehicle to cloud connectivity takes advantage of V2N connections to wideband mobile networks, aiming to exchange data with the cloud. Several methods and approaches have been proposed about V2N and vehicle to cloud communications. We review some of them as follows.

He et al. in [34] proposed an innovative multi-layered vehicular data cloud framework utilizing IoT technologies and cloud computing. Two novel vehicular data cloud systems for vehicle warranty processing in the IoT environment have also been introduced: a vehicular data mining cloud system and a smart parking cloud system. Two updated data mining methods, a Nave Bayes method, and a Logistic Regression method were thoroughly investigated for the vehicular data mining cloud system.

Pillmann et al. in [35] concentrated on estimating the accessible data rate by using an analytical method based on experiential measurements. A Common Vehicle Information Model (CVIM) is amalgamated with a vehicle simulator to generate CVIM compatible data streams, as a consequence of the individual behavior of each car (speed, the activity of steering, the activity of brake, and so on). Consequently, a novel vehicle-to-cloud communication framework has been developed, which measures the data rate of collected vehicle-to-cloud data generated by vehicles based on present traffic conditions (traffic jams and the free traffic flow).

Guldenring et al. in [36] presented a novel Multi-Radio Access Technology (Multi-RAT) sharing method which helps the vehicle sensors to upload data more efficiently and faster. This method makes use of various network interfaces and integrates them into a single coherent communication link. Data uploading may be postponed to take advantage of better channel conditions and prevent uploading when the quality of the channel is low. The simulation reports and assessments showed that the presented method is appropriate and efficient for vehicular data uploading.

3.4   Vehicle-to-Pedestrian (V2P)

Vulnerable Road Users (VRUs) include pedestrians, cyclists, and drivers of motorized two-wheelers. V2P is a general term that refers to all forms of communication between VRUs and vehicles. By implementing V2P for VRUs, they will become an active member of ITS and allow a variety of safety, comfort, and functionality ITS applications. Various traffic safety systems are introduced to enhance pedestrian safety to minimize VRUs fatalities. We will discuss some of them in the following.

Wu et al. in [37] developed a V2P platform for pedestrians based on DSRC. This system employs a smartphone as a VRU device and utilizes sensors of the smartphone to maximize the delivery of safety messages. The vehicle and the VRU device both transmit safety messages containing information about their direction, location, situation, distance, and speed.

Anaya et al. in [38] introduced a system that leverages iBeacon and Bluetooth technologies to notify vehicles about the existence of cyclists. The vehicle is provided with a V2X system which is equipped with a Bluetooth interface. The iBeacon notifications sent by cyclists can be received by that Bluetooth interface.

He et al. in [39] proposed a generalized system that consists of a responsive control mechanism, a stochastic model, and generic V2P communication scenarios (that were suggested for improving pedestrian safety). The responsive control model was used to enhance the safety of pedestrians under V2P communication circumstances. The presented stochastic model formularized multiple consequences of uncertainty in a V2P communication network. The results revealed that using either wireless local area network (Wi-Fi) or Bluetooth technologies with a long installation time is insufficient for V2P communication, while DSRC satisfies the requirements and has low latencies. In conclusion, by using the presented method and the responsive control method, DSRC incorporated with Bluetooth technology will be useful for effective pedestrian safety.

Zadeh et al. in [40] suggested a new warning-based system for protecting VRUs. This new system, which can be installed on the smartphone, utilizes

4G wireless communication and GPS technology for implementation. The system includes three steps: activation, forecasting, and alert step. The zone for sending alerts is limited during the activation step. The forecasting step recognizes the danger of a crash based on effective factors such as car and pedestrian speeds, car acceleration, driver reflex time, and time of collision of the vehicle and pedestrian. A fuzzy inference algorithm is used in the alert step to categorize real situations into low, middle, and high warnings depending on the severity of threats. These alerts lead to circumstances of no danger, being cautious, and braking, respectively.

4 Discussion

According to the aforementioned methods, there are many efforts to design more efficient V2X communication approaches. In this work some of them have been discussed based on their characteristics.

V2V enables vehicles to quickly transfer and receive information and messages, resulting in a perfect "awareness" of all vehicles in the vicinity. The range of communication signals is around 300 m, and they can detect hazards that are hidden by terrain, traffic, or weather. V2I minimizes traffic congestion and maximizes the utility of established infrastructure and facilities. The data aggregated and produced by the smart infrastructure can be used to effectively predict and model the traffic flow in real-time and in the context of long-term requirements. Onboard systems can send data to a server over a cellular network by using V2N communication. Based on the obtained data, the server produces a virtual environment, processes it using some developed frameworks, and transmits it to the connected cars and vehicles. V2P includes a direct connection between VRUs and vehicles which are close together. V2P is carried out directly or through utilizing network substructure. It can make it easier to warn pedestrians about arriving vehicles and to warn vehicles about VRUs' existence. The identified V2X scenarios and related Key Performance Indicators are summarized and shown in Table 2, which is extracted from those works that we have investigated in this paper.

Table 2. Configuration of the major V2X fragments

V2X category	Communication type	Latency	Data rate	Reliability
Safety and traffic efficiency	V2V,V2P	100 ms	Not a concern	Not yet explicated
Autonomous driving	V2V,V2N,V2I	1 ms	10 Mb/s	Nearly 100%
Teleoperator driving	V2N	20 ms (end-to-end)	25 Mb/s	99.999%
Vehicular internet and infotainment	V2N	100 ms (for web browsing)	0.5 Mb/s up to 15 Mb/s	Not a concern
Remote diagnostic and management	V2I, V2N	Not a concern	Not a concern	Not a concern

5   Conclusion

VANET is an important and new research topic with innovations in the vehicle industries and wireless networks. VANET communications paradigms have a promising future in smart transportation systems. Recently, V2X paradigms have been considered by many researchers who have been trying to propose more efficient and improved algorithms for them. What V2X technology adds to the autonomous driving system is safety and efficiency, as it constructs communication between vehicles, infrastructure, etc. Some survey papers have been published in the context of V2X communication scenarios, but it is hard to find an article that covers all scenarios together. Hence with this motivation, we decided to investigate all V2X communication paradigms together in a single paper. In this work, we reviewed some of the most important algorithms about V2V, V2I, V2N, and V2P scenarios and we discussed their positive and negative points. Several applications and challenges in this area have been investigated as well. V2X technology helps us to make roads safer, increase traffic and fuel efficiency, and decrease the number of car accidents, fatalities, and injuries. Many research works have been done in these areas, particularly about V2V and V2I algorithms, but there are still a lot of things to be done.

References

1. Kwatirayo, S., Almhana, J., Liu, Z.: Adaptive traffic light control using VANET: a case study. In: 9th International Wireless Communications and Mobile Computing Conference (IWCMC) on Proceedings, Sardinia, Italy, pp. 752–757. IEEE (2013)
2. Bouk, S.H., Ahmed, S.H., Kim, D.: Vehicular content centric network (VCCN): a survey and research challenges. In: 30th Annual ACM Symposium on Applied Computing on Proceedings, Salamanca, Spain, pp. 695–700. ACM (2015)
3. Bouk, S.H., Ahmed, S.H., Kim, D., Song, H.: Named-data-networking-based ITS for smart cities. IEEE Commun. Mag. **55**(1), 105–111 (2017)
4. Ferreira, M., Fernandes, R., Conceição, H., Viriyasitavat, W., Tonguz, O.K.: Self-organized traffic control. In: ACM 7th International Workshop on Vehicular Internetworking on Proceedings, pp. 85–90, Chicago, USA. ACM Digital Library (2010)
5. Wang, J., Shao, Y., Ge, Y., Yu, R.: A survey of vehicle to everything (v2x) testing. Sensors **19**(2), 334 (2019)
6. Kenney, J.B.: Dedicated short-range communications (DSRC) standards in the United States. Proc. IEEE **99**(7), 1162–1182 (2011)
7. Araniti, G., Campolo, C., Condoluci, M., Iera, A., Molinaro, A.: LTE for vehicular networking: a survey. IEEE Commun. Mag. **51**(5), 148–157 (2013)
8. Toukabri, T., Said, A.M., Abd-Elrahman, E., Afifi, H.: Cellular Vehicular Networks (CVN): ProSe-based ITS in advanced 4G networks. In: IEEE 11th International Conference on Mobile Ad Hoc and Sensor Systems (MASS) on Proceedings, Philadelphia, USA, pp. 28–30. IEEE (2014)
9. Feng, Y., He, D., Niu, L., Yang, M., Guan, Y.: The overview of Chinese cooperative intelligent transportation system; vehicular communication; application layer specification and data exchange standard. In: 2nd International Conference on Information Technology and Intelligent Transportation Systems (ITITS) on Proceedings, Beijing, China, pp. 528–616. Springer (2017)

10. Hamida, E.B., Noura, H., Znaidi, W.: Security of cooperative intelligent transport systems: standards, threats analysis and cryptographic countermeasures. Electronics **4**(3), 380–423 (2015)
11. Karagiannis, G., Altintas, O., Ekici, E., Heijenk, G., Jarupan, B., Lin, K., Weil, K.: Vehicular networking: a survey and tutorial on requirements, architectures, challenges, standards and solutions. IEEE Commun. Surv. Tutorials **13**(4), 584–616 (2011)
12. Chen, S., Hu, J., Shi, Y., Zhao, L.: LTE-V: a TD-LTE-based V2X solution for future vehicular network. IEEE Internet Things J. **3**(6), 997–1005 (2016)
13. RoselinMary, S., Maheshwari, M., Thamaraiselvan, M.: Early detection of DOS attacks in VANET using Attacked Packet Detection Algorithm (APDA). In: International Conference on Information Communication and Embedded Systems (ICICES) on Proceedings, Chennai, India, pp. 237–240. IEEE (2013)
14. Mejri, M.N., Ben-Othman, J., Hamdi, M.: Survey on VANET security challenges and possible cryptographic solutions. Veh. Commun. **1**(2), 53–66 (2014)
15. Gross, J., Punyal, O., Pereira, C., Aguiar, A.: Experimental characterization and modeling of RF jamming attacks on VANETs. IEEE Trans. Veh. Technol. **64**(2), 524–540 (2015)
16. Al-Terri, D., Otrok, H., Barada, H., Al-Qutayri, M., Al Hammadi, Y.: Cooperative based tit-for-tat strategies to retaliate against greedy behavior in VANETs. Comput. Commun. **104**(15), 108–118 (2017)
17. Ghosal, A., Conti, M.: Security issues and challenges in V2X: A survey. Comput. Netw. **169**, Article 107093 (2020)
18. Hasrouny, H., Samhat, A.E., Bassil, C., Laouiti, A.: VANet security challenges and solutions: a survey. Veh. Commun. **7**(1), 7–20 (2017)
19. Anaya, J.J., Talavera, E., Jimenez, F., Zato, J.G., Gomez, N., Naranjo, J.E.: GeoNetworking based V2V mesh communications over WSN. In: 16th International IEEE Conference on Intelligent Transportation Systems (ITSC) on Proceedings, The Hague, The Netherlands, pp. 2421–2426. IEEE (2013)
20. Dong, E., Zhang, L.: Vehicle stability control system of emergency brake on split-mu road. In: 9th International Conference on Intelligent Human-Machine Systems and Cybernetics (IHMSC) on Proceedings, Hangzhou, China, pp. 252–255. IEEE (2017)
21. Tornell, S.M., Patra, S., Calafate, C.T., Cano, J., Manzoni, P.: A novel on-board unit to accelerate the penetration of ITS services. In: 13th IEEE Annual Consumer Communications Networking Conference (CCNC) on Proceedings, Las Vegas, USA, pp. 467–472. IEEE (2016)
22. Boban, M., d'Orey, P.M.: Exploring the practical limits of cooperative awareness in vehicular communications. IEEE Trans. Veh. Technol. **65**(6), 3904–3916 (2016)
23. Ali, G.G.M.N., Noor-A-Rahim, M., Rahman, M.A., Samantha, S.K., Chong, P.H.J., Guan, Y.L.: Efficient real-time coding-assisted heterogeneous data access in vehicular networks. IEEE Internet Things J. **5**(5), 3499–3512 (2018)
24. Ali, G.G.M.N., Noor-A-Rahim, M., Chong, P.H.J., Guan, Y.L.: Analysis and improvement of reliability through coding for safety message broadcasting in urban vehicular networks. IEEE Trans. Veh. Technol. **67**(8), 6774–6787 (2018)
25. Azimi, S.R., Bhatia, G., Rajkumar, R., Mudalige, P.: Vehicular networks for collision avoidance at intersections. SAE Int. J. Passeng. Cars-Mech. Syst. **4**(1), 406–416 (2011)

26. Sepulcre, M., Gozalvez, J.: Experimental evaluation of cooperative active safety applications based on V2V communications. In: 9th ACM International Workshop on Vehicular Inter-Networking. Systems, and Applications on Proceedings, Low Wood Bay Lake District, UK, pp. 13–20. ACM (2012)
27. Boban, M., D'Orey P.M.: Measurement-based evaluation of cooperative awareness for V2V and V2I communication. In: IEEE Vehicular Networking Conference (VNC) on Proceedings, Paderborn, Germany pp. 1–8. IEEE (2014)
28. Bazzi, A., Zanella, A., Masini, B.M.: A distributed virtual traffic light algorithm exploiting short range V2V communications. Ad Hoc Netw. **49**(1), 42–57 (2016)
29. Sepulcre, M., Gozalvez, J., Altintas, O., Kremo, H.: Context-aware heterogeneous V2I communications. In: 7th International Workshop on Reliable Networks Design and Modeling (RNDM) on Proceedings, Munich, Germany, pp. 295–300. IEEE (2015)
30. Wuthishuwong, C., Traechtler, A., Bruns, T.: Safe trajectory planning for autonomous intersection management by using vehicle to infrastructure communication. EURASIP J. Wirel. Commun. Netw. **2015**(1), 1–12 (2015). https://doi.org/10.1186/s13638-015-0243-3
31. Mohammed, M., Ke, Y., Gao, J., Zhang, H., El-Basyouny, K., Qiu, T.Z: Connected vehicle V2I communication application to enhance driver awareness at signalized intersections. In: 11th International Transportation Specialty Conference (CSCE) on Proceedings, London, UK, pp. 1–12. CSCE (2016)
32. Gheorghiu, R.A., Minea, M.: Energy-efficient solution for vehicle prioritisation employing ZigBee V2I communications. In: International Conference on Applied and Theoretical Electricity (ICATE) on Proceedings, Craiova, Romania, pp. 1–6. IEEE (2016)
33. Al-qutwani, M., Wang, X.: Smart traffic lights over vehicular named data networking. Information **10**(3), 83 (2019)
34. He, W., Yan, G., Xu, L.D.: Developing vehicular data cloud services in the IoT environment. IEEE Trans. Indus. Inform. **10**(2), 1587–1595 (2014)
35. Pillmann, J., Sliwa, B., Schmutzler, J., Ide, C., Wietfeld, C.: Car-to-Cloud Communication Traffic Analysis Based on the Common Vehicle Information Model. In: IEEE 85th Vehicular Technology Conference (VTC) on Proceedings, Sydney, Australia, pp. 1–5. IEEE (2017)
36. Guldenring, J., Wietfeld, C.: Scalability analysis of context-aware multi-RAT Car-to-Cloud communication. In: IEEE 92nd Vehicular Technology Conference (VTC2) on Proceedings, Victoria, Canada, pp. 1–6. IEEE (2020)
37. Wu, X., et al.: Cars talk to phones: a DSRC based vehicle-pedestrian safety system. In: 80th Vehicular Technology Conference (VTC) on Proceedings, Vancouver, Canada, pp. 14–17. IEEE (2014)
38. Anaya, J.J., Talavera, E., Giménez, D., Gómez, N., Jiménez, F., Naranjo, J.E.: Vulnerable road users detection using V2X communications. In: 18th International Conference on Intelligent Transportation Systems on Proceedings, Las Palmas, Spain, pp. 107–112. IEEE (2015)
39. He, S., Li, J., Qiu, T.Z.: Vehicle-to-pedestrian communication modeling and collision avoiding method in connected vehicle environment. Transp. Res. Rec. **2621**(1), 21–30 (2017)
40. Zadeh, R.B., Ghatee, M., Eftekhari, H.R.: Three-phases smartphone-based warning system to protect vulnerable road users under fuzzy conditions. IEEE Trans. Intell. Transp. Syst. **19**(7), 2086–2098 (2018)

Privacy-Preserving Credit Scoring via Functional Encryption

Lorenzo Andolfo[1], Luigi Coppolino[1], Salvatore D'Antonio[1],
Giovanni Mazzeo[1(✉)], Luigi Romano[1], Matthew Ficke[2], Arne Hollum[2],
and Darshan Vaydia[2]

[1] Department of Engineering, University of Naples 'Parthenope', Naples, Italy
{lorenzo.andolfo,luigi.coppolino,salvatore.dantonio,giovanni.mazzeo,
luigi.romano}@uniparthenope.it
[2] X-Margin Inc., 141 Nantucket Cove, San Rafael, CA 94901, USA
{matthew,arne,darshan}@xmargin.io

Abstract. The majority of financial organizations managing confidential data are aware of security threats and leverage widely accepted solutions (e.g., storage encryption, transport-level encryption, intrusion detection systems) to prevent or detect attacks. Yet these hardening measures do little to face even worse threats posed on *data-in-use*. Solutions such as Homomorphic Encryption (HE) and hardware-assisted Trusted Execution Environment (TEE) are nowadays among the preferred approaches for mitigating this type of threats. However, given the high-performance overhead of HE, financial institutions —whose processing rate requirements are stringent— are more oriented towards TEE-based solutions. The *X-Margin Inc.* company, for example, offers secure financial computations by combining the Intel SGX TEE technology and HE-based *Zero-Knowledge Proofs*, which shield customers' *data-in-use* even against *malicious insiders*, i.e., users having privileged access to the system. Despite such a solution offers strong security guarantees, it is constrained by having to trust Intel and by the SGX hardware extension availability. In this paper, we evaluate a new frontier for *X-Margin*, i.e., performing privacy-preserving credit risk scoring via an emerging cryptographic scheme: *Functional Encryption (FE)*, which allows a user to only learn a function of the encrypted data. We describe how the *X-Margin* application can benefit from this innovative approach and —most importantly— evaluate its performance impact.

Keywords: Credit scoring · Data privacy · Functional encryption · Machine learning

1 Introduction

Data confidentiality has significant relevance in the financial field. The disclosure of sensitive information such as credit scoring or exchange apikeys, can lead to, e.g., learn about users' credit risk —and therefore decide whether to lend money— or ultimately money theft. A data breach inevitably leads to serious consequences

© Springer Nature Switzerland AG 2021
O. Gervasi et al. (Eds.): ICCSA 2021, LNCS 12956, pp. 31–43, 2021.
https://doi.org/10.1007/978-3-030-87010-2_3

affecting the reputation of the financial institution. The importance of cyber-security is even more crucial for the cryptocurrency industry, whose current valuation —1.8\$ trillion in 2021— attracts a rapidly increasing number of hackers. Only in the last two years, four large hacks occurred in the digital currency space[1].

Companies are therefore pushing on equipping their platforms with state-of-the-art security mechanisms. There are widely accepted solutions such as storage encryption, transport-level encryption, intrusion detection systems, firewalls, IP white-listing, which are used and help in preventing common cyber-attacks. However, there are still open issues —especially in terms of *data-in-use* protection against privileged attackers (e.g., a *malicious insider*)— that requires more advanced approaches. Companies aim for methods where the customer does not need to trust them. There are technologies and cryptography schemes that can be leveraged for this purpose. In this regard, the adoption of hardware-assisted Trusted Execution Environments (TEE) (e.g., Intel SGX) [15] and Homomorphic Encryption (HE) [12] is making its way into the industrial community to ensure this kind of protection. HE is extremely powerful since it enables arbitrary computations on ciphered data and allows the user to trust no one. A TEE such as SGX provides also strong security guarantees enabling the execution of sensitive code in an isolated and measurable area of CPUs, with the only limitation that the user needs to trust the hardware manufacturers such as Intel and that the application's state is sealed in the hardware [6]. Unfortunately, the exclusive use of HE is not doable since it is affected by a non-negligible execution time overhead, and by a large cipher text expansion. Moreover, a major problem of HE is the so-called unverifiable conditional issue, which forces a program running on a third-party host, and processing homomorphically encrypted data, to request that a client decrypts intermediate functional results to proceed further in the execution [7]. This introduces additional synchronization points and performance overhead, and increases the risk of information disclosure (e.g. via side channel analysis of the program workflow). For this reason, the trend for the majority of financial companies is to prefer TEEs.

The *X-Margin Inc.*[2] company, instead, uses both security mechanisms. It offers secure credit risk scoring by shielding computations in Intel SGX enclaves and performs HE-based *Zero-Knowledge Proofs* to offer cryptographic Proof of Security, Computation and Encrypted Input. In this paper, we explore an innovative approach for *X-Margin* which would allow to replace the use of SGX, thus removing Intel from the chain-of-trust and being hardware agnostic: *Functional Encryption* (FE) [5]. This is a cryptographic scheme similar to HE that does both evaluation and decryption of the *result of a function* at the same time, without leaking the private key for data decryption and without leaking information about the plaintexts. This means that —unlike HE— there is no need anymore of doing synchronizations between the client and the computation entity for intermediate results. In a FE model, there are special "evaluation keys" that only allow the functional evaluation of ciphered data. An additional advantage given

---

[1] https://www.investopedia.com/news/largest-cryptocurrency-hacks-so-far-year/.
[2] https://xmargin.io/.

by the FE scheme is that it enables *Attribute-based encryption* (ABE) schemes, where the encrypted data is linked with a set of attributes and secret keys along with certain policies that allow to control which ciphertexts can be decrypted depending on the possessed attributes. Unlike the classical encryption systems, where *"access to the encrypted data is all or nothing, one can either decrypt and read the entire plain or one learns nothing at all about the plain other than its length"*, FE tries to change this paradigm allowing a more fine-grained access to encrypted data and improving its flexibility. We describe how FE can be leveraged for *X-Margin* financial computations and —most importantly— evaluate the performance impact of this innovative scheme. We overview a solution that computes credit risk from an encrypted borrower's data with the FE, thus preserving data privacy in a cloud environment even from the company itself. As a first step, we implemented an ad-hoc neural network for the purpose of credit risk scoring, which acts as a binary classifier saying whether a loan defaults. The training is conducted on a plain dataset. The resulting weight configuration downstream the training step is saved for the second step. We built the functional encryption scheme using the weights configuration obtained during the first step. We used a symmetric private key quadratic multivariate polynomial scheme called SGP [8]. As from the definition of functional encryption, the result of decryption is not the record itself, but the evaluation of a function of it, that is represented by the credit risk associated to the borrower. At the end, we computed the credit risk via two FE functions: one that computes the score to say whether the borrower defaults, and the other one that computes the score whether the borrower doesn't default. Then, the final result is normalized among the scores in order to provide the probability of default. Results from experimental evaluation show that the FE entails a non-negligible overhead on the classification time. Using 20 attributes, the application took 17.3 s to compute the score with 200 borrowers in the system. It is important to notice that the scoring classification job is highly parallelizable, thus performance can be improved using multiple nodes.

The rest of this paper is organized as follows: In Sect. 2, we provide a background on credit scoring and on the FE scheme. Afterwards, in Sect. 3, the X-Margin case study is presented. In Sect. 4, the architecture of the proposed solution is discussed. Section 5 presents results from the experimental evaluation. Finally, Sect. 6 concludes the document.

2 Background

In this section, we provide a background on the two main elements covered in this work, i.e., credit scoring and functional encryption.

2.1 Principles of Credit Scoring

Credit scoring is a method that is historically used by banks to estimate the risk of lending money to an individual. It determines the ability of a person to repay the debts. The higher is the credit score, the higher is the probability of obtaining a loan with low interest rates. On the other hand, people with a lower credit score must pay higher interest rates on their loans. The process of giving a loan is influenced by many factors: characteristics of borrowers in terms of who they are, their economic situation, the amount of the requested loan, its purpose, and the collateral type. The risk is estimated using elements of quantitative and qualitative analysis. The quantitative analysis takes into account an assessment of the financial standing of customers. It could also consider cash flow analysis of customers' accounts together with their credit history. While the qualitative assessment includes other information such as the education, employment, industry in which they operate, or the way of keeping accounts.

2.2 Fundamentals of Functional Encryption

Functional encryption (FE) is relatively a new encryption technique, which was introduced by Amit Sahai and Brent Water in 2008 [16]. FE enables selective access control of sensitive data d basing on specific functions $f(d)$. In an FE scheme, a decryption key $sfKey(f)$ is associated with the function f. Therefore, the decryption of an encrypted data d through $sfKey(f)$, provides the function evaluation $f(d)$, and nothing more about d. Concerning differences between FE and FHE, from one side they result similar, because once the message has been encrypted, both evaluate a function of the message. However, FHE suffers from to the additional step of decrypting the evaluation of the function, since the result of its computation is still an encrypted result. With FE instead, the result of the decryption already represents the evaluation of the function. FE has been successfully applied to cloud environments and to obfuscation mechanisms [9], that can be useful for example to protect intellectual property. Unfortunately, up to now, industries seldom adopt such advanced cryptography technologies: the majority of cryptography technologies used by industries were developed in early 2000s [14]. Only recently, thanks to the ambitious project FENTEC (Functional ENcryption TEChnologies)[3], there has been a tentative to propose FE solutions for privacy preserving in a wide range of sectors from clinical data[4], to public transportation[5].

There are several types of schemes that can be assimilated to the FE, these are: attribute-based encryption (ABE) [3,10,13], identity-based encryption (IBE) [4], the ones that implement inner product functions [1,2] and nonlinear (at most quadratic) polynomials. In this work, the focus is on a symmetric private key FE scheme called SGP, that implements a two dimensional quadratic polynomial function.

$$f(x,y): \sum_{i=1,j=1}^{m,n} f_{i,j}x_iy_j = \underset{1\times m}{X^T} \cdot \underset{m\times n}{F} \cdot \underset{n\times 1}{Y} \tag{1}$$

---

[3] https://fentec.eu/.
[4] https://github.com/fentec-project/Selective-Access-to-Clinical-Data.
[5] https://github.com/fentec-project/FE-anonymous-heatmap.

Here, X and Y represents the vectors we want to encrypt, while F is a custom matrix. The result of decryption in this case will be the evaluation of the function above.

Regarding security, it provides an adaptive security under chosen-plaintext attacks (IND-CPA security) which is based on bilinear pairings, with the following primitives:

1. $msk \leftarrow GenerateMasterKey()$: generates a secret key for the SGP scheme.
2. $c \leftarrow Encrypt(X, Y, msk)$: encrypts input vectors X and Y with the secret key msk and returns the appropriate ciphertext c.
3. $feKey \leftarrow DeriveKey(msk, F)$: given in input a custom matrix F and the secret key msk, derives the FE key $feKey$.
4. $X^T \cdot F \cdot Y \leftarrow Decrypt(c, feKey, F)$: given in input the ciphertext c the FE key $feKey$ and the custom matrix F, gets the evaluation of $f(x, y)$ that is $X^T \cdot F \cdot Y$.

3   The X-Margin Case Study

X-Margin Inc. provides privacy-preserving credit scoring in the crypto-currency credit market. With over \$100B of crypto-collateral being used to generate over \$1.25B of interest on a quarterly basis, credit is one of the most rapidly growing sectors of the emerging crypto-currency finance ecosystem. *X-Margin* allows borrowers to supply lenders with real-time portfolio risk metrics, while preserving the privacy of trades, positions, and other sensitive information. Borrowers benefit from improved lending terms, as they can display their risk in real-time and assure lenders they are trading responsibly. Lenders benefit from increased visibility and real-time information. *X-Margin* calculates a variety of Risk Metrics on each user's portfolio, including Equity, Balance, Margin Usage, Maximum Loss (SPAN or VaR calculations), Aggregate absolute Delta, and the company uses Zero Knowledge technology to ensure that the credit scoring system is functioning in an unbiased and privacy preserving way, and as the users expect.

X-Margin leverages TEE technologies, along with HE-based cryptographic Proof of Security, Computation and Encrypted Input, to ensure the privacy of users' sensitive data and guarantee risk analysis. Intel Software Guard Extensions (SGX), is the enabling TEE technology that is currently used to protect and attest the sensitive computations. SGX is a recent extension of modern CPUs, which ensures confidentiality even against super-privileged users running as *root*. *X-Margin* uses HE-based schemes for Proof of Computation including a Proof of Encrypted Input. Together, the proofs demonstrate that a given function being executed within the SGX enclave corresponds exactly to a symbolic representation stored in the server, outside the enclave —the untrusted 'host'— and that the data on which the function operates is received encrypted from an external source. *X-Margin* proves that the functions the system is instructed to run are run in the enclave, without revealing the functions themselves. The Proof of Computation & Encrypt ed Input uses the Enhanced Skyline protocol, which is a proprietary protocol developed by *X-Margin*'s team of cryptographers. Figure 1 shows the current architecture of the *X-Margin* solution. There is a SGX-based Key Management System (KMS) that holds users' apikeys, and a CScore unit where the actual private computation takes place, protected by the SGX secure enclave, and proven by cryptographic proofs. It queries spot/derivative exchanges and provide risk score metrics to a Time Series Database (TSDB).

The goal of the company is to further improve their solution by raising the concept of *trust* to a higher level. In the current situation, in fact, its customers must trust the hardware manufacturer, i.e., *Intel*. It would be ideal for the company to remove also Intel from the *chain-of-trust*. Furthermore, in the current status, the credit scoring application is strictly bounded to a particular hardware where the SGX ISA extension —and the related motherboard support— is available. This also entails migration constraints because the application's state is sealed in the hardware. *X-Margin*'s R&D is therefore exploring new innovative security techniques to cope with the mentioned limitations.

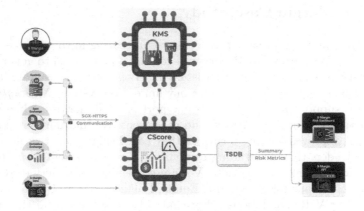

Fig. 1. The *X-Margin* architecture

4   The FE-Based Credit Scoring Solution

The functional encryption paradigm represents an opportunity to overcome limitations posed by the SGX-based credit scoring solution. It ensures security properties similar to HE but with the advantage that it allows to learn specific functions of the encrypted data. Overall, the FE-based credit scoring works as follows. In a first phase, the neural network is trained leveraging plain datasets in *X-Margin*'s premises. This is acceptable since the training process does not use any customers' sensitive data but it is conducted on anonymous data. At the end of this learning phase, coefficients needed to compute the credit risk of a given borrower are obtained. These are then used to generate keys. In this regard, according to the FE scheme principles, a trusted *key authority* receives the coefficients and generates two types of keys, i.e.: public/private keys for the encryption/decryption of data, and operational keys needed to perform the functional computation on encrypted data, which can only be used to decrypt the result of the computation but not the data itself. At the end of this phase, the *X-Margin* credit scoring application is finally configured. From now on, the customer will encrypt the data along with the public keys received by the authority. The ciphered information is then sent to the untrusted *X-Margin* premises running on cloud. Here, the credit risk associated to the borrower is computed on ciphered data. It is important to notice that the computation of the credit risk associated to the borrower does not include any confidential borrower's data. Only the result of this computation (i.e., the scoring evaluation) will be accessible to *X-Margin*.

4.1 Architecture

Figure 2 shows the overall architecture of the FE-based credit scoring solution, together with the steps performed during normal functioning.

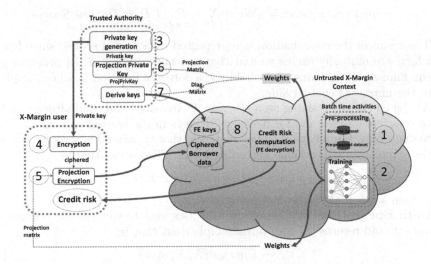

Fig. 2. The credit risk score architecture

1. **Data pre-processing**: At startup, *X-Margin* performs a pre-processing activity on the data-set that will be used during the training phase. Modifications to the dataset are needed to adapt the subsequent computation to the FE requirements, and also to improve the accuracy of the neural network model, such as:
   (a) Removes columns and rows containing null values, discard columns with a high percentage of null values, as well as rows with null values inside.
   (b) Removes outliers.
   (c) Adapt timestamps
   (d) Scales and normalizes columns.

(e) Replaces object columns with dummy variables and one-hot encodes the output.
(f) Transform data in integer form in order to ensure compatibility with the FE scheme properties,

2. **Neural Network Training:** In this phase, the training phase takes place using clear data. This is acceptable given that the leveraged dataset contains anonymous entries. An ad-hoc neural network was defined. We leveraged and adapted the *Adam optimization algorithm*, with a learning rate of 10^{-4} and a batch size of 32. Training epochs have been set to 50. The neural network has a single hidden layer and its activation layer is represented by a *square element-wise*, instead of *sigmoid*. This choice will be better explained in the rest of this section.

Let $\underset{1\times n}{X}$ be our input vector, that is the borrower's record, $\underset{n\times d}{Pr}$ be the weight matrix of the first layer and $\underset{d\times l}{D}$ be the weight matrix of the hidden layer. In our case, $n = 130$, $d = 20$ and $l = 2$. The output of the neural network is:

$$prediction : \text{squareElemWise}(\underset{1\times n}{X} \cdot \underset{n\times d}{Pr}) \cdot \underset{d\times l}{D} = \underset{1\times l}{DefaultScores}.$$

The result of the classification is represented by a pair of scores, since $l = 2$, which are mutually exclusive and that are not normalized. In order to get the final result in terms of probability, a softmax function has been applied in the untrusted context side.

At the end of the training step, Pr and D are saved and used afterwards for the encryption task and for deriving FE keys in the trusted context.

3. **Secret Key Generation.** The trusted authority generates a secret key for the symmetric SGP scheme according to the FE scheme, that is:

$$msk \leftarrow GenerateMasterKey() \tag{2}$$

It then sends msk to the *X-Margin* user.

4. **Data Encryption.** The X-margin user uses msk to encrypt the borrower's data X and returns the appropriate ciphertext that is:

$$c \leftarrow Encrypt(X, X, msk) \tag{3}$$

Here, respect to the classical SGP scheme, we have replaced the parameter Y by X.

5. **Encryption Projection.** The *X-Margin* user takes the encryption c and weight matrix Pr obtained at step 2 to produce a projection of c, that is:

$$ProjC \leftarrow projectEncryption(c, Pr) \tag{4}$$

$ProjC$ represents the encryption of $(Pr \cdot X)$, that is sent to the untrusted context.

6. **Secret Key Projection.** The trusted authority takes the secret key msk obtained at step 3 and the weight matrix Pr obtained at step 2 to get a projection of the secret key:

$$ProjSecKey \leftarrow projectSecKey(msk, Pr) \tag{5}$$

$ProjSecKey$ represents the secret key for encryption of $(Pr \cdot X)$.

7. **FE Key Generation.** The trusted authority provides also the FE keys to the untrusted party to compute the credit risk of the borrower. There are two FE keys: one used to decrypt the score of default and one used to decrypt the score of not default of the borrower. Therefore, each FE key is used to decrypt a different output i of the neural network:

$$feKey_i \leftarrow DeriveKey(ProjSecKey, Diag_i) \forall i \in l \qquad (6)$$

$DeriveKey$ accepts as parameter the secret key $ProjSecKey$, obtained at the previous step, and the diagonal matrix $Diag_i$, that is the diagonalized version of D_i, that represents the $i - th$ row of the matrix D. It should be noted that D_i is the vector containing the weights connected to a single label. Then, the trusted authority sends the obtained FE keys to the untrusted context.

8. **Credit Score Computation.** The untrusted context, computes the credit risk scores of the borrower through the FE key provided by the trusted authority at the previous step. This means that for each label i it evaluates the function of $(Pr \cdot X)$, that is $(Pr \cdot X)^T \cdot Diag_i \cdot (Pr \cdot X)$. In order to do that, it exploits the following decryption primitive of the SGP scheme:

$$defaultScore_i = (Pr \cdot X)^T \cdot Diag_i \cdot (Pr \cdot X) \qquad (7)$$
$$\leftarrow Decrypt(ProjC, feKey_i, Diag_i) \forall i \in l$$

For each label i, $Decrypt$ accepts $ProjC$, that as we saw represents the encryption of $(Pr \cdot X)$ sent by the $X\text{-}Margin$ user, the derived FE key $feKey_i$ and the diagonal matrix $Diag_i$ sent by the trusted authority.

Since $l = 2$, there are two functions: one that computes the score that the borrower defaults and one that he/she doesn't default. Such scores can be seen as mutually exclusive, therefore we can apply the soft max function on them in order to normalize the results and obtain the related probabilities.

$$DefaultProbabilities_{1 \times l} = \text{softMax}(Scores_{1 \times l}) \qquad (8)$$

Finally, the untrusted context sends back to the $X\text{-}Margin$ user the score obtained at 8.

4.2 Details on the FE Scheme for Credit Risk Scoring

The aim of this section is to draw connections between the neural network output function provided at 2 and the FE function at 1, so as to understand what is the information needed to build the FE scheme.

Given the FE function at 1, we can transform it from a multivariate to a single variable function.

$$f(k) : K^T_{1 \times d} \cdot F_{d \times d} \cdot K_{d \times 1} \qquad (9)$$

From the other side, we can see the neural network function at 2 as the result obtained for each single label:

$$defaultScore_i : \text{squareElemWise}(\underset{1\times n}{X} \cdot \underset{n\times d}{Pr}) \cdot \underset{d\times 1}{D_i} \forall i \in l. \qquad (10)$$

where D_i is a vector containing the weights connected to a single label i, X is the borrower's vector and Pr is the weight matrix associated to the first layer. Applying the following manipulation to each function i obtained in 10, it is possible to get the FE function at 9:

$$defaultScore_i : \text{squareElemWise}(X \cdot Pr) \cdot D_i \qquad (11)$$
$$= ((Pr)^T \cdot (X)^T)^T \cdot Diag_i \cdot ((Pr)^T \cdot (X)^T)$$
$$= K^T \cdot Diag_i \cdot K$$
$$\forall i \in l.$$

Here, we have transformed the first matrix product, switching the operands and applying the transpose on them. Indeed, we have removed the square element-wise operation on it and, in order to keep the equality we have replaced D_i with its diagonalized version $Diag_i$ and we have multiplied by the product $((Pr)^T \cdot (X)^T)$. Finally, we have replaced the products with the obtained vector K in order to highlight the equivalence with the 9. The custom matrix F is the diagonal matrix $Diag_i$ that is different for each label, while the other parts of the function don't change.

We have shown that such neural network architecture computes the FE function 9, for each label l. Each function has, as variable, the matrix product $((Pr)^T \cdot (X)^T)$ named K, and produces as output respectively the score that a borrower defaults and not. From now on $((Pr)^T \cdot (X)^T)$ will be indicated without the transpose operations inside, in order to not burden the discussion.

5   Experimental Performance Evaluation

We conducted an experimental evaluation of the privacy-preserving scoring solution. The goal was to estimate the performance overhead given by the adoption of the FE-based processing. More precisely, our focus was on the execution time needed to encrypt borrowers' data, and to compute the credit risk score, i.e., the evaluation of the functional decryption occurring on X-$Margin$ premises. These tests did not take into account the classification algorithm accuracy since our main goal is to focus on the sole performance.

We have evaluated our model on a Windows 10 machine equipped with an AMD Ryzen 3600X with 6-Core Processor at 3.80 GHz and 16 GB of RAM. Execution times (in ms) are the average of 5 repeated tests.

As a first experiment, we evaluated the encryption phase (i.e., steps 4 & 5) by increasing the number of users in the system up to 1000 borrowers, and also varying the number of borrowers' attributes (in the range [5,25]).

Figure 3 shows the outcomes of the evaluation. It can be noticed that the encryption is not significantly time consuming. The encryption of one borrower in what we defined the worst situation —i.e., characterized by 50 attributes— takes on average 52.3 ms, while in the best situation —i.e., 5 attributes— it takes 14.3 ms. The execution time increases linearly with the number of borrowers.

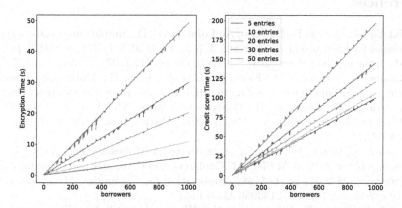

Fig. 3. Encryption and credit scoring performance

The second evaluation we made refers to the FE-based scoring computation time, which is critical for the actual usability of the proposed solution. It is important to notice that this operation includes both the actual functional computation and the final result decryption. Figure 3 shows that the overhead is significant, reaching in the worst condition —i.e., 50 attributes and 1000 users— a computation time of 170 s. It must be noticed that in real situations, the number of attributes is lower, in the order of 20. Nevertheless, performance are still not acceptable for the adoption in real contexts such as the *X-Margin* one. However, the type of job we implemented with FE is highly parallelizable, and the deployment on multiple nodes could make the adoption of the FE-based credit scoring solution acceptable.

6   Conclusion

In this paper, we presented an innovative solution for privacy-preserving credit risk scoring, which leverages the emerging *Functional Encryption* cryptography that allows to learn the result of a specific function using only encrypted data. We built a credit risk model using the quadratic polynomial FE symmetric scheme SGP for the X-Margin Inc. company, whose case study was used to validate the effectiveness of the proposed approach. Results from the experimental campaign show that the solution performs well under certain conditions, but the overhead needs to be properly managed in case of a real production deployment. We discovered that with a limited number of borrowers' attributes (e.g. < 20) the encryption time and the classification time are acceptable. Future developments of the current solution will be focused on improving performance by evaluating new public key quadratic schemes (e.g., [11]), and setting up a multi-node parallel architecture.

References

1. Abdalla, M., Bourse, F., De Caro, A., Pointcheval, D.: Simple functional encryption schemes for inner products. In: Katz, J. (ed.) PKC 2015. LNCS, vol. 9020, pp. 733–751. Springer, Heidelberg (2015). https://doi.org/10.1007/978-3-662-46447-2_33
2. Abdalla, M., Catalano, D., Fiore, D., Gay, R., Ursu, B.: Multi-input functional encryption for inner products: function-hiding realizations and constructions without pairings. In: Shacham, H., Boldyreva, A. (eds.) CRYPTO 2018. LNCS, vol. 10991, pp. 597–627. Springer, Cham (2018). https://doi.org/10.1007/978-3-319-96884-1_20
3. Agrawal, S., Chase, M.: Fame: fast attribute-based message encryption. In: Proceedings of the 2017 ACM SIGSAC Conference on Computer and Communications Security, CCS 2017, pp. 665–682. Association for Computing Machinery (2017). https://doi.org/10.1145/3133956.3134014
4. Boneh, D., Boyen, X.: Efficient selective-ID secure identity-based encryption without random Oracles. In: Cachin, C., Camenisch, J.L. (eds.) EUROCRYPT 2004. LNCS, vol. 3027, pp. 223–238. Springer, Heidelberg (2004). https://doi.org/10.1007/978-3-540-24676-3_14
5. Boneh, D., Sahai, A., Waters, B.: Functional encryption: definitions and challenges. In: Ishai, Y. (ed.) TCC 2011. LNCS, vol. 6597, pp. 253–273. Springer, Heidelberg (2011). https://doi.org/10.1007/978-3-642-19571-6_16
6. Campanile, F., et al.: Cloudifying critical applications: a use case from the power grid domain. In: 2017 25th Euromicro International Conference on Parallel, Distributed and Network-based Processing (PDP), pp. 363–370 (2017). https://doi.org/10.1109/PDP.2017.50
7. Coppolino, L., D'Antonio, S., Formicola, V., Mazzeo, G., Romano, L.: VISE: combining intel SGX and homomorphic encryption for cloud industrial control systems. IEEE Trans. Comput. **70**(5), 711–724 (2020). https://doi.org/10.1109/TC.2020.2995638
8. Dufour-Sans, E., Gay, R., Pointcheval, D.: Reading in the dark: classifying encrypted digits with functional encryption. Cryptology ePrint Archive, Report 2018/206 (2018). https://eprint.iacr.org/2018/206
9. Garg, S., Gentry, C., Halevi, S., Raykova, M., Sahai, A., Waters, B.: Candidate indistinguishability obfuscation and functional encryption for all circuits. SIAM J. Comput. **45**(3), 882–929 (2016)
10. Garg, S., Gentry, C., Halevi, S., Sahai, A., Waters, B.: Attribute-based encryption for circuits from multilinear maps. In: Canetti, R., Garay, J.A. (eds.) CRYPTO 2013. LNCS, vol. 8043, pp. 479–499. Springer, Heidelberg (2013). https://doi.org/10.1007/978-3-642-40084-1_27
11. Gay, R.: A new paradigm for public-key functional encryption for degree-2 polynomials. In: Kiayias, A., Kohlweiss, M., Wallden, P., Zikas, V. (eds.) PKC 2020. LNCS, vol. 12110, pp. 95–120. Springer, Cham (2020). https://doi.org/10.1007/978-3-030-45374-9_4

12. Gentry, C.: Fully homomorphic encryption using ideal lattices. In: Proceedings of the Forty-First Annual ACM Symposium on Theory of Computing, STOC 2009, New York, NY, USA, pp. 169–178. ACM (2009). https://doi.org/10.1145/1536414.1536440

13. Goyal, V., Pandey, O., Sahai, A., Waters, B.: Attribute-based encryption for fine-grained access control of encrypted data. In: Proceedings of the 13th ACM Conference on Computer and Communications Security, CCS 2006, New York, NY, USA, pp. 89–98. Association for Computing Machinery (2006). https://doi.org/10.1145/1180405.1180418

14. Green, M.: A few thoughts on cryptographic engineering. https://blog.cryptographyengineering.com/2017/07/02/beyond-public-key-encryption/ (2017)

15. McKeen, F., et al.: Innovative instructions and software model for isolated execution. In: Proceedings of the 2Nd International Workshop on Hardware and Architectural Support for Security and Privacy, New York, NY, USA, HASP 2013, pp. 10:1–10:1. ACM (2013). https://doi.org/10.1145/2487726.2488368

16. Sahai, A., Waters, B.: Slides on functional encryption. http://www.cs.utexas.edu/~bwaters/presentations/files/function.ppt (2008)

Privacy-Preserving Access
for Multi-Access Edge Computing (MEC)
Applications

Gizem Akman[1,2](✉)📶, Philip Ginzboorg[3,4]📶, and Valtteri Niemi[1,2]📶

[1] University of Helsinki, Helsinki, Finland
{gizem.akman,valtteri.niemi}@helsinki.fi
[2] Helsinki Institute for Information Technology (HIIT), Helsinki, Finland
[3] Huawei Technologies, Helsinki, Finland
philip.ginzboorg@huawei.com
[4] Aalto University, Helsinki, Finland

Abstract. Multi-Access Edge Computing (MEC) is one of the emerging key technologies in Fifth Generation (5G) Mobile Networks, providing reduced end-to-end latency for applications and reduced load in the transport network. This paper is about user privacy in MEC within 5G. We consider a basic MEC usage scenario, where the user accesses an application hosted in the MEC platform via the radio access network of the Mobile Network Operator (MNO). First, we create a system model based on this scenario, then define the adversary model and privacy requirements for this system model. Second, we introduce a privacy-preserving access solution for the system model and analyze the solution against the privacy requirements.

Keywords: MEC · 5G · Privacy · Unlinkability

1   Introduction and Related Work

The European Telecommunication Standards Institute (ETSI) initiated standardization for bringing cloud computing to the edge of the network in 2014. Since 2017 the name for this initiative is Multi-Access Edge Computing (MEC). Edge computing is described by the 3rd Generation Partnership Project (3GPP) as an enabling technology that hosts operator and third-party services near the access point of the user to provide efficient service with reduced end-to-end latency and load in transportation network [1]. MEC can be deployed either by Mobile Network Operator (MNO) or by private cloud service providers, such as Amazon AWS and Google [2]. Base stations and access points are some examples of possible deployment locations of MEC servers [3,4].

The Fifth Generation (5G) mobile networks are designed with the goal to provide improved quality of service and quality of experience compared to legacy networks. A 5G mobile network is expected to provide high bandwidth (e.g., 10 Gbps) and very low latency (e.g., 1 ms) at a low operational cost. It should also be able to

© Springer Nature Switzerland AG 2021
O. Gervasi et al. (Eds.): ICCSA 2021, LNCS 12956, pp. 44–59, 2021.
https://doi.org/10.1007/978-3-030-87010-2_4

serve a large number of Internet of Things (IoT) devices, which can communicate in real-time effectively and work reliably and affordably [5]. MEC is considered to be a key technology for 5G development as MEC provides an effective solution for the high demands of 5G [6].

MEC is already deployed in 4G [7], but the new architecture and new features of 5G support a new approach for MEC deployment in 5G architecture, as specified in [1]. The communication between MEC and 5G network is provided through the User Plane Function (UPF). A schematic illustration of the network after the deployment of MEC is shown in Fig. 1.

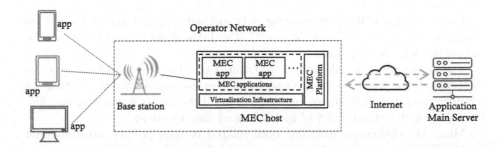

Fig. 1. Overview of network after deployment of MEC, adapted from [3,8].

Services that may be provided by the MEC applications include computational offloading, distributed content delivery and caching, IoT and big data, smart city services [2], and vehicle-to-everything (V2X) [9].

Privacy concerns arise because MEC usage involves a large amount of data that may be sensitive and personal. The MNO, MEC host, and MEC application may belong to different companies or they can belong to the same company. Regardless of the ownership, personal data related to the user is passing through MNO and MEC host towards the MEC application. Analysis of the data related to MEC application usage may be useful for various purposes. We discuss this issue further in Sect. 3.1.

We focus on three notions related to privacy: identity confidentiality, data confidentiality, and unlinkability.

Confidentiality, in general, is *"the act of preventing unauthorized entities from reading or accessing sensitive materials"* [10]. It is identity confidentiality if the sensitive material is the identity of the user. The user would have several identifiers for MNO and MEC application during the process of using the MEC application. These identifiers should be shared only with the parties who really need to know them. In addition, these identifiers should not be eavesdropped on during the communication on the radio access link [11].

International Mobile Subscriber Identity (IMSI) is the permanent identifier of the subscriber in a mobile network. In legacy mobile networks, the IMSI is sent over the radio access link as rarely as possible, and a randomly generated temporary identifier is sent instead. This randomly generated identifier is called

Temporary Mobile Subscriber Identity (TMSI) in 2G and 3G systems, and Globally Unique Temporary Identifier (GUTI) in the 4G system. In the 5G system, the temporary user identity is called 5G-GUTI, and the permanent user identity is called Subscription Permanent Identifier (SUPI). The 5G network never sends SUPI in the clear over the radio access link. Besides, the 5G system enhances user identity confidentiality with a mechanism, where SUPI can be encrypted by the User Equipment (UE) with the public key of the home network of the subscriber before the UE sends it over the radio access link [1, 12]. For simplicity, we will use the terms IMSI and TMSI to designate the permanent and the temporary identities of the mobile user in the rest of this paper, even when the discussion is about 5G.

Data confidentiality is *"protecting data against unintentional, unlawful, or unauthorized access, disclosure, or theft"* [13]. Data should be accessed only by the parties who actually need it.

The definition of unlinkability is given in [14]: *"unlinkability of two or more items of interest from an attacker's perspective means that within the system, the attacker cannot sufficiently distinguish whether these items are related or not"*. We focus on the unlinkability of messages and user identities.

Many 5G challenges, including ones related to user privacy, are presented in [15]. The survey [10] explains background information of MEC with security and privacy issues in MEC. The focus in [16] is on MEC for heterogeneous IoT. Privacy issues in MEC are identified, and machine learning privacy is examined for MEC. The survey [17] focuses on the security and privacy of 5G technologies, including MEC. In [18], privacy concerns related to cellular networks are raised, and a solution for protecting the network privacy of the mobile user by using MEC is provided.

Our ideas are related to the concepts of Virtual Private Network (VPN) and Onion Routing (OR). The VPN provides a private and secure channel over the public network. This secure channel is obtained by the tunneling protocol between two entities [19]. Onion Routing provides anonymous communication by routing encrypted traffic over several different routers [20].

Our system model is introduced in Sect. 2. We define the adversary model in Sect. 3. Then, we list requirements that will minimize the exposure of private data of the users in Sect. 4, and introduce a solution for privacy-preserving access to MEC applications in Sect. 5. We also show how the solution meets privacy requirements. The paper ends with the conclusion and future work in Sect. 6.

2   System Model

Our system model is based on the following scenario. Alice is a subscriber of a Mobile Network Operator, MNO. In the rest of the paper, Alice without quotes refers to the person while we denote her real name by "Alice". Alice wants to use a MEC application, which is called APPIFY. In order to use APPIFY, the messages of Alice should go through both the network of MNO and the MEC host. The traffics between Alice and the MNO network, between the MNO network and MEC host, and between the MEC host and APPIFY are secured. However, the MNO and the MEC host can see the message flow between Alice and APPIFY. Still, Alice wants to communicate with APPIFY without revealing the identity of APPIFY and the content of the messages to MNO. Alice also wants to be anonymous towards the MEC host. For example, the MEC host should not learn the IMSI of Alice.

We build an abstract model with the four parties involved in this scenario: Alice, MNO, MEC, and APPIFY. Please note that APPIFY represents a generic MEC application in the model, similarly as Alice takes the role of a generic user. This model is visualized in Fig. 2. Next, the elements of the model are described in more detail.

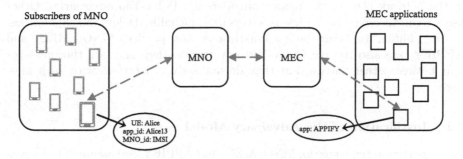

Fig. 2. Elements of the system model.

Mobile Network Operator (MNO) provides services to Alice and other subscribers. IMSI is the identifier of Alice for MNO. In addition to IMSI, MNO may know other information related to Alice, such as her phone number, home address, email address, social security number, etc.

Recall that the MEC host is deployed in MNO, and MEC applications are running in the MEC host. In our model, we call the MEC host simply as MEC. It transfers messages of users between MNO and MEC applications. During this process, MEC does not share any dedicated identifiers with users. Our model does not depend on any specifics of the 5G network, and it also applies to the 4G network.

APPIFY is one of the MEC applications in the MEC host. Typically, the data in the MEC application residing in the MEC host is synchronized regularly with the main server (see Fig. 1) to provide up-to-date service to its users [21]. Both Alice and APPIFY communicate with the main server of APPIFY when it is necessary. For simplicity, we do not include the main server of the application in our model.

There are many other subscribers in addition to Alice; similarly, there are many MEC applications in addition to APPIFY. From the point of view of Alice communicating with APPIFY, these other subscribers and MEC applications are outsiders.

3   Adversary Model

After defining the system model, we now move to security and privacy aspects. First, we identify potential types of adversaries relevant to the model. These types are honest-but-curious adversary and Dolev-Yao adversary.

Honest-but-curious adversary is defined as *"a legitimate participant in a communication protocol who will not deviate from the defined protocol but will attempt to learn all possible information from legitimately received messages"* [14]. In our scenario, we assume that MNO, MEC, and APPIFY are honest-but-curious adversaries. They are acting according to the protocol, but on the side, they are collecting information.

Dolev-Yao adversary can see, delete, replay, reroute, and reorder all messages in the network [22]. In the model, outsiders are Dolev-Yao adversaries. Other users than Alice may be malicious adversaries, including Dolev-Yao capabilities.

In addition to being honest-but-curious, the parties, MNO, MEC, and APPIFY, are also passive Dolev-Yao adversaries: they may see the messages sent between other parties, but they do not actively interfere with such messages.

3.1   Justification of the Adversary Model

Three parties in the scenario, MNO, MEC, and APPIFY, are assumed to be passive Dolev-Yao and honest-but-curious adversaries. They are passive Dolev-Yao because they are assumed to be able to see all the messages. However, they are honest and do not interfere in the communication by deleting, replaying, rerouting, and reordering the messages. It makes sense to assume that these parties are honest because they do business and provide services for their customers. If they misuse their powers, e.g., by selling customer data to third parties, it could be possible that this abnormal behavior is detected. As a result of the malicious action, they can get a bad reputation and lose the trust of the customers; an example case can be found in [23]. Therefore, they are likely to follow the rules.

MNO, MEC, and APPIFY can get curious about their customers while providing services to them. MNO and MEC carry messages between Alice and APPIFY. If MNO and MEC get curious, they can capture the messages they forward. They can learn how the customers use services, which services they prefer, how often they use these applications, and many other details related to customers. So they can analyze the needs of their clients. This analysis provides companies with an understanding of what customers want based on their previous behaviors [24]. Similarly, APPIFY may be interested to learn more about its customers than what they intentionally share with APPIFY.

Outsiders are full Dolev-Yao adversaries. An outsider is any party other than Alice, MNO, MEC, and APPIFY. Outsiders include other users that are subscribers of the same MNO or customers of APPIFY, or both. These other users could be malicious because anybody could get a subscription, and there typically is no reputation that could be lost either.

Alice is not an adversary in the model because it is her identities and data we try to protect.

4 Privacy Requirements

As explained in Sect. 2, Alice, MNO, MEC, and APPIFY are the parties of the system model. Alice is the user, and the rest are providing services to Alice. Each party sends and receives messages, and these messages include information that is necessary for the service.

Three properties were taken into consideration while determining the privacy requirements: data confidentiality, identity confidentiality, and unlinkability.

Data confidentiality-related requirements, which we label by D, aim to keep information private for parties who need the information. In other words, each party should only know the information that is necessary for them to provide the service and not reveal this information to the other parties. Identity confidentiality-related requirements (I) are for protecting the identities of the user. One party should not learn the identifier by which the other party knows the user because learning this information is not needed by the first party to provide the service. Unlinkability-related requirements (U) aim to prevent distinguishing whether any two messages belong to the same user, same destination, or have the same identifier.

Next, we give the full list of privacy requirements.

R1-MNO-D: MNO should not learn what content Alice sends to and receives from APPIFY.

R2-MNO-D: MNO should not learn which MEC application Alice is using.

R3-MNO-I: MNO should not learn that Alice13 is the identifier of Alice for APPIFY.

R4-MNO-U: MNO should not be able to distinguish whether two messages go to the same MEC application.

R5-MNO-U: MNO should not be able to distinguish whether two messages are related to the same user identifier for the MEC application.

R6-MEC-D: MEC should not learn the content that Alice sends to and receives from APPIFY.

R7-MEC-I: MEC should not learn that identities "Alice", Alice13, or IMSI are relevant to the messages.

R8-MEC-U: MEC should not be able to distinguish whether two messages are related to the same user, same IMSI, or same user identifier for a MEC application.

R9-APP-D: APPIFY should not learn anything related to Alice if Alice does not provide such information.

R10-APP-I: APPIFY should not learn that "Alice" or IMSI is related to Alice13.

R11-APP-U: APPIFY should not distinguish whether two messages are coming from the same device.

R12-APP-U: APPIFY should not distinguish whether two messages are related to the same IMSI.

R13-OUT-D: Outsiders should not learn which MEC application Alice is using.

R14-OUT-D: Outsiders should not learn the content of what Alice is sending and receiving.

R15-OUT-I: Outsiders should not learn anything related to the identities of Alice.

R16-OUT-U: Outsiders should not be able to distinguish whether two UEs use the same MEC application.

R17-OUT-U: Outsiders should not be able to distinguish whether two messages are related to the same MEC application.

In the rest of this section, we justify these requirements. While defining the requirements, it is assumed that the parties are independent, i.e., they do not share information other than what is necessary for interoperability. The parties are typically independent if they belong to different companies. In our system model, these companies work together and use services of each other, but they should not share confidential information related to their business and customers.

If some parties are dependent, i.e., they share more information with each other than what is necessary for interoperability, some of the privacy requirements do not apply. For the most part, this makes it easier to fulfill the remaining privacy requirements. However, there are also some cases where the solution presented later in this paper does not as such fulfill all of the remaining requirements. Due to the limitation of space, we do not discuss dependent cases further.

Some of our requirements, especially for unlinkability, may look strict. The reason for strictness is that we cannot predict all the ways of how information is used in the future.

Requirements about MNO (R1-R5): Alice is a subscriber of MNO; therefore, her personal information can be found in the database of MNO. The MEC application that Alice is using and the content that she gets are private to Alice. Also, MNO should not learn about Alice13, the identifier of Alice for APPIFY. The MNO should not be able to distinguish whether two messages are sent to the same MEC application or include the same user identifier for the MEC application.

In order to provide services to Alice, MNO does not need to know the application details, such as the name of the MEC application, the messages between Alice and APPIFY, or the identifier for APPIFY. Distinguishing two messages with the same destination or identifier reveals the frequency of the usage of the application. If MNO learns these kinds of information, then, for example, Alice may receive unwanted advertisements or special offers. Therefore, the name of the application, the content, or the frequency of usage should not be learned by MNO.

Requirements about MEC (R6-R8): MEC is transferring messages between MNO and APPIFY, and MEC does not have other tasks in the model. Therefore, there is no need for MEC to know the content of the messages or details of the sender, such as the identifiers of Alice for other parties. It is enough for MEC to know that a subscriber of MNO is using APPIFY.

MNO and APPIFY do the authorization of Alice, and MEC does not need to worry about Alice being unauthorized. MNO checks whether Alice is a valid subscriber, and APPIFY checks whether Alice13 is registered. "Alice" might be known, if necessary, by MNO and APPIFY. However, MEC does not need to know this information in order to operate.

Requirements about APPIFY (R9-R12): The APPIFY in MEC is responsible for providing service to Alice. In order to do this, APPIFY might request information or verification of identity from Alice, which APPIFY either asks directly from Alice or uses a verification method that Alice agrees with. Either way, APPIFY should not request information from MNO or MEC. Alice can provide her real name or a fake name, phone number, location, etc., to APPIFY. However, APPIFY should not learn anything unless Alice provides it herself. There is some information that APPIFY learns automatically because of the setting. An example is the approximate location of Alice since it is close to the location of MEC.

APPIFY should not distinguish whether the messages are coming from the same device or the same IMSI. Let us take a concrete example to highlight this point. Bob is another user with APPIFY identity Bob57. APPIFY may be used in an IoT device of Bob, which is connected to the mobile device of Alice. Now, the IMSI for Bob would be the same IMSI that Alice is using. If APPIFY learns that Alice13 and Bob57 share the same IMSI, then it shows that either the two users are together or the identifiers belong to the same person. APPIFY does not need to know this.

APPIFY might want to learn which type of device Alice and Bob are using if this helps APPIFY to provide its service. However, knowing exactly which devices Alice and Bob are using is not necessary for that purpose. Furthermore, this information can reveal whether one person uses the identifiers Alice13 and Bob57 or two different users are sharing the same device.

Requirements about Outsiders (R13-R17): Unlike MNO, MEC, and APPIFY, outsiders are not involved in providing services to Alice. Therefore, they do not need to learn anything, e.g., the MEC application that Alice is using, the content of this communication, and the identifiers that Alice is using for MNO and APPIFY. In general, outsiders should not be able to distinguish whether two messages of different users are sent to the same MEC application.

5   Privacy-Preserving Access to MEC Application

In this section, we present a solution that aims to provide privacy-preserving communication between Alice and APPIFY. Later, we show how this solution meets privacy requirements.

5.1 Solution

We assume that the main server of APPIFY has public and private verification and signature key pair (VK_{main}, SK_{main}). The main server also has a (potentially self-signed root) certificate for public verification key $cert(VK_{main})$. The main server of APPIFY sends this certificate to the APPIFY in MEC.

The main server of APPIFY issues a certificate $cert(APPIFY)$ for APPIFY in the MEC host. This certificate is given to APPIFY when deployed in MEC and will be used to authenticate APPIFY to Alice.

We also assume that MNO has public and private verification and signature key pair (VK_{main}, SK_{main}). The MNO has a (potentially self-signed root) certificate for public verification key $cert(VK_{MNO})$. The MNO sends $cert(VK_{MNO})$ to its subscribers, including Alice.

The MNO issues a certificate $cert(MEC)$ for MEC when MEC is deployed to MNO. This certificate will be used later for authenticating MEC to Alice.

Before Alice can access APPIFY in MEC, she has to register with the main server of APPIFY. During the registration, Alice chooses her user id (Alice13) and password (psw). The main server of APPIFY issues a certificate $cert(Alice13)$. This certificate includes the information that Alice13 is a valid user and which services Alice is authorized to get. The main server of APPIFY sends the certificates $cert(Alice13)$ and $cert(VK_{main})$ to Alice after the registration is completed successfully.

Once Alice is done with the registration, Alice can start using APPIFY in MEC. When there is no suitable MEC deployed near Alice, the service is provided by the main server of APPIFY, which means that the user cannot take advantage of the proximity of the MEC host. For simplicity, we assume below that a suitable MEC host is deployed near the user.

The 5G system, similarly to the earlier mobile systems, includes a secure channel between UE and MNO. We also assume there are secure channels between MNO and MEC, as well as between MEC and APPIFY.

Our solution includes two additional secure (authenticated, confidential, and integrity-protected) channels: outer and inner. The outer channel is between UE and MEC, and the inner channel is between UE and APPIFY. The UE-to-MEC part of the inner channel runs inside the outer channel. The solution can be realized in several ways, depending on the choice of protocols for those two channels. Below we describe a variant where Datagram Transport Layer Security (DTLS) [25] (run on top of UDP) is used for the outer channel and Transport Layer Security (TLS) 1.3 [26] (run on top of TCP) for the inner channel.

The DTLS handshake includes server authentication based on the certificate of the server, MEC. The TLS handshake includes server authentication based on the certificate of the server, APPIFY. The client, Alice, is authenticated towards the TLS server, APPIFY, after the handshake using the Post-Handshake Client Authentication extension of TLS 1.3. As a result, Alice and APPIFY will have a mutually authenticated TLS connection.

The procedure for accessing APPIFY in local MEC is summarized in Fig. 3 and explained step-by-step in the following.

1. The UE of Alice and MNO run 5G Authentication and Key Agreement (AKA) procedure, resulting from which they establish a secure connection. At this point, Alice and MNO share a Temporary Mobile Subscriber Identity (TMSI) for further identification of Alice to MNO.
2. Alice sends a DTLS communication request (over UDP) for MEC to MNO.
3. If MEC is not deployed in MNO, then MNO returns an error message to Alice. In this case, Alice connects to the main server of APPIFY. If MEC is deployed in MNO, then MNO replies with the IP address of MEC.
4. DTLS handshake is done between Alice and MEC. During the handshake, MEC sends $cert(MEC)$ to Alice, and she verifies the certificate with the verification key of MNO, VK_{MNO}. After the handshake is completed successfully, the DTLS connection is established between Alice and MEC.
5. Alice sends a communication request for APPIFY to MEC through the DTLS channel.
6. If MEC does not host APPIFY, then MEC returns an error message to Alice. In this case, Alice begins to establish a connection to the APPIFY main server over the Internet. If MEC does host APPIFY, then MEC sets a session number N and links this number with the DTLS channel and APPIFY.
7. MEC confirms that it hosts APPIFY.
8. After receiving confirmation that MEC hosts APPIFY, Alice opens TLS/TCP connection to APPIFY. Upon receiving this message, MEC inserts its internal label N and forwards the resulting message to APPIFY. The APPIFY will include N in its messages towards Alice. MEC will use N for directing them to the appropriate DTLS channel but strip N before the message goes into the DTLS channel. We do not go further into the details of communication inside the MEC host.
   During the TLS handshake, the APPIFY sends $cert(APPIFY)$ to Alice, and she verifies the certificate with the verification key of the main server of APPIFY, VK_{main}. After the handshake is completed successfully, the TLS connection is established between Alice and APPIFY.
9. At this point, Alice knows that she is talking to the correct entity. Alice reveals her identity to APPIFY by initiating a Post-Handshake Client Authentication with APPIFY. Alice sends $cert(Alice13)$ to APPIFY, and APPIFY verifies it with the verification key of the main server of APPIFY, VK_{main}.
10. Alice sends a service request to APPIFY through the TLS connection.
11. APPIFY replies with the service response to Alice through the TLS connection.
12. The communication between Alice and APPIFY continues as in Steps 10. and 11.

The DTLS and TLS connections stay open during the session. When the session ends, both DTLS and TLS connections should be terminated. If Alice13 wants to contact APPIFY again after the session is closed, the procedure should start again from Step 1 or Step 2.

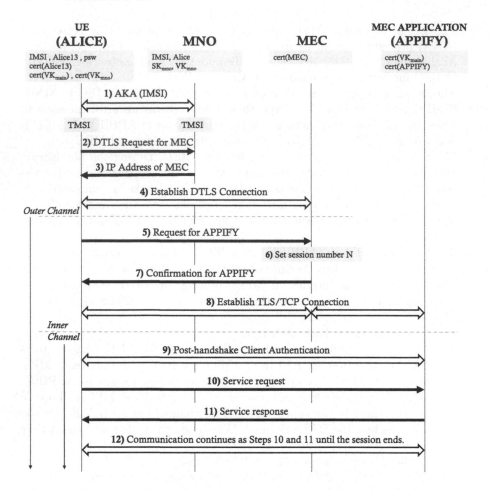

Fig. 3. Communication flow of the MEC access.

5.2 Analysis

Our solution follows one of the principles of Onion Routing (OR) [20]: the communication channels from UE to MNO, and from UE to MEC can be seen as the first and the second routes of OR, respectively. However, a path in OR is random and includes typically (at least) three intermediate nodes, which are chosen from a pool of onion routers. We have a single path with two nodes: MNO and MEC. While adding a third intermediate node on the path between UE and MEC would better protect user privacy against, e.g., colluding MNO and MEC, it would also increase the communication delay and make the solution more complex.

Different protocol choices for outer and inner channels would result in different variants of the solution. The variant presented above, where both outer and inner channels are based on standard, widely used protocols (respectively,

DTLS/UDP and TLS/TCP), has the advantage that the solution is easier to deploy than variants based on custom-made protocols. It has been shown that an arrangement where TCP runs on top of DTLS is feasible [27]. On the other hand, a solution based on custom-made protocols could potentially be more efficient than variants based on standard protocols.

The deployed solution needs to have measures against Denial of Service (DoS) attacks that try to overload the servers by opening many DTLS connections towards the MEC host or TLS connections to APPIFY. Various mechanisms to prevent DoS attacks exist [25,26,28,29] but we do not discuss those further.

Now, we analyze how the solution in Sect. 5.1 meets the privacy requirements defined in Sect. 4. We will see that we can fulfill most of the requirements by using the outer and inner channels and partially fulfill the rest of the requirements. Better coverage of the requirements could be potentially achieved with more sophisticated mechanisms, e.g., a fully-fledged Onion Routing between the parties. However, this would increase the complexity and cost of the solution, making it less likely to be deployed. Throughout this section, we use the assumption that all three network-side parties are honest-but-curious.

Data and Identity Confidentiality: As explained in Sect. 5.1, we use secure channels between UE and MNO, MNO and MEC, and MEC and APPIFY. Hop-by-hop protection of the path between UE and APPIFY protects the traffic against outsiders. Thus, the requirements R14-OUT-D and R15-OUT-I are fulfilled. This hop-by-hop protection is not enough to protect against the honest-but-curious parties who are nodes in the traffic path.

The request for APPIFY in Step 5 of the procedure, see Fig. 3, and subsequent messages between Alice and APPIFY are delivered inside the DTLS channel. This prevents MNO from learning the identities, APPIFY and Alice13, as well as the content of messages exchanged between Alice and APPIFY. The MNO can only observe that Alice is using some MEC application. We can conclude that the requirements R1-MNO-D and R3-MNO-I are fulfilled.

Alice does not send any messages to APPIFY, which includes her personal information, until the TLS handshake between UE and APPIFY is completed. After the handshake, all communication between Alice and APPIFY is concealed by the TLS channel. Alice introduces herself as Alice13 by sending $cert(Alice13)$ to APPIFY inside a secure channel to perform Post-Handshake Client Authentication. This way, APPIFY authenticates Alice13, and MEC does not learn the identity Alice13. The real identity of Alice is not used in any messages of the procedure, and it is only known by MNO. The IMSI is only used between Alice and MNO. Therefore, MEC cannot learn any of these identifiers. We can conclude that the requirements R6-MEC-D and R7-MEC-I are fulfilled.

APPIFY is at the end of the communication path. Since all the information between Alice and APPIFY, similarly as between MEC and APPIFY, is transferred inside an integrity-protected channel, APPIFY receives only the information that other parties have intended for it. Therefore, APPIFY cannot learn more information than what Alice provides. Similarly, as we explained earlier for MEC, we can conclude that neither APPIFY learns the identifiers "Alice" or IMSI. Therefore, APPIFY cannot relate these identifiers with Alice13. Thus, the requirements R9-APP-D and R10-APP-I are fulfilled.

Outsiders and MNO cannot see the identifier of APPIFY because it is carried inside secure channels. Still, traffic analysis may help in identifying the MEC application in use; see [30,31]. For that reason, our solution does not fully meet the requirements R2-MNO-D and R13-OUT-D. However, if the application cannot be recognized by studying encrypted traffic patterns, then R2-MNO-D and R13-OUT-D are met.

Unlinkability: The requirements about unlinkability are partially met with our solution. In Step 6, MEC creates a one-to-one mapping from the DTLS session between Alice and MEC to the TLS session between Alice and APPIFY. This means that anybody who is able to recognize that two messages belong to the same DTLS session (or the same TLS session), also learns that these messages are between the same user and the same MEC application. There are many ways how even an outsider could find out that two protected messages belong to the same (D)TLS session (see, for example, [32]). Therefore, we limit the discussion of unlinkability requirements to the case where the two messages under consideration belong to two different DTLS or TLS sessions.

Our solution generates a new TLS channel from scratch for every new connection between the user and APPIFY. Therefore, only Alice and APPIFY can link different TLS channels to each other.

As explained earlier, the MNO learns neither APPIFY nor Alice13. When a new DTLS connection is established, MNO cannot know whether this connection is for the same MEC application as an earlier connection, except by analyzing traffic patterns. Thus, requirement R4-MNO-U is partially met. MNO could assume that if the same UE connects to the same MEC application, then the identifier of the user towards that application is also the same. However, MNO cannot know this for sure. For example, the UE could be a hotspot and be shared by several users. We conclude that the requirement R5-MNO-U is partially met.

Similar reasoning as for MNO and R4-MNO-U above can be carried out for the case of outsiders. Therefore, the outsider could learn that two UEs use the same MEC application from traffic analysis only, hence requirement R16-OUT-U is partially met. Also, it is only by traffic analysis that the outsider can learn that two messages from two different DTLS sessions relate to the same MEC application. Therefore, also requirement R17-OUT-U is partially met.

When establishing the outer DTLS channel, Alice authenticates MEC, but MEC does not authenticate Alice. This prevents MEC from linking Alice to APPIFY. In the established session, MEC knows which MEC application is used, but the identity of Alice is not revealed to MEC. However, the IP addresses in the messages might reveal that the same device is used in two different DTLS connections. In that case, these two connections are likely from the same user. Still, MEC cannot be sure about that, as explained above for the case of MNO. We can conclude that the requirement R8-MEC-U is partially fulfilled.

We now discuss the unlinkability requirements R11-APP-U and R12-APP-U for APPIFY in the case where two messages are from two different TLS sessions.

In that case, APPIFY can conclude that the user is probably using the same device if the user sends the same certificate to APPIFY in both TLS sessions. On the other hand, having different certificates does not imply that different devices are used. We can conclude that requirement R11-APP-U is partially met.

Typically there is a one-to-one mapping between the user device and IMSI. However, there may be several SIM cards in a single device, and the same SIM card could be moved from one device to another. The APPIFY cannot distinguish between any of these cases. We can conclude that R12-APP-U is partially met.

In summary, our solution meets the privacy requirements well, except for the unlinkability. An adversary may recognize that messages belong to the same DTLS or TLS session and carry out traffic analysis. However, similar arguments against unlinkability can be made in the setting where applications are used without the help of MEC technology.

6   Conclusion and Future Work

This paper sheds light on the privacy challenges related to MEC usage in 5G. We consider a basic MEC usage scenario, where the user accesses an application hosted in the MEC platform via the radio access network of MNO. We first create a system model of the scenario. Second, we identify an appropriate adversary model covering all parties. Third, privacy requirements are defined for all parties in the system model. Finally, based on those requirements and the adversary model, a privacy-preserving solution is introduced to access the MEC application. The solution is analyzed against the privacy requirements. The scope of our study is restricted to the basic MEC usage scenario. Another limitation of this study is that our solution has not been verified experimentally.

Future work could include experimentation and formal verification for our solution. It could also cover user privacy protection in more complicated scenarios, e.g., when the communication parties include multiple MNOs. This is the case in a roaming situation. Also, user might need to switch from one MEC to another, e.g., when the user is moving fast. Privacy-preserving protocols could be developed for those more complicated scenarios.

Acknowledgements. The authors would like to thank Sami Kekki and Andrey Krendzel for helpful comments.

References

1. 3GPP TS 23.501 V16.5.0: System architecture for the 5G System (5GS) (2020)
2. Taleb, T., Samdanis, K., Mada, B., Flinck, H., Dutta, S., Sabella, D.: On multi-access edge computing: a survey of the emerging 5G network edge cloud architecture and orchestration. IEEE Commun. Surv. Tutorials **19**(3), 1657–1681 (2017). https://doi.org/10.1109/COMST.2017.2705720

3. Pham, Q., et al.: A survey of multi-access edge computing in 5G and beyond: fundamentals, technology integration, and state-of-the-art. IEEE Access **8**, 1–44 (2020). https://doi.org/10.1109/ACCESS.2020.3001277
4. Parada, C., Fontes, F., Marque, C.S., Cunha, V., Leitão, C.: Multi-access edge computing: a 5G technology. In: European Conference on Networks and Communications (EuCNC), Ljubljana, Slovenia, pp. 277–281. IEEE (2018). https://doi.org/10.1109/EuCNC.2018.8442492
5. Porambage, P., Okwuibe, J., Liyanage, M., Ylianttila, M., Taleb, T.: Survey on multi-access edge computing for Internet of Things realization. IEEE Commun. Surv. Tutorials **20**(4), 2961–2991 (2018). https://doi.org/10.1109/COMST.2018.2849509
6. Okwuibe, J., Liyanage, M., Ahmad, I., Ylianttila, M.: Cloud and MEC security. A comprehensive Guide to 5G security, pp. 373–397. Wiley (2018). https://doi.org/10.1002/9781119293071.ch16
7. ETSI White Paper No. 28: MEC in 5G Networks; First Edition (2018)
8. ETSI GS MEC 002 V2.1.1: Multi-access Edge Computing (MEC); Phase 2: Use Cases and Requirements. Group Specification (2018)
9. ETSI GS MEC 030 V2.1.1: Multi-access Edge Computing (MEC); V2X Information Service API. Group Specification (2020)
10. Ranaweera, P., Jurcut, A.D., Liyanage, M.: Survey on multi-access edge computing security and privacy. IEEE Commun. Surv. Tutorials (2021). https://doi.org/10.1109/COMST.2021.3062546
11. 3GPP TS 33.102 V16.0.0: 3G Security; Security architecture (2020)
12. 3GPP TS 33.501 V16.3.0: Security architecture and procedures for 5G system (2020)
13. University of Delaware, Secure UD: Managing data confidentiality. https://www1.udel.edu/security/data/confidentiality.html. Accessed 28 July 2020
14. Paverd, A.J., Martin, A., Brown, I.: Modelling and automatically analyzing privacy properties for honest-but-curious adversaries. Technical report (2014)
15. Ahmad, I., Kumar, T., Liyanage, M., Okwuibe, J., Ylianttila, M., Gurtov, A.: Overview of 5G security challenges and solutions. IEEE Commun. Stand. Mag. **2**(1), 36–43 (2018). https://doi.org/10.1109/MCOMSTD.2018.1700063
16. Du, M., Wang, K., Chen, Y., Wang, X., Sun, Y.: Big data privacy preserving in multi-access edge computing for heterogeneous internet of things. IEEE Commun. Mag. **56**(8), 62–67 (2018). https://doi.org/10.1109/MCOM.2018.1701148
17. Khan, R., Kumar, P., Jayakody, D., Liyanage, M.: A survey on security and privacy of 5G technologies: potential solutions, recent advancements, and future directions. IEEE Commun. Surv. Tutorials **22**(1), 196–248 (2020). https://doi.org/10.1109/COMST.2019.2933899
18. Zhang, P., Durresi, M., Durresi, A.: Mobile privacy protection enhanced with multi-access edge computing. In: IEEE 32nd International Conference on Advanced Information Networking and Applications (AINA), pp. 724–731 (2018). https://doi.org/10.1109/AINA.2018.00109
19. Alshalan, A., Pisharody, S., Huang, D.: A survey of mobile VPN technologies. IEEE Commun. Surv. Tutorials **18**(2), 1177–1196 (2016). https://doi.org/10.1109/COMST.2015.2496624
20. Chauhan, M., Singh, A.K., Komal: Survey of onion routing approaches: advantages, limitations and future scopes. In: Pandian, A., Palanisamy, R., Ntalianis, K. (eds.) Proceeding of the International Conference on Computer Networks, Big Data and IoT (ICCBI - 2019). ICCBI 2019. LNDECT, vol. 49, pp. 686–697. Springer, Cham (2019). https://doi.org/10.1007/978-3-030-43192-1_76

21. Ojanperä, T., van den Berg, H., IJntema, W., de Souza Schwartz, R., Djurica, M.: Application synchronization among multiple MEC servers in connected vehicle scenarios. In: 2018 IEEE 88th Vehicular Technology Conference (VTC-Fall), Chicago, IL, USA, pp. 1–5. IEEE (2018). https://doi.org/10.1109/VTCFall.2018.8691039
22. Herzog, J.: A computational interpretation of Dolev-Yao adversaries. Theor. Comput. Sci. **340**(1), 57–81 (2005). https://doi.org/10.1016/j.tcs.2005.03.003
23. ICO (Information Commisioners' Office) News: Estate agency fined & #x00A3;80,000 for failing to keep tenants' data safe (2009). https://ico.org.uk/about-the-ico/news-and-events/news-and-blogs/2019/07/estate-agency-fined-80-000-for-failing-to-keep-tenants-data-safe/. Accessed 22 April 2021
24. Freedman, M.: How businesses are collecting data (and what they're doing with it) (2020). https://www.businessnewsdaily.com/10625-businesses-collecting-data.html. Accessed 22 Apr 2021
25. IETF RFC 6347: Datagram Transport Layer Security Version 1.2 (2012)
26. IETF RFC 8446: The Transport Layer Security (TLS) Protocol Version 1.3 (2018)
27. Reardon, J., Goldberg, I.: Improving TOR using a TCP-over-DTLS tunnel. In: Proceedings of the 18th Conference on USENIX Security Symposium (SSYM 2009), USA, pp. 119–134 (2009). https://doi.org/10.5555/1855768.1855776
28. IETF RFC 5246: The Transport Layer Security (TLS) Protocol Version 1.2 (2008)
29. Feng, W., Kaiser, E., Luu, A.: Design and implementation of network puzzles. Proc. IEEE Infocom **2005**(4), 2372–2382 (2005). https://doi.org/10.1109/INFCOM.2005.1498523
30. Taylor, V.F., Spolaor, R., Conti, M., Martinovic, I.: Robust smartphone app identification via encrypted network traffic analysis. IEEE Trans. Inf. Forensics Secur. **13**(1), 63–78 (2018). https://doi.org/10.1109/TIFS.2017.2737970
31. Saltaformaggio, B., et al.: Eavesdropping on fine-grained user activities within smartphone apps over encrypted network traffic. In: Proceedings of the 10th USENIX Conference on Offensive Technologies (WOOT 2016), pp. 69–78 (2016). https://doi.org/10.5555/3027019.3027026
32. Pironti, A., Strub, P.Y., Bhargavan, K.: Identifying website users by TLS traffic analysis: new attacks and effective countermeasures, Rev. 1. INRIA Paris (2012)

A Conceptual Model for the General Data Protection Regulation

Pasquale Cantiello[1]([✉])(ID), Michele Mastroianni[2](ID), and Massimiliano Rak[2](ID)

[1] Osservatorio Vesuviano, Istituto Nazionale di Geofisica e Vulcanologia, Napoli, Italy
pasquale.cantiello@ingv.it
[2] Dipartimento di Ingegneria, Università degli Studi della Campania, Aversa, Italy
{michele.mastroianni,massimiliano.rak}@unicampania.it
http://www.ingv.it, http://www.unicampania.it

Abstract. The widespread diffusion of Cloud paradigm and its approach based on delegation of resources to service providers, improved greatly the need of protecting personal data. Accordingly, in recent years, governments are going to define and apply new rules, that aims at protecting the personal space of each individual. From 2018, General Data protection Regulation (GDPR) applies in Europe, giving specific rights to each individual and imposing procedures to protect personal data. GDPR addresses a clear need of our social network-based society, but has the side effect of outlining the incapability of many actual enterprises, especially small and medium ones, to address such new requirements. In this paper the new Regulation is described with a conceptual map approach.

Keywords: GDPR · Privacy · Cloud

1 Introduction

In recent years, governments are going to define and apply new rules, that aims at protecting the personal space of each individual. In fact, from 2018, General Data protection Regulation (GDPR) [6] applies in Europe, it defines new rights for each European citizen, related to the control over their own personal data, as an example a citizen has the right to know who hosts his own personal data and ask for their deletion.

GDPR addresses a clear need of our *social network*-based society, but has the side effect of outlining the incapability of many actual enterprises, especially small and medium ones, to address such new requirements. As an example, GDPR imposes that service provider should perform a dedicated risk analysis (compiling a report named Data privacy Impact Assessment, DPIA) and select according the appropriate mechanisms. But the DPIA is not a simple analysis to carry out, and for proper evaluation of risks, is mandatory for data controllers to demonstrate that all security measures, both organisational and technical, are taken at state of the art level.

© Springer Nature Switzerland AG 2021
O. Gervasi et al. (Eds.): ICCSA 2021, LNCS 12956, pp. 60–77, 2021.
https://doi.org/10.1007/978-3-030-87010-2_5

The work proposed in this paper aims at addressing a very specific issue: the selection of countermeasures needed to demonstrate compliance to GDPR. We propose to address such an issue using standard security controls, in order to have a solution that can be transparently applied to different contexts. Accordingly, this paper proposes the following original and innovative results:

- A GDPR Conceptual map, that summarizes the main concepts of GDPR and will drive us in demonstrating compliances granted by security controls.
- A Mapping among standard security controls and GDPR concepts, in order to identify sets of security controls that grant compliances with GDPR requests.

The reminder of this paper is structured as follows. Section 2 describes the known issues related to GDPR adoption and to privacy management in general, outlining existing results. The following Sect. 3 describes the new Regulation and our innovative conceptual map over GDPR concepts, while Sect. 4 describes the relationship among the standard NIST security controls and GDPR articles. Section 5 summarizes our conclusions and a proposed set of future work.

2   Related Works

An interesting example that integrates semantic techniques for GDPR compliance was the approach proposed by [11,12]: they developed an integrated, semantically rich Knowledge Graph (or Ontology) to represent the rules mandated by both PCI DSS[1] and EU GDPR.

Another interesting research line is the one proposed in [7] which aims at semantically enrich BPMN (Business Process Model and Notation) with concepts related to GDPR, in order to support risk analysis and compliance verification.

An approach also based on ontologies may be found in [14]. In this paper is introduced PrOnto (Privacy Ontology for Legal Reasoning), which aims to provide a legal knowledge modelling of the privacy agents, data types, types of processing operations, rights and obligations, using a methodology used based on legal theory analysis joined with ontological patterns.

The results described in [1–3] (all produced by the same research team), focuses on the idea of Privacy Level Agreements (PLAs), proposed by CSA (Cloud Security alliance) [5]. The authors propose a PLA metamodel in [3], relating together the concepts of privacy, the security requirements and trying to understand how to address GDPR rules using such a metamodel to express both user needs and providers capabilities.

The idea of using standard security controls in order to address privacy requirements was explored by Rios et al. [15], trying to apply the concepts and results of the MUSA project, which suggests a development flow to address security requirements, involving Security Service Level Agreement all over the

---

[1] PCI DSS: Payment Card Industry Data Security Standards - https://www.pcisecuritystandards.org/.

development process. Such a research line differs from the approaches proposed in this paper because the compliance aspect is not the core of the technique, which, mainly, aims at relating Security SLAs and privacy.

The work in [10] proposes to use ISO27000 controls as a way to address GDPR compliance. The authors identify a set of controls in the ISO27000 framework and for each of them they suggest how to interpret/apply them in order to respect GDPR constraints. The approach proposed reminds our one, even if the procedure for the controls selection was not explained in detail (offering a limited grant about the completeness of the procedure), and there is no support for automating the process and its application when concretely applying the results in the process of GDPR compliance verification. The same team explored GDPR compliance in different contexts (public administration and crowdsourcing), even if experimenting different and less formal techniques in [9] and in [8].

3   A Conceptual Model for GDPR

The GDPR (General Data Protection Regulation), has been adopted on April 27 of 2016 by the European Parliament and the Council *to protect the natural persons with regard to the processing of personal data and on the free movement of such data* [6]. Its birth has been mainly driven by the necessity to harmonize the different regulations about the privacy in the countries of the EU, by focusing on the rights of the european citizens to protect and control their personal data. At the same time it allows the circulation of the data in the current digital society in a protected way. Since the GDPR has the form of a regulation, it is adopted and has effects on each country of the EU with no further actions required, neither it can be modified by a single country.

In this paper the new Regulation is described with a conceptual map approach. The global conceptual map is shown in Fig. 6. Eight core concepts of the GDPR have been outlined and shown in Fig. 1a. They are described here along with their relationships with further topics.

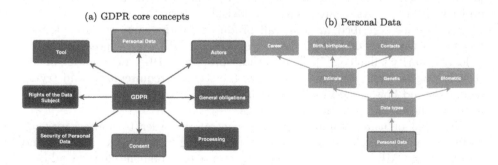

Fig. 1. GDPR core concepts and personal data

3.1   Personal Data

Personal Data, as defined in the article 4 of the Regulation, is any information relating to an identified or identifiable natural person *("Data subject")*. According to the Regulation, the identifiability of a natural person derives not only from common factors as names, identification numbers, locations or IP addresses, but also from factors specific to the *physical, physiological, genetic, mental, economic, cultural or social identity of that natural person.*

A further classification of Personal Data, as shown in Fig. 1b, can lead to the following three sub-types:

- *Personal:* these are the data commonly known as personal, such as name, birth place and date, addresses, contacts (email, phone number), career and work experiences;
- *Genetic:* these are data relating to the characteristics (inherited or acquired genetic) of a natural person derived from the biological analysis (e.g.: DNA, RNA) which can give unique information about the physiology or the health of that natural person;
- *Biometric:* data resulting from specific technical processing (on physical, physiological or behavioural characteristics of a natural person), which can lead to the unique identification of that natural person;

3.2   Actors

Several actors are involved in the GDPR, each with his rights or obligations. In the conceptual model proposed here, as in Fig. 2a, we have identified the following:

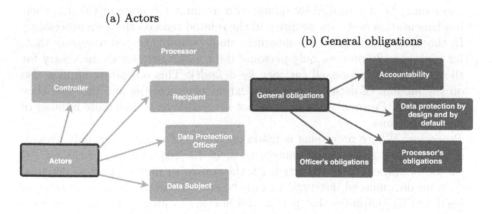

(a) Actors

(b) General obligations

Fig. 2. Actors and General obligations

- *Controller:* A physical or legal person, a public authority, or any other service or organization that by itself, or in cooperation with others, defines the purposes and the methods of personal data processing.
- *Processor:* A physical or legal person, a public authority, or any other service or organization that processes personal data on behalf of a controller.
- *Recipient:* A physical or legal person, a public authority, or any other service or organization that receives communications with personal data.
- *Data Protection Officer (DPO):* A professional with specific knowledge about regulations and practice on personal data processing.
- *Data Subject:* A person to whom personal data is processed.

3.3   General Obligations

As described in Sect. 1 of Chapter IV of the GDPR, in order to guarantee the rights and freedoms of natural persons, several technical and organisational measures must be implemented, reviewed and updated where necessary. On our conceptual model, these obligations are classified, as shown in Fig. 2b, in the following four concepts:

- *Responsibility of the controller (Accountability):* As stated in the article 24 of the GDPR, the measures implemented by the controller serve to ensure (and to demonstrate) the compliance, according to the Regulation, of the processing on the data. Also any adherence to approved codes of conduct or to approved certification mechanisms, may be used to prove that compliance.
- *Data protection by design and by default:* The controller shall implement (article 25 of the Regulation) appropriate technical and organisational measures, since the planning stages of the data processing (*privacy by design*), to ensure data-protection principles and protect the rights of data subjects. These measures must be determined by taking into account the state of the art, their implementation costs, the nature and the related risks on the data processing. In the same way appropriate measures shall be implemented to ensure that, for each specific process, only personal data which are strictly necessary for the purpose are processed (*privacy by default*). This obligation applies also on the amount of data collected, the extent of processing and the time they are retained. Personal data must be not accessible to an indefinite number of natural persons.
- *Processor:* Where processing is made on behalf of a controller, only processors providing sufficient guarantees to meet the requirements of the GDPR should be chosen. As in the article 28, the controller must: i) process personal data on documented instruction from the controller and under a contract or legal act; ii) guarantee that persons authorised to process the data act with confidentiality or under an obligation of confidentiality; iii) take all security measures required.
- *Protection Officer:* The DPO has several obligations (Article 39) and in particular she/he must: i) inform and support the controller, the processor and the employees who process personal data about their obligations deriving from

the Regulation; ii) monitor compliance with the Regulation of the controller and the processor about protection of personal data; iii) provide advice, upon request, about DPIA (see Sect. 3.6) iv) have due regard to the risk associated with processing operations, considering the nature, scope, purposes and context of processing.

3.4 Processing

Personal Data Processing, as defined in the Article 4 of the Regulation generally means any operation or set of operations which is performed on personal data. In our model, shown in Fig. 3, we have identified two concepts: typology of personal data processing and principles applicable to them.

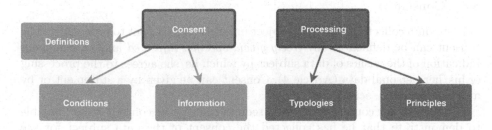

Fig. 3. Processing and consent

- *Typologies:* Several typologies of data processing operations are identified in the GDPR. In particular: i) *collection* is the starting point of the processing consisting in the acquisition of the data; ii) *recording* of the data on any kind of support for further processing; iii) *organisation* represents a classification of data in predefined way; iv) *structuring* consists in data distribution according to suitable schemas; v) *storage* of the data on any kind of support; vi) *adaptation* or *alteration* means any operation made on data to modify them in order to do a correlation with other data; vii) *retrieval* is the activity to find and retrieve any stored data; viii) *consultation* is the reading of the data, even in a simple form like visualisation; ix) *use* is a generic activity that involves any utilization of the data; x) *disclosure* is the transmission of data to different subjects; xi) *dissemination* regards the making available of the data as on public social networks; xii) *alignment* or *combination* of multiple data to get new structured information; xiii) *restriction* as partially hiding of entire classes or only parts of the personal data; xiv) *erasure* is data deletion using electronic tools; xv) *destruction* means the permanently deletion of that data.
- *Principles:* Every processing must be carried out in compliance with the principles of the Article 5 of the GDPR. These are: i) *lawfulness, fairness* and *transparency* of the processing in relation to the data subject; ii) *purpose*

limitation or that no further processing on the data is done other than the specified, explicit and legitimate purposes; iii) *data minimisation* is that the collected data must be adequate, relevant and limited to only what is strictly necessary to the specific purposes; iv) *accuracy* means the data must be accurate and kept up to date, and any personal data that are inaccurate are promptly erased or rectified; v) *storage limitation* of the data for no longer than what is necessary for the purposes of the processing; vi) *integrity* and *confidentiality* or that data must be processed to ensure appropriate security and protection against unauthorised processing and against accidental loss or modification by using appropriate technical or organisational measures; vii) *accountability* these principles must be followed by the controller, and he/she must be able to prove it (Article 24, par. 1).

3.5   Consent

Prior to data collection, the data subject must give his consent to processing. The consent can be defined as any *freely given, specific, informed* and *unambiguous* indication of the wishes of data subject by which he/she agrees to the processing of his/her personal data (Article 4). Consent can be given by a statement or by a clear affirmative action.

Conditions for consent (Article 7) require that: i) the controller shall be able to demonstrate that he has collected the consent of the data subject for the specific processing; ii) if the consent has been given in a written declaration with other matters, the request shall be presented in an easily accessible form, with clear and plain language; iii) the consent can be easily withdrawn by the data subject easily at any time and this shall stop any further processing on his/her data; iv) in order to assess if the consent is freely given, must be verified if the performance of a contract is conditional on consent to the processing of unnecessary personal data.

At the time when personal data are obtained from a data subject, and before performing any processing, the controller shall provide the data subject with all of the following information (Article 13): i) identity and contact details of the controller and possible representative; ii) contact details of the Data Protection Officer, where applicable; iii) the purposes and legal basis of the processing for which the personal data will be collected; iv) if the processing is related to the legitimate interests pursued by the controller or by a third party (Article 6(1)(f)); v) the recipients or categories of them that will receive personal data; vi) the reference to suitable safeguards if the collector means to transfer data in third part countries, along with the means by which the data subject can obtain a copy of them.

3.6   Security of Personal Data

In order to guarantee a level of security of the collected personal data (Article 32), the controller and the processor shall implement appropriate organisational and technical measures. These must be chosen taking into account: state of the art, costs of implementation, nature, scope, context and purposes of processing, the risk related on the processing. In the conceptual model of this work, the related part is shown in Fig. 4.

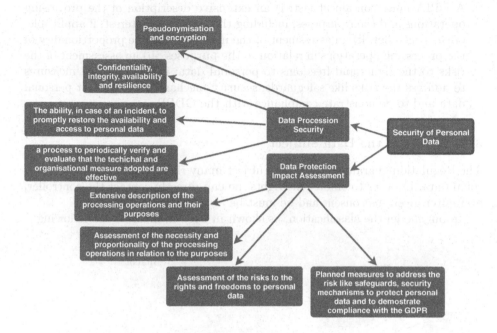

Fig. 4. Personal data security

We have done the following classification:

– *Data Processing Security:* the Article 32 of the Regulation identifies inter-alia the following measures: i) pseudonymisation and encryption of personal data, in order to delete or hide any reference to the data subject they belong; ii) the ability to ensure confidentiality, integrity, availability and resilience of all the systems and services involved in the personal data processing; iii) the ability, in case of an incident, to promptly restore the availability and access to personal data; iv) a process to periodically verify and evaluate that the technical and organisational measure adopted are effective.
– *Data Protection Impact Assessment:* Where a processing, especially when using new technology, may result in a high risk to the rights and freedoms of natural person, prior to that processing, an assessment of the impact of the processing on the protection of personal data must be carried out by the controller. This assesment is defined in Article 35 as *Data Protection Impact Assesment* (DPIA) and can be carried out on multiple similar processing operations that present similar risks. The decision to conduct a DPIA is leaved on risk evaluation by the controller, but is required in the case of

an evaluation of personal aspects relating to natural persons conducted systematically and extensively done by using exclusively automated processing, including profiling, and on which decision are based that can produce effects on or affect natural persons.

A DPIA must contain at last: i) an extensive description of the processing operations and their purposes, including the legitimate interest, if applicable, of the controller. ii) an assessment of the necessity and the proportionality of the processing operations in relation to the purposes; iii) an assessment of the risks to the rights and freedoms to personal data; iv) the planned measures to address the risks like safeguards, security mechanisms to protect personal data and to demonstrate compliance with the GDPR.

3.7   Rights of the Data Subject

The Regulation guarantees the Data Subject many rights regarding his/her personal data. In order to enforce his rights, he can directly contact the controller, even after given his consent and he must be able to revoke it.

In our model the classification, as shown in Fig. 5a, includes the following:

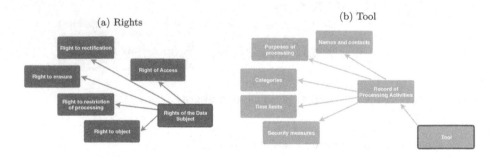

Fig. 5. Rights and tool

- *Right of access:* The Data Subject can ask the controller and has the right to obtain the confirmation about any personal data processing concerning him (Article 15 of GDPR). In that case, he has the right to access to the personal data, to know the purposes of the processing, to know the concerning categories of personal data and any recipients to whom this data will be disclosed. The Data Subjects can also have a copy of all his personal data processed.
- *Right to rectification:* The data subject has the right (Article 16) to obtain from the controller the rectification of any inaccurate personal data concerning him or her. The data subject has also to right to complete any personal data that is not complete regarding the purposes of the processing. The controller must comply without undue delay.

– *Right to erasure* or *right to be forgotten:* As guaranteed by the Article 17, the data subject can obtain by the controller that any data concerning him/her, that are no longer necessary for the reason they are collected and processed, must be erased. He/she can also obtain the erasure upon withdrawing of the consent, or if that data are unlawfully processed.
– *Right to restriction of processing:* The Article 18 guarantees the data subject that he/she can restrict the processing if, among the others: accuracy of personal data is contested by the data subject, or the process is unlawful and the subject opposes the erasure of the data, or the personal data are no longer necessary for the processing.
– *Right to object:* This right (Article 21 of GDPR), ensures that the data subject can object, at any time, to the processing of data concerning him or her, including profiling. This can be related to his or her particular situation. This right is different from the erasure one.

3.8   Tool

A fundamental tool required by the Regulation is the *Record of Processing Activities* described in the Article 30 of the GDPR. This is important to map all flows inside the organization, and is considered a best practice in data processing for the accountability of the controller. The record should be maintained by the controller and by any controller's representative, if present. The record is also useful for risk analysis and processing planning.

The representation is shown in Fig. 5b and the informations that should contained in the record, are:

– *Name and contacts* of controller, the joint controller (if present), the controller's representative and the Data Protection Officer.
– *Purposes of processing:* a description of the purposes of processing for each of the typologies and natures (e.g.: accounting, selling, payroll).
– *Categories:* a description of categories of data subject, personal data processing and categories of recipient.
– *Time limits:* where possible, the envisaged time limits for erasure of data, including any legal statement.
– *Security measures:* technical and organisational measures to enforce security on processing of personal data.

4   Compliance Verification Through Standard Security Control

Demonstrating compliance to GDPR is, nowadays, a complex issue that opens a lot of concerns, especially to SMEs. In this paper we focuses mainly on article 25 which imposes Data protection by design and by default (article 25) and that data processing should respect all the principles listed in article 5 (see Sect. 3 for

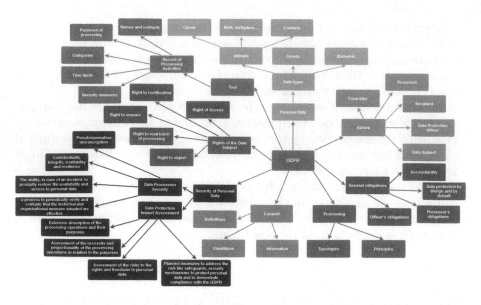

Fig. 6. GDPR global map

more details). GDPR, being a regulation, expresses the constraints (which are reasonable), but does not give a unique solution to implement them and gives freedom (and the duty) to Data Controller to identify the technical solutions. In any case, GDPR starts from the assumption that it is impossible to grant in absolute that a security breach will never happen, but imposes to Data Controller to implements all the countermeasures reasonably needed. In details, article 32 of the GDPR cites the criteria for processing security, while article 33 describes the behaviour to be followed in case of data breach [4]. As a drawback, it is up to Data Controller the role of demonstrating that he has applied all due diligence to grant correctness of behaviour. Section 2 outlined that, at best of authors' knowledge, no concrete solutions are available at state of the art.

The idea we propose relies on building a Security policy in terms of standard countermeasures that helps to systematically verify the compliance to GDPR, demonstrating the required *due diligence*. Accordingly, our solution relies on few key concepts:

- A **Security Policy** should describe all the organizational and technical procedures in order to demonstrate the correctness of systems behaviour
- The Security Policy should be expressed in terms of **standard security controls**, which are system and technology independent
- Security controls selection should be documented and clearly related to GDPR rules in order to both enable a basis for security assessment and offer a clear demonstration of compliance to the regulation

In order to grant the first point, we adopted the NIST security control framework [13], described in the following subsection. To address the second point, instead, we systematically analysed the control framework, in order to create a detailed mapping of security controls and GDPR articles. The result is a pretty complex *mapping table* available on request to the authors and for which we report in this paper only some example rows. It is worth noticing that NIST security control framework contains (in the Appendix I) a table that relates each security control to controls in international standard (e.g. ISO 27000). Accordingly, our approach can be extended to such standard with a limited effort, this will be subject to a future work from our team. Last but no least, to document and assess the security policy for a specific infrastructure we defined a simple process to derive the security controls that each component of the infrastructure should respect, building a dedicated set of security controls for each of them.

4.1   NIST Security Controls

As outlined above, in order to grant well known, accepted and reusable security countermeasures, we adopted the NIST control framework, a catalogue of security controls. It is worth noticing that we adopted the revision 5 of the control framework, released in September 2020; this revision completely change the approach to privacy controls respect to the previous versions, adding new control families and outlining, for each control, if it affects or not privacy requirements. Alternative frameworks exist in literature, proposed by standardization bodies and/or by industry-oriented organizations, such as the ISO/IEC 27002 specification [10], CIS (Center for Internet security) security controls and the Cloud Security Alliance's (CSA) Cloud Control Matrix. Appendix I of NIST SP-800-53 outlines the relationship among the proposed controls and the international standards. Alternative mappings are offered by CIS and CSA among the controls they propose and NIST Framework. Being the NIST framework openly accessible, we choose to adopt it as a reference for our work.

A security control, according to NIST, can be defined as follows: *Security Controls are safeguards or countermeasures prescribed for an information system or an organization designed to protect the confidentiality, integrity, and availability of its information and to meet a set of defined security requirements.*

A system security policy can be expressed in the form of *capabilities*, which are themselves expressed in terms of a list of standard *security controls*. NIST lists several security controls, addressing different security domains and are related to both technical and organization aspects. As an example, the NIST Security Control Framework (currently supported by our process) lists more than 900 controls belonging to 18 different *control families*, including access control (AC), identification and authentication (IA), physical and environmental protection (PE) and awareness and training (AT).

Security controls are organized in Families, listed in Table 1 Each security control family has a name, that intuitively identify the capabilities addressed by the controls, and an acronym, used to identify the Family.

Table 1. NIST security controls families

ID	Name	ID	Name
AC	Access control	PE	Physical and environmental protection
AT	Awareness and training	PL	Planning
AU	Audit and accountability	PM	Program management
CA	Assessment, authorization, and monitoring	PS	Personnel security
CM	Configuration management	PT	PII processing and transparency
CP	Contingency planning	RA	Risk assessment
IA	Identification and authentication	SA	System and services acquisition
IR	Incident response	SC	System and communications protection
MA	Maintenance	SI	System and information integrity
MP	Media protection	SR	Supply chain risk management

NIST framework describes security controls in natural language, but adopting a fixed structure and with fixing naming rules. Each Security Control has a name, which summarize the control behaviour and an identifier, made of the family acronym followed by an incremental number (e.g. AC-1). The First security control of each family is always an organizational prescription, that requires the documentation and the description of the practice related to the family. It acts even as a description of the generic characteristics of the control family. The description of the control is offered in natural language and describes the prescription that should be done to correctly implement the countermeasure it refers to. A *supplemental guide* section describes additional actions and supports (human) operators that have the role of verifying the correct implementation of the control. The description of the control ends with a list of *Related controls* that directly impact or support the implementation of that control. Security Controls description may include *Control Enhancements*. Control Enhancements are themselves security controls that increase the strength of the base control. Their identifiers are formed by the ID of the security control they enhance, followed by an additional incremental value, commonly reported in parenthesis, e.g. AC-2(1).

As an example, the security control **IR-6**, named **INCIDENT REPORT-ING** has the following description[2]: *i) Require personnel to report suspected security and privacy incidents to the organizational incident response capability within [Assignment: organization-defined time-period]; and ii) Report security, privacy, and supply chain incident information to [Assignment: organization-defined authorities].* An example of enhancement is **IR-6 (1)** Automated Reporting, that imposes to automate the process of reporting. For brevity's sake we have not reported the full control and control enhancement descriptions, we invite the interested reader to check the NIST document for further details.

---

[2] The following text is directly extracted from NIST document.

4.2 How to Relate Security Controls and GDPR

NIST security control framework contains almost a thousand of security controls, considering even the enhancements, accordingly the control selection process (tailoring) can be very hard to perform. NIST suggests the adoption of their risk-based procedure and offers a referring baseline which outlines the level of risk for which each control should be considered.

For what regards privacy, NIST framework adopts, as a reference, the U.S laws (i.e. the FIPP standard) that differs from the EU regulation. In order to help tailoring process and identification of controls related to privacy, the latest version of the security control framework contains dedicated table that outlines: i) if a security control is privacy related and ii) if the security control is implemented by a system according to technical or organizational means.

It is worth noticing that we aim at adopting the control framework in an innovative way, suggesting a new process for security control tailoring, focused on EU legislation. Accordingly we had to make a dedicated analysis throughout all the framework, comparing it against the EU regulation. A detailed analysis of the full framework is a long and error-prone activity, so we proceeded in a systematic way, building a list of security controls, that we consider relevant for the GDPR. We built such a list following the procedure here described:

1. Starting from the Conceptual Map of the GDPR (illustrated in Sect. 3 and reported in Fig. 6) we assigned to each GDPR article a label to outline if it affects Technical (T) or Organizational (O) means
2. We selected all controls labeled as privacy-related, selected if they are Technical or Organizational ones and checked one by one against the GDPR articles of the same type. If we considered the control able to grant compliance to the regulation article, we:
   - describe how the security control grants compliance to the GDPR article;
   - describe the limit of such compliance, i.e. what the control, as it is, cannot grant respect to GDPR constraints;
   - outline if the control relates to System, Data or Organizational means;
   - outline the list of security control enhancement needed to grant compliance to the regulation.
3. Once the privacy-related controls (together with their enhancements) were analysed, we restarted the process for all the security controls that are listed in the *related controls* of the controls selected, and for each of them:
   - if we consider the security control relevant respect to the GDPR compliance, we applied the process in step 2
   - if we consider the security control an alternative and or a useful improvement, we added the id of the control in the description of the control that suggested this one
   - if we consider the security control useless respect to GDPR compliance, we simply neglect it
4. we analysed all the security controls that were not yet analysed and, if needed, we applied the process described in step 2, analysing consequently the related controls

5. we made a final review of the full framework

Note that, at end, we analysed the full framework, but the process adopted helped us in granting coherence in the analysis and limits the possible errors. Table 2 describes briefly each field of the final mapping table, in order to help the reader to correctly interpret the result.

Table 2. NIST-GDPR mapping table fields

Field	Values	Description
Art.	Number	Article number of GDPR
Title	Text	Title of GDPR Article
Type	T, O	**T**echnical or **O**rganizational prescription
Notes	Text	Notes about the article
Control	NIST ID	NIST Security Control Identification in the format <Family>-<Number>
Motivation	Text	Description of how the security control covers the article prescription
Limits	Text	Description of the article prescription that the security control cannot grant
Target	D, S, O	The article and the control are related to **D**ata, **S**ystem or **O**rganization
En.	NIST ID	The ID of security control enhancement needed to cover the article prescription, in the format <Family>-<Number>-<Number>
Related	NIST ID	Identification of the NIST security controls related to the one discussed, needed to cover article prescription, in the format <Family>-<Number>

In order to illustrate the result of the mapping process, offering a guide to its interpretation, we briefly illustrate it for the case of article 7 (related to the consent) and 33 (related to notification) of the GDPR. We cannot report a full description of each law article and mapping due to space constraints, the full map can be requested to the authors. A piece of the table was reported in Table 3. As outlined in Sect. 3, article 7 relates to the *Conditions for Consent*, which we consider a technical measure (consent must be collected, maintained in the system and must contain a clear set of data). Accordingly we identified six different standard security controls that regulates the consent management process: IP-2, PA-4, AC-3, IP.4, PA-2 and IP-5. They are listed in the fifth column of the table and briefly described in the sixth one. It is worth noticing that the first one (IP-2) relates to data (and governates the conditions of the consent). In fact it is classified as *Data Oriented Target(D)*. Such control, moreover has two enhancements that we suggest to adopt (IP-2(1) and IP-2(2)) and a related security control IP-4, that, in fact, we included in the list of supported controls.

The AC-3 control is a system related control, we suggest it due to the AC-3(8) enhancement, which is specific for consent revocation (needed by GDPR). The last three security controls (IP-4, PA-2 and IP-5) relate to the *Organization (O)*, so they do not affect directly our systems, but should be implemented through the internal procedures adopted in the organization. As illustrated, a detailed analysis of the table enables to identify the security controls to be implemented and, accordingly, it supports an internal self-assessment oriented to grant (and demonstrate) compliance to GDPR.

It is worth noting that not always a control exists that enables to correctly implement all the law prescriptions. As an example Article 33 imposes to notify to supervisory authority that a personal data breach has happened and imposes a time constraint (2 weeks) for such a notification. However, even if security control IR-6 (together with enhancement IR-6(2)) matches with the requirement of notification, there is no enhancement and/or additional control that imposes the two weeks limit. In such a case we report such a limitation of the suggested control in column 7. DPO should outline to Data Controller to apply an additional check.

Table 3. The section of NIST-GDPR mapping table related to art. 7 and 33

Art.	Title	Type	Notes	Ctrl	Motivation	Limits	T	En.	Rel.
7	Conditions for consent	T	Consent from the data subject to personal data processing	IP-2	Consent		D	IP-2(1) IP-2(2)	IP-4
				PA-4	Ensures that information sharing is authorized respecting the purpose		D		PA-1
				AC-3	Allows consent revocation		S	AC-3(8)	
				IP-4	Notifies privacy authorization		O	IP-4(1)	
				PA-2	Determines the authority that allows data collection		O		
				IP-5	Helps understanding the actions to be performed on the data collected from the user		O		
33	Notification of a personal data breach to the supervisory authority	O		IR-6	TBC	Time constraints for notification are missing		IR-6(2)	

5 Conclusions and Future Work

The effort needed by Enterprises, in particular SMEs, to grant compliance to GDPR is time- and cost- expensive. Moreover it involves specialized competences, including, but not limited to, the technical skills on security and privacy.

Among the issues opened by GDPR implementation, this paper focuses on the selection of countermeasures needed to demonstrate compliance to GDPR. As we outlined in the paper, this technical problem implies the definition of a security policy that grants compliance to the regulation on one side and that could be concretely assessed on the other side.

We proposed a concrete technique that helps the security administrator to define a security policy in terms of standard countermeasures and outline how such policy addresses GDPR constraints, offering a simple way to support GDPR compliance verification.

Standard security controls are commonly adopted in certification processes and in security assessment procedures, offering enough technical details to enable the technical personnel to verify their correct implementation with an acceptable effort. This paper offers two concrete results: (i) a conceptual map of the GDPR, and (ii) the mapping among GDPR articles and the security controls.

The solution has the great advantage of offering a technical base to demonstrate compliance and offer a clear support to DPO, Data Controller and Data Processor to verify the correct implementation of security countermeasures.

We aims at extending the methodology in the near future, fully automating the process of countermeasures selection and comparison and generating a report that outlines how countermeasures addresses GDPR requirements. Moreover, we aims at integrating existing risk analysis tools, in order to relate the proposed countermeasures directly to the DPIA (Data Protection Impact Analysis) prescribed by the GDPR.

Acknowledgement. This work was partially supported by the Project SSCeGov, funded by University of Campania Luigi Vanvitelli, under Program VALERE.

References

1. Ahmadian, A.S., Coerschulte, F., Jürjens, J.: Supporting the security certification and privacy level agreements in the context of clouds. In: Conference of 5th International Symposium on Business Modeling and Software Design, BMSD 2015, 6 July 2015 Through 8 July 2015, Conference Code: 176459, pp. 80–95 (2016). https://doi.org/10.1007/978-3-319-40512-4_5
2. Ahmadian, A.S., Strüber, D., Riediger, V., Jürjens, J.: Supporting privacy impact assessment by model-based privacy analysis. In: Proceedings of the 33rd Annual ACM Symposium on Applied Computing, New York, NY, USA, pp. 1467–1474, SAC 2018. Association for Computing Machinery (2018). https://doi.org/10.1145/3167132.3167288

3. Ahmadian, A., Jurjens, J.: Supporting model-based privacy analysis by exploiting privacy level agreements, Conference of 8th IEEE International Conference on Cloud Computing Technology and Science, CloudCom 2016, pp. 360–365. IEEE Computer Society (2016). https://doi.org/10.1109/CloudCom.2016.0063. 12 December 2016 Through 15 December 2016; Conference Code: 126112
4. Article 29 Working Party: guidelines on personal data breach notification under Regulation 2016/679 (wp250rev.01) (2018). https://ec.europa.eu/newsroom/article29/item-detail.cfm?item_id=612052
5. Cloud Security Alliance (CSA): Privacy level agreement outline for the sale of cloud services in the European union, p. 21 (2013). https://downloads.cloudsecurityalliance.org/initiatives/pla/Privacy_Level_Agreement_Outline.pdf
6. Council of European Union: General Data Protection Regulation (2016). https://eur-lex.europa.eu/eli/reg/2016/679/oj
7. Di Martino, B., Mastroianni, M., Campaiola, M., Morelli, G., Sparaco, E.: Semantic techniques for validation of GDPR compliance of business processes. In: Barolli, L., Hussain, F.K., Ikeda, M. (eds.) CISIS 2019. AISC, vol. 993, pp. 847–855. Springer, Cham (2020). https://doi.org/10.1007/978-3-030-22354-0_78
8. Diamantopoulou, V., Androutsopoulou, A., Gritzalis, S., Charalabidis, Y.: An assessment of privacy preservation in crowdsourcing approaches: towards GDPR compliance, vol. 2018, pp. 1–9 (2018). IEEE Computer Society (2018). https://doi.org/10.1109/RCIS.2018.8406643
9. Diamantopoulou, V., Pavlidis, M., Mouratidis, H.: Privacy level agreements for public administration information systems, p. 8 (2017)
10. Diamantopoulou, V., Tsohou, A., Karyda, M.: From ISO/IEC 27002:2013 information security controls to personal data protection controls: guidelines for GDPR compliance. In: Katsikas, S., et al. (eds.) CyberICPS/SECPRE/SPOSE/ADIoT -2019. LNCS, vol. 11980, pp. 238–257. Springer, Cham (2020). https://doi.org/10.1007/978-3-030-42048-2_16
11. Elluri, L., Joshi, K.P.: A knowledge representation of cloud data controls for EU GDPR compliance. In: 2018 IEEE World Congress on Services (SERVICES), pp. 45–46. IEEE, July 2018. https://doi.org/10.1109/SERVICES.2018.00036, https://ieeexplore.ieee.org/document/8495788/
12. Elluri, L., Nagar, A., Joshi, K.P.: An integrated knowledge graph to automate GDPR and PCI DSS compliance. In: 2018 IEEE International Conference on Big Data (Big Data), pp. 1266–1271. IEEE, December 2018. https://doi.org/10.1109/BigData.2018.8622236, https://ieeexplore.ieee.org/document/8622236/
13. Joint Task Force Interagency Working Group: Security and Privacy Controls for Information Systems and Organizations. Technical report, National Institute of Standards and Technology, September 2020. https://doi.org/10.6028/NIST.SP.800-53r5, https://nvlpubs.nist.gov/nistpubs/SpecialPublications/NIST.SP.800-53r5.pdf. Edition: Revision 5
14. Palmirani, M., Martoni, M., Rossi, A., Bartolini, C., Robaldo, L.: PrOnto: privacy ontology for legal reasoning. In: Kő, A., Francesconi, E. (eds.) EGOVIS 2018. LNCS, vol. 11032, pp. 139–152. Springer, Cham (2018). https://doi.org/10.1007/978-3-319-98349-3_11
15. Rios, E.: Service level agreement-based GDPR compliance and security assurance in (multi)cloud-based systems. IET Softw. 13(3), 213–222 (2019). https://doi.org/10.1049/iet-sen.2018.5293

Toward a Design of Blood Donation Management by Blockchain Technologies

Nga Tang Thi Quynh[1], Ha Xuan Son[2], Trieu Hai Le[3], Hung Nguyen Duc Huy[4], Khanh Hong Vo[4], Huong Hoang Luong[4], Khoi Nguyen Huynh Tuan[4], Tuan Dao Anh[4], The Anh Nguyen[4], and Nghia Duong-Trung[5(✉)]

[1] National Taiwan University of Science and Technology, Taipei, Taiwan
[2] University of Insubria, Varese, Italy
sha@uninsubria.it
[3] Can Tho University of Technology, Can Tho city, Vietnam
[4] FPT University, Can Tho city, Vietnam
{khanhvh,huonglh3}@fe.edu.vn,
{khoinhtce140133,tuandace140502,anhntce160237}@fpt.edu.vn
[5] Technische Universität Berlin, Berlin, Germany
nghia.duong-trung@tu-berlin.de

Abstract. Nowadays, due to rapid changes in the population structure, which results in lower fertility rates and rapid aging, the demand for blood supply is increasing a lot. In most countries, blood quality and origin are managed by blood management information systems, such as national institutions. However, the existing system lacks limitations in that it lacked detailed blood information, which causes difficulties in managing blood quality, supply, and demand. Therefore, to solve this problem, this paper proposes an innovative system that supports managing the blood information, providing more detailed blood information such as blood consumption and disposal. A blockchain is currently a standard tool implemented in research, especially in supply chain management such as the medical field or financial system. Notably, private blockchain techniques with limited participants are relatively fast and reliable, making them suitable for B2B (Business-to-Business) transactions. Therefore, the proposed system is based on the architecture of Hyperledger Fabric. Moreover, the recorded information in blockchain technology will support dealing with the supply and demand of blood in the national institutions so that it is easier for national institutions to solve emergencies.

Keywords: Blood donation management · Blockchain · Hyperledger fabric · Blood quality · Information visibility

1 Introduction

Blockchain technology and distributed ledgers are gaining massive attention and are the main factor triggering multiple projects and research worldwide [12, 13]. On top of that, healthcare is seen as a significant industry and a primary user

O. Gervasi et al. (Eds.): ICCSA 2021, LNCS 12956, pp. 78–90, 2021.
https://doi.org/10.1007/978-3-030-87010-2_6

of using the blockchain concept. This is not only because the most well-known application of this technology is the cryptocurrency Bitcoin, but sustainable process inefficiencies also drive it, and a massive cost base issue specifically in this industry [25]. On top of this industry, blood directly linked to human life is extremely vital because of the specificity of the storage, supply condition, origin, and blood quality. Globally, blood is banned from commercial distribution, and indeed, due to the complexity of blood management, building a blood supply chain system is extraordinarily vital and necessary. It is even more of a problem for the healthcare industry if the blood donator and blood receiver do not know anything about the quality and origin of blood they will give and take.

Consequently, the problem of clarifying all detailed information about blood donations in a supply chain system for every participant is already becoming a critical aspect of healthcare services. WHO (World Health Organization), which pays attention to this problem, already has a specific definition of a blood cold chain management system. It is referred to as a system that stores and transports blood at precise temperatures and conditions, from donors to the final transfusion site [10]. This system focuses on emphasizing the collection sites, storing sites, and distribution sites of the blood. However, none of the papers has investigated applying Blockchain technologies in finding blood origin and accessing the blood quality. In many countries, the blood donation system has been established due to its scarcity of blood resources for patients.

Nevertheless, few countries have a sound blood supply chain management system. In Korea, the Korean Red Cross Blood Service Headquarters, which contains fifteen blood banks, three blood inspections is established in 1958 [4]. This system is operated to collect, store, and distribute the blood only and has not well-evaluated blood quality and origin. Blockchain technologies are today's right solution for providing helpful information to blood ownership, hospital, and recipients. Blockchain performs the transparency and privacy of each involved party along the blood donation supply chain. Blockchain technologies promise to resolve the critical aspects in the healthcare industry, which have not been investigated before, representing "a shift from trusting people to trusting math," which plays an essential role in the evolution of the blood donation system.

In the current blood management system, there are two significant problems. Firstly, the flow of information from blood collection sites to consumption or disposal is not clear. Since blood donors are willing to give their blood for the lofty purposes of saving human life, they are perplexed about the information that their blood is ultimately used for medical purposes. In a centralized blood management system, it is tough to pinpoint the cause of blood disposal in many medical institutions. Therefore, how to improve the blood quality in some resources is becoming a challenging problem.

Moreover, some donors do not know about their health situation, which is represented in blood quality. If they have infectious diseases but do not know, it becomes a severe problem for both blood donors and receivers. Thus, having information transparency in the blood management system is becoming mandatory for the involved party to know their health better and receivers will feel guaranteed about the blood source. Secondly, since some hospital under centralized blood supply system has not controlled the supply and demand of blood types, the unbalanced between the supply and demand of blood types and the poor management of blood also causes unclear reasons for blood disposal. Moreover, the lack of necessary blood types in emergencies is hazardous to the patients' lives, so it is essential to have a platform that helps improve the blood management system and reduce the differences between supply and demand.

Therefore, this paper proposed blockchain-based blood donation management and provided a critical understanding for readers about how the process works. In the blood donation process with preliminary information about blood origin and quality, complex storage, and transportation conditions, the blockchain technologies can generate traceability by storing all information in the platform. Everyone has their private rights to access the system and sees the necessary information. Existing blood management system reports only information about the amount of blood collection but lacks information about the demand of patients; Blockchain will clarify the specific management problems that can deal with suddenly increased needs of particular blood types in a region or medical institutions in an area emergencies. By using a blockchain-based health care system, not only the involved party receives beneficiary for improving their health, but it also stabilizes blood supply and demand even in extraordinary situations.

2   Related Work

2.1   Blood Supply Chain Management System

Supply chain management integrates core business processes and information. The process goes through many steps, including customers and retailers, and wholesalers, manufacturers, and suppliers, which add value to customers and other stakeholders [18]. The system incorporates a highly complex process that requires synchronization of various activities resulting in randomness and supply chain risk [20,26]. Regarding the blood supply chain system, Nagurney et al. [24] proposed a model to minimize cost and risk by representing the decay characteristics of blood as an arc multiplier. Armaghan and Pazani [3] suggested a blood supply chain to handle urgent requests from blood units in the earthquake. It is a multi-level, multi-objective model to minimize the cost of blood supply chain networks and maximize the reliability of the selected routes for blood transportation. Eskandari-Khanghahi et al. [11] developed a supply model incorporating mixed-integer linear programming that simultaneously considers location, allocation, inventory, and delivery. Delen et al. [7] sought to support the decision-making process in the blood supply chain using both a geographic information system and data mining techniques. The blood supply chain can store and distribute blood. Still, it is also a vital issue to pay attention to regarding the medical field, especially to a patient's life. Thus, designing a system to improve information sharing in a blood supply chain is very mandatory and vital. Finding a better method by using blockchain technology to cope with urgent demand and tracking blood origin, and accessing blood quality is worth researching.

2.2 Application of Blockchain Technologies to Supply Chain Management

Blockchain is a state sharing and consensus-building technique that fulfills transaction record retention and synchronization of distributed network participant systems [6]. Without having a centralized server, transaction records are recorded, shared on the distributed ledger, and is organized into blocks when a new transaction is generated. According to blockchain structure, it is classified into three main types: public, private, and consortium with base technologies, including Bitcoin Core, Ethereum, Hyperledger Fabric, etc. Hyperledger Fabric is a Linux Foundation project that was launched with 17 member companies in December 2015. It is an open-source distributed ledger platform design for developing permission applications enterprise-grade. Fabric provides a platform to build fast, efficient, and secure enterprise blockchain applications. It is characterized as being suitable with B2B transactions, and its membership services have limitations to the entry of unauthorized participants [35]. Because of having a node for verifying the transactions during transaction processing, it is possible to remove uncertain transactions early and fast. Due to these benefits, we intend to design a Hyperledger Fabric architecture-based system for managing blood quality.

The benefits of using Blockchain are expected to improve the visibility of the product supply chain and streamline work among participants through real-time tracking capability and smart contract-based characteristics. Blockchain can be used in many industries to track the origin and quality of other products. One of the Blockchain-based supply chain projects is the case of China's Walmart and IBM affiliated in 2016, aiming at guaranteeing consumers' confidence in food safety [14]. Using this blockchain technology, consumers can track the food's origin, freshness, the authenticity of its certifications, such as whether the information of the source, production sites, and distribution process is transparent or not. Another project, the Counterfeit Medicines Projects, is one of the projects in the Hyperledger Research Network, which displays the timestamp for each drug to prevent the production of counterfeit medicines [23]. Blockchain technology can be applied in various fields. It can be used to track and classify forgery, quality degradation, and theft by following drug production time and location and clarifying their origin. It can also help to improve safety and reduce costs relating to medical sectors.

On the other hand, researches on blood supply chain management have been conducted by several approaches. Blockchain application in the healthcare supply chain is not as common as others; they are considered vital. Blockchain solutions are more suitable for healthcare supply chains; however, there are not yet that using blockchain solutions for healthcare. Although researches investigated applying Blockchain in this sector is increasing, it is mainly used for data sharing and recording data, while using it for supply chain management is rare [16]. Some companies, like Imperial Logistics and FarmaTrust, use Blockchain to manage pharmaceutical supply chains [1]. Other experimental projects such as OrganTree and Dhonor Blockchain also use this technology to connect organ donors, recipients, and practitioners by using incentives such as paying for funeral cost [2]. Several articles have investigated blood donation tracking. BloodChain and SmartBag focus on preventing contamination in the supply chain and reducing the spread of HIV in developing countries [34]. Another project, which is called BLOODCHAIN, focusing on motivating blood donors by giving monetary returns. Wust and Gervais (2018) have proposed a flow chart to emphasize the importance of Blockchain application in blood tracking origin [32]. The model is presented and discussed in the paper to see whether Blockchain should solve the problem; however, the situation has not been solved well.

2.3   Limitation of Existing Research

This study overcomes the restriction of the prevailing research and methods regarding blood information systems and blood supply chain management. The proposed approach can secure the transparency of blood information management by using real-time information recording. When focusing on this point, the system has the advantages of clarifying blood types, such as blood types, origin, quality. In terms of blood supply and demand, this system can cope with emergencies when there is a sudden increase in blood demand in a specific region. Moreover, the Blockchain is actively investigated in the supply chain and healthcare sectors. This research contributes further to the scope of investigations in the healthcare system, especially in the blood supply chain, which blockchain technologies have not yet recovered.

3   Design of the Blood Donation Management Using Blockchain

In this paper, the design of a blood donation management using Hyperledger Fabric is proposed. This system can detect various problems related to blood donation supply chains such as blood origin or quality, especially for emergency blood requests. The most crucial issue to deal with in this system is the concern with the blood quality and tries to manage the supply and demand of the blood by transactions recorded in the blockchain technology. The procedure below shows the process of how our proposed system works.

As can be seen from Fig. 1, several steps in the system are performed. After donations from the volunteers, blood will be stored at the healthcare center; these blood samples are determined based on the ID of each volunteer. This blood data is only accessible by the facility's medical staff to prevent unauthorized exploitation of information from outside individuals. The blood samples will be shipped to other medical facilities or hospitals after the test is completed. After changing the storage location, data for each blood sample will be updated with the respective medical facility. The inquiry of staff at the new medical facility is also recorded in the system to help monitor and manage better; of course, the querying of information is only done by the staff of the new medical facility. Besides, blood using data such as emergency care, blood transfusion is also recorded to determine which patients have used blood samples donated by volunteers. In many cases, when the donated blood samples have problems or are of poor quality, recording the data also helps in better traceability of the blood so that health facilities can know which volunteers are in poor health and how much blood did they donate at which health facilities.

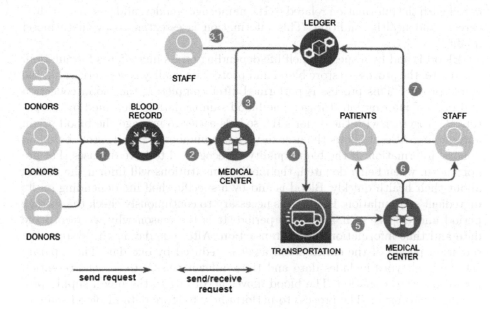

Fig. 1. Architecture of blood donation chain.

One of the important reasons to implement our proposed system in Blockchain is information visibility. Many medical institutions wherein blood transfusions are made generate data that records when the final blood is used or disposed of, which can improve blood inventorying as well as blood-demand predictability. The participant consensus algorithm of Hyperledger Fabric sequentially records transactions over time and manages information transparently so as to prevent forgery or alteration.

4   Implementation of the Blood Donation Management

In the proposed system, we have several algorithms to operate the system. The proposed method in this paper uses Hyperledger Fabric to conduct transactions. This tool, based on JavaScript, uses the blockchain network because it is suitable for a private business environment.

The participants in the blood management system are defined in the code below. There are five main participants in this system: Staff, Donors, Transporter, Medical center, and Patient. His/her corresponding ID identifies each participant in the process. Besides, the information about the participants is also stored to support the data query and tracking purposes.

The donors who perform the blood donation are the first participants of the process. Information of this user group is collected after the blood donation procedure is completed, and it is stored together with the data of the blood sample collected from that donor. The code below describes donors' reports in detail with the information related to ID, name, age, gender, address, nationality, career, and health condition. This information is essential to evaluate blood quality.

Blood is and by a specific shelf life depending on its ingredients formulation. Therefore, the process to store blood and protect its quality is very critical in the whole process. This process is performed after completing the blood collection and donors' information storage. The blood sample data is identified by a separate ID, together with the donor's ID, so it is easier to manage the blood origin and quality. Also, it allows the user to view the number of blood assets based on donors' information. If the blood quality is recognized to have diseases that are not known when being donated, the medical institutions will inform the donors about their health quickly. Blood is and by a specific shelf life depending on its ingredient's formulation. Hence, it is necessary to continuously check the storage period and dispose of it after that period. It is the reason why we record the date and time information in the transaction. After one day in the system, the retention period of the entire blood asset is reduced by one day. The separate ID of blood types includes date and time, allowing users to see the retention period of blood donation. The blood moves according to the blood supply process for transfusion. The process to perform how to store data of blood samples is presented in the structure bellows.

```
{
  "donorID":"dn001",
  "name":"Jame Morrison",
  "age":"32",
  "gender":"female",
  "address":"Taipei",
  "nationality":"Italy",
  "career":"student",
  "healthcondition:"good"
}
```

The movement state is defined to indicate whether the blood is currently moving or within the organ. In addition, the blood ownership information is defined. Managing the blood process includes transportation, which is defined as one of the important steps in the whole process. Consequently, the information related to the shipping company is also needed to be stored in the system.

```
{
  "bloodsampleID":"bs001",
  "donorID":"dn001",
  "type":"AB",
  "date":"09/20/2020",
  "time":"11:45",
  "location":"Taipei",
  "medicalcenter":"Taipei"
}
```

As can be seen from the structure of the process to record blood sample information, the information of the delivery company is also recorded to serve the purpose of verification during the transport of blood samples. The information recorded in the system includes ID company (name of delivery company), ID delivery (name of delivery worker), name of delivery man, age, phone number, address of the delivery man. This info is structured in the process of recording transportation.

```
{
  "companyID":"company001",
  "deliveryID":"delivery001",
  "name":"deliverer001",
  "age":"30",
  "number":"12345678",
  "address":"Tainan"
}
```

The information of patient who receive donation blood is recorded in the system under the structure.

```
{
  "patientID":"volunteers001",
  "bloodsampleID":"bs001",
  "name":"John",
  "age":"20",
  "address":"Taipei",
  "medicalstatus":"status record 001"
}
```

Patient and medical personnel information is also created and stored to determine which patients have received which units of blood and determine whether healthcare staff has access to blood data. The information recorded in the system consists of six components, such as patients' ID, blood sample, name, age, address, medical status. The sample information can be seen clearly in the structure bellows.

```
{
  "staffID":"staff001",
  "name":"Jenny",
  "age":"25",
  "number":"+88 22334455",
  "gender":"female",
  "address":"Taipei",
  "workingStatus":"active"
}
```

5 Algorithms

In addition to the implementation of information is recorded in the system, several algorithms are also performed to illustrate how the system works. The system consists of two main algorithms, including Algorithms 1 (to describe the mechanism to store blood samples of donors) and Algorithms 2 (which summarizes delivering blood samples from the donation place to the medical center).

Algorithm 1 consists of five main steps. It describes the mechanism to store blood samples of donors. Blood samples, once collected, will be identified with the IDs of the respective donors. Each blood sample will have a separate ID to avoid duplication of data inside the ledger; after being donated, the blood will be stored at the medical facility. The blood samples will also be stored in the ledger.

Algorithm 1: storing blood samples of donors

1: Input: donors ID, name, age, date of birth, blood type, amount of blood unit
2: Output: data of donors and their blood is stored into ledger
3: **for** unit of blood **do**
4:     storing data of donors and blood to ledger
5: **end for**

Algorithm 2 summarizes delivering blood samples from the donation place to the medical center via ten main steps. In the donation place, after storage, the blood samples will be transported to different medical facilities. Before shipping, the carrier information will be stored in the ledger to determine which company transports the blood and how many units of blood have been transported. The process's input is the data of the delivery unit, and the output of the algorithm is the data of delivery and the new medical center, which receives the blood from donors. Its corresponding ID further identifies each step.

Moreover, the authors provide the sources codes for the proof of concept, instruction of installation. Interesting readers might refer to our GitHub repository[1].

---

[1] https://github.com/Masquerade0127/bloody-blockchain.

Algorithm 2: transportation of blood samples from donation places to medical center

---

1: Input: data of delivery unit
2: Output: data of delivery is stored to ledger, new medical center also updated
3: **for** delivery unit **do**
4:   **for** blood samples **do**
5:     storing ID of blood unit with correspondence ID of delivery unit
6:   **end for**
7:   **for** blood samples **do**
8:     update location of new medical center of blood samples
9:   **end for**
10: **end for**
11: **return** Encrypted hash

---

6 Security and Privacy Discussion

The blockchain plays a vital role in the modern system; this model meets the transparency and availability requirements for the supply chain [5, 19, 30]. However, the blockchain-based system still has some problems that are listed in [17], especially in the security and privacy aspect. To improve the security and privacy issues in the blockchain-based blood donation system, we consider the authorization for the parties in the same transaction and the flexibility in the medical environment.

For the authorization aspect, we will exploit attribute-based access control (ABAC) [15, 29] to manage the access control process. The main benefit of this model is only the authorized users can access the release data. Besides, the query rewriting can apply for the complex context where the release data can be shared to multiple users [28, 33]. Finally, some approaches split the original policy into sub-policy [27, 31] (i.e., public and private policy) to ensure the data is only accessed via permission even the parties in the same transaction.

For the flexibility aspect, we should embed the blood donation management system in the larger environment (e.g., medical, healthcare) were combining with the other supply chain [21, 22] as well as connecting with the other smart things [8, 9].

7 Conclusion

In this paper, we designed and implemented a blood donation management based on the private Blockchain technology to obtain several goals: blood secure information visibility and guarantee the blood quality for both receivers and donors. The real-time recording and sharing of information as blood is donated, classified, consumed in distributed ledgers enables efficient management of blood. The information among participants is transparent, which helps participants track the source of blood quality easily. In addition, this system, which prevents forgery and information tampering, will make the blood management operation more transparent by solving problems that may occur in medical institutions and with medical staff, such as missing inputs of entry, exit, band errors. Besides, the system, which supports blood transactions between medical institutions, can manage blood quality. This function is beneficial for both receivers and donors because, for receivers, they feel safe when the blood quality is ensured, and for donors, they know their health situation.

At present, the use of blockchain technology in the medical field is actively discussed, but no previous relevant studies or application samples are dealing with blood origin or quality. To realize the blockchain network proposed by this paper, consideration should be given to the coordination of interests among participants in the blood chain system and the infrastructural, legal, institutional, and technical aspects.

Although this study proposes an innovative method for blood supply chain management and implementation of a prototype system, there is insufficient verification of the proposed approach. Hence, a thorough evaluation study will be performed to prove the effectiveness of the proposed scheme by integrating the proposed system with the existing blood information system. Furthermore, we will consider the proposed design's cost and network configuration and view the additional information, block size, and hacking-prevention potential required for actual hospital blood transactions.

References

1. Farmatrust report (2019). https://www.farmatrust.com/
2. Organ tree (2019). https://.organ-tree.com
3. Armaghan, N., Pazani, N.: A model for designing a blood supply chain network to earthquake disasters (case study: Tehran city). Int. J. Qual. Res. **13**(3), 605–624 (2019)
4. Baek, E.J., Kim, H.O., Kim, S., Park, Q.E., Oh, D.J.: The trends for nationwide blood collection and the supply of blood in Korea during 2002–2006. Korean J. Blood Transfus. **19**(2), 83–90 (2008)
5. Campanile, L., Iacono, M., Levis, A.H., Marulli, F., Mastroianni, M.: Privacy regulations, smart roads, blockchain, and liability insurance: putting technologies to work. IEEE Secur. Priv. **19**, 34–43 (2020)
6. Crosby, M., Pattanayak, P., Verma, S., Kalyanaraman, V., et al.: Blockchain technology: beyond bitcoin. Appl. Innov. **2**(6–10), 71 (2016)
7. Delen, D., Erraguntla, M., Mayer, R.J., Wu, C.N.: Better management of blood supply-chain with GIS-based analytics. Ann. Oper. Res. **185**(1), 181–193 (2011)
8. Duong-Trung, N., Son, H.X., Le, H.T., Phan, T.T.: On components of a patient-centered healthcare system using smart contract. In: Proceedings of the 2020 4th International Conference on Cryptography, Security and Privacy, pp. 31–35. Association for Computing Machinery, New York (2020). https://doi.org/10.1145/3377644.3377668
9. Duong-Trung, N., Son, H.X., Le, H.T., Phan, T.T.: Smart care: integrating blockchain technology into the design of patient-centered healthcare systems. In: Proceedings of the 2020 4th International Conference on Cryptography, Security and Privacy, ICCSP 2020, pp. 105–109. Association for Computing Machinery, New York (2020). https://doi.org/10.1145/3377644.3377667

10. Emmanuel, J.C.: The blood cold chain. WHO report (2017)
11. Eskandari-Khanghahi, M., Tavakkoli-Moghaddam, R., Taleizadeh, A.A., Amin, S.H.: Designing and optimizing a sustainable supply chain network for a blood platelet bank under uncertainty. Eng. Appl. Artif. Intell. **71**, 236–250 (2018)
12. Ha, X.S., Le, H.T., Metoui, N., Duong-Trung, N.: Dem-cod: novel access-control-based cash on delivery mechanism for decentralized marketplace. In: 2020 IEEE 19th International Conference on Trust, Security and Privacy in Computing and Communications (TrustCom), pp. 71–78. IEEE (2020)
13. Ha, X.S., Le, T.H., Phan, T.T., Nguyen, H.H.D., Vo, H.K., Duong-Trung, N.: Scrutinizing trust and transparency in cash on delivery systems. In: Wang, G., Chen, B., Li, W., Di Pietro, R., Yan, X., Han, H. (eds.) SpaCCS 2020. LNCS, vol. 12382, pp. 214–227. Springer, Cham (2021). https://doi.org/10.1007/978-3-030-68851-6_15
14. Hackius, N., Petersen, M.: Blockchain in logistics and supply chain: trick or treat? In: Digitalization in Supply Chain Management and Logistics: Smart and Digital Solutions for an Industry 4.0 Environment. Proceedings of the Hamburg International Conference of Logistics (HICL), vol. 23, pp. 3–18. epubli GmbH, Berlin (2017)
15. Hoang, N.M., Son, H.X.: A dynamic solution for fine-grained policy conflict resolution. In: Proceedings of the 3rd International Conference on Cryptography, Security and Privacy, pp. 116–120 (2019)
16. Hölbl, M., Kompara, M., Kamišalić, A., Nemec Zlatolas, L.: A systematic review of the use of blockchain in healthcare. Symmetry **10**(10), 470 (2018)
17. Joshi, A.P., Han, M., Wang, Y.: A survey on security and privacy issues of blockchain technology. Math. Found. Comput. **1**(2), 121 (2018)
18. Kim, D.: An integrated supply chain management system: a case study in healthcare sector. In: Bauknecht, K., Pröll, B., Werthner, H. (eds.) EC-Web 2005. LNCS, vol. 3590, pp. 218–227. Springer, Heidelberg (2005). https://doi.org/10.1007/11545163_22
19. Kshetri, N.: Blockchain's roles in strengthening cybersecurity and protecting privacy. Telecommun. Policy **41**(10), 1027–1038 (2017)
20. Lavastre, O., Gunasekaran, A., Spalanzani, A.: Effect of firm characteristics, supplier relationships and techniques used on supply chain risk management (SCRM): an empirical investigation on French industrial firms. Int. J. Prod. Res. **52**(11), 3381–3403 (2014)
21. Le, H.T., Le, N.T.T., Phien, N.N., Duong-Trung, N.: Introducing multi shippers mechanism for decentralized cash on delivery system. Money **10**(6), 590–597 (2019)
22. Le, N.T.T., et al.: Assuring non-fraudulent transactions in cash on delivery by introducing double smart contracts. Int. J. Adv. Comput. Sci. Appl. **10**(5), 677–684 (2019)
23. Mettler, M.: Blockchain technology in healthcare: the revolution starts here. In: 2016 IEEE 18th International Conference on E-health Networking, Applications and Services (Healthcom), pp. 1–3. IEEE (2016)
24. Nagurney, A., Masoumi, A.H., Yu, M.: Supply chain network operations management of a blood banking system with cost and risk minimization. Comput. Manag. Sci. **9**(2), 205–231 (2012)
25. Nofer, M., Gomber, P., Hinz, O., Schiereck, D.: Blockchain. Bus. Inf. Syst. Eng. **59**(3), 183–187 (2017)
26. Shahbaz, M.S., RM, R.Z., Bin, M.F., Rehman, F.: What is supply chain risk management? A review. Adv. Sci. Lett. **23**(9), 9233–9238 (2017)

27. Son, H.X., Chen, E.: Towards a fine-grained access control mechanism for privacy protection and policy conflict resolution. Int. J. Adv. Comput. Sci. Appl. **10**(2), 507–516 (2019)
28. Son, H.X., Dang, T.K., Massacci, F.: Rew-smt: a new approach for rewriting xacml request with dynamic big data security policies. In: International Conference on Security, Privacy and Anonymity in Computation, Communication and Storage. pp. 501–515. Springer (2017)
29. Son, H.X., Hoang, N.M.: A novel attribute-based access control system for fine-grained privacy protection. In: Proceedings of the 3rd International Conference on Cryptography, Security and Privacy, pp. 76–80 (2019)
30. Son, H.X., Le, T.H., Quynh, N.T.T., Huy, H.N.D., Duong-Trung, N., Luong, H.H.: Toward a blockchain-based technology in dealing with emergencies in patient-centered healthcare systems. In: Bouzefrane, S., Laurent, M., Boumerdassi, S., Renault, E. (eds.) MSPN 2020. LNCS, vol. 12605, pp. 44–56. Springer, Cham (2021). https://doi.org/10.1007/978-3-030-67550-9_4
31. Thi, Q.N.T., Dang, T.K., Van, H.L., Son, H.X.: Using JSON to specify privacy preserving-enabled attribute-based access control policies. In: Wang, G., Atiquzzaman, M., Yan, Z., Choo, K.-K.R. (eds.) SpaCCS 2017. LNCS, vol. 10656, pp. 561–570. Springer, Cham (2017). https://doi.org/10.1007/978-3-319-72389-1_44
32. Wüst, K., Gervais, A.: Do you need a blockchain? In: 2018 Crypto Valley Conference on Blockchain Technology (CVCBT), pp. 45–54. IEEE (2018)
33. Xuan, S.H., Tran, L.K., Dang, T.K., Pham, Y.N.: Rew-xac: an approach to rewriting request for elastic abac enforcement with dynamic policies. In: 2016 International Conference on Advanced Computing and Applications (ACOMP). pp. 25–31. IEEE (2016)
34. Yaga, D., Mell, P., Roby, N., Scarfone, K.: Blockchain technology overview. arXiv preprint arXiv:1906.11078 (2019)
35. Yoshiharu, A., et al.: Blockchain structure and theory. Wikibooks (2017)

International Workshop on Processes, Methods and Tools Towards RE-Silient Cities and Cultural Heritage Prone to SOD and ROD Disasters (RES 2021)

Resilience of Urban Mobility Systems: Combining Urban Subsystems and Threats with a System Dynamics Approach

Daniela Vanessa Rodriguez Lara[(✉)] ⓘ and Antônio Nélson Rodrigues da Silva ⓘ

São Carlos School of Engineering, University of São Paulo, São Carlos, Brazil
daniela.lara@usp.br, anelson@sc.usp.br

Abstract. Urban systems are dynamic, complex, and often involve multiple stake-holders, resulting in responses with distinct time lags. A resilient urban mobility system should be able to neutralize the effects of disruptive events (threats) while maintaining its essential state of functionality. Given the lack of studies addressing threats to urban mobility and the concurrent impacts on the urban mobility system, a holistic analysis considering key elements of transport systems and their interactions is necessary. Thus, this study aims to describe and analyze the dynamics involved in a resilient urban mobility system using qualitative system dynamics modeling. We start by identifying the main system components, threats, interrelations, and interconnections. Then, we create causal loop diagrams (CLD) of the urban mobility system under different conditions: (i) in the essential state of functionality, (ii) affected by a disruptive event and (iii) still functioning due to its resilience. Analyzing the CLDs indicated that the dynamics involved in a resilient urban mobility system have a preventive nature as it reflects the importance of transport policies considering climate change and disaster prevention policies/measures. In addition, the results showed that public opinion and incentives to use sustainable transport play an important role in balancing the system. Therefore, the negative effects of threats on the system, such as deaths, damage to transport infrastructures, and collapse of mobility performance, can be prevented. The outcomes of this study may be used to support the process of planning and building resilient cities.

Keyword: Urban resilience · Urban mobility systems · System dynamics · Causal loop diagrams · Threats to urban systems

1 Introduction

Cities are complex and self-organized systems with nonlinear behavior and dynamic properties [1], which can be further divided or aggregated into other systems. Disruptions, disturbances, or shock events that occur in one part of the system may lead to difficulties elsewhere [2, 3] and eventually impact the whole system. Urban mobility systems are subject to frequent and continuous disruptive events (threats), which compromise not only the satisfactory functioning but also the integrity of infrastructures, resulting in multiple negative impacts [1, 4, 5].

© Springer Nature Switzerland AG 2021
O. Gervasi et al. (Eds.): ICCSA 2021, LNCS 12956, pp. 93–108, 2021.
https://doi.org/10.1007/978-3-030-87010-2_7

The ability of cities or urban systems to resist, adapt or transform themselves in the face of shock and stressful events is known as urban resilience [6]. A resilient urban transport system should be able to neutralize the effects of threats while maintaining its essential state of functionality, reconciling the reduction of its ecological footprint while improving the quality of life [1]. Although some studies have addressed combined threats to all elements of urban systems [7, 8], most strategies to quantify urban resilience consider the particularities and scales of different urban subsystems separately [1, 9]. A wide range of studies has also addressed the impacts of climate change and extreme weather on transport systems [10–13], but few are related to urban mobility. There is also a lack of studies addressing the threats to urban mobility and their concurrent impacts on the system.

Given that transport systems are essentially dynamic in time and in space, a systematic analysis framework that integrates different stakeholders and/or agents is advantageous. Problems with these characteristics fit precisely into System Dynamics (SD) modeling. SD is based on Causal Loop Diagrams (CLD), whose (qualitative) representation indicates how a change in one variable affects other variables, which in turn affect the initial variable again. System components can be added in the form of mathematical rules that can explain and predict their evolution in the short and long term. SD can help to understand decision-making mechanisms in complex situations (e.g., how policy targets, strategies, incentives, or penalties in one part of the system influence other subsystems and eventually change the behavior of the whole system [14]). SD models can help to properly manage and control transport systems and provide plausible solutions to many transportation problems [2], such as threats to urban mobility and the resilience of urban mobility when faced with a threat [15–18].

In addition, an in-depth qualitative analysis of the dynamics in a system allows visualization of the system's hypothesized structure, and the proper construction of quantitative models [19]. Hence, the proposed research investigates the components of urban, transport and urban mobility systems, aiming at describing and analyzing the resilience of urban mobility in the face of its main threat (or eventually threats), through qualitative system dynamics modeling. We intend to answer the following questions: What are the main components of and threats to urban mobility systems? What are the dynamics involved in urban mobility systems in their essential state of functionality and when exposed to the main threat? How resilient are urban mobility systems in the face of the main threat (or threats)?

This section introduced the importance of modeling the resilience of urban mobility system using a conceptual analysis of system dynamics. The remainder of this paper is organized into four additional sections. Section 2 presents a brief background on urban mobility systems and resilience. In Sect. 3, we describe the qualitative system dynamics models used for characterizing the resilience of urban mobility systems. Section 4 discusses the results. Finally, the conclusions and suggestions for future works are presented in Sect. 5.

2 Theoretical Background

In this section, we present a brief literature review on urban mobility systems and resilience. We investigate the components of the systems found in the literature and propose a standardized nomenclature and a division into subsystems. Furthermore, we introduce the concepts and threats to characterize the resilience of urban mobility systems.

2.1 Urban Mobility Systems

A system is a set of elements that are interrelated and interconnected forming a complex whole [20]. An urban system is a complex and adaptive interdependent network consisting of different subsystems [21, 22] which can be further divided or aggregated into larger and more complex systems depending on the context of the study [23], such as urban transport and urban mobility systems.

Stefaniec et al. [24] divided transport systems into three subsystems: environmental, economic, and social. Environmental is related to resources, land-use, and ecological issues, such as waste and pollution. Economic includes the movement of people and goods, economic development, and measures to avoid the economic vulnerability of society. Social corresponds to safety, human health, social interactions, and equity. Lopes et al. [25] identified three transport subsystems: transported people and goods, means or services of transportation, and network through which movements happen.

In general, the divisions and nomenclatures of the subsystems diverge in most of the studies we found. The studies conducted by [21, 26–28] are comprehensive and addressed several elements. Therefore, based on the studies presented, we propose dividing urban mobility systems into eight subsystems, as indicated in Table 1.

Table 1. Urban mobility subsystems

Subsystem	Urban mobility subsystems
Institutional	Governance and policies (local norms, customs, and laws), actors and institutions (governmental and nongovernmental)
Social	Communities, people, demographics, justice and equity, safety, human health, social interactions, social movements, right to urban mobility
Economic	Development of societies and economies, monetary capital, measures to avoid economic vulnerability of society, transport infrastructure investment
Material and energy flows	Materials produced or consumed in or by a system (energy)
Infrastructure	Infrastructures and built environment, land use and structural design, network through which movements happen, transportation infrastructure
Natural	Natural includes ecology, environment, natural resources, estimated vehicle emissions, and geographical conditions
Demand	Transported people and goods, movement of people and goods, attitude/mobility options, origin, and destinations
Transport mode	Movement of people and goods, means or services of transportation, traffic congestion, transport modes, public transportation, private transportation, attractiveness

2.2 Resilience: Concepts and Threats

The concept of resilience has increasingly been applied in urban transport studies and has drawn the attention of urban and transport planners. Urban resilience refers to the ability of an urban system - and all its constituent socio-ecological and socio-technical networks across temporal and spatial scales - to maintain or rapidly return to desired functions [21], to absorb the first damage, to reduce the impacts from a disturbance [29], to adapt to change, and to quickly transform systems that limit current or future adaptive capacity [21, 29].

Fernandes et al. [27, 28] adapted the concept of resilience of Folke et al. [30] to urban mobility. The authors defined persistence as the potential of an individual or group to maintain existing mobility patterns, possibly affecting their socioeconomic conditions, but without compromising their quality of life. Adaptability corresponds to the potential to adopt different alternatives to the essential mobility patterns, also without compromising the quality of life. Transformability is the potential to create new conditions for adaptability and persistence in the face of future threats. In addition, Roy et al. [31] defined mobility resilience as the ability of a mobility infrastructure system (for people's trips) to manage shocks and return to a steady state in response to extreme events, such as hurricanes, earthquakes, terrorist attacks, winter storms, wildfires, floods, and others.

The concept of resilience we selected for this study is specific regarding urban mobility, but also considers the interactions and interconnections with other system components. Thus, the resilience of an urban mobility system corresponds to the ability to maintain the current conditions or rapidly return to the original mobility status (persistence), to absorb the first damage and to reduce the impacts from a disturbance by adopting different alternatives to the essential mobility conditions (adaptability); or to adapt to change (transformability) across temporal and spatial scales.

After an extensive search in the literature on threats that specifically affect the resilience of urban, transport, and urban mobility systems, we identified 37 types of threats. We then aggregated similar threats into common names that are representative of the original individual meanings. For instance, terrorism, targeted destructions, malevolent attacks, and pranks were called malicious hazards. The final list was reduced to 17 threats. Natural disasters (39.4%), climate change (15.5%), malicious hazards (9.9%), and technical failures (8.5%) were the most frequent threats, whereas peak oil (5.6%) and increased fuel price (4.2%) were the least frequent.

The investigation of threats to urban mobility systems is important to characterize the system responses before, during and after shock events, so that proper frameworks for measuring and characterizing resilience could be designed. In the studies analyzed, we observed that the methods and variables used to describe resilience vary according to the threat outlined. Therefore, we identified threats to the urban mobility system and segregated them according to the subsystem affected. The studies more frequently address increased fuel prices (33.3%), peak oil (29.6%), and disrupted fossil fuel supply (14.8%) as threats to the urban mobility system. The *Social* and *Economic* subsystems were most often associated with these threats.

3 Method

After conducting a comprehensive literature review on urban mobility systems and resilience, we identified the main subsystems, threats, and variables. Considering these subsystems, we proposed a method to describe the dynamics involved in an urban mobility system in its essential state of functionality and in the face of threat(s). Finally, we built models, using causal loop diagrams (CLD), illustrating the resilience of an urban mobility system in the face of a major threat. The method follows these steps:

1. Characterization, based on the literature review, of interrelations and interconnections between the elements of an urban mobility system: identification of cause and effect relationships (and feedbacks) [32] between the main system elements. Moreover, identifying the boundaries of the system (resilience of what) [17–19], and time horizons [17, 18].
2. Qualitative modeling describing the system in the essential state of functionality: investigation of the causal beliefs [15], creation of CLD, structure and feedback processes [33, 34].
3. Qualitative modeling of the system when affected by one or more disruptive events: creation of CLD, structure and feedback processes in the face of threat(s).
4. Qualitative modeling of the system facing one or more disruptive events but still functioning due to its resilience: creation of CLD, structure and feedback processes describing persistence, adaptability, and transformability of an urban mobility system in the face of threat(s).

CLD models comprise a graphic tool used for better understanding the cause and effect relationships between the components of a system [20]. Cause and effect relationships are graphically represented by an arrow and a sign (positive or negative). When components or variables are directly proportional, that is, when the growth in one variable (cause) produces an increase in another variable (effect), it is stated that the causal relationship between the variables is positive. In contrast, when the variables are inversely proportional, that is, when the growth in one variable (cause) produces a decrease in another variable (effect), the causal relationship between the variables is negative.

Causal relationships help the development of positive (or reinforcing) feedback loops, negative (or balancing) feedback loops, and archetypes. Reinforcing loops lead to an exponential growth of the system, while balancing loops lead to stabilization. Archetypes comprise common system structures that produce characteristic behavior patterns [35]. More specifically, archetypes are composed of specific combinations of reinforcing and balancing loops [14].

Qualitative models provide an in-depth understanding of the dynamics involved in a system, allowing a global view of the entire functioning of the system. This is particularly important to identify the impacts of decision-making processes that might run counterintuitively, worsening functionalities, or intensifying the malfunction of the system. Models are validated through careful examination of their internal consistency and their realistic representation of critical aspects of the problem [14, 15, 20]. To do this, case studies to establish realistic databases are needed. In this study, we focus on identifying cause and effect relationships that have already been validated by researchers from several areas of knowledge. Model validation and quantitative system dynamics modeling using case studies will be the focus of future investigations.

4 Results and Discussions

The first step of the method corresponds to identifying interrelations and interconnections between system elements. We identified 118 variables used to characterize urban mobility subsystems and their associations. However, to include only variables in the CLD that are relevant to describe the system behavior, we aggregated similar variables and selected the most relevant to characterize the causal relationships, as presented in Table 2.

Table 2. Variables for characterizing subsystems

Subsystem	Variables
Institutional	Land-use policies, Private motorized transport policies, Priorities of policymakers to transport policies, Active and public transport policies, Technological strengths [1, 13, 16, 36], Disaster prevention policies/measures, Segregated housing or relocation programs
Social	Deaths, Employment, Health issues, Safety, Urban segregation, Vulnerable social groups [12, 16, 32, 33, 36–43]
Economic	Economy, Trip costs [1, 12, 16, 39, 40, 43, 44]
Material and energy flows	Fuel consumption [3, 16, 36, 43]
Infrastructure	Compact urban form and structure, Transport infrastructure investments, Green infrastructures, Impervious area, Transport infrastructure recovery [1, 16, 17, 36, 39, 40, 45], Transport infrastructure maintenance, Infrastructure conservation status
Natural	Climate change, Flooding, GHG emissions [1, 33, 39, 42, 44, 45], Environmental issues
Demand	Private motorized travel demand, Population, Active and public travel demand, Public awareness and willingness to change [17, 36, 37, 40, 43–45]
Transport mode	Efficiency of vehicles, Mobility performance, Transport mode attractiveness, Travel time, Traffic congestion, Travel distance, Technological strengths [3, 12, 13, 16, 17, 36, 37, 42–45]

Based on the variables selected, we built qualitative models to represent an urban mobility system under different conditions: (i) in the essential state of functionality, (ii) affected by a disruptive event and (iii) still functioning due to its resilience. The essential state corresponds to common system structures that represent the system's behavior during a typical day, that is, the essential state is an archetype of the urban mobility system. The CLD, in this case, resulted in fourteen feedback loops, in which ten are reinforcing (R1 to R10) and four are balancing (B1 to B4) loops, as depicted in Fig. 1. A schematic representation of reinforcing feedback loops (R), in which the most frequent variables are underlined, correspond to:

(R1) PRIVATE MOTORIZED TRANSPORT POLICIES $\xrightarrow{-}$ TRIP COSTS $\xrightarrow{-}$ TRANSPORT MODE ATTRACTIVENESS $\xrightarrow{+}$ PRIVATE

MOTORIZED TRANSPORT DEMAND [$\xrightarrow{-}$ ACTIVE AND PUBLIC TRAVEL DEMAND $\xrightarrow{+}$ ACTIVE AND PUBLIC TRAVEL POLICIES

$\xrightarrow{-}$] $\xrightarrow{+}$ PRIVATE MOTORIZED TRANSPORT POLICIES

(R2) PRIVATE MOTORIZED TRANSPORT POLICIES $\xrightarrow{+}$ TRANSPORT INFRASTRUCTURE INVESTMENTS $\xrightarrow{+}$ MOBILITY

PERFORMANCE $\xrightarrow{-}$ TRAVEL TIME $\xrightarrow{-}$ TRANSPORT MODE ATTRACTIVENESS $\xrightarrow{+}$ PRIVATE MOTORIZED TRANSPORT DEMAND

[$\xrightarrow{-}$ ACTIVE AND PUBLIC TRAVEL DEMAND $\xrightarrow{+}$ ACTIVE AND PUBLIC TRAVEL POLICIES $\xrightarrow{-}$] $\xrightarrow{+}$ PRIVATE MOTORIZED

TRANSPORT POLICIES

(R3) ACTIVE AND PUBLIC TRANSPORT POLICIES $\xrightarrow{-}$ TRIP COSTS $\xrightarrow{-}$ TRANSPORT MODE ATTRACTIVENESS $\xrightarrow{+}$ ACTIVE AND

PUBLIC TRAVEL DEMAND $\xrightarrow{+}$ ACTIVE AND PUBLIC TRANSPORT POLICIES

(R4) ACTIVE AND PUBLIC TRANSPORT POLICIES $\xrightarrow{+}$ TRANSPORT INFRASTRUCTURE INVESTMENTS $\xrightarrow{+}$ MOBILITY

PERFORMANCE $\xrightarrow{+}$ TRAVEL TIME [$\xrightarrow{+}$ TRIP COSTS] $\xrightarrow{-}$ TRANSPORT MODE ATTRACTIVENESS $\xrightarrow{+}$ ACTIVE AND PUBLIC

TRAVEL DEMAND $\xrightarrow{+}$ ACTIVE AND PUBLIC TRANSPORT POLICIES

(R5) ACTIVE AND PUBLIC TRAVEL DEMAND $\xrightarrow{-}$ PRIVATE MOTORIZED TRAVEL DEMAND [$\xrightarrow{+}$ TRAFFIC CONGESTION] $\xrightarrow{-}$

MOBILITY PERFORMANCE $\xrightarrow{-}$ TRAVEL TIME [$\xrightarrow{+}$ TRIP COSTS] $\xrightarrow{-}$ TRANSPORT MODE ATTRACTIVENESS $\xrightarrow{+}$ ACTIVE AND

PUBLIC TRAVEL DEMAND

(R6) ACTIVE AND PUBLIC TRAVEL DEMAND $\xrightarrow{-}$ FUEL CONSUMPTION $\xrightarrow{+}$ TRIP COSTS $\xrightarrow{-}$ TRANSPORT MODE

ATTRACTIVENESS $\xrightarrow{+}$ ACTIVE AND PUBLIC TRAVEL DEMAND

(R7) ACTIVE AND PUBLIC TRANSPORT DEMAND $\xrightarrow{-}$ PRIVATE MOTORIZED TRANSPORT DEMAND $\xrightarrow{-}$ ACTIVE AND PUBLIC

TRANSPORT DEMAND

(R8) ECONOMY $\xrightarrow{+}$ PRIORITIES OF POLICYMAKERS TO TRANSPORT POLICIES $\xrightarrow{+}$ ACTIVE AND PUBLIC TRANSPORT POLICIES

$\xrightarrow{+}$ TRANSPORT INFRASTRUCTURE INVESTMENTS $\xrightarrow{+}$ MOBILITY PERFORMANCE [$\xrightarrow{-}$ TRAFFIC CONGESTION $\xrightarrow{-}$] $\xrightarrow{+}$

ECONOMY

(R8') ECONOMY $\xrightarrow{+}$ PRIORITIES OF POLICYMAKERS TO TRANSPORT POLICIES $\xrightarrow{+}$ PRIVATE MOTORIZED TRANSPORT

POLICIES $\xrightarrow{+}$ TRANSPORT INFRASTRUCTURE INVESTMENTS $\xrightarrow{+}$ MOBILITY PERFORMANCE [$\xrightarrow{-}$ TRAFFIC CONGESTION $\xrightarrow{-}$] $\xrightarrow{+}$

ECONOMY

(R9) MOBILITY PERFORMANCE $\xrightarrow{-}$ TRAFFIC CONGESTION $\xrightarrow{-}$ MOBILITY PERFORMANCE

(R10) FUEL CONSUMPTION $\xrightarrow{+}$ GHG EMISSIONS $\xrightarrow{-}$ POPULATION $\xrightarrow{+}$ VULNERABLE SOCIAL GROUPS $\xrightarrow{-}$ PRIVATE MOTORIZED

TRAVEL DEMAND $\xrightarrow{+}$ FUEL CONSUMPTION

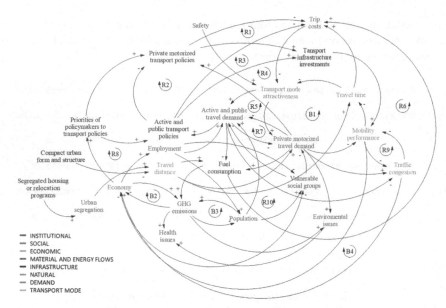

Fig. 1. Causal loop diagram for urban mobility system in its essential state of functionality

The separate loops can be interpreted as follows. In reinforcing loop R1, for example, an increase in policies aimed at private motorized transport decreases costs incurred by private motorized trips, which increases the transport mode attractiveness, increasing private motorized transport demand (which decreases active and public travel demand, reducing policies on active and public transport, which increases policies on private motorized transport), which in turn increases policies related to private motorized transport. As the interpretation of the other loops follows a similar logic, we will not explain them in detail, except for loop R8.

Reinforcing loop R8 indicates that an increase in the economy leads to more priorities of policymakers towards active and public transport policies, which increases investments in active and public transport infrastructures. An increase in transport infrastructure investments leads to more mobility performance (which decreases traffic congestion), which in turn increases the economy. Reinforcing loop R8' is equal to R8, but instead of the variable active and public travel policies, it refers to the variable private motorized transport policies.

A schematic representation of the balancing feedback loops (B) from Fig. 1, in which the most frequent variables are underlined, correspond to:

(B1) PRIVATE MOTORIZED TRAVEL DEMAND [→ TRAFFIC CONGESTION]⁺ → MOBILITY PERFORMANCE⁻ → TRAVEL TIME⁻

[→ TRIP COSTS]⁺ → TRANSPORT MODE ATTRACTIVENESS⁻ → PRIVATE MOTORIZED TRAVEL DEMAND⁺

(B2) ECONOMY⁺ → GH EMISSIONS⁻ → ECONOMY

(B3) POPULATION⁺ → GH EMISSIONS⁻ → POPULATION

(B4) ECONOMY⁺ → EMPLOYMENT⁻ → VULNERABLE SOCIAL GROUPS⁻ → PRIVATE MOTORIZED TRAVEL DEMAND⁻ →

MOBILITY PERFORMANCE [→ TRAFFIC CONGESTION⁻→]⁻ ⁺→ ECONOMY

In general, *Social*, *Transport mode* and *Institutional* subsystems have a greater influence over the CLD regarding the essential state of functionality, as they represent 58.3% of the variables. The CLD is general and does not consider the dynamics over time, that is, there are links and loops that can occur at different times, producing different impacts on the general system. For instance, the variable mobility performance is affected by several variables that tend to stabilize (balancing loop B1) or generate an exponential growth over it (reinforcing loop R9).

Additionally, Fig. 1 illustrates that the priorities of the public authorities for directing policies aimed at active, public, or private motorized transport are related to economic interests. Thus, although there are dynamics that pressure the implementation of public policies favoring a particular travel mode, these policies only occur if there is a convergence of the priorities of policymakers with economic interests. In addition, loop R10 indicates that a decrease in vulnerable social groups (e.g., low-income population) leads to an increase in fuel consumption. This is because there is an increase in the population traveling by private motorized vehicles, which means an increase in private motorized travel demand. However, loop R10 has no other balancing loops acting to stabilize it, thus an exponential growth in fuel consumption is observed.

Therefore, urban mobility in its essential state of functionality is driven by economic interests, whereby mobility performance and travel demand have dynamics with exponential growth, as well as stabilizing dynamics that can lead to balanced feedback loops. Furthermore, measures must be taken to stabilize fuel consumption as the functioning of the system exponentially aggravates environmental issues and is exposed to fuel restrictions.

We observed in the literature review that natural disasters and climate change are more often indicated as threats to urban systems, while increased fuel prices and peak oil are more frequently indicated as threats to urban mobility. Hence, a gap in studies addressing climate change impacts on urban mobility was noted. For this reason, we also built a CLD representing the system behavior when threatened by natural disasters and climate change. The diagram resulted in eleven feedback loops, in which five are reinforcing (Rt1 to Rt5) and six are balancing (Bt1 to Bt6) loops (Fig. 2). The interpretation of reinforcing and balancing feedback loops in Fig. 2 follows the same logic explained for the causal loop diagram regarding the system in its essential state of functionality.

In general, when the system is under threat, new variables, links, and loops are created and rearranged in response. The system response depends on the intensity of the shock and the intrinsic characteristics of the system, for instance, the existence of disaster prevention policies. Our model considers a variety of these possibilities, resulting in an increase in the participation of the number of variables that comprise the *Infrastructure* and *Institutional* subsystems (from 8.3% to 16.7% and from 16.7% to 19.4%, respectively), in relation to the essential state. *Institutional, Transport mode, Social,* and *Infrastructure* subsystems have a greater influence over the CLD as they represent 72.2% of the variables.

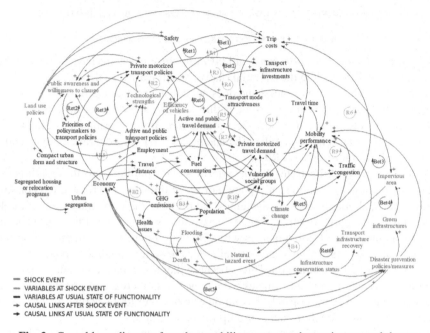

Fig. 2. Causal loop diagram for urban mobility system under environmental threats

Additionally, Fig. 2 indicates that the priorities of policymakers for directing transport policies are not only a consequence of economic interests, but also of public opinion (Rt3). Reinforcing feedback loop Rt3 pressures policymakers towards sustainable travel modes, stabilizing loops with private motorized travel policies. On the other hand, there are dynamics that reinforce or balance climate change, as can be observed in loops Rt5, Rt6 and Bt5. Mobility performance affects economy (Rt5) and private motorized travel demand (Rt6), causing an exponential increase in climate change. In loop Bt5, disaster prevention policies/measures affect fatalities, flooding, and infrastructure conservation status, stabilizing fuel consumption, GHG emissions, and, consequently, climate change. Loops Bt1 and Bt2 balance private motorized policies through technological strengths, such as innovation, smart city strategies, intelligent transportation systems (ITS), electric vehicles, alternative fuels, and energy efficiency (fuels and vehicles). In contrast, loop Rt6 is counterintuitive, as measures for the recovery of private motorized infrastructures may, in fact, increase private motorized demand, aggravating climate change.

Therefore, an urban mobility system threatened by climate change is driven by interests of the economy and public opinion, especially with regard to encouraging the use of sustainable transport. Furthermore, technological strengths, energy efficiency of vehicles and disaster prevention play an important role in stabilizing fuel consumption, mobility performance, private motorized demand, and climate change. These findings are important to support and guide decision-making processes in low-carbon policies and smart cities paradigms, for instance.

Finally, in the last part of our analysis, we built a CLD for the resilience of urban mobility system based on the analysis of several attributes proposed by Fernandes et al. [28] and Folke et al. [30]: persistence, adaptability, and transformability. The CLD representing a resilient urban mobility system resulted in eleven feedback loops, in which five are reinforcing (Rr1 to Rr5) and six are balancing (Br1 to Br6) loops. The interpretation of reinforcing and balancing feedback loops in Fig. 3 follows the same logic explained for the causal loop diagram regarding the system in its essential state of functionality.

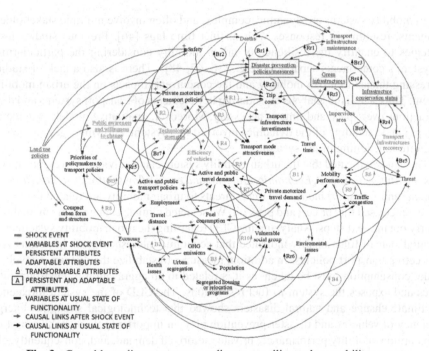

Fig. 3. Causal loop diagram corresponding to a resilient urban mobility system

In general, a resilient urban mobility system should have attributes that allow the system to maintain its current conditions (persistence), to absorb the first damage and reduce impacts (adaptability), or to adapt to change, and to quickly transform subsystems (transformability) after a shock event. Analyzing the system under threat (Fig. 2) made it possible to identify variables, links, and feedback loops that are important to describe a resilient system. Thus, the CLD from Fig. 3 showed that the *Institutional, Infrastructure, Transport mode*, and *Social* subsystems have a greater influence over the diagram, as they represent 75.0% of the variables.

Additionally, Fig. 3 indicates that the CLD for a resilient system is slightly similar to the CLD for the system under threat, however, there is an important difference between the two diagrams. In the CLD under threat, the dynamics have a reactive pattern, while in the resilient CLD they have a preventive pattern, as can be seen in feedback loops Rr1 to Rr5, in which transport policies provide for the planning of disaster prevention policies/measures. In addition, loop Rr6 strengthens the dynamics aimed at controlling fuel consumption and climate change, strengthening the economy and disaster prevention policies/measures. On the other hand, loops Br1 to Br7 tend to stabilize threats and the effects of threats to the system, such as deaths, infrastructure conservation status, and fuel consumption. Besides that, it can be observed that public opinion plays an important role in balancing the system, as well as encouraging the use of sustainable transport.

5 Conclusions

Urban mobility systems are dynamic, complex, and often involve multiple stakeholders or agents, resulting in responses with distinct time lags [46]. Previous studies used strategies to quantify the resilience of urban mobility considering the particularities of system's components separately (e.g., [36, 47, 48]). There is also a lack of studies addressing threats to urban mobility and the concurrent impacts on the urban mobility system. Thus, a holistic analysis considering key elements of transport systems and their interactions over space and time is necessary. Moreover, qualitative models provide an in-depth understanding of the dynamics involved in a system, allowing a global view of the entire functioning of the system.

This study indicated that the urban mobility system can be divided into eight subsystems: *Institutional, Social, Economic, Material and energy flows, Infrastructure, Natural, Demand* and *Transport mode.* The main threats to urban mobility are related to climate change, increased fuel prices, and peak oil. We selected climate change as the main threat to carry out the next steps. Analyzing the CLD regarding the urban mobility system in its essential state of functionality indicated that economic interests play an important role in directing transport policies. In addition, measures to stabilize the dynamics involved in fuel consumption must be taken, as it is related to an aggravation of environmental issues and exposes the system to fuel restrictions. The CLD of the system threatened by climate change and natural disasters showed that technological strengths, energy efficiency of vehicles and disaster prevention play an important role in stabilizing fuel consumption, mobility performance, private motorized demand, and, consequently, climate change. Furthermore, the system is driven by interests of the economy and public opinion, especially with regard to encouraging the use of sustainable transport.

The CLD of the resilience of the urban mobility system is similar to the CLD of the system under threat. However, the dynamics of the system under threat have a reactive pattern, while in a resilient system they have a preventive pattern. This can be seen through the dynamics concerning transport policies that provide for the planning of disaster prevention policies/measures and strengthening of the dynamics aimed at controlling fuel consumption and climate change. Thus, the economy and disaster prevention policies/measures are reinforced, preventing the negative effects of threats to the system (deaths, infrastructure conservation status, and mobility performance). Besides that, public opinion and incentives to use sustainable transport play an important role in balancing the system.

The study characterized the dynamics involved in urban mobility system in its essential state of functionality, under natural hazards and under resilient functioning. Considering this, the study helps to develop holistic quantitative models to determine the resilience of urban mobility using a system dynamics approach. Thus, besides answering the questions formulated in the introductory section, this study proposes a new division of subsystems and addresses a threat to urban mobility that has been scarcely explored in the literature using holistic qualitative models. The model shows that the elements of the urban system are strongly connected, generating effects in different parts of the system.

Thus, when analyzing urban mobility considering the threat of climate change, we are faced with other threats already mentioned in the literature (e.g., flooding, natural disasters, GHG emissions, population growth, vehicle demand, etc.). However, most of the studies we found analyze only one effect at a time, not considering the dynamics that lead to its appearance, or its interconnections with other subsystems, that is, cause and effect relations are not always considered.

The proposed method can support the development of integrated urban and transport management, in which the consequences of policies and actions carried out in one part of the system can be identified and have effects on other predicted parts. In addition, the study can be adapted to different urban systems and even other situations that have systemic characteristics, such as smart cities and Industry 4.0. Thus, the outcomes of this study may be used to support the process of planning and building resilient cities.

This study provides an in-depth understanding of the dynamics involved in the urban mobility system through qualitative models (CLD). However, the models do not allow a local analysis and do not consider the dynamics over time. For future work, we suggest extending this study for quantitative models based on stock and flow diagrams. To do this, it would be necessary to validate the model through case studies, for example. In addition, other threats could be explored, such as increased fuel prices, and peak oil. Consequently, an integrated analysis considering several threats, as well as the resilience of urban mobility systems under concomitant threats could be carried out.

Acknowledgment. . This study was financed in part by the Coordenação de Aperfeiçoamento de Pessoal de Nível Superior - Brasil (CAPES) - Finance Code 001.

References

1. Zhao, P., Chapman, R., Randal, E., Howden-Chapman, P.: Understanding resilient urban futures: a systemic modelling approach. Sustainability **5**, 3202–3223 (2013). https://doi.org/10.3390/su5073202
2. Abbas, K.A., Bell, M.G.H.: System dynamics applicability to transportation modeling. Transp. Res. Part A **28**, 373–390 (1994). https://doi.org/10.1016/0965-8564(94)90022-1
3. Lovelace, R., Philips, I.: The "oil vulnerability" of commuter patterns: a case study from Yorkshire and the Humber UK. Geoforum **51**, 169–182 (2014). https://doi.org/10.1016/j.geoforum.2013.11.005

4. Srivastav, R.K., Simonovic, S.P.: Simulation of dynamic resilience: A railway case study, Ontario, Canada (2014)
5. Cantillo, V., Macea, L.F., Jaller, M.: Assessing vulnerability of transportation networks for disaster response operations. Netw. Spat. Econ. **19**(1), 243–273 (2018). https://doi.org/10.1007/s11067-017-9382-x
6. Leichenko, R.: Climate change and urban resilience. Current Opinion Environ. Sustain. **3**, 164–168 (2011). https://doi.org/10.1016/j.cosust.2010.12.014
7. Cavallo, A., Ireland, V.: Preparing for complex interdependent risks: a system of systems approach to building disaster resilience. Int. J. Disaster Risk Reduct. **9**, 181–193 (2014). https://doi.org/10.1016/j.ijdrr.2014.05.001
8. Esposito, D., Cantatore, E., Sonnessa, A.: A multi risk analysis for the planning, management and retrofit of cultural heritage in historic urban districts. In: La Rosa, D., Privitera, R. (eds.) Innovation in Urban and Regional Planning. INPUT 2021. Lecture Notes in Civil Engineering, vol. 146, pp. 571–580. Springer, Cham (2021). https://doi.org/10.1007/978-3-030-68824-0_61
9. Amoaning-Yankson, S., Amekudzi-Kennedy, A.: Transportation system resilience opportunities to expand from principally technical to sociotechnical approaches. Transp. Res. Rec. 28–36 (2017). https://doi.org/10.3141/2604-04
10. Chopra, S.S., Dillon, T., Bilec, M.M., Khanna, V.: A network-based framework for assessing infrastructure resilience: a case study of the London metro system. J. R. Soc. Inter. **13** (2016). https://doi.org/10.1098/rsif.2016.0113
11. Duy, P.N., Chapman, L., Tight, M.: Resilient transport systems to reduce urban vulnerability to floods in emerging-coastal cities: a case study of Ho Chi Minh City Vietnam. Travel Behav. Soc. **15**, 28–43 (2019). https://doi.org/10.1016/j.tbs.2018.11.001
12. Mattsson, L.-G., Jenelius, E.: Vulnerability and resilience of transport systems - a discussion of recent research. Transp. Res. Part A Policy Pract. **81**, 16–34 (2015). https://doi.org/10.1016/j.tra.2015.06.002
13. Mostafavi, A., Inman, A.: Exploratory analysis of the pathway towards operationalizing resilience in transportation infrastructure management. Built Environ. Project Asset Manag. **6**, 106–118 (2016). https://doi.org/10.1108/BEPAM-03-2015-0011
14. Nabavi, E., Daniell, K.A., Najafi, H.: Boundary matters: the potential of system dynamics to support sustainability? J. Clean. Prod. **140**, 312–323 (2017). https://doi.org/10.1016/j.jclepro.2016.03.032
15. Rich, E., Gonzalez, J.J., Qian, Y., Sveen, F.O., Radianti, J., Hillen, S.: Emergent vulnerabilities in Integrated Operations: a proactive simulation study of economic risk. Int. J. Crit. Infrastruct. Prot. **2**, 110–123 (2009). https://doi.org/10.1016/j.ijcip.2009.07.002
16. Moradi, A., Vagnoni, E.: A multi-level perspective analysis of urban mobility system dynamics: what are the future transition pathways? Technol. Forecast. Soc. Chang. **126**, 231–243 (2018). https://doi.org/10.1016/j.techfore.2017.09.002
17. Suryani, E., Hendrawan, R.A., Adipraja, P.F.E., Indraswari, R.: System dynamics simulation model for urban transportation planning: a case study. Int. J. Simul. Model. **19**, 5–16 (2020). https://doi.org/10.2507/IJSIMM19-1-493
18. Suryani, E., Hendrawan, R.A., Adipraja, P.F.E., Wibisono, A., Dewi, L.P.: Urban mobility modeling to reduce traffic congestion in Surabaya: a system dynamics framework. J. Model. Manag. **6**(1), 37–69 (2021). https://doi.org/10.1108/JM2-03-2019-0055
19. Tenza, A., Perez, I., Martinez-Fernandez, J., Gimenez, A.: Understanding the decline and resilience loss of a long-lived socialecological system: insights from system dynamics. Ecol. Soc. **22** (2017). https://doi.org/10.5751/ES-09176-220215
20. Sterman, J.D.: System dynamics: systems thinking and modeling for a complex world. Massachusetts Institute of Technology, Working Paper Series ESD-WP-2003-01.13 (2002)

21. Meerow, S., Newell, J.P., Stults, M.: Defining urban resilience: a review. Landsc. Urban Plan. **147**, 38–49 (2016). https://doi.org/10.1016/j.landurbplan.2015.11.011
22. Rus, K., Kilar, V., Koren, D.: Resilience assessment of complex urban systems to natural disasters: a new literature review. Int. J. Disaster Risk Reduct. **31**, 311–330 (2018). https://doi.org/10.1016/j.ijdrr.2018.05.015
23. Tobey, M.B., Binder, R.B., Yoshida, T., Yamagata, Y.: Urban systems design applicability case study: Applying urban systems design framework to North Sumida Ward Tokyo. In: 16th International Conference on Computers in Urban Planning and Urban Management, Wuhan, China, pp. 555–570 (2019)
24. Stefaniec, A., Hosseini, K., Xie, J., Li, Y.: Sustainability assessment of inland transportation in China: a triple bottom line-based network DEA approach. Transp. Res. Part D Transp. Environ. **80**, 102258 (2020). https://doi.org/10.1016/j.trd.2020.102258
25. Lopes, A.S., Cavalcante, C.B., Vale, D.S., Loureiro, C.F.G.: Convergence of planning practices towards LUT integration: seeking evidences in a developing country. Land Use Policy **99**, 104842 (2020). https://doi.org/10.1016/j.landusepol.2020.104842
26. Ostadtaghizadeh, A., Ardalan, A., Paton, D., Jabbari, H., Khankeh, H.R.: Community disaster resilience: a systematic review on assessment models and tools. PLoS Currents **7** (2015). https://doi.org/10.1371/currents.dis.f224ef8efbdfcf1d508dd0de4d8210ed
27. Fernandes, V.A., Rothfuss, R., Hochschild, V., da Silva, W.R., Santos, M.P. de S.: Resiliência da mobilidade urbana: Uma proposta conceitual e de sistematização. Revista Transportes **25**, 147–160 (2017). https://doi.org/10.14295/transportes.v25i4.1079
28. Fernandes, V.A., et al.: Urban resilience in the face of fossil fuel dependency: the case of Rio de Janeiro's urban mobility. URBE-Revista Brasileira de Gestão Urbana **11** (2019). https://doi.org/10.1590/2175-3369.011.e20180160
29. Ribeiro, P.J.G., Pena Jardim Gonçalves, L.A.: Urban resilience: a conceptual framework. Sustain. Cities Soc. **50**, 101625 (2019). https://doi.org/10.1016/j.scs.2019.101625
30. Folke, C., Carpenter, S.R., Walker, B., Scheffer, M., Chapin, T., Rockström, J.: Resilience thinking: integrating resilience, adaptability and transformability. Ecol. Soc. **15** (2010). https://doi.org/10.5751/ES-03610-150420
31. Roy, K.C., Cebrian, M., Hasan, S.: Quantifying human mobility resilience to extreme events using geo-located social media data. EPJ Data Sci. **8**, 1–15 (2019). https://doi.org/10.1140/epjds/s13688-019-0196-6
32. Joakim, E.P., et al.: Using system dynamics to model social vulnerability and resilience to coastal hazards. Int. J. Emergency Manage. **12**, 366–391 (2016). https://doi.org/10.1504/IJEM.2016.079846
33. Feofilovs, M., et al.: Assessing resilience against floods with a system dynamics approach: a comparative study of two models. Int. J. Disast. Resil. Built Environ. **11**, 615–629 (2020). https://doi.org/10.1108/IJDRBE-02-2020-0013
34. Menezes, E., Maia, A.G., de Carvalho, C.S.: Effectiveness of low-carbon development strategies: Evaluation of policy scenarios for the urban transport sector in a Brazilian megacity. Technol. Forecast. Soc. Chang. **114**, 226–241 (2017). https://doi.org/10.1016/j.techfore.2016.08.016
35. Meadows, D.: Thinking in systems. Chelsea Green (2000)
36. Leung, A., Burke, M., Cui, J.: The tale of two (very different) cities - mapping the urban transport oil vulnerability of Brisbane and Hong Kong. Transp. Res. Part D - Transp. Environ. **65**, 796–816 (2018). https://doi.org/10.1016/j.trd.2017.10.011
37. Dodson, J.: Suburbia under an energy transition: a socio-technical perspective. Urban Stud. **51**, 1487–1505 (2014). https://doi.org/10.1177/0042098013500083
38. Macmillan, A.K., et al.: Controlled before-after intervention study of suburb-wide street changes to increase walking and cycling: Te Ara Mua-Future Streets study design. BMC Public Health. **18** (2018). https://doi.org/10.1186/s12889-018-5758-1

39. Song, K., You, S., Chon, J.: Simulation modeling for a resilience improvement plan for natural disasters in a coastal area. Environ. Pollut. **242**, 1970–1980 (2018). https://doi.org/10.1016/j.envpol.2018.07.057

40. Xie, X.-F., Wang, Z.J.: Examining travel patterns and characteristics in a bikesharing network and implications for data-driven decision supports: case study in the Washington DC area. J. Transp. Geogr. **71**, 84–102 (2018). https://doi.org/10.1016/j.jtrangeo.2018.07.010

41. Cao, M., Hickman, R.: Urban transport and social inequities in neighbourhoods near underground stations in Greater London. Transp. Plan. Technol. **42**, 419–441 (2019). https://doi.org/10.1080/03081060.2019.1609215

42. Williams, D.S., Manez Costa, M., Sutherland, C., Celliers, L., Scheffran, J.: Vulnerability of informal settlements in the context of rapid urbanization and climate change. Environ. Urban. **31**, 157–176 (2019). https://doi.org/10.1177/0956247818819694

43. Pfaffenbichler, P., Emberger, G., Shepherd, S.: A system dynamics approach to land use transport interaction modelling: the strategic model MARS and its application. Syst. Dyn. Rev. **26**, 262–282 (2010). https://doi.org/10.1002/sdr.451

44. Chaves, G. de L.D., Fontoura, W.B., Ribeiro, G.M.: The Brazilian urban mobility policy: the impact in São Paulo transport system using system dynamics. Transp. Policy **73**, 51–61 (2019). https://doi.org/10.1016/j.tranpol.2018.09.014

45. Philp, M., Taylor, M.A.P.: Research agenda for low-carbon mobility: issues for New World cities. Int. J. Sustain Transp. **11**, 49–58 (2015). https://doi.org/10.1080/15568318.2015.1106261

46. Shepherd, S.P.: A review of system dynamics models applied in transportation. Transportmetrica B Transp. Dyn. **2**, 83–105 (2014). https://doi.org/10.1080/21680566.2014.916236

47. Santos, T., Silva, M.A., Fernandes, V.A., Marsden, G.: Resilience and vulnerability of public transportation fare systems: the case of the city of Rio De Janeiro, Brazil. Sustainability. **12** (2020). https://doi.org/10.3390/su12020647

48. Martins, M.C. da M., Rodrigues da Silva, A.N., Pinto, N.: An indicator-based methodology for assessing resilience in urban mobility. Transp. Res. Part D Transp. Environ. **77**, 352–363 (2019). https://doi.org/10.1016/j.trd.2019.01.004

Knowledge and Big Data: New Approaches to the Anamnesis and Diagnosis of the Architectural Heritage's Conservation Status. State of Art and Future Perspectives

Laura Morero[1](✉) [iD], Antonella Guida[1] [iD], Vito Porcari[1] [iD], and Nicola Masini[2] [iD]

[1] DiCEM - Department of European and Mediterranean Culture: Architecture, Environment and Cultural Heritage, University of Basilicata, 75100 Matera, Italy
{laura.morero,antonella.guida,vito.porcari}@unibas.it
[2] CNR - National Research Council of Italy, ISPC - Institute of Cultural Heritage Sciences, 85100 Potenza, Italy
nicola.masini@cnr.it

Abstract. Italy holds the international record for Cultural Heritage and Unesco sites' number but, in the face of this wealth, a number of criticalities emerge as it cannot be a mere passive location; Cultural Heritage needs protection, conservation and valorization through direct interventions such as restoration and maintenance, and indirect interventions such as the deepening and dissemination of knowledge. Strengthening the knowledge chain means, in fact, increasing the possibility of preserving Historical Buildings by developing a culture of protection and conservation.

The study, systematization, digitization and the possibility of making the totality of information on the Architectural Heritage accessible online is a fundamental means of disseminating knowledge about them.

Direct access to the information system can significantly increase the quality of the design and execution of conservation work on historic buildings.

Digital systematization therefore represents an urgent priority not only for the dissemination of cultural contents but, especially, for the executive guarantee of correct interventions on the Heritage in accordance with the provisions dictated by the national protection system according to which every action must be aimed at the conservation of the Heritage.

This contribution constitutes an overview of the digital tools related to the Architectural Heritage existing today in Italy. The peculiarities and gaps of each one are identified, in order to achieve the methodological definition of a new and improved approach based on the awareness that the digitization and dissemination of these contents are, to all intents and purposes, processes for the enhancement of Cultural Heritage.

Keywords: Architectural Heritage · Big data · Digital knowledge

© Springer Nature Switzerland AG 2021
O. Gervasi et al. (Eds.): ICCSA 2021, LNCS 12956, pp. 109–124, 2021.
https://doi.org/10.1007/978-3-030-87010-2_8

1 Introduction

In a historical period when access to places of culture, such as archives and libraries, is subject to severe restrictions, it is necessary to ask ourselves about the different ways of dealing with Cultural Heritage, without precluding the possibility of conducting studies, research and projects remotely.

The current pandemic situation has highlighted the need to deal with the digital world and its countless potentialities, which is also well suited to the collection and dissemination of cultural content.

With respect to historical studies of architectural heritage, the main documentary sources are not, in most cases, easily available because they are not published or are stored in diverse archives of different institutions and are not always quickly and easily accessible.

Systematizing and making all this historical and technical information directly available for study and consultation is, therefore, a useful tool both for scientific research and for cultural dissemination. It is also a training and planning/decision-making support for professionals in the Cultural Heritage sector, since direct access to this body of information will facilitate and qualitatively improve the conservation and enhancement work carried out by architcts, engineers and technicians.

Often, in the case of historical buildings and monuments, it is not possible to reconstruct their construction history due to the lack of sources and knowledge of archivals. To make the work of the architectural historian even more difficult is the fact that the documentation is often not inventoried, in many cases dismembered, and stored in various cultural sites.

Rethinking this system, by channeling all the data into a single reference tool, can therefore allow for a complete knowledge and anamnesis of the Heritage, avoiding the risk of making incorrect planning choices because they lack an adequate knowledge base of the Heritage on which we are going to intervene.

The availability of this information is, therefore, a fundamental aid to research and to the definition of restoration and maintenance interventions, as it would guarantee the easy retrieval of general and specific information on the building under study or intervention.

The structuring of online Information Technology (IT) platforms that can be implemented with continuously updated data (such as works in progress or monitoring campaigns) represents an extraordinary tool for the knowledge and dissemination of the Heritage, for the restoration works to be planned and, to avoid the dispersion of known and unknown data.

2 State of Art

2.1 The Italian Context

The critical and cognitive examination of the Architectural Heritage and the necessary comparison with the digital in terms of applications for the management, conservation and use of the Heritage, has animated several national and regional initiatives [1].

As regards the definition of specific platforms generally related to the Architectural Heritage, we can distinguish between national digital tools and additional tools developed autonomously by the regions. At national level, the following platforms are included:

- General Catalogue of Cultural Heritage [2]

Database of catalogued Cultural Heritage in Italy. Each file contains photos, typological and cultural definition, qualification, denomination, geographical-administrative location, historical information, plan, structural and material information, state of conservation, uses, legal status and constraints, sources and reference documents.

- MiC, Online Constraints [3]

National Protection System for Cultural Heritage. A file on an Architectural Heritage contains general information, constraints, photos, documentation, location, competent Institution and recorder, historical period, cadastral data, geographical information, state of conservation and seismic risk.

- The Churches of the Italian Dioceses [4]

Data bank with in-depth and census sheets containing: typology and qualification, names, historical information, description, Diocese, photos, geographical and ecclesiastical location, map of buildings belonging to the same ecclesiastical Institution.

- Beweb [5]

Census' platform of Historical and Artistic, Architectural, Archival and Book Heritage conducted by Italian Dioceses and ecclesiastical cultural Institutes.
A typical file of an Architectural Heritage contains photo, historical-architectural description, map, Diocese, address, plan, sources, liturgical adaptation, and devotions.

- The spaces of madness' Portal [6]

Atlas of asylum Heritage between the nineteenth and twentieth centuries with five setions: identification, history and architectur, iconography, bibliography and sources.

- MiC, National census of Architecture of the second half of 20th century [7]

Census of the most recent Architectural Heritage. For each building, there are four main sections (work, details, sources/annexes, and map) and in-depth sections.

- MiC, Information System for Restoration worksites (SICaR) [8]

System dedicated to restoration that geo-references graphic, photographic and alphanumeric documentation. The data are grouped in general and external data, scientific project/consultation, diagnostics, interventions, architectural archaeology, photos [9].

– Ecole Française de Rome, Census of Christian Sanctuaries in Italy [10]

Census of all existing and disappeared Christian sanctuaries in Italy. A typical sheet contains name, geographical location, Diocese and parish, dedication, objects of worship, life cycle of the sanctuary, type of worship, building, foundation legend, traditions, events and chronological data, official recognition, jurisdiction, patronage, architectural type, information on the structure, ex-votos, pilgrimages, miracles, rituals, bibliography.

As far as the individual regions are concerned, it should be noted, first of all, that the regions of Umbria, Abruzzo and Molise do not have any online platform and that the only information about their Cultural Heritage can be found by consulting the above-mentioned national tools.

Below are the digital initiatives undertaken by the remaining Italian regions.

– Valle D'Aosta - Cultural Heritage Catalogue System [11]

Integrated and geo-referenced relational database accessible only upon request.

– Piedmont - Digital Ecosystem of Cultural Heritage [12]

The system is divided into three sections: Mèmora, Librinlinea, and Journals of Piedmont. The Mèmora platform is available only to property owners and operators.

– Piedmont - Metropolitan City of Turin [13]

Collection of municipal files describing the Cultural Heritage catalogued to date.

– Valle D'Aosta, Piedmont - Cities and Cathedrals [14]

Digital portal of restoration and valorisation projects carried out in cooperation between Dioceses, Regions and Superintendencies.

– Lombardy - Lombardy Cultural Heritage [15]

Portal of Lombardy's Cultural Heritage with four main sections: Cultural Heritage, History and Documents, Places of Culture and Special Projects.

The Architectures sub-section contains synthetic and complete files.

– Liguria - Catalogue Inventory of Liguria's Cultural Heritage [16]

A central database that makes available files on Archaeological, Environmental and Architectural, Ethno-Anthropological, Historical and Artistic, and Natural Heritage. Now there is no file available on Architectural Heritage.

– Trentino Alto Adige - MonumentBrowser [17] and Archaeobrowser

Monumentbrowser provides an up-to-date list of all Architectural Heritage in South Tyrol. Archaeobrowser is the analogous information system by geo-referenced portal.

– Veneto - Veneto Region Cultural Heritage Catalogue [18]

Technological platform of the regional Cultural Heritage.

– Friuli Venezia Giulia - Regional Information System of Friuli Venezia Giulia's Cultural Heritage [19]

Web-based database and computerised cartography. Three sections are available for each building: file, contained Cultural Heritage, map.

– Veneto, Friuli Venezia Giulia - Regional Institute for Venetian Villas [20]

An on-line catalogue allowing consultation of the cataloguing data sheets of the Architectural and Environmental Heritage of the Veneto and Friuli Venezia Giulia regions.

– Emilia Romagna - PatER Catalogue of Cultural Heritage [21]

Portal that unites and integrates the digital resources of the regional system of Museums and Cultural Heritage.

– Emilia Romagna - Webgis Emilia-Romagna's Cultural Heritage [22]

A platform that represents the protection system in the region according to whether it is Architectural, Archaeological or Landscape Heritage, with a specific section for Architectural Heritage and the 2012 earthquake.

– Tuscany - Research System of the Cultural Heritage and Landscape [23]

A system for searching the regional territory for protection measures depending on whether they are Architectural, Archaeological or Landscape Heritage.

– Tuscany - Architecture in Tuscany from 1945 until today [24]

A platform that collects information on a selection of works of major historical and artistic interest from the 20th century.

– Tuscany - Places of Faith [25]

Platform of historical-religious buildings surveyed during the project for the enhancement of Cultural Heritage carried out by the Region between 1995 and 2000.

The data sheets are brief; only for some buildings considered to be of particular importance are there more detailed descriptions.

– Tuscany - Directory of Civil Architecture in Florence [26]

Census project of the civil buildings in the UNESCO site area.

– Marche - Marche Cultural Heritage [27]

Regional information portal on Cultural Heritage.

– Lazio - Geographical Information System [28]

Collection of georeferenced cards for the Cultural and Environmental Heritage of Lazio. The site is open but searches do not produce any results. However, there is a list of fact sheets compiled for the Architectural Heritage up to 2014.

– Campania - Campania Region, Digital ecosystem for culture [29]

A project not yet complete, the publication of the platform was anticipated to provide online cultural content during the health emergency by Covid-19.

In particular, the platform provides information, cataloguing sheets and other multimedia services related to the Activities and Cultural Heritage in the area.

– Puglia - CartApulia [30]

Territorial information system for research, valorisation and monitoring of regional Cultural Heritage.

– Basilicata - Digital Atlas of Basilicata's Castles - Basilicastle

WebGis of the Basilicata's fortified Heritage on an app fort the smartphone.

– Basilicata - Webgis Basilicata Regional Landscape Plan [31]

This platform represents the protection system in the Region, depending on whether the Heritage is Architectural or Landscape.

– Basilicata - Homepage SABAP Basilicata [32]

Information site about the Architectural Heritage of Potenza and Matera.

– Basilicata - Smart cities and Communities and Social Innovation "Product and process innovation for sustainable and planned maintenance, conservation and restoration of Cultural Heritage" [33–36]

He Ma In (Heritage Maintenance Innovation) technological platform for the programming of maintenance interventions.

– Calabria - Atlas of Calabria's Cultural Heritage [37]

Atlas collecting data from the census of Cultural Heritage. The database is freely accessible and allows for interaction with other sites or studies and publications [38].

– Sicily - ICCD, Cultural Itineraries of the Sicilian Middle Ages [39]

Portal divided into three themes: Religious and Civil Architecture, Paintings and Mosaics, Rock sites. The number of files present is small.

– Sardinia - Region of Sardinia, Catalogue of Cultural Heritage [40]

A regional catalogue containing the results of the cataloguing of the island's cultural and identity Heritage carried out by the Region since 1996.

Table 1 gives a summary overview about the contents of each platform described.

2.1.1 Italian Associations Active in the Protection and Conservation of Cultural Heritage

There is also a very active sector of associations in Italy, through foundations or private organizations, with artistic, research and cultural Heritage conservation objectives.

Among the most established experiences, which have created their own digital database of the Architectural Heritage or a census, we can mention:

– DOCOMOMO Italy ONLUS [41]

A continuously updated catalogue of the most relevant architecture of the modern movement in order to preserve and document it. The online inventory of Italy currently contains 50 files containing photos, names, location, classification, legal status, historical information, designers, interventions, use, general and technical description, bibliographic and archival references.

– FAI - Italian Environmental Fund [42]

Individual files of historical-artistic or landscape Heritage owned by FAI or received in concession from a public body or on loan from a private individual or through a sponsorship agreement aimed at protection and enhancement.

For each built there is an extensive description and individual thematic details, photos, events, news and links to the corresponding social pages.

Table 1. Data contained in Italian cultural heritage platforms

	Identification	Unused Historical Sites	Localization	Historical information	Description	Previous interventions	State of conservation	Legal status and constraints	2d/3d drawings	Photos	Attached documents	Georeferenced map	In-depth information	Cadastre and cartography	Type and technology	Quantitative data and indicators	Sources and bibliography	External links (national,regional websites)
Cultural Heritage Catalogue System	•				•	•	•	•				•	•					
Digital Ecosystem of Cultural Heritage											•	•	•		•		•	
Metropolitan City of Turin	•	•	•		•			•				•			•	•		
Cities and Cathedrals				•	•									•		•		
Lombardy Cultural Heritage		•	•	•	•			•				•	•			•	•	•
Catalogue Inventory of Liguria's Cultural Heritage																		
MonumentBrowser and Archaeobrowser	•	•			•		•			•	•			•				
Veneto Region Cultural Heritage Catalogue		•	•	•			•	•		•			•	•	•	•	•	•
Regional Information System of Friuli Venezia Giulia's Cultural Heritage	•	•	•		•								•	•				•
Regional Institute for Venetian Villas	•	•	•	•	•		•			•					•			•
PatER Catalogue of Cultural Heritage	•		•	•						•			•		•			•
Webgis Emilia-Romagna's Cultural Heritage	•	•	•		•		•			•	•	•	•			•	•	•
Research System of the Cultural Heritage and Landscape of the Region of Tuscany	•	•	•		•									•				•
Architecture in Tuscany from 1945 until today	•		•		•					•	•	•					•	
Tuscany - Places of Faith	•		•	•	•					•								
Tuscany - Directory of Civil Architecture in Florence	•		•	•	•		•	•					•				•	•
Marche - Marche Cultural Heritage	•	•	•		•					•			•					
Lazio - Geographical Information System																		
Campania Region, Digital ecosystem for culture	•	•	•		•					•		•						
Puglia - CartApulia	•	•	•	•	•	•	•	•				•				•	•	•
Basilicata - Digital Atlas of Basilicata's Castles	•	•	•	•	•					•		•	•					
Webgis Basilicata Regional Landscape Plan	•	•	•		•		•											•
Homepage SABAP Basilicata	•		•		•		•			•				•	•			
Basilicata - He Ma In	•		•	•	•	•	•		•	•		•		•	•	•	•	
Atlas of Calabria's Cultural Heritage	•	•	•	•	•							•	•			•	•	•
Sicily - Cultural Itineraries of the Sicilian Middle Ages	•		•	•	•	•	•					•	•				•	
Region of Sardinia, Catalogue of Cultural Heritage	•	•	•	•	•			•				•	•	•		•	•	

– Italia Nostra ONLUS [43]

This is one of the oldest Italian associations for the protection of Cultural Heritage.
Among the various activities undertaken over the years, of great importance for the subject matter is the national "Red List" campaign, a tool for collecting, by means of a

report, all architectural, archeological and landscape assets in a state of abandonment or in need of protection, historic site, castles and individual monuments in danger.

The list is available on an online map and for each listed built there is a photographic and descriptive file highlighting the reasons for its inclusion on the list.

– ADSI - Association of Italian Historic Houses [44]

The ADSI brings together owners of historic properties throughout Italy with the aim of helping them to defend, preserve and enhance their heritage.

A list and photographic reference of all the Italian houses whose owners have joined the initiative is available online, as well as in-depth historical descriptions of some of them.

– Association Archeologiaindustriale.net [45]

Cultural Association founded with the mission of promoting and enhancing industrial culture and its material and immaterial heritage at local, national and international level.

Among its activities is the networking, which is constantly updated, of the Italian and foreign industrial Heritage. Photos, historical and technical descriptions, in-depth information on machinery and bibliographical references are available for each artefact.

2.2 International Experiences

The research focuses on the Italian situation, reserving its implementation in the future, also taking into account international experiences; in-depth analysis that is the most necessary in light of the fact that the digitization and dissemination of knowledge related to Heritage goes well with the strategies indicated by the European Community and, in particular, with the Digital Agenda for Europe.

As early as 2006, the European Community invited Member States to implement an optimization of the cultural and economic potentials linked to Cultural Heritage, indicating which were the recommendations [46] to be followed in the areas of digitization and online accessibility of documentary sources linked to the European Heritage, seeing digitization as a fundamental tool for conservation purposes.

With the strategic action plan Digital Agenda for Europe 2010–2020 [47], the European Union relaunches the potential of a sustainable digital economy that makes the most of information and communication technologies in favor of knowledge, innovation, growth and progress.

Specifically linked to the reference theme is the promotion of policies for access to online content, giving a central role, both in the field of scientific and technological research, to the use of ICT (Information and Communication Technologies) which, through targeted digital actions, would allow the cultural memory of Europe to be preserved and handed down.

It is considered important to mention at least one of the most important responses to European dictates in the field of digitization; the establishment by the French Government of the Mérimée platform; a database on French National Monuments [48].

Mérimée has put on-line all the data of the French Architectural Heritage which includes civil, religious, military, funerary, industrial architecture and historic gardens using the support of the MAP (Médiathèque de l'architecture et du patrimoine) and the General Inventory.

The platform consists of three main sections:

– Historical Monuments: technical data sheets of buildings protected under the Historical Monuments Act of 1913 with the registration and classification decrees
– Inventory: technical sheets of everything that has been inventoried by the regional General Inventory;
– Architecture: 20th century Heritage data sheets.

The data sets of Mérimée Historical Monuments are accessible and downloadable from the government platform and include photos, name, location, cadastral references, historical description, constraint measures and specific provisions, legal status, bibliographical references, year of compilation and author.

3 Critical Reflections on Contemporary Needs and Requirements

The research carried out on the digital tools that, in Italy, investigate the Architectural Heritage has highlighted that, while there are a large number of online tools, the information provided is almost always partial, dispersed as it is disseminated over several platforms (the region of Tuscany, for example, boasts a number of four digital platforms). In some cases the information are complete but, only if referred to specific areas (predominance of portals focusing on religious architectural Heritage).

These observations are accompanied by the fact that some portals are not directly accessible. The Memora platform of the Piedmont region, for example, is for the exclusive use of the owners of the building and ministerial operators, the Catalogue System of the Cultural Heritage of the Valle d'Aosta region is accessible only upon request and only in the regional offices in charge.

Some portals are not functioning or up-to-date, such as the Lazio tool; which does not produce searches and whose last update is dated 2014.

On the other hand, an accurate historical-critical survey, together with technical-constructive information and information on the state of conservation, can be found in the Veneto Region Catalogue of Cultural Heritage platform and in the CartApulia platform of the Puglia region (see Fig. 1). In both, however, there is no two- and three-dimensional comparison with the possibility of investigating the buildings by following the actual survey of the state of art.

This possibility is instead found in the Lucanian platform He Ma In - Heritage Maintenance Innovation (see Fig. 1), where it is also possible to assess the progress of maintenance work through a network of sensors and instruments for in situ and ex situ measurements (see Fig. 2).

Two- and three-dimensional data can also be found in the National Information System for Restoration Sites SICaR for use by Superintendencies.

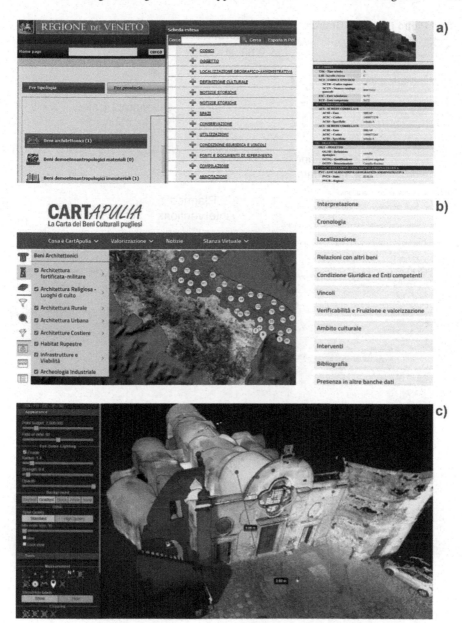

Fig. 1. Extracts of Veneto Region Catalogue of Cultural Heritage platform a), CartApulia platform b) and platform He Ma In - Heritage Maintenance Innovation c)

Both platforms, which are quite complete from the point of view of the information provided, probably because they have been in use for a relatively short time, investigate a small number of Architectural Heritage but, especially, follow an inverse principle to that which animates the research project described.

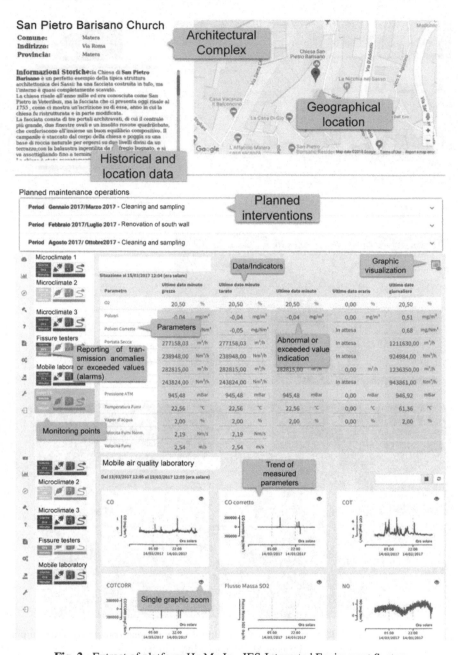

Fig. 2. Extract of platform He Ma In - IES-Integrated Enviroment System

They are conceived as platforms to be implemented at the time of the intervention on the buildings, therefore dissemination and catalyzing of all known information on a single reference tool, but only during the restoration or maintenance project to which the building is subjected.

Therefore, at the moment in Italy there is no synthesis product that integrates all the information needed for the drafting of a restoration or maintenance project, overcoming the difficulties related to accessibility, availability and all the limitations that, especially at this precise moment in history, compromise the study, in-depth study and, consequently, the protection of the Cultural Heritage.

4 Future Perspectives

The national state of the art has highlighted the lack of a single reference tool to act as the driving force behind a new approach based on the awareness that knowledge of the Heritage is essential to the planning dimension and can guide and direct it.

At the same time, that the complete recognition and dissemination of information is a guarantee of the conservation and enhancement of the Heritage itself.

In view of these considerations, the best step to be investigated is that of a single digital platform to support the activities of knowledge, analysis and planning of interventions based on a new approach. This new approach is based on the interoperability between the anamnesis of the building, intended as a catalyst of historical-constructive data, and the diagnosis, i.e. the set of data coming from dedicated sensors.

The result would be twofold: on the one hand, the design and prototyping of an integrated system that, starting from historical data collected in the field, makes it possible to manage and make available all the information known about the building. On the other hand, the possibility of implementing and modifying in real time with new data obtained from experimental surveys, monitoring and ongoing interventions.

The platform will therefore support the activities of acquisition, documentation, cataloguing, digitisation and dissemination of Heritage.

The aim is to catalogue and disseminate contents by exploiting the combination of new technologies, digital interactions and Cultural Heritage in order to foster the knowledge of historical and architectural Heritage through the exclusive use of open products and technologies, new immersive virtual and augmented reality systems that can involve not only professionals but also communities and visitors.

In particular, the technological platform thus conceived will make it possible to convey different types of data (see Fig. 3) and, specifically:

- The classification of the Cultural Heritage, mapped on a geographical basis, in all their components (general, historical, architectural, material, constructional, technological) and the archiving and management of the detailed information in formats that are easy to consult (documents, archive materials, photo, 2D and 3D models, plans, graphs, etc.).
- It will be advisable to develop a standardized model for data, which will always be able to be integrated and modified.
- The graphic interface should be designed to guide and facilitate this process;
- Monitoring of control parameters, acquired in real time (such as indoor and outdoor indicators of thermo-hygrometric characteristics, illuminance, exposure, and other parameters useful for analysing the state of conservation).
- The parameters deriving from the survey will be available in a special section where it will be possible to view the trend over time;

– Cataloguing and management of the activity plan of activities carried out, in progress and planned, and thus not only document and share the activities carried out, but information regarding chronology, progress, details and outcomes.

The platform will have to be designed in such a way as to allow access to different types of users through specific authorization profiles. This will make it possible to overcome the problem of finding material related to the Architectural Heritage by facilitating processes and digitizing data, which is now more essential than ever; and to encourage collaboration and the exchange of opinions, experiences and cross-sectoral learning between the various technical professions. At the same time, thanks to an online open data resource, the platform will be able to reach a large participatory community in accordance with Italian and European Commission guidelines.

A context where both research and experimentation activities could be carried out, aimed at defining prototype systems for the monitoring and conservation of Heritage,

IDENTIFICATION

- DEFINITION
- GEO-REFERENCED MAPPING
- LEGAL STATUS AND CONSTRAINTS
- PHOTO GALLERY
- EXTERNAL LINKS

ANAMNESIS

- HISTORICAL DATA
- ARCHITECTURAL DATA
- TECHNOLOGICAL DATA
- MATERIAL AND CONSTRUCTION DATA

- ARCHIVE DOCUMENTATION
- STUDIES, RESEARCH, THESES
- HISTORICAL ICONOGRAPHY
- SOURCES AND BIBLIOGRAPHY

- 2D GRAPHIC DESIGNS
- 3D MODEL
- HBIM MODEL
- THEMATIC IN-DEPTH ANALYSIS

+

DIAGNOSIS

- CONSERVATION STATUS
- FORMS OF DECAY AND INSTABILITY
- PREVIOUS INTERVENTIONS
- WORK IN PROGRESS

- DIAGNOSTIC CAMPAIGNS
- MULTI-TEMPORAL MONITORING
- MAINTENANCE PROJECT
- RESTORATION PROJECT

= DIGITAL, OPEN AND INTERACTIVE SOFTWARE

Fig. 3. The architecture of the proposed platform

and at developing digital-interactive approaches for the integrated management, sharing and communication of Heritage on a geographical basis.

References

1. Bonacini, E.: Nuove tecnologie per la fruizione e la valorizzazione del patrimonio culturale, Aracne, Roma (2011)
2. ICCD Homepage. http://www.catalogo.beniculturali.it. Accessed 28 Mar 2021
3. Vincoli online Homepage. http://vincoliinrete.beniculturali.it. Accessed 28 Mar 2021
4. Churches in Italian Dioceses Homepage. http://www.chieseitaliane.chiesacattolica.it. Accessed 28 Mar 2021
5. Beweb Homepage. https://www.beweb.chiesacattolica.it. Accessed 28 Mar 2021
6. Madness' places portal Homepage. http://www.spazidellafollia.eu. Accessed 28 Mar 2021
7. Census of late 20th century Architecture Homepage. http://architetturecontemporanee.benicu lturali.it. Accessed 28 Mar 2021
8. SICaR Homepage. https://sicar.beniculturali.it. Accessed 28 Mar 2021
9. Fabiani, F., Grilli, R., Musetti, V.: Verso nuove modalità di gestione e presentazione della documentazione di restauro: SICaR web la piattaforma in rete del Ministero dei Beni e delle Attività Culturali e del Turismo. In: Bollettino Ingegneri, n. 3 (2016)
10. Census of Christian Sanctuaries in Italy Homepage. http://www.santuaricristiani.iccd.benicu lturali.it. Accessed 28 Mar 2021
11. Valle d'Aosta Cultural Heritage Catalogue System Homepage. https://beniculturali.regione. vda.it. Accessed 28 Mar 2021
12. Mèmora Homepage. https://www.memora.piemonte.it. Accessed 28 Mar 2021
13. Metropolitan City of Tourin Homepage. http://www.cittametropolitana.torino.it. Accessed 28 Mar 2021
14. Cities and Cathedrals Homepage. https://www.cittaecattedrali.it. Accessed 28 Mar 2021
15. Lombardia Cultural Heritage Homepage. http://www.lombardiabeniculturali.it. Accessed 28 Mar 2021
16. ICBC Homepage. http://catalogobeniculturali.regione.liguria.it. Accessed 28 Mar 2021
17. MonumentBrowser Homepage. http://www.provincia.bz.it/arte-cultura/beni-culturali/mon umentbrowser-ricerca.asp. Accessed 28 Mar 2021
18. Veneto Region Cultural Heritage Catalogue Homepage. https://catalogo.regione.veneto.it. Accessed 28 Mar 2021
19. IPAC Homepage. http://www.ipac.regione.fvg.it. Accessed 28 Mar 2021
20. IRVV Homepage. http://irvv.regione.veneto.it. Accessed 28 Mar 2021
21. PatER Homepage. https://bbcc.ibc.regione.emilia-romagna.it. Accessed 28 Mar 2021
22. Webgis Emilia Romagna Homepage. https://www.patrimonioculturale-er.it/webgis/. Accessed 28 Mar 2021
23. Research System of the Cultural Heritage and Landscape of the Tuscany Region Homepage. http://www502.regione.toscana.it. Accessed 28 Mar 2021
24. Architecture in Tuscany from 1945 to today Homepage. http://www.architetturatoscana.it. Accessed 28 Mar 2021
25. Places of Faith Homepage. http://web.rete.toscana.it. Accessed 28 Mar 2021
26. Directory of Civil Architecture in Florence Homepage. http://www.palazzospinelli.org. Accessed 28 Mar 2021
27. Marche Cultural Heritage Homepage. http://www.beniculturali.marche.it. Accessed 28 Mar 2021
28. SIT Lazio Homepage. http://dati.lazio.it. Accessed 28 Mar 2021

29. Digital ecosystem for Culture Homepage. https://cultura.regione.campania.it/sistema-inform ativo-culturale. Accessed 28 Mar 2021
30. CartApulia Homepage. http://www.cartapulia.it. Accessed 28 Mar 2021
31. Webgis Basilicata Homepage. http://rsdi.regione.basilicata.it. Accessed 28 Mar 2021
32. SABAP Basilicata Homepage. http://www.vincolibasilicata.beniculturali.it. Accessed 28 Mar 2021
33. He Ma In Homepage. https://smartcities.tabsrl.com/piattaforma/#/main/gestione-beni. Accessed 28 Mar 2021
34. Guida, A., Porcari, V.D.: Innovation of the management process for the recovery and maintenance of cultural heritage. In: Congresso Euro - Americano Reha - Bend, Patología de la Construcción, Tecnología de la Rehabilitación y Gestión del Patrimonio, pp. 2572–2580 (2018)
35. Bernardo, G., Guida, A., Porcari, V.D.: Processi innovativi di manutenzione Smart del patrimonio architettonico. In: ReUSO 18, vol. 2 Conservación y Contemporaneidad, Granada, pp. 507–514 (2017)
36. Guida, A., Porcari, V.D.: Prevention, monitoring and conservation for a smart management of the cultural heritage. Int. J. Herit. Architect. 1, 71–80 (2018). Wessex WIT Print
37. Calabria's Atlas of Cultural Heritage Homepage. http://atlante.beniculturalicalabria.it. Accessed 28 Mar 2021
38. Scaduto, R.: Tutela e restauri in Sicilia e in Calabria nella prima metà del novecento. Istituzioni, protagonisti e interventi. Aracne editrice (2015)
39. Cultural Itineraries of the Sicilian Middle Ages Homepage. http://iccdold.beniculturali.it. Accessed 28 Mar 2021
40. Sardinia's Catalogue of Cultural Heritage Homepage. http://catalogo.sardegnacultura.it. Accessed 28 Mar 2021
41. DOCOMOMO Italy ONLUS Homepage. https://www.docomomoitalia.it/catalogo/. Accessed 15 June 2021
42. FAI Homepage. https://fondoambiente.it/luoghi/beni-fai/. Accessed 15 June 2021
43. Red List Italia Nostra Homepage. https://www.italianostra.org/le-nostre-campagne/la-lista-rossa-dei-beni-culturali-in-pericolo/. Accessed 15 June 2021
44. ADSI Homepage. https://www.associazionedimorestoricheitaliane.it/dimore/. Accessed 15 June 2021
45. Archeologiaindustriale.net Homepage. https://archeologiaindustriale.net/category/il-patrimonio-in-italia/. Accessed 15 June 2021
46. Commission Recommendation of 24 August 2006 on the digitisation and online accessibility of cultural material and digital preservation. https://eur-lex.europa.eu/eli/reco/2006/585/oj. Accessed 14 Apr 2021
47. Digital Agenda for Europe Homepage. https://digital-agenda-data.eu/. Accessed 14 Apr 2021
48. Mérimée Homepage. https://www.pop.culture.gouv.fr/search/list?base=%5B%22Patrimo ine%20architectural%20%28M%C3%A9rim%C3%A9e%29%22%5D. Accessed 14 Apr 2021

Built Environments Prone to Sudden and Slow Onset Disasters: From Taxonomy Towards Approaches for Pervasive Training of Users

Fabio Fatiguso[1]([✉]) [iD], Silvana Bruno[1] [iD], Elena Cantatore[1] [iD], Letizia Bernabei[2] [iD],
Juan Diego Blanco[3] [iD], Giovanni Mochi[2] [iD], Graziano Salvalai[3] [iD], Edoardo Currà[4] [iD],
and Enrico Quagliarini[5] [iD]

[1] Polytechnic University of Bari, Bari, Italy
{fabio.fatiguso,silvana.bruno,elena.cantatore}@poliba.it
[2] University of Perugia, Perugia, Italy
{letizia.bernabei,giovanni.mochi}@unipg.it
[3] Politecnico di Milano, Milan, Italy
{juandiego.blanco,graziano.salvalai}@polimi.it
[4] "La Sapienza" University of Rome, Rome, Italy
edoardo.curra@uniroma1.it
[5] Polytechnic University of Marche, Ancona, Italy
e.quagliarini@staff.univpm.it

Abstract. The assessment of resilience for the Built Environment (BE) and humans exposed to SUdden Onset and SLow Onset Disasters (SUOD and SLOD) is possible when simulations are performed to predict and analyze what can succeed, and awareness and preparedness are consolidated among human users. These two steps require the representation of the Built Environment (BE), in its spatial, geometric and informative features, in order to be perceived by users. Nevertheless, different objectives and available economic, hardware/software and human resources will determine the selection of the methodological workflow and the software products chain. Thus, the research examines disruptive technologies for the creation of Digital Built Environments to highlight the potentialities of Virtual Reality in improving expert knowledge acquisition and awareness gathering. Particularly, the use of Digital Models, BIM and Virtual Tour based, supports analytical and parametric simulations and pervasive training, respectively. This last objective can be perceived through smart and inclusive Digital solutions, mostly shared via web applications, to reach a wider audience.

Keywords: Built Environment · Digital models · Human awareness · Pervasive training

1 Introduction

Resilience of the Built Environment (BE), comprehending human users, can be pursued both simulating human behavior in multi-hazard scenarios where Slow and Sudden Onset

O. Gervasi et al. (Eds.): ICCSA 2021, LNCS 12956, pp. 125–139, 2021.
https://doi.org/10.1007/978-3-030-87010-2_9

Disasters (SLOD and SUOD) can occur and providing risk maps within the real world after computing level of risks with quantitative or qualitative methods. These risk assessment and behavioral models are substantial for understanding which knowledge should be shared through training sessions to enhance urban resilience and human preparedness to catastrophic events against multiple risks [1]. Effective training is achievable with structured tools able to widespread and consolidate this knowledge reaching a wider audience. In this regards, disruptive technologies have been investigating for these goals in training, such as Virtual Reality (VR) and Augmented Reality (AR), which demonstrated high retention, self-efficacy and involvement, rather than traditional training material, such as slides, paper and video [2].

Describing VR or Virtual Environment (VE), it reproduces reality with specific devices after its acquisition or reconstruction in digital contents and allows an immersive experience within a digitalized environment that could not be necessarily close to the users [3]. Thus, in VR the interaction between user and environment is guaranteed by the use of traditional interfaces (monitors, keyboards and mouse) or by sophisticated devices (helmets, visors and motion sensors), able to transform the created environment from the virtual to the immersive level, enhancing perception and participation. VR applications address several purposes as they allow the visualization of reality data capture and/or the reproduction of building environment typologies, from territorial to building/element scale. As the built environment concerns, the VR aims to communicate, disseminate and enhance as well as manage and share data, information and knowledge about single buildings, system or parts to support interdisciplinary studies.

Whereas, AR uses mobile devices to superimpose elaborated digital contents to the reality when users activate specific applications, leaving user not isolated in the context [4]. AR implementations mostly address touristic application to augment monuments with supplementary information [5] or help users in finding touristic places with GPS, providing specific information. The AR technology is also being used for urban planning to overlay of new masterplan on the existing landscape, in project and construction to consult drawings and administrative and technical documents, during maintenance to retrieve instructions [6].

Among all the available techniques for the creation of VEs, Virtual Tours (VT) are identified as a smart and fast technique because of the use of panoramic images. The continuous representation and visualization of the BE are ensured by rotations of each scene linked with others [7]. Here, the sharing knowledge, as a technical discussion of the BE, is ensured by means of external data, properly organized and referenced in the visualized VE [8]. Also Building Information Modelling (BIM) could be employed for VR applications as extensive models [9]. BIM is an approach for generating, storing, managing, exchanging and sharing information about the BE during the life cycle [10, 11] with the capability of computing inserted parameters and collaboration among process figures. This thanks to ontological representation and data structure of geometry and information of elements, permitting some operations of query, filtering, extraction and computing of parameters.

The baseline for training objectives is the reconstruction of the BE that can be obtained with the previously described technologies, with the aim to recognize, represent and characterize it according to the granular decomposition of the BE for risk assessment scopes, as defined in the BE S²ECURE project [12]. Indeed, this research started with the definition of typologies, elements and parameters at urban and architectural scale, focusing on the disaster events occurring in open spaces OS (such as squares and streets) and affecting humans, including the BE immediately surrounding the OS, defined as frontiers (Sect. 2). The hierarchy decomposition of the BE can be reconstructed with reality-capture techniques, BIM and GIS approach and navigated with AR/VR. In this research, where urban tissue is the baseline for multi-risk assessment, GIS may be useful to implement in the process. Recently, GIS transits from 2D GIS to 3D GIS and is combined with reality-capture, 3D City and BIM models for three-dimensional and semantic models of terrestrial surface and buildings in order to obtain a different level of detail, according to a specific use and thanks to exchange standards (i.e. cityGML and ifc) [13].

Moreover, these digital models of the BE can be navigated with fast VR/AR-oriented representations. In this perspective, the research will examine the above-mentioned disruptive technologies for pervasive training of users, to be distinguished by specific training for experts, aiming at increase resilience and preparedness against SLODs and SUODs, enhancing an aware knowledge of the BE and suggesting safe human behaviours. In particular, available methods and tools for analytical and parametric simulations and virtual training will be compared in terms of required economic, hardware/software and human resources in order to determine the selection of the methodological workflow for pervasive training, illustrated in Sect. 3. This last objective can be perceived through smart and inclusive Digital solutions (Sect. 4), mostly shared via web applications, to reach a wider audience anywhere at any time and that can be easily managed by local authorities.

2   BE and Parameters Involved in SLODs and SUODs

The BE characterisation represents the first step toward the definition of the risk level of an urban settlement prone to SUODs and SLODs and the development of effective mitigation strategies [14]. Particularly, how risk factors interfere with BE elements, modifying their setting and usability during disasters, and which BE characteristics lead to higher impacts [1]. In this regard, meso-scale risk assessments allow addressing all the aspects related to the elements of the BE, which belonging to the OS frontiers, the elements content in the OS itself and the OS users in a holistic perspective [1]. According to previous analysis, OSs can be categorized into different main type of AS and LS according to morphological approaches [15, 16]. Such configurations influence the evacuation aspects during SUODs, since LSs act as rescue roads and ASs as temporary outdoor gathering areas for the stricken population [17], while, determine the exposure risk factor for SLODs depending on factors related to the solar radiation, natural ventilation and pollutant concentration [18]. For example, shapes of AS tending to quadrangular or circular guarantee the same proximity to escape routes and, the central point may be the safest place in case of fronts overturning due to earthquakes; contrary, when such configurations favour large areas exposed to intense and direct solar radiation, heat entrapment, wind block and air pollutants concentration [18]. LS types are distinguished according to the level of vehicular and pedestrian traffic [15]. In fact, the simultaneous presence of vehicles and pedestrian determines risk factors: in the case of SLODs, influences air quality due to pollutant concentration; during SUODs, it can be dangerous for the evacuation during an earthquake, or even, it may represent a terrorist threat to people. Moreover, the dimension regarding the maximum height of the OS frontiers (H_{max} built front) is also relevant for estimating the possibility of path blockage from debris due to buildings collapse, and, the canyon effect thus reducing pollutants dispersion through ventilation and the risk of solar radiant exposure [18].

The definition of the OS geometry is provided by the types of elements of the OS frontiers and the OS itself. The permeability of the OS in terms of number, width and position of the accesses affect both SUODs and SLODs: multiple accesses enhance the evacuation process avoiding overcrowding; good permeability increases the ventilation. The greenery and water bodies presence and position within the OS influence the physical vulnerability for exclusively SLODs risks: they can mitigate the increasing temperatures and air pollution. On the other hand, the presence of special buildings, town walls, porches mainly interact with the SUODs risks: such constructions have more structural weaknesses (i.e. typical failure mechanisms) in response to earthquake [16]; buildings belonging to cultural heritage are more prone to overcrowding since being tourist attractions [19]. In addition, other elements content in the OS that involve a 3D spatial modification, such as fountains, monuments and quote differences, can be considered as obstacles for users during the post-earthquake emergency phase. Regarding terrorism, fixed or mobile elements in contents [20] represent the main elements that should enhance the vulnerability to a terrorist attack. Most of these parameters can be obtained directly from 2D or 3D models. In addition, either GIS or BIM tools can help enrich the quality and quantity of data collected to be used for studying the BE.

The constructive features of OS frontiers and the materiality of the OS itself influence the response to both SUODs [16] and SLODs [21]. In case of earthquakes, constructive features define the vulnerability in terms of structural performance and damage suffered by buildings that could determine the path blockages by debris, thus affecting the safety of OS users and preventing access to rescue [16, 22, 23]. The materiality and finishing of façades and OS pavement influence the heat balance, determining the façades and pavement surface capacity for capturing, releasing or emitting heat; thus, making its surroundings warmer or cooler.

Characteristics of use of the OS itself and the functions of the facing buildings provide the exposure risk factor of both earthquakes and terrorism by determining the number of OS users and the potential crowding conditions over the time which may increase disasters' casualties. Moreover, overcrowding may hinder the evacuation process and influence the behaviour and the motion of evacuees, especially of those that have no familiarity with the urban layout (i.e. tourists). Specifically, buildings of political, religious or cultural value (e.g. parliament, churches, monuments, museums, theaters) and specific uses of the outdoor space (e.g. nocturnal attraction for young people, special events) suggest the evaluation of the "exposed value" since they represent sensitive targets for terrorist acts [19]. Regarding SLODs, the space use and functions determine only crowding levels and type of users; however, these exposures shall be constant or recurrent, for the BE users, to generate significant health deterioration. The definition of the spatio-temporal users' pattern and the availability of database integrated with

Table 1. Summary of the main BE parameters described, specifying if they affect the whole OS or buildings (Bs) and the relation with Seismic (S) or Terrorism (T) SUOD, as well as Heat wave (H) or air pollution (P) SLOD

Macro-area for BE classification	Criteria	OS	Bs	Risk/s related			
				S	T	H	P
MAIN TYPE							
	Prevalent shape	x					
	Dimension	x					
	H_{max} built front		x				
	H_{min} built front		x				
CHARACTERISTICS OF GEOMETRY AND SPACE							
	Structural Type (SA/SU)		x				
	Accesses	x	x				
	Special buildings		x				
Frontier	Town walls	x					
	Porches	x	x				
	Water	x					
	Quote differences	x					
	Green area	x	x				
	Special buildings		x				
	Canopy	x					
	Fountain	x					
	Monuments	x					
Content	Dehors	x					
	Quote difference	x					
	Archaeological sites	x					
	Green area	x					
	Underground park	x					
	Underground cavities	x					
CONSTRUCTIVE CHARACTERISTICS							
	Homogeneity of built environment age		x				
Frontier	Homogeneity of constructive techniques		x				
	Urban furniture/obstacles	x					
	Pavement/Surface materials	x					
Content	Pavement lying	x					
	Pavement/Surface finishing	x					
	Urban furniture/obstacles	x					
CHARACTERISTICS OF USE							
	Daily crowding	x	x				
	Sensitive target to terroristic attack	x	x				

(*continued*)

Table 1. (*continued*)

	Vehicular accessibility	x					
	Pedestrian accessibility	x					
	Type of users	x	x				
ENVIRONMENTAL CHARACTERISTICS							
	Climatic zone	x					
	Type of infrastructures	x					
	Permanent elements (natural and man-made)	x					
	Hazard assessment	x					

GIS/BIM tools would enable a more precise and constantly updated definition of the real impacts [24, 25].

Finally, the characteristics of the environment where the OS is located contribute to the definition of the hazard level of SLODs according to the climate zone (e.g. maximum seasonal temperatures). Moreover, specific hazard that may affect the area (e.g. tsunami, landslide, wildfire, storm/tornado, etc.) and, the presence of strategic infrastructural network that may be susceptible to damage, are also considered as additional risk elements of both SLODs and SUODs.

All the described BE elements are then summarized in Table 1, relating to single SLOD and SUOD and highlighting the relevance with the scale of detail.

3 Approaches for the Pervasive Training in Virtual BE

Approaches and materials to enhance recognition and knowledge of BE elements that influence multi-risk scenarios, as screened above, will be investigated in this section to provide innovative and interactive VR tools for knowledge dissemination and pervasive training. The virtual training via VR can be implemented in several modalities, but the first objective to structure an effective tool is the reconstruction of the BE with different accessibility and fruition modes of the digital reality. The training material should be prone to web publication in order to reach the goal of widespread (pervasive) training materials for expert and non-expert users.

In the VTs, the VE is based on indoor and outdoor spherical images or videos, maintaining real colours and elements, linked together to re-create the building morphology [8] through locomotion switches. After the preparation of the baseline VT, this can be augmented with external media, in several common use formats, attached to interactive popups, called hotspots or widgets.

Nevertheless, VT can comprehend panoramas exported by 3D models, such as CAD and BIM. Moreover, BIM models themselves can be navigated in VR (both display-based and immersive), sometimes with the opportunity to query parameters added to each element, in remote mode or on-site using QRcodes and tags. The continuous digital flow from BIM and VR/AR applications requires the acceptance of shared languages (standards and exchange formats) for unique understanding among the software products, and interoperability when possible both on-desk and on-line applications. The transition from architectural to urban scale is supported by GIS models for which interoperability with BIM is created developing the open standard cityGML, after the conversion of IFC data from BIM models [26–28]. Moreover, the use of Reality capture outputs (meshes or point clouds) in 3D city models increases the recognition of each BE element affecting risk scenarios due to a higher level of detail and accuracy.

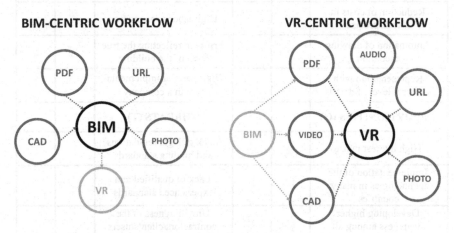

Fig. 1. BIM-centric and VR-centric data and information schema (authors)

According to the analysis of available approaches for VR, two typologies of workflows can be defined to link and read information and data (Fig. 1):

1. BIM-centric workflow: BIM modelling software products are mainly used to represent, analyse risks and then navigated in VR for training.
2. VR-centric workflow: virtual tours with 360° photos or videos acquired by cameras are the main tools for virtual training, immediately available for adding external information contents such as digitalized paper documents, video, and web pages, and progressively implemented with panoramas and 3D models from BIM or CAD and assessment outcomes, such as risk maps and evacuation simulations.

The selection of the methodological workflow for pervasive training is guided by the comparison of available tools and methods for analytical and parametric simulations and virtual training in terms of required economic, hardware/software and human resources.

The assessment of the different tools for training, BIM and VR, is carried out through the SWOT analysis which identifies strengths, weaknesses, opportunities and threats of each one beyond risk and resilience management purposes (Table 2).

Table 2. SWOT analysis between BIM (BIM-Centric) and VR (VR-Centric) workflows in representing Built Environments.

STRENGTHS (S)	BIM	VR	WEAKNESS (W)	BIM	VR
Better documentation	■	■	No universal software platform		■
Reduction of costs in overall process	■	■	High labor consumption	■	
Automation of drawing execution	■		Errors in reflecting the true form of the building	■	■
Representation with different level of details	■	■	High costs of implementation in a company	■	
OPPORTIUNITIES (O)			**THREATS (T)**		
High interest in use	■	■	Lack of legal regulations and binding standards		■
Implementation of the technologies in many countries	■	■	Lack of qualified and experienced standards	■	
Developing higher awareness among all stakeholders	■	■	Unwillingness of the contractors/clients/users to employ	■	■
Educating students	■	■			

The VR-centric workflow based on VTs demonstrates advantages in representation and usability capability via interrelated data sources built on top of a reality-based, comprehensive and rapid reconstruction of the BE through spherical panoramas or video. The most effective potentialities of VR-centric against BIM-centric workflows regard the usability features such as possible involvement of users with low expertise in software usage, lightweight outputs/file, ease of widespread, reduced cost for acquiring software, reduced cost for user software training. The use of spherical photos is an inexpensive technique because of the low costs of required tools (spherical head, tripod and remote control for remote photo shooting) and smartness in creating spherical images themselves. In fact, those are the result of a processing phase (acquisition of wide-angle images, alignment of them and photo-stitching) usually performed by the camera. In addition, the parameters related to the BEs can be modifiable over time, thus efficiency and low time consuming in updating BE representation may be investigated. According to this requirement, the most rapid updating and efficient management of VT emerge against time consuming and expensive modelling and arranging the reality in BIM and GIS applications, and this can be very useful for public authorities called to manage pervasive training tools. On the other hand, BIM-centric workflow allows a parametric modelling of objects with a structured and well-defined architecture to consult them with their properties, but the BE reconstruction can be very labor intensive because of the element-by-element modelling and expensive in terms of human resources to create it, software and hardware. This can lead organisations to select traditional approaches with CAD and documentation to disseminate knowledge about risk assessment. Nevertheless, BIM can be effective if it is selected for specific simulations and assessment, such as human behaviour modelling and risk indices and maps calculations. In this situation, the BIM deliverable identified as training material can be easily added to the VT, as an example, the videos of evacuation paths simulations.

For Macro-scale representation, 3DCity Models are configured as a powerful tool for the management and integration of multidisciplinary data, that can integrate BIM, VR and AR technologies. Moreover, the WebGIS solutions offer an intuitive, innovative and challenging way to incorporate, explore and analyse information in a pervasive manner of digital models of the BE via web. As the VT is a web-based tool, it can be loaded in a webGIS platform to create a network of cities where risk assessment and virtual training products have been configured. In webGIS can converge BIM models as well, if they have been created for specialist analysis of risk assessment. Thus, the 3D city model can be featured by all the potentialities and criticalities highlighted for VR and BIM-centric approaches due to the process of its implementation.

4 VR-Centric Approach Applied to BE Prone to SLODs and SUODs

Resulting from the previous discussion, the VR-centric approach has been examined in depth for the BE representation towards the main aim of pervasive training. In detail, the main features of VE based on VR-centric approach are declined to the BE and elements introduced for the risk assessment (Sect. 2).

In a VR-centric workflow, BE reconstruction for training can be conducted in three levels of representation (LoR):

A. n spherical photos (scenes) interlinked by switch hotspots;
B. n hotspot plans;
C. n hotspots.

The Virtual Tour created with n spherical photos, reality-based or model-based, (LoR A) can make immediately viewable the physical appearance in W direction (vertical axis), only with n scenes interlinked by shift hotspots, thus after the project of an acquisition plan. Major details of BEs can be obtained with minor distance between each 360° photos (in X, Y and W directions) and between camera and object. Each element of the frontier and the content of the OS (accesses, special buildings, town walls, porches, water, and so on) is easily and vividly recognized and identified within the 360° photos.

The perception of the morphological configuration of the OS is guaranteed by adding the n hotspot plans (LoR B), as they are 2D drawings and follow the user's movements, showing his/her field of view. Moreover, the number of scenes, enclosed in the plans, directly reflects the morphological features of BE, as well as influences the acquisition plans. In fact, the n hotspot plans also add visual perception (in X and Y directions), while the presence of several levels of acquisition in the same point of acquisition gives back the dimension of buildings heights (W direction) or relative differences between horizontal and vertical dimensions (Fig. 2). The higher level of detail is strictly related to the representation scale and representation accuracy of each hotspot plans.

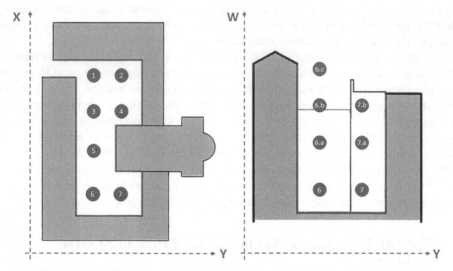

Fig. 2. Acquisition plan of spherical photos (scenes) in X, Y and W directions

The third level of representation C, in VR-centric workflows, consists of inserting hotspots to dynamically show additional and detailed information about the BE. After the insertion and augmentation of hotspots with external data, the BE can be fully reconstructed and training material can be shared. The external data to be shared and communicated can be derived from different sources and exchanged in different file formats (pdf, URL, videos, pictures, audio media, etc.) (Fig. 3). These media can describe the BE and its intrinsic and extrinsic features such as the analysis of morphological configuration, dimensions, structural type, special buildings, porches, slope and green, and so on (Table 3).

The BIM, when employed for risk assessment, can be integrated in the VR-centric workflow in each level of representation (A, B and C). Specifically, external data produced within a BIM-based approach are specified in Table 4.

The VT created for recognizing and disseminating BE criteria will configure material for pervasive training to be shared via web, supported also by tags in the real world, and navigated on displays or headsets. The pervasive training is based on web-based 3D city models (3D GIS) for navigating Virtual Tours, augmented with informative data about the BE, guidelines and procedures, in form of digital contents derived from BIM-centric workflows, useful to support public administrations in the risk management and widely enhance the preparedness of users with self-training.

Table 3. LoR of the entire set of BEs parameters in VR-centric workflow

Macro-area for BE classification	Criteria	LoR in VR		
		A	B	C
MAIN TYPE				
	Prevalent shape		■	■
	Dimension			■
	H_{max} built front	■		■
	H_{min} built front	■		■
CHARACTERISTICS OF GEOMETRY AND SPACE				
Frontier	Structural Type (SA/SU)	■		
	Accesses	■		
	Special buildings	■		
	Town walls	■		
	Porches	■		
	Water	■		
	Quote differences	■		
	Green area	■		
Content	Special buildings			■
	Canopy			■
	Fountain			■
	Monuments			■
	Dehors			■
	Quote difference			■
	Archaeological sites			■
	Green area			■
	Underground park			■
	Underground cavities			■
CONSTRUCTIVE CHARACTERISTICS				
Frontier	Homogeneity of built environment age			■
	Homogeneity of constructive techniques			■
	Urban furniture/obstacles		■	■
Content	Pavement/Surface materials			■
	Pavement lying			■
	Pavement/Surface finishing			■
	Urban furniture/obstacles		■	■
CHARACTERISTICS OF USE				
	Daily crowding			■
	Sensitive target to terroristic attack	■		■
	Vehicular accessibility			■
	Pedestrian accessibility	■		■
	Type of users			■
ENVIRONMENTAL CHARACTERISTICS				
	Climatic zone			■
	Type of infrastructures			■
	Permanent elements (natural and man-made)	■		■
	Hazard assessment			■

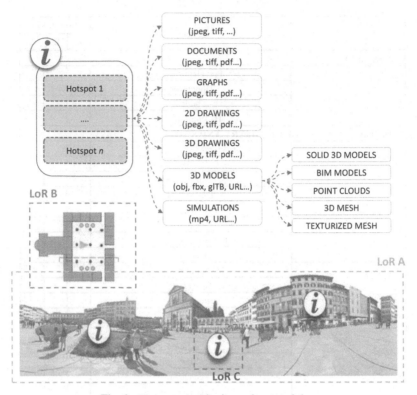

Fig. 3. Hotspots typologies and external data

Table 4. Specification of external data derived by BIM approach for VR-centric workflow

LoR	EXTERNAL DATA SPECIFICATION FROM BIM
A	Spherical photos from BIM models
B	Hotspot plan as exported BIM plan view
C	Graphical drawing exported by BIM models (plans, elevations, sections, 3D views, constructive details, …)
	Documentation exported by BIM models (reports, data sheets, graphs, …)
	BIM models as obj/fbx file or URL, after publication on a web viewer
	Simulations generated with BIM models exported as video

5   Remarks and Conclusions

The three-dimensional reconstruction of a real environment provides a higher analysis and perception. Navigating within a virtual environment, the user has the opportunity to move freely approaching the architectural elements, obtaining detailed information equal to the vision that will be obtained nearby, but staying a few kilometres away from the Built Environment.

The critical analysis conducted highlights that BIM and GIS are employed to produce and edit contents that describe BEs' and real case studies' parametric modelling, while Virtual Tours work as an easy-to-use and easy-to-update platform for full-scale representation of the BE. This study leads to distinguish two levels of training workflows for the enhancement of resilience in the BE, including humans. These training methods will fulfil a relevant objective of BE S^{2}ECURe project, as the outlining of a holistic framework able to involve experts in risk management and reach a wider group of users, firstly providing a taxonomy about Built Environments prone to Sudden and Slow Onset disasters within disruptive technologies. The specific training is based on BIM-centric simulation and modelling, aimed at testing the behavioural design within the BE at micro/meso/macro scale thanks to different scenarios simulations for technical users and professionals. The parametric tools such as BIM and GIS (2D and 3D GIS) are more suitable for simulation and analysis of real events. Indeed, parametric modelling can be employed for multiple analytical modelling and analysis, aimed at deriving risk matrix and indicators, creating several alternative scenarios for identifying risk mitigation measures, guidelines and strategies to SUOD and SLOD within a risk management plan.

As the VR-centric approach is a smart tool, it will be employed for pervasive training, due to capabilities of sharing, communication, education, collaboration and dissemination. Indeed, selected results/deliverable of simulation and analysis will be located on a represented built environment - as it is seen by humans – with reliable spherical photos for disseminating acquired knowledge in a friendly and accurate manner. Hotspots would be inserted for sharing deliverables provided by other processes/analysis phases on the Built Environment, as drawings, images, spreadsheets, multimedia file such as video. The creation and next maintenance of Virtual Tour are effective for editors, also if they are without expert skills, because the acquisition of spherical photos is rapid and it does not create unresolvable interferences with users and spaces. These can be managed within a basic 2D or 3D GIS web-based platform for geographical localization. The use of 3D City model will be a collecting tool for the representation, exploration and analysis of heterogeneous georeferenced spatial information to provide immediate and intuitive use of all the intrinsic and extrinsic information of the Built Environment with effects on risk scenarios.

Acknowledgements. This work was supported by the MIUR (the Italian Ministry of Education, University, and Research) Project BE S2ECURe - (make) Built Environment Safer in Slow and Emergency Conditions through behavioUral assessed/designed Resilient solutions (Grant number: 2017LR75XK).

References

1. Bernabei, L., et al.: Human behaviours and BE investigations to preserve the heritage against SUOD disasters. In: Amoêda, R., Lira, S., Pinheiro, C. (eds.) HERITAGE 2020 Proceedings of the 7th International Conference on Heritage and Sustainable Development, pp. 187–197. Green Lines Institute for Sustainable Development, Barcelos (2020)

2. Lovreglio, R.: Virtual and augmented reality for human behaviour in disasters: a review. In: Fire and Evacuation Modeling Technical Conference (FEMTC) 2020 Online Conference, September 9–11 (2020)
3. De Paolis, L.T.: Applicazione interattiva di realtà aumentata per i beni culturali. SCIRES-IT-SCI. Res. Inf. Technol. **2**, 121–132 (2012)
4. Billinghurst, M., Clark, A., Lee, G.: A survey of augmented reality. Found. Trends® Hum.-Comput. Interact. **8**(2–3), 73–272 (2015)
5. Tian, F., Xu, F., Fu, J.: Augmented reality technology overview for tourism app development. In: 2013 International Conference on Machine Learning and Cybernetics, pp. 1483–1489. IEEE, Tianjin (2013)
6. Palmarini, R., Erkoyuncu, J.A., Roy, R., Torabmostaedi, H.: A systematic review of augmented reality applications in maintenance. Robot. Comput.-Integr. Manuf. **49**, 215–228 (2018)
7. Cardaci, A., Versaci, A., Fauzia, L.R.: Nuove tecniche fotografiche per la documentazione, la valorizzazione e la divulgazione del patrimonio culturale: high dynamic range imaging, photo stitching e virtual tour. In: IX Conferenza del Colore. Maggioli, pp. 270–281 (2013)
8. Cantatore, E., Lasorella, M., Fatiguso, F.: Virtual reality to support technical knowledge in cultural heritage. The case study of cryptoporticus in the archaeological site of Egnatia (Italy). The International Archives of the Photogrammetry, Remote Sensing and Spatial Information Sciences, XLIV-M-1-2020, pp. 465–472 (2020)
9. Currà, E., D'Amico, A., Angelosanti, M.: Representation and knowledge of historic construction: HBIM for structural use in the case of Villa Palma-Guazzaroni in Terni. TEMA **7**, 8–20 (2020)
10. Sacks, R., Eastman, C., Lee, G., Teicholz, P.: BIM Handbook: A Guide to Building Information Modeling for Owners, Managers, Designers, Engineers and Contractors, 3rd edn. Wiley, New Jersey (2018)
11. Azhar, S., Hein, M., Sketo, B.: Building information modeling (BIM): benefits, risks and challenges. In: Proceedings of the 44th ASC Annual Conference (2008)
12. Stadler, A., Kolbe, T.H.: Spatio-semantic coherence in the integration of 3D city models. In: Proceedings of the 5th International ISPRS Symposium on Spatial Data Quality, ISSDQ 2007 in Enschede, The Netherlands, 13–15 June (2007)
13. BE S^{2}ECURe. www.bes2ecure.net. Accessed 14 June 2021
14. Rus, K., Kilar, V., Koren, D.: Resilience assessment of complex urban systems to natural disasters: a new literature review. Int. J. Disaster Risk Reduct. **31**, 311–330 (2018)
15. Russo, M., et al.: Morphological systems of open spaces in built environment prone to sudden-onset disasters. In: Littlewood, J., Howlett, R.J., Jain, L.C. (eds.) Sustainability in Energy and Buildings 2020. Smart Innovation, Systems and Technologies, vol. 203. Springer, Singapore (2021). https://doi.org/10.1007/978-981-15-8783-2_27
16. Bernabei, L., et al.: Human behaviours and BE investigations to preserve the heritage against SUOD disasters. In: Amoeda, R., Lira, S., Pinheiro, C. (eds.) HERITAGE 2020. Proceedings of the 7th International Conference on Heritage and Sustainable Development, pp. 187–197. Green Lines Institute for Sustainable Development, Barcelos (2020)
17. Sharifi, A.: Urban form resilience: a meso-scale analysis. Cities **93**, 238–252 (2019)
18. Salvalai, G., Quagliarini, E., Cadena, J.D.B.: Built environment and human behavior boosting slow-onset disaster risk. In: Amoeda, R., Lira, S., Pinheiro, C. (eds.) HERITAGE 2020. Proceedings of the 7th International Conference on Heritage and Sustainable Development, pp 199–209. Green Lines Institute for Sustainable Development 2020 (2020)
19. Woo, G.: Understanding the principles of terrorism risk modeling from Charlie Hebdo attack in Paris. Def. Against Terror. Rev. **7**(1), 33–46 (2015)
20. Quagliarini, E., Fatiguso, F., Lucesoli, M., Bernardini, G., Cantatore, E.: Risk reduction strategies against terrorist acts in urban built environments: towards sustainable and human-centred challenges. Sustainability **13**(2), 901 (2021)

21. Salvalai, G., Moretti, N., Blanco Cadena, J.D., Quagliarini, E.: SLow onset disaster events factors in italian built environment archetypes. In: Littlewood, J., Howlett, R.J., Jain, L.C. (eds.) Sustainability in Energy and Buildings 2020. SIST, vol. 203, pp. 333–343. Springer, Singapore (2021). https://doi.org/10.1007/978-981-15-8783-2_28
22. Giuliani, F., De Falco, A., Cutini, V.: The role of urban configuration during disasters. A scenario-based methodology for the post-earthquake emergency management of Italian historic centres. Saf. Sci. **127**, 104700 (2020)
23. Bernardini, G., Lucesoli, M., Quagliarini, E.: Sustainable planning of seismic emergency in historic centres through semeiotic tools: comparison of different existing methods through real case studies. Sustain. Cities Soc. **52**, 101834 (2020)
24. De Lotto, R., Pietra, C., Venco, E.M.: Risk analysis: a focus on urban exposure estimation. In: Misra, S., et al. (eds.) ICCSA 2019. LNCS, vol. 11620, pp. 407–423. Springer, Cham (2019). https://doi.org/10.1007/978-3-030-24296-1_33
25. Li, J., Li, J., Yuan, Y., Li, G.: Spatiotemporal distribution characteristics and mechanism analysis of urban population density: a case of Xi'an, Shaanxi, China. Cities **86**, 62–70 (2019)
26. Dore, C., Murphy, M.: Integration of HBIM and 3D GIS for Digital Heritage Modelling, Digital Documentation, 22–23 October, 2012 Edinburgh, Scotland (2012)
27. Jusuf, S.K., Mousseau, B., Godfroid, G., Hui, V.S.J.: Integrated modeling of CityGML and IFC for city/neighborhood development for urban microclimates analysis. Energy Procedia **122**, 145–150 (2017)
28. de Laat, R., van Berlo, L.: Integration of BIM and GIS: the development of the CityGML GeoBIM extension. In: Kolbe, T., König, G., Nagel, C. (eds.) Advances in 3D Geo-Information Sciences. Lecture Notes in Geoinformation and Cartography. Springer, Heidelberg (2011). https://doi.org/10.1007/978-3-642-12670-3_13

Multi-instrumental Analysis of the Extreme Meteorological Event Occurred in Matera (Italy) on November 2019

Virginia Coletta[1,3]([✉])[iD], Alessandra Mascitelli[2][iD], Alessandra Bonazza[4][iD], Alessandro Ciarravano[3][iD], Stefano Federico[3][iD], Fernanda Prestileo[3][iD], Rosa Claudia Torcasio[3][iD], and Stefano Dietrich[3][iD]

[1] Geodesy and Geomatic Division, University of Rome "La Sapienza", Rome, Italy
virginia.coletta@uniroma1.it
[2] Department of Geosciences, University of Padova, Padova, Italy
alessandra.mascitelli@unipd.it
[3] CNR-ISAC, The Institute of Atmospheric Sciences and Climate, Rome, Italy
[4] CNR-ISAC, The Institute of Atmospheric Sciences and Climate, Bologna, Italy

Abstract. Most of the municipalities of the Italian territory are located in areas of high hydrogeological risk, i.e. exposed to flooding and landslides. Consequently, part of the existing cultural heritage on the national territory is located in areas subject to flood risk, which compromises the accessibility, preservation and integrity of cultural heritage. As an example, we consider a single flood event that occurred in southern Italy on November 11th and 12th, 2019, which mainly affected the city of Matera and its surroundings. This episode appears to be significant for the violence of the phenomenon that led to considerable quantities of water flowing inside the city, a UNESCO World Heritage Site, causing damage to buildings, including historical ones. The event has been analysed using both meteorology and geomatic technologies, to have an overview on spatial and temporal evolution of the phenomenon. Global Navigation Satellite System Zenith Total Delay (GNSS-ZTD) data obtained by receivers located around the city of Matera, were compared with measurements from ground-based devices (i.e. weather stations), Numerical Weather Prediction (NWP) models, and ERA5 reanalysis. To assess the extent of the flood and show the flooded areas, the images provided by the Sentinel-1 Synthetic Aperture Radar (SAR) were used, isolating and analyzing the images captured before and after the event. Finally, through a digital terrain model, developed using Agisoft Metashape software from satellite images, the morphology of Matera was recreated to evidence the areas of accumulation of water. Once all the information was obtained, the data correlated showed an overall view of the event.

Keywords: Photogrammetry · GNSS · Meteorology · Cultural heritage · Flooding

O. Gervasi et al. (Eds.): ICCSA 2021, LNCS 12956, pp. 140–154, 2021.
https://doi.org/10.1007/978-3-030-87010-2_10

1 Introduction

In recent years there are increasingly violent and frequent flood events that cause physical and economic damage to entire countries and cities. Cultural heritage is not unaffected by these hazards that compromise their integrity and appropriate conservation [6,9,14]. In recent years, several World Heritage Sites have been exposed to high-intensity flooding events that have caused the loss of inestimable assets or have simply led to their closure. Technological advances are bringing great support in the study of floods. The advent of satellites has allowed post-event study without coming into direct contact with the area by evaluating the first estimate of damage and possible emergency plans to save the population [1,2,11]. Increasingly accurate weather models permit short-term forecasts with high accuracy. These can be useful for the creation of evacuation and risk prevention strategies for the protection of people and the safety of cultural heritage [20,30]. In this study, the flood event that occurred in the town of Matera, Basilicata Region (Italy), on November 11th and 12th, 2019 is examined with the aim of assessing the importance of the meteorological event that affected the city. The historic centre of Matera is characterised by a rupestrian habitat, consisting of dwellings and places of worship dug into the soft calcareous stone and open to the free air with a built part, known throughout the world as the *"Sassi di Matera"* [10]. The *Sassi* were inscribed on the UNESCO World Heritage List in 1993 after a long process of urban and socio-cultural recovery [19]. In this investigation, interdisciplinary work was carried out including a combination of meteorological methodologies and geomatic technologies. In this sense, in order to analyse the event as comprehensively as possible, a multi-instrumental approach was performed. The meteorological aspect was studied using a dataset from different techniques (GNSS, NWP models, ERA5 and weather station) described more in depth in the following section. Assessing the expansion of a flood event through satellite imagery is possible with synthetic aperture radar (SAR) spectral satellites, that are not dependent on weather and time conditions [35]. In recent years, images provided by SAR satellites are used very frequently for the construction of flooding maps during or immediately after the flood event [3,13,27,36]. In this paper, we have used the images provided by the Sentinel-1 satellites. These satellites are part of the Sentinel family developed by the European Space Agency (ESA) to support the operational requirements of the Copernicus program. The Sentinel-1 mission is composed of two satellites that provide continuous images (day, night, and in all weather conditions) [38]. For the processing of these images was used the Google Earth Engine (GEE) platform, this platform provides a very rich data set and allows their elaboration in remote accelerating the process [12,16,26].

Two different digital elevation models (DEMs) have been considered to better evaluate the pathways and areas of water accumulation. The first one is a digital terrain model (DTM), the WWF HydroSHEDS with lower spatial resolution, present in the GEE dataset having quasi-global scale [40]. The second one is a digital surface model (DSM), with high spatial resolution, that is developed only for the historical centre of Matera [28].

2   Case Study: Matera the City of *Sassi*

The city of Matera (coordinates 40° 40' N 16° 36' E; altitude 401 m a.s.l.; area 392.09 km²), located near the Ionian coast in the North-Eastern corner of the Basilicata Region (Italy), is considered one of the oldest cities in the world, a veritable open-air museum that has been continuously inhabited for 7000 years, bearing witness to the presence of man from the Palaeolithic to the present day [18, 19, 32–34]. In the terraced plateaus formed by limestone, the Murge of Lucania and Apulia, the gravines are a spectacular example of erosion valleys, geological features rich in carsic phenomena (underground water circulation, dolinas, gorges, caves), used for this purpose since the earliest times by humanity. While part of the town spreads out across the Murgia plateau, the famed *Sassi di Matera*, the old center of the town, comprises cave dwelling built on and dug into the side of the *Gravina Gorge* which drops vertiginously away beneath it (Fig. 1).

Fig. 1. View of the *Sassi di Matera*: the *Sasso Barisano* with the *Civita* and the Cathedral (photo by Fernanda Prestileo©, May 2018)

The *Sassi di Matera*, or cliffs and stones, are an architectural and urban ensemble of exceptional quality, a living system built in the geological material itself, the *Gravina Calcarenite* (a soft calcareous rock known locally as "tuff", which is of Upper Pliocene-Pleistocene age, easy to excavate while ensuring high stability) along the slopes of a deep and grandiose *Gravina Gorge* [32–34]. Over the centuries, the slopes of the *Gravina of Matera* were excavated by man, drilled and sculpted to create tunnels, cisterns and underground architectural environments. The excavated materials, cut into quadrangular "tufa" blocks, were used to build dry walls, terraces, roads and stairways in an architecture that responds perfectly to the climatic conditions, composing an original urban fabric. The city develops vertically on the two natural amphitheatres of *Sasso Caveoso* and *Sasso Barisano*, with the *Civita* in the centre. The dwellings carved into the rock face with deep underground chambers open up to the outside with terraces and hanging gardens. An extraordinary and prolonged example of symbiosis between the natural site and human intervention, like many others in the Mediterranean Basin and the Near East, the

Sassi find their originality in the ability to create architecture with few means and sustainable use of available resources. Also used in modern times as dwellings in which people and animals often lived together, in conditions of extreme degradation and poverty until after the Second World War, the *Sassi*, following a national law, were subjected to an operation of eviction for reasons of health and hygiene, which from the 1960s onwards saw the relocation of the population (about 15,000 people) in accommodation built in the new districts of the city. Thus the *Sassi* were marked in Italy as one of the "national shames" of the South. The *Sassi* so remained a mysterious and fascinating historic centre, uninhabited and abandoned until the 1970s, when a slow but important programme of urban recovery and restoration of the houses and prestigious places of worship, many of which are adorned with prestigious but much-deteriorated pictorial wall decorations from the early Middle Ages (there is evidence of Longobard, Byzantine and Benedictine art), was initiated by illuminated citizens and experienced Lucanian professionals [18,19]. This long and complex process of urban and socio-cultural recovery allowed the *Sassi di Matera* to be included in the UNESCO World Heritage List in 1993, even amidst the incredulity and scepticism of some of the local population. From that date onwards, Matera will no longer stop its process of urban recovery and socio-cultural enhancement, with important benefits in the economic sector, especially tourism, which sees the proliferation of accommodation facilities in the *Sassi*. The continuous restoration of the main monuments in and around the city, as well as the increased hotel accommodation, means that it is even more visited by tourists from all over the world. Another important recognition, further proof of this unstoppable process of redemption, was Italy's nomination of Matera as European Capital of Culture in 2019 thanks to its rich history and cultural diversity [18].

3   Data and Methods

3.1   Dataset Description

The first technique applied is GNSS (Global Navigation Satellite Systems), which defines all the constellations of artificial terrestrial satellites for positioning and navigation. In this section we will focus on the added value that this technology brings to the meteorological field [8,23,25,31], referring essentially to the tropospheric delay parameter, Zenith Total Delay (ZTD), and to the Precipitable Water Vapor (PWV) [7,21,24] content derived from it [4,17,22]. In this specific case study GNSS data, from November 8th to 15th, 2019 referred to 11 geodetic receivers located around Matera (Fig. 2) were processed.

To compute GNSS-ZTD values, starting from dual-frequency observational files (RINEX Version 3 format), a multi-constellation PPP processing [37] was applied by goGPS software [15,29], using precise products provided by Center for Orbit Determination in Europe (CODE) and applying ionosphere-free combination to estimate GNSS-ZTD values for each epoch, by daily processing sessions. The conversion from GNSS-ZTD to GNSS-PWV was carried out using data from the empirical model GPT (Global Pressure and Temperature) [5].

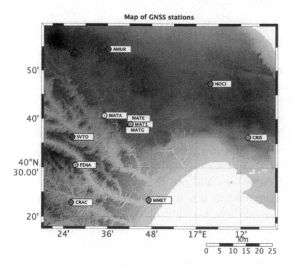

Fig. 2. GNSS receivers location around Matera (Table 1)

Table 1. Data features

Technique	Box latitude	Box longitude	Source
GNSS	$39N < \varphi < 41N$	$16E < \lambda < 18E$	Kindly provided by GReD srl
ERA5	$39N < \varphi < 43N$	$10E < \lambda < 20E$	https://cds.climate.copernicus.eu
Rain gauge	$\varphi = 40.64N$	$\lambda = 16.70$	Civil Protection Department

In order to compare our results with a renown dataset, ERA5 has been employed. ERA5 is the fifth generation of meteorological reanalyses issued by ECMWF. Reanalysis combines the background field, provided by the IFS (Integrated Forecasting System) model, with observations to give the best estimate of the atmospheric state. ERA5 dataset offers hourly estimates of a large number of atmospheric, land and oceanic climate variables. The data cover the whole Earth and resolve the atmosphere in the vertical using 137 levels from the surface up to a height of 80 km. The horizontal resolution of the model used in ERA5 is about 30 km. For this paper, we used the following parameter of ERA5 reanalyses: Total Column Water Vapour (TCWV) [kg m^2], which represents the total amount of water vapour in a column extending from the surface of the Earth to the top of the atmosphere (i.e. the area-averaged value for a grid box).

To assess the extent of flood areas, in this work, images captured by the Sentinel 1 satellites were used. The Sentinel-1 mission comprises a constellation of two satellites in polar orbit, operating day and night performing C-band synthetic aperture radar imaging, allowing them to acquire images regardless of weather and time conditions. Sentinel-1A and Sentinel-1B satellites share the same quasi-polar heliosynchronous orbit but are 180° out of phase; a cycle for one satellite lasts 12 days, considering both is 6 days. Sentinel-1 satellites are equipped with a C-band synthetic aperture radar that supports dual-polarization operations including four different choices: HH, VV, HV, VH. The main acquisition modes are Interferometric Wide swath (IW) and Wave mode (WV), the first is the default mode for acquisition on the Earth's surface and meets almost all service requirements, the second is used in open sea [38]. To assess flooded areas the Interferometric Wide swath has been used as an acquisition mode, which has a spatial resolution of 5 × 20 m, with VH polarization, this is widely suggested for flood mapping, since it is more sensitive to changes on the Earth's surface. The images captured by the Sentinel 1 satellites were not downloaded but processed directly on the online platform Google Earth Engine (GEE) in which you can work on the images directly in the cloud. GEE has an extensive library and for processing, it is possible to use the programming languages Javascript and Python.

Two different digital elevation models (DEMs) have been considered to better evaluate the pathways and areas of water accumulation. The first one is a digital terrain model (DTM), the WWF HydroSHEDS with lower spatial resolution, present in the GEE dataset having quasi-global scale [40]. The second one is a digital surface model (DSM), with high spatial resolution, that is developed only for the historical centre of Matera [28].

3.2 Operative Workflow

The operational workflow adopted was summarized in Fig. 3.

Different techniques and methodologies were adopted to provide a comprehensive analysis of the flood event studied. Moreover, the techniques applied in this case study provided an overview of the event, integrating satellite and ground-based information and facilitating a survey of both the state of the atmosphere and the flood condition.

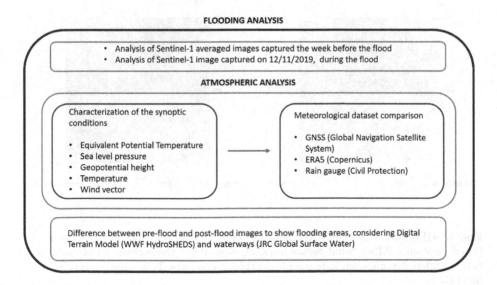

Fig. 3. Operative workflow

4   Results and Discussion

4.1   Synoptic Conditions of the Matera Case Study

To characterize the synoptic conditions of the Matera case study we used the ECMWF operational analyses at 00 UTC on 12th November 2019 (Fig. 4). The surface map shows a low pressure (994 hPa) over the southern Tyrrhenian Sea, between the Italian mainland, Sardinia and Sicily. With this baric situation, winds are advected from the Ionian Sea towards Calabria and Basilicata Regions, bringing warm and unstable air masses over southern Italy. This is shown by the equivalent potential temperature, which is larger than 330 K over the Ionian Sea. Also, surface winds (10 m above the surface) in this sector are sustained, being larger than 20 m/s.

At 500 hPa (Fig. 4.b) it is apparent a deep wave trough, extending from polar latitude towards the Central Mediterranean Sea. The trough developed a cut-off downwind of the Atlas Mountains, which is over Tunisia at the time of Fig. 4.b. The cut-off determines a diffluent flow over southern Italy, which favours the sustainment of convection. An important ingredient of the Matera case is the atmospheric river of large water vapour values advected from the tropical latitudes over the Central Mediterranean Sea, especially towards Calabria and Basilicata. The storm circulation conveyed considerable amounts of water vapour over southern Italy determining favourable humidity conditions to trigger and sustain the convection at all tropospheric levels.

So, the meteorological analysis of the Matera case shows that the event occurred in a favourable synoptic environment characterized by a cyclone evolving into the Mediterranean Sea, reinforced by the interaction between the atmo-

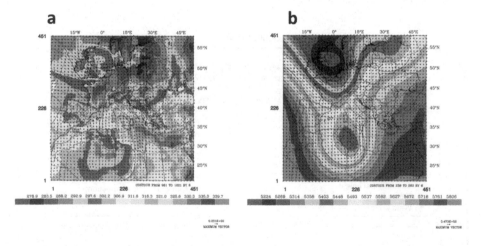

Fig. 4. a) Equivalent potential temperature (filled contours, [K]), sea level pressure (black contours, [hPa]), wind vector [m/s] at 19 m above the surface; **b)** Geopotential height (filled contours, [m]), temperature (black contours [K]), wind vector [m/s] at 500 hPa

spheric flow and the Atlas Mountains. The circulation close to the surface advected warm and unstable air masses over Italy forcing the development of convection. In addition, the circulation at mid and high tropospheric levels conveyed a water vapour plume from tropical latitudes towards the Mediterranean.

4.2   Meteorological Dataset Comparison

In order to characterise the phenomenon identified as a case study, the trends of the GNSS-ZTD parameter were examined with specific attention to an area including the city of Matera (Fig. 2). The whole dataset is internally consistent, indicating that the convective event affected the entire area covered by the receiver network; Fig. 5, indeed, shows the maximum peak of the week during the day of November 12th, followed by a sudden decrease of the parameter.

At this point, moving to a more local level, a single receiver (closest to the event) was analysed. In this case, the analysis of the observations of the meteorological variables was carried out mainly by direct comparison on a weekly dataset of the GNSS-PWV pattern, referred to the GNSS receiver located in Matera (MATE), with the data recorded by a nearby rain gauge. Results, given in Fig. 6, show excellent consistency between the two sets of data, also highlighting how the extreme event under study is immediately identifiable as a function of both the amount of GNSS-PWV and the precipitate rate.

A further step was made in order to compare the observed data with the ERA5 one. In this case, as previously mentioned, a map containing at each pixel the corresponding ERA5-TCWV (Total Column Water Vapour) value, at the time of the event (7.00 UTC), was plotted. From Fig. 7.a it is clear the agreement between the two sets of data that, at the Matera coordinates, show an ERA5-TCWV of comparable amount with the observed GNSS-PWV.

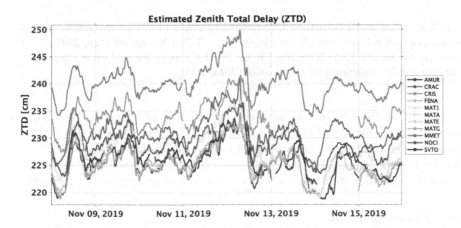

Fig. 5. GNSS-ZTD from November 8th to 15th, 2019 referred to 11 geodetic receivers located around Matera

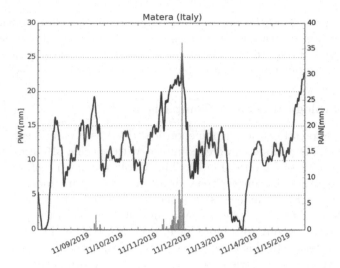

Fig. 6. Weekly comparison between GNSS-PWV at MATE receiver and rain data from a close weather station

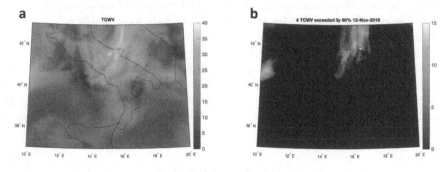

Fig. 7. a) Amount of ERA5 Total Column Water Vapor (TCWV) at the time identified by peak of GNSS-PWV and of rain gauge: 7.00 UTC of November 12th, 2019; **b)** How often on November 12th, 2019 the ERA5 Total Column Water Vapor exceeded the 90th percentiles computed on three years (2018–2020)

Finally, at the end of this analysis, the number of times on 12th November that the 90 percentile calculated over the three-year period 2018–2020 was exceeded was plotted for each pixel. As can be seen from Fig. 7.b, the event that took place in southern Italy is not an ordinary case study and is therefore certainly interesting from the point of view of analysing extreme weather events.

4.3 Flooding Areas

In order to assess the extent of flooded areas as a first step the Sentinel 1 images were imported to GEE and the area of interest was cropped. As mentioned earlier the IW mode with VH bias was considered. An approach was chosen that shows the change between two images collected on different days, before and after the flooding event that occurred on 11th November 2019. In this case, the satellite flew over the area of interest on 6th November (Fig. 8.a) and 12th November (Fig. 8.b).

Different pre-processing steps would need to be performed before using the images: noise removal, radiometric calibration and terrain correction; but on GEE the available images are already pre-processed. We have operated only on the smoothing filter to reduce the speckle effect associated with radar images. In order to evaluate the change that occurred between the two temporal instants in which the images were acquired, the colour difference between two corresponding pixels, i.e. including the same portion of terrain, was considered. High values (bright pixels) indicate a high change, low values (dark pixels) indicate a minimal change. Several additional datasets were used to eliminate possible interpretation errors. The JRC Global Surface Water dataset is used to mask all areas covered by water for more than 10 months per year. The dataset has a resolution of 30 m and was last updated in 2018. To remove areas with a slope greater than 5%, a digital elevation model (WWF HydroSHEDS) was chosen, based on SRTM data, and has a spatial resolution of 3 arc-seconds, available on GEE. The analysis has shown, in accordance with meteorological data, that the southern area of the Basilicata Region has been severely affected by this event. Focusing on the city of Matera we can see that the flood has mainly affected the area north-east of the city, where "The Murgia National Park" is located, added to the UNESCO World Heritage List in 1993, creating numerous flood areas, blue areas in the (Fig. 9). On the other hand, there are no particular accumulations of water in the historical part of the city the *Sassi*. In order to investigate this phenomenon, a DSM with a very high spatial resolution, equal to 0.5 m, was used, relative only to the historical centre of Matera [28]. The area is morphologically very complex, being composed of erosive inci-

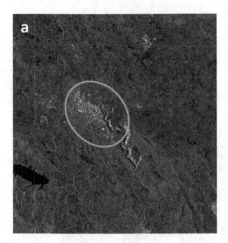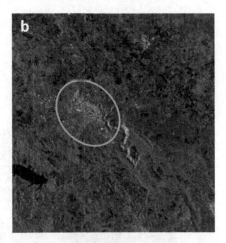

Fig. 8. a) Image captured by Sentinel 1 on 6th November 2019, Before Flooding, in IW/VH mode; **b)** Image captured by Sentinel 1 on 12th November 2019, After Flooding, in IW/VH mode

Fig. 9. Flooding Areas in blue, obtained from the color difference between the pixels of the images captured by Sentinel 1 before and after the flood event (Color figure online)

sions similar to canyons, typical carsic morphologies of the Murgia (Fig. 10). This particular morphology has contributed to generate a flow of water that has flowed inside the archaeological areas (Fig. 11), without creating areas of accumulation, exposing the heritage present to very strong and sudden stress and consequently to significant damage.

Fig. 10. View of the *Sassi* Area showing the particularity of morphology (photo by Fernanda Prestileo©, May 2018)

Fig. 11. View of a street of the *Sassi* Area flooded during the event examined. Image is taken from the newspaper *Quotidiano Nazionale* of the day 12/11/2019 [39]

5 Conclusion

The aim of this work was to analyze, using an interdisciplinary approach, the flood that affected the Region of Basilicata (Italy) in November 2019, especially the city of Matera. This event was significant both for its meteorological characteristics, which are not ordinary and for the uniqueness of the site involved. The flood event has been studied by combining geomatic technologies with meteorological methodologies in order to have a complete description of the event. From the meteorological point of view a multi-instrumental approach has been performed using datasets from different techniques (GNSS, NWP models, ERA5 and meteorological station). In this specific case study, GNSS data, from November 8th to 15th, 2019, referred to 11 geodetic receivers located around Matera were processed. The meteorological analysis shows that the event occurred in a favourable synoptic environment characterized by a cyclone evolving towards the Mediterranean Sea, reinforced by the interaction between the atmospheric flow and the Atlas Mountains. In order to characterize the phenomenon identified as a case study, the GNSS-ZTD parameter trends have been examined with specific attention to an area including the city of Matera. The entire dataset is internally consistent, showing the maximum peak of the week during the day of November 12th, followed by a sudden decrease of the parameter. Moving to a more local level, a direct comparison was made on a weekly dataset of the GNSS-PWV pattern, referred to the GNSS receiver located in Matera, with the data recorded by a rain gauge nearby, showing a very good consistency between the two datasets. Finally, the number of times the 90th percentile calculated over the three-year period 2018–2020 was exceeded on November 12th, was plotted for each pixel, and it was found that the event had characteristics out of the ordinary. To assess the extent of the flood, images transmitted by the Sentinel-1 SAR satellites were used. By comparing the images from the days immediately before the flood with the images transmitted by the satellite the days immediately after the flood, it was possible to highlight the flooded areas. In total agreement with the meteorological data, it has been highlighted that the flooding has affected the southern area of the Basilicata Region. In particular, in the area of Matera the most flooded areas are located in the North-Eastern part of the city, where "The Murgia National Park" is located. Instead, in the historical part, characterized by morphologically very complex areas, the water has run in the *Sassi* damaging significantly cultural heritage unique in the world. In the future, more resolute digital terrain models will be used, to improve the analysis of satellite images. In addition, hydrogeological studies will be conducted, in order to project possible protections and increase the resilience of the city.

Acknowledgements. In this work the raw GNSS data were kindly provided by Geomatics Research & Development Srl (GReD), developer of the goGPS software. We would like to thank Valeria Belloni, Lorenzo Lastilla and Roberta Ravanelli for having made available to the research the DSM they developed. We would like to thank Civil Protection Department for providing us the rainfall data.

References

1. Adeleke, O.O., Jimoh, Y.A., Ayanshola, A.M., Aremu, A.S.: Role of geomatics in the management of disasters and infrastructural failures. Ethiop. J. Environ. Stud. Manag. **6**(2), 143–148 (2013)
2. Aicardi, I., et al.: A didactic project for landscape heritage mapping in post-disaster management. Appl. Geomat. **7**(1), 49–60 (2015)
3. Ajmar, A., Boccardo, P., Broglia, M., Kucera, J., Giulio-Tonolo, F., Wania, A.: Response to flood events: the role of satellite-based emergency mapping and the experience of the Copernicus emergency management service. Flood Damage Surv. Assess. New Insights Res. Pract. **228**, 213–228 (2017)
4. Bevis, M., Businger, S., Herring, T.A., Rocken, C., Anthes, R.A., Ware, R.H.: GPS meteorology: remote sensing of atmospheric water vapor using the global positioning system. J. Geophys. Res.: Atmos. **97**, 15787–15801 (1992). https://doi.org/10.1029/92JD01517
5. Böhm, J., Heinkelmann, R., Schuh, H.: Short note: a global model of pressure and temperature for geodetic applications. J. Geod. **81**(10), 679–683 (2007)
6. Bonazza, A., Maxwell, I., Drdácký, M., Vintzileou, E., Hanus, C.: Safeguarding cultural heritage from natural and man-made disasters: a comparative analysis of risk management in the EU (2018)
7. Campanelli, M., et al.: Precipitable water vapour content from ESR/SKYNET sun-sky radiometers: validation against GNSS/GPS and AERONET over three different sites in Europe. Atmos. Meas. Tech. **11**(1), 81–94 (2018)
8. D'Adderio, L.P., Pazienza, L., Mascitelli, A., Tiberia, A., Dietrich, S.: A combined IR-GPS satellite analysis for potential applications in detecting and predicting lightning activity. Remote Sens. **12**(6), 1031 (2020)

9. Drdácký, M.F.: Flood damage to historic buildings and structures. J. Perform. Constr. Facil. **24**(5), 439–445 (2010)

10. Fatiguso, F., De Fino, M., Cantatore, E., Caponio, V.: Resilience of historic built environments: inherent qualities and potential strategies. Procedia Eng. **180**, 1024–1033 (2017)

11. Fattore, C., Abate, N., Faridani, F., Masini, N., Lasaponara, R.: Google earth engine as multi-sensor open-source tool for supporting the preservation of archaeological areas: the case study of flood and fire mapping in Metaponto, Italy. Sensors **21**(5), 1791 (2021)

12. Gorelick, N., Hancher, M., Dixon, M., Ilyushchenko, S., Thau, D., Moore, R.: Google earth engine: planetary-scale geospatial analysis for everyone. Remote Sens. Environ. **202**, 18–27 (2017)

13. Greifeneder, F., Wagner, W., Sabel, D., Naeimi, V.: Suitability of SAR imagery for automatic flood mapping in the Lower Mekong Basin. Int. J. Remote Sens. **35**(8), 2857–2874 (2014)

14. Herle, I., Herbstová, V., Kupka, M., Kolymbas, D.: Geotechnical problems of cultural heritage due to floods. J. Perform. Constr. Facil. **24**(5), 446–451 (2010)

15. Herrera, A.M., Suhandri, H.F., Realini, E., Reguzzoni, M., de Lacy, M.C.: goGPS: open-source matlab software. GPS Solut. **20**(3), 595–603 (2016)

16. Huang, H., et al.: Mapping major land cover dynamics in Beijing using all Landsat images in Google Earth Engine. Remote Sens. Environ. **202**, 166–176 (2017)

17. Kleijer, F.: Troposphere modeling and filtering for precise GPS leveling. Ph.D. thesis, Delft University of Technology (2004)

18. Laureano, P.: Matera, la sfida della memoria, Architettura della fusione. Lett. Internazionale **118**, 44–47 (2013)

19. Laureano, P.: Giardini di Pietra: I Sassi di Matera e la Civiltí Mediterranea. Bollati Boringhieri, Torino, Italy, 2019 II edn. (2019)

20. Mahmood, S., Sajjad, A., Rahman, A.U.: Cause and damage analysis of 2010 flood disaster in district Muzaffar Garh, Pakistan. Nat. Hazards **107**(2), 1681–1692 (2021)

21. Mascitelli, A., et al.: Data assimilation of GPS-ZTD into the RAMS model through 3D-Var: preliminary results at the regional scale. Meas. Sci. Technol. **30**(5), 055801 (2019)

22. Mascitelli, A.: New applications and opportunities of GNSS meteorology. Ph.D. thesis, Sapienza University of Rome (2020). http://hdl.handle.net/11573/1378843

23. Mascitelli, A., Federico, S., Torcasio, R.C., Dietrich, S.: Assimilation of GPS Zenith Total Delay estimates in RAMS NWP model: impact studies over central Italy. Advances in Space Research (2020)

24. Mascitelli, A., Barindelli, S., Realini, E., Luini, L., Venuti, G.: Precipitable water vapor content from GNSS/GPS: validation against radiometric retrievals, atmospheric sounding and ECMWF model outputs over a test area in Milan. In: Parente, C., Troisi, S., Vettore, A. (eds.) R3GEO 2019. CCIS, vol. 1246, pp. 27–34. Springer, Cham (2020). https://doi.org/10.1007/978-3-030-62800-0_3

25. Meroni, A.N., et al.: On the definition of the strategy to obtain absolute InSAR Zenith total delay maps for meteorological applications. Front. Earth Sci. **8**, 359 (2020)

26. Mutanga, O., Kumar, L.: Google earth engine applications (2019)

27. Ohki, M., et al.: Flood area detection using ALOS-2 PALSAR-2 data for the 2015heavy rainfall disaster in the Kanto and Tohoku area, Japan. J. Remote Sens. Soc. Japan **36**(4), 348–359 (2016)

28. Lastilla, L., Belloni, V., Ravanelli, R., Crespi, M.: DSM generation from single and cross-sensor multi-view satellite images using the new Agisoft Metashape: the case studies of Trento and Matera (Italy). Remote Sens. **13**(4), 593 (2021)
29. Realini, E., Reguzzoni, M.: goGPS: open source software for enhancing the accuracy of low-cost receivers by single-frequency relative kinematic positioning. Meas. Sci. Technol. **24**(11), 115010 (2013)
30. Sonnessa, A., Cantatore, E., Esposito, D., Fiorito, F.: A multidisciplinary approach for multi-risk analysis and monitoring of influence of SODs and RODs on historic centres: the ResCUDE project. In: Gervasi, O., et al. (eds.) ICCSA 2020, Part IV. LNCS, vol. 12252, pp. 752–766. Springer, Cham (2020). https://doi.org/10.1007/978-3-030-58811-3_54
31. Tiberia, A., et al.: Time evolution of storms producing terrestrial gamma-ray flashes using ERA5 reanalysis data, GPS, lightning and geo-stationary satellite observations. Remote Sens. **13**(4), 784 (2021)
32. Tropeano, M.: Aspetti geologici e geomorfologici della Gravina di Matera "Parco Archeologico Storico Naturale delle Chiese Rupestri del Materano". Itinerari Speleologici, II **6**, 19–33 (1992)
33. Tropeano, M.: Regional geology and stratigraphy of Matera and surroundings. In: IGCP 369 Perimediterranean Palaeogeography Workshop, IGCP, Matera, Italy (1999)
34. Tropeano, M., Sabato, L., Pieri, P.: The quaternary "post-turbidite" sedimentation in the South-Apennines Foredeep (Bradanic Trough-Southern Italy). Bollettino Soc. Geol. Ital. **121**(1), 449–454 (2002)
35. Uddin, K., Matin, M.A., Meyer, F.J.: Operational flood mapping using multi-temporal sentinel-1 SAR images: a case study from Bangladesh. Remote Sens. **11**(13), 1581 (2019)
36. Voormansik, K., Praks, J., Antropov, O., Jagomägi, J., Zalite, K.: Flood mapping with TerraSAR-X in forested regions in Estonia. IEEE J. Sel. Top. Appl. Earth Obs. Remote Sens. **7**(2), 562–577 (2013)
37. Zumberge, J.F., Heflin, M.B., Jefferson, D.C., Watkins, M.M., Webb, F.H.: Precise point positioning for the efficient and robust analysis of GPS data from large networks. J. Geophys. Res.: Solid Earth **102**(B3), 5005–5017 (1997)
38. ESA sentinel1. https://sentinel.esa.int/web/sentinel/missions/sentinel-1
39. QuotidianoNazionale.   https://www.quotidiano.net/meteo/maltempo-oggi-calabria-puglia-1.4881718
40. WWF hydrosheds. https://www.hydrosheds.org/

Resilient Improvement of Historic Districts via Digital Tools. The Virtualization of Energy Retrofit Actions Using Simplified CityGML-Based Plans

Elena Cantatore(✉) ⓘ, Margherita Lasorella ⓘ, and Fabio Fatiguso ⓘ

Department of Civil, Environmental, Building Engineering and Chemistry (DICATECh),
Polytechnic University of Bari, 70126 Bari, Italy
{elena.cantatore,margherita.lasorella,fabio.fatiguso}@poliba.it

Abstract. The management of the built environment directly exposed to the effect of climate change and the assessment of buildings for their participation in such environmental processes are part of the main challenges in scientific, technical and administrative fields. On the other hand, the increasing endorsement of IT expertise and tools in traditional processes offers the opportunity to manage specific knowledge and relations using Digital Models. As unusual parts, historic centers represent unconventional districts of cities in treating mitigation and adaptation strategies, because of their overordered system of preservation normative framework and inherent formal and technical variabilities. Historic centers, as well as Cultural Heritage, require specific plans of actions for their resilient improvement to climate change. In that sense, the paper discusses and tests a simplified Digital Model based on the CityGML standard for the creation of a virtual recovery plan of historic districts, starting from previous results in supporting their management in an energy-resilient perspective. The Model has been conceived as a structured system of technical and scientific knowledge, re-organized according to the IT structure of CityGML to support public administration in managing adaptive and mitigative actions and practitioners in choosing compatible technical solutions.

Keywords: Digital model · Historic district · Energy-resilient and virtual plan

1 Introduction

Climate change and its unpredictability are, until now, a paramount challenge for technicians, scientists and administrators, above all in relating quantitative certainties on the effects, from natural eco-systems to anthropic systems as the cities. On the other hand, recent effects confirm the necessity to move towards strong and coherent actions that support mitigation on the climate change process and adaptability to the exposed systems. In cities, the built environment and the building sector represent the most challenging targets due to the dealings with urban users and energy relevance. In Europe, the building sector affects more than 40% of energy sources but just 1% of building stock

© Springer Nature Switzerland AG 2021
O. Gervasi et al. (Eds.): ICCSA 2021, LNCS 12956, pp. 155–172, 2021.
https://doi.org/10.1007/978-3-030-87010-2_11

is involved in renovation processes, delaying mitigation and adaptation goals expected in 2030 for this sector. This is widely recognized by the European Commission that announced the European Green Deal [1] to support the European transition towards climate-neutrality. As extensively highlighted in the document, climate neutrality can be supported by long-term combined strategies of mitigation and adaptation actions, increasing the resilience of cities.

The concept of resilient cities is linked to the necessity to analyse and manage cities prone to all the risk related to natural and anthropic hazards, also involved in climate-changing. However, the concepts of preparedness and readiness are fully implied in the resilient perspective, both for urban users and stakeholders. Thus, the management of wide territories requires the use of smart tools and systems. In fact, if the implementation of energy systems with ICTs can enhance the fast management of efficient supplies and control specific issues for urban or built environments, the digitalization of cities, in all their components, supports their knowledge by major public administrators of cities and wider territories. The concept of "Smart Cities" recently evolves towards the Urban "Digital Twin" (DT) as a digitalized version where different actors of the built environment study and manage urban challenges. Moreover, due to their nature, the use of digitalized cities and their parts allows sharing information, strategies, solutions and results among technicians and local administrations, overcoming the administrative borders of the single city landscape as required by the European Green Deal [1].

In the complex system of the urban built stock, historic buildings and landscape Heritage are part of an intricate and semi-paradoxical process of management. Such buildings require a depth transformation aimed at solving energy deficiencies, however, the necessity to preserve their social, cultural and environmental values limits the interventions. In the European frame, the management of Cultural and Landscape heritage is entrusted to the national authorities which provide their research and listing and define the national legislative frame of conservation and preservation, according to previous "Charters" [2]. However, near to the listed buildings, directly recognized as "Cultural Heritage", buildings in historic districts represent part of Landscape Heritage and usually still require primary recovery on the district, i.e., methane supplies, and building levels, e.g., static recovery [3]. Here, the normative frame is related to the regional landscape plans. Due to the nature of normative constraints, these buildings are not directly listed as single buildings but by means of regulations aimed at preserving them as a *unicum* of the district. Due to that, previous scientific experience in managing historic districts highlighted the use of "building types", as recurrent combinations of morpho-typological, constructive and material features [4], to overgo the singularities of traditional artefacts and to recognize the recurrent aesthetic and cultural values to preserve. Besides, this approach is in line with traditional planning instruments ("Recover plans for ancient core") for the management of such districts. Here, the process of recovery combines the relevance of values widely present in the ancient core to the system of suitable and allowed actions, in compliance with the overordered Authorities for their preservation. Moreover, such traditional buildings include some inherent features linked to the *genius loci* experiences; here, the resolution of residential needs and geo-morphological adaptation to local environmental features are part of inherent values to preserve as cultural and historical traces of human abilities to adapt to external stresses.

In the light of resilient management of such Heritage prone to the climate change process, the assessment of these buildings requires a coherent analysis of the described cultural and aesthetic values declined to the current challenges and constraints. These buildings are part of the existent stock that participates in the increasing CO_2 emissions and suffers the exposure of the consequent effects. However, specific strategies for their resilient improvement are still incomplete due to the inherent complexity derived by the preservation actions required, as well as in extending strategies and solutions overcoming the traditional process of refurbishment for single cases of listed buildings.

All the described issues involving the historic districts that are already solved by the authors in previous work [5], combining previous experiences of managing buildings in such part of cities. Here, a structured set of actions and solutions are identified for a representative case study as the result of the combined assessment of inherent adaptation capacities and energy deficiencies identified in a multi-scale approach.

The present work aims to complete the previous one by discussing and testing a structured database for sharing data and results based on its Digital Model. In detail, the work uses the CityGML database as a smart tool to generate a digitalized 3D district, organizing the resulted actions and solutions according to the "building type" scheme of analysis and creating a georeferenced database of buildings. These goals are planned in order to propose a system of technical actions that will support all the stakeholders involved in the management of such parts of cities; among them are included i) the increasing IT relevance in managing digitalized models, ii) technical and scientific knowledge for the management of district behaviour according to the discussed methodology, iii) public administrator in managing priority of interventions and compatible actions to suggest to iv) technical practitioners involved in designing final solutions.

2 CityGML Applications to the Cultural Heritage and Historic Urban Districts

Digital Twin is not a recent concept. However, the first applications were found in manufacturing and industrial sectors where the concept of "Industry 4.0" easily involved the creation of the Digitalized Model (DM) to control and assess processes and products [6]. Cities are the latest application for DM that follows the increasing trend in associating smart technologies aimed at monitor environmental or managing processes to the digitalized models, ensuring automatic dialogue among urban actors and digitalized city, as well as between digitalized and real city [7]. Moreover, DMs require to be structured in order to include and share all the virtualized parts or elements in the same platform as well as to have common tools for their interactions [8]. Today, all the created DMs are conceived aiming at the creation of Digital Twins applied to cities, districts or single buildings, encompassing several of their abilities [9]: i) import and observe sensing data in the real world and define the specific process of monitoring actions (related to the goals, i.e., pollution); ii) integrate and share data and knowledge according to structured and georeferenced data (i.e. geometric information and building properties and performances); finally, iii) simulate, predict and optimize urban behaviours in compliance with single domain (e.g. energy) or combined ones. If BIM architecture is the widest tool in treating buildings according to the DT concept, the CityGML architecture represents the most complete tool used by academia for the digitalization of cities or their part, correlating semantic and geographical data.

CityGML is an open data model based on an XML format adopted by the Open Geospatial Consortium (OGC). The main purposes of such IT architecture refer to the modelling, storage and exchange of virtual and semantic 3D city models and all the information related [10]. Finally, its structure is in line with the Geography Markup Language version 3.1.1 (GML3), the extendible international standard for spatial data exchange issued by the Open Geospatial Consortium (OGC) and the ISO TC211.

All the DMs represented in CityGML requires the association of real properties to specific feature classes in the models, as pre-organized in a proper structure. In detail, these are referred to i) geometric and topological information that includes spatial properties of single city objects and ii) thematic and semantic information aimed at improving the city objects and their properties considering the relations among them. The system of relations and classes of properties, as well as classes of city objects, are already determined in the CityGML standards that are applicable all-around the issues [11]. However, CityGML is an "extensible" architecture thanks to its implementable system of properties [12]. It is an enclosed property of the database which allows improving several classes of parameters with the "Generic" module according to which for any City object a set of wider properties can be related. On the other hand, when specific classes of properties and relations were already structured and validated by the OCG, CityGML can be improved by means of Application Domain Extensions (ADEs). Furthermore, the detail of the representation of city objects is another paramount issue in the CityGML standard. To very detailed geometric data correspond more detailed semantic features to associate specific classes of properties to single parts of city objects. In detail, five Levels of Detail (LODs) are determined referring to the LOD 0 up to LOD 4, moving from Regional to Interior model ("walkable" architecture) models [12].

Main characteristics and field of applications were discussed in [13] recognizing i) simulations on the noise spread and its mapping in cities, ii) energy assessment of buildings based on sensing tools and energy (cadastral) certificates, iii) urban and landscape planning, iv) various application in managing cadastral 3D data and v) disasters on the large scale and vi) vehicular and pedestrian traffic modelling and simulations [13].

As far as the goal of this work is concerned, in this section, a brief state of the art of CityGML applications to the historic district is discussed, in order to highlight common point of application and novelty. In detail, a selected number of previous works is chosen in the SCOPUS database, applying the filter "CityGML; AND Cultural Heritage; OR historic AND districts; AND application" to research papers (excluding reviews). The searching phase shown firstly 18 results, reduced to 17 for the availability of documents. Table 1 reports details of the analysed applications.

As far as the review is concerned, recurrent points of discussion are highlighted.

Table 1. Applications of CityGML structure on Cultural Heritage and Historic Districts. Reference reports the year of publication, the scale of application (S-BS for Sub-part of Building; SB Building scale; DS District Scale; CS City scale) and LoD for the cases (1 to 4), the aim of application and the type of extensibility (ADE, Generic enrichment G, any detail)

Ref.	Year	Application Scale - LOD	Aim of application – (type of extensibility)
[14]	2020	DS - LOD1; BS - LOD3	Analysis of historical evolution of the pilot historic district; insertion of a high-resolution 3D construction (any detail)
[15]	2020	BS - LOD3	Correlation between HBIM and CityGML ontologies to implement a 3D model in CityGML-based one (any detail)
[16]	2019	BS - LOD3	Reference for LOD, any CityGML integration (any detail)
[17]	2019	BS - LOD3	Correlation between HBIM and CityGML ontologies to implement a 3D model in CityGML-based one (G)
[18]	2019	BS - LOD4	Correlation between HBIM and CityGML ontologies to implement a 3D model in CityGML-based one (New ADE)
[19]	2018	BS - LOD4	Creation of 3D high-level-of-detail data harmonized with CityGML existing structure (new ADE)
[20]	2018	DS - LOD2	Assessment of parameters involved in Energy Conservation Measures for listed and common buildings in the historic district for the creation of an automatic generation of classes of priority for energy retrofitting (New ADE)
[21]	2018	DS - LOD1-2	Platform creation for the creation of a district CityGML-based model enriched with detailed point clouds of buildings (G)
[22]	2017	S-BS, LOD3	Semantic enrichment of LOD3 for ancient Chinese-style architectural roof styles (new ADE)
[23]	2017	SB - LOD3	Geometric data enrichment for texturized facade elements (G)
[24]	2016	DS - LOD1	Assessment of reduced parameters involved in planning management for energy retrofit priority for buildings in historic districts for the creation of a web-based platform (G)

(*continued*)

Table 1. (*continued*)

Ref.	Year	Application Scale - LOD	Aim of application – (type of extensibility)
[25]	2015	DS - LOD2	Geometry semantics analysis for landscape heritage visual protection (any detail)
[26]	2013	SB - LOD3	Coordination of 3D model semantics and CH class (New ADE)
[27]	2013	Any	Web application based on CityGML ontologies (any detail)
[28]	2010	Any	Creation of CityGML-based APP applied to CH aiming at the import and visualize detailed 3D models (New ADE)
[29]	2010	Any	Creation of CityGML-based APP applied to CH aiming at the import and visualize detailed 3D models (New ADE)
[30]	2010	Any	Enrichment of semantics for archaeological sites combining CityGML and CIDOC-CRM (G)

CityGML applied to CH and historic districts is part of a recent issue of analysis that covers the last 12 years in the scientific world. Near to that, applications moved from the large scale of 3D models on the district scale to the single building one. Here, the use of the large scale for models is not an overcome issue for scientists and technicians but the attention is moved towards the HBIM and BIM model implementation in CityGML-based ones as the result of the increasing trend in using high-resolution models for the management of listed buildings.

All the analysed works focus on the necessity to balance the proper LOD to the semantic issues of the model. Obviously, to the high level of representation corresponds more information details that involve both geometric and technical data. When high-resolution models have been discussed for CityGML implementation the system of ontologies required to be enriched according to the relative modelled structure (as building) or parts (i.e., walls, roofs). Nevertheless, for all the cases, basic ontologies for CityGML are implemented according to the nature of the real environment, as well as to the real aim of the representation. Thus, if for BS cases the main goal is the identification of a structured system of properties and processes aimed at importing high-resolution model (HBIM/BIM-based) and maintaining the native ontologies by means of the semantic implementation of CityGML ontologies, for large scale of representation (DS) CityGML ontologies requires to be reorganized and structured according to the main aim of the representation and goals. Here, the main classes of ontologies are referred to medium scale of details for historic buildings, including both geometric and semantic data for their conservation. In that sense, all the works highlighted the necessity to determine and use a homogeneous system of ontologies for CH, as a proper ADE, or when it cannot be possible, structure a coherent system of features classes.

3 The Energy-Resilient Management for Historic Districts by Means of CityGML-Based Models

3.1 Background on the Methodological Frame in Managing the Built Stock in Historic Districts

As discussed in Sect. 1.1, the present work is related to a previous one presented by the authors, where a structured methodology for the management of energy-resilient retrofit actions for buildings in historic districts that combine their inherent adaptability and transformability capacities [5]. These are based on a multi-scale approach based on the theories of "resilient thinking" according to which every system exposed to external stress can be assessed focusing on its aptitude to transform and adapt itself. Borrowing it for the urban systems of historic districts, the transformation ability (or transformability level) consists in the building attitude to be modified without altering its historical and architectural features as inherent results of technological construction features (and relative preservation level) and state of disrepair, analysed for each sub-component of the envelope. Furthermore, the adaptability of such buildings includes classes of positive effects in energy consumption derived by boundary conditions (e.g. shading effects for the compact arrangement of blocks) and technical solutions at building scale (e.g. massive walls, stack effect) that are associated to inherent bioclimatic features in the traditional built environment. These classes of transformability and adaptability are useful in assessing the built stock according to combination classes of such capabilities, identified as MUERIs (Minimum Units of Energy-Resilient Intervention). Finally, for all of them, a system of solutions is provided as guidelines for technical practitioners including materials and technics compatible with the existing solutions. MUERIs are identified for each "building type" as recurrent combinations of technical, material features and main morpho-typologies of buildings. Combining administrative features for such buildings and major experimental results, recurrent geometric features and specific semantic data should be collected and organized. Specifically, for the geometric details, the footprint and the height of buildings are required to define the virtual geometry of 3D buildings. On the other hand, semantic information can be structured according to six main classes: i) administrative data; ii) directly derived from onsite measures, or iii) indirectly from normative preservation framework (city or regional); iv) external measures; v) final data for the management of energy transformation. Specifically, Table 2 reports the details of required features, classified according to the described classes and specified according to the inherent meaning (description).

3.2 Technical Approach for the Web-Service Development

The creation of a CityGML as a web-service instrument can be based on interoperable tools. Notably, among the other, four tools are identified for the creation of the free web server based on CityGML architecture.

Safe FME (Feature Manipulation Engine) is a Spatial ETL (Extract Transform Load) software used for the conversation of main data in proper format files, including spatial and semantic information. It is based on a graphical interface that allows a simplified

Table 2. Classification of collected features in GIS, highlighting classes of data and description

Data classes	Feature	Description
Geometric data		
	Height [He]	Height of building
	Building footprint [BF]	Geometric data inherent in the .shp file
	Number of Floors [F]	Number of floors
Semantic data		
Administrative data	Cadastral data [CD]	Administrative information of buildings
	Construction Period [CP]	Referred to the historic development of district
	Construction class [CC]	Class of construction artefacts (church, castle)
	Property [PP]	Type of properties (public or private)
	Use of Building [UB]	Main Uses for buildings (residential, touristic)
Normative framework	Preservation codes [PC]	System of compatible actions for each type of dispersant surface
	Preservation restriction [PR]	Listed buildings according to the national or regional framework
Onsite survey	State of maintenance [SM]	Referred to each dispersant surface
	Morpho-typology [MT]	Recurrent building types (tower, palace houses, etc.)
External measures	Classes of dispersant surfaces [CS]	For each dispersant surface, materials and technologies involved in the construction
Data for the management of energy transformations	Transformation levels [TL]	For each relevant sub-system, the level of transformability
	Adaptability levels [AL]	For each relevant sub-system of the envelope, the level of adaptability
	System of actions [SA]	For each relevant sub-system of the envelope, the system of technical solutions
	MUERI code [MUERI]	Identified for each Building type, a technical sheet of compatible resilient solutions

conversion of data based on specific categories of functions [31]. FME also supports the validation of the CityGML schema, thus, to check semantics and their relations.

Near to that, the online "Val3dity" tool is chosen to validate 3D primitives according to the international standard ISO 19107 [32].

3D City Database (3DCityDB) is an open-source software based on and structured according to the CityGML structure. The database architecture supports ORACLE Spatial and PostgreSQL/PostGIS relations and it is based on the CityGML v.2.0 for LODs up to 4. The 3DCity database is equipped with the 3DCityDB Import/Exporter tool, useful for the creation of semantic relations between the starting database and the CityGML standards, including geometric and semantic features. Moreover, the software allows to import CityGML data and export KML/COLLADA/gITF data, to integrate and manage data through external spreadsheets and ADE structures [33].

Finally, the 3DCityDB Web-Map-Client is a free viewer based on a simple web-browser (APACHE structure), structured as an extension of Virtual Globe CesiumJS WebGL. The Web-Map-Client aims at the visualization of the virtualized city models and properties in the webpage, importing them following the CityGML standards. The easily use help users in interacting with the DMs showing the structured details. It is fully compatible with KML/gITF files exported from the 3DCityDB Import/Exporter tool. The upload of model databases can be available for two classes of users: end-users that can just upload and visualize the data and overarched-users able to manage the contents of databases. It is possible thanks to the management of thematic features through external sheets (i.e. Spreadsheet Google API or PostgreSQL REST API) [34], restricting accesses to a limited number of users.

3.3 Method for a Simplified CityGML-Based Plan for Historic Districts

Due to the methodological background and the aim of the work, the DM could support public administrators, in managing acceptable transformations, and practitioners, in choosing relevant and compatible solutions. Thus, the model cannot automatically qualify the required solutions, but it is proposed as a digitalized version of the traditional energy plans for historic districts as the results of external analyses made by technical and IT expertise. The creation of the interactive web service is based on the tools described in previous sub-section. However, it requires a structured system of actions for the digitalization of real cases and the organization of semantic data, considering specialistic capacities and functional activities. In detail, the model is structured according to the CityGML structure of data based on LOD1 ("block model") and the information required for the aim. Method, tools and data are summarized in Fig. 1.

Phase 1 consists in the processing and translation data stage. All the collected data in GIS (.shp file), concerning geometric and sematic features (see Table 1), are translated according to the CityGML standard (.gml file). The process follows the specific workflow ETL in FME in order to create the system of (vertical) relations between single city objects to attributes, as well as (horizontal) relations among them. In detail, aims and tools are described as follows:

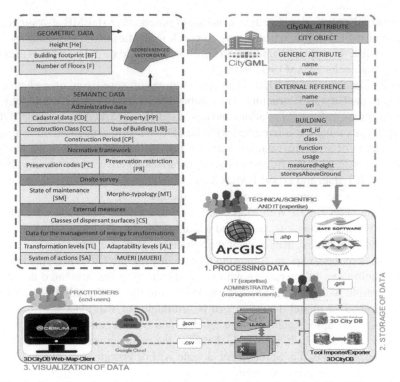

Fig. 1. Process and tools involved in the creation of the simplified CityGML model

- geometric information is processed extruding the footprint using the height of buildings derived by DSM, for the full representation in LOD1 (transformer: Extruder);
- Codification of buildings according to the Cadastral information; all the extruded buildings are associated to a specific alphanumeric ID that includes the cadastral data (transformer: UUIDGenerator and String Concatenator), aiming at supporting final activities of searching and visualization of objects and data;
- Generation of CityGML attributes, where all the .shp features are translated in the CityGML standard (script: AttributeCreator);
- Identification of relations between geometric building and attributes, aiming at the enrichment of extruded buildings with sematic information (CityGML LOD Name: Lod1MultiSurface; FeatureRole: cityObjectMember);
- Creation of CityGML model and concordance with thematic classes; here, all the data are related to the features of "building" classes, when already structured with the CityGML standard, or to the "_genericAttribute" and "ExternalReferences" as a conclusive semantic enrichment. Specifically, an ExternalReference defines a hyperlink from a _CityObject to a corresponding object in another information system. Each of them includes the name of the external information system, represented by a URI, and the reference of the external object, given either by a string or by a URI.

In this phase the validation of the model is included, by means of the CityGML writer option included in the FME Workbench, as well as the geometric validation of features using the Val3dity tool. In this stage are included the scientific and technical expertise resulting from the analysis of the districts as i) the critical management of semantic data derived resulting from external calculations, ii) the critical reading of buildings properties (onsite surveys, external measures) and iii) the normative framework for the preservation of the site. Other geo-topological information (construction classes and cadastral ID), as well as the functional ones (property, use), include technical information organized to solve the administrative level of knowledge. At the same time, guidelines for practitioners are created using specific sheets, including all the descriptions.

Phase 2 aims at the storage of a queryable and editable database with conditional accesses. Here, the structure of features is imported in the 3DCityBD using the relational database based in PostgreSQL/PostGIS that can be readable by means of a specific graphical interface. The process requires a medium-high level of IT support (expertise) due to the programming procedure. In fact, in this phase the database is also prepared for the management of data between final users (administrative and technical). In that sense, .csv files can be created from the database to be shared with different levels of accessibility in the Google Cloud Platform by means of Google sheets API.

Phase 3 consists in the visualization of data in the front-end webpage. Particularly, the model is queryable for cadastral information of buildings and all the related semantic data are shown in the specific pop-windows. The importing process for the visualization by the authorized users requires both .json file and data, organized in sheets in the previous phase. The use of Google sheets allows the visualization of thematic data, while only administrative ones are authorized to modify and manage the contents.

4   Application to the Case Study

According to the work aim, this section presents the experimental proposal of the web-service. Due to the big amount of data required for the creation of the database, the application is traced for the case study presented and validated for the management of the built stock in the historic district in previous work. Particularly, it is the case of the ancient core of Molfetta, a city located in the south of Italy in the Apulia region.

This urban district has a medieval foundation featured by a regular structure in building arrangement, organized in long blocks. These are organized shaping narrow streets canyons and creating consequent compactness of the district. The historical and slow process of recovery plans created local variations in such inherent enclosed structure, generating local exceptions to the main feature (i.e., squares and garden).

In addition to special buildings as churches, the building stock is featured by two main typologies, tower and palace houses, mainly used for residential aims that differ from the orientation of living spaces. As common geometric features, all the buildings are classified for the number of floors and heights for them, to create the simplified building models. For both the typologies, the built stock is analysed summarizing technologies and materials involved in dispersant surfaces, organizing them for recurrent typologies (e.g. wooden, concrete roofs or vaults) and consequent thermal and optical properties directly involved in the energy assessment. For each of them, an alphanumeric

Table 3. Relation of collected attributes and CityGML semantics for the case study

Class of feature	Title of attribute	Data type	Name of attribute	Class of city object
Height [He]	Height	gml::LenghtType	measuredHeight	Building
Building footprint [BF]	Floor extension	xs::string gml::MeasureType	name value	genericAttribute
Number of Floors [F]	Floors	xs::nonNegativeInteger	storeysAboveGround	Building
Cadastral data [CD]	Sheet_Parcel	xs::string	gml_id	Building
Construction Period [CP]	Constr_period	xs::string	name value	genericAttribute
Construction class [CC]	Constr_class	gml::CodeType	class	Building
Property [PP]	Property	gml::CodeType	usage	Building
Use of Building [UB]	Building_use	gml::CodeType	function	Building
State of maintenance [SM]	SM_wall SM_roof	xs::string	name value	genericAttribute
Morpho-typology [MT]	Building_Type	xs::string	name value	genericAttribute
Classes of dispersant surfaces [CS]	Wall_Type_code Roof_Type_code	xs::string	name value	genericAttribute
Preservation codes [PC]	Pres_Code_wall Pres_Code_roof Pres_Code_window Pres_Code_groundfloor Pres_Code_Basement	xs::string	name value	genericAttribute

(continued)

Table 3. (*continued*)

Class of feature	Title of attribute	Data type	Name of attribute	Class of city object
Preservation restriction [PR]	Listed_building	xs::string	name value	genericAttribute
Transform. levels [TL]	Transf_Wall Transf_Roof	xs::string	name value	genericAttribute
Adaptability levels [AL]	Adapt_wall Adapt_roof	xs::string	name value	genericAttribute
System of actions [SA]	Action_Code_Wall_therm Action_code_Roof_therm Action_code_Roof_opt Action_code_Roof_inert	xs::string	name value	genericAttribute
Description of actions	Action_link	xs::string xs:anyURI	name uri	ExternalReference
MUERI [Mx]	MUERI	xs::string xs:anyURI	name uri	ExternalReference

code is associated to simplify the codification in the database. Moreover, linking them to the district recovery plan (developed by urban administration) and strategies for the preservation of landscape protection (identified at regional scale), the equivalent system of preservation alphanumeric codes is generated. This process is based on the qualification of multiple combinations of techniques, materials and building typologies and supported the creation of a simplified database in the GIS model. The external analysis focused on inherent energy deficiencies for dispersant surfaces. Major relevance is associated to roofs and walls, considering the combination of thermal, optical and inertial deficiencies and only thermal one, respectively. Moreover, due to the compactness of the district, walls are also analysed for the assessment of inherent qualities derived by compact cities. In detail, vertical components are assessed to evaluate bioclimatic consequences of the high shading between buildings, take into account i) the variation of air temperatures along the narrow street canyons and large squares and ii) the energy effects derived by direct solar radiations on vertical surfaces. Finally, "transformation levels" and "adaptability levels" are associated to walls and roofs. All the described information was implemented in the GIS model by means of a .shp file and it constitutes the main system of features to transform in the CityGML attribute. In particular, Table 3 summarizes .shp attributes and the transformed ones in the CityGML standard, according to the method. The 3D model has been created using geometric information derived from the DSM of Molfetta (LIDAR based, resolution of grid 2×2) obtained by the Italian Geoportale [35], featured by a planar and height accuracy of 0.3 m and 0.15 m. Finally, the created model has been geometrically and semantically validated according to the method.

Following phases 2 and 3, the 3DCityDB web-map client has been designed in order to visualize contents and manage accesses (Fig. 2). The use of cadastral data as ID of buildings helps technicians in searching for the specific building in the web-map, highlighting the searched building in the virtual model (Fig. 2). Specifically, the ID name is identified by combining Cadastral Sheet and Parcel according to the Italian structure.

As far as the visualization of information is concerned, at the right of Fig. 2, the pop-windows shows all the catalogued and structured data for the selected building. Special attention is given to the "Action_link" and "MUERI" attributes. For them, the database is structured using a website link (.http) that allows users to show the specific sheet of detailed actions in separated webpages (Fig. 3). Here, the complete sheet of MUERI information and detail of compatible actions are described as technical details to support the final solutions of practitioners. In detail, in Fig. 3 technical sheets of MUERI 1 and detailed information of actions are reported (Fig. 3a and Fig. 3b, respectively).

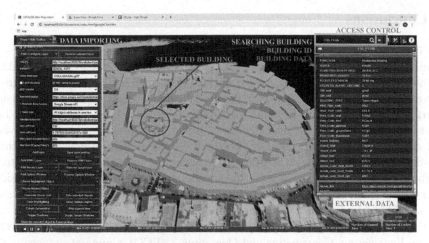

Fig. 2. Web-page structure and details of information and data

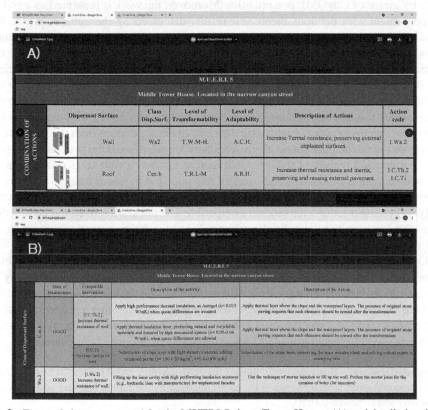

Fig. 3. External sheets generated for the MUERI 5 about Tower Houses (A) and detailed actions for the practitioners (B)

5 Conclusions

The increasing use of virtual models to manage cities moved the IT experiences in creating tools and system to support multiple aims. Today, BIM and CityGML-based are the most used tools for the representation and management of buildings and city/districts with their parts, respectively. However, the virtualization process requires coherent and severe structure to correlate the data visualization to the correlated information. When these tools are applied to the management of urban infrastructures, relations between data and users involved became complex, both for the amount of data and relations as well as for the expertise. It is exasperated when the infrastructure is the Cultural Heritage in all its macro-classes. Here, the knowledge of such buildings has to consider several technicians and an over-ordered normative framework, requiring that collected data should be translated in a universal language to be shared with all the users.

This work is part of the structured application of digitalized knowledge for Architecture, Engineering, Construction and Operations (AECO), aiming at supporting the management of data for historic districts with specific application to the energy-resilient plans by means of CityGML potentialities. Moreover, the work is presented as a coherent *continuum* with previous theoretical results discussed by the authors, where the creation of a digitalized recovery plan for building in historic districts support the share knowledge between users and stakeholders involved in the process. According to the increasing trend in modelling and sharing data for CH, CityGML represents an efficient tool in managing high-resolution models derived by BIM, as a spreading request for the public buildings. However, the CityGML does not present a parallel tool to achieve the experimental results but a system to collect all the data, coherently with the traditional systems of "recovery plans" for historic districts. In detail, starting from the structure of objects and semantic data, the work presents how knowledge can be structured in order to be harmonized with the CityGML architecture towards a web-service for the goal. The main attention is set to the end-users of this plan, public administrators and private technicians, allowing the management and the visualization of design choices, respectively, following a set of over-ordered compatible solutions. Moreover, the application offers the opportunity to test the shared knowledge for future scenario application, as well as to join it freely and available anywhere and any time.

Despite the enclosure of CityGML structures for attributes, the process highlighted a convenient and compatible system of data organization, bypassing the necessity to create an ADE. However, it represents a future scenario for the work. In this attempt, the proposal will be tested with final users of the platform, also creating a proper manual of instruction as well as a specific sheet to help the data reading, as fundamental elements for the translation of technical and IT knowledge in real actions of practitioners.

Acknowledgements. This research is funded under the project "AIM1871082-1" of the AIM (Attraction and International Mobility) Program, financed by the Italian Ministry of Education, University and Research (MUR).

References

1. Commission European Communication from the Commission to the European Parliament, the European Council, the Council, the European Economic and Social Committee and the Committee of the Regions. The European Green Deal. COM/2019/640 final (2019)
2. De Naeyer, A., Arroyo, S.P., Blanco, J.R.: Krakow charter 2000: principles for conservation and restoration of built heritage (2000)
3. Cantatore, E., Fatiguso, F.: Riabitare il patrimonio edilizio dei centri storici come strategia di retrofit energetico – un caso studio. In: D'Andria, P.F.E. (ed.) Small towns… from problem to resource Sustainable strategies for the valorization of building, landscape and cultural heritage in inland areas, pp. 1193–1201. FrancoAngeli, Milano (2019)
4. Cyx, W., Renders, N., Van Holm, M., Verbeke, S.: IEE TABULA-typology approach for building stock energy assessment. Mol, Belgium (2011)
5. Cantatore, E., Fatiguso, F.: An energy-resilient retrofit methodology to climate change for historic districts. Application in the mediterranean area. Sustainability **13**(3), 1422 (2021)
6. Tao, F., Zhang, H., Liu, A., Nee, A.Y.C.: Digital twin in industry: state-of-the-art. IEEE Trans. Ind. Informatics **15**, 2405–2415 (2018)
7. Fuller, A., Fan, Z., Day, C., Barlow, C.: Digital twin: enabling technologies, challenges and open research. IEEE Access **8**, 108952–108971 (2020)
8. Jones, D., Snider, C., Nassehi, A., Yon, J., Hicks, B.: Characterising the digital twin: a systematic literature review. CIRP J. Manuf. Sci. Technol. **29**, 36–52 (2020)
9. Boje, C., Guerriero, A., Kubicki, S., Rezgui, Y.: Towards a semantic construction digital twin: directions for future research. Autom. Constr. **114**, 103179 (2020)
10. Gröger, G., Kolbe, T.H., Nagel, C., Häfele, K.-H.: OGC city geography markup language (CityGML) encoding standard (2012)
11. Stadler, A., Kolbe, T.H.: Spatio-semantic coherence in the integration of 3D city models. In: Proceedings of the Proceedings of the 5th International ISPRS Symposium on Spatial Data Quality ISSDQ 2007 in Enschede, The Netherlands, 13–15 June 2007 (2007)
12. Kolbe, T.H.: Representing and exchanging 3D city models with CityGML. In: Lee, J., Zlatanova, S. (eds.) 3D geo-information sciences, pp. 15–31. Springer, Heidelberg (2009). https://doi.org/10.1007/978-3-540-87395-2_2
13. Gröger, G., Plümer, L.: CityGML–interoperable semantic 3D city models. ISPRS J. Photogramm. Remote Sens. **71**, 12–33 (2012)
14. Pepe, M., Costantino, D., Alfio, V.S., Angelini, M.G., Garofalo, A.R.: A CityGML multiscale approach for the conservation and management of cultural heritage: the case study of the old town of taranto (Italy). ISPRS Int. J. Geo-Information **9**, 449 (2020)
15. Colucci, E., De Ruvo, V., Lingua, A., Matrone, F., Rizzo, G.: HBIM-GIS integration: from IFC to cityGML standard for damaged cultural heritage in a multiscale 3D GIS. Appl. Sci. **10**, 1356 (2020)
16. Hejmanowska, B., et al.: The comparison of the web GIS applications relevant for 4D models sharing. In: Proceedings of the IOP Conference Series: Earth and Environmental Science, vol. 362, p. 12158. IOP Publishing (2019)
17. Matrone, F., Colucci, E., De Ruvo, V., Lingua, A., Spanò, A.: HBIM in a semantic 3D GIS database. Int. Arch. Photogramm. Remote Sens. Spat. Inf. Sci. **42**(2), W11 (2019)
18. Yaagoubi, R., Al-Gilani, A., Baik, A., Alhomodi, E., Miky, Y.: SEH-SDB: a semantically enriched historical spatial database for documentation and preservation of monumental heritage based on CityGML. Appl. Geomat. **11**(1), 53–68 (2018). https://doi.org/10.1007/s12518-018-0238-y
19. Noardo, F.: Architectural heritage semantic 3D documentation in multi-scale standard maps. J. Cult. Herit. **32**, 156–165 (2018)

20. Egusquiza, A., Prieto, I., Izkara, J.L., Béjar, R.: Multi-scale urban data models for early-stage suitability assessment of energy conservation measures in historic urban areas. Energy Build. **164**, 87–98 (2018)
21. Prieto, I., Izkara, J.L., Mediavilla, A., Arambarri, J., Arroyo, A.: Collaborative platform based on standard services for the semi-automated generation of the 3D city model on the cloud. In: Proceedings of the eWork and eBusiness in Architecture, Engineering and Construction: Proceedings of the 12th European Conference on Product and Process Modelling (ECPPM 2018), Copenhagen, Denmark, 12–14 September 2018, p. 169. CRC Press (2018)
22. Li, L., Tang, L., Zhu, H., Zhang, H., Yang, F., Qin, W.: Semantic 3D modeling based on CityGML for ancient Chinese-style architectural roofs of digital heritage. ISPRS Int. J. Geo-Information **6**, 132 (2017)
23. Slade, J., Jones, C.B., Rosin, P.L.: Automatic semantic and geometric enrichment of CityGML building models using HOG-based template matching. In: Abdul-Rahman, A. (ed.) Advances in 3D Geoinformation. LNGC, pp. 357–372. Springer, Cham (2017). https://doi.org/10.1007/978-3-319-25691-7_20
24. Egusquiza, A., Prieto, I., Izkara, J.L.: Web-based tool for prioritization of areas for energy efficiency interventions in historic districts. In: Proceedings of the Euro-American Congress REHABEND 2016, May 24–27, 2016. Burgos, Spain (2016)
25. Rubinowicz, P., Czynska, K.: Study of city landscape heritage using LiDAR data and 3D-city models. Int. Arch. Photogramm. Remote Sens. Spat. Inf. Sci. **40**, 1395 (2015)
26. Costamagna, E., Spanò, A.: CityGML for architectural heritage. In: Rahman, A.A., Boguslawski, P., Gold, C., Said, M.N. (eds.) Developments in multidimensional spatial data models, pp. 219–237. Springer Berlin Heidelberg, Berlin, Heidelberg (2013). https://doi.org/10.1007/978-3-642-36379-5_14
27. San Jose, J.I., et al.: An open source software platform for visualizing and teaching conservation tasks in architectural heritage environments. Int. Arch. Photogramm. Remote Sens. Spat. Inf. Sci. **5**, W2 (2013)
28. Finat, J., Delgado, F.J., Martinez, R., Hurtado, A.: GIRAPIM A 3D information system for suveying cultural heritag environments. Int. Arch. Photogramm. Remote Sens. Spat. Inf. Sci. (2010)
29. Delgado, F., Martínez, R., Hurtado, A., Finat, J.: Extending functionalities of management systems to CityGML. eWork Ebus. Archit. Eng. Constr. 409–415 (2010)
30. Felicetti, A., Lorenzini, M., Niccolucci, F.: Semantic enrichment of geographic data and 3D models for the management of archaeological features. In: Proceedings of the Proceedings of the 11th International conference on Virtual Reality, Archaeology and Cultural Heritage, pp. 115–122 (2010)
31. Safe Software FME. www.safe.com/fme
32. Ledoux, H.: val3dity: validation of 3D GIS primitives according to the international standards. Open Geospatial Data Softw. Stand. **3**(1), 1–12 (2018). https://doi.org/10.1186/s40965-018-0043-x
33. Yao, Z., et al.: 3DCityDB-a 3D geodatabase solution for the management, analysis, and visualization of semantic 3D city models based on CityGML. Open Geospatial Data Softw. Stand. **3**, 1–26 (2018)
34. Chaturvedi, K., Yao, Z., Kolbe, T.H.: Web-based Exploration of and interaction with large and deeply structured semantic 3D city models using HTML5 and WebGL. In: Proceedings of the Bridging Scales-Skalenübergreifende Nah-und Fernerkundungsmethoden, 35. Wissenschaftlich-Technische Jahrestagung der DGPF (2015)
35. Italian Minister for Ecological Transition Geoportale Nazionale. http://www.pcn.minambiente.it/mattm/servizio-wms/. Accessed 30 May 2021

International Workshop on Risk, Resilience and Sustainability in the Efficient Management of Water Resources: Approaches, Tools, Methodologies and Multidisciplinary Integrated Applications (RRS 2021)

An Indicator of Boarded Staff Good Practices About Waste Management

M. Filomena Teodoro[1,2]([envelope]) [iD], José B. Rebelo[1], and Suzana Lampreia[1] [iD]

[1] CINAV, Center of Naval Research, Naval Academy,
Portuguese Navy, 2810-001 Almada, Portugal
maria.alves.teodoro@marinha.pt
[2] CEMAT, Center for Computational and Stochastic Mathematics,
Instituto Superior Técnico, Lisbon University, 1048-001 Lisboa, Portugal

Abstract. In this manuscript, is complemented a study that carried out an analysis of the waste management system of the Portuguese Navy ships (earlier presented in [14]). This study, restricted to the pollution contemplated in Annexes I, IV and V of Marpol 73/78 [3] (namely hydrocarbons, sewage and all types of garbage), analyzed the methods and types of storage and disposal of ship waste to verify the existing equipment, operating conditions and on-board waste management plans. The evaluation of knowledge and cooperation of the military people on board and their contribution to the sustainability and environmental protection was also investigated. With such purpose, a questionnaire was created and implemented for the garrison of some NRP warships, after legal authorization. In [14] we were able to use Exploratory Factor Analysis (EFA) to identify important queries to identify the latent variables that take into account waste management skills. In the present manuscript it is proposes an indicator of good practices about environmental issues between embarked staff. Analysis of variance techniques were used to relate the proposed indicator with some explanatory variables.

Keywords: Waste management · Navy and environment · Pollution of ships · Literacy · Questionnaire · Statistical analysis · ANOVA

1 Introduction

Since the Navy has a very close relationship with the marine environment, it is a continuous concern to reduce the environmental impact of ships in their missions. Under the keywords of environmental protection and sustainability, know how waste treatment is handled on Portuguese Navy ships is an important issue. Implementing a waste management system (WMS) correctly on board helps to minimize the ecological footprint, which must comply with national and international regulations that cover the entire process from collection, separation and treatment types to discharges or storage of produced waste. Given that the Portuguese Navy has some aged ships in its fleet, the current study is to find out under what conditions the WMS is implemented, when possible. This study takes interest on the garrison's status in terms of training and environmental awareness. It

© Springer Nature Switzerland AG 2021
O. Gervasi et al. (Eds.): ICCSA 2021, LNCS 12956, pp. 175–188, 2021.
https://doi.org/10.1007/978-3-030-87010-2_12

is important to note that ships are the main focus of this study, we have visited several ships and other ground support units and collected data in interview mode and applying questionnaires.

This work started from [8], where the author resumed the specific regulations about the topic. In addition, in the same monograph, we implemented a questionnaire to assess knowledge, attitudes and practice (KAP) in waste management during boarding time for NRP ships. Using an incomplete sample of the embarked staff, a preliminary statistical analysis was performed on [10,11] to be used as a support for the current work. In this manuscript, we continued the statistical approach proposed in [9,14,15].

This article consists of an introduction, results and concluding remarks sections, a Sect. 2 where we present some motivations and references to the legal regulation of waste management in the marine environment. Section 3 has some details about the methodology. Empirical application can be found in Sect. 4.

2   Preliminaries

In accordance with the principles of sustainable development, the most important legal tool for dealing with marine environmental issues with regard to the management of ship-generated waste and cargo residues in EU ports is an important element to be studied. Receiving waste and cargo residues from ports is especially important for organization. In [2] the author describes the existing environmental tax system, the basis for calculating such taxes, several ports in Europe, namely Rotterdam, Antwerp, Klaipeda, Szczecin.

Another issue related with waste management is the life cycle of ships with age restrictions related to their operations. When the ship is no longer economically profitable, it is recycled or thrown away. Abandoned ships contain many hazardous materials, so special care must be taken to handle waste in accordance with national and internationally available rules. In this connection, dismantling and ship clothing, ship recycling facilities for recycling machinery and infrastructure must be well designed to comply with all regulations so as not to generate contaminated waste that is harmful to humans and the environment. The authors of [12] promoted a study to design an environmentally friendly ship recycling workshop, a pilot project that predicted the rise of old used merchant ships.

In [2], the authors placed particular emphasis on the legal provisions of international law that define how waste and exhaust gases are treated on ships (MARPOL Appendices 5 and 6). Due to the standardization and automation of the handling of shipping, shipping orders and documents are issued in accordance with classification societies in certain countries. In Fig. 1 we can find a generic scheme of a WMS installed in a ship.

The Portuguese navy has been trying to become more and more green in recent years. The Navy's Admiral Chief of Staff has defined the security and health policy for the Navy's work and environment, where there are environmental guidelines on land and ships to which all military, military and civilian work and contribute for good waste management and environmental protection. In [4] the author gives a good description of this effort. This work has completed these studies in order to

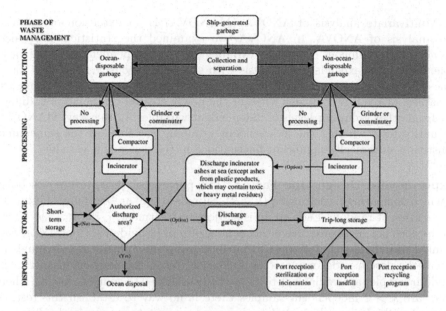

Fig. 1. Scheme of a Waste Management System. Source: [1].

carry out a waste management analysis of Portuguese naval ships and restricts the study to the residues mentioned in Annexes I, IV and V of Marpol 73/78. For this analysis, a questionnaire with relevant questions about knowledge, practice and attitudes was completed and implemented on the crew of the NRP ships to gather the information necessary about the waste management.

3   Methodology

3.1   Analysis of Variance

Experimental design is primarily due to *Sir* Fisher in designing a methodology for agricultural experiments. The main purpose of these methods is to

- assess how a set of qualitative explanatory variables, factors, affect the answer variable,
- discern the most important factors,
- select the best combination of factors to optimize the response,
- fit a model that can make predictions and/or adjust controllable factors to maintain the response variable in the proposed objective.

Noise factors (uncontrollable) that condition the response variable will not be considered. The different values of a factor are called levels. A combination of levels of different factors is denominated treatment. If there is only one factor, each level is a treatment. This work considers only two distinct cases: one-factor and two-factor experimental design [5, 6].

Multivariate analysis of ANOVA (MANOVA) is an extension of univariate analysis of ANOVA. In ANOVA, we examined the statistical difference between the continuous dependent variable and the independent grouping variable. MANOVA expands this analysis with several consecutive dependent variables in mind and groups them into weighted linear combinations or complex variables. MANOVA compares whether the newly created combination is different from other groups or levels of independent variables. In this way, MANOVA primarily tests whether the independent grouping variables at the same time constitute statistically significant fluctuations in the dependent variable.

Experimental Design One Factor. The purpose of these techniques boils down to comparing k treatments ($k \geq 2$). Suppose there are k groups of individuals chosen at random. Each group is subject to treatment, i, $i = 1, \ldots, k$. Each group does not necessarily have the same group of individuals. Consider n_i the number of individuals in group i. If in each group the number of individuals is equal, the design is denominated as balanced. When two independent ($k = 2$) random samples are available, t-tests can be established to compare means, when there are $k > 2$ independent samples there is no way to establish this test to proceed with their analysis. It is necessary to resort to a completely different technique known as analysis of variance. The data of k samples are generally presented as y_{ij}, the response of individual j in sample i.

Theoretical Model. Formal inference to compare means of different treatments implies the definition of probabilistic models [7,13]. It is assumed that the relative data on the $i - th$ treatment have a normal distribution of mean μ_i and variance σ^2. If Y_{ij} is a random variable (rv) associated to the observed value y_{ij} the theoretical model can be represented by (1)

$$Y_{ij} = \mu_i + \epsilon_{ij}, \, (\, j = 1, \ldots, n_i, \, i = 1, \ldots, k), \tag{1}$$

with ϵ_{ij} rv's independents and Gaussian

$$\epsilon_{ij} \cap N(0, \sigma^2). \tag{2}$$

The model can be rewritten as (3)

$$Y_{ij} = \mu + \alpha_i + \epsilon_{ij}, \, (i = 1, \ldots, k, \, j = 1, \ldots, n_i). \tag{3}$$

We are able to obtain confidence intervals at $(1 - \alpha) \times 100\%$ for each μ_i. Since $\hat{\mu}_i = \overline{y}_i$ and from (1) and (2) we can conclude

$$\overline{y}_i \cap N(\mu_i, \sigma^2) \tag{4}$$

following

$$\frac{\overline{y}_i - \mu_i}{\sigma/\sqrt{n_i}} \cap N(0, 1) \tag{5}$$

or, if σ is unknown,

$$\frac{\overline{y}_i - \mu_i}{S/\sqrt{n_i}} \cap t_{[N-k]}. \tag{6}$$

The confidence intervals (CI) considering a confidence level $(1 - \alpha) \times 100\%$ for each μ_i are given by (7)

$$\overline{y}_i - t_{[N-k;1-\alpha/2]}\frac{s}{\sqrt{n_i}} \leq \mu_i \leq \overline{y}_i + t_{[N-k;1-\alpha/2]}\frac{s}{\sqrt{n_i}}. \tag{7}$$

To investigate whether the treatments have identical means or not can be tested the hypothesis (8) using as statistical test the formula (6)

$$H_0 : \mu_1 = \cdots = \mu_k \text{ versus } H_1 : \text{ some } \mu_i \text{ are not equal.} \tag{8}$$

A rejection of H_0 means that there is experiential evidence that treatments differ from each other. In terms of the effect of treatment α_i, the above hypothesis can be described as

$$H_0 : \alpha_1 = \cdots = \alpha_k = 0 \text{ versus } H_1 : \text{ some } \alpha_i \text{ are not null.} \tag{9}$$

To perform the test defined by (9) it is necessary to calculate the total variability of $\widehat{\mu}_i = \overline{y}_i$ around $\widehat{\mu} = \overline{y}$ given by the sum of squares of treatment deviations (16)

$$SS_{TREAT} = \sum_{i=1}^{k} n_i \left(\overline{y}_i - \overline{y}\right)^2. \tag{10}$$

A large SS_{TREAT} suggests that the treatments are distinct. It is necessary to take its average value, dividing by the degrees of freedom (11)

$$MS_{TREAT} = \frac{\sum_{i=1}^{k} n_i \left(\overline{y}_i - \overline{y}\right)^2}{k - 1} \tag{11}$$

and compare with the variability of each observation within the sample, i.e., with the mean sum of squared errors defined as (12)

$$MSE = s^2 = \frac{\sum_{i=1}^{k} \sum_{j=1}^{n_i} \left(y_{ij} - \overline{y}_i\right)^2}{N - k} = \frac{SSE}{N - k}. \tag{12}$$

The F test statistic associated to test hypothesis (9) is given by (14)

$$F = \frac{\text{average sum of squares due to treatments}}{\text{mean sum of squares of residuals}} \tag{13}$$

$$= \frac{MS_{TREAT}}{MSE} \cap F(k - 1, n - k). \tag{14}$$

The critical region of test (9), for significance level α is given by (15)

$$F_{|H_0} > F_{(k-1,n-k,1-\alpha)}. \tag{15}$$

The total variability SST (16) is measured by the squared mean of the deviations of each observation from the overall mean

$$SST = \sum_{i=1}^{k} \sum_{j=1}^{n_i} \left(y_{ij} - \overline{y}\right)^2 \tag{16}$$

and can be decomposed by the sum of two terms: the inter-group variability given by SS_{TREAT} and a variability within each group SSE, given by (17)

$$SST = SS_{TREAT} + SSE. \tag{17}$$

This relationship is generally presented in tabular form, the ANOVA table.

4   Empirical Application

4.1   The Data

We have focused the study to ships. Under such aim, several visits to ships were performed, the questionnaires were applied and some data collection was done in interview mode. After the adequate approval, data collection was conducted through a questionnaire for the crew of each licensed vessel (see Fig. 2). The questionnaire is divided into two parts. The first part contains socio-demographic variables and personal data (detailed in Table 1).

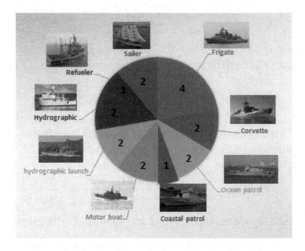

Fig. 2. Selected ships (after authorization by the Surface Fleet Commander from Portuguese Navy).

The second part of questionnaire is composed with questions that allow to evaluate KAP about waste management (detailed in Table 2).

The major number of questions from second part use of Likert scale with four levels from 1 to 4 (1 - Totally Disagree, 2 - Partially Disagree, 3 - Partially agree, 4 - Totally Agree; also some questions have a "yes" or "No" answer. Question related to identifying the factors that contribute to poor waste management has an open answer.

Table 1. Questionnaire questions. Questions about the socio-demographic information of each participant.

- $Q1_1$ - "'Gender."'
- $Q1_2$ - "'Age."'
- $Q1_3$ - "'Grade."'
- $Q1_4$ - "'Have you ever attended an environmental training course?"'
- $Q1_{41}$ "'If you answered "Yes" in the previous question, it was in Navy."'
- $Q1_5$ "'Do you recycle at home?"'

4.2 Sample Characterization

The collection of data was done taking into consideration that we are interested to know how waste treatment is carried out on Portuguese Navy ships, if there exists a waste treatment plan adapted to the characteristics and needs of each ship and which are the conditions, how is condition of the equipment on board for processing waste and if the garrisons are aware of the importance of minimizing the environmental impact of ships. Were performed fifteen interviews to on board Waste management Officers to understand the application of a WMS; there were 241 participants from garrisons that responded the questionnaires; the chief of the port support service and the head of financial management and supply section were also interviewed (Fig. 3). In this manuscript we have focused our attention in questionnaires data set.

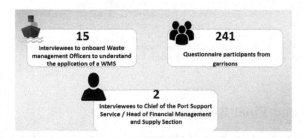

Fig. 3. Collection data.

The questionnaire answers are described as follows. In Fig. 4, the distributions of gender and age are summarized. The sample is composed by 64% of men and 36% of women. People at almost 46% are under 30, and between 38% between 30 and 40. The oldest participant is 51 years old. Information about the environmental issues training and recycling at the home can be found in Fig. 3. Approximately one third of the participants (36%) performed environmental education training. About 68% of participants recycle at home.

Table 2. Questionnaire questions. Questions about the knowledge, Attitude and Practice of each participant about waste management.

- $Q2_1$ -"'The environmental concern on board is always present in my daily life."'
- $Q2_2$ - "'I consider good waste management practice on board ships important."'
- $Q2_3$ - "'There are regular lectures on board on waste management ."'
- $Q2_4$ "'Sometimes I dump small waste into the sea."'
- $Q2_5$ - "'I think there is a good waste management policy on board ships."'
- $Q2_6$ -"' There are some types of waste that we can discharge into the sea."'
- $Q2_7$ - "' The glass can be discharged into the sea, as it ends up in the bottom of the sea, having no interaction with the environment."'
- $Q2_8$ - "'Paper and cardboard can be discharged at sea because they easily degrade."'
- $Q2_9$ "'Proper packaging of waste contributes to the welfare, hygiene and safety of the trim."'
- $Q2_{10}$ - "'Waste storage space is adequate."'
- $Q2_{11}$ - "'The conditions of shipboard equipment allow for the treatment of different types of waste."'
- $Q2_{12}$ - "'Even if conditions are not adequate, there is an effort and concern from the trim to minimize the environmental impact of the ship."'
- $Q2_{13}$ - "'The educational offer of the Navy in the environment preservation is sufficient."'
- $Q2_{14}$ - "'The Navy promotes, with its military staff, the preservation of the environment."'
- $Q2_{15}$ -"' There has been an increase in people's awareness of environmental preservation ."'
- $Q2_{16}$ - "' I know the Navy Environmental Policy and I know where I can consult it."'
- $Q2_{17}$ - "'I am aware of national and international regulations for reducing environmental impact."'
- $Q2_{18}$ - "'Sometimes on board, environmentally harmful acts are performed due to lack of waste treatment conditions."'
- $Q2_{19}$ - "'Feels that their role in minimizing waste generation on board is important for good waste management in the organization."'
- $Q2_{20}$ - "'On board are used environmentally friendly consumables."'
- $Q3$ - "'Has the waste generated on board ever compromised your well-being?."'
- $Q4$ - "'elect from 1 to 2 factors that undermine the proper functioning of onboard waste management."'
- $Q5$ - "'As the Navy is a military organization, do you consider your concern about the ecological footprint at sea important?"'

4.3 Results and Final Remarks

In [9, 14], the statistical analysis of the questionnaire was performed. The alpha-Cronbach coefficient was coherent to a good internal consistency. We have measured the homogeneity and internal consistence of questionnaire and respective validation.

A preliminary data analysis using the questionnaire data set and taking into account the non-quantitative nature of the relevant variables, we have computed some measures of association between the distinct questions: the non-parametric Spearmann correlation coefficient and Friedman's non-parametric test for samples [10, 14]. Both tests were significant ($p - value < 0.001$) meaning that, in general, questions have not the same distribution Fig. 5.

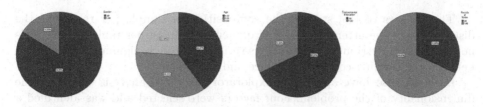

Fig. 4. Sample distribution per gender, per age, pe renvironmental education training attendance, per use of recycling at home. Left: Gender (male/female); Center left: Age; Center right: environmental training (no/yes); Right: Recycling use (no/yes). Source [8].

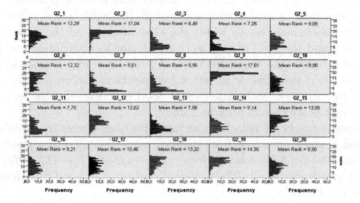

Fig. 5. Sample distribution of ranks $Q2_1 - Q2_{20}$. Source [9].

The paired T-test, McNemar's test for frequencies comparison, Crochan's Q test for binary variables comparison[1] were applied. Also were performed the Friedman test (p-value < 0.001) and kendalls coefficient of concordance test ($p-value < 0.001$). All tests conduced to the same conclusion: the distributions of considered questions are distinct [11].

In [14] were also performed unilateral tests for median considering each question $Q2_1 - Q2_{20}$, the Wilcoxon test and the signal test. We can say that more than 50% of participants have declared that there exists the daily environmental care, consider it an important procedure, also consider that some waste can be left in sea, the waste storage contributes to welfare, security and hygiene of staff. Also consider that the existent equipment to process waste is not enough. The staff declares to know the internal and external rules but claims that there is not a good offer of formation in environmental education. Also we could confirm that environmental awareness is increasing.

---

[1] When the Crochan's Q test for binary variables is applied, we associate to insuccess the first and second levels of the Likert scale, the third and fourth levels of the Likert scale contribute to success.

The authors of [15] studied the composition of sample per rank and the distribution of the attendance of environmental training per rank. Clearly, it is not uniformely distributed. The authors verified a strongly significant correlation between the training course attendance and the rank.

In [8] we also have applied an exploratory factorial analysis to reduce the dimensionality of the problem. Four factors were selected and was identified a meaning for each: F_1 combines variables that characterize *Awareness*, F_2 combines variables from *Hygiene and Safety*, F_3 combines variables from *Practice*. This new variables were introduced as independent variables in a ANOVA unidimensional model in [14]. The factor associated with *Hygiene and Safety* issues conduced a significant model where the kind of ship is the explanatory variable.

In [15] was built a model with a global F test with a $p - value = 0.073$, using a two dimensional anova where the kind of ship and the first interaction between rank and the kind of ship were significant as covariates to explain the *Awareness* variable (the dominant factor $F1$ obtained in [9] by EFA).

We also could establish some strong correlations between some questions associated to awareness and some uses of good practices and the age and rank of participants as we can identify in Table 3.

In the present work we have built an indicator of *goodpractices* combining the information of some questions from questionnaire identified as a good practice. Basically we have defined $goodpractices = Q2_3 + Q2_5 + Q2_{10} + Q2_{11} + Q2_{12} + Q2_{18}$ as the indicator under study. The sample distribution of good practices variable is displayed in Fig. 6.

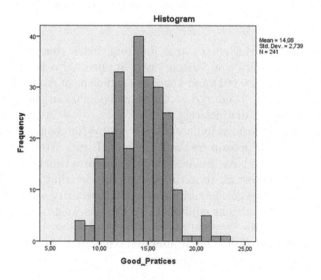

Fig. 6. Distribution of good practices indicator.

Table 3. Correlation between some awareness and good practices questions with age and rank.

Correlations

		Rank	The environmental concern on board is always present in my daily life.	Do you recycle at home?	I consider good waste management practice on board ships important.	Age
Kendall's tau_b	Rank	1,000	,099	-,124*	-,178**	,118*
			,091	,044	,003	,043
		241	241	241	241	241
	The environmental concern on board is always present in my daily life.	,099	1,000	,138*	,166**	,196**
		,091		,024	,006	,001
		241	241	241	241	241
	Do you recycle at home?	-,124*	,138*	1,000	,081	,117
		,044	,024		,203	,055
		241	241	241	241	241
	I consider good waste management practice on board ships important.	-,178**	,166**	,081	1,000	,004
		,003	,006	,203		,945
		241	241	241	241	241
	Age	,118*	,196**	,117	,004	1,000
		,043	,001	,055	,945	
		241	241	241	241	241
Spearman's rho	Rank	1,000	,110	-,130*	-,189**	,131*
			,090	,043	,003	,043
		241	241	241	241	241
	The environmental concern on board is always present in my daily life.	,110	1,000	,146*	,177**	,216**
		,090		,024	,006	,001
		241	241	241	241	241
	Do you recycle at home?	-,130*	,146*	1,000	,082	,124
		,043	,024		,204	,055
		241	241	241	241	241
	I consider good waste management practice on board ships important.	-,189**	,177**	,082	1,000	,004
		,003	,006	,204		,945
		241	241	241	241	241
	Age	,131*	,216**	,124	,004	1,000
		,043	,001	,055	,945	
		241	241	241	241	241

The good practices indicator seems to be related with the kind of ship when we observe the box-plots of indicator depending on the ship (see Fig. 7).

We used the ANOVA approach to confirm that the kind of ship is a good explanatory variable of the proposed indicator. The Levene test has $p-value = 0.05$, confirming the variances homogeneity. In Table 4, we get a $p-value = 0.09$ for the global F test defined by expression (9). The kind of ship is statistically significant for a significant level of 10%.

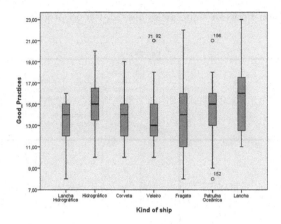

Fig. 7. Distribution of good practices indicator per kind of ship.

Table 4. Analysis of variance. Dependent variable: Indicator of good practices. Explanatory variable: Kind of ship.

ANOVA

Good_Pratices

	Sum of Squares	df	Mean Square	F	Sig.
Between Groups	81,505	6	13,584	1,849	,090
Within Groups	1718,835	234	7,345		
Total	1800,340	240			

It means that at least one level of kind of ship has different effects in the indicator than other distinct level, i.e. the difference between the mean estimate per level with the global average is not the same for all levels (see Fig. 8).

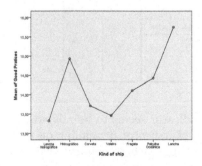

Fig. 8. Effects of the kind of ship in the good practice indicator.

Some ships of Portuguese Navy are previous to the recent environmental concern and a plan of waste management was not a rule, other ships are very small, usually perform short trips, not needing a WMS. The majority of ships have a WMS, but some of them have few space to store the waste or the equipment is not recent. All this details contribute to distinct effects in the good practices indicator.

Acknowledgements. This work was supported by Portuguese funds through the *Center of Naval Research* (CINAV), Portuguese Naval Academy, Portugal and *The Portuguese Foundation for Science and Technology* (FCT), through the *Center for Computational and Stochastic Mathematics* (CEMAT), University of Lisbon, Portugal, project UID/Multi/04621/2019.

References

1. https://intlreg.org/2019/08/05/options-for-shipboard-handling-and-discharge-of-garbage/. Accessed 24 Aug 2021
2. Deja, A.: Organization of the reception of ship-generated wastes and cargo residues illustrated by selected examples of European union seaports. Sci. J. **33**(105), 16–21 (2013)
3. Consolidated Edition: MARPOL 73/78. Regulation (2002)
4. Monteiro, J.: Poluição. Marítima; Normas e Controlo nos meios Navais das Forças Armadas. Monography, Instituto Universitário Militar (2016)
5. Montgomery, D.: Design and Analysis of Experiments, 5th edn. Wiley, New York (2001)
6. Moore, D., McCabe, G.: Introduction to the Practice of Statistics, 4th edn. W H Freeman & Co., New York (2003)
7. Morgado, L., Teodoro, F., Perdicoulis, T.: Métodos Estatísticos em Ciências Biomédicas. Universidade de Trás-os-Montes e Alto Douro (UTAD), Vila-Real, Portugal (2010)
8. Rebelo, J.: Impacto Ambiental da Marinha Portuguesa. Análise e resolução da Gestão de Resíduos no mar. Master thesis, Escola Naval (2019)
9. Rebelo, J., Jerónimo, J., Teodoro, M., Lampreia, S.: Literacy about the waste management in boarded staff. In: Proceedings of EUROGEN 2019, 12nd–14th September, Guimarães (2019)
10. Rebelo, J., Jerónimo, J., Teodoro, M., Lampreia, S.: Modeling the waste management in NRP ships. In: Entrepreneurial Ecosystems and Sustainability. Proceedings of Regional Helix 2019 (2019). ISBN 978-989-98447-7-3
11. Rebelo, J., Jerónimo, J., Teodoro, M., Lampreia, S.: Preliminary reflexion about waste management plan in NRP ships. In: Simos, T., et al. (eds.) Computational Methods in Science and Engineering, vol. 2186, pp. 183–188. AIP (2019)
12. Sunaryo, S., Pahalatua, D.: Green ship recycle yarn design. J. Nav. Archit. Mar. Eng. **12**(1), 15–20 (2015)
13. Tamhane, A., Dunlop, D.: Statistics and Data Analysis: From Elementary to Intermediate. Prentice Hall, New Jersey (2001)

14. Teodoro, M.F., Rebelo, J.B., Lampreia, S.: Waste management and embarked staff. In: Gervasi, O., et al. (eds.) ICCSA 2020. LNCS, vol. 12251, pp. 492–503. Springer, Cham (2020). https://doi.org/10.1007/978-3-030-58808-3_36
15. Teodoro, M.F., Rebelo, J.B., Lampreia, S.: Modeling waste management and boarded personnel KAP. In: Machado, J., Soares, F., Trojanowska, J., Ivanov, V. (eds.) icieng 2021. LNME, pp. 257–270. Springer, Cham (2022). https://doi.org/10.1007/978-3-030-78170-5_23

Discounting for Economic Analysis of Long-Lived and Short-Lived Water Resource Investments

Gabriella Maselli(✉) 🄳 and Antonio Nesticò 🄳

Department of Civil Engineering, University of Salerno, Fisciano, SA, Italy
{gmaselli,anestico}@unisa.it

Abstract. With reference to the Cost-Benefit Analysis (CBA) of water resource projects, this paper intends to show the effects of discounting cash flows on the evaluation results. These are projects that commonly involve the use of unique and irreplaceable natural sites, often with potentially irreversible consequences and considerable effects on the community. Therefore, in the analyses it is of absolute importance to give the right "weight" to costs and benefits progressively more distant in time. In other words, the Social Discount Rate (SDR) must be chosen correctly. In this way, decision-makers can orientate themselves towards investment choices aimed at safeguarding the proper management of water resources.

This research proposes a discounting approach that distinguishes between long-lived and short-lived water projects. Specifically: (i) a constant and dual discounting approach for interventions with a useful life of 30 years or more; (ii) a declining dual discounting approach for investment decisions with very long lifespan. The main novelty is the introduction in the logical-mathematical structure of the SDR of the environmental quality, expressed as a function of the Water Resource Index.

An application compares the CBA results obtained both using the discount rates proposed here and the constant discount rates suggested by the European Commission. The substantial differences obtained show the importance of the defined model on the whole process of allocation of resources to water projects.

Keywords: Cost-benefit analysis · Dual discounting · Economic evaluation · Water projects

1 Introduction

Balancing consumption with supply is a key challenge for effective water management worldwide. The rapid population growth of recent decades will result in a 40% shortfall between projected demand and available water supply by 2030. In addition, feeding 9 billion people by 2050 will require a 60% increase in agricultural production – which today consumes 70% of resources – and a 15% increase in water withdrawals. In addition, estimates indicate that 40% of the world's population lives in water-scarce areas and

G. Maselli, A. Nesticò—The paper is attributed equally to the two authors.

© Springer Nature Switzerland AG 2021
O. Gervasi et al. (Eds.): ICCSA 2021, LNCS 12956, pp. 189–201, 2021.
https://doi.org/10.1007/978-3-030-87010-2_13

about ¼ of the world's GDP is exposed to this challenge [1]. The Global Risk Perception Survey, conducted among 900 experts recognised by the World Economic Forum, found that water crises will generate the largest level of social impact over the next 10 years [2]. In other words, water scarcity, hydrological uncertainty and extreme weather events are seen as threats to wealth and global stability.

Water management issues are increasingly becoming a priority political issue at international level. The United Nations recognises water management as the core of sustainable development. In fact, the United Nations Sustainable Development Goal (SDG) 6 on water and sanitation - adopted as part of the 2030 Agenda - provides the blueprint for ensuring availability and sustainable management of water and sanitation for all. According to the third United Nations World Water Development Report (UN WWAP, 2009), both economic development and security are put at risk by poor water management [3]. The UN WWAP (2014) also pointed out that the water-energy nexus is playing an increasingly crucial role. So, concern about a global energy crisis is now matched by worry about a looming global water crisis [4].

Promoting water security in a scenario of increasing water demand but decreasing water supply requires investment in the development and careful management of natural and man-made infrastructure. Governmental instruments such as legal and regulatory frameworks, water pricing and incentives are required to better allocate, manage and conserve water resources [5–7].

Therefore, there is a clear need to characterise new methodologies able to guide the policymakers towards more sustainable investment choices in the water sector. In this respect, environmental discounting is a potentially relevant research area for water resources management. While the importance of the Social Discount Rate (SDR) for the assessment of problems with environmental effects has been widely acknowledged, the choice of SDR is rarely discussed when policy objectives must be translated into actions and intervention strategies [8–10]. In other words, it is underestimated that the outcome of a Cost-Benefit Analysis (CBA) is markedly influenced by the value of the discount rate used in the assessment.

The aim of the paper is to suggest the Social Discount Rate (SDR) to be used in the water resource investment analyses, distinguishing between long-lived and short-lived water projects. This can be done by first analysing the emerging discounting approaches (Sect. 2). Then, by defining an innovative model for estimating discount rates for water investments (Sect. 3). Finally, showing how discount rates estimated with the proposed model can guide decision-making towards investment choices aimed at preserving the sustainable water management of water resources.

2 Literature Review

Discounting is a mathematical procedure used to make costs and benefits that occur at different instants in time economically comparable. Dasgupta points out that there are many reasons for discounting [11]. The first is that individuals expect their level of consumption to increase over time and that, consequently, the marginal utility of consumption tends to decrease. Because of this expectation, individuals are willing to give up a unit of consumption today only if they can get a higher reward in the future. The second explanation is that individuals are generally "impatient" or "myopic" because of the risk of not being alive in the future and, for this reason, always tend to attach greater weight to current consumption.

It follows that, to choose between alternative projects, it is necessary to estimate the current value of the future flow of net benefits that the different investment alternative generates [12–14]. Discounting is therefore a mathematically step of the Cost-Benefit Analysis (CBA) needed to compare the Cash-Flows of a proposed investment project [15–17].

The choice of the Social Discount Rate is a crucial step in CBA, as small variations in it significantly influence the outcome of the evaluation. This is particularly true for projects with environmental impacts, which tend to occur over long-time intervals [18]. Like forestry, fisheries and climate change applications, water resource investments represent decisions that generate intergenerational effects. In addition, water resource investments commonly involve the use of irreplaceable natural sites, often with potentially irreversible consequences [19]. Choosing the right discount rate can lead to more sustainable project choices. In this regard, the literature is almost unanimous in excluding the use of exponential discount procedures. In fact, the use of constant discount rates underestimates the environmental effects that occur in a period distant from that of the evaluation.

According to Emmerling et al. [8], the climate targets of the Paris Agreement (2015) can only be achieved by using lower discount rates than those suggested by governments, such as the one proposed by Stern [20]. van den Bijgaart et al. [21] and van der Ploeg and Rezai [22] show that the discount rate is a crucial determinant of the Social Cost of Carbon.

In the case of projects with long-term effects, other scholars believe that time-declining rates should be used to give greater weight to events that are progressively more distant in time [23, 24].

According to a recent branch of the literature, the discounting of environmental components should instead take place at a different and lower "environmental" rate than the "economic" one, the latter being useful to evaluate strictly financial cash flows [25, 26].

Finally, other scholars estimate specific rates for environmental categories and services. Just to mention a few, Vazquez-Lavín et al. [27] propose a declining discount rate for eco-system services, with particular attention to projects aimed at preserving biodiversity in marine protected areas in Chile. Muñoz-Torrecillas et al. [28] evaluate a SDR to be applied in US afforestation project appraisal.

In practice, while the European Commission recommends the use of exponential discounting also for long-term valuations [29], France and the UK have decided to use time-declining discount rates. The UK Green Book proposes a decreasing sequence of rates for projects with impacts over more than 30 years [30]. In France, the discount rate has been increased from 8% to 4%, suggesting a decreasing discount rate down to 2% for very long-term assessments [31].

The aim of this research is to define a new approach for the estimation of SDR to be used in the analysis of water resource investments, distinguishing between long-lived and short-lived projects. To give the right weight to the environmental effects, a dual discounting model is proposed, which allows to evaluate a different economic discount rate than the one useful for the environmental components.

3 The Social Discount Rate for Water Resource Investments

Water is fast becoming a scarce resource in almost every country in the world. This scarcity makes water both a social and an economic good used for multiple purposes.

Therefore, it is essential to assess the sustainability of Water Supply Projects (WPs) so that planners, policy makers, water companies and consumers are aware of the true economic cost of scarce water resources and the appropriate levels of tariff needed to financially sustain it [32].

In this perspective, the choice of the Social Discount Rate becomes essential to correctly assess the economic performance of water projects. Thus, we define: (i) a constant dual discounting approach for water projects, whose useful life is at most 30 years (Sect. 3.1); (ii) a declining dual discounting approach for investment decisions with very long lifespan (Sect. 3.2).

3.1 A Discounting Approach for Short-Lived Water Projects

In the case of water projects with a useful life of thirty years or more, it is considered coherent to give the right weight to the financial and extra-financial effects of the investment using a constant and dual discounting approach. In fact, for short-lived water projects, the contraction of the present value of cash flows over time can be considered acceptable. However, as the environmental effects are not negligible, it is necessary to discount them at a lower rate than the economic rate.

In order to estimate a double discount rate, i.e. an economic one for the strictly financial terms, and an environmental one for the extra-financial effects, the environmental quality is introduced in the logical-mathematical structure of the Social Discount Rate. This can be done by assuming that: (i) any improvement in environmental quality will matter more to future generations than to current ones, as the environment tends to deteriorate over time; (ii) the utility of society $U(c_{1t}, c_{2t})$ is a function of both consumption c_{1t} and environmental quality c_{2t}, where the availability of the two goods varies over time; (iii) the utility or "happiness" function $U(c_{1t}, c_{2t})$ is of the Cobb-Douglas type, increasing and concave; (iv) environmental quality and consumption are two mutually substitutable goods; (v) environmental quality increases less quickly than consumption [24].

If we assume that consumption and environmental quality are correlated according to a deterministic function such as $c_{2t} = f(c_{1t})$, then two discount rate functions are obtained:

i. deriving $U(c_{1t}, c_{2t})$ compared to consumption c_{1t}, we obtain the equation describing the "economic" discount rate r_{ECt}:

$$r_{ECt} = \delta + \left[\gamma_1 + \rho(\gamma_2 - 1)\right] \cdot \left[g_1 - 0.5(1 + \gamma_1\rho(\gamma_2 - 1)\right] \cdot \sigma_{11} \qquad (1)$$

ii. deriving instead $U(c_{1t}, c_{2t})$ with respect to environmental quality c_{2t} we obtain the equation describing the "ecologic" discount rate r_{ENt}:

$$r_{ENt} = \delta + \left[(\rho \cdot (\gamma_2 + \gamma_1 - 1)\right] \cdot \left[g_1 - 0.5(\rho\gamma_2 + \gamma_1)\right] \cdot \sigma_{11} \qquad (2)$$

Where:

- δ is the rate of time preference;
- γ_1 the risk aversion parameter of income inequality;
- γ_2 the degree of environmental risk aversion;
- g_1 the growth rate of consumption;
- ρ the elasticity of environmental quality to changes in the growth rate of consumption g_1;
- σ_{11} the uncertainty of the consumption growth rate in terms of the mean square deviation of the variable.

Main novelty of this research concerns the modelling of the ρ parameter, which makes it possible to assess how environmental quality changes as consumption varies. Specifically, environmental quality is expressed as a function of the "Water and Sanitation" index, which makes up the Environmental Performance Index (EPI). This composite index makes it possible to establish how close countries are to achieving the UN's 2015 Sustainable Development Goals [33].

Consider c_1 equal to a country's GDP per capita and c_2 its environmental index. The correlation between the two parameters gives the value ρ:

$$c_1 = x + \rho \cdot c_2 + \varepsilon \tag{3}$$

In (3) x is the intercept of the line on the axis y, ρ is the inclination of the line and ε the statistical error of the regression.

Table 1 summarises the formulas for estimating the economic, social, and environmental parameters of (1) and (2).

3.2 A Discounting Approach for Long-Lived Water Projects

In the case of water projects with intergenerational impacts a dual and declining discounting approach is defined. This means that we estimates two discount rates, economic and environmental, both with a declining structure over time. In this way, greater weight is given to environmental costs and benefits progressively more distant.

The idea is to characterize a stochastic model, in which the growth rate of the consumption g_1 of (1) and (2) is modelled as an uncertain variable. This is a crucial parameter for the evaluation. In fact, since $q_t = f(c_t)$, from g_1 depends on both the value of the economic discount rate r_c and the value of the environmental discount rate r_q. The growth rate of consumption g_1 is an uncertain parameter, so it is modelled as a stochastic variable. This means that from the trend analysis of g_1, we first estimate a probability function to be associated with the parameter itself. Then, from the probability function thus obtained, implementing the Monte Carlo simulation, a set of possible values is obtained to associate with the rate g_1 and, consequently, with the unknow value of r_{EC} and r_{EN}.

Table 2 summarises the rationale and practical steps of the model.

Table 1. Methods for estimating the parameters of (1) and (2).

Parameter	Formula
δ = the rate of time preference	$\delta = l + r$ l = average mortality rate of a country r = pure time preference rate, $0\% < r < 0.5\%$
γ_1 = the risk aversion parameter of income inequality	$\gamma_1 = \dfrac{\log(1-t)}{\log\left(1-\frac{T}{Y}\right)}$ t = marginal tax rate; T/Y = average tax rate
g_1 = the growth rate of consumption	g_1 is approximated to the average growth rate of a country's GDP per capita
γ_2 = the degree of environmental risk aversion	$\gamma^* = \dfrac{\gamma_2-1}{\gamma_1+\gamma_2-2}$ γ^* = expenditure on environmental quality $(10\% < \gamma^* < 50\%)$
σ_{11} = uncertainty of the consumption growth rate	mean square deviation of the variable g_1
ρ = elasticity of environmental quality to changes in the growth rate of consumption g_1	$c_1 = x + \rho \cdot c_2 + \varepsilon$ x = intercept of the line on the axis y; ρ = inclination of the line; ε the statistical error

Table 2. Operational phases of the discounting model for long-lived water projects.

Step 1	Estimation of the constant parameters of (1) and (2)
Step 2	Estimation of the probability distribution of the consumption growth rate g_1 and, consequently, of the "economic" and "environmental" discount rates r_{EC} and r_{EN} implementing Monte Carlo analysis
Step 3	Estimate of "economic" and "environmental" certain-equivalent discount factors $E_{EC}(P_t)$ e $E_{EN}(P_t)$ $E_{EC}(P_t) = E_{EC}[\exp(-\sum_{i=1}^{m} p_{1i} \cdot r_{1i}) \cdot t] \cdot E_{EN}(P_t) = E_{EN}[\exp(-\sum_{i=1}^{m} p_{2i} \cdot r_{2i}) \cdot t]$ r_{1i} = i-th economic discount rate (from r_{EC} of step 2) p_{1i} = probability of the i-th value of the economic rate r_1 occurring probability r_{2i} = i-th economic discount rate (from r_{EN} of step 2) p_{1i} = probability of the i-th value of the economic rate r_2 occurring probability t = time variable m = number of intervals in which the functions of r_{EC} and r_{EN} are discretized
Step 4	Estimating the declining "economic" discount rate $\tilde{r}_{ECt}$ and the declining "environmental" discount rate $\tilde{r}_{ENt}$ $\dfrac{E_{EC}(P_t)}{E_{EC}(P_t+1)} - 1 = \tilde{r}_{ECt}$ $\dfrac{E_{EN}(P_t)}{E_{EN}(P_t+1)} - 1 = \tilde{r}_{ENt}$

4   Estimation of Social Discount Rate for Water Projects in Italy

The approaches defined in Sect. 3 are implemented to estimate:

i.   constant economic and environmental discount rates to be used for short-lived water projects in Italy (Sect. 4.1);
ii. declining economic and environmental discount rates for long-lived water projects in Italy (Sect. 4.2).

4.1   Estimation of r_{EC} and r_{EN} for Short-Lived Water Projects

The implementation of the approach described in Sect. 3.1 returns the results summarised in Table 3. The economic, social, and environmental parameters of formulas (1) and (2) were estimated using the methods shown in Table 1.

Figure 1 returns the regression analysis result delivered by (3), in which $\rho = 0.61$.

Table 3. Estimation of the r_{EC} and r_{EN} for short-lived water projects.

Parameter	Value	Source
l = average mortality rate of a country	1.00%	*World Bank*, time frame 1991–2020
r = pure time preference rate	0.30%	Evans and Kula [34]
δ = time preference rate	1.30%	–
γ_1 = risk aversion parameter of income inequality	1.34	Organization for Economic Cooperation and Development Countries (OECD)
g_1 = consumption growth rate	1.22%	World Bank, time frame 1980–2019
γ_2 = degree of environmental risk aversion	1.15	$\gamma^* = 30\%$ [35, 36]
σ_{11} = uncertainty of the consumption growth rate	0.03%	–
ρ = elasticity of environmental quality to changes in the growth rate of consumption	0.61	–
r_{EC}	3.0%	–
r_{EN}	2.4%	–

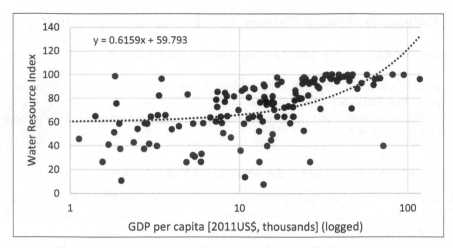

Fig. 1. Relationship between Water Resource Index and GDP per capita.

4.2 Estimation of r_{ECt} and r_{ENt} for Long-Lived Water Projects

To estimate time-declining discount rates r_{ECt} and r_{ENt} for long-lived water projects in Italy, the steps described in Table 2 are followed.

Step 1. For the estimation of the constant parameters, δ, γ_1, γ_2, σ_{11} e ρ, reference is made to the values in Table 3.

Step 2. At this point, it is essential to obtain the probability distribution that best describes the historical series of g_1. From this, by implementing the Monte Carlo technique, it is possible to forecast all the values that the rates r_{EC} and r_{EN} can have.

Figure 2 illustrates the probability distribution of g_1 that best approximates the historical data, i.e. the Weibull distribution. Figures 3 and 4 show the probability distributions of r_{EC} and r_{EN}, of which only positive values are considered, since the discount rate has a logical-mathematical meaning only if it is greater than zero.

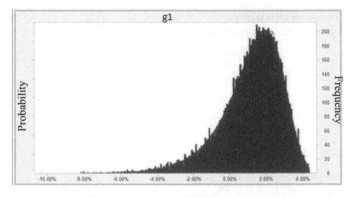

Fig. 2. Probability distribution of g_1.

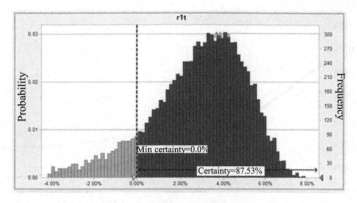

Fig. 3. Probability distribution of r_{EC}.

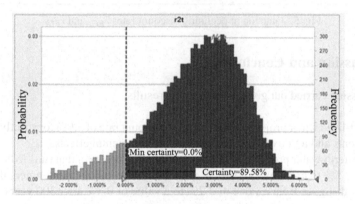

Fig. 4. Probability distribution of r_{EN}.

Step 3. At this stage, using approach of the Expected Net Present Value (ENPV), we move from the uncertain and constant discount rate to the certain but decreasing discount rate with a "certainty equivalent". This requires estimating the economic discount factors $E_{EC}(P_t)$ and ecological $E_{EN}(P_t)$ for each future instant t according to the mathematical formulations shown in Table 2.

Step 4. From the time trend of each of the two discount factors, it is possible to estimate the values of the declining economic discount rate $\tilde{r}_{ECt}$ and the declining environmental discount rate $\tilde{r}_{ENt}$ according to the formulations in Table 2 for step 4.

Figure 5 summarises the results of the elaborations.

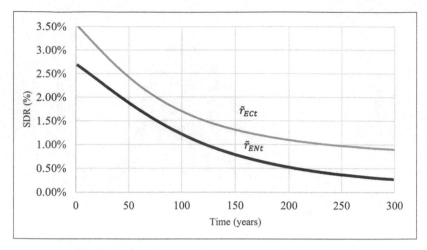

Fig. 5. Function of declining discount rates $\tilde{r}_{ECt}$ and $\tilde{r}_{ENt}$.

5 Discussion and Conclusions

The processing carried out gives the following results.

- For short-lived water projects in Italy: a r_{ECt} discount rate of 3.0% for strictly financial components and a rate of 2.4% to discount environmental effects.
- For long-term water projects: an economic discount rate r_{ECt} that runs from an initial value of 3.5% to a value of about 1% after 300 years; and an environmental discount rate r_{ENt} that goes from a value of 2.7% to a value of 0.3% after 300 years.

The results obtained by implementing the two approaches are consistent with each other. In fact, the average r_{ECt} value for the first 30 years is 3.1%, which corresponds roughly to the 3.0% r_{EC} value obtained by implementing the determination approach. Similarly, the average value of r_{ENt} for the first 30 years is 2.4%, which corresponds to the value estimated for short-lived projects.

The value obtained for the economic discount rate is also in line with the 3.0% discount rate suggested by the European Commission for countries outside the Cohesion Fund [19].

In order to understand how the results obtained may influence the outcome of an economic assessment of a water resources investment, we show how the discount factor $F_S = 1/(1 + r)^t$ varies as time t.

increases in two cases:

1. Using the constant discount rate of 3.0%, suggested by the European Commission;
2. Using a double declining discount rate, with $r_{ECt} < r_{ECt}$.

Figure 6 shows the relationship between discount factor F_D and time t, with $1 < t < 100$ years.

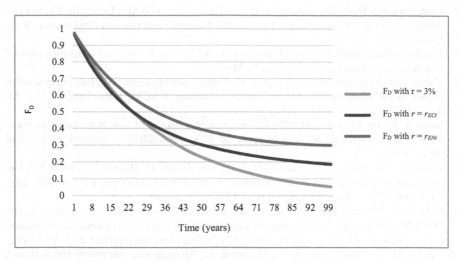

Fig. 6. Relationship between $F_{D-}t$.

Two main findings emerge from the analysis:

1. For periods of analysis up to thirty years, it can be considered consistent not to use a declining logic. However, using a double discount rate also for short-lived water projects allows to give more weight to environmental effects which are often not negligible already at the beginning of the assessment;
2. For periods of analysis longer than thirty years, the use of a constant discount rate would halve the "weight" of the environmental effects compared to a declining environmental rate. After one hundred years, using a constant SDR would mean not considering at all the environmental damages and benefits that the project is able to generate.

In conclusion, the repercussions that the choice of discount rate can have on the whole decision making process are extremely important. The study shows that the use of dual and declining discounting approaches specific to water resources investment can guide the analyst towards more sustainable investment choices, both in the short and long term.

References

1. Cosgrove, W.J., Loucksb, D.P.: Water management: current and future challenges and research directions. Water Resour. Res. **51**, 4823–4839 (2015). https://doi.org/10.1002/201 4WR016869
2. World Economic Forum (2015). http://www3.weforum.org/docs/WEF_Global_Risks_ 2015_Report15.pdf. Accessed 20 Mar 2021
3. United Nations World Water Assessment Programme (UN WWAP): The United Nations World Water Development. In: Water in a Changing World, Report 3, Earthscan, London, UK, 380p. (2009)

4. United Nations World Water Assessment Programme (UN WWAP): Facing the Challenges, Water and Energy, United Nations Educational, Scientific and Cultural Organization, Paris (2014)
5. The World Bank: Water Resources Management (2017). https://www.worldbank.org/en/topic/waterresourcesmanagement. Accessed 20 Mar 2021
6. Macchiaroli, M., Pellecchia, V., D'Alpaos, C.: Urban water management in Italy: an innovative model for the selection of water service infrastructures. WSEAS Trans. Environ. Dev. **15**, 463–477 (2019)
7. Nesticò, A., De Mare, G., Maselli, G.: An economic model of risk assessment for water projects. Water Sci. Technol. Water Supply **20**, 2054–2068 (2020). https://doi.org/10.2166/ws.2020.093
8. Emmerling, J., Drouet, L., van der Wijst, K.-I., Van Vuuren, D., Bosetti, V., Tavoni, M.: The role of the discount rate for emission pathways and negative emissions. Environ. Res. Lett. **14**, 104008 (2019). https://doi.org/10.1088/1748-9326/ab3cc9
9. Calabrò, F.: Integrated programming for the enhancement of minor historical centres. The SOSTEC model for the verification of the economic feasibility for the enhancement of unused public buildings. ArcHistoR **13**(7), 1509–1523 (2020). https://doi.org/10.14633/AHR280
10. Della Spina, L., Lorè, I., Scrivo, R., Viglianisi, A.: An integrated assessment approach as a decision support system for urban planning and urban regeneration policies. Buildings **7**(4), 85 (2017)
11. Dasgupta, P.: Discounting Climate Change. J. Risk Uncertain. **37**(2–3), 141–169 (2008)
12. Nesticò, A., Somma, P.: Comparative analysis of multi-criteria methods for the enhancement of historical buildings. Sustainability **11**(17), 4526 (2019). https://doi.org/10.3390/su11174526
13. Dolores, L., Macchiaroli, M., De Mare, G.: A dynamic model for the financial sustainability of the restoration sponsorship. Sustainability **12**(4), 1694 (2020). https://doi.org/10.3390/su12041694
14. Calabrò, F., Cassalia, G., Lorè, I.: The economic feasibility for valorization of cultural heritage. The restoration project of the reformed fathers' convent in Francavilla Angitola: the Zibìb territorial wine cellar. In: Bevilacqua, C., Calabrò, F., Della Spina, L. (eds.) NMP 2020. SIST, vol. 178, pp. 1105–1115. Springer, Cham (2021). https://doi.org/10.1007/978-3-030-48279-4_103
15. Nesticò, A., Maselli, G.: A protocol for the estimate of the social rate of time preference: the case studies of Italy and the USA. J. Econ. Stud. **47**(3), 527–545 (2020). https://doi.org/10.1108/JES-02-2019-0081
16. Troisi, R., Alfano, G.: Towns as safety organizational fields: an institutional framework in times of emergency. Sustainability **11**(24), 7025 (2019)
17. Nesticò, A., Guarini, M.R., Morano, P., Sica, F.: An economic analysis algorithm for urban forestry projects. Sustainability **11**(2), 314 (2019). https://doi.org/10.3390/su11020314
18. Nesticò, A., Maselli, G.: Declining discount rate estimate in the long-term economic evaluation of environmental projects. J. Environ. Account. Manag. **8**(1), 93–110 (2020). https://doi.org/10.5890/JEAM.2020.03.007
19. U.S. Department of the Interior Bureau of Reclamation Technical Service Center: Discounting for Long-Lived Water Resource Investments. Science and Technology Report, U.S. Department of the Interior Bureau of Reclamation Technical Service Center Denver, Colorado (2014)
20. Stern, N.: Stern Review: The Economics of Climate Change. HM Treasury, London (2006)
21. van den Bijgaart, I., Gerlagh, R., Liski, M.: A simple formula for the social cost of carbon. J. Environ. Econ. Manag. **77**, 75–94 (2016)
22. van der Ploeg, F., Rezai, A.: Simple rules for climate policy and integrated assessment. Environ. Resour. Econ. **72**, 77–108 (2019)

23. Arrow, K.J., et al.: How Should Benefits and Costs Be Discounted in an Intergenerational Context? The Views of an Expert Panel. Resources for the Future Discussion Paper, pp. 12–53 (2013)
24. Newell, R.G., Pizer, W.A.: Discounting the distant future: how much do uncertain rates increase valuations? J. Environ. Econ. Manag. **46**(1), 52–57 (2003)
25. Gollier, C.: Ecological discounting. J. Econ. Theory **145**, 812–829 (2010)
26. Weikard, H.P., Zhu, X.: Discounting and environmental quality: when should dual rates be used? Econ. Model. **22**, 868–878 (2005)
27. Vazquez-lavin, F., Oliva, R.D.P., Hernandez, J.I., Gelcich, S., Carrasco, M., Quiroga, M.: Exploring dual discount rates for ecosystem services: evidence from a marine protected area network. Resour. Energy Econ. **55**, 63–80 (2019)
28. Muñoz Torrecillas, M.J., Roche, J., Cruz Rambaud, S.: Building a social discount rate to be applied in US afforestation project appraisal. Forests **10**(5), 445 (2019). https://doi.org/10.3390/f10050445
29. European Commission, Directorate General Regional Policy: Guide to Cost-Benefit Analysis of Investment Projects: Economic Appraisal Tool for Cohesion Policy 2014–2020, Bruxelles (2014)
30. Her Majesty's (HM) Treasury: The Green Book: Appraisal and Evaluation in Central Government. HM Treasury, London England (2003)
31. Commissariat Général Du Plan: Révision du Taux d'Actualisation des Investissements Publics. Rapport du Groupe d'Experts, Présidé par Daniel Lebègue (2005)
32. Asian Development Bank: Handbook for the Economic Analysis of Water Supply Projects. ADB, Manila, Philippines (1999)
33. Wendling, Z.A., Emerson, J.W., Esty, D.C., Levy, M.A., de Sherbinin, A., et al.: Environmental Performance Index. Yale Center for Environmental, Law & Policy, New Haven (2018). https://epi.yale.edu/
34. Evans D.J., Kula, E.: Social Discount Rates and Welfare Weights for Public Investment Decisions under Budgetary Restrictions: The Case of Cyprus. VIII Milan European Economic Workshop, University of Milan, Working Paper 19 (2009)
35. Hoel, M., Sterner, T.: Discounting and relative prices. Climate Change **84**, 265–280 (2007)
36. Sterner, T., Persson, M.: An Even Sterner Report: Introducing Relative Prices into the Discounting Debate. Rev. Environ. Econ. Policy **2**(1) (2008)

Energy Efficiency in the Management of the Integrated Water Service. A Case Study on the White Certificates Incentive System

Maria Macchiaroli [iD], Luigi Dolores [iD], Luigi Nicodemo[✉], and Gianluigi De Mare [iD]

University of Salerno, Via Giovanni Paolo II, 132, Fisciano, SA, Italy
lnicodemo@unisa.it

Abstract. Energy Efficiency Certificates (TEEs, also called White Certificates) are tradable certificates certifying the achievement of energy savings in energy end-use through energy efficiency improvement measures and projects. Electricity and natural gas distributors (obliged parties) can achieve their energy efficiency improvement targets either by implementing energy efficiency projects (and earning TEEs) or by purchasing TEEs from other parties. Voluntary actors can also participate in the mechanism, typically Energy Service Companies (ESCo) or companies that have appointed an energy management expert (EGE). Voluntary actors are those operators who freely choose to carry out energy end-use reduction measures.

In this work, the TEE mechanism is applied to the Integrated Water Service to reduce energy consumption. To date, it is noted that few projects relating to the Integrated Water Service have been presented for the issue of TEEs. The proposed application aims at verifying the financial convenience in using the tool both for the service provider and for those external subjects (e.g., ESCo) that support the provider in carrying out an energy efficiency intervention. The results show the impact of TEEs on the financial sustainability of projects in the water sector.

Keywords: Economic evaluation of projects · Financial sustainability · Energy efficiency certificates · Discounted cash-flow methods · Integrated urban water management

1 Introduction

The European Union has addressed the issue of energy efficiency since 2006 with the first "Action Plan for Energy Efficiency" (COM 2006/0545). The aim of the action plan was to mobilize civil society, policy makers, and market participants to transform the internal energy market, to provide EU citizens with high levels of energy efficiency in relation to:

- Infrastructures, through distribution systems and building performance.

All authors contributed in equal parts to this work.

© Springer Nature Switzerland AG 2021
O. Gervasi et al. (Eds.): ICCSA 2021, LNCS 12956, pp. 202–217, 2021.
https://doi.org/10.1007/978-3-030-87010-2_14

- Products, through appliances, automobiles, and machinery.
- Territorial systems, through connected networks, organization, and territorial governance [1].

The first Energy Efficiency Directive (2012/27/EU) imposed requirements and the Member States and entered into force in December 2012. The directive requires the definition of indicative national energy efficiency targets to ensure the overall objective of reducing energy consumption by 20% by 2020. This means that the EU's total energy consumption should not exceed 1483 million tonnes of oil equivalent (Mtoe) of primary energy or 1086 Mtoe of final energy. Member States are free to adopt stricter minimum requirements to promote energy-saving and establish legally binding rules for end-users and energy suppliers. The first amendment was the "Clean Energy for All Europeans" package. Under the amending directive, countries can achieve new energy savings of 0.8% each year of final energy consumption for the period 2021–2030, except for Cyprus and Malta which is achieved 0.24% annually. The Commission has pledged to review existing legislation to meet the 2030 greenhouse gas emissions target. "The Green new deal", in the impact assessment accompanying the Communication on the Climate Target Plan, proposes an emission reduction target of at least 55% net.

Italy, to align itself with the European objectives, adopted two measures in 2014, inserting energy-saving objectives set for 2020:

- Legislative Decree no. 102/2014, which transposes the EU directive and establishes a framework of measures for the promotion and improvement of efficiency aimed at reducing primary energy consumption by 20 million tonnes of oil equivalent (Mtoe) by 2020.
- Action Plan for Energy Efficiency (PAE), which from a strategic and regulatory point of view aims to remove the barriers that delay the spread of energy efficiency, both nationally and locally.

The action plan for energy efficiency imposes a mix of fiscal, economic, regulatory, and programmatic instruments, calibrated mainly by sectors of intervention and typology of recipients. However, the plan will favour the integration of energy efficiency into policies and measures with main purposes to optimize the relationship between costs and benefits of the actions. From this point of view, the great potential for efficiency of the construction sector can be better exploited with interventions that pursue energy redevelopment together with seismic improvement and the aesthetic renovation of buildings and neighbourhoods, in line with the real estate redevelopment strategy at 2050. Italy intends to pursue an indicative target of reducing consumption by 2030 equal to 43% of primary energy and 39.7% of final energy compared to the PRIMES 2007 reference scenario[1]. 2030, Italy pursues a target of 132 Mtoe of primary energy and 103.8 Mtoe of final energy, with the trajectory shown in Fig. 1, starting from the estimated consumption in 2020 [2].

---

[1] As a partial equilibrium model for the European Union energy markets, PRIMES is used for forecasting, scenario construction and policy impact analysis.

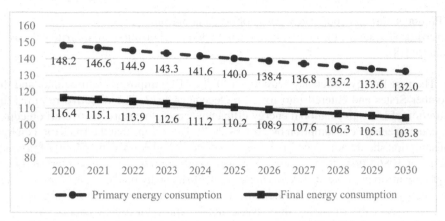

Fig. 1. Expected trend of primary and final energy consumption 2020–2030. Source: Action Plan for Energy Efficiency (PAE).

Therefore, to fulfil the obligation, the plan promotes a reduction in final energy consumption from active policies of approximately 9.3 Mtoe/year by 2030, with the annual objectives shown in Table 1 [3].

Table 1. Savings to be achieved in 2020–2030. Source: Ministry of Economic Development (MISE).

Year	Annual saving	Annual energy savings										Tot
2021	0.80%	0.935										0.935
2022	0.80%	0.935	0.935									1.870
2023	0.80%	0.935	0.935	0.935								2.805
2024	0.80%	0.935	0.935	0.935	0.935							3.740
2025	0.80%	0.935	0.935	0.935	0.935	0.935						4.675
2026	0.80%	0.935	0.935	0.935	0.935	0.935	0.935					5.610
2027	0.80%	0.935	0.935	0.935	0.935	0.935	0.935	0.935				6.545
2028	0.80%	0.935	0.935	0.935	0.935	0.935	0.935	0.935	0.935			7.480
2029	0.80%	0.935	0.935	0.935	0.935	0.935	0.935	0.935	0.935	0.935		8.415
2030	0.80%	0.935	0.935	0.935	0.935	0.935	0.935	0.935	0.935	0.935	0.935	9.350
Total Cumulative saving 2021–2030												51.425

To achieve the 2021–2030 energy-saving objectives, pursuant to article 7 of the Energy Efficiency Directive - EED (and estimated at 51.4 Mtoe), Italy makes use of various support tools, such as:

- The mechanism of White Certificates.
- Tax deductions for energy efficiency interventions and recovery of existing buildings (Ecobonus DL 104/2020).
- The National Energy Efficiency Fund.
- Measures contained in the "Thermal Account" incentives.

This paper focuses on the first line of action, namely the White Certificate mechanism for financing energy efficiency projects.

The European Directive on Energy Efficiency in End-Use and Energy Services (2006/32/EC) of 5 April 2006 introduces and defines White Certificates as documents issued by independent certification bodies that certify the energy savings of market players because of measures to improve energy efficiency.

According to Italian laws, the obliged actors of the White Certificate mechanism are the distributors of electricity and natural gas with more than 50,000 registered customers; these utilities can achieve their energy efficiency improvement objectives both by implementing energy efficiency projects and earning TEE (direct interventions) and by purchasing TEE from other subjects (indirect interventions) [4, 5]. White Certificates must certify the amount of savings achieved and can be purchased by obliged subjects to fulfil the obligations imposed by law because these companies often consider a direct intervention not advantageous.

In addition to energy distributors, other voluntary subjects can also participate in the mechanism, typically energy service companies (ESCos) or companies that have appointed a certified energy management expert (EGE). The voluntary subjects are all the operators who freely choose to carry out interventions to reduce consumption in the final uses of energy, and who are granted the right to receive the corresponding quantity of White Certificates.

The operating rules of White Certificates were updated with the decrees of January 2017 and May 2018; instead, with the decree of April 2019, the "Operating Guide to promote the identification, definition, and presentation of projects within the framework of the White Certificates mechanism" was approved. The Guide, drawn up by the GSE (Head of Energy Services), contains useful information for the preparation and presentation of requests for access to incentives as well as indications on the potential for energy savings deriving from the application of the best technologies available in the main production sectors. The system introduced in January 2017 caused the price of White Certificates to rise during the first year of adoption. Therefore, the government tried to limit the price of the certificates by implementing further constraints and, after the publication of the corrective decree in May 2018, the price of the certificates stabilized at $250 \div 260$ €/TEE [6].

The civil sector is the main actor of efficiency interventions, with a reduction in energy consumption of about 5.7 Mtoe compared to the BASIC scenario in 2030. In particular, the residential sector contributes 3.3 Mtoe to this reduction, while the tertiary sector its consumption projections are reduced by 2.4 Mtoe thanks to building redevelopment and installation of heat pumps, as well as a strong efficiency of end-use devices [7–9].

As for the Integrated Water Service (SII), it is one of the most energy-intensive systems. Based on the data collected by Terna for the year 2019, only the activities of the Integrated Water Service consumed 5,964 GWh of electricity, approximately 2% of the total national energy requirement equal to 301,803 GWh [10]. As regards the aqueduct service, in Italy an average of 0.45 kWh is consumed per cubic meter of water introduced into the pipeline: 9.9 kWh per km of network and 58.5 kWh per inhabitant. As the population density of the areas served increases, the energy consumption per km of piping tends to increase, while the unit consumption per cubic meter of water introduced into the pipeline decreases. The highest energy consumption is recorded in the South of the country, unlike what happens instead for the sewing service. Finally, as regards the purification service, the average energy consumption is equal to 0.29 kWh per cubic meter treated [11, 12].

In this work, the White Certificate mechanism is applied to the Integrated Water Service to reduce energy consumption. They could generate TEEs by financing interventions on the water network or the replacement of machinery.

This document compares the cost of TEE in the virtual market with the possibility of earning TEE by investing in the energy efficiency of the water service [13]. The results show the impact of TEE on the financial sustainability of the project in the water sector and the range of acceptable value for project financing.

Among the volunteers, to date, it is noted that few projects relating to the Integrated Water Service have been presented for the issue of White Certificates. The proposed application, therefore, has the objective of verifying the financial convenience in using the tool both for the service managing body and for those subjects (for example energy service companies) who possibly support the operator in carrying out an energy efficiency intervention.

2 White Certificate Mechanism in the Integrated Water Service

The Integrated Water Service (SII) represents the set of public services for the collection, supply, and distribution of water for civil use, sewerage, and wastewater purification. So, it is the set of complex processes that provide a service such as water delivered to the user or wastewater treatment returned to the environment[2]. These services are associated with directly connected services (quality of drinking water or discharged wastewater, quantity, and continuity of service), indirectly connected services (service information, billing, customer care), and other services for the community (improvement of hygienic-sanitary conditions, protection of the environment from civil and industrial discharges, etc.) [14–16]. The energy consumption of the water service is essentially related to:

- Pumping systems. Energy consumption depends on numerous variables such as the flow rates, the orography of the territory, the types of pipelines, the type of operation, the interconnections between the pipelines, the number, and type of collection tanks, and the distribution.
- Wastewater treatment plants. Energy consumption depends on the influence of the qualitative characteristics of the water (higher or lower concentration of substances to be removed, presence of micropollutants), on the complexity of the treatment plant.

---

[2] Art. 142, co. 2, Legislative Decree n. 152/06.

– Drinking water systems. Energy consumption is independent of the qualitative characteristics of the water subjected to purification, as they are identical for all users of the service.

Electricity, which represents one of the main cost items for water operators, is between 10% and 30% of the total costs of the water service. The average value of the incidence of electricity costs on turnover can be considered equal to 15%[3]. From the analysis of the water service data collected by the ARERA (Authority for Energy, Networks, and the Environment) in 2020, it is noted that 30% of the energy consumption of the SII is attributable to purification systems alone [17].

The interventions aimed at improving energy efficiency in the Integrated Water Service, and which can therefore allow the obtaining of TEE, can be grouped into 3 categories:

1. Punctual interventions. Punctual interventions consist of the replacement of specific components or machinery within networks or systems with components that guarantee greater energy efficiency under the same plant and engineering conditions.
2. Interventions on processes. Process interventions consist of increasing the energy efficiency of a plant section that performs a specific function. The effectiveness of the intervention is evaluated based on the comparison between the post-intervention energy consumption and a baseline made up of other similar plant components used to carry out the same process.
3. System interventions. System interventions consist of intervening on different processes or functional parts of the system, improving its general energy efficiency. The effectiveness of the intervention is evaluated based on the comparison of the energy consumption of the entire system before and after the intervention.

The first approach to evaluate an investment in energy efficiency is the analysis of basic consumption. There can be two different situations: installation of a new system or renovation of an existing system. In the case of the construction of a new plant, the reference consumption is obtained from the market analysis, or from the most common systems in the period considered. In the case of renovation of an existing plant, the reference baseline is the performance before the intervention, obviously considering the condition of maximum efficiency of the plant and the regulations in force.

As previously stated, according to ARERA the most energy-consuming part of the system is wastewater treatment. Considering that half of the purification plants use traditional aeration technologies[4], attributing 50% of the total consumption of the wastewater treatment plants to the energy consumption of the aeration, we obtain that the savings of the sector at the national level are equal to:[5]

$$Re = 7062 \; GWh \times 0.30 \times 0.50 \times 0.50 \times 0.40 = 211.5 \; GWh \qquad (1)$$

---

[3] ENEA, "White Certificates - Operational Guide for the Integrated Water Service", 2014.

[4] GSE, "White Certificates - Sectoral Guides: The Integrated Water Service", 2019.

[5] ENEA, "White Certificates - Operational Guide for the Integrated Water Service", 2014.

Treated wastewater often has a variability of flow rate and concentration of pollutants that must be made as persistent as possible. The correction of the variability of the flow is called equalization, while homogenization is the concentration of pollutants. To ensure these conditions and to avoid the sedimentation of suspended solids in the wastewater, large storage tanks equipped with agitation and mixing devices are required. For old plants, which have installed low-yield machines, it is possible to replace the mixers present in the homogenization, equalization, and activated sludge treatment phases to obtain primary energy savings that can be translated into White Certificates [18].

This article analyses two mixer replacement interventions, within two different wastewater treatment plants.

The study estimates the achievable energy savings, the resulting TEEs, and the profitability of the proposed project solutions through the main economic performance indicators: the net present value (NPV) and the internal rate of return (IRR).

3 Materials and Methods

In this paper, we intend to make the wastewater disposal system more efficient from an energy point of view through appropriate plant investments. The sector under analysis has multiple similarities with that of gas distribution (it is no coincidence that they share the same regulator, the Regulatory Authority for Energy, Networks, and the Environment - ARERA) [19–21]. For this reason, the project managers for the purification service can evaluate the investment performance through methods like those used for the gas sector.

To make the wastewater disposal system energy-efficient, it is assumed that the mixer must be replaced in a purification plant. The evaluation of the energy efficiency project is based on 4 phases:

- Analysis of the energy absorption of the plant installed before the project (calculation of the consumption baseline, monitoring of consumption with two daily measurements for 3 months).
- Calculation of the average absorbed energy and the average absorbed power of the systems and analysis of the standard deviation for the measurement data.
- Evaluation of the total energy saving.
- Calculation of the TEE generated by the system.

The study considers two plants:

1. Plant A - the system has 7 mixers divided as follows:

    - 5 mixers with 2.9 kW absorbed power from data sheet.
    - 2 mixers with 1.5 kW.

The analysis of the previous years (2017 and 2018) shows that the energy absorbed by the set of 7 mixers represents approximately 28% of the total electrical consumption of the system. During the monitoring period, there was an average daily flow in the plant of 2.08 m^3 of wastewater and 3.5 mm of average daily precipitation.

2. Plant B - the system has 5 mixers divided as follows:

   - 3 mixers with 5.5 kW absorbed power from data sheet.
   - 2 mixers with 2.8 kW.

The analysis of the previous years (2017 and 2018) shows that the energy absorbed by the set of 5 mixers represents approximately 31% of the total electrical consumption of the system. During the monitoring period, there was an average daily flow in the plant equal to 1.74 m^3 of wastewater and 3.1 mm of average daily precipitation.

As for the new mixers to be installed, it is assumed that the water operator has identified two possible estimates from suppliers, or two alternative types of mixer:

- Solution 1 - Adaptive compact submersible mixer, IE4 class efficiency. This permanent magnet synchronous motor can be used in all tanks from the plants in question, allowing a lower capital investment in parts and spare parts (see Table 2).

Table 2. Solution 1. Power installed plant A and plant B.

PLANT A	Power installed by each machine [kW]			Absorbed power [kW]
	Mixer 1	Mixer 2	Mixer 3	kW
Equalization	0.35	0.35	0.35	1.05
Model 1	0.30	0.30		0.60
Model 2	0.41	0.41		0.82
Total absorbed power				2.47
PLANT B	Power installed by each machine [kW]			Absorbed power [kW]
	Mixer 1	Mixer 2	Mixer 3	kW
Equalization	1.07	1.07	1.07	3.21
Model 1	0.49			0.49
Model 2	0.79	0.79		1.58
Total absorbed power				5.28

- Solution 2 - Compact submersible mixers, IE3 class efficiency. This solution involves the installation of permanent magnet motors controlled by a frequency converter (VFD) with nominal powers between 3 and 5 kW (see Table 3).

Table 4 shows the installation cost for the two plants.

For the calculation of the reference baseline, the legislation provides for a period of monitoring consumption before the intervention of at least 12 months, with daily measurements. In some cases, however, it is possible to submit projects that have a shorter monitoring period to the GSE, demonstrating that this is sufficient and representative of

Table 3. Solution 2. Power installed plant A and plant B.

PLANT A	Power installed by each machine [kW]			Absorbed power [kW]
	Mixer 1	Mixer 2	Mixer 3	kW
Equalization	1.87	1.87	1.87	5.61
Model 1	1.87			1.87
Model 2	3.64			3.64
Total absorbed power				11.12
PLANT B	Power installed by each machine [kW]			Absorbed power [kW]
	Mixer 1	Mixer 2	Mixer 3	kW
Equalization	2.39	2.39		4.79
Model 1	1.35			1.35
Model 2	3.64	3.64		7.28
Total absorbed power				13.42

Table 4. Cost of installation (€).

	Solution 1	Solution 2
PLANT A	61,011 €	26,343 €
PLANT B	52,295 €	34,577 €
TOTAL	113,306 €	60,921 €

actual consumption. In this case, a period of about 3 months was considered, sufficient for the definition of a reliable consumption baseline.

For the calculation of the saved energy (RISP) the equation used is the following:

$$RISP = P_{pre} \cdot h_{post} - E_{post} [kWh] \qquad (2)$$

with:

- P_{pre}: Basic power before surgery in relation to daily monitoring.
- h_{post}: Operating time in hours after installation.
- E_{post}: Total amount of energy absorbed by the mixers in each system, measured after replacement.

The conversion factor used for the TEP assessment is shown in the following equation:[6]

$$fe = 0.187 \cdot 10^{-3} \ tep/kWh \tag{3}$$

Following the analysis of the technical data, the two investment proposals (Solution 1 and Solution 2) are evaluated through the Discounted Cash-Flow considering three different scenarios [22]:

- Scenario 1: Sustainability of the investment project for the Integrated Water Service operator. The NPV and IRR performance indicators are estimated according to the point of view of the Managing Body (public or private entity).
- Scenario 2: Sustainability of the investment project for the eventual purchaser of the TEEs. In this scenario, it is assumed that an Energy Service Company (ESCo) or another private investor will finance the energy efficiency project. It is assumed that the necessary capital is disbursed to the operator of the Integrated Water Service by means of a French loan. Another source of income for the investor consists in the sale of White Certificates earned by making the service more efficient.
- Scenario 3: direct involvement of investors (ESCo or other private entity) with sharing of costs and risk. Assuming that the operator of the Integrated Water Service is a public body, for example, a Municipality, it is assumed that the latter entrusts it to a private person through a public-private partnership, sharing risks, costs, and cash flows with it. In this scenario, we intend to evaluate the convenience of the investment for both actors involved [23–27].

In all three scenarios, the analyses are conducted without considering the effects of positive and negative externalities on the environment and the social context. The analysis conducted focus solely on the financial, or monetary, aspects of the hypothesized investments, neglecting further economic assessments.

4 Results and Discussion

As previously anticipated, the first step of the energy efficiency project is to monitor consumption and define the power of the two plants. The following table shows the value of the average installed power before the intervention and the results of the consumption monitoring (Table 5).

The second phase is the calculation of the installed power after the intervention for both solutions. These data are based on information certified by suppliers and simulations of the application of technologies on the two plants considered in analysis with the aid of specific technical software for energy calculations. It is assumed that the pre-intervention working conditions are the same as the post-intervention ones (Table 6).

Total amount of savings estimated for each plant are reported in Table 7. The number of TEEs obtainable for each solution is evaluated using Eq. (2). The results are shown below.

---

[6] Resolution EEN 3/08 of 20 March 2008.

Table 5. Consumption analyses (MWh/year) and power installed (kW).

	Power installed	Annual consumption
PLANT A	17.5 kW	130.3 MWh/year
PLANT B	22.1 kW	164.5 MWh/year
TOTAL	39.0 kW	294.8 MWh/year

Table 6. Post intervention data, powers estimated by the suppliers applied on plant system.

	Solution 1	Solution 2
PLANT A	2.47 kW	11.12 kW
PLANT B	5.286 kW	13.42 kW
TOTAL	7.98 kW	24.53 kW

Table 7. Total amount of savings estimated for each plant.

	Solution 1	Solution 2
PLANT A	111.91 MWh	67.14 MWh
PLANT B	90.95 MWh	46.96 MWh
TOTAL	7.98 MWh	24.53 MWh

$$\text{RISP}_1 = 37.93 \text{ TEP/year} \cong 38 \text{ } TEE \tag{4}$$

$$\text{RISP}_2 = 21.33 \text{ TEP/year} \cong 21 \text{ } TEE \tag{5}$$

For the estimate of the NPV, a time horizon of $n = 5$ years is considered[7], with a discount rate i $= 4\%$, as suggested by the European commission and other authors for similar investments in the Integrated Water Service sector [28, 29]. For each year it is assumed that the energy-saving remains constant without changing the characteristics of both the plant and the reference area.

The cost of energy is estimated at Cee $= €\,0.16/kWh$ for the first year, equal to the average cost of electricity in 2019 for non-domestic consumers. The tariff is made up of the sum of the sales tariff (TV), the network services (SR), the system charges (OS), and the taxes (I):

$$TEE = TV + SR + OS + I \tag{6}$$

---

[7] SACE, Table attached 1 types of interventions. https://www.sacee.it/wp-content/uploads/2019/02/Tipologie-di-interventi-per-certificati-bianchi.pdf.

If the volumes of water treated are approximately constant over the years, the consumption of electricity can be considered constant for each year of the reference time horizon.

Below are the NPV and IRR obtained for each scenario.

Scenario 1. In the scenario in which the sustainability of the investment project is assessed for the Integrated Water Service operator, the values of the performance indicators shown in Table 8 are obtained:

Table 8. Financial assessment from the point of view of the Service Operator.

	Solution 1	Solution 2
NPV	€ 29,988	€ 19,574
IRR	13%	11%

Scenario 2. In the scenario in which the sustainability of the project is assessed for the lender who obtains the White Certificates, the efficiency of the investment depends on the number of TEEs acquired and their market value. Table 9 shows the NPV and the estimated IRR considering the same time horizon and a discount rate of Scenario 1.

Table 9. Financial assessment from the investor's point of view (ESCo or another lender).

	Solution 1	Solution 2
NPV	€ 55,260	€ 33,771
IRR	23%	18%

Scenario 3. Finally, we consider the case in which both the managing body and the private entity (ESCo) finance the energy efficiency interventions. It is assumed that the operator invests directly in the project covering 30% of the initial costs and that the ESCo finances the remainder with a French mortgage as in the previous scenario. Table 10 shows the investment performance indicators estimated for the first mixer solution selected with respect to both economic actors involved.

Table 11 shows the investment performance indicators estimated for the second solution of the selected mixer.

Also, in this case the discount rate and time horizon are assumed to be similar to those of the previous scenarios. For all three scenarios, a decrease in the price of energy of 2% per year is assumed (a more conservative and high-risk situation). For the first year, the price of the White Certificates is set at € 250/TEE (market value 2019 according to ARERA resolutions 270/2020/R/EFR). For the following years, a decrease of 2% per

Table 10. SOLUTION 1, financial evaluation for a shared project.

	Operator	ESCo
NPV	€ 24,309	€ 16,661
IRR	24%	11%

Table 11. SOLUTION 2, financial evaluation for a shared project.

	Operator	ESCo
NPV	€ 21,160	€ 11,302
IRR	29%	13%

year is considered. The impact generated by the reduction of both the energy price and the TEE on the sustainability of the project is therefore considered.

The comparative analysis of the three scenarios shows that for the water service operator the most advantageous solution is the first of scenario 1. Instead, for a possible external investor, the best solution is the first of scenario 2. However, solution 2 of scenario 3 allows the service provider to obtain a much higher expected return of the discount rate than the other possible solutions, even though the NPV is slightly lower than that of solution 1 of scenario 1.

The convenience of directly financing the project (scenario 1) may depend on various parameters, such as the virtual market price of White Certificates (subject to monthly variation), the mortgage interest rate, the forecast of energy costs, and the lack of skills in the management. To avoid that these parameters have a negative impact, it is advisable that the Integrated Water Service operator opts for the risk-sharing solution (scenario 3) to obtain levels of NPV and IRR that are acceptable for both economic actors.

5 Conclusions

To promote energy efficiency interventions, several operational tools have recently been introduced in the community. Among these, an important role is assumed by the Energy Efficiency Certificates (TEE), also called White Certificates. In this case, these are negotiable securities that certify the achievement of savings in the final uses of energy through interventions to increase energy efficiency. One certificate is equivalent to saving one Ton of Oil Equivalent (TOE). In addition to energy distributors, other voluntary subjects can also participate in the mechanism, including the operators of the Integrated Water Service. The aim of this paper is to clarify the operating mechanism of the White Certificates in the case of investments in energy efficiency aimed at reducing consumption for the treatment of industrial and domestic wastewater. The incentive mechanism was then applied to a case study, providing for three investment scenarios.

In the first scenario, the financial sustainability of the investment project for the service operator is assessed. In the second, the convenience of the investment is assessed from the point of view of the investor (ESCo or another lender) who supports the service operator in the implementation of the energy efficiency project. Finally, the third scenario is assumed that the operator covers 30% of the costs and the remaining share is up to the ESCo, with a view to sharing both risks and benefits. For each scenario, two design alternatives are considered. In terms of net present value, the most advantageous solution for the managing body is alternative 1 of scenario 1 (NPV = € 29'988). Instead, alternative 1 of scenario 2 is the most advantageous for the investor. However, by resorting to solution 1 of scenario 3, which provides for the sharing of the risk with the investor, the service operator is entitled to a slightly lower NPV than that of the first solution of scenario 1. And in fact, in this case, the operator obtains the highest IRR among the different scenarios and possible solutions. In this scenario, it would be desirable to implement risk management models [30, 31] that could be used to evaluate investments in energy efficiency considering all the critical variables related to the project, such as the price of energy and the variability of the value of the TEEs.

Although in practice, market operators tend to be more involved in direct investments (generally to have energy savings of 5–10%) rather than resorting to the exchange of White Certificates on the virtual market, the model demonstrates the validity of a shared project between the managing body of the service and the Energy Service Company.

References

1. Ciucci, M.: Energy efficiency, Fact sheets on the European Union (2020). https://www.eur oparl.europa.eu/factsheets/it/sheet/69/efficienza-energetica. Accessed 07 May 2021
2. Action Plan for Energy Efficiency (PAE). https://ec.europa.eu/energy/sites/ener/files/docume nts/2014_neeap_it_italy.pdf. Accessed 07 May 2021
3. Ministry of the Environment and Protection of Natural Resources and the Sea, Ministry of Infrastructure and Transport, Integrated national plan for energy and climate (2019). https://www.mise.gov.it/images/stories/documenti/it_final_necp_main_en.pdf. Accessed 07 May 2021
4. Venturini, V.: Il meccanismo dei certificati bianchi in Europa, Report ricerca sul sistema elettrico, FIRE (2010)
5. ENEA, I Titoli di Efficienza Energetica: Cosa sono e come si ottengono i Certificati Bianchi. Guida Operativa (2011)
6. GSE: Annual report of white certificates (2020). https://www.gse.it/documenti_site/Doc umenti%20GSE/Rapporti%20Certificati%20Bianchi/Rapporto%20Annuale%202020.pdf. Accessed 07 May 2021
7. ENEA, National Agency for New Technologies, Energy and Sustainable Economic Development: ANNUAL REPORT 2019 - TAX DEDUCTIONS for energy efficiency and the use of renewable energy sources in existing buildings (2019). ISBN 978-88-8286-383-8
8. Nesticò, A., De Mare, G., Fiore, P., Pipolo, O.: A model for the economic evaluation of energetic requalification projects in buildings. A real case application. In: Murgante, B., et al. (eds.) Computational Science and Its Applications – ICCSA 2014. LNCS, vol. 8580, pp. 563–578. Springer, Cham (2014). https://doi.org/10.1007/978-3-319-09129-7_41

9. Nesticò, A., Macchiaroli, M., Pipolo, O.: Historic buildings and energetic requalification a model for the selection of technologically advanced interventions. In: Gervasi, O., et al. (eds.) ICCSA 2015. LNCS, vol. 9157, pp. 61–76. Springer, Cham (2015). https://doi.org/10.1007/978-3-319-21470-2_5

10. Terna Group. https://download.terna.it/terna/6-CONSUMI_8d8e25a62c1cdf5.pdf. Accessed 07 May 2021

11. Buratto, A., D'Alpaos, C.: Optimal sustainable use of drinking water sources and interactions between multiple providers. Oper. Res. Lett. **43**(4), 389–395 (2015)

12. Utilitatis: BlueBook (2017). ISBN 978-88-6121-007-3

13. Grimaldi, M., Sebillo, M., Vitiello, G., Pellecchia, V.: Planning and managing the integrated water system: a spatial decision support system to analyze the infrastructure performances. Sustainability **12**(16), 6432 (2020). https://doi.org/10.3390/su12166432

14. De Mare, G., Nesticò, A., Macchiaroli, M., Dolores, L.: Market prices and institutional values. In: Gervasi, O., et al. (eds.) ICCSA 2017. LNCS, vol. 10409, pp. 430–440. Springer, Cham (2017). https://doi.org/10.1007/978-3-319-62407-5_30

15. Canesi, R., D'Alpaos, C., Marella, G.: Foreclosed homes market in Italy: bases of value. Int. J. Hous. Sci. Appl. **40**(3), 201–209 (2016)

16. Sbandati, A.: Servizi ecosistemici, servizio idrico integrato e componenti tariffarie: l'opportunità dei Payments for Ecosystem Services (2020). http://hdl.handle.net/20.500.12010/17532. Accessed 27 Mar 2021

17. Autorità per l'Energia Elettrica, il Gas e il Sistema Idrico (ARERA): Sintesi relazione annuale (2020). https://www.arera.it/allegati/relaz_ann/20/ra20_sintesi.pdf

18. GSE S.p.A. Gestore dei Servizi Energetici: Certificati Bianchi – Guida operative. https://www.mise.gov.it/images/stories/documenti/Allegato%201%20-%20Guida%20operativa.pdf. Accessed 07 May 2021

19. D'Alpaos, C.: The value of flexibility to switch between water supply sources. Appl. Math. Sci. **6**(125–128), 6381–6401 (2012)

20. D'Alpaos, C.: The privatization of water services in italy: make or buy, capability and efficiency issues. In: Mondini, G., Fattinnanzi, E., Oppio, A., Bottero, M., Stanghellini, S. (eds.) SIEV 2016. GET, pp. 223–231. Springer, Cham (2018). https://doi.org/10.1007/978-3-319-78271-3_18

21. Macchiaroli, M., Pellecchia, V., D'Alpaos, C.: Urban water management in Italy: an innovative model for the selection of water service infrastructures. WSEAS Trans. Environ. Dev. **15**, 463–477 (2019)

22. De Mare, G., Granata, M.F., Forte, F.: Investing in sports facilities: the Italian situation toward an Olympic perspective. In: Gervasi, O., et al. (eds.) ICCSA 2015. LNCS, vol. 9157, pp. 77–87. Springer, Cham (2015). https://doi.org/10.1007/978-3-319-21470-2_6

23. Dolores, L., Macchiaroli, M., De Mare, G.: A model for defining sponsorship fees in public-private bargaining for the rehabilitation of historical-architectural heritage. In: Calabrò, F., Della Spina, L., Bevilacqua, C. (eds.) ISHT 2018. SIST, vol. 101, pp. 484–492. Springer, Cham (2019). https://doi.org/10.1007/978-3-319-92102-0_51

24. De Mare, G., Di Piazza, F.: The role of public-private partnerships in school building projects. In: Gervasi, O., et al. (eds.) ICCSA 2015. LNCS, vol. 9156, pp. 624–634. Springer, Cham (2015). https://doi.org/10.1007/978-3-319-21407-8_44

25. Dolores, L., Macchiaroli, M., De Mare, G.: A dynamic model for the financial sustainability of the restoration sponsorship. Sustainability **12**(4), 1694 (2020). https://doi.org/10.3390/su12041694

26. Nesticò, A., Somma, P.: Comparative analysis of multi-criteria methods for the enhancement of historical buildings. Sustainability **11**(17), 4526 (2019). https://doi.org/10.3390/su11174526

27. Dolores, L., Macchiaroli, M., De Mare, G.: Sponsorship's financial sustainability for cultural conservation and enhancement strategies: an innovative model for sponsees and sponsors. Sustainability **13**(16), 9070 (2021). https://doi.org/10.3390/su13169070
28. European Commission, Directorate General Regional Policy: Guide to cost-benefit analysis of investment projects: Economic appraisal tool for Cohesion Policy 2014–2020, Bruxelles (2014)
29. Nesticò, A., Maselli, G.: Declining discount rate estimate in the long-term economic evaluation of environmental projects. J. Environ. Account. Manag. **8**(1), 93-110 (2020). L&H Scientific Publishing, LLC. https://doi.org/10.5890/JEAM.2020.03.007
30. Benintendi, R., De Mare, G.: Upgrade the ALARP model as a holistic approach to project risk and decision management. Hydrocarb. Process. **9**, 75–82 (2017)
31. Maselli, G., Macchiaroli, M.: Tolerability and acceptability of the risk for projects in the civil sector. In: Bevilacqua, C., Calabrò, F., Della Spina, L. (eds.) NMP 2020. SIST, vol. 178, pp. 686–695. Springer, Cham (2021). https://doi.org/10.1007/978-3-030-48279-4_64

Water and Land Value in Italy

Paolo Rosato[1], Lucia Rotaris[2], and Raul Berto[1]([✉])

[1] Department of Engineering and Architecture, University of Trieste, Trieste, Italy
rberto@units.it
[2] Department of Economics, Business, Mathematics and Statistics, University of Trieste,
Trieste, Italy

Abstract. Irrigation water in Italy, as in all Mediterranean countries, is of great importance for soil productivity and, therefore, its presence has a high impact on its value.

Irrigation water is not just a factor of production but its availability has generated new territorial systems, significantly different from those that would have developed in its absence; subsequently, these systems have evolved from traditional agricultural to industrial and tertiary ones.

The article presents research aimed at estimating the effect of the presence of irrigation water on the value of agricultural soils. The assessment was carried out by hedonic approach using the quotations (Average Agricultural Values) of the soils carried out by the provincial commissions, established pursuant to Article 41 of the Presidential Decree of 08/06/2001 No. 327, to determine the compensation for expropriation for public utility. The study briefly illustrates the hedonic method and its use in the evaluation of water resources and presents some econometric models developed to identify the contribution of water availability to the value of the soil.

Keywords: Water · Land value · Hedonic land pricing

1 Introduction

Since ancient times, the availability of water for agricultural and civil uses has been of great importance in Italy, as in all Mediterranean countries. As a matter of fact, the first examples of artificial use of water for agricultural production in the peninsula date back to the Etruscan civilization. However, it is thanks to the Benedictine monks that, around the year one thousand, it began to improve and spread to central and northern Italy. Subsequently, the Renaissance lords and the pre-unification States promoted important irrigation works, especially in northern Italy. At the end of the nineteenth century, in Italy, there were about 1.5 million hectares equipped for irrigation, but the real explosion of irrigation took place in the first half of the last century, thanks to the virtuous combination of adequate national laws (RD 1775/33 and LN 215/33) and local collective initiatives

---

Research funded by INEA - MiPAAF, INEA executive project "Research activities and technical support for the definition of a cost policy for the irrigation use of water".

O. Gervasi et al. (Eds.): ICCSA 2021, LNCS 12956, pp. 218–235, 2021.
https://doi.org/10.1007/978-3-030-87010-2_15

(Reclamation and Irrigation Consortia). In less than a century, the area equipped for irrigation doubled, reaching almost 3.1 million hectares [1]. The massive expansion of irrigation in the last century took place essentially to respond to the growing demand for agricultural products from a very high population compared to the little fertile land available. Currently, there are nearly 400,000 farms involved in irrigation, equal to 25% of the total amount [2]. The regularly irrigated area exceeds 2.4 million hectares (19%), while that equipped for irrigation is over three million hectares [3]. Overall, it has been estimated that irrigation involves 11 billion cu. m. of water [2].

Irrigation has not been, and is not, just a mere factor of production but, by profoundly modifying the production techniques, the use of the soil and its productivity, it has actually generated new agricultural and territorial systems, significantly different from those that would have been developed in its absence. In addition, the availability of irrigation has led to the adoption of investments that have changed, along with profitability, also the landscape and the value of the soils.

Soils are a complex primary production resource whose market value depends on multiple factors. Therefore, by observing the variation in the value of soils as a function of their characteristics, which also include the presence of irrigation water, it is possible to derive the contribution to the market value.

The hypothesis underlying the adopted method (Hedonic Land Price) is that buyers and sellers of agricultural land are able to evaluate the effect of the various characteristics of the soil on future profits and that this effect is incorporated into the purchase and sale value. In this case, the values reflect market preferences for the particular productive characteristics of the soils.

The evaluation of the effect of the presence of irrigation water was carried out starting from the quotations of agricultural land carried out by the provincial commissions established pursuant to Article 41 of the Presidential Decree 327/2001 for the determination of the expropriation compensation for public utility: the Average Agricultural Values (AAV). The AAV of a soil is determined "taking into account the crops actually practiced on the land and the value of the building structures legitimately built, also in relation to the operation of the farm, without evaluating any possible or actual use other than agricultural", DPR 327/2001 art. 40–42. Basically, the AAVs, although not market prices, are conditioned exclusively by agricultural production characteristics and, therefore, can be assimilated to capitalization values of the income deriving from cultivation.

The use of AAVs, compared to other sources, has some advantages:

1. they are available for the whole national territory in a homogeneous way;
2. they refer only to agricultural use and, therefore, are not influenced by urban rents;
3. they refer to codified and transparent economic and productive conditions;
4. they are available for homogeneous territorial areas (Agricultural Regions).

The contribution is divided into four parts.

The first and second are dedicated to a concise description of the theoretical approach and the hedonic method. The third explores its use in assessing the impact of irrigation water on land values and illustrates the characteristics of the data.

The fourth is dedicated to the development of econometric models at an aggregate level (national), by geographical area (Northern, Central and Southern Italy), by crop used and to the discussion of the results obtained.

Finally, some concluding remarks are proposed.

2 Water and Land Value

The land value as a function of its profitability (income value) can be assimilated to an investment value by a farmer. This places the value on a different level from that of the current market value which can also be influenced by aspects other than those considered by the agricultural entrepreneur, such as those due to urban rents connected with the potential transformation to civil uses (residential, industrial and commercial). That said, the agricultural plot value derives from the rent collectable through land property and embedded investments.

Indeed, with reference to agricultural land, the value is calculated with the following equation:

$$V_a = \frac{B_f}{r_{cf}} = \frac{R_f + K_f \cdot r_f}{r_{cf}} \tag{1}$$

Where

V_a Value of agricultural land;
B_f Land benefit (income resulting from the land property);
r_{cf} Land incomes capitalization rate;
R_f Ricardian land rent;
K_f Value of land investments;
r_i Price-earnings rate of land investments.

Equation (1) shows that the value, at least in lands with low investments (extensive latifundia), is due to the rent, which is to say to the revenue deriving from the mere property. Indeed, in the past, it was connected to the privilege of landowners, which derived from the possession of the most productive lands, and prospered thanks to the work of the rural population.

The availability of irrigation water affects the income of the owner (B_f) of the soil both in terms of size and composition.

In particular, the presence of water influences "natural" productivity and, therefore, the "pure land rent" (R_f) but also conditions the presence of (fixed) land investments (K_f).

To assess the impact of water availability on the value of soils in Italy, it is necessary to investigate the ways in which the producer has available water for irrigation, which are different from those in use in other countries, such as the USA, where the water is a normal production factor that can be purchased in a special market.

In Italy, water can be considered a public state property and can be used through a specific authorization, its amount is often fixed and commensurate not with the quantity of water available (which may vary according to the seasonal weather and climate) but to the potentially irrigable surface. The cost of irrigation water, therefore, can be broken down into three components: the first, fixed, is equal to the contribution that the owner of the land must pay to the consortium that takes care of the derivation of water from the river and delivery to the company; this cost is fixed and commensurate with the total annual management cost of the consortium and the benefit brought to farmers. The second is the cost incurred by the farmer for the distribution of irrigation water and can be further divided into a variable cost commensurate to the volumes of water distributed and a fixed amount relating to any fixed systems incorporated into the company grounds.

Therefore, the impact of water availability on the value of an agricultural fund can be evaluated using the following equation:

$$V_w = \frac{B_f^c}{r_{cf}^c} - \frac{B_f^s}{r_{cf}^s} = \frac{R_f^c + (K_w + K_{f \neq w})r_i}{r_{cf}^c} - \frac{R_f^s + K_{f \neq w}r_i}{r_{cf}^s} \tag{2}$$

Where:

V_w Value of water;
B_f Land benefit with (c) and without (s) irrigation water;
r_{cf} Land incomes capitalization rate with (c) and without (s) irrigation water;
R_f Ricardian land rent with (c) and without (s) irrigation water;
K_w Value of irrigation investments;
r_i Price-earnings rate of land investments.

Assuming:

$$r_{cf}^c = r_{cf}^s = r_i = r_{cf} \tag{3}$$

Equation (2) becomes:

$$V_w = \frac{R_f^c - R_f^s}{r_{cf}} + K_w \tag{4}$$

Therefore, the effect of the availability of irrigation water on the value of the soil is given by the capital value of the Ricardian rent difference produced and by the value of the irrigation investments incorporated into the soil.

3   The Hedonic Land Price Method

The hedonic method is based on the assumption that economic goods are aggregates of different characteristics whose status affects the market value [4]. If some of these characteristics are separable from the asset in question then they have their own market value. If, on the other hand, they are incorporated into the asset, they cannot be sold/purchased separately and have no individual prices. In the land market, for example, it is not possible to buy separately the texture of the land, the position or the agricultural hydraulic arrangement; in our case, it is assumed that the possibility of irrigation is not separable from the soil but is inherent in a place where it is available naturally or provided by an irrigation consortium. The hedonic method allows, starting from the market value of a private good, to estimate the implicit prices of the individual characteristics. The method has several variations and the best known, and most used, is the one that uses the price of the properties as a reference value. In particular, the hedonic land price estimates the value of the characteristics of landed assets (tangible and intangible), starting with the variations induced in their market price [5]. The hypothesis is that the different characteristics may affect the value of the land and, therefore, that the economic value of these characteristics can be traced back to the price differences of the soils, obviously without the effect of all other specificities. The hedonic approach has the advantage of being based on actual values, rather than on investigations of hypothetical choices or production simulations.

Rosen [6], who assumes a competitive market and, therefore, provides for the simultaneous estimation of supply and demand functions, rigorously formulated the theory on which hedonic methods are based. Originally, the approach was developed to estimate the consumer's rent deriving from attributes of consumer goods and was subsequently adapted by Palmquist [7] to the demand for factors of production.

From a theoretical point of view, the problem can be illustrated by considering a producer with an availability of resources equal to y and with a company described by a vector of technical characteristics (a), who uses its resources by choosing a soil, defined by a vector of characteristics $z = (z_j)$, and by a level of expenditure x in other factors of production.

The problem that the producer must solve is the maximization of the following production function:

$$MaxP = f(z_j, x, a) \ \ with \ \ x + v(z_j) \le y \tag{5}$$

where $v(z_j)$ represents the value (V) of the soil as a function of its productive characteristics, that is the hedonic function to be estimated.

The solution of the previous model is obtained when the weighted marginal productivity of all the factors of production used in the production process are equalized, including the production characteristics of the fund (z_j).

$$\frac{dP/dz_j}{dv/dz_j} = \frac{dP/dx}{dV/dx} \tag{6}$$

The value of a land can, therefore, be expressed by the present value of the income (B_f) that it can provide over time (t) given a certain discount rate (r):

$$V = f(z_j) = \int_0^\infty B_f(z_j) \cdot e^{-rt} dt \tag{7}$$

Or, with reference to constant, discontinuous annual, deferred and unlimited income:

$$V = f(z_j) = \frac{B_f(z_j)}{r} \tag{8}$$

The value of a certain z characteristic will be commensurate with the contribution made to the income. In other words, under perfectly competitive market conditions, the value of the characteristic will be equal, in the case of a factor of production, to the value of its marginal profitability.

The estimate of the value function of the private good is normally obtained by applying the statistical method of multiple regression to a significant sample of goods sold. By using this method, the market value (V) is related to a series of explanatory variables that represent the different characteristics of the asset itself.

In this way, each characteristic of the asset is associated with a parameter (β_j) of the function which, having satisfied the conditions illustrated above, represents its implicit price and, consequently, the impact on value. By adopting a linear function, we have that:

$$V = \alpha + \sum_{j=1}^{k} \beta_j z_j + \varepsilon \ \text{ with } \ \beta_j = dV/dz_j \tag{9}$$

In other words, β_i represents the implicit marginal price of one unit of the characteristic z_i. If, as in this case, the characteristic (presence of irrigation water) is represented by a dummy variable (0/1), β_j represents its total value per unit of surface.

The hedonic method presents, alongside undoubted potential, some limitations attributable to compliance with a series of rather restrictive hypotheses [8] which, if not verified, can compromise the quality of the estimates.

First, it is assumed that the market is in equilibrium, that is, that the supply of goods with a certain characteristic is equal to the corresponding demand. Second, which all combinations in the characteristics required by the market are available on the market. Freeman [8] envisions the market as a vast warehouse with various baskets (the complex goods), each filled with various combinations of characteristics. The buyer chooses among the available baskets the one that maximizes its utility (production), in other words, the one that contains a combination of characteristics such that their weighted marginal utilities (productivity) are equal. Third, the reference market must have good transparency on the prices and characteristics of the goods sold and there must be no transaction costs. Fourth, all observations come from a homogeneous market. The presence of a segmented market will result in clearly different supply and/or demand functions and, consequently, in different marginal prices. Finally, prices must not be influenced by expected changes in the characteristic under consideration[1]. The real land market has undoubted limits compared to the prerequisites described above. However, the use of the AAV as a reference value allows these limits to be mitigated since the determination of these values is formulated for territorially homogeneous market segments and with reference only to agricultural productivity. Finally, they are formulated starting from a deep knowledge of the land market which, in this case, can be defined as substantially transparent.

4 Irrigation Water and Land Value

As previously illustrated, the effect of the presence of water for irrigation on the value of the soils was estimated using an econometric approach by relating the AAV of the soils

---

[1] For example, if the values of the soils in an area reflect the expectations of introducing irrigation resulting from a consortium investment, the implicit prices obtained with the Hedonic method underestimate the current economic value of the presence of irrigation.

and the possibility of irrigating them. As a matter of fact, the hedonic analysis could also be applied to rents. If the market values reflect the rents, it doesn't matter is one uses rents or values. In Italy, the rental of agricultural land is highly regulated and current rents cannot be considered "market" rents and, therefore, it is appropriate to refer to the values of the land and not to the rents.

Obviously, if the market value exceeds the present value of future income deriving from the fund (land benefit), the value of the land does not reflect agricultural productivity, but incorporates future income from non-agricultural uses. In this case, the market values of the soils cannot be used to derive the value of the productive characteristics. The use of the AAV allows to reduce the distorting effect of extra-urban annuities.

In the literature there are not many contributions on the evaluation of irrigation with this approach, although in recent years there has been a growing interest, perhaps due to the greater availability of market data, the growing conflicts around the uses of the water resource and the possible effects of climate change.

To our knowledge, the first articles that explore the possibility of using the values of agricultural soils to estimate the value of irrigation water date back to the late 1950s with Renshaw [9] and Milliman [10]. In particular, Milliman observes how the assessment of water resources is particularly complex to estimate directly (budget approach) since water is often allocated with mechanisms other than that of the market. The indirect estimate, on the other hand, collides with the lack of adequate market information. Hartman and Anderson [11], relying more on the value of soils as the basis for estimating the value of irrigation and analyzing the effect of a federal irrigation project in Colorado on the sales values of 44 farms, identified a positive effect on the value of the soils of the availability of irrigation water. Twenty-five years later, Crouter [12], drawing inspiration from earlier works by Brown et al. [13] and Anderson [14], carried out similar evaluations with reference to 53 companies in Colorado, confirming the positive effect of the quantities of water available on the value of the soils and, at the same time, the difficulties of activating an efficient irrigation water market due to the high transaction costs.

Torell, Libbin and Miller [15] investigated the effects of a drastic reduction in the amount of water derived from the Ogallala Aquifer in the western United States, noting a consequent decrease in the market value of soils from 30 to 60%. King and Sinden [16], in a study aimed at identifying the main factors affecting the market value in New Wales and South Australia, found that the proximity of the soil to a river, with the consequent possibility of irrigation, is positive but not significant. On the contrary, Faux and Perry [17] focused on the value of irrigation water in Oregon in relation to the productivity of the soil: in the most productive lands the value of water is equal to about three € cent/cu. m. while, in the less fertile ones, the value drops to less than one € cent.

Arias [18], in the province of Leon in Spain, estimates that the value of irrigated arable land is about three times that of non-irrigated arable land while in the meadow it is about double. The value ratio in the Chalkidiki region, a typical rural area in Greece, is equal to two [19] and rises to 2.7 in the Great Plains region of the USA [20].

Petrie and Taylor [21] evaluated water use permits in Georgia starting from the effect of their restriction on the market values of farms. They found that the difference in values between irrigated and non-irrigated soils becomes significant after the introduction of a moratorium on the issuance of new water derivation permits and that the difference is approximately 30% (1,240 €/ha).

Thompson and Johnson [22] estimate the impact of irrigation on the market value of soils in Nebraska at about 290 €/ha, much lower than that estimated by the "Annual Residual Rent Method" according to which it would be worth about 600 €/ha. The difference, according to the authors, lies in the higher rate of capitalization with which the income from irrigated land is discounted compared to non-irrigated land, due to the uncertainty affecting the future availability of water for irrigation.

Yoo et al. [23] investigate the effect of irrigation in relation to the degree of urbanization of agricultural areas in some areas of Arizona and find that, in absolute terms, the effect is greater in peri-urban areas (€ 15,000/ha against € 14,000/ha) while it is lower in percentage terms (28% against 58.5%).

Buck et al. [24] return to the difficulty of estimating the value of irrigation water and, using panel data on repeated farmland sales in California (San Joaquin valley), find that the capital value of the right of use incorporated in that of the land is equal to 6, 2 €/cu. m., so, if the owner has the perpetual possibility to use 2,000 m³/year of water, the value of the land increases by 12,400 €/ha.

Swanepoel et al. [25] studied the value of irrigation water from underground sources in Phillis County in Colorado. The study found that the average value of is equal to 2.2 € cents/cu. m. but that it varies a lot depending on the depth of the supply wells (extraction cost).

Joshi et al. [26] studied the effect of access to irrigation in Nepal, highlighting that it affects the average value of soils by 46%; in addition, the presence of multiple sources of supply and a structured distribution system increase its effect.

Sampson et al. [27] estimated that the presence of irrigation affects the value of soils in the High Plains of Kansas to the extent of 53% and that the effect from 1988 to 2015 increased by 1%/year.

From the analysis of the main contributions published, some obvious trends can be identified:

1. the value of irrigation water seems to increase over time;
2. the value increases in the areas where it is scarcer and where the investments made to distribute it are greater;
3. the value increases where the most profitable crops are grown (horticulture and orchard);
4. the value increases in areas with greater urban development.

Ultimately, water availability is a very important factor in the enhancement of agricultural soils as it affects both the extent and variability of production.

5 Results

The evaluation of the effect of the presence of irrigation water on the value of the soils was performed using linear regression models with fixed effects:

$$V_i = \alpha_i + \beta_{1i} z_{1i} + \sum_{j=2}^{k} \beta_{ji} z_{ji} + \varepsilon_i \tag{10}$$

where:

V_i represents the AAV per hectare measured in the i-th territorial area;
z_{1i} the presence of irrigation water;
z_{ji} represents the value that the j variables (altimetry, location, crop, etc.) assume within the territorial area i;
β_{1i} represents the effect of irrigation on the soil AAV;
β_{ji} represent the effect of the other z_{ji} variables on the AAV, α_i represents a constant that expresses the effect on the AAV of the variables that have not been included in the model and that characterize the territorial scope i and ε_i represents the idiosyncratic error. The estimation of the parameters of these models (α_i and β_{ji}) is usually carried out with the least squares method.

The peculiarity of fixed effects models consists in the inclusion of as many constants αi as there are territorial areas considered (minus one) in order to avoid the distortions of the estimates caused by the possible omission of relevant explanatory variables. The constant will, therefore, capture the effect of all the factors that influence the AAV in the particular territorial area but which, due to the unavailability of the data, it was not possible to include in the database and, therefore, in the regression model.

The analysis was performed on both average data at a national level and on homogeneous geographical partitions (North, Center, South). The study by homogeneous partition of the database allowed to obtain models characterized by a greater interpretative capacity of the data used.

As mentioned above, the values of the soils were assumed to be equal to the average agricultural values (pursuant to art.16, LN 865/71) since, although they are not market values, they are transparent, they refer only to agricultural production characteristics, they are available uniformly throughout the national territory and for predefined crop types, they are averaged by agricultural region and therefore are more stable and little affected by specific contingent situations (urban rents). The evaluation involved a representative sample of all Italian regions (one representative province per region) for a total of 166 Agricultural Regions and 1368 municipalities.

The data used for the evaluation is:

- AAV of the Agricultural Region to which it belongs, distinguished by type of crop (lawn, arable land, orchard, vegetable garden) and by the presence/absence of an irrigation system (Source: Revenue Agency, 2013);
- Structure of agricultural activities: average size of farms; % of agricultural area with valuable crops; use of third parties (Source: VI Agricultural Census, 2010);
- Type and source of irrigation (Source: VI Agricultural Census, 2010);
- Geographical and climatic characterization: altimetric zone; hydro-climatic balance values (Source: ISTAT; Agrometeorological database of CRA-CMA);
- General economic characterization: agricultural labor; industry employees; service personnel (Source: VI Agricultural Census 2010; Industry, Commerce and Handicraft Census, 2011);
- Demographic characterization: population; population density (Source: Population Census 2011).

Overall, the variables taken into consideration provide a sufficient framework to outline the structure of the agricultural sector, the climatic and socio-economic characteristics of the territorial areas considered.

The average AAV of the most important crops from an economic point of view (arable land, orchard, vegetable garden and lawn) is around 40 thousand €/ha, with a maximum of 52 thousand €/ha in the north and a minimum of 20 thousand €/ha in the center (Fig. 1). The presence of irrigation significantly discriminates the AAV by introducing an average difference between irrigated and non-irrigated equal to 13.5 thousand €/ha. In percentage terms, this difference is higher in the center-south (60–80%) than in the north (39%) due to the known climatic differences.

The benefit produced by irrigation differs not only by geographic distribution (latitude), but also by the most widely practiced crops. On average, in areas where arable land predominates, the increase in value attributable to irrigation is approximately 27%. The maximum contribution is recorded for soils located in areas suitable for specialized crops: orchards (+35%) and vegetable garden (+82%). The contribution made to the value of lawn areas, which, even in the north, require high volumes of irrigation water, is also significant (+48%).

Basically, by comparing the AAVs in the different geographic areas it is clear that the contribution of irrigation to the value increases with the value of the crops grown and with the average value of the soils.

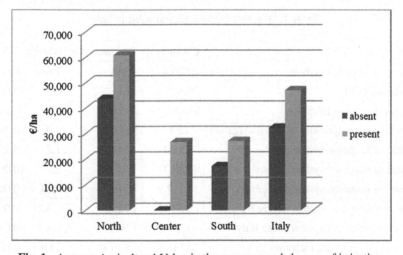

Fig. 1. Average Agricultural Value in the presence and absence of irrigation.

These first results are confirmed by the econometric analysis which identifies, net of all the other characteristics that may affect the land value, the contribution attributable to the possibility of irrigation in the sample of municipalities considered.

Two main investigations were carried out: the first to verify whether or not the contribution of irrigation to the agricultural value was statistically significant, the second to identify the factors that most affected this contribution, both in the first instance and interacting with other characteristics.

Analysis confirm that the AAV of the soils (Table 1) is significantly and positively influenced by the possibility of irrigation (+€ 9,520/ha), by the diffusion of irrigation at the local level and by the presence of a structured (consortium) water supply system. Irrigation plays a decisive role in the formation of value, especially in the presence of consolidated irrigation territorial systems.

The effect of advanced irrigation techniques (sprinkler or micro-irrigation) is apparently counterintuitive, perhaps due to their higher operating costs.

The value of the soils, in addition to the presence of irrigation, is significantly connected with the crops practiced: taking as a reference basis the value of the grass soils, arable crops involve an increase in value of 16k €/ha, horticultural ones of 18.8k €/ha and fruit crops of 31.2k €/ha.

The greater contribution of orchards to the value is due to the huge land investments present.

Compared to lowland AAVs, mountain and hilly ones are significantly penalized (−6.2k €/ha and - 3.1k €/ha).

Finally, the average agricultural value of the soil is negatively influenced by the average company size (−33.9 €/ha per hectare of average company size) and positively by the density of the population and the outsourcing of the economy. Ultimately, the value of land for exclusive agricultural use is positively linked to general factors of economic and urban development.

Table 1. The average agricultural value in Italy.

Variable	Coefficient	Standard error	b/St.Er	P[|Z|>z]
Presence of irrigation system	9.520,4	1.254,1	7,6	0,00
Irrigated area (%)	78,8	12,1	6,5	0,00
Consortium source of supply	856,8	533,0	1,6	0,11
Irrigation system: sprinkler or micro irrigation	−12,7	595,0	0,0	0,98
Presence of irrigation system arable	1.751,2	1.511,5	1,2	0,25
Presence of irrigation system orchard	8.780,3	1.542,0	5,7	0,00
Presence of irrigation system vegetable	17.217,9	1.516,8	11,4	0,00
Presence of irrigation system Centre Italy	−3.974,7	1.225,5	−3,2	0,00
Presence of irrigation system South Italy	−8.775,9	1.006,3	−8,7	0,00
Type of arable crop (vs. meadow)	16.118,6	1.080,8	14,9	0,00
Type of crop orchard (vs. meadow)	31.246,3	1.103,2	28,3	0,00
Type of vegetable garden (vs. meadows)	18.840,1	1.084,3	17,4	0,00
Valuable crops: vegetable garden and orchard (%)	124,9	12,9	9,6	0,00
Altimetric area mountain (vs. plain)	−6.187,0	1.169,2	−5,3	0,00

(*continued*)

Table 1. (*continued*)

Variable	Coefficient	Standard error	b/St.Er	P[IZI>z]
Altitude hill area (vs. plain)	−3.150,5	796,2	−4,0	0,00
Average size of agricultural holdings (UAA ha / az.)	−33,9	16,6	−2,0	0,04
Main use of subcontractors (% of shares)	19,6	14,5	1,3	0,18
Agriculture employees (%)	0,9	0,4	2,6	0,01
Industry employees (%)	−1,0	0,4	−2,5	0,01
Service employees (%)	0,3	0,2	2,0	0,04
Common population (inhab.)	0,0	0,0	−0,5	0,60
Population density (inhab./sq. km)	1,7	0,6	3,0	0,00

R-squared = .71
Adjusted R-squared = .71
Akaike Info. Criter. = 19.5
AAV dependent variable (€/ha)
UAA: utilized agricultural area

Table 2 deepens the analysis by reporting three models developed without including the interactions between the presence of irrigation and the geographical area. The first of the models was estimated with reference to the entire national territory and the other two on the opposite realities from a climatic point of view: the northern and southern agricultural regions. In principle, these models confirm the main results obtained with the model shown in Table 1.

The presence of irrigation ensures a higher value of 9 thousand €/ha, with a slight prevalence in the southern regions (+10 thousand €/ha) compared to the northern ones (+9 thousand €/ha). The AAVs appear to be influenced, even in these models, by crop destination. In particular, arable crops, orchards and horticultural crops have a significant effect compared to the lawn in all the considered territorial realities. Taking into consideration the differences between the agricultural regions of northern and southern Italy, it is noted that:

- fruit crops induce a greater effect in the northern regions;
- the mountain location uniformly penalizes the AAVs of the peninsula;
- the hilly location penalizes the AAVs of the Southern Agricultural Regions the most;
- the availability of agricultural labor has a positive effect on AAVs, particularly in the north;
- population density positively influences AAV, especially in the North;
- the effect of the interaction with the presence of irrigation is always positive for vegetable crops while for fruit crops it is positive only in the agricultural regions of the north.

Table 2. The Average Agricultural Value by geographical areas in Italy.

Variable	Italy		North		South	
	Coeff.	t-ratio	Coeff.	t-ratio	Coeff.	t-ratio
Presence of irrigation system	8,965.58	7.13	9,127.33	5.58	10,179.10	4.59
Type of arable crop (vs. meadow)	17,652.40	16.50	15,122.10	9.95	13,009.80	7.92
Type of crop orchard (vs. meadow)	32,669.60	29.86	38,504.70	24.61	23,481.10	14.23
Type of vegetable garden (vs. meadows)	20,388.00	18.98	17,675.20	11.62	15,891.40	9.68
Average size of agricultural holdings (UAA ha/az.)	−33.94	−2.03	−4.37	−0.18	−9.30	−0.52
UAA valuable crops (%)	124.87	9.59	183.45	7.84	10.58	1.20
Prevailing use of the CT (%) of the shares)	19.55	1.34	35.62	1.31	−44.17	−4.70
UAA Irrigated (%)	78.78	6.46	69.56	3.65	17.79	1.91
Irrigation system: sprinkler or micro-irrigation	−12.70	−0.02	601.97	0.56	−334.10	−0.88
Supply source: aqueduct, consortium or other entity with delivery in turn or on demand	856.81	1.60	2,130.99	2.47	−766.00	−1.98
Altimetric area mountain (vs. plain)	−6,187.02	−5.26	−11,407.80	−3.59	−10,083.60	−14.27
Altitude hill area (vs. plain)	−3,150.49	−3.94	−1,905.62	−1.49	−6,108.98	−10.94
Agricultural labor (number of people)	0.92	2.59	2.36	2.65	0.45	2.24
Industry employees (number of people)	−0.98	−2.45	−1.55	−2.25	1.11	1.92
Service employees (number of people)	0.33	2.03	0.56	2.08	−0.30	−1.52
Municipalities population	−0.02	−0.52	−0.09	−1.07	0.00	0.15
Density (inhab./sq. km)	1.67	2.97	6.31	2.42	1.08	4.58
Presence of irrigation system_arable	−1,316.48	−0.89	−1,452.48	−0.68	−2,928.39	−1.29

(*continued*)

Table 2. (*continued*)

Variable	Italy		North		South	
	Coeff.	t-ratio	Coeff.	t-ratio	Coeff.	t-ratio
Presence of irrigation system_orchard	5,933.61	3.94	10,641.70	4.87	−2,298.82	−1.01
Presence of irrigation system_vegetable garden	14,122.10	9.55	20,206.20	9.49	3,918.53	1.73
R-squared	0.71		0.71		0.83	
Adjusted R-squared	0.71		0.71		0.83	
Akaike Info. Criter	19.59		19.58		17.56	

Table 3 shows the results obtained by taking into account, at national level, the effect of irrigation on the AAV of the main crops. In addition, in this case, the fixed effects models confirm, on average, the results of the analysis illustrated above. The effect of irrigation on the value of the soils is positive for all crops examined. The increase in value is particularly evident in orchard soils (+€ 15.4 thousand) and more contained in vegetable gardens (+€ 9.6 thousand), lawn (+€ 9 thousand) and arable land (+7, € 6 thousand). Another significant element is that the AAV is always penalized by mountainous and hilly locations, except for fruit crops.

Table 3. The Average Agricultural Value by crop in Italy.

Variable	Crop							
	Arable		Orchard		Vegetable		Garden	
	Coeff.	t-ratio	Coeff.	t-ratio	Coeff.	t-ratio	Coeff.	t-ratio
Presence of irrigation system	7,612.49	33.17	15,394.00	8.26	9.59	32.72	8,965.58	21.90
Average size of agricultural holdings (UAA ha/az.)	7.17	0.77	−66.50	−0.35	18.23	1.33	32.62	2.31
UAA valuable crops (%)	46.33	6.49	338.90	7.01	8.34	0.96	18.29	1.37
Prevailing use of the CT (%) of the shares)	14.55	1.86	71.90	1.14	0.24	0.02	−12.83	−0.81
UAA Irrigated (%)	14.80	2.17	305.40	6.01	−7.71	−0.75	30.48	2.59

(*continued*)

Table 3. (*continued*)

Variable	Crop							
	Arable		Orchard		Vegetable		Garden	
	Coeff.	t-ratio	Coeff.	t-ratio	Coeff.	t-ratio	Coeff.	t-ratio
Irrigation system: sprinkler or micro-irrigation	514.45	1.62	−2,078.90	−0.71	−363.62	−0.84	−1,555.93	−2.49
Supply source: aqueduct, consortium or other entity with delivery in turn or on demand	389.76	1.34	2,663.90	1.14	−185.01	−0.43	28.10	0.05
Altimetric area mountain (vs. plain)	−9,170.25	−14.64	8,205.10	1.43	−14,715.60	−9.09	−5,126.45	−1.58
Altitude hill area (vs. plain)	−5,594.53	−12.62	6,20580	2.11	−4,718.86	−7.47	−1,761.75	−1.94
Agricultural labor (number of people)	0.66	3.54	2.60	1.92	0.09	0.32	0.51	0.99
Industry employees (number of people)	−0.47	−2.27	−3.30	−1.85	0.20	0.39	−1.06	−1.64
Service employees (number of people)	0.10	1.17	1.00	1.76	−0.23	−0.75	0.46	1.59
Municipalities population	0.00	−0.05	−0.10	−0.52	0.04	0.82	−0.07	−0.87
Density (inhab./sq. km)	2.39	8.15	1.10	0.63	0.26	0.91	4.41	32.44
Number of observs	810.0		810.00		810.00		810.00	
R-squared	0.93		0.78		0.95		0.87	
Adjusted R-squared	0.93		0.77		0.95		0.86	
Akaike Info. Criter	7.19		20.43		16.32		17.37	

The estimates of the effect of irrigation on the AAV of the soils in relation to the crops grown, the geographical location and the structural characteristics of agriculture allow an initial estimate of the total value of irrigation at the national level. This estimate was made starting from the extent of the irrigated area, the use of the land and its main characteristics. The calculated value varies, depending on the econometric model adopted, between € 25.8 and € 28.6 billion, with an average of € 27.2 billion (the highest value was obtained by extending the estimates made at national level with the model shown in Table 2, which includes the effect of the interaction between the presence of irrigation and the geographical location of the soil. The lowest value is obtained using the estimates obtained by type of crop (Table 3).

This is a rather variable estimate but, nevertheless, useful for providing an order of magnitude of the contribution of irrigation to the value of the land and to agricultural income.

6 Conclusions

The study presented above applied the hedonic method to evaluate the effect of the availability of water for irrigation on the value of agricultural soils in Italy. The study made it possible to highlight the effect of irrigation and the other main variables that characterize the soils and the socio-economic context where they are located. The overall effect at the national level was estimated at approximately € 27.2 billion, equal to € 8,770/ha. Assuming that the total annual volume of water used for irrigation is equal to 11 billion cu. m./year, a greater value of the irrigated land is obtained equal to 2.5 €/cu. m. of usable water per year. Approximately 5 € cents/cu. m. is obtained by extending the estimates to the value of the water.

These estimates are consistent with what has been observed in the literature.

Furthermore, the results allow to highlight some important (and not always obvious) issues:

1. The values consistent with the reasonable a priori that can be formulated on the main effects of irrigation on the value and on agricultural income.
2. Irrigation contributes significantly to the agricultural value, and, therefore, to the income of all the main crops grown in Italy and at all latitudes.
3. Irrigation contributes not only to the amount of income but also to its stability over time, decreasing the economic risk at the level of the agricultural enterprise.
4. Irrigation is essential for the survival of agricultural systems based on specialized crops in all Italian areas, in the north as well as in the south.
5. The unit volumes used in agriculture (on average 3,500 cu. m./ha) are high and give a glimpse of ample room for improvement in the efficiency of water use in agriculture with the possibility of reducing the significant conflicts in place with competing uses.

However, the analysis carried out has some obvious limitations deriving from the database used (AAV) and from the fact that only some sample provinces were considered and not the entire national universe. Some limits could be easily overcome by re-estimating the effect of irrigation on a larger database and integrating the AAVs with direct observations on the real estate market.

References

1. Antonietti, A., D'Alanno, A., Vanzetti, C.: Carta delle irrigazioni d'Italia (1965)
2. ISTAT National Institute of Statistics: Agricultural statistics: Years 2001–2002 (2006)
3. Zucaro, R., Pontrandolfi, A., Dodaro, G.M., Gallinoni, C., Pacicco, C.L., Vollaro, M.: Atlante nazionale dell'irrigazione. INEA (2011)
4. Rosato, P., Stellin, G.: La valutazione economica dei beni ambientali (1998)
5. Hanley, N., Spash, C.: Cost benefit analysis and the environment (1996)
6. Rosen, S.: Hedonic prices and implicit markets: product differentiation in pure competition. J. Polit. Econ. **82**, 34–55 (1974)
7. Palmquist, R.B.: Land as a differentiated factor of production: a hedonic model and its implications for welfare measurement. Land Econ. **65**, 23–28 (1989)
8. Freeman, M.: The Measurement of Environmental and Resource Values: Theory and Methods. Resources for the Future, Washington, D.C. (1992)
9. Renshaw, E.F.: Cross-sectional pricing in the market for irrigated land. Agric. Econ. Res. **10**, 14–19 (1958)
10. Milliman, J.W.: Land values as measures of primary irrigation benefits. J. Farm Econ. **41**, 234–243 (1959)
11. Hartman, L.M., Anderson, R.L.: Estimating the value of irrigation water from farm sales data in Northeastern Colorado. J. Farm Econ. **44**, 207–213 (1962)
12. Crouter, J.P.: Hedonic estimation applied to a water rights market. Land Econ. **63**, 259–271 (1987)
13. Brown, L., McDonald, B., Tysseling, J., DuMars, C.: Water reallocation, market proficiency, and conflicting social values. Water Agric. West. U. S. Conserv. Reallocation, Mark. Westview Press. Boulder Color. 1982, pp. 191–255, 2 tab, 147 ref. (1982)
14. Anderson, T.L.: Water Crisis: Ending the Policy Drought. The Johns Hopkins University Press, Baltimore (1983)
15. Torell, L.A., Libbin, J.D., Miller, M.D.: The market value of water in the Ogallala Aquifer. Land Econ. **66**, 163–175 (1990)
16. King, D.A., Sinden, J.A.: Price formation in farm land markets. Land Econ. **70**, 38–52 (1994)
17. Faux, J., Perry, G.M.: Estimating irrigation water value using hedonic price analysis: a case study in Malheur County. Oregon. Land Econ. **75**, 440–452 (1999)
18. Sampedro, C.A.: Estimación del valor del regadío a partir del precio de la tierra. Econ. Agrar. y Recur. Nat. **1**, 115–123 (2001)
19. Latinopoulos, P., Tziakas, V., MallIos, Z.: Valuation of irrigation water by the hedonic price method: a case study in Chalkidiki, Greece. Water Air Soil Pollut. Focus **4**, 253–262 (2004)
20. Jenkins, A., Elder, B., Valluru, R., Burger, P.: Water rights and land values in the West-Central Plains. Gt. Plains Res. **17**, 101–111 (2007)
21. Petrie, R.A., Taylor, L.O.: Estimating the value of water use permits: a hedonic approach applied to farmland in the southeastern United States. Land Econ. **83**, 302–318 (2007)
22. Thompson, C.L., Johnson, B.B.: The value of water in agriculture land markets: the Nebraska case. J. ASFMRA. 20–28 (2012)
23. Yoo, J., Simonit, S., Connors, J.P., Maliszewski, P.J., Kinzig, A.P., Perrings, C.: The value of agricultural water rights in agricultural properties in the path of development. Ecol. Econ. **91**, 57–68 (2013)
24. Buck, S., Auffhammer, M., Sunding, D.: Land markets and the value of water: hedonic analysis using repeat sales of farmland. Am. J. Agric. Econ. **96**, 953–969 (2014)
25. Swanepoel, G.D., Hadrich, J., Goemans, C.: Estimating the contribution of groundwater irrigation to farmland values in Phillips County, Colorado. J. ASFMRA (American Soc. Farm Manag. Rural Apprais.) 166–179 (2015)

26. Joshi, J., Ali, M., Berrens, R.P.: Valuing farm access to irrigation in Nepal: a hedonic pricing model. Agric. water Manag. **181**, 35–46 (2017)
27. Sampson, G.S., Hendricks, N.P., Taylor, M.R.: Land market valuation of groundwater. Resour. Energy Econ. **58**, 101120 (2019)

Water Losses and Maintenance Investment. An Econometric Model for the Sustainable Management of Water Services

Luigi Dolores(✉) , Maria Macchiaroli , and Gianluigi De Mare

University of Salerno, Via Giovanni Paolo II, 132, Fisciano, SA, Italy
{ldolores,mmacchiaroli,gdemare}@unisa.it

Abstract. In Italy, there is a large gap between the water supplied to the distribution networks and the water delivered to users. Reducing the dispersion along the aqueduct network has several advantages for water service operators, such as reducing the production and distribution costs of the resource, limiting the volumes of water purchased wholesale, and improving the users' perception of the service. The aim of the paper is to define an econometric model that allows water utilities to determine the optimal budget to be used to finance the maintenance work required to reduce water losses. The model, which uses a Cobb-Douglas production function with increasing returns to scale, identifies the maximum level of profit that the manager can obtain by investing the optimal amount. The higher profits obtained can be used to self-finance new maintenance. A key parameter is the coefficient of return-on-investment α, which is a measure of the degree of user satisfaction with the service offered. The water tariff is dependent on financial (capital and operating), environmental and resource costs. The model is applied to a water utility in the Campania region (Italy).

Keywords: Water service management · Water losses · Maintenance investment · Econometric model · Financial sustainability · Cobb-Douglas function

1 Introduction

Water is the natural element that makes human development possible. The water resource is the main constituent of both the planet and our organism, both of which are composed of approximately 70% water. Of the water on Earth, about 97.5% is found in the oceans and seas, 2% comes from glaciers and polar ice caps, and only 0.5% is available to humans for sustenance. But the percentage of freshwater that is drinkable and not contaminated is even lower and is unevenly distributed over the surface of the planet. Although water is a scarce resource, it is thanks to the water that human beings have achieved the conditions necessary for development. Worldwide, 70% of the water available to man is used for food and in the primary sector, 22% to produce consumer goods and 8% for domestic

---

The three authors contributed in equal parts to this work.

© Springer Nature Switzerland AG 2021
O. Gervasi et al. (Eds.): ICCSA 2021, LNCS 12956, pp. 236–253, 2021.
https://doi.org/10.1007/978-3-030-87010-2_16

use [1]. The exploitation of the resource is rapidly leading to the irreversible degradation of aquifers. Today, more than 4 billion people live in conditions of water scarcity for at least one month a year and around 500 million people live in places where annual water consumption is double the amount that can be replenished by rainfall [2]. In large parts of the world, water infrastructures are unable to meet the growing need for water. The remarkably low price of water, often below the cost of production, is encouraging the wasteful use of the resource and dampening the inflow of financial capital needed to maintain existing facilities and build new infrastructure [3]. In addition to direct consumption of the resource for domestic and industrial purposes, recent climate change, periods of drought, environmental pollution and hydraulic load losses along distribution networks are contributing strongly to the reduction of drinking water availability. In particular, the issue of water losses is receiving increasing interest from the scientific community [4]. Water losses represent one of the main obstacles to achieving quantitative standards of access and availability of the resource. In any country and network, water loss is a phenomenon that can hardly be eliminated in its entirety. This is because its causes can be multiple (age of plants, pipeline failures, unauthorised withdrawals, measurement errors) and not always easy to predict [5]. In this sense, it is estimated that in Europe, leakages in water networks, leakages from taps and the lack of water-saving facilities are among the main causes of dispersion of about 20–40% of available water resources. The overall percentage of water losses is unevenly distributed across the European Union. In fact, a 2015 CENSIS study reveals that in Germany, network losses amounted to 6.5%, in the UK to 15.5%, in France to 20.9%, and in Italy, they exceeded 50% [6].

The problem of water losses is particularly felt in Italy. Therefore, the aim of this work is to propose an operational tool to support Italian Integrated Water Services operators in defining the budget for investments to limit water losses. Specifically, an econometric model is proposed, whose objective is to establish the optimal annual budget that the individual water service manager should invest in maintenance interventions aimed at reducing water losses of the supply and distribution networks. This budget allows the operator to maximise the operating profit, i.e., to achieve an optimal balance between annual turnover and production costs. The higher profits obtained, some of which are usually set aside in the form of reserves for subsequent years, could be used to finance new maintenance work. The operator can thus resort to self-financing and guarantee the financial sustainability of future investments. Such investments not only lead to an increase in total production costs, but also to an increase in turnover. This is because, as required by the relevant national and EU regulatory framework, water tariffs are defined in such a way as to comprehensively cover all cost components (operating costs, capital costs, environmental costs, and resource costs). As a result, as total production costs increase, the average tariff increases accordingly. In the model, the effects on the user of the service generated by investments aimed at reducing water losses are also considered. These investments contribute to the reduction of environmental and resource costs, which in budgetary terms translate into higher revenues for the operator. This is because increased sensitivity to the ecosystem and improved service can generate increased demand. Some of the users who are dissatisfied with the management of the water resource may change their perception of the managing company. This can be translated into a reduction in the risk of insolvency for the operator and a consequent increase in turnover [7–9].

The document is structured as follows: Sect. 2 defines the main managerial and financial characteristics of the Italian water services to be considered in the model characterization phase; Sect. 3 describes the econometric model; in Sect. 4 the model is applied to an Integrated Water Service manager in the Campania region (Italy) and the main results are presented; in Sect. 5 the results obtained are commented on and interpreted from an economic-financial point of view; Sect. 6 contains the concluding remarks.

2 Overview of the Italian Water Service Management

As mentioned, the Italian situation regarding water losses is particularly serious. In 2018, high losses were recorded along the water networks of provincial capitals: about 44 cubic metres per day per kilometre of the network. In these municipalities, 37.3% of the volume of water injected into the networks did not reach users due to leakage (39% in 2016). With respect to supply interruptions, worrying levels of dissatisfaction on the part of households were recorded in Calabria (36.8%), Sicily (32.4%) and Sardinia (25.6%). In one out of three Italian municipalities, overall losses of more than 45% were recorded. On the contrary, only in one municipality out of five total water losses were below 25% [10]. The need for infrastructure investments in the water supply sector is strongly felt in Italy. The current infrastructural heritage, developed in parallel with the urban and industrial development of the 20th century, is very diverse and has a different residual useful life. For this reason, the investments to be made concern both the construction of new infrastructures and the continuous and constant maintenance of existing ones. To reach acceptable European standards, investments of at least 80 euros per inhabitant would be necessary [11].

In Italy, the financing methods for the construction and maintenance of the infrastructure of the Integrated Water Service are mainly linked to revenues from tariffs and public funds. The latter, which come from European, national, and regional funding as well as from loans granted to local authorities, should represent a decreasing item within the budgets for infrastructure investments since they should be reflected in the tariff according to the principle of full cost recovery. However, flows derived from user payments are still far from adequate thresholds to meet today's needs. Indeed, Italian water tariffs are currently among the lowest in Europe, averaging €1.87 per cubic metre (far from France's €3.67 and Germany's €4.98). On the one hand, low water tariffs encourage wastage of the resource (average annual consumption of about 160 cubic metres of drinking water per inhabitant is estimated), while on the other hand, they limit the scope for investments not financed by the public funds. As a result, the level of investment in water infrastructure is also among the lowest in Europe (e.g., only around 30% of that in the UK). The high levels of losses in Italian distribution networks are therefore mainly due to the reduced availability of financial capital to invest in the maintenance/replacement of existing infrastructure [12].

In Italy, the low flow of investments to improve the efficiency of water networks is partly due to the complex regulatory and legislative framework that characterises the

Integrated Water Service and the model for determining water tariffs. Until 2012, the Ministry of the Environment and Protection of Land and Sea (Ministero dell'Ambiente e della Tutela del Territorio e del Mare - MATTM) defined the cost components for determining the tariff for water services for the various sectors of water use (aqueduct, sewerage, and purification). Today, however, it is an independent administrative authority - the Regulatory Authority for Energy, Networks, and the Environment (Autorità di Regolazione per Energia Reti e Ambiente - ARERA) - which exercises regulatory powers over the Integrated Water Service determines the national method of calculating tariffs and approves them on the proposal of the Ambit Management Body (dell'Ente di Gestione d'Ambito - EGA). The latter is a local body, with a legal personality, which organises, entrusts, and controls the work of the individual water service managers within an Optimal Territorial Ambit (Ambito Territoriale Ottimale - ATO), which represents the minimum territorial unit of reference. The tariffs that each management must apply are therefore proposed by the EGAs based on a technical, economic, and financial planning tool, the Area Plan (Piano d'Ambito - PdA), and subsequently approved by ARERA. All the portions of the tariff for the Integrated Water Service are in the nature of a fee. In fact, the tariff regulations contained in the Consolidated Environmental Act (Testo Unico dell'Ambiente, Legislative Decree 152/2006) state that the tariff is determined considering the quality of the water resource and the service provided, the necessary works, the management costs of these works, and a share of the operating costs of the Ambit Authority. This ensures full coverage and recovery of investment and operating costs according to the polluter pays principle. This is in accordance with the Water Framework Directive promulgated by the European Commission (2000/60/EC), which introduces the concept of full cost recovery, according to which the tariffs charged to users must cover operating, capital costs, and environmental costs [13].

In a similar way to the model for defining water tariffs, the service management model should have followed the approach prevailing in Europe. In fact, in the initial intentions, the reform of the Italian regulations in matters of Integrated Water Service should have been inspired by the management models of England and Wales. In this sense, the main objectives that should have been pursued are the concentration of management (in particular, hoping for the presence of a single manager for each ATO) and the start of an entrepreneurial organisation of the sector to make the service financially autonomous as regards investments in infrastructure. However, the current management model that has emerged from the regulations that have followed over the years has taken on a different physiognomy from the English one. Therefore, the Italian model has appeared in the European panorama as a hybrid model. In fact, the legislator, considering the vast administrative, technical, and political apparatus operating in public enterprises, has in fact accepted the compromise of optional privatisation, leaving the possibility of a public presence in management. At present, an industrial type of management can only be found in a few areas of the country (mostly in the centre-north, in Puglia and Basilicata), while in the south and on the islands, it is almost always the municipalities that manage water services on a tight budget [14].

Significant economies of scale and scope emerge only for a few medium and large-scale management (in terms of employees and catchment area), mostly private and multi-service. In contrast to the small operators, these companies are more financially self-sufficient, in some cases managing to finance their investments from tariff revenues. However, even for these companies, there is enormous room for improvement. Hence the need to propose innovative models and instruments that allow operators to increase the financial sustainability of their investments, especially those necessary for the maintenance of existing plants and the construction of new infrastructure [15–19]. A crucial issue is the definition of the optimal budget to be allocated to these investments, considering both the most efficient technical solution in terms of reducing environmental costs and satisfying the service users and the financial impact in terms of company profits. In the present work, the attention is focused on the maintenance interventions of the aqueduct plants necessary to reduce water losses. In this regard, an innovative model is introduced in the next chapter whose objective is to establish the optimal budget that the managing body should allocate to maintenance interventions to maximise profits. In the following sections, the model will be applied retrospectively on the investments made by the managing body in the last ten years to understand how much the adopted strategy differs from the optimal one.

3   Characterization of the Financial Sustainability Model

In microeconomic terms, water utilities operate under a natural monopoly. This is for several reasons. First, the water network for technical reasons can only be unique. Secondly, the production costs incurred by a single company to provide the required volumes of water are lower than if several companies were operating on the market. Finally, being a public economic activity, the natural monopoly reduces the risk of market failure, guaranteeing the uninterrupted supply of the resource to citizens and industries [20]. In a monopoly market, the inverse market demand for the year $t_0 \leq t \leq t_f$ can be represented through the following functional relationship:

$$p_{(t)} = a - b\,q_{(t)} + c\,C_{T\,(t)} \tag{1}$$

where p is the average water tariff (i.e., the average of the different tariffs by user type and consumption bands, including the fixed fee), q is the quantity of water demanded and C_T is the total production costs. The parameters a, b and c are constants. In particular, a identifies the intercept of the price plane with the Cartesian price axis, while b and c represent the slope of this plane with respect to the same axis. A linear relationship is assumed between the variables. Initially, a relationship of inverse proportionality between p and q was assumed, being the quantity demanded not being independent of the price (and vice versa) as in perfect competition. Therefore, in terms of inverse demand, as the quantity demanded decreases, the average water tariff should increase. For this reason, in (1) the parameter a is preceded by a minus sign. The monopoly company can therefore carry out a policy of both price (in compliance with the maximum tariffs defined by ARERA Resolution 665/2017/R/idr of 28 September 2017 [21]) and quantity. The relationship between p and C_T is, instead, of direct proportionality based on the full cost recovery principle. Therefore, as total production costs increase, the average tariff increases. However, in accounting terms, and therefore in the income statements of the managing bodies, the production cost does not include the following two types of cost:

- Environmental costs: negative externalities arising from the damage that water use causes to the environment, ecosystems, and users (reduction in the ecological quality of water ecosystems, salinisation, degradation of productive land, etc.) [22, 23]. To calculate environmental costs, it is also necessary to consider the mere abstraction of water and, especially, water losses that, in addition to reducing the availability of the resource, do not contribute to an increase in productivity.
- Resource costs: costs arising from the use of the water resource for a specific use rather than for alternative uses (opportunity cost of the resource).

On the other hand, production costs include a large part of financial costs, such as operating costs (raw material costs, service costs, personnel costs, ordinary maintenance), depreciation costs (depreciation allowances, extraordinary maintenance), while capital costs (interest to be paid on investments made) are excluded. In order to follow the full cost recovery principle to the letter, environmental and resource costs must also be considered. The investments made by the managing body that contribute to the reduction of these costs are rewarded by the national regulator (ARERA) through the increase of the water tariff [24, 25]. Virtually, the tariff increase is equivalent to a reduction in the quantity demanded. If the positive effects on the price generated by the investments exceed the negative effects generated by the increase in demand, then it is possible to change the sign of the a coefficient in (1). The change of sign from negative to positive is also justifiable for a second reason. The increasing sensibility of the managing body for environmental sustainability (manifested, for example, through investments finalized to the reduction of the water losses) is often welcomed by the users, also by those less satisfied with the offered service. In particular, it is among the latter that there is the highest percentage of insolvents, i.e., those who use the service without paying. Investments to reduce environmental and resource costs can lead to dissatisfied users having a favourable perception of management, helping to reduce the risk of insolvency. Again, this translates into higher revenues for the authority, which can be justified by a change in the sign of the a coefficient. The payment of interest to the financing bodies can generate a similar effect, contributing to an increase in the positive opinion of management. The same applies to the reduction of operational costs of drawing the resource at the source obtained by containing water losses. All these elements can result in a change of sign of the a coefficient, so (1) can be rewritten as follows:

$$p_{(t)} = a + b\,q_{(t)} + c\,C_{T\,(t)} \tag{2}$$

The average tariff p is obtained by dividing the production revenues (R) by the volumes of water supplied to users (q):

$$p_{(t)} = \frac{R_{(t)}}{q_{(t)}}. \tag{3}$$

Parameters a, b and c can be estimated using multiple linear regression and considering the time series of p, q, and C_T. As we shall see, when applying the model, the regression confirmed the positivity of parameter a.

Similarly to the assumptions made by the authors in other application areas [26–28], supply is defined by means of the following Cobb-Douglas production function at increasing returns to scale [29]:

$$q_{(t)} = K_{I(t)}^{\alpha} L_{(t)}^{\beta} \; con \; \alpha + \beta = 1.4 > 1, 0 < \alpha < 1 \; e \; 0 < \beta < 1, \tag{4}$$

where $q_{(t)}$ is the quantity offered, $K_{I(t)}$ is the stock of investments accumulated over time and aimed at reducing water losses, $L_{(t)}$ is the labour input. The capital at the disposal of the managing body is not considered among the production factors, as these activities do not contribute directly to production (a building owned, for example, does not directly affect the distribution of water to users). In $K_{I(t)}$, on the other hand, are included the installations of the entire aqueduct network, which is assumed to be publicly owned and managed by the water manager. Each investment $I_{(t)}$ made in the time unit t contributes to the increase of the capital stock $K_{I(t)}$. The exponential coefficients α and β represent the rate of change of the (decreasing) marginal return on capital ($K_{I(t)}$) and labour ($L_{(t)}$), respectively. In particular, the parameter α incorporates within it those intangible aspects that can directly affect productivity, such as the level of user satisfaction with the service offered. As regards the hypothesis of increasing returns to scale ($\alpha + \beta = 1.4 > 1$), it is supported by the reference literature on the Integrated Water Service [30, 31]. This is because it has been empirically demonstrated that the productivity of jointly employed production factors increases exponentially as the size of the management increases. In fact, it is much more difficult for management on a tight budget to achieve high output levels than industrial management with a larger catchment area. Following industry surveys, it was considered acceptable to set $\alpha + \beta = 1.4$ following the national trend in the water services market. Exploiting the log-linearity property of the Cobb-Douglas function and solving the following system it is possible to calculate the values of α and β:

$$\begin{cases} \alpha = 1.4 - \beta \\ \beta = \frac{\ln q - \log K_{I(t)}}{\ln L_{(t)} - \log K_{I(t)}} \end{cases}, \tag{5}$$

Total production costs can be defined as follows:

$$C_{T(t)} = C_A + I_t, \tag{6}$$

where I_t is the cost of the investment to reduce water losses in year t and C_A represents the remaining production costs (including personnel costs). The stock of investments accumulated up to year t can be defined as the sum of the investment I_t with the stock of investments accumulated up to year $t - 1$:

$$K_{I(t)} = I_t + K_{I(t-1)}. \tag{7}$$

In turn, $K_{I(t-1)}$ includes the loss of value suffered by the investment stock over time due to technical and functional obsolescence [32, 33]. By virtue of this, we can estimate $K_{I(t-1)}$ as follows:

$$K_{I(t-1)} = K_{I(t_0)} + \sum_{t_1}^{t-1}(I_t - v_i) \; con \; v_i = \frac{(t-1) - t_1}{U} 100 \; e \; t_0 \le t \le t_f, \tag{8}$$

where $K_{I(t_0)}$ is the value of the entire aqueduct network at year t_0 (i.e., at the beginning of the period under analysis), v_i is the age coefficient applied to the network and U is its useful life, which usually is set at 40 years. Having defined the main variables, it is possible to write the profit function $\pi_{(t)}$ as follows:

$$\pi_{(t)} = \left\{ a + bK_{I(t)}^{\alpha}L_{(t)}^{\beta} + c[C_A + (K_{I(t)} - K_{t-1})] \right\} K_{I(t)}^{\alpha}L_{(t)}^{\beta} - C_A - K_{I(t)} + K_{I(t-1)}.$$

(9)

Under monopoly, entrepreneurial profit is maximised when marginal revenues equal marginal costs. Specifically, the first-order condition is met if the derivative of profits with respect to the stock of investment at time t is zero (i.e., $\frac{\partial \pi_t}{\partial S_{I(t)}} = 0$). We take for granted the second-order condition (downward concavity of the total profits function) [34]. We can therefore write:

$$\left(\beta b K_{I(t)}^{(\alpha-1)}L_{(t)}^{\beta} + c \right)K_{I(t)}^{\alpha}L_{(t)}^{\beta} + \left\{ a + bK_{I(t)}^{\alpha}L_{(t)}^{\beta} + cC_A + cK_{I(t)} - cK_{t-1} \right\}\beta K_{I(t)}^{(\alpha-1)}L_{(t)}^{\beta} - 1 = 0 \quad (10)$$

from which we obtain the objective function to be maximised:

$$2\beta b L_{(t)}^{\beta}K_{I(t)}^{2(\alpha-1)} + (1+\beta)cL_{(t)}^{\beta}K_{I(t)}^{(\alpha)} + (a + cC_A - cK_{t-1})\beta b L_{(t)}^{\beta}K_{I(t)}^{(\alpha-1)} - 1 = 0.$$

(11)

Finally, by posing:

$$\begin{cases} 2\beta b L_{(t)}^{\beta} = A \\ (1+\beta)cL_{(t)}^{\beta} = B \\ (a + cC_A - cK_{t-1})\beta b L_{(t)}^{\beta} = C \end{cases},$$

(12)

we obtain:

$$AK_{I(t)}^{2(\alpha-1)} + BK_{I(t)}^{(\alpha)} + CK_{I(t)}^{(\alpha-1)} - 1 = 0.$$

(13)

Equation (13), which is of degree $(\alpha - 1)$, can be easily solved using the Excel solver for each $t_0 \le t \le t_f$. In solving Eq. (13), since the average tariff increases as the investment increases, the following constraint must be introduced: the tariff $p(t)$ cannot exceed a maximum value p_{MAX} set by the standard. Specifically, this threshold was set at 4.80 €/m³ (national average value of the third-class excess tariff including a representative share of fixed costs [21]). It is thus possible to obtain $K_{I(t)}$*, i.e., the optimal stock of investment that should be accumulated at time t to maximise the entrepreneurial profit. The optimal investment at time t can be calculated as follows:

$$I_t^* = K_{I(t)}^* - K_{I(t-1)}.$$

(14)

Finally, the maximum achievable profit at time t is obtained from the following equation:

$$\pi_{MAX(t)} = \left\{ a + bK_{I(t)}^{*\alpha}L_{(t)}^{\beta} + c[C_A + (K_{I(t)}^* - K_{I(t-1)})] \right\} K_{I(t)}^{*\alpha}L_{(t)}^{\beta} - C_A - K_{I(t)}^* + K_{I(t-1)} \quad (15)$$

In the next section, the model is applied to a manager of the Integrated Water Service in the Campania region (Italy) with the aim of estimating the annual investment that would have allowed him in each of the ten years of the reference time horizon (2010–2019) to maximise entrepreneurial profit.

4 Application and Results

The managing body selected for the case study offers a plurality of services. In addition to services related to the management of the public aqueduct (collection, adduction, and distribution of water for domestic, commercial, and industrial use), it also offers non-water services, such as gas distribution, maintenance of public green spaces and, ordinary and extraordinary maintenance of roads. Sewerage and purification services, which are further characteristic activities of the Integrated Water Service, are instead offered in the municipality by two other companies. The aqueduct service covers the entire municipal territory, serving a population of approximately 12,000 inhabitants and 5,500 users. The aim of the company is to manage the aqueduct service as well as the construction of the related plants and their consequent maintenance in the municipality where it is managed. The tariffs for the sewerage and purification services are collected by the manager of the aqueduct service, who then distributes them among the other managers. The financial sustainability model was applied using as variables the financial statement data for the last ten years of management available (financial years 2010 to 2019), i.e., published by the Chamber of Commerce, Industry, Crafts and Agriculture.

Since we are interested in analysing only the profits related to the aqueduct service, the balance sheet items were reclassified by compartments (aqueduct, sewerage, purification, other water activities, miscellaneous activities) according to the scheme proposed by AEEGSI (now ARERA) with Resolution 137/2016/R/com [35]. For example, those revenues attributable to the collection of sewerage and purification service tariffs that have not yet been credited to other managing bodies in the year of reference have been subtracted from the value of production. Similarly, the financial statements were purged of revenues and costs relating to gas distribution activities and the maintenance of roads and public parks. In the case of operational functions and activities shared between several different compartments, the individual revenue or cost item has been broken down through a driver as suggested by the standard. Table 1 shows the balance sheet data of the aqueduct sector and the other economic-management data necessary for the application of the model. For each year t, the average water tariff was obtained from (3), while the investment stock was estimated by applying (7) and (8).

Parameters a, b and c were estimated using multiple linear regression (R multiple 0.876, R^2 0.732, R^2 corrected 0.542, standard error 0.014). The values obtained are $a = 0.9389474385$, $b = 0.0000000271$ and $c = 0.0000002999$. Having calculated the natural logarithms of $q_{(t)}$, $K_{I(t)}$ and $L_{(t)}$, it was possible to estimate the α and β constants (shown in Table 2) of the Cobb-Douglas function for each t from (5).

Using the solver function it is possible to estimate the value of $K_{I(t)}$ that makes the objective function (13) converge to zero for each t. Applying (14) and (15) we obtain the optimal investment $I_{(t)}$ and the maximum feasible tariff π_{MAX} (see Table 3).

The profits obtained can be further increased by subtracting the cost of purchased wholesale water. In fact, in the real scenario, the resource withdrawn at source net of water losses did not meet the demand for any of the years considered. For each t, the quantity demanded q (volumes of water sold to users) is equal to the volumes withdrawn (w_w) minus the water losses (w_l) plus the volumes purchased (w_p). Water losses (w_l) are equal to the difference between the volumes withdrawn (w_w) and the volumes distributed to users (w_d). In ten years, these losses amounted to about 45% of the volumes withdrawn,

Table 1. Data required for the application of the financial sustainability model.

Years	2010	2011	2012	2013	2014	2015	2016	2017	2018	2019
q (m³)	947,154	961,157	878,672	903,895	1,102,665	1,138,847	1,147,958	1,068,113	1,108,036	1,088,074
p (€/m³)	1.55	1.12	1.10	1.08	1.37	1.41	1.25	1.40	1.31	1.33
R (€)	1,469,821	1,072,524	962,930	975,564	1,506,094	1,609,456	1,438,085	1,494,373	1,452,822	1,442,152
CT (€)	971,947	704,656	773,741	660,010	1,111,738	1,111,738	1,319,984	1,398,322	1,361,337	1,393,245
π (€)	497,874	367,869	189,189	315,554	394,356	497,718	118,101	96,051	91,484	48,907
Ca (€)	919,026	684,115	747,463	528,071	1,014,330	1,018,580	1,259,690	1,313,878	1,269,694	1,340,686
I (€)	52,921	20,540	26,278	31,939	97,408	93,158	60,294	84,444	91,643	52,559
L (cad)	15	15	15	15	13	12	12	12	12	12
K_I (€)	1,052,921	1,072,138	1,096,580	1,126,025	1,220,141	1,307,572	1,359,810	1,434,691	1,514,659	1,553,252

Table 2. Estimation of the α and β constants of the Cobb-Douglas function.

dati	2010	2011	2012	2013	2014	2015	2016	2017	2018	2019
α	0.89344	0.89331	0.88350	0.88394	0.90155	0.90239	0.90004	0.88975	0.88876	0.88532
β	0.50656	0.50669	0.51650	0.51606	0.49845	0.49761	0.49996	0.51025	0.51124	0.51468

Table 3. Results of the optimisation problem.

t_i (years)	K_I* (€)	I* (€)	q* (m^3)	C_T* (€)	p* (€/m^3)	R* (€)	π_{MAX} (€)
2010	1,967,844	967,844	1,656,056	1,886,870	1.85	3,056,073	1,169,203
2011	2,818,240	850,396	2,278,980	2,449,434	1.67	3,816,784	1,367,350
2012	3,532,622	2,460,484	2,469,990	3,207,947	1.87	4,616,278	1,408,331
2013	3,547,787	2,451,208	2,492,756	3,079,278	1.85	4,606,106	1,526,828
2014	2,090,327	964,301	1,791,552	1,978,632	1.64	2,946,185	967,553
2015	2,080,817	860,676	1,731,967	1,879,256	1.66	2,874,125	994,870
2016	2,547,074	1,239,502	2,019,502	2,499,193	1.63	3,291,694	792,501
2017	2,986,017	1,626,208	2,050,474	2,940,085	1.89	3,871,330	931,245
2018	3,266,615	1,831,924	2,193,854	3,101,619	1.86	4,085,923	984,304
2019	3,519,823	2,005,164	2,244,883	3,345,850	1.94	4,360,190	1,014,340
average	2,835,717	1,525,771	2,093,001	2,636,816	2	3,752,469	1,115,653

in line with the average regional figure for 2015 (middle year of the time horizon) [36]. Similar percentages can be found for other Campania utilities of a similar size to the one under study.

It is found that about 15% of the water sold to users was purchased by the manager at wholesale at a unit price (p_p) of €/m^3 0.2697. The cost of the wholesale purchased water (Cw) for each t is equal to the product of p_p and w_p. Table 4 shows the volumetric data and the cost of wholesale purchased water for the real scenario. For this scenario, the available data show that with an average annual investment of €61,118, water losses are reduced by an average of 1.24% per year. Proportionally, the optimal average annual investment of €1,617,263 (see Table 3) should allow the operator to reduce leakage by an average of 32.78% per year.

Furthermore, if we assume a direct proportionality relationship between volumes demanded by users (q) and volumes withdrawn at source (w_w), then known q* it is easy to obtain the withdrawn volumes for the optimal scenario (w_{w*}). From these it is possible to estimate all other volumes for the optimal scenario (see Table 5).

Table 4. Volumetric data and cost of water purchased in bulk: real scenario.

Years	2010	2011	2012	2013	2014	2015	2016	2017	2018	2019
w_w (€/m³)	1,373,373	1,393,678	1,274,074	1,310,648	1,598,864	1,651,328	1,664,539	1,548,764	1,606,651	1,577,708
w_d (€/m³)	805,081	816,983	746,871	768,311	937,265	968,020	975,764	907,896	941,830	924,863
w_l (€/m³)	568,292	576,694	527,203	542,337	661,599	683,308	688,775	640,868	664,821	652,845
w_p (€/m³)	142,073	144,174	131,801	135,584	165,400	170,827	172,194	160,217	166,205	163,211
q (€/m³)	947,154	961,157	878,672	903,895	1,102,665	1,138,847	1,147,958	1,068,113	1,108,036	1,088,074
C_w (€)	38,317	38,884	35,547	36,567	44,608	46,072	46,441	43,211	44,826	44,018

Table 5. Volumetric data and cost of water purchased in bulk: optimal scenario.

Years	2010	2011	2012	2013	2014	2015	2016	2017	2018	2019
w_w* (€/m³)	2,401,281	3,304,521	3,581,485	3,614,497	2,597,751	2,511,353	2,928,277	2,973,187	3,181,089	3,255,081
w_d* (€/m³)	1,733,387	2,385,400	2,585,329	2,609,159	1,875,211	1,812,844	2,113,805	2,146,223	2,296,299	2,349,711
w_l* (€/m³)	667,894	919,121	996,156	1,005,338	722,540	698,509	814,473	826,964	884,790	905,370
w_p* (€/m³)	−77,332	1−06,420	−115,339	−116,402	−83,659	−80,876	−94,303	−95,749	−102,445	−104,828
q* (€/m³)	1,656,056	2,278,980	2,469,990	2,492,756	1,791,552	1,731,967	2,019,502	2,050,474	2,193,854	2,244,883
C_w* (€)	−20,856	−28,701	−31,107	−31,394	−22,563	−21,812	−25,434	−25,824	−27,629	−28,272

For each year, the optimal investment generates an increase in demand, as users have a better perception of the service. Together with demand, the volumes of water extracted at the source increase proportionally. Although water losses also increase, they increase less than proportionally to demand, due to improvements in the water systems. As a result, the volumes supplied to users exceed demand. Rather than buying wholesale water, the operator could sell excess water to further increase revenues or, alternatively, reduce the water supply by reducing the cost of extracting the resource. If we add to C_A (production cost net of investment I^*) the cost Cw^* (which is negative), we get a new adjusted production cost (C_{R*}) which if inserted in (15) returns an even higher maximum profit (see Table 6).

Table 6. Adjusted results of the optimization problem (without wholesale purchase).

t_i (years)	K_I^* (€)	I^* (€)	q^*_{ADJ} (m^3)	C_{T}^* ADJ (€)	p^* ADJ (€/m^3)	R^* ADJ (€)	$\pi_{MAX, ADJ}$ (€)
2010	1,967,844	967,844	1,656,056	1,866,014	1.84	3,045,716	1,179,703
2011	2,818,240	850,396	2,278,980	2,420,733	1.67	3,797,170	1,376,438
2012	3,532,622	2,460,484	2,469,990	3,176,840	1.86	4,593,238	1,416,398
2013	3,547,787	2,451,208	2,492,756	3,047,885	1.84	4,582,640	1,534,756
2014	2,090,327	964,301	1,791,552	1,956,069	1.64	2,934,064	977,995
2015	2,080,817	860,676	1,731,967	1,857,443	1.65	2,862,797	1,005,354
2016	2,547,074	1,239,502	2,019,502	2,473,759	1.62	3,276,292	802,533
2017	2,986,017	1,626,208	2,050,474	2,914,262	1.88	3,855,452	941,190
2018	3,266,615	1,831,924	2,193,854	3,073,989	1.85	4,067,747	993,758
2019	3,519,823	2,005,164	2,244,883	3,317,578	1.93	4,341,159	1,023,581
average	2,835,717	1,525,771	2,093,002	2,610,457	2	3,735,628	1,125,171

The results obtained will be commented on in the next section.

5 Discussion

To understand the advantages obtained by increasing the investments aimed at reducing water losses by the right amount, it is necessary to compare the real investment and profit levels with the optimal ones. Figure 1 shows the evolution of I and I^* over time.

In contrast to the investments actually made by the manager, which follow an almost linear trend and remain more or less constant over time, the optimal investments, in addition to being significantly higher, show a cyclical pattern. Figure 2 shows the time trend of π and π_{MAX}.

The maximum profits are parallel to those actually pursued only in some years, namely between 2012 and 2013 and then between 2014 and 2016. For the other years π_{MAX} and π have a mirror-image trend.

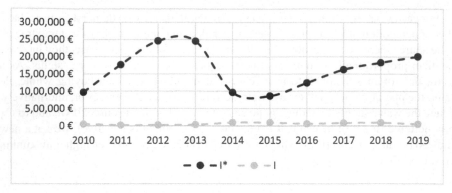

Fig. 1. Evolution of I and I* over time.

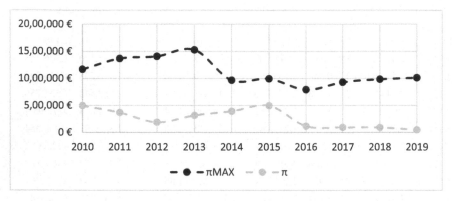

Fig. 2. Evolution of π e π_{MAX} over the time.

6 Conclusions

In Italy, Europe's leading country in terms of water withdrawals for drinking, there is a wide gap between the water resources fed into the distribution networks and those supplied to users. This is especially true in the South, where water losses are around 46% [37]. In addition to the damage inflicted on the environment, water losses are also a problem for water utilities. Although the complete elimination of leakages is impossible, the objective of any efficient operator is to limit losses of the distribution network. This has several benefits, including reducing production and distribution costs, limiting the volume of water purchased in bulk and improving the perception of the service by users. On the latter point, the impact that the losses reduction has on the users can affect water tariffs. This effect is crucial for those services under management concession that use tariff leverage, by foregoing part of the profit, to self-finance investments aimed at reducing water losses [31]. It is, therefore, necessary to assess the limits and benefits of such investments using appropriate models.

The aim of this work is to define an econometric model that allows water utilities to establish the optimal budget to be used to finance the maintenance work required to reduce water losses. The model identifies the maximum level of profit that the operator can pursue by investing the right amount of money. A key parameter is a coefficient that measures the rate of change of the investment return (α), which incorporates those intangible aspects that affect productivity, such as user perception of the service. A similar function is performed by the (a) coefficient in the price equation. According to this equation, the average tariff depends on financial costs (capital and operating costs), environmental costs and resource costs. In addition, it is possible to include in the model the profit effects generated by the decrease in wholesale water purchase costs following maintenance interventions.

References

1. Sparano, E.: Obiettivo acqua. Educazione, etica e valori alla base dello sviluppo sostenibile. Culture e Studi del Sociale **5**(1), 101–118 (2020)
2. RINNOVABILI.IT   Homepage.   https://www.rinnovabili.it/ambiente/scarsita-acqua-pro blema-grave-333/. Accessed 03 July 2021
3. Piotti, A., Ronco, G.: Alcune considerazioni sulla distribuzione e sul consumo dell'acqua potabile. L'ACQUA - Rivista bimestrale dell'Associazione Idrotecnica Italiana **1** (2007)
4. Dono, G., Marongiu, S., Severini, S., Sistu, G., Strazzera, E.: Studio sulla gestione sostenibile delle risorse idriche: analisi dei modelli di consumo per usi irrigui e civili. ENEA, Collana Desertificazione – Progetto RIADE (2008)
5. Vitiello, M.: Il sistema idrico italiano: un confronto con i principali Paesi europei. Tesi di Laurea in Economia e gestione dei servizi di pubblica utilità, Luiss Guido Carli, relatore Simona D'Amico, p. 49 (2020)
6. Censis: Quarantottesimo rapporto sulla situazione sociale del Paese. Franco Angeli (2014)
7. González-Méndez, M., Olaya, C., Fasolino, I., Grimaldi, M., Obregón, N.: Agent-based modeling for urban development planning based on human needs. Conceptual Basis Model Formulation. Land Use Policy **101**, 105110 (2021). https://doi.org/10.1016/j.landusepol.2020. 105110
8. Grimaldi, M., Sebillo, M., Vitiello, G., Pellecchia, V.: Planning and managing the integrated water system: a spatial decision support system to analyze the infrastructure performances. Sustainability **12**(16), 6432 (2020). https://doi.org/10.3390/su12166432
9. Sebillo, M., Vitiello, G., Grimaldi, M., De Piano, A.: A citizen-centric approach for the improvement of territorial services management. ISPRS Int. J. Geo Inf. **9**(4), 223 (2020). https://doi.org/10.3390/ijgi9040223
10. ISTAT: Le statistiche dell'Istat sull'acqua - anni 2018–2019 (2020)
11. Macchiaroli, M., Pellecchia, V., D'Alpaos, C.: Urban water management in Italy: an innovative model for the selection of water service infrastructures. WSEAS Trans. Environ. Dev. **15**, 463–477 (2019)
12. LA REPUBBLICA Homepage. https://www.repubblica.it/economia/2019/11/09/news/ acqua_rubinetto_ambrosetti-240292743/. Accessed 14 August 2020
13. Cauduro, A.: Il ruolo pubblico nella determinazione della tariffa del servizio idrico integrato. Politica del diritto **2**, 229–258 (2020)
14. Muraro G.: La gestione del servizio idrico integrato in Italia, tra vincoli europei e scelte nazionali. Mercato Concorrenza Regole **2** (2003)
15. Nesticò, A., Somma, P.: Comparative analysis of multi-criteria methods for the enhancement of historical buildings. Sustainability **11**(17), 4526 (2019). https://doi.org/10.3390/su1117 4526

16. Nesticò, A., Maselli, G.: Declining discount rate estimate in the long-term economic evaluation of environmental projects. J. Environ. Acc. Manag. **8**(1), 93-110 (2020). https://doi.org/10.5890/JEAM.2020.03.007

17. De Mare, G., Granata, M.F., Forte, F.: Investing in Sports Facilities: The Italian Situation Toward an Olympic Perspective. In: Gervasi, O., et al. (eds.) ICCSA 2015. LNCS, vol. 9157, pp. 77–87. Springer, Cham (2015). https://doi.org/10.1007/978-3-319-21470-2_6

18. Benintendi, R., De Mare, G.: Upgrade the ALARP model as a holistic approach to project risk and decision management. Hydrocarb. Process. **2017**(9), 75–82 (2017)

19. De Mare, G., Di Piazza, F.: The role of public-private partnerships in school building projects. In: Gervasi, O., et al. (eds.) ICCSA 2015. LNCS, vol. 9156, pp. 624–634. Springer, Cham (2015). https://doi.org/10.1007/978-3-319-21407-8_44

20. Castoldi, F.: Il servizio idrico nazionale: problematiche attuali e prospettive di riforma. PhD Thesis, University of Milan - Bicocca, Milan, Italy (2010)

21. Autorità di Regolazione per Energia Reti e Ambiente: Testo Integrato Corrispettivi Servizi Idrici (TICSI), deliberazione 665/2017/R/idr del 28 settembre 2017, Allegato A (2017). https://www.arera.it/it/docs/17/665-17.htm

22. Salvo, F., Morano, P., De Ruggiero, M., Tajani, F.: Environmental health valuation through real estate prices. In: Bevilacqua, C., Calabrò, F., Della Spina, L. (eds.) NMP 2020. SIST, vol. 178, pp. 768–778. Springer, Cham (2021). https://doi.org/10.1007/978-3-030-48279-4_72

23. Salvo, F., Zupi, M., De Ruggiero, M.: Land consumption and urban regeneration. evaluation principles and choice criteria. In: Calabrò, F., Della Spina, L., Bevilacqua, C. (eds.) ISHT 2018. SIST, vol. 100, pp. 582–589. Springer, Cham (2019). https://doi.org/10.1007/978-3-319-92099-3_65

24. Boggia, A, Rocchi, L.: Applicazione del "costo pieno" dell'acqua (Direttiva 2000/60/CE) in un'azienda dell'alto Tevere umbro. In: Casini, L., Gallerani, V. (eds.) Acqua, agricoltura e ambiente nei nuovi scenari di politica comunitaria, Franco Angeli, Milan, Italy (2008)

25. Sbandati, A.: Servizi ecosistemici, servizio idrico integrato e componenti tariffarie: l'opportunità dei Payments for Ecosystem Services (2020). http://hdl.handle.net/20.500.12010/17532. Accessed 27 Mar 2021

26. Dolores, L., Macchiaroli, M., De Mare, G.: A dynamic model for the financial sustainability of the restoration sponsorship. Sustainability **12**(4), 1694 (2020). https://doi.org/10.3390/su12041694

27. Dolores, L., Macchiaroli, M., De Mare, G.: Sponsorship's financial sustainability for cultural conservation and enhancement strategies: an innovative model for sponsees and sponsors. Sustainability **13**(16), 9070 (2021). https://doi.org/10.3390/su13169070

28. Dolores, L., Macchiaroli, M., De Mare, G.: A model for defining sponsorship fees in public-private bargaining for the rehabilitation of historical-architectural heritage. In: Calabrò, F., Della Spina, L., Bevilacqua, C. (eds.) ISHT 2018. SIST, vol. 101, pp. 484–492. Springer, Cham (2019). https://doi.org/10.1007/978-3-319-92102-0_51

29. Cobb, C.W., Douglas, P.H.: A theory of production. Am. Econ. Rev. **18**, 139–165 (1928). https://www.jstor.org/stable/1811556

30. Bianco, G., Cecati, P.: Costi di produzione ed erogazione di acqua potabile. Una proposta di analisi dell'efficienza. Economia pubblica (1–2), 79–116 (2008)

31. Bazzurro, N., Mazzola, M.: Aspetti economici nelle strategie di gestione delle perdite idriche. In: Brunone, B., Ferrante, M., Meniconi, S., (eds.) Ricerca e controllo delle perdite nelle reti di condotte, pp. 3–44. Città Studi Edizioni, Turin, Italy (2008)

32. Nesticò, A., De Mare, G., Frusciante, B., Dolores, L.: Construction costs estimate for civil works. a model for the analysis during the preliminary stage of the project. In: Gervasi, O., et al. (eds.) ICCSA 2017. LNCS, vol. 10408, pp. 89–105. Springer, Cham (2017). https://doi.org/10.1007/978-3-319-62404-4_7

33. De Mare, G., Nesticò, A., Macchiaroli, M., Dolores, L.: Market prices and institutional values. In: Gervasi, O., et al. (eds.) ICCSA 2017. LNCS, vol. 10409, pp. 430–440. Springer, Cham (2017). https://doi.org/10.1007/978-3-319-62407-5_30

34. Varian, H.R.: Microeconomia. 7th edn. Libreria Editrice Cafoscarina, Venezia, Italy (2011). ISBN 9788875433079

35. Autorità per l'Energia Elettrica, il Gas e il Sistema Idrico: Testo integrato delle disposizioni dell'AEEGSI in merito agli obblighi di separazione Contabile (TIUC), deliberazione 2016137/2016/R/com del 24 marzo 2016, Allegato A (2016). https://www.arera.it/it/docs/16/137-16.htm

36. Istituto Nazionale di Statistica (ISTAT): le statistiche dell'istat sull'acqua - anni 2018–2020. https://www.istat.it/it/archivio/255596#:~:text=Nel%202018%2C%20non%20sono%20collegati,abbastanza%20soddisfatta%20del%20servizio%20idrico. Accessed 07 Mar 2021

37. Legambiente: Acqua e ambiente: criticità e opportunità per migliorarne la gestione in Italia. https://www.legambiente.it/wp-content/uploads/2021/03/Acque-in-rete_dossier-2021.pdf. Accessed 07 Mar 2021

How Substrate and Drainage Layer Materials Affect the Hydrological Performance of Green Roofs: CHEMFLO-2000 Numerical Investigation

Roberta D'Ambrosio[1]([✉]), Mirka Mobilia[1], Irandyk Fanilevich Khamidullin[2], Antonia Longobardi[1], and Alexey Nikolaevich Elizaryev[2]

[1] Department of Civil Engineering, University of Salerno, Via Giovanni Paolo II, Fisciano, 132 84084 Salerno, Italy
robdambrosio@unisa.it
[2] Ufa State Aviation Technical University, st. Karl Marx, 12, 450077 Ufa, Republic of Bashkortostan, Russia

Abstract. Green Roofs (GRs) are a promising solution for the reduction of flooding risk in urban areas. Reproducing on the traditional roofs the drainage pattern typical of natural soils, these infrastructures are able to mitigate the stormwater discharged into sewers. Their retention capacity depends on both climate and design variables, among which the substrate and drainage materials seem to play a fundamental role in the enhancement of the efficiency of the roof. This research aimed at analyzing the hydrological behavior of five 15-cm GRs modules, characterized by different substrate and drainage layers soil composition and thickness, using CHEMFLO-2000. Specifically, among the substrate materials particular attention was paid to the biochar, a fertilizer known for its ability to filter pollutant, to assess its effect on the green roof retention capacity. Simulations under different rainfall inputs were carried out to compare the performance of each system.

Keywords: Green Roofs · Technological properties · Retention capacity

1 Introduction

Worldwide, integrated approaches involving Sustainable Drainage Systems (SuDS) are increasingly spreading to support traditional infrastructures in the urban flooding management [1]. Among the types of SuDS, green roofs (GRs) allows making the best use of the roofs waterproof surface, reproducing the drainage pattern typical of natural soil and reducing stormwater runoff [2–4]. It is widely known that technological features affect the performance of these systems. Specifically, researchers worldwide agree in recognizing the influence of the GR substrate and drainage materials on the ability of the roof to retain and detain stormwater, consequently reducing peak flows and discharged volumes [5, 6]. However, the variety of soils that make up green roofs with their different characteristics, thickness and disposal may lead to a great variety of findings.

© Springer Nature Switzerland AG 2021
O. Gervasi et al. (Eds.): ICCSA 2021, LNCS 12956, pp. 254–263, 2021.
https://doi.org/10.1007/978-3-030-87010-2_17

Hence, this study aims at investigating the hydrological performance of five GRs stratigraphic models of 15-cm height, characterized by different substrate and drainage layers soil composition and thickness. In particular, the analyses focused on the assessment of the biochar, a carbonaceous material commonly used as fertilizer and renowned for its ability to filter pollutants and improving the quality of stormwater discharged [7, 8]. The purpose is to understand weather this material, if implemented in GRs, also manages achieving significant results in term of reduction of stormwater quantity as stated by several studies [9–11]. To this end, CHEMFLO-2000 simulations helped quantify the hydrological response of the mentioned GR configurations, two of which involving biochar, under four rainfall inputs, characterized by different durations and designed according to the mean precipitation extremes registered at the University of Salerno campus, Italy, where a GR experimental site was set up in 2017. Simulation results were compared in terms of retention capacity.

2   Materials and Methods

2.1   Case Study

The hydrological response of five GR types to four different precipitation inputs was compared in the present study. In general, a green roof is made up of several overlapping layers. In the basic configuration, the system consists of four components including, from the top to the bottom, a vegetation layer, a substrate to support plant growth, a non-woven filter fabric that prevent substrate dropping into the underlying drainage layer and a drainage/storage layer with the function of detaining rainwater (Fig. 1).

PLANTS

GROWING MEDIUM

FILTER CLOTH

DRAINAGE LAYER

Fig. 1. The composition of a GR system

The five GR configurations selected in the present study differ in terms of composition and depth of the substrate and storage layers (Fig. 2) even if, in each case, the total thickness of the roof is set on 15 cm. In details, they consist of:

1) 10 cm depth loam substrate with an underlying 5-cm depth expanded clay storage layer (GR1);
2) 10 cm depth loam substrate with an underlying 5-cm depth sand storage layer (GR2);
3) 15-cm depth loam substrate (GR3);
4) 5 cm depth loam and 5-cm depth biochar substrate with an underlying 5 cm depth expanded clay storage layer (GR4);

5) 7 cm depth loam and 3-cm depth biochar substrate with an underlying 5 cm depth expanded clay storage layer (GR5);

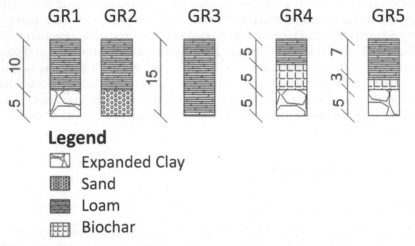

Legend

⊠ Expanded Clay

▒ Sand

▬ Loam

⊞ Biochar

Fig. 2. Composition and depth of the layers of the five GR systems. In the figure, the metric unit of length is centimetre.

In this study, the vegetation, whose role is not so decisive during the precipitation event as during the inter-storm period, was not examined.

2.2 Description of CHEMFLO-2000, Initial Setting and Input Data

Among the several software used to model the behavior of the GRs [12, 13], CHEMFLO-2000 was chosen in the present work to simulate the hydrological response of the five different GR configurations (Fig. 2) to several rainfall events. CHEMFLO-2000 [14] is an interactive software for simulating water and chemical movement in unsaturated soils developed by the Department of Plant and Soil Sciences of the Oklahoma State University. The governing equation used in this software to describe the one-dimensional water movement in the soils is the partial differential equation proposed by Richards in 1931 [15] that can be expressed as:

$$\frac{\partial \theta}{\partial t} = \frac{\partial}{\partial x}\left[K(h)\left(\frac{\partial h}{\partial x} - \sin(A)\right)\right] \tag{1}$$

Where $\theta = \theta(h)$ is the volumetric water content, $h = h(x, t)$ is the matric potential, x is the position coordinate parallel to the direction of the flow; t is the time; $\sin(A)$ is the sine of the angle A between the direction of flow and the horizontal direction; $K(h)$ is the hydraulic conductivity of the soil at matric potential h; and C (h) is the specific water capacity. In this study, to simulate the vertical flow with x increasing in the downward direction an angle A equal to 90° was chosen.

Among the different possibilities given by the model, van Genuchten [16] mathematical equations were chosen to describe soil water content θ(h) and hydraulic conductivity K(h):

$$\theta(h) = \begin{cases} \frac{\theta_s - \theta_r}{(1+(\alpha|h|)^n)^m} + \theta_r & if h < 0 \ and \ m = 1 - 1/n \\ \theta_s & if \ h \geq 0 \end{cases} \tag{2}$$

$$K(h) = \begin{cases} \frac{\left\{1-(-\alpha h)^{n-1}[1+(-\alpha h)^n]^{-m}\right\}^2}{[1+(-\alpha h)^n]^{m/2}} & if h < 0 \ and \ m = 1 - 1/n \\ K_s & if \ h \geq 0 \end{cases} \tag{3}$$

Where θ_r [v/v] is the residual water content, θ_s [v/v] is the saturated water content, K_s [cm/h] is the saturated hydraulic conductivity and α [1/cm] and n [-] are both empirical constant representative respectively the inverse of the air-entry suction and the pore-size distribution.

In this modeling study, the upper boundary condition at the beginning of the simulation was controlled by the rainfall rate (cm/h). Subsequently, in order to study the water movement since the end of the precipitation, a new condition was established with a constant flux density equal to zero. A free-drainage was chosen to describe the bottom boundary conditions. Initial values of uniform volumetric water content (cm³/cm³) (SWC) of 0.10, 0.15 and 0.25 were set in each model to test the effect of this variable on overall performance of the GR configurations. These values, never below residual water content θ_r [v/v] and never exceeding saturated water content θ_s [v/v], were selected among the soil moisture contents in-between the wilting point and the field capacity of the substrate layer, thus simulating the best condition for plant growth.

The van Genuchten functions parameters (Table 1) for modeling loam and sand used in this study are those suggested by Carsel and Parrish (1988) [17] and they are the default parameters of CHEMFLO-2000 for van Genuchten functions. The parameters for the expanded clay and Biochar were respectively provided by [18] and [19].

Table 1. The used van Genuchten model parameters

Soil name	θr	θs	A	n	Ks
	[-]	[-]	[1/mm]	[-]	[mm/h]
Biochar	0.07	0.66	0.0124	1.82	444.6
Expanded clay	0.045	0.43	0.0145	2.68	6.3
Loam	0.078	0.43	0.0036	1.56	10.4
Sand	0.045	0.43	0.0145	2.68	297

For each GR configuration, the model was run using four precipitation inputs different for duration, intensity and cumulative rainfall. The durations selected are representative of the rainfall events registered at the University of Salerno campus, Italy, where an experimental GR was set up in 2017, having the same soil layer composition as the GR1 of the current study. This site is equipped with a meteorological station. From a statistical analysis of precipitation records observed since 2017, rainfall duration according to the maximum, the mode, the mean and median durations were taken into account (respectively 76 h, 1 h, 10 h and 6 h). Cumulate rainfalls corresponding to the selected durations are reported in Table 2. Intensity-duration-frequency curves characteristics of Fisciano in Southern Italy were used to estimate intensities and rainfall amounts associated to the mentioned durations (Table 2).

Table 2. Rainfall characteristics

	R1	R2	R3	R4
Duration (h)	1	6	10	76
Cumulate rainfall (mm)	26.50	47.78	56.52	110.2

2.3   Retention Capacity of the GR Configurations

The output file of each of the 60 simulations (5 configuration under 4 rainfall scenarios and under 3 Initial Soil Water Contents) was analysed specifically investigating the cumulative flux (runoff) at x = 15 cm at 24 h from the rainfall end. For each modelled GR configuration, the hydrological performance in term of retention capacity (RC) was then computed as follows [20]:

$$1 - C^* = RC \tag{4}$$

Where C^* is the discharge coefficient, computed as the ratio between the cumulative observed runoff depth and the cumulative observed rainfall depth at the event scale.

3   Results and Discussions

Overall, under 10% initial soil water content (SWC), retention capacity assessment confirm reasonably good performances of all the GRs configurations, achieving an average value of 64.07%. Values range from a minimum of 23.28%, reached in GR2 under the highest intensity rainfall (26.50 mm/h), to a maximum of 99.83%, reached in GR3 under the lowest intensity rainfall (1.45 mm/h). The good efficiency of the modelled grs stratigraphic columns is mainly due to the low initial soil moisture content, close to the wilting point of the loam and set in CHEMFLO-2000 equal to 10%. Looking at Table 3 it is possible to observe that GR4 and GR5, both characterized by the presence of biochar, reached the highest retention performances (69.15 and 66.90% on average respectively). These results proved the potential of this fertilizer, already experienced for improving water quality, in the reduction of stormwater volumes. GR2, characterized by 10-cm loam soil layer and 5-cm sand drainage layer, showed the worst retention performance, still achieving an average retention performance of 55.05%. Comparing this result with those reached by GR1 (65.29% on average), which differ from the previous one just for the drainage material (clay), it is clear that the drainage layer characteristics play a fundamental role in the retention performance of the roof, as stated by several authors [21]. In particular, as it can be observed from Table 1, expanded clay (parameterized according to literature) and sand just differ for k_s, saturated conductivity, substantially lower in the first drainage material.

Table 3. RC (%) of different GRs configurations under 10% soil moisture content

		R1	R2	R3	R4	Mean
GR 1	10loam + 5clay	99.82	70.73	59.79	30.83	65.29
GR 2	10loam + 5sand	97.99	53.24	45.70	23.28	55.05
GR 3	15loam	99.83	67.59	58.90	29.48	63.95
GR 4	5loam + 5biochar + 5clay	99.82	78.58	65.49	32.70	69.15
GR 5	7loam + 3biochar + 5clay	99.82	73.60	62.23	31.93	66.90
Mean		99.46	68.75	58.42	29.65	64.07

Moreover, the relation between Retention Capacity and rainfall amount was investigated (Fig. 3) to understand weather and to what extent rainfall severity could affect the behaviour of each of the observed GR configurations. Examining Fig. 3 it appears that the GRs retention capacities decrease as the rainfall amount increase. The regression analysis, in fact, found a negative linear relationship between the retention coefficients and the rainfall cumulative.

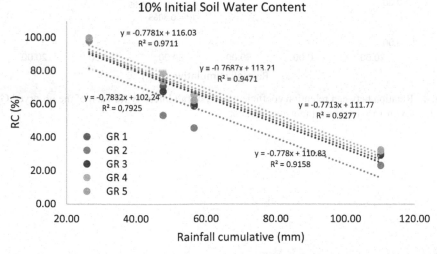

Fig. 3. Relation between retention coefficient and rainfall intensity for each of the observed GR modules with 10% initial soil moisture content

With the increase of the initial SWC to 15% and 25%, a decrease of the retention performance of the GR configurations can be observed with average values of 54.73% and 33.29% respectively. Even if the negative linear relationship between RC and rainfall cumulative still exists, a larger scattering of the values and consequently lower coefficients of determination can be pointed out (Fig. 4 and Fig. 5). Moreover, the assessment found GR2 much more sensitive than the other configurations to the initial SWC changes with an average RC decrease of 24.48% and 78.11% switching from 10% SWC to 15% and 25% respectively.

The analysis of the runoff delay, representative of the time at which the runoff starts, failed to achieve successful results. Specifically, even if GR2 appears characterized by the lowest delay time and so characterized by a faster stormwater runoff occurrence, no great differences between the configurations under varying rainfall inputs can be detected. The reason behind this can be ascribed to the limits of the software, whose numerical models assume a strictly one-dimensional water flow in the soil.

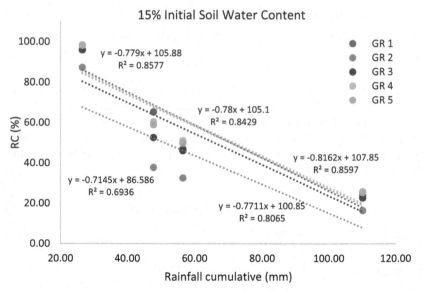

Fig. 4. Relation between retention coefficient and rainfall intensity for each of the observed GR modules with 15% initial soil moisture content

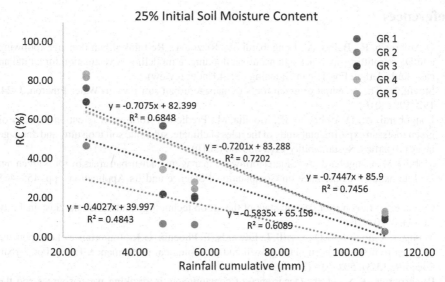

Fig. 5. Relation between retention coefficient and rainfall intensity for each of the observed GR modules with 25% initial soil moisture content

4   Conclusions

In this paper, the performance of five 15-cm GR modules different for substrate and drainage layer characteristics was investigated under varying rainfall inputs and initial SWC to understand how technological parameters and rainfall characteristics could affect their hydrological performance. Even if all the configurations achieved good performances (64.07% on average under 0.10 SWC), soil characteristics seem to play a fundamental role in the enhancement of GRs performance. Specifically substrate involving the fertilizer biochar reached the highest values of retention capacity (69.15 and 66.90% under 0.10 SWC) confirming that this material, already known for the enhancement of water quality, could be a valid solution also for the reduction of stormwater volumes. Moreover, drainage layers made by expanded clay are for sure preferable to those made by sand, exceeding of about the 10% their RC. In addition, the results of the modeling assessment showed that the total rainfall amount seem to affect GRs RC that decrease with the increase of precipitation amount.

The implementation of multi-dimensional models in the future analyses is essential for simulating a more realistic water movement in the soil. Moreover, the possible occurrence and effect of a capillary barrier between the substrate (finer material) and the drainage layer (coarse material) should also be investigated. Several studies borrowed from other scientific fields, in fact, demonstrated that when a capillary barrier effect acts, there is an inhibition of deep drainage and an increase in water storage [22].

Nonetheless, additional research supported by experimental studies is foreseen to confirm the model-based results obtained so far and to improve the hydrological performance investigation of the GRs.

References

1. D'Ambrosio, R., Balbo, A., Longobardi, A., Rizzo, A.: Re-think urban drainage following a SuDS retrofitting approach against urban flooding: a modelling investigation for an Italian case study. Urban For. Urban Greening (2014,Under review)
2. Stovin, V.: The potential of green roofs to manage urban stormwater. Water Environ. J. **24**, 192–199 (2010)
3. Longobardi, A., D'Ambrosio, R., Mobilia, M.: Predicting stormwater retention capacity of green roofs: an experimental study of the roles of climate, substrate soil moisture, and drainage layer properties. Sustainability **11**(24), 6956 (2019)
4. Mobilia, M., Longobardi, A.: Smart stormwater management in urban areas by roofs greening. In: International Conference on Computational Science and Its Applications, pp. 455–463 (2017)
5. Cascone, S.: Green roof design: state of the art on technology and materials. Sustainability **11**(11), 3020 (2019)
6. Young, T., Cameron, D.D., Sorrill, J., Edwards, T., Phoenix, G.K.: Importance of components of green roof substrate on plant growth and physiological performance. Urban For. Urban Greening **13**(3), 507–516 (2014)
7. Palansooriya, K.N., et al.: Occurrence of contaminants in drinking water sources and the potential of biochar for water quality improvement: a review. Crit. Rev. Environ. Sci. Technol. **50**(6), 549–611 (2019)
8. Blanco-Canqui, H.: Biochar and water quality. J. Environ. Qual. **48**(1), 2–15 (2019)
9. Kuoppamäki, K., Hagner, M., Lehvävirta, S., Setälä, H.: Biochar amendment in the green roof substrate affects runoff quality and quantity. Ecol. Eng. **88**, 1–9 (2016)
10. Qianqian, Z., Liping, M., Huiwei, W., Long, W.: Analysis of the effect of green roof substrate amended with biochar on water quality and quantity of rainfall runoff. Environ. Monit. Assess. **191**(5), 1–11 (2019). https://doi.org/10.1007/s10661-019-7466-4
11. Beck, D.A., Johnson, G.R., Spolek, G.A.: Amending green roof soil with biochar to affect runoff water quantity and quality. Environ. Pollut. **159**(8–9), 2111–2118 (2011)
12. Krasnogorskaya, N., Longobardi, A., Mobilia, M., Khasanova, L.F., Shchelchkova, A.I.: Hydrological modeling of green roofs runoff by Nash cascade model. Open Civil Eng. J. **13**(1) (2019)
13. Mobilia, M., Longobardi, A.: Event scale modeling of experimental green roofs runoff in a mediterranean environment. In: Frontiers in Water-Energy-Nexus–Nature-Based Solutions, Advanced Technologies and Best Practices for Environmental Sustainability, pp. 153–156 (2020)
14. Nofziger, D.L., Wu, J.: CHEMFLO-2000: Interactive Software for Simulating Water and Chemical Movement in Unsaturated Soils. U.S. Environmental Protection Agency, Washington (2003)
15. Richards, L.A.: Capillary conduction of liquids through porous mediums. J. Appl. Phys. **1**, 318–333 (1931)
16. Van Genuchten, M.T.: A closed-form equation for predicting the hydraulic conductivity of unsaturated soils. Soil Sci. Soc. Am. J. **44**, 892–898 (1980)
17. Carsel, R.F., Parrish, R.S.: Developing joint probability distributions of soil water characteristics. Water Resour. Res. **24**, 755–769 (1988)
18. Mobilia, M., Longobardi, A.: Impact of rainfall properties on the performance of hydrological models for green roofs simulation. Water Sci. Technol. **81**(7), 1375–1387 (2020)
19. Phillips, C.L., Meyer, K.M., Trippe, K.M.: Is biochar applied as surface mulch beneficial for grassland restoration? Geoderma **375**, 114457 (2020)

20. Mobilia, M., D'Ambrosio, R., Longobardi, A.: Climate, soil moisture and drainage layer properties impact on green roofs in a mediterranean environment. In: Naddeo, V., Balakrishnan, M., Choo, K.H. (eds.) Frontiers in Water-Energy-Nexus–Nature-Based Solutions, Advanced Technologies and Best Practices for Environmental Sustainability Advances in Science Technology and Innovation, pp. 169–171 (2020)
21. Baryla, A.M.: Role of drainage layer on green roofs in limiting the runoff of rainwater from urbanized areas. J. Water Land Dev. 12–18 (2019)
22. Reder, A., Pagano, L., Picarelli, L., Rianna, G.: The role of the lowermost boundary conditions in the hydrological response of shallow sloping covers. Landslides **14**(3), 861–873 (2016). https://doi.org/10.1007/s10346-016-0753-z

Rainfall Extraordinary Extreme Events (EEEs) Frequency and Magnitude Assessment: The EEE Occurred on 14th–15th October 2015 in Benevento Area (Southern Italy)

Anna Pelosi[1]([⊠]) [iD], Paolo Villani[1], and Giovanni Battista Chirico[2] [iD]

[1] University of Salerno, Via Giovanni Paolo II, 84084 Fisciano, SA, Italy
apelosi@unisa.it
[2] University of Naples "Federico II", Via Università 100, 80055 Portici, NA, Italy

Abstract. The identification of suitable statistical models of rainfall maxima at regional scale is a key element for the definition of reliable flood and landslide risk mitigation plans and for the design and security evaluation of high hazard strategic engineering structures. The ability to develop such models is highly dependent on a rain gauge monitoring network able to observe the extreme events that occurred in a region for several decades. In Italy, the density of the monitoring network and the time series lengths are often inadequate to capture some of the rainfall extreme events (referred to as extraordinary extreme events - EEEs), characterized by very low frequencies and spatial extent scales much smaller than those of rainfall ordinary maxima. In recent years, new operational statistical approaches were proposed to properly retrieve the EEEs frequency from the available database. However, the meteorological patterns of the EEEs are still poorly known, due to the limited number of documented cases studies available. The post-event rainfall analysis of observed EEEs and the evaluation of the efficiency of the monitoring network in detecting their magnitude and spatial properties may certainly help to improve the interpretation of the phenomena and their probabilistic modeling. In this study, new insights about the characteristics of EEEs are retrieved by analyzing data collected by different automatic rain gauge networks operating in Campania region (Southern Italy) from year 2001 to 2020. In this time frame, the extreme rainfall event occurred on 14th–15th October 2015 in Benevento area is the only daily EEE observed. The analyses show the capability of different monitoring networks to observe the phenomenon and the impact of different statistical regional models of rainfall maxima in assessing its frequency.

Keywords: Extraordinary Extreme Event (EEE) · Extreme rainfall · Rain gauge network density

1 Introduction

The ability to develop suitable statistical models of rainfall maxima at regional scale is highly dependent on a rain gauge monitoring network that has been effectively able

© Springer Nature Switzerland AG 2021
O. Gervasi et al. (Eds.): ICCSA 2021, LNCS 12956, pp. 264–278, 2021.
https://doi.org/10.1007/978-3-030-87010-2_18

to capture the main spatial features of the extreme events that occurred in a region for several decades [1, 2].

Rossi et al. [3] introduced the Two-Component Extreme Value (TCEV) distribution for modeling rainfall maxima, since they observed the existence of two independent meteorological processes generating rainfall extremes in Italy. The TCEV distribution describes the frequency distribution of maxima as a mixture of two independent populations of random variables, represented respectively by an ordinary component, more frequent and less severe in intensity, and an outlying component, which produces the higher, although rare, values. The use of TCEV in the regional frequency analysis for the statistical assessment of hydrological extremes has become very popular in Italy after it was implemented in the national reference procedure for flood hazard assessment [4].

Later, Pelosi et al. [5] showed that the density of the monitoring network and the length of the observed rainfall time series are often inadequate to capture some extraordinary extreme rainfall events (EEEs), characterized by very low frequencies and spatial extent scales much smaller than those of ordinary maxima. Stemming from a data-driven analysis, the occurrence of EEEs at daily scale was identified by a lower threshold of 250 mm day^{-1}. Then, it was proved that regional statistical analyses, even those that implement mixture models like TCEV, tend to underestimate EEEs probability of occurrence due to the limitations of the observational dataset that not consistently reflects the spatial occurrence of the extreme rainfall patterns in a region. This circumstance can deteriorate the reliability of flood and landslide risk mitigation plans as well as the design and security evaluation of high hazard strategic engineering structures, such as dam spillways. Therefore, a new operational statistical approach was proposed to properly retrieve the EEEs frequency from the available database and thus to avoid dramatic underestimations of the rainfall depth at very high return periods.

However, the meteorological patterns of the EEEs are still poorly known, due to the limited number of documented cases studies available. The post-event rainfall analysis of observed EEEs and the evaluation of the efficiency of the monitoring network in detecting their magnitude and spatial properties may certainly help to improve the interpretation of the phenomena and their probabilistic modeling at regional scale.

A recent study proposed the use of reanalysis data for classifying and analyzing heavy rainfall precipitation patterns and their synoptic evolution [6]. Nevertheless, this approach may not give interesting information on the rainfall patterns when the spatial extent scales of the rainfall events are smaller than the spatial resolution of the numerical grids of the reanalysis models that may varies from about 31 km, for the case of the most efficient European global reanalysis model, such as ERA5 [6] to about 9 km for its downscaled land application, i.e. ERA5-Land, whose performances have been already verified in Southern Italy for other hydrological applications [7].

In this study, new insights about the characteristics of EEEs are retrieved by analyzing data collected by automatic rain gauge networks that have been operating in Campania region (Southern Italy) from year 2001 to 2020. In this time frame, the extreme rainfall event occurred on 14th–15th October 2015 in Benevento area is the only daily EEE observed in the region. In Sect. 2, the study area and the available rainfall data are presented. In Sect. 3, the identified EEE is described. The ability of the rain gauge network to detect such type of events is discussed, along with an analysis of the network efficiency, by comparing the spatial density of the rain gauge and the spatial extent scale of these extreme rainfall pattern.

2 Study Area and Data

2.1 Topographic and Meteorological Description of the Study Area

The study area is part of the Campania region, located in Southern Italy (Fig. 1). The extension of the whole region is of about 14000 km^2 placed between the Tyrrhenian Sea and the Apennines. The complex topography of the region strongly influences the weather [8] and the rainfall patterns that widely vary along the region with relevant local effects due to the presence of orography [9, 10] and the proximity of the sea.

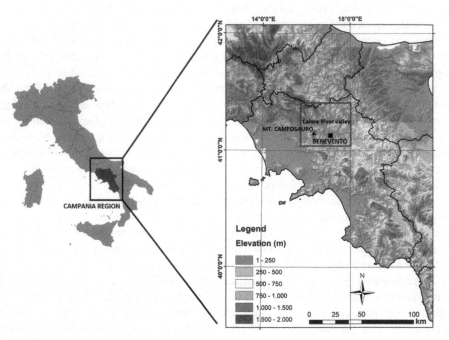

Fig. 1. Elevation map of the Campania region (Southern Italy) and overview of the study area (Benevento area – in the blue square). (Color figure online)

At regional scale, rainfall extremes are caused by atmospheric processes of very different characteristics and length scales. It is possible to identify three main mechanisms that generate maxima [5, 11]: (i) frontal systems, associated to baroclinic extratropical cyclones with a spatial domain greater than 10^4 km^2 and lifetimes greater than 12 h, (ii) convective systems with spatial domains less than 10^2 km^2 and lifetimes of several hours, (iii) "medicanes", from Mediterranean hurricanes, or TLC (tropical-like cyclones) that usually interest an area of 10^2–10^3 km^2 for several hours (~6–12 h, <24 h) with a combination of intense winds and heavy precipitation. The first two reported mechanisms (i.e., convective and frontal) may also co-exist and one may trigger and influence the other in a complex way [12]. The latter represents a very rare [13] but strongly intense cause of extreme rainfall.

The focus area has an extent of about 2000 km^2 in the upper-eastern part of Campania region (see blue rectangle in Fig. 1), near the city of Benevento. The main river of the area is the Calore River flowing at the foot of the northern slope of Mt. Camposauro (1390 m a. s. l) that is the main relief of the area.

2.2 Rain Gauge Monitoring Networks and Available Rainfall Data

In Italy, the rain gauge monitoring network was controlled by the National Hydrographical Service (SIMN) for water management and scientific purposes until the late 1990s. The SIMN was also responsible for publishing hydrological annals, containing all the hydrological and rainfall observations in a year and some brief considerations, elaborations, and summaries.

However, after the end of the last century, the management of the ground-based network and rainfall data was progressively assigned to different regional agencies. In Campania, the maintenance and the development of the monitoring network was assigned to the Hydro-Meteorological Service of the regional Civil Protection Department, which also guarantees activities of supervision, alert and mitigation against flood and landslide risks generated by hydrometeorological events. In the transition from the management of the SIMN to the regional Civil Protection Department, the historical network (Fig. 2 – green squares) was partly abandoned and partly re-designed for the new functions, that are primarily directed towards civil protection purposes.

Currently, in Campania there are about 200 rain gauges operated by the regional Civil Protection Department (hereinafter, referred as CP network), with a mean coverage of one station per 70 km^2. However, the density of the network is quite uneven over the region: in the study area, we found 14 rain gauge stations in about 2000 km^2 that means the half of the expected number of stations. Moreover, these stations are distributed with a clear asymmetry that leaves the central portion of the area completely uncovered. Figure 2 shows the rain gauge stations in the study area with red triangles and a progressive code, with the prefix CP. Figure 2 also shows the rain gauges stations formerly managed by SIMN that have been either dismissed or re-placed.

In addition, there is an auxiliary network managed by the same regional Civil Protection Department but not still operationally used for the civil protection activities since its rain gauges have been installed at the beginning of 2015. These rain gauges are shown in Fig. 2 with blue circles and a progressive code with the prefix V. This auxiliary network has been designed to fill the well-known lack of rainfall data in mountainous sites [14, 15]: from Table 1 that reports some specifications of the rain gauge stations, it is possible to verify that all these rain gauges are indeed installed at an elevation above 350 m a. s. l.

Finally, beside these networks managed by the regional Civil Protection Department, there is another rain gauge network installed at the end of the 1990s and managed by the Regional Agrometeorological Service for the specific tasks of water management and support to agricultural, forestry and land policies and activities in the region [16, 17]. This network is made of 37 rain gauges distributed all over the region (on average:

one station per 380 km^2) but with a very uneven and irregular spatial distribution that reflects the peculiar purposes for which it has been designed.

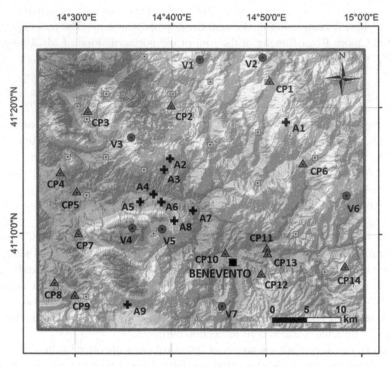

Fig. 2. Monitoring rain gauge networks managed by (i) the regional Civil Protection Department - in operation (CP – red triangles) and (ii) the Agrometeorological regional service (A – black crosses). The blue circles (V) represent an auxiliary network managed by the regional Civil Protection Department, not operationally used for civil protection. The green squares (with no assigned codes) are the rain gauges managed by the SIMN - in operation until the late 1990s. For the legend of the digital elevation model, please refer to Fig. 1. (Color figure online)

Figure 2 shows the nine rain gauge stations in the study area belonging to the agrometeorological network with black crosses and a progressive code starting with the letter A. These agrometeorological stations were installed to serve an area (i.e., the study area) where about the 50% of the regional wine is produced (i.e., Solopaca, S. Agata dei Goti, Torrecuso, Mt. Taburno) so that the number of stations in the study area is more than twice as expected and most of them (i.e., A2-A8) are in an area of 150 km^2 inside the zone of interest.

Table 1 provides a complete list of the rain gauge stations along with their spatial coordinates and elevation: in summary, in the study area, there are 14 stations managed by the regional Civil Protection Department, plus seven auxiliary stations and nine stations of the agrometeorological network.

Table 1. List of the rain gauge stations in the study area

Code	Name	Latitude (° N)	Longitude (° E)	Elevation (m)
CP1	Colle Sannita	41° 22′ 10.40′	14° 50′ 21.67″	777
CP2	Morcone	41° 20′ 9.90″	14° 39′ 57.63″	630
CP3	Cusano Mutri	41° 19′ 42.20″	14° 31′ 13.90″	364
CP4	S. Salvatore Telesino METEO	41° 14′ 51.49″	14° 28′ 22.09″	167
CP5	Sorgenti Grassano	41° 13′ 21.79″	14° 30′ 5.90″	52
CP6	Pago Veiano	41° 15′ 37.99″	14° 53′ 51.38″	259
CP7	Melizzano	41° 10′ 4.88″	14° 30′ 18.90″	190
CP8	S. Agata dei Goti Isclero	41° 6′ 11.08″	14° 27′ 50.29″	65
CP9	S. Agata dei Goti	41° 5′ 11.17″	14° 29′ 57.70″	153
CP10	Benevento	41° 8′ 33.78″	14° 45′ 44.65″	119
CP11	Paduli	41° 8′ 56.18″	14° 50′ 5.27″	130
CP12	Benevento METEO	41° 6′ 56.78″	14° 49′ 30.06″	236
CP13	Ponte Valentino	41° 8′ 32.58″	14° 50′ 9.67″	139
CP14	Rocchetta	41° 7′ 31.18″	14° 58′ 14.69″	670
V1	S. Croce del Sannio	41° 23′ 48.29″	14° 43′ 0.40″	827
V2	Castelpagano	41° 23′ 59.78″	14° 49′ 37.56″	819
V3	Cerreto Sannita	41° 17′ 35.37″	14° 35′ 45.39″	648
V4	Vitulano (Camposauro)	41° 10′ 28.33″	14° 35′ 55.44″	1124
V5	Vitulano	41° 10′ 23.75″	14° 39′ 2.12′	419
V6	Buonalbergo	41° 13′ 3.57″	14° 58′ 24.70″	432
V7	S. Leucio del Sannio	41° 4′ 19.90″	14° 45′ 24.14″	356
A1	S. Marco dei Cavoti	41° 18′ 50.88″	14° 52′ 5.92″	725
A2	Casalduni	41° 15′ 55.20″	14° 39′ 51.60″	482
A3	S. Lupo	41° 15′ 3.93″	14° 39′ 14.00″	346
A4	S. Lorenzo Maggiore	41° 13′ 7.60″	14° 38′ 8.40″	174
A5	Vitulano	41° 12′ 32.00″	14° 36′ 44.40″	96
A6	Paupisi	41° 12′ 31.50″	14° 38′ 56.80″	183
A7	Torrecuso	41° 11′ 51.70″	14° 42′ 19.00″	172
A8	Torrecuso	41° 11′ 3.50″	14° 40′ 19.00″	507
A9	Airola	41° 04′ ′ 25.73″	14° 35′ 26.02″	270

3   Rainfall Event Occurred on 14th–15th October 2015

This section describes the properties of the extraordinary extreme rainfall event (EEE) occurred on 14th–15th October 2015 in Benevento area. The descriptions are made for evaluating the monitoring network efficiency in the detection of EEEs. An assessment of this efficiency is conducted considering the CP network.

In particular, the focus is on the efficiency of the current CP network that is operationally used for civil protection and represents the reference network for the hydrological extreme analyses in the region since it replaced the SIMN network. For the scope, Fig. 3 and Fig. 4 show the evolution of the rainfall spatial patterns obtained by using the inverse distance weighting (IDW) method for interpolating all the available rain gauge observations in the study area. However, only the CP network is displayed on the maps, to evidence how a coarse network may not detect the occurrence of an EEE. Moreover, Fig. 5 shows the 24 h accumulated rainfall computed by considering all the observations available from all the monitoring networks (on the left) in comparison with the 24 h accumulated rainfall measured only at the CP network (on the right). Further comments on this are provided in the following Section and in the Discussion and Conclusions Section.

3.1 Meteorological Description of the Event

On 14th October 2015, at about 8 pm, a mesoscale convective rainfall began to hit the study area in the southwestern-northeastern direction and, at 10:30 pm, reached an intensity up to 20 mm in 30 min at CP9 station (Fig. 3a) and up to 24 mm in 30 min at V4 station. In the subsequent hours (Fig. 3b-c-d), the center of the more intense rainfall proceeded slightly moving toward east and clearly increasing its intensity along the northeastern direction, then reaching 32 mm in 30 min at CP9 station, more than 40 mm in 30 min at A9 and V4 stations, and about 56 mm in 30 min at A6 station.

On 15th October at 12:30 am (Fig. 3e), the intensity reached 80 mm in 30 min at V4 station. This intensity is the highest that has ever been observed in Campania. At the same time, the intensities in the southwestern tail of the storm were already decreased, with a residual storm cell (that waned in the next 2 h as the main cell) observed at CP8 station with an intensity up to 34 mm in the same interval. Another cell developed around CP6 station where about 30 mm in 30 min were registered. Then, at 1 am, about 75 mm were measured in 30 min at A6 station while the other stations belonging to the agrometeorological network located in the center of the storm (i.e., A2, A3, A4, A5) observed intensities greater than 50 mm in 30 min. At the same time, the CP network observed the maximum intensity at CP6 station with a value of more than 30 mm in 30 min while at the other rain gauges no more than 15 mm in 30 min were measured, besides the active isolated storm cell at CP8 station.

On 15th October at 1:30 am (Fig. 4a), the rainfall intensity recorded by A6 station was above 60 mm in 30 min, while stations A2, A3, A4, A5, A7 and A8 recorded around 30 mm in 30 min. Rainfall in 30 min was around 50 mm at V4 station and above 30 mm at V5 station. At 2 am, A6 station recorded 45 mm in 30 min while the other stations in the center of the storm (i.e., A2, A3, A4, A5) observed values around 30 mm. Another cell with enhanced intensity developed at the northeastern tail of the storm, as registered by CP1 station, with about 30 mm in 30 min. The cell was detected by CP6 station with the same intensity.

In the time between 2:30 and 3:00 (Fig. 4c-d), the center of the storm moved in the southeastern direction with residual intensities around 30 mm in 30 min registered by the CP network (i.e., CP6, CP11, CP13) and by V6 station.

After 3 am, the rainfall persisted for more than ten hours with ordinary intensities.

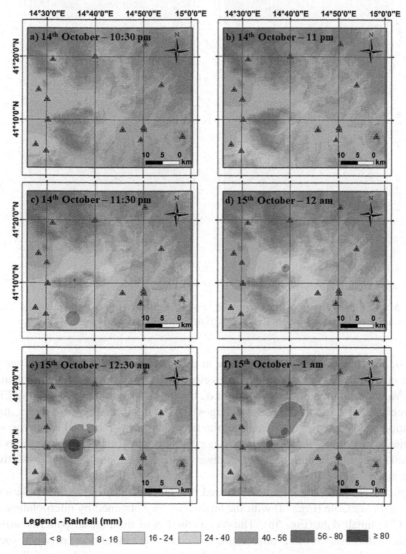

Fig. 3. Maps of the evolution of the event with rainfall aggregated into 30-min intervals. The red triangles are the rain gauges belonging to the CP network. (Color figure online)

The lifetime of the entire event was about 24 h. The 24 h accumulated rainfall values do not show a significative relation with elevation but a clear development along the southwestern-northeastern direction. Table 2 shows the 24 h accumulated rainfall values

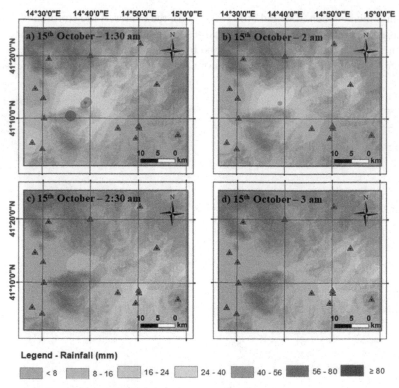

Fig. 4. Maps of the evolution of the event with rainfall aggregated into 30-min intervals. The red triangles are the rain gauges belonging to the CP network. (Color figure online)

at the stations that measured values close to and greater than 200 mm. Only two rain gauges of the CP network measured values close to 200 mm, but never greater than this value. Values even greater than 250 mm i.e., the lower threshold characterizing EEEs, were recorded at other sites. The two largest 24-h rainfall depths were 363.1 mm at V4 station and 415.4 mm at A6 station: the two stations were located along the same line oriented according the southwestern-northeastern direction. The two stations also recorded the highest rainfall depths ever observed in the region in 30 min: respectively, 80 mm and 75 mm.

Figure 5 compares the 24 h accumulated rainfall map retrieved by interpolating all rainfall data available (Fig. 5a) with the analogous map obtained by interpolating only at the CP rainfall data (Fig. 5b). The reconstruction of the rainfall patterns strongly depends on the observations available, and it is clear how a monitoring network, such as the CP network, too coarse with respect to the spatial properties of the rainfall pattern, is not able to assess the actual magnitude of the event and is not able to detect the occurrence of EEEs. These limitations can have severe impact of the reliability of long-term probabilistic predictions of extreme rainfall at regional scale [5].

Figure 5 also shows the characteristic lengths of the occurred phenomena compared with the size of the CP monitoring network. In particular, the EEE (24 h accumulated

Table 2. 24 h accumulated rainfall for values close to and greater than 200 mm.

Code	Name	Elevation (m)	24-h rainfall (mm)
CP6	Pago Veiano	259	201.0
CP8	S. Agata dei Goti Isclero	65	197.6
V4	Vitulano (Camposauro)	1124	363.1
V5	Vitulano	419	229.5
V6	Buonalbergo	432	199.8
A2	Casalduni	482	247.0
A3	S. Lupo	346	238.6
A4	S. Lorenzo Maggiore	174	267.6
A5	Vitulano	96	270.4
A6	**Paupisi**	**183**	**415.4**
A7	Torrecuso	172	229.6
A8	Torrecuso	507	222.0
A9	Airola	270	194.8

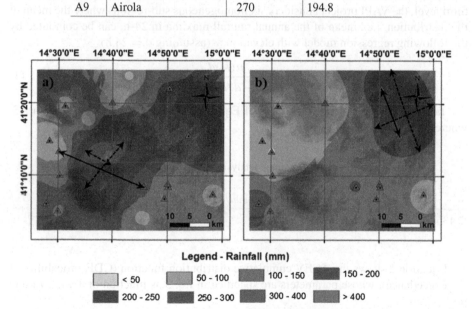

Fig. 5. Maps of the 24 h accumulated rainfall computed by IDW interpolation of **a)** all the stations and **b)** only the stations belonging to the CP network (red triangles). (Color figure online)

rainfall > 250 mm) was identifiable by an extent of about 9 km per 15 km (see the dashed arrows in Fig. 5a) that was not detected by a network made of rain gauge stations with a spacing of about 25 km in that specific zone (see the solid arrow in Fig. 5a). The

CP network detected just marginal fraction of the rainfall pattern, characterized by 24 h accumulated values larger than150 mm but smaller than 200 mm. This sub-event was located on the upper right corner of the study area and it was identifiable by an extent of about 17 km per more than 22 km (see the dashed arrows in Fig. 5b).

3.2 Statistical Description of the Event

Let consider the random variable, X, indicating the annual rainfall maxima in 24-h. According to the VAPI (VAlutazione delle Plene) project that provides the national reference procedure for flood hazard assessment in Italy [4], X can be modeled by the TCEV distribution, and its parameters can be regionally estimated through a three-level hierarchical procedure [18]. Then, the regional model is a simple model of homogeneous regions where parameters can be assumed constant at each level: at the first level, it deals with the estimation of the shape parameters of the distribution (i.e., skewness $\theta*$ and kurtosis $\lambda*$); at the second level, the scale parameter λ_1 is computed and, finally, at the third level, regression models for the mean (μ) estimation are provided, since the mean is strongly dependent from the elevation (z).

At first and second levels, the whole Campania region can be considered homogeneous, with the shape and scale parameters that assume unique values everywhere. Table 3 provides the values of $\theta*$, $\lambda*$ and λ_1 for the region, also valid for the study area. At the third level, the VAPI project considers six homogeneous sub-regions where the mean of the distribution, i.e., mean of the annual rainfall maxima in 24-h, can be computed by the following regression model with elevation, z (assuming d = 24 h):

$$\mu = \frac{\mu(I_0)d}{(1 + d/d_c)^{C-Dz}} \tag{1}$$

Table 3 also reports the parameters of Eq. 1 for the homogeneous sub-region A3, where the study area is located.

Table 3. Parameters for the regional analysis of rainfall extremes in the study area

$\theta*$	$\lambda*$	λ_1	α	$\mu(I_0)$ (mm/h)	d_c (mm)	C	D (m)
2.136	0.224	41	4.688	117	0.0976	0.736	$8.730 \cdot 10^{-5}$

Equation 2 shows the TCEV cumulative distribution function (CDF, probability of not exceedance), whose parameters are specified in Eq. 3 as function of $\theta*$, $\lambda*$, λ_1 and μ.

$$F_X(x) = exp\left[-\lambda_1 exp(-x/\theta_1) - \lambda_2 exp(-x/\theta_2)\right], x \geq 0 \tag{2}$$

$$\theta_1 = \frac{\mu}{\alpha}; \theta_2 = \theta*\theta_1; \lambda_2 = \lambda*\lambda_1^{1/\theta*} \tag{3}$$

However, Pelosi et al. [5] proposed a new probabilistic model for annual rainfall maxima in 24-h, in regions where the presence of EEEs enhances the hazard. In these regions, the at-site parameter estimation and the regional hierarchical approach have been replaced operationally by the definition of a support area around the monitoring stations, whose characteristic dimension has been estimated to be 20 km. This support area was employed to define the probability that an EEE (i.e., rainfall depths greater than 250 mm) occurs in any point belonging to that area. This probability is certainly more representative for the frequency assessment of EEEs than the probability estimated regionally in a point by using TCEV.

The cumulative distribution function of rainfall annual maxima in 24-h, above the threshold (x_0) of 250 mm, according to the new formulation becomes:

$$G_X(x) = 1 - p_E exp[(x - x_0)/\beta], x \geq 250 \tag{4}$$

where β is equal to 68 mm as reference national value while p_E varies regionally and it is equal to 0.1 in the study area [5].

Table 4 shows the probability of exceedance expressed through the definition of return period (Eq. 5), of the two highest 24 h accumulated rainfall depths registered at V4 and A6 stations during the 14th–15th October 2015 event. Those values represent annual rainfall maxima in 24-h for each station in year 2015.

$$T = \frac{1}{P[X > x]} \tag{5}$$

Table 4 compares the return periods of the observed maxima obtained by using the TCEV model with the return periods obtained using the model proposed by Pelosi et al. [5]. It is clear how the TCEV tends to dramatically underestimate the probability of exceedance (i.e., to overestimate return periods) of the event in all the station where EEEs are observed.

Table 4. Return periods associated to the occurred EEE

Code	Name	24-h rainfall (mm)	μ (mm)	T (years) TCEV	T (years) Pelosi et al. [5]
V4	Vitulano (Camposauro)	363.1	83.6	10809	52
A6	Paupisi	415.4	53.2	21906106	112

4 Discussion and Conclusions

The availability of long time series of hydrological data has been always considered a critical aspect for providing reliable estimates of the frequency distribution of extremes, such as rainfall maxima and floods [19]. This aspect is even more relevant in studies aiming at assessing signals of climate change effects in hydrological processes [20].

Mapping the frequency distribution of rainfall maxima in a region is often essential for predicting flood extremes, since flow data are very poor and not representative of the catchment response at all spatial scales of interest. It is also important to predict hydrological hazards generated at hillslope or small catchments scales, such as shallow landslides and debris flows [21, 22].

However, when dealing with regional analysis of rainfall extremes, the spatial density of the rainfall network can be as much important as the length of the time series. Indeed, the spatial scale of the monitoring systems should be comparable with the spatial scale of the rainstorm cells generating the related hydrological hazards. The spatial scales of a monitoring systems can be described by the well-known scale triplet [1]: i) the spacing between the measurements; ii) the support i.e., the spatial dimensions of the measurements; iii) the extent i.e., the dimension of the region covered by the monitoring system. In the case of rainfall network, the support corresponds to dimension of the rain gauge bucket and thus can be considered punctual, while the spacing is the average distance between adjacent rain gauges. If the rainstorm cells generating the extremes are smaller than the rain gauge spacing, the number of missed events in a region can be important over a long period of time. This issue was theoretically proved by Pelosi et al. [5] when looking at extraordinary extreme events (EEEs) in Mediterranean Regions, which probability of occurrence can be dramatically underestimated when the frequency distribution are retrieved by means of regional analysis that are based on time series of rain gauge networks with a spacing much larger than 20 km, which is the characteristic dimension of rainstorm cells producing relevant hydrological hazards, such as flood and shallow landslides.

This paper provides a clear example about how the occurrence of a EEEs and their actual magnitude can be completely missed if observed with a rain gauge network with a common spatial spacing. The examined event produced intense sheet and channelized flow along slopes as well as debris transport, causing severe losses at the toe of a massif located in the central portion of the Calore river valley, in Benevento province of Southern Italy [23]. The rainfall data detected by the automatic rain gauge network operated for early warning of hydrological hazards could not justify the physical evidence of an intense flow and debris transport along slopes, especially if compared with what was observed in adjacent similar slopes, which were apparently subjected to the same amount of rainfall. The actual magnitude of the event and its EEE features could be retrieved by only integrating data of other rain gauges operating in the surroundings.

This study also evidences how the frequency of the event could be completely mislead if it is computed with frequency distributions retrieved with the traditional regional analyses, which do not account for the mismatch between the spacing of the rain gauges and the spatial scales of the EEEs.

Pelosi et al. [5] proposed a theoretical framework for overcoming the scale mismatch for EEEs, characterized by return periods larger than 50 years and causing dramatic effects from the hillslope to the small catchment scale (i.e., of the order of 1–500 km^2). The return period estimated for the examined event would be of thousands of years according to the reference regional frequency analysis, while of the order of 50–100 years according to Pelosi et al. [5] probabilistic model.

This study also outlines the importance of having rain gauge networks designed with optimal criteria [24] and, even better, auxiliary distributed monitoring systems, such as meteorological radars, which eliminate the issue of the mismatch in the spatial spacing of the point rainfall observation, with a spatial support scale (i.e., the radar image resolutions) smaller than the spatial dimensions of the rainstorm cells of interest. However, dense rain gauge networks are still fundamental for an effective assessment of the rainfall maps from radar reflectivity maps [25].

References

1. Blöschl, G., Sivapalan, M.: Scale issues in hydrological modelling – a review. Hydrol. Process. **9**(3–4), 251–290 (1995). https://doi.org/10.1002/hyp.3360090305
2. Zoccatelli, D., Borga, M., Chirico, G.B., Nikolopoulos, E.I.: The relative role of hillslope and river network routing in the hydrologic response to spatially variable rainfall fields. J. Hydrol. **531**, 349–435 (2015). https://doi.org/10.1016/j.jhydrol.2015.08.014
3. Rossi, F., Fiorentino, M., Versace, P.: Two-component extreme value distribution for flood frequency analysis. Water Resour. Res. **20**(2), 847–856 (1984)
4. Rossi, F., Villani, P.: A project for regional analysis of flood in Italy. In: Rossi, G., Harmancioglu, N., Yevjevich, V. (eds.) Coping with Floods, pp. 227–251, Pre-proceedings of NATO - ASI, Kluwer Academic, Dordrecht (1994)
5. Pelosi, A., Furcolo, P., Rossi, F., Villani, P.: The characterization of extraordinary extreme events (EEEs) for the assessment of design rainfall depths with high return periods. Hydrol. Process. **34**(11), 2543–2559 (2020). https://doi.org/10.1002/hyp.13747
6. Greco, A., De Luca, D.L., Avolio, E.: Heavy precipitation systems in Calabria Region (Southern Italy): high-resolution observed rainfall and large-scale atmospheric pattern analysis. Water **12**, 1468 (2020). https://doi.org/10.3390/w12051468
7. Pelosi, A., Terribile, F., D'Urso, G., Chirico, G.B.: Comparison of ERA5-Land and UERRA MESCAN-SURFEX reanalysis data with spatially interpolated weather observations for the regional assessment of reference evapotranspiration. Water **12**, 1669 (2020). https://doi.org/10.3390/w12061669
8. Pelosi, A., Medina, H., Villani, P., D'Urso, G., Chirico, G.B.: Probabilistic forecasting of reference evapotranspiration with a limited area ensemble prediction system. Agric. Water Manag. **178**, 106–118 (2016). https://doi.org/10.1016/j.agwat.2016.09.015
9. Roe, G.H.: Orographic precipitation. Annu. Rev. Earth Planet. Sci. **33**, 645–667 (2005)
10. Furcolo, P., Pelosi, A., Rossi, F.: Statistical identification of orographic effects in the regional analysis of extreme rainfall. Hydrol. Process. **30**(9), 1342–1353 (2015). https://doi.org/10.1002/hyp.10719
11. De Luca, C., Furcolo, P., Rossi, F., Villani, P., Vitolo, C.: Extreme rainfall in the Mediterranean. In: Proceedings of the International Workshop: Advances in Statistical Hydrology, Taormina, Italy (2010)
12. Houze, R.A., Jr.: Stratiform precipitation in regions of convection: a meteorological paradox? Bull. Am. Meteor. Soc. **78**, 2179–2196 (1997)
13. Cavicchia, L., von Storch, H., Gualdi, S.: A long-term climatology of medicanes. Clim. Dyn. **43**(5–6), 1183–1195 (2013). https://doi.org/10.1007/s00382-013-1893-7
14. Prudhomme, C., Reed, D.W.: Mapping extreme rainfall in a mountainous region using geostatistical techniques: a case study in Scotland. Int. J. Climatol. **19**, 1337–1356 (1999)
15. Pelosi, A., Furcolo, P.: An amplification model for the regional estimation of extreme rainfall within orographic areas in Campania Region (Italy). Water **7**(12), 6877–6891 (2015). https://doi.org/10.3390/w7126664
16. Preti, F., Forzieri, G., Chirico, G.B.: Forest cover influence on regional flood frequency assessment in Mediterranean catchments. Hydrol. Earth Syst. Sci. **15**, 3077–3090 (2011). https://doi.org/10.5194/hess-15-3077-2011

17. Pelosi, A., Villani, P., Falanga Bolognesi, S., Chirico, G.B., D'Urso, G.: Predicting crop evapotranspiration by integrating ground and remote sensors with air temperature forecasts. Sensors **20**, 1740 (2020). https://doi.org/10.3390/s20061740
18. Fiorentino, M., Gabriele, S., Rossi, F., Versace, P.: Hierarchical approach for regional flood frequency analysis. In: Singh, V.P. (Ed.) Regional Flood Frequency Analysis, pp 35–49. D. Reidel, Norwell (1987)
19. Hall, J., et al.: A European flood database: facilitating comprehensive flood research beyond administrative boundaries. In: Changes in Flood Risk and Perception in Catchments and Cities at the 26th IUGG General Assembly, vol. 370, pp 89–95 IAHS-AISH Proceedings and Reports, Prague, Czech Republic (2015). https://doi.org/10.5194/piahs-370-89-2015
20. Longobardi, A., Villani, P.: Trend analysis of annual and seasonal rainfall time series in the Mediterranean area. Int. J. Climatol. **30**(10), 1538–1546 (2010). https://doi.org/10.1002/joc.2001
21. Santo, A., Santangelo, N., Di Crescenzo, G., Scorpio, V., De Falco, M., Chirico, G.B.: Flash flood occurrence and magnitude assessment in an alluvial fan context: the October 2011 event in the Southern Apennines. Nat. Hazards **78**(1), 417–442 (2015). https://doi.org/10.1007/s11069-015-1728-4
22. Rogger, M., et al.: Impact of mountain permafrost on flow path and runoff response in a high alpine catchment. Water Resour. Res. **53**, 1288–1308 (2017). https://doi.org/10.1002/2016WR019341
23. Santo, A., Santangelo, N., Forte, G., De Falco, M.: Post flash flood survey: the 14th and 15th October 2015 event in the Paupisi-Solopaca area (Southern Italy). J. Maps **13**(2), 19–25 (2017). https://doi.org/10.1080/17445647.2016.1249034
24. Fattoruso, G., et al.: Evaluation and design of a rain gauge network using a statistical optimization method in a severe hydro-geological hazard prone area. In: Ntalianis, K. (ed.) 1st International Conference on Applied Mathematics and Computer Science, ICAMCS 2017, AIP Conference Proceedings, vol. 1836, 020055. American Institute of Physics Inc. (2017)
25. Piccolo, F., Chirico, G.B.: Sampling errors in rainfall measurements by weather radar. Adv. Geosci. **2**, 151–155 (2005). https://doi.org/10.5194/adgeo-2-151-2005

Compensation Valuation Due to Hydraulic Constraints

Francesca Salvo$^{(\boxtimes)}$, Manuela De Ruggiero, and Daniela Tavano

Department of Environmental Engineering, University of Calabria, Via P. Bucci Cubo 46,
87036 Rende, Italy
francesca.salvo@unical.it

Abstract. This work aims to valuate the benefits and/or damages related to the apposition of hydraulic constraints, considering the economic aspects and the appraisal ones. From an appraisal point of view, the valuation of hydraulic damage considers the *ex ante* compensation: for the imposition of the hydraulic constraint and for the preventive compensation of future damages. The constraint can probably produce a loss in terms of income and assets, but also a decrease in hydraulic risk and consequent economic benefits. Compensation for future damage concerns random events and expresses the variation in the hydraulic risk for the land subject to restriction. If the change in hydraulic risk produces a reduction in risk (due to less probability and/ or less damage), then the measure of the damage is negative and it corresponds to a surplus value of lands. The proposed methodological process essentially aims to define the function of the *ex post* damage and to identify the criteria and the procedural process in order to valuate the damage caused to land as a result of the imposition of the hydraulic constraint and future damage avoided which have to be indemnified in advance (*ex ante*).

Keywords: Hydraulic risk · Hydrogeological constraint · Compensation appraisal

1 Introduction

Floodings are a central issue in public opinion and governance attention, both for an increased cultural emancipation and a more mature awareness of the related risk, and for the worsening of hydrographic basins instability caused by the lack of controls on the land use [1]. This phenomenon affects the territory at a widespread level, prefiguring the occurrence of risk situations almost everywhere. It is clear that the prevention of emergencies connected to the occurrence of flooding must be an imperative both under the socio-political profile, of the involvement of public institutions, and under the more strictly technical profile, in relation to the choice and planning of interventions aimed at flood defense [2–4].

Regarding the technical aspects, a fundamental role in the planning of the hydraulic works for rivers, streams, entire catchment areas, is played by the economic assessment of damage from flooding [5]. This is preliminary to the design of the interventions, since

© Springer Nature Switzerland AG 2021
O. Gervasi et al. (Eds.): ICCSA 2021, LNCS 12956, pp. 279–288, 2021.
https://doi.org/10.1007/978-3-030-87010-2_19

the works, in the absence of budgetary constraints, must be sized so that the marginal variation of the potential damage is equal to the marginal construction cost; and it is also preliminary to the economic evaluation of the interventions, matching the extent of the damage to the benefits obtainable with the implementation of the works, to be offset against the construction costs.

The problem of hydraulic risk mitigation is particularly significant in Italy. The Higher Institute for Environmental Protection and Research (ISPRA) report on the Italian hydrogeological instability provides a reference framework on the risk of landslides and floods on the national territory and on other risk indicators relating to population, buildings and cultural heritage [6].

91.1% of Italian municipalities are located in an area where the risk of hydrogeological instability is considerable. The surface of the areas classified as dangerous by medium-high landslides and/or medium intensity hydraulic landslides amounts to a total of 50,117 square kilometers, and is equal to 16.6% of the national territory. These are areas in which, following very heavy rainfall, landslides or floods, even of large dimensions, can occur. Considering that every year about a hundred landslides occur on the Italian national territory, which cause victims, injuries, evacuations and damage to buildings, cultural assets and infrastructures, it can be said that these are not only isolated events caused by particular atmospheric conditions or seismic events.

The report shows that over 7 million Italians reside in vulnerable areas, but potentially the number could be higher. Analyzing the risk from the point of view of the population, it turns out that 2.2% of the Italian population (from 2011 Istat census), resides in areas deemed to be at high and very high landslide risk, for a total of over one million inhabitants (1,281,970).

The population exposed to high flood risk is equal to 3.5% of the population (2,062,475 inhabitants), while those exposed to a scenario of average danger (with a return time between 100 and 200 years) reaches 10. 4% of Italian citizens (6,183,364 inhabitants).

The only way to reduce the damage caused by floods and landslides remains the most obvious, but also the least used: prevention. Prevention is possible by activating territorial monitoring and hydrogeological risk mitigation projects [7].

2 The Hydrogeological Constraint and the Hydrogeological Structure Plan (PAI)

The Italian law evolution about hydrogeological risk is extremely vast because of breadth and variety of all environmental cases.

The Royal Decree (R.D.) n. 3918/1877, still in force, among the others is the first regulatory interventions on specific restrictions for the protection of forests, summarized within the term 'forest restriction'. It defines the concept of hydrogeological constraint, which subjects land of any nature and destination to "constraint for hydrogeological purposes"(art. 1).

The main purpose of the hydrogeological constraint is to preserve the physical environment and therefore to ensure that all interventions that interact with the territory do not compromise its stability, nor trigger erosive phenomena, etc., with the possibility of damage. public, especially in hilly and mountainous areas.

The hydrogeological constraint therefore concerns land of any nature and destination, but is mainly located in the mountainous and hilly areas and may concern wooded or non-wooded areas. In this regard, it should be noted that the hydrogeological constraint does not coincide with the wood or forest one, always governed originally by the R.D.L. 3267/1923.

The hydrogeological constraint in general does not preclude the possibility of intervening on territory, but it makes interventions in these areas subject to the obtaining of a specific authorization (art. 7 of the Royal Decree no. 3267/1923).

The hydrogeological constraint has the nature of a "conformative" constraint of private property aimed at protecting a public interest (in this case the conservation of the good water regime, the stability and hydrogeological defense of the territory) and, that is, it can be imposed on all properties that have certain characteristics, with the consequence that it does not imply forms of compensation for the owners, as is the case for landscape, historical-artistic, park / protected area restrictions, etc.

The hydrogeological constraint does not entail the absolute urbanization of the area, so the interventions allowed by the urban planning instrument can be carried out if they do not damage or endanger the protected environmental values. The presence of the constraint imposes on the owners the obligation to obtain, before carrying out the intervention, the release of the specific authorization from the competent administration, in addition to the building permit.

In the Italian legislation, due to to Law Decree 11.06.1998 n. 180, the hydrogeological risk means both the hydraulic and the geomorphological ones; in simplified terms, the first is linked to a flood event in a watercourse, the second to the movement of a mass of earth, rock, or debris along a slope, both often caused by persistent precipitation of high intensity that characterize that particular area. Therefore, careful monitoring becomes fundamental in order to prevent and reduce the extent of these types of risk and to build adequate warning systems.

The hydrogeological risk assessment method has been identified in 1998 with Prime Minister's decree DPCM of 29.09.1998 [8]; it is structured in such a way as to allow a qualitative assumption of the essential risk factors, through which it is possible to reach a gradation in classes that depends on the combination of the danger of the area and related land use:

- R1: moderate risk;
- R2: medium risk;
- R3: high risk;
- R4: very high risk.

The purpose of this classification is essentially to identify riskier areas than others, even if they have the same hazard, depending on physical and anthropogenic elements found on them. In fact, according to the R level of risk degree, areas with a greater human presence are associated with high hydrogeological criticalities and, consequently, those to be defended as a priority. The identification of areas with different hazards, as well as the subsequent calculation of the risk, is instead essentially aimed at providing the basic elements for the subsequent planning and design activities of new construction in order to prevent the creation of new risk areas.

The identification of hydrogeological risk areas leads to the drafting of the hydrogeological risk map which is an elaboration foreseen in the excerpt planning of each Basin Authority. The hydrogeological risk map provides for the definition of some risk classes by crossing the hazard classes with the risk elements deriving from the land use map. The Hydrogeological Plan (P.A.I.) has essentially three functions:

1) the cognitive function, which includes the study of the physical environment and the anthropic system, as well as the recognition of the forecasts of urban planning tools and hydrogeological and landscape constraints;
2) the regulatory and prescriptive function, intended for activities related to the protection of the territory and water, the assessment of the hydrogeological risk and the consequent constraint activity in both extraordinary and ordinary regime;
3) the programmatic function, which provides the possible intervention methods aimed at mitigating the risk, it determines the necessary financial commitment and the temporal distribution of the interventions.

In the R4 risk areas, the PAI pursues the objective of guaranteeing hydraulic safety conditions, ensuring the free flow of the flood with a return time of 20 - 50 years, as well as the maintenance and recovery of the dynamic equilibrium conditions of the riverbed.

In the aforementioned areas all works and activities related to urban, territorial and building nature are prohibited, with the exclusive exception of those of demolition without reconstruction, adaptation or maintenance, making the assets and areas safe, practices for correct agricultural activity, provided that the morphology of the territory is not changed; there is greater flexibility for public infrastructures referring to essential and non-delocalizable services, but always subject to authorization by the Basin Authority.

In the R3 risk areas, PAI pursues the objective of guaranteeing hydraulic safety conditions, maintaining or increasing the flooding conditions with a return time of 200 years, together with the conservation and improvement of the natural environmental characteristics. In these areas all works and activities related to urban, territorial and building nature are prohibited, except all interventions allowed in R4 risk area, expansion interventions of existing buildings for hygienic-sanitary adaptation needs, of temporary deposits resulting from and connected to authorized mining activities, to be carried out in accordance with the procedures prescribed by the authorization devices.

In the R2 and R1 risk areas, the construction of underground and/or semi-terraced rooms for residential and commercial use is not permitted.

3   Methodology. The Damage Appraisal

The study examines the damage in its sense of *ex post* and *ex ante* valuation, with reference to the imposition of hydraulic constraints.

The topic of *ex post* compensation is proposed in the form of an income statement intended to quantify the reintegration for the loss resulting from the damage.

The valuation of the *ex ante* damage, in planning of hydraulic interventions, regards the imposition of the hydraulic constraint and the future damage avoided, to be compensated in advance. The appraisal of the *ex ante* damage, more specifically, concerns the evaluation of the indemnity, which means the measure of the damage linked to the variation in income and assets following the imposition of the constraint (land hydraulic arrangement land and related costs, loss of potential buildings, etc.)

The issue of compensation for *ex post* damage in private relationships is well stated in literature review [9, 10] and it follows the principle of reintegration of the property affected by the damage (once it has occurred). In the plumbing project, the preliminary valuation of the cost of compensation for any damage arises as a problem of the valuation of the *ex ante* compensation, paid in advance and one-off. The problem can be treated in terms of appraisal but it requires legal and political investigations for the justification of the indemnity.

Hydraulic damage has the following characteristics [11]:

- a harmful event that has occurred or to occur;
- the cause-effect link that allows the identification and delimitation of the damage;
- the presence of at least two subjects in antithetical garments;
- a situation prior to the damage (or initial);
- a situation subsequent to the damage (or final) that allows the differential measurement;
- the existing structure of property and use rights that attributes responsibilities and promotes compensation between private (or public in private relations) subjects.
- The damage exists only in the case in which the posterior situation is worse than the anterior one, otherwise there is an advantage.

3.1 *Ex post* Damage Appraisal

The compensation valuation follows a theoretical criterion that sets out the principle of reintegration of assets for the loss resulting from the damage, and a practical criterion that provides for the appraisal of the monetary amount [11].

The theoretical criterion considers the loss in value of lands submerged by water (temporary or permanent loss).

The practical criterion concerns the analysis of the events and responsibilities of the occurrence of damage, which can be sought in the following components:

- natural component, linked to the occurrence of the adverse event;
- administrative/technical component, attributable to poor management of resources and lack of or inadequate planning;
- management component, due to the presumed inefficient management of any hydraulic measures present;
- private component, linked to any conduct not aimed at containing the damage once it has occurred.

If we indicate with α the rate of damage caused by nature, β the rate of damage caused by political and technical contingencies, with γ the rate of damage caused by bad management and maintenance and δ is the rate of damage caused by the anomalous behavior of the owners, the unit damage is equal to:

$$Unitary\ damage\ =\ \alpha + \beta + \gamma + \delta\ =\ 1. \tag{1}$$

In summary, the problem of *ex post* compensation can be proposed in the form of an economic account Table 1.

Table 1. Ex post damage - Economic account

To give	To have
To private owners, according to the practical criterion for the rate γ	- from the natural component (natural adversity) for the α rate
	- from the administrative / technical component (political risk) for the β rate - from the management component for the disservice part for the rate γ; - from the private owners for the part of unsuitable practices for the δ rate

3.2 *Ex ante* Damage Appraisal

When planning hydraulic interventions, the valuation of damage caused to lands concerns the imposition of the hydraulic constraint and the future damage avoided, to be compensated in advance (*ex ante*).

Hydraulic Constraint
The theoretical criterion suitable to valuate the *ex ante* compensation for the imposition of hydraulic constraints regards the extent of the damage linked to the change in income and assets resulting from the imposition of the constraint. If this change results in a loss of income and/or capital value, then the relative measure corresponds to the permanent loss of market value of the asset, otherwise it is a capital gain. For the purposes of compensation, this means that this can be canceled or hypothetically give rise to a withdrawal. The loss of value is estimated from the difference between the condition prior to the project and the following one (the first ascertained, the second assumed).

The difference between the previous situation and the following one expresses the change in the value of the real estate assets following the imposition of the hydraulic constraint as perceived by the market (buyers and sellers).

The practical criterion for appraise the *ex ante* compensation for the imposition of constraints may concern:

a) the plant species, indicating R_a and R_p the net annual incomes respectively in the situations before and after the imposition of the restriction and with P_a and P_p

the current values of the multi-year annuities adjusted respectively in the situations before and after the imposition of the constraint [12]:

$$P_a = \frac{\sum_{s=1}^{m} R_{a_s} \cdot (1 + i_P)^{-s}}{1 - (1 + i_P)^{-m}}, \tag{2}$$

$$P_p = \frac{\sum_{s=1}^{q} R_{p_s} \cdot (1 + i_P)^{-s}}{1 - (1 + i_P)^{-q}}, \tag{3}$$

where m and q are the durations of the multi-year crop cycle respectively in the situations prior to and following the imposition of the constraint; i_P is the capitalization rate of tree crops;

b) the hydraulic works (for example, drainage ditches, drains) and the related costs C_s;
c) the loss of the land building potential; the permanent damage E for the loss of building potential is equal to the difference between the value of the building land in the previous situation and the value of the agricultural land in the situation following the feared damage:

$$E = \left[(p - c) \cdot e - p_A \right] \cdot S, \tag{4}$$

where p is the unit price of the building ($€/m^3$), c is the unit construction cost, e is the building index (m^3/m^2), S is the land area (m^2), p_A ($€/m^2$) is the unit price of agricultural land [13].

Future Damage
The theoretical criterion for the *ex ante* compensation related to future damages considers the extent of the damage linked to the variation of hydraulic risk in the area. This risk is related to the change in the probability of the adverse event and the change in the extent of the damage. If this variation results in an increase in risk (due to greater probability and/or greater damage), then the relative measure corresponds to the loss in value of the asset (temporary or permanent). If the change in hydraulic risk translates into a reduction in risk (due to lower probability and/or less damage), then the relative measure corresponds to a surplus value of lands. The loss or increase in value is estimated from the difference between the situation prior to the damage and the following one (the first ascertained, the second supposed).

The practical criterion for estimating the *ex ante* compensation for future damages may concern the losses of crop products and real estate assets following the occurrence of the damage:

a) the loss of the annual income of the herbaceous crops R_a and R_p respectively in the situations before and after the damage and the relative current values of the multi-year annuities P_a and P_p respectively in the situations before and after the damage;
b) the loss of land investments (for example rural and industrial buildings, roads, industrial buildings) and the related restoration costs C;

c) the loss of buildings (rural, industrial or residential ones) of value V_f.

At the time of the harmful event, the extent of damages D_a and D_p in the preceding and following situations is equal to:

$$D_a = R_a + P_a + C_a + V_{f_a}, \qquad (5)$$

$$D_p = R_p + P_p + C_p + V_{f_p}. \qquad (6)$$

At the present time, the amount of the damage related to the imposition of constraints and for future damages Δ is equal to conditions ascertained before and after the event:

$$\Delta = \frac{R_a - R_p}{i_R} + \frac{P_a - P_p}{i_P} + E + C_s - \left[\frac{D_a}{(1+i)^{n_a} - 1} - \frac{D_p}{(1+i)^{n_p} - 1} \right], \qquad (7)$$

where i_R is the capitalization rate of herbaceous crops [14, 15], n_p and n_a the return times of the harmful event in the situations preceding and following the damage respectively.

According to the report, therefore, the damage is equal to the loss of income from agricultural crops and buildability and the cost of company accommodation, decreased by the reduction of hydraulic risk measured by the amount of the damage and its probability. The damage occurs if the loss of income and buildability is greater than the risk avoided.

In areas with little or no building susceptibility, if the implementation of the project involves maintaining the same crops and arranging the land at the expense of the institution, then it is possible to have net advantages if the hydraulic risk decreases. This means that there is an equilibrium point for which a certain rate of damage due to the imposition of constraints is offset by the lower hydraulic risk.

4 Conclusion

From an appraisal point of view, the valuation of the hydraulic damage in a hydraulic project takes into account the *ex ante* compensation: for the imposition of the constraint and for the preventive compensation of future damages.

The constraint can probably produce a loss in terms of income and assets but also a decrease in hydraulic risk and so that consequent advantages. The fact that the constraint places a burden on the landowners (losers) to the advantage of the external owners (gainers), requires that the advantage of the external owners is equal to or greater than the disadvantage of the imposition of the constraint on the owners of properties characterized by hydrogeological risk but also by potential advantages of proximity. The supply and demand of these lands considers the advantages and disadvantages of this position in the market price.

Compensation for future damage relates to random events and expresses the variation in the hydraulic risk for land falling within the risk area. This risk is related to the change in the probability of the adverse event and the extent of the damage produced. If the change in hydraulic risk translates into a reduction in risk (due to lesser probability and/or less damage), then the extent of the damage is negative and corresponds to a surplus value of the agricultural land of the area. It should be noted that there is likely to be a decrease in the hydraulic risk for the land outside the area due to the damage avoided. If the damage avoided to external land is greater than any damage caused to the land in the area, then there are the conditions to justify the hydraulic intervention project, and for the external owners to hypothetically compensate the owners of the area [16–18].

Finally, it should be noted that the realization of hydraulic protection works may entail compensation for the temporary occupation of the areas, intended for example to receive excavation and processing materials. In these circumstances, the compensation is equal to the loss of income for the period of occupation and the costs of restoring the areas intended to receive the material, referring to the end of the occupation.

References

1. Green, C.H., Tunstall, S.M., Fordham, M.H.: The risks from flooding: which risks and whose perception? Disasters **15**(3), 227–236 (1991)
2. Macchiaroli, M., Pellecchia, V., D'Alpaos, C.: Urban water management in Italy: an innovative model for the selection of water service infrastructures, WSEAS Trans. Environ. Dev. **15**, 463–477 (2019). ISSN 1790-5079
3. Driessen, P.P., et al.: Toward more resilient flood risk governance. Ecol. Soc. **21**(4) (2016)
4. Benintendi, R., De Mare, G.: Upgrade the ALARP model as a holistic approach to project risk and decision management. Hydrocarb. Process. **9**, 75–82 (2017)
5. Johnson, C., Penning-Rowsell, E., Tapsell, S.: Aspiration and reality: flood policy, economic damages and the appraisal process. Area **39**(2), 214–223 (2007)
6. ISPRA. https://www.isprambiente.gov.it/it/banche-dati. Accessed 27 Apr 2021
7. Brandolini, P., Cevasco, A., Firpo, M., Robbiano, A., Sacchini, A.: Geo-hydrological risk management for civil protection purposes in the urban area of Genoa, Liguria, NW Italy. Nat. Hazard. **12**(4), 943–959 (2012)
8. https://www.gazzettaufficiale.it/atto/serie_generale/caricaDettaglioAtto/originario?atto. dataPubblicazioneGazzetta=1999-01-05&atto.codiceRedazionale=98A11189&elenco30g iorni=false. Accessed 27 Mar 2021
9. Bowman, M., Boyle, A.E. (eds.): Environmental damage in international and comparative law: problems of definition and valuation. Oxford University Press on Demand (2002)
10. Salvo, F., Morano, P., De Ruggiero, M., Tajani, F.: Environmental health valuation through real estate prices. In: International Symposium: New Metropolitan Perspectives, pp. 768-778. Springer, Cham (2020). https://doi.org/10.1007/978-3-030-48279-4_72
11. Simonotti, M.: Introduzione alla valutazione del danno da inquinamento all'agrosistema, La Nuovagrafica, Catania (1982)
12. Ciuna, M., Pesce, S.: Il saggio di capitalizzazione della terra e dei miglioramenti fondiari, Rivista dell'agenzia del territorio, 1 (2008)
13. Ciuna, M., Pesce, S.: Il saggio di sconto variabile nella stima analitica delle colture arboree coetanee, Genio rurale - Estimo e Territorio, 2 (2003)
14. Simonotti, M.: L'analisi finanziaria del saggio di capitalizzazione, Genio rurale, 12 (1983)
15. Simonotti, M.: Ricerca del saggio di capitalizzazione nel mercato immobiliare, Aestimum, 59 (2011)
16. Kaldor, M.: Welfare propositions of economics and interpersonal comparison of utility. Economics J. **49**, 549–552 (1939)

17. De Mare, G., Nesticò, A., Macchiaroli, M., Dolores, L.: Market prices and institutional values comparison for tax purposes through GIS instrument. Lecture Notes in Computer Science, vol. 10409, pp. 430-440 (2017). https://doi.org/10.1007/978-3-319-62407-5_30
18. Hicks, J.: The foundations of welfare economics. Econ. J. **49**, 549–552 (1939)

Social Choices and Public Decision-Making in Mitigation of Hydrogeological Risk

Chiara D'Alpaos[1]([⊠]) [iD] and Gianpaolo Bottacin[2]

[1] Department of Civil, Architectural and Environmental Engineering, University of Padova,
via Venezia 1, Padova, Italy
chiara.dalpaos@unipd.it
[2] via Cavour 24, Miane (Treviso), Italy
gianpaolo.bottacin@regione.veneto.it

Abstract. Due to climate change effects, the EU is experiencing heavier rainfalls and storms and sea level rising, which resulted at local and regional level in an increasing intensity and frequency of flooding. Increasing territories resilience and mitigating hydrogeological risk have become, therefore, one of the greatest challenges that our society is facing today. In this context, the successfulness of public decision processes play a key role. Due to the dramatic complexity of these decision process, which involve different stakeholders and actors, whose stakes are high and who may have conflicting objectives, policy-makers and planners require robust, transparent and coherent decision tools to support them in pursuing their arduous task. In this paper, we propose a methodological approach, which aims at increasing legitimation, accountability and transparency in public decision-making related to prioritization of hydrogeological risk mitigation strategies, by creating consensus via a participative approach. In detail, we discuss the potential of absolute AHP models in the prioritization of hydrogeological risk mitigation strategies. We argue that, due to the specific characteristics of absolute AHP measurement, once the hierarchy of criteria has been set and weights have been determined, the absolute model can be implemented on any set of alternatives, which does not need to be defined a priori, but can evolve over time, thus accounting for changes in single-criterion valuation of alternatives, contingent to variations in boundary conditions of the decision environment.

Keywords: Mitigation of hydrogeological risk · Social choices · Public decision process · Multicriteria decision aid

1 Introduction

Due to climate change effects, the EU is experiencing heavier rainfalls and storms and sea level rising, which resulted at local and regional level in an increasing intensity and frequency of flooding [1–3]. According to the 2018 European Court of Auditors (ECA) report, the costs of hydrogeological events across the EU territory amounted to €166 billion in the period 1980–2017 [4]. In a business-as-usual scenario, costs of damages have risen from €7 billion per year in the control period 1981–2010 to €20 billion

© Springer Nature Switzerland AG 2021
O. Gervasi et al. (Eds.): ICCSA 2021, LNCS 12956, pp. 289–300, 2021.
https://doi.org/10.1007/978-3-030-87010-2_20

per year by the 2020s, and will rise to €46 billion per year by the 2050s [4]. In this context, it is undoubtful the ever growing attention to mitigation of hydrogeological risks paid by Member States. Floods can cause loss of life, significant economic costs and damage to the natural and built environment, including cultural heritage assets. Due to climate change, floods are becoming more frequent and severe. In recent years, the number of medium to large magnitude flash floods has become twice as great than those recorded in the Eighties [4]. In response to the challenges posed by the rising incidence of flooding, in 2007 the EU enacted Directive 2007/60/EC, better known as Floods Directive, which focuses on effective flood prevention and mitigation, and mobilizes support from Member States in the event of a major emergency. In this respect, the Floods Directive recognizes the role of Civil Protection in providing assistance to affected populations and improving preparedness and resilience. Flood risk management plans should include interventions meant to prevent and reduce damage to human health, the environment, cultural heritage and economic activities. To a broad extent, increase in resilience and mitigation of risk are one of the most important challenges that our society is facing today [5]. In this context, the successfulness of public decision processes play a key role in the implementation of risk mitigation measures and the increase in resilience of urban and rural areas. Therefore, due to the severe complexity of public decision processes, which involve different stakeholders and actors, whose stakes are high and who may have conflicting objectives, policymakers and planners require robust, transparent and coherent decision tools to support them in pursuing their arduous task.

This complexity is aggravated by stringent budget constraints and lack of financial resources, which affect public administrations and governments both at local and national level. To favor the implementation of cost-effective mitigation strategies of hydrogeological risk, policymakers and public decision-makers must take into consideration along with social costs and benefits, EU directives and regulations, territories' current residual resilience and environmental concerns [6–9]. In a dichotomous vision of human nature and behavior, it is often argued whether economic activities must be sacrificed tout court with respect to safety and avoidance of human losses, or whether there exists an acceptable risk, that can be tolerated and can be assumed as the decision variable in the process of finding a compromise solution, which accounts for human life, economy and the environment.

This paper contributes to this debate. We argue that multiple criteria approaches provide a proper theoretical and methodological framework to address the complexity of economic, physical, social, cultural and environmental factors, which characterize the design of hydrogeological risk mitigation strategies and policies.

Within academic literature, collaborative governance, which bases on the ability of multiple stakeholders and actors to share information and learn from best practices in the achievement of common societal goals, has emerged as a potential approach to the management of complex systems that involve society, economy and the environment [10, 11]. This is apparently in contrast with Arrow's impossibility theorem, according to which, when voters have three or more distinct alternatives, there is not a voting electoral system, which can convert the ranked preferences of individuals into a community-wide (complete and transitive) ranking, which satisfies the requirements of unrestricted domain, non-dictatorship, Pareto efficiency, and independence of irrelevant alternatives

[12]. The need for aggregating preferences emerges indeed in many disciplines ranging from welfare economics, where the aim is to identify an economic outcome deemed to be as acceptable and stable, to decision theory, where rational choices have to be made based on several criteria, and to electoral systems, in which a governance-related decision has to be extracted from a large number of voters' preferences. The apparently opposing positions, which inflames academic debate, can be reconciled, if we consider that, unlike traditional optimization approaches, in the presence of multiple criteria, there is not an objective definition of "best solution".

In this paper, we propose a methodological approach, which aims at increasing legitimation, accountability and transparency in public decision-making related to prioritization of hydrogeological risk mitigation strategies, and creating consensus via a participative approach and the involvement of relevant stakeholders. In this context, by creating consensus we intend finding common ground and solutions that are acceptable to all and best for the group, for which decision aiding is provided. We discuss, in fact, that the informed participation of public bodies, the private sector and civil society may be a cornerstone of efficient policy-making processes.

The remainder of the paper is organized as follows. In Sect. 2 we briefly illustrate the basics of public decision processes and decision aiding, and we discuss the role of multiple criteria decision aiding in supporting public decisions; Sect. 3 discusses a methodological approach, based on multicriteria decision aiding principles, for the prioritization of hydrogeological risk mitigation strategies; Sect. 4 concludes.

2 Public Decision Processes and Multiple Criteria Decision Aiding

Due to the growing mistrust between public opinion, experts and politicians, policymakers and public decision-makers feel the need for legitimation in their policy making and decision process. In the emergent information society [13, 14], the widespread of information and communication technologies has resulted in a rapid growth of information availability and circulation, which is somehow forcing a change in a variety of sectors, such as education, economy, health, welfare and governance, which in turn may impose a turning point in the concept of democracy. In addition, social fragmentation and the dichotomy between short-term agendas and long-term concerns contribute to making public decision processes more complex than ever. In a public decision process, due to the variety of stakeholders, there is somehow a distributed decision power and there seem to emerge different rationalities, expressed by different actors (e.g., politicians, who have short-term political agendas, and experts, who have mid-term knowledge based agendas) and different stakes (ranging from opportunistic stakes, to long-term stakes or stakes affecting large areas and populations), which are often conflicting in the allocation of heterogeneous resources (e.g., money, knowledge, land, etc.). This leads, on the one side, to conflicting opinions, actions and priorities, and on the other to conflicting information and interpretations, which mostly depend on different languages and communication patterns [15–17]. It is therefore crucial that public decision processes move from and account for core values such as accountability, legitimation, consensus and evidence. In detail, voting theory and preference modeling are extremely relevant for governance related problems and underlie theories of fair representation, participation in democracy and transparency of public decision processes

[18, 19][1]. It is fundamental as well to adopt formal models in public policy assessment, as they are grounded in a common formal language, which reduces ambiguity of communication, contributes to improving accountability and represents the basis for participative decision processes [16, 20, 21]. Nonetheless, it can be argued that formal models can generate a reduction in creative thinking, are costly to implement and not easily understandable by everyone. There is consequently a trade-off in implementing formal models between the above advantages and potential drawbacks. Once again, in order to find a compromise solution, great equilibrium and balance, together with focused vision and stated clear objectives are mandatory.

In this respect, it essential to share a common view on what is evaluation and on its role in public decision processes. In measurement theory and decision theory, evaluation means basically measuring values [15, 22, 23]. This gives rise in turn to other issues on what we mean by measure and what we mean by value (e.g., value of what, for whom, etc.).

According to measurement theory, when we measure we construct a function from a set of objects, which comes from the real world, to a set of measures, which derive from empirical observations on some attributes of the objects under investigation, by implicitly assuming that there are specific conditions under which relations among numbers can be used to express relations among objects. In this framework, objects which are indifferent, and are stated as indifferent by means of trade-offs, can be considered as of the same value. There is no doubt, that the cornerstone in measuring is related to how we construct and define the above mentioned function, starting from observations [22–24]. In addition, as different measurement scales (i.e., nominal, ordinal, ratio, interval, and absolute scales) convey different empirically significant information [25, 26], scales cannot be used indifferently and are distinguished by the transformations they can undergo without loss of empirical information. As an example, all proportional transformations on ratio scales will provide the same information, whereas all affine transformations on interval scales will provide the same information, and ordinal scales admit of any transformation as long as it is a monotonic and increasing function. Consequently, on an ordinal scale such as the Mohs scale of mineral hardness, we just know that 1 represent the softest mineral and 10 represents the hardest mineral, but there is no empirical significance to equality among intervals or ratios of those numbers [27]. Therefore, the meaningfulness of the measurement scale is a prerequisite for the meaningfulness of measures and value assessment.

It is consequently crystal clear, that based on the above considerations, evaluating is less intuitive than usually expected, and it can be considered indeed an activity within the domain of decision aiding. Decision aiding is grounded in the consensual construction of shared cognitive artifacts and can be defined as the interactions between someone involved in a decision process and a specialist able to support him/her in the decision process, of which decision aiding is part [15, 22, 23, 28–32]. The act of deciding implies that a specific decision problem is stated, a decision-maker is identified, and a specific

---

[1] It is worth noting that, in the Condorcet voting model, alternatives are pair-compared, preferences are stated and the corresponding graph defines the tournament. Nonetheless, it is not straightforward to identify the Condorcet winner in most of real world situations.

decision process is structured and implemented. This obviously requires cognitive efforts and responsibility.

The main objective of decision aiding is to aiding to decide, not to deciding, and it comprises four main phases: providing a comprehensive representation of the problem situation, formulating the problem, constructing or co-constructing the evaluation model and providing final recommendations to the decision maker [15, 33–35].

In the first phase, participants, stakeholders, concerns, stakes, potential resources and commitments involved are identified and described:

$$P = \langle A, O, R \rangle \tag{1}$$

where

A: actors, participants, stakeholders
O: objects, concerns, stakes
R: resources, commitments.

In the second phase, by adopting a model of rationality, actions (i.e., objects under evaluation) and points of view are identified and the problem is stated:

$$\Gamma = \langle \alpha, v, \Pi \rangle \tag{2}$$

where

α: actions, objects
v: points of view
Π: problem statement.

Subsequently, the evaluation model is developed according to objectives and criteria previously set, and preferences and preference structures are modelled and aggregated via preference models, based on specific procedure, algorithms or protocols:

$$M = \langle \alpha', D, E, H, U, R' \rangle \tag{3}$$

where

α': alternatives, decision variables
D: dimensions, attributes
E: scales associated to attributes
H: criteria, preference models
U: uncertainty
R': procedures, algorithms, protocols.

In order to assess values, which depend on preferences, we need to take into account values and preferences of relevant stakeholders, individual vs social values, experts' and politicians' judgements.

Finally, in the fourth phase, final recommendations are established and a discussion on their validity and legitimation is set in place, by verifying whether information have been correctly used and are meaningful with respect to Measurement Theory, the decision process and the decision-maker.

The most relevant issues in any decision aiding process are related *de facto* to preference and preference structures. The key questions concern how to learn, model and aggregate preferences as well as how to use preference information to provide recommendations. Preferences are indeed binary relations, and a preference structure can be viewed as a collection of binary relations. The problem is therefore searching for an overall preference relation, which is representative of the different preferences. According to Social Choice Theory, preferences can be aggregated via majority voting, where each voter has equal importance and they are interviewed as many voters as necessary. By contrast, in multiple criteria decision aiding (MCDA) comparisons are based on a finite set of criteria, reflecting the preferences of one or multiple actors for whom the decision aiding process is implemented, and each criterion has a variable (relative) importance. Consequently, the nature and quantification of preference information required to formulate comprehensive comparisons is fundamental and may affect results [36–38]. This implies that information needs to be manipulated in a consistent and coherent way, in order to be useful for whom is using it and for the purpose for which the decision process has been designed.

Evaluating a performance and aggregating evaluations play a central role in evaluation and decision models. Comparing differences in evaluation is at the core of modeling and aggregating preferences to build an informed decision process [17, 22, 23, 34]. Preference models can be distinguished in two main typologies: preference models based on utility (value) functions, in which preferences are a weak order (i.e., transitive and complete preference), vs preference models, which accounts for incomparability and/or intransitivity [22, 32, 35].

When considering multi-dimensional (i.e., multiple-criteria) evaluations of actions and alternatives, specifically in public decision processes, it is likely that decision-makers call for a one-dimensional synthesis. This synthesis should reflect the value of actions and alternatives on a synthetic global evaluation scale, which in turn reflects the decision-maker's value system and his/her preferences, and it is grounded in the assumption that the decision-maker maximizes his/her utility or value, where the former is mostly referred to decision under risk, whereas the latter refers to the deterministic case [23, 24, 37]. Accordingly, alternative a is preferred to alternative b:

$$a \precsim b \; iff \; u(a) \geq u(b) \tag{4}$$

where
$\precsim$: preference relation
u: utility
and u is a function of evaluations based on n criteria g_k, i.e. $\{g_k(a), k = 1,.....n\}$.
If function u is linear, we obtain an additive utility (value) model:

$$u(a) = \sum_{k=1}^{n} u_k(g_k(a)) \tag{5}$$

where
u_k: single-attribute value function.
In case of a linear combination of g_k, (5) results into a weighted sum model:

$$u(a) = \sum_{k=1}^{n} w_k(g_k(a)) \tag{6}$$

where
w_k: weight (i.e., relative importance) of criterion k.

Although the additive value model is one of the most widely adopted in real world situations, it is worth noting that there are conditions under which the preferences of a decision-maker cannot be described by an additive value function model. These conditions are those in which compensation among criteria is not accepted. It is therefore of primary importance to verify whether the decision-maker's value system (i.e., preference system) can be described by an additive model. If not, other models should be implemented, e.g., multiplicative or non-independent models, which accounts more specifically for imprecisions [39, 40].

The additive multi-attribute value model is indeed satisfactory, when stakeholders actively participate in the decision process and accept its formulation. It provides in fact a direct and easy-to-understand interpretation of results in terms of decision: the best alternative is the one, which exhibits the highest model value [23, 24, 37].

3 Prioritization of Hydrogeological Risk Mitigation Strategies

Public decision-making in mitigation of hydrogeological risk is a challenging and complex task, which is evermore submitted to verification, monitoring and transparency.

As above discussed, decision aiding provides both a theoretical and methodological framework that can be implemented to different contexts of decision-making, and a formal preference theory [32, 38, 41]. Within the context of decision aiding, in this section we propose a methodological approach meant to increase legitimation, accountability and transparency in prioritization of hydrogeological risk mitigation strategies, and to embed some participatory decision-making elements, such as consensus.

The occurrence of natural disasters, such as river flooding, represents a worldwide challenge, due to more frequent extreme weather events and storm surges, which have made territories more vulnerable to floods and have produced severe economic impacts [42]. River discharges have increased as a consequence of climate change, urban sprawl and lack of maintenance of riverbeds and hydraulic infrastructures, which in turn caused more frequent levee failures and, consequently, further increased risk of flooding [43].

In this respect, the Veneto Region has suffered from many flooding events in the past and in recent years. The event that occurred in 1966 is the most worldwide known. Although it affected the entire Veneto Region, the images of the high water event (acqua alta), which occurred in Venice on November 4 1966, when an exceptional occurrence of high tides, rain-swallen rivers and a strong scirocco-wind caused the canals to rise to a height of 194 cm (measured with respect to the reference sea level at Punta della Salute), impressed and shocked the world. More recently, it is worth mentioning the occurrence of two extreme events in 2010 and 2018, respectively. Between the end of October 2010 and the beginning of November 2010, the effects of extreme meteorological conditions involved 130 municipalities, more than 500,000 inhabitants and caused the flooding of 140 km^2 of rural and urban areas in the provinces of Vicenza, Padova, Verona and landsides in the provinces of Treviso and Belluno. In addition, in 2018 the so-called Vaia storm (namely a hurricane) caused significant damages to forests (more than 8 million cubic meters of standing trees), buildings and infrastructures and impacted severely and unprecedentedly protection against landslides, avalanches and floods, as well as biodiversity. The consequences of Vaia storm affected not only natural resources and the environment, but also the local and regional economy and local communities, caused two deaths and the isolation of entire communities for weeks [44]. Key lessons have been learnt from these two events in terms of both territorial planning and management and policy interventions, in order to mitigate hydrogeological risk and increase the territory resilience. In 2011 the Veneto Region approved a comprehensive master plan of interventions ("Piano delle azioni e degli interventi di mitigazione del rischio idraulico e geologico"-Deliberazione della Giunta Regionale n. 1643 del 11 ottobre 2011) for a total amount of €2,731,972,000 of public works and infrastructures, considered as structural measures, and €5,422,600 of non-structural measures (e.g., efficient flood forecast-warning systems, flood risk assessment, etc.). In addition, in 2019 the Veneto Region approved an additional plan of interventions for a total amount of about €928,000,000 ("DPCM 27 febbraio 2019" and "DPCM 4 aprile 2019").

Due to high upfront and investment costs and to the chronic lack of public financial resources, these masterplans are implemented by sequential phases and their implementation requires a clear and informed identification of priorities, which should account not only for technical issues and concerns, but also for economic, social and environmental ones. In this context, in which high stakes and stochastic future implications are involved, multicriteria approaches provide formal decision-making models to assess a finite set of criteria, perform evaluation of alternatives based on each single criterion, and finally aggregate these evaluations to rank alternatives with respect to the specific objective of identifying priority of intervention [7, 45–50].

In detail, we discuss the potential of a novel application of the Analytic Hierarchy Process [51–53] in the solution of this ranking problem and in the improvement of public decision-making in terms of legitimation, accountability and transparency. The Analytic Hierarchy Process (AHP) is indeed a well-established multi-criteria approach, based on experts' judgements. It has been largely adopted by scholars and practitioners to systematize a wealth of decision problems, and proved to be effective when quantitative information on the effects of action is limited [6, 48, 54–57].

The AHP allows for ordering a finite number of actions A_i, with respect to a finite number k of attributes/criteria a_j ($j = 1, ..., k$), each of which is assigned a judgment score qualifying its performance according to Saaty's semantic scale [58]. The AHP implement a weighted sum model and is grounded in the construction of a hierarchy, where the main goal of the decision problem (i.e., the prioritization of risk mitigation strategies) is placed at the top of the hierarchy, whereas criteria and sub-criteria are positioned at lower levels, and alternatives/actions are at the bottom level. We deem that to structure the specific decision problem under investigation and provide a valid support to the decision-maker, it should be developed and implemented an absolute AHP model, in which each independent alternative at a time is ranked in terms of rating of intensities with respect to each criterion/sub-criterion. In an absolute model, the hierarchy is decomposed as usual into criteria and sub-criteria, which are further decomposed to the bottom level, which accounts indeed for intensities through ratings [59, 60].

According to [61], rating categories can be established for each criterion and the typology (i.e., qualitative or quantitative) and number of ratings can vary contingent on different criteria/sub-criteria, which are evaluated by an "intensity", identified by a numerical variation range. Subsequently, available information can be used to assess relative importance of criteria and sub-criteria through pairwise comparisons performed by the interviewed panel of experts, and priorities (i.e., weights) are determined according the eigenvalue approach. Absolute measurement AHP compares pairwise indicator categories (i.e., high, low, etc.) to an ideal preference synthesis, as alternatives are compared to standard levels and are measured on an absolute scale.

In the context of prioritization of hydrogeological risk mitigation strategies, it is of paramount importance the representativeness of the group of experts, which should include representatives of the three main perspectives involved in a public decision process: knowledge, government and business. It is worth noting that group decision-making benefits from capturing as much diversity of thinking as possible, in order to reach consensus on the final ranking in a systematic and transparent way [62]. Via focus groups and dynamic discussion, consensus on criteria, sub-criteria and ratings can be created, experts' judgements obtained and the hierarchy can be validated.

Thanks to the absolute AHP model peculiar characteristics, once the hierarchy of criteria has been set and weights have been determined, the model can be implemented on any set of alternatives, which does not need to be defined a priori, as in relative AHP models, but can evolve over time. This guarantees the possibility of including straightforward additional alternatives or accounting for changes in single-criterion valuations of alternatives, contingent to variations in boundary conditions of the decision environment, which may stochastically evolve over time (e.g., due to climate change effects, variations in terrain slope stability, etc.). Furthermore, such a model could be easily coupled to existing monitoring systems and prediction models, thus providing some dynamics in public decision processes and contributing to the fulfillment of Directive 2007/60/EC requirements in terms of flood risk management and flood prevention, protection and mitigation.

4 Conclusions

The mitigation of hydrogeological risk is a challenging and complex task, which includes the reduction of damages to human health, the environment, cultural heritage and economic activities. Public decision-making in this context is evermore submitted to verification, monitoring and transparency and, as any other decision process, calls for legitimation due to the growing mistrust between public opinion, experts and politicians.

Investments in structural and non-structural measures to reduce hydrogeological risk and increase territories resilience involve large investment and upfront costs. Due to the dramatic and ever-growing lack of public financial resources, these investments are necessarily implemented by sequential phases, thus requiring an informed identification of priorities, which should account for technical, economic, social and environmental issues and concerns. In this respect, multicriteria approaches provide valuable formal models to identify a priority ranking and improve the legitimation, accountability and transparency of public decision-making. Specifically, in this paper we discussed the potential of an absolute AHP model *ad hoc* developed to support public decision-makers in the ranking process, when quantitative information on the effects of actions may be limited. Thanks to the specific characteristics of absolute AHP measurement, once the hierarchy of criteria has been set and weights have been determined, the model can be implemented on any set of alternatives, which can evolve over time, thus accounting for changes in single-criterion valuation of alternatives, contingent to variations in boundary conditions of the decision environment.

References

1. Jongman, B.: Effective adaptation to rising flood risk. Nat. Commun. **9**, 1986 (2018). https://doi.org/10.1038/s41467-018-04396-1
2. Paprotny, D., Sebastian, A., Morales-Nápoles, O., Jonkman, S.N.: Trends in flood losses in Europe over the past 150 years. Nat. Commun. **9** (2018). https://doi.org/10.1038/s41467-018-04253-1.
3. Dottori, F., et al.: Increased human and economic losses from river flooding with anthropogenic warming. Nat. Clim. Change **8**, 781–786 (2018). https://doi.org/10.1038/s41558-018-0257-z
4. European Court of Auditors (ECA): Floods Directive: Progress in Assessing Risks, While Planning and Implementation Need to Improve (2018). https://www.eca.europa.eu/Lists/ECA Documents/SR18_25/SR_FLOODS_EN.pdf. Accessed 4 May 2021
5. Piazza, A.: Collective responsibility in the cooperative governance of climate change. Sustainability **13**, 4363 (2021)
6. D'Alpaos, C., Bragolusi, P.: Multicriteria prioritization of policy instruments in buildings energy retrofit. Valori Valutazioni **21**, 15–25 (2018)
7. Pluchinotta, I., Pagano, A., Giordano, R., Tsoukiàs, A.: A system dynamics model for supporting decision-makers in irrigation water management. J. Environ. Manage. **223**, 815–824 (2018)
8. Pluchinotta, I., Giordano, R., Zikos, D., Krueger, T., Tsoukiàs, A.: Integrating problem structuring methods and concept-knowledge theory for an advanced policy design: lessons from a case study in cyprus. J. Compar. Policy Anal. Res. Pract. **22**(6), 626–647 (2020)
9. Daniell, K.A., White, I., Ferrand, N., Tsoukiàs A., Burn, S., Perez, P.: Towards an art and science of decision aiding for water management and planning: a participatory modelling process. In: 30th Hydrology and Water Resources Symposium, HWRS 2006 (2020)
10. Ansell, C., Gash, A.: Collaborative governance in theory and practice. J. Public Adm. Res. Theory **18**, 543–571 (2008)
11. Bodin, Ö.: Collaborative environmental governance: achieving collective action in social-ecological systems. Science **357**(6352), eaan11 (2017)
12. Arrow, K.J.: A difficulty in the concept of social welfare. J. Polit. Econ. **58**(4), 28–346 (1950). https://doi.org/10.1086/256963
13. Webster, F.: Theories of the Information Society. Routledge, Cambridge (2002)
14. Webster, F.: What is an information society? In: Webster, F. (ed.) Theories of the Information Society, 3rd edn., pp. 15–31. Routledge, New York (2007)
15. Tsoukiàs, A.: On the concept of decision aiding process. Ann. Oper. Res. **154**, 3–27 (2007)
16. Tsoukiàs, A.: From decision theory to decision aiding methodology. Eur. J. Oper. Res. **187**(1), 138–161 (2008)
17. Meinard, Y., Tsoukiàs, A.: On the rationality of decision aiding processes. Eur. J. Oper. Res. **273**(3), 1074–1084 (2019)
18. Roberts, F., Tsoukiás, A.: Voting theory and preference modeling. Math. Soc. Sci. **57**(3), 289–291 (2009)
19. Young, H.P.: Condorcet's theory of voting. Am. Polit. Sci. Rev. **82**(4), 1231–1244 (1988)
20. Mari, L.: Epistemology of measurement. Measurement **34**, 17–30 (2003)

21. Giordani, A., Mari, L.: Measurement, models, and uncertainty. IEEE Trans. Instrum. Meas. **61**(8), 2144–2152 (2012)
22. Vincke, P.: Multicriteria Decision-Aid. Wiley, Chichester (1992)
23. Bouyssou, D., Marchant, T., Pirlot, M., Perny, P., Tsoukiàs, A., Vincke, P.: Evaluation and Decision Models: A Critical Perspective. Kluwer Academic Publishers, Dordrecht (2000)
24. Bouyssou, D., Marchant, T., Pirlot, M., Tsoukias, A., Vincke, P.: Evaluation and Decision Models with Multiple Criteria: Stepping Stones for the Analyst. Kluwer Academic Publishers, Dordrecht (2006)
25. Stevens, S.S.: On the theory of scales of measurement. Science **103**, 677–680 (1946)
26. Stevens, S.S.: Mathematics, measurement, psychophysics. In: Stevens, S.S. (ed.) Handbook of Experimental Psychology, pp. 1–49. Wiley & Sons, New York (1951)
27. Tabor, D.: The hardness of solids. Rev. Phys. Technol. **1**(3), 145–179 (1970)
28. Roy, B.: Science de la décision ou science de l'aide à la décision? Technical Report, Cahier du LAMSADE No 97. Université ParisDauphine, Paris (1990)
29. Roy, B.: Decision science or decision-aid science? Eur. J. Oper. Res. **66**, 184–203 (1993)
30. Ostanello, A., Tsoukiás, A.: An explicative model of public interorganizational interactions. Eur. J. Oper. Res. **70**, 67–82 (1993)
31. Fishburn, P.C.: Preference structure and their numerical representations. Theoret. Comput. Sci. **217**, 359–383 (1999)
32. Öztürk, M., Tosukias, A., Vincke, P.: Preference modeling. In: Ehrgott, S., Figueira, J., Greco, S. (eds.) State of the Art in Multiple Criteria Decision Analysis. Springer, Berlin (2005)
33. Colorni, A., Tsoukiàs, A.: What is a decision problem? Preliminary statements. In: Perny, P., Pirlot, M., Tsoukiàs, A. (eds.) ADT 2013. LNCS (LNAI), vol. 8176, pp. 139–153. Springer, Heidelberg (2013). https://doi.org/10.1007/978-3-642-41575-3_11
34. Bouyssou, D., Marchant, T., Pirlot, M., Tsoukiàs, A., Vincke, P.: Aiding to decide: concepts and issues. In: Bisdorff, R., Dias, L.C., Meyer, P., Mousseau, V., Pirlot, M. (eds.) Evaluation and Decision Models with Multiple Criteria. IHIS, pp. 17–34. Springer, Heidelberg (2015). https://doi.org/10.1007/978-3-662-46816-6_2
35. Bouyssou, D., Marchant, T., Pirlot, M., Tsoukiàs, A., Vincke, P.: Building recommendations. In: Bisdorff, R., Dias, L.C., Meyer, P., Mousseau, V., Pirlot, M. (eds.) Evaluation and Decision Models with Multiple Criteria. IHIS, pp. 89–113. Springer, Heidelberg (2015). https://doi.org/10.1007/978-3-662-46816-6_4
36. Bouyssou, D., Pirlot, M.: Preferences for multi-attributed alternatives: traces, dominance, and numerical representations. J. Math. Psychol. **48**(3), 167–185 (2004)
37. Bouyssou, D., Marchant, T., Pirlot, M., Tsoukiàs, A., Vincke, P.: Modelling preferences. In: Bisdorff, R., Dias, L.C., Meyer, P., Mousseau, V., Pirlot, M. (eds.) Evaluation and Decision Models with Multiple Criteria. IHIS, pp. 35–87. Springer, Heidelberg (2015). https://doi.org/10.1007/978-3-662-46816-6_3
38. Moretti, S., Öztürk, M., Tsoukiàs, A.: Preference modelling. Int. Ser. Oper. Res. Manage. Sci. **233**, 43–95 (2016)
39. Krantz, D.H., Luce, R.D., Suppes, P., Tversky, A.: Foundations of Measurement, Vol. 1: Additive and Polynomial Representations. Academic Press, New York (1971)
40. Luce, R.D., Krantz, D.H., Suppes, P., Tversky, A.: Foundations of Measurement, Vol. 3: Representation, Axiomatisation and Invariance. Academic Press, New York (1990)
41. Ouerdane, W., Maudet, N., Tsoukiàs, A.: Argumentation theory and decision aiding. In: Ehrgott, M., Figueira, J., Greco, S. (eds.) Trends in Multiple Criteria Decision Analysis. International Series in Operations Research & Management Science, vol. 142, pp. 177–208. Springer, Boston (2010). https://doi.org/10.1007/978-1-4419-5904-1_7
42. Ward, P.J., et al.: A global framework for future costs and benefits of river-flood protection in urban areas. Nat. Clim. Change **7**, 642–646 (2017)

43. Mel, R.A., Viero, D.P., Carniello, L., D'Alpaos, L.: Optimal floodgate operation for river flood management: the case study of Padova (Italy). J. Hydrol. Reg. Stud. **30**, 100702 (2020)
44. Bottacin, G.: I giorni di Vaia. Diario dal campo. Cleup: Padova (2019).
45. De Mare, G., Nesticò, A., Macchiaroli, M., Dolores, L.: Market prices and institutional values. In: Gervasi, O., et al. (eds.) ICCSA 2017. LNCS, vol. 10409, pp. 430–440. Springer, Cham (2017). https://doi.org/10.1007/978-3-319-62407-5_30
46. Macchiaroli, M., Pellecchia, V., D'Alpaos, C.: Urban water management in Italy: an innovative model for the selection of water service infrastructures. WSEAS Trans. Environ. Develop. **15**, 463–477 (2019)
47. D'Alpaos, C., Andreolli, F.: Urban quality in the city of the future: a bibliometric multicriteria assessment model. Ecol. Indicat. **117**, 106575 (2020)
48. D'Alpaos, C., Valluzzi, M.R.: Protection of cultural heritage buildings and artistic assets from seismic hazard: a hierarchical approach. Sustainability **12**(4), 1608 (2020)
49. Dolores, L., Macchiaroli, M., De Mare, G.: A dynamic model for the financial sustainability of the restoration sponsorship. Sustainability **12**(4), 1694 (2020)
50. Nesticò, A., Macchiaroli, M., Maselli, G.: An innovative risk assessment approach in projects for the enhancement of small towns. Valori Valutazioni **25**, 91–98 (2020)
51. Saaty, T.L.: A scaling method for priorities in hierarchical structures. J. Math. Psychol. **15**, 234–281 (1977)
52. Saaty, T.L.: The Analytic Hierarchy Process: Planning, Priority Setting, Resource Allocation. McGraw-Hill, New York (1980)
53. Saaty, T.L.: Fundamentals of Decision Making and Priority Theory with the Analytic Hierarchy Process. RWS Publications, Pittsburgh (2000)
54. De Felice, F., Petrillo, A.: Absolute measurement with analytic hierarchy process: a case study for Italian racecourse. Int. J. Appl. Dec. Sci. **6**(3), 209–227 (2013)
55. Ferreira, F.A., Santos, S.P., Dias, V.M.: An AHP-based approach to credit risk evaluation of mortgage loans. Int. J. Strateg. Prop. Manag. **18**, 38–55 (2014)
56. Canesi, R., D'Alpaos, C., Marella, G.: Foreclosed homes market in Italy: bases of value. Int. J. Hous. Sci. Appl. **40**(3), 201–209 (2016)
57. Bottero, M., D'Alpaos, C., Oppio, A.: Multicriteria evaluation of urban regeneration processes: an application of PROMETHEE method in northern Italy. Adv. Oper. Res. **2018**, 9276075 (2018)
58. Saaty, T.L.: The analytic hierarchy process in conflict management. Int. J. Confl. Manag. **1**, 47–68 (1990)
59. Saaty, T.L.: Absolute and relative measurement with the AHP. The most livable cities in the United States. Socio-Econ. Plan. Sci. **20**, 327–331 (1986)
60. Saaty, T.L.: Rank from comparisons and from ratings in the analytic hierarchy/network processes. Eur. J. Oper. Res. **168**, 557–570 (2006)
61. Saaty, T.L.: Decision-making with the analytic hierarchy process. Int. J. Serv. Sci. **1**, 83–98 (2008)
62. Senge, P.M.: The Fifth Discipline: The Art & Practice of the Learning Organization. Currency Doubleday, NewYork (2006)

Water Distribution Network Perspective in RAFAEL Project, A System for Critical Infrastructure Risk Analysis and Forecast

Antonia Longobardi[1]([✉]) [iD], Grazia Fattoruso[2], Guido Guarnieri[2], Antonio Di Pietro[3], Luigi La Porta[3], Alberto Tofani[3] [iD], and Maurizio Pollino[3] [iD]

[1] Department of Civil Engineering, University of Salerno, 84084 Fisciano, Italy
antonia.longobardi@unisa.it
[2] ENEA, TERIN-FSD-SAFS Laboratory, Portici Research Centre, 80055 Portici, NA, Italy
{grazia.fattoruso,guido.guarnieri}@enea.it
[3] ENEA, TERIN-SEN-APIC Lab, Casaccia Research Centre, Rome, Italy
{antonio.dipietro,luigi.laporta,maurizio.pollino}@enea.it

Abstract. RAFAEL is the acronym for "system for Risk Analysis and Forecast for critical infrastructure in ApenninEs dorsaL regions" project (PNR 2015–2020 Italian Ministry of University and Research). As part of technological developments undertaken over the last few years, it aims at integrating ad hoc technologies, developed within the project, into a platform, the CIPCast Decision Support System (DSS), which will become the reference platform to support the critical infrastructures (CI) protection and risk analysis, in favour of the Operators and the Public Administration. RAFAEL deals with the management of numerous CI evaluating the damages of natural disastrous on individual elements. the impacts on the services and the consequences on the interdependent CIs. The water supply network issue is approached in the presented research, by means of a heuristic approach. The relevant impacts on the water distribution system have been investigated through the combination of a hydraulic simulation model and a reliability analysis of the hydraulic parameters. The methodology has been applied to the Castel San Giorgio water distribution network.

Keywords: Numerical modelling · Optimal sampling design · Water network · Critical infrastructure protection · CIPCast

1 Introduction

In accordance with art. 2 of Directive 2008/114 / EC of the Council of the European Union, a critical infrastructure is meant as "an element, a system or part of this located in the Member States that is essential for the maintenance of the vital functions of society, health, safety and the economic and social well-being of citizens whose damage or destruction would have a significant impact in a Member State due to the impossibility of maintaining these functions". Critical Infrastructure Systems (CI) particularly include utility networks such as energy, water, telecommunications and transportation

© Springer Nature Switzerland AG 2021
O. Gervasi et al. (Eds.): ICCSA 2021, LNCS 12956, pp. 301–310, 2021.
https://doi.org/10.1007/978-3-030-87010-2_21

systems, i.e. discrete critical facilities such as hospitals, ports and airports among others. For economic, social, political and technological reasons these infrastructures have become increasingly complex and interdependent [1–3]. While this has made it possible to improve the quality of the services provided and contain costs, it has nevertheless induced a high level of vulnerability to a series of natural or non-natural events that can cause damage or destruction [4]. For the protection of critical infrastructures, governmental, individual and academic world actions, are necessary within a security-oriented culture, converging towards the development of new approaches and methodologies to reduce vulnerabilities and face new threats to which these complex systems, increasingly indispensable for our daily life and the security and prosperity of a country, are subject.

A focus of both EU and national legislation is on the energy and transport sectors. In the energy sector, the electricity system (ECI) - Infrastructures and plants for the production and transmission of electricity for the supply of electricity - represents one of the three sub-sectors.

ECIs play a vital role in supporting modern society and are critical for the smooth delivery of critical services such as health, water, wastewater and telecommunications, among others. [5]. In particular as regards the water supply and distribution networks intended for domestic, irrigation and industrial consumption, there are numerous devices that require an electrical power supply for the relative functioning of the water service. This circumstance places a strong dependence of CI water on CI electricity.

In the current literature there are quite a number of studies that illustrate the effect of natural phenomena on ECIs. History teaches that natural disasters related to climate change, such as floods and anomalous heat waves, are critical elements with respect to the functioning of ECIs. A substantial review of the impacts associated with climate change is illustrated in Varianou Mikellidou et al. [6]. The effects that earthquakes have on ECIs are also studied in the literature [7]. What are the effects that critical situations in ECIs can cause in strongly interconnected systems such as those dedicated to the water service are not as well understood [8, 9].

After an introduction of the RAFAEL project (PNR 2015–2020 Italian Ministry of Education, University and Research), which deals with the management of critical infrastructures predicting the relevant impact of natural disastrous events, the current paper presents a methodology to quantitatively assess the interdependence between the electrical and water supply networks at the city scale. An application is presented for the Castel San Giorgio water distribution network, one of the pilot cases study selected by the RAFAEL project. The methodology represents a planning tool for the mitigation of power supply failure events on the water distribution system. It is grounded on a hydraulic simulation model, for which proper calibration a network of sensors must be designed, providing hydraulic pressure at each node and water flow at each pipe of the network as a function of network components relying on power supply. In the end, in a reliability analysis, failures in the power supply network are related to failures in the water supply system.

2 The Context of Application: RAFAEL Project

The study and the related applicative case study presented in this paper have been carried out in the framework of the RAFAEL Project [10]. RAFAEL is the acronym for "system for Risk Analysis and Forecast for critical infrastructure in ApenninEs dorsaL regions" project (co-funded by the Italian Ministry of Research, Grant no. ARS01_00305, scheduled to end in November 2021). Starting from technological developments carried out during over the last few years, the Project aims at integrating ad new technologies and approaches, developed within its activities, into a Decision Support System (DSS), [11] the CIPCast platform (described in the next section). One of the main goals of RAFAEL is related to the risk analysis and the management of numerous Cis, by evaluating the potential harms from natural disastrous events and assessing the likelihood of individual elements being damaged, also considering the impact on the services and the consequences on the interdependent networks and technological system. In particular, CIPCast will become the reference platform to provide services to CI operators and to the Public Administration, by relying on the EISAC.IT programme, which will carry out its operational deployment in Italy.

2.1 The CIPCast Platform

The CIPCast platform is a decision support tool developed for supporting risk analysis and CI protection in the case of natural hazardous events [11]. CIPCast can run both in operational mode (on a 24/7 basis, as an alert system) and in off-line mode as a simulator of events. In the first case, CIPCast gathers data from many different sources (e.g. seismic network surveys, outputs from meteo/hydrological models, etc.), in order to provide a comprehensive overview of the current conditions of the CIs monitored [12]. In case of (predicted/occurred) hazardous event, it produces an expected "damage scenario" for each element of the CI, depending on the type of event expected (and its intensity) and considering the specific vulnerabilities of infrastructure elements (pipes, substations, etc.). In the simulation mode, CIPCast can be used as a stress tester, in order to set-up and run simulations of synthetic natural hazards (e.g. earthquakes) and, consequently, assessing the resulting damages and consequences [13, 14].Such specific application devoted to the earthquake simulation and risk analysis is called CIPCast-ES (Earthquake Simulator). Moreover, CIPCast has been customised to interactively support multi-criteria decision processes [15]. All the CIPCast services and capabilities are accessible by means of its geographical interface (WebGIS application), which can be used as graphical front end of data and information provided and/or produced (Fig. 1).

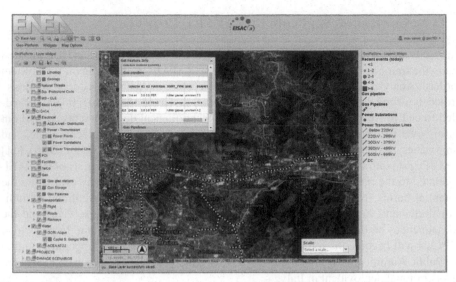

Fig. 1. CIPCast WebGIS interface: example of visualisation of the water distribution network (blue polylines) along with other CIs present in the same area (power and gas networks)

3   Water Supply Network Tools Within RAFAEL

A synthetic description of the case study is preliminarily provided. Following, the methodology aimed at the analysis of the quantitative interdependence between the power and water supply network is detailed.

3.1   The Case Study

The Castel San Giorgio water distribution network (WDN) was selected as the water critical infrastructure to be investigated within the RAFEL project (Fig. 2). The WDN is located in the Campania Region (Southern Italy) and it serves about 14,000 inhabitants, on an area of about 13 km^2. It distributes about 60 l/s every day, provided by three boreholes that guarantee the whole required water resource, through a path line made up of about 60 km of pipelines. More information on the characteristics of the network is detailed in Ottobrino et al. [16].

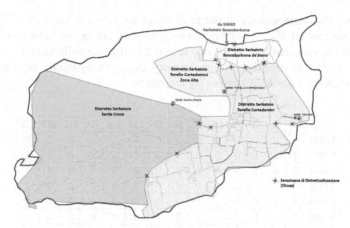

Fig. 2. Castel San Giorgio municipality water distribution network.

3.2 Optimal Sampling Design of the CIs Water

CIs water modeling can be an effective way to analyses the effects on network hydraulics and pinpoint customers who will be negatively affected, by the critical situations in ECIs. In fact, events eventually occur as reservoir shutdowns as well as low storage-tank levels can be predicted and appropriate solutions can be determined.

Modelling capabilities enable operators to manage their water supplies and distribution systems more efficiently and also to take rapid, informed actions to minimize the impact on the customer service during critical situations. These models allow the operators to control network during critical failures, optimize emergency response and consequence management plans.

However, before using these models, it has to be ensured that they predict the behavior of the real network with reasonable accuracy [17, 18]. Several factors can affect the prediction accuracy such as model structure, state and parameters. The input parameters (e.g. pipe roughness) of the model are among these ones, though an effective calibration process can significantly reduce the uncertainty of model predictions.

A calibration process needs a collection of data measured in various points of the real system and over time. The model calibration accuracy is directly dependent on the sampling scheme ie. the quantity and the spatial distribution of measurements/devices to be optimally located along the water distribution network.

For this scope, a sampling design (SD) procedure that determine optimal sensor location schemes has been developed as one of the RAFAEL Project tasks. This procedure uses a stochastic approach where the SD problem is formulated and solved as a two-objective optimization problem under parameter uncertainty intended to assess the Pareto front for trade-offs between sensor cost and the resulting accuracy of hydraulic model [19, 20].

The hydraulic model prediction accuracy has been qualified by a FOSM (First Order Second Moment) method, approximating the relevant parameter and prediction covariance matrices. The optimization problem has been solved by using a multi-objective genetic algorithm.

Applying this methodology at the pilot water distribution network of Castel San Giorgio, a scheme of $N_{max} = 13$ possible sensor locations, including main critical points of the network, has been evaluated referred to the hydraulic model.

In Fig. 3, it is evident that the uncertainty φ_{hydra} in hydraulic head predictions decreases when the number of sensors N_S increases.

φ_{idra}	N_s	S1	S2	S5	S6	S7	S8	S9	S10	S14	S15	S16	S17	S18
1.7629	1	0	1	0	0	0	0	0	0	0	0	0	0	0
0.7911	2	1	1	0	0	0	0	0	0	0	0	0	0	0
0.4431	3	1	1	0	0	0	0	0	0	0	0	0	0	1
0.4158	4	1	1	1	0	0	0	0	0	0	0	0	0	1
0.3833	5	1	1	1	1	0	0	0	0	0	0	0	0	1
0.3699	6	1	1	1	1	0	0	0	0	1	0	0	0	1
0.3527	7	1	1	1	1	0	0	0	0	1	1	0	1	0
0.3292	8	1	1	1	1	0	0	1	0	1	1	0	1	0
0.2950	9	1	1	0	1	1	1	1	0	1	1	0	1	0

Fig. 3. Pareto optimal solutions (φ_{hydra}, N_S) and related schemes of optimal water sensors locations L_{Ns} as sequence of 0,1 where 1 means location to be monitored and 0 to be not monitored.

By analysing the table of Fig. 3 it is possible to observe that the uncertainty value corresponding to the 2-sensors scheme decreases about 45% compared to 1-sensor scheme and the value corresponding to the 3-sensors scheme further decreases about 56%. While, by increasing the sensor number ($N_s > 3$), the model calibration accuracy increases more slowly.

Anyway optimal 9-sensors scheme given by the sequence $\{S_1, S_2, S_6, S_7, S_8, S_9, S_{14}, S_{15}, S_{17}\}$ reduces significantly the pressure predictions uncertainty.

Through the proposed SD procedure, the water supplier of the pilot network Castel San Giorgio knows the optimal scheme for an effective monitoring of hydraulic parameters along the water distribution network.

3.3 Interdependence Between Power and Water Supply Networks

The analysis of the interdependence between the electricity power supply network and the water distribution network is conducted through a heuristic approach, according to which specific "cases" are accounted for and analysed. On the basis of the results related to these, an explanation or a general rule is sought. The "cases" that are selected are identified as failure scenarios of the power supply network. The impacts that these determine on the water distribution system are then investigated through the combination of a hydraulic simulation model and a reliability analysis of the hydraulic parameters.

In a water distribution network it is possible to identify a set of physical components (pipes, valves, reservoirs, tanks). Among these, there are some that require electrical power for their operation, in particular pumps. The latter can be used as a connection between the different tanks located in a city network, or as machines necessary for the extraction of the volumes of water from wells and aquifers. Pumps operation is schematized, together with that of the pipes, valves and tanks, as part of a hydraulic simulation model that allows to assess how the regular operation of the pumps affects the hydraulic behaviour of the network. This is generally pursued by a critical link analysis, that is by studying the distribution of pressures in the nodes of the water supply network and of the flow rates within the network pipes. Hydraulic pressure must be contained within certain limits, minimum and maximum, so that it can be said that the operation of the network is reliable. Flow rate must, on the one hand, satisfy the users' water demand, and on the other provide the distribution of flow velocity within the network, which is another parameter used to measure the reliable hydraulic behaviour.

Through an appropriately calibrated hydraulic simulation model, it will then be possible to verify how a failure of a component that requires electrical power supply, e.g. a pump, affects the hydraulic behaviour of the network. The quantitative assessment of the interdependence between the two critical infrastructures arises from the comparison between the distributions of nodes hydraulic pressures and pipes flow rates in the case of the ordinary scenario (when no failure of the power supply is accounted for) and those relating to the particular failure scenario studied.

With reference to the case study of the Castel San Giorgio network, the water distribution network is fully fed by three boreholes, for which pumps operation are required (Fig. 4). Additional pumps are also located on the connections between some of the tanks belonging to the water supply network. The system is therefore extremely vulnerable to failures in the power supply infrastructure. This consideration is also the reason why the case study was selected for the applications related to the RAFAEL project.

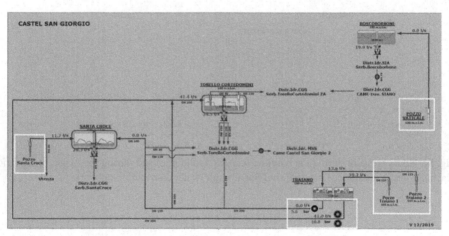

Fig. 4. Castel San Giorgio municipality water distribution network remote control. The location of pumps is highlighted by yellow boxes.(Color figure online)

Among the numerous scenarios of power supply failure, the one involving to a general and total interruption of the power supply would be associated to the largest impact. This scenario is identified as "black out 6–16", meaning with this wording that the pumps are out of operation from hours 6 to 16 of the day, or for a period which, compared with the filling times of the network tanks, it can be considered quite long.

In this scenario, therefore, the filling of the tanks by the boreholes does not take place, causing a significant reduction in the available water resources volume to be supplied to the municipality.

As an example, the results of the hydraulic simulations, carried out with the software EPANET2.0 software (United States Environmental Protection Agency), are reported in relation to a non-dimensional index which represents the availability of hydraulic pressure relative to the assigned water demand. Figure 5 illustrates the trends of the index, DC, for two different network nodes. In particular, a "baseline" scenario, i.e. of ordinary operation, is compared with the "blackout 6–16" which we have said is the heaviest of the possible failure scenarios. The DC index ranges between 0 and 1, which correspond respectively to no or maximum reliability in the operation of the network. In the case of the ORC24857 node (Fig. 5 right panel), the DC index in the baseline simulation assumes rather high values, between 1 and 0.94, indicating a node whose hydraulic pressure can be considered almost stationary and optimal during the day. On the contrary, the node OCR23478 (Fig. 5 left panel), already in the baseline simulation, shows rather low and highly variable values during the day, ranging between 0.54 and 0.76. While in the case of the ORC24857 node the blackout simulation, while determining a maximum reduction of the index of 11%, at 3 pm, leads to DC values that are still adequate for reliable operation, in the case of the OCR23478 node, the simulation of blackout leads to maximum reductions in the index equal to 13% (comparable with node ORC24857), but probably inadequate for the reliable performance of the service, or for the supply of the given water demand.

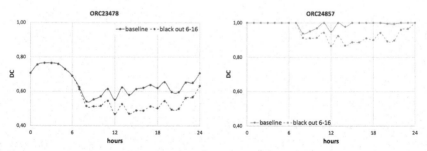

Fig. 5. Nodal pressure during the baseline scenario (solid line) and during the blackout scenario (dashed lines) at two nodes of the Castel San Giorgio water distribution network.

4 Conclusions

RAFAEL on-going activities deal with the risk analysis and protection of numerous CI. The CIPCast platform has been exploited to produce expected damage scenarios for the monitored CIs, both in operational and simulation modes [21]. In particular, CIPCast outputs can be used to produce critical scenarios focusing on cascading effects, in order to evaluate how a failure power network could impact on the operational level of the WDN.

To this end, the water supply network issue has been approached in the presented research with a specific reference to the interdependence between the power supply and the water distribution networks at the city scale. The presented methodology consists of a heuristic approach, according to which specific "cases", e.g. failure scenarios of the power supply network, are accounted for and the relevant impacts that these determine on the water distribution system are then investigated through the combination of a hydraulic simulation model and a reliability analysis of the hydraulic parameters. The methodology has been applied to the Castel San Giorgio water distribution network and, as an example, summary results for the most severe scenario were presented. By comparing failure scenarios with a baseline scenario, describing an ordinary operation case, the reported methodology represents a planning tool for the design of management rules devoted to the mitigation of power supply failure events on the water distribution system.

Acknowledgments. The research activities described in the present paper have been carried out in the framework of the RAFAEL project, co-funded by Italian Ministry of University and Research, MUR, Grant no. ARS01_00305.

References

1. Baloye, D.O., Palamuleni, L.G.: Urban critical infrastructure interdependencies in emergency management: findings from Abeokuta Nigeria. Disaster Prev. Manage. **26**(2), 162–182 (2017)
2. Griot, C.: Modelling and simulation for critical infrastructure interdependency assessment: a meta-review for model characterization. Int. J. Crit. Infrastruct. **6**(4), 363–379 (2010)
3. Chou, C.-C., Tseng, S.-M.: Collection and analysis of critical infrastructure interdependency relationships. J. Comput. Civ. Eng. **24**(6), 539–547 (2010)
4. Moriconi, C., Pollino, M., Rosato, V.: La protezione delle Infrastrutture Critiche e il controllo del territorio. Energia ambiente e innovazione **1**, 52–57 (2017)
5. Luiijf, E., et al.: Empirical findings on critical infrastructure dependencies in Europe. **5508**(2009), 302–310 (2009)
6. Varianou Mikellidou, C., Shakou, L.M., Boustras, G., Dimopoulos, C.: Energy critical infrastructures at risk from climate change: a state of the art review. Safety Sci. **110**, 110–120 (2018)
7. Rosato, V., Di Pietro, A., La Porta, L., Pollino, M., Tofani, A., Marti, J.R., Romani, C.: A decision support system for emergency management of critical infrastructures subjected to natural hazards. In: Panayiotou, C.G.G., Ellinas, G., Kyriakides, E., Polycarpou, M.M.M. (eds.) Critical Information Infrastructures Security. LNCS, vol. 8985, pp. 362–367. Springer, Cham (2016). https://doi.org/10.1007/978-3-319-31664-2_37
8. Omidvar, B., Hojjati Malekshah, M., Omidvar, H.: Failure risk assessment of interdependent infrastructures against earthquake, a Petri net approach: case study-power and water distribution networks. Nat. Hazards **71**(3), 1971–1993 (2014)
9. Fattoruso, G., et al.: Modeling electric and water distribution systems interdependences in urban areas risk analysis. In: COWM 2nd International Conference Citizen Observatories for Natural Hazards and Water Management, Venice, pp. 222–225 (2018)
10. RAFAEL. https://www.progetto-rafael.it/. Accessed 12 May 2021

11. Di Pietro, A., Lavalle, L., La Porta, L., Pollino, M., Tofani, A., Rosato, V.: Design of DSS for supporting preparedness to and management of anomalous situations in complex scenarios. In: Setola, R., Rosato, V., Kyriakides, E., Rome, E. (eds.) Managing the Complexity of Critical Infrastructures. SSDC, vol. 90, pp. 195–232. Springer, Cham (2016). https://doi.org/10.1007/978-3-319-51043-9_9

12. Taraglio, S.: A Lombardi: decision support system for smart urban management: resilience against natural phenomena and aerial environmental assessment. Int. J. Sustain. Energy Plann. Manage. 24 (2019)

13. Matassoni, L., Giovinazzi, S., Pollino, M., Fiaschi, A., La Porta, L., Rosato, V.: A geospatial decision support tool for seismic risk management: florence (Italy) case study. In: Gervasi, O. (ed.) Computational Science and Its Applications – ICCSA 2017. LNCS, vol. 10405, pp. 278–293. Springer, Cham (2017). https://doi.org/10.1007/978-3-319-62395-5_20

14. Gervasi, O. (ed.): Computational Science and Its Applications – ICCSA 2017. LNCS, vol. 10404. Springer, Cham (2017). https://doi.org/10.1007/978-3-319-62392-4

15. Modica, G., et al.: Land suitability evaluation for agro-forestry: definition of a web-based multi-criteria spatial decision support system (MC-SDSS): preliminary results. In: Gervasi, O. (ed.) Computational Science and Its Applications -- ICCSA 2016. LNCS, vol. 9788, pp. 399–413. Springer, Cham (2016). https://doi.org/10.1007/978-3-319-42111-7_31

16. Ottobrino, V., Esposito, T., Locoratolo, S.: Towards a smart water distribution network for assessing the effects by critical situations in electric networks. the pilot case of Castel San Giorgio. In: 21th International Conference on Computational Science and its Application, RRS2021 Workshop, Cagliari, Italy (2021)

17. Agresta, A., et al.: Applying numerical models and optimized sensor networks for drinking water quality control. Proc. Eng. 119, 918–926 (2015). ISSN 1877-7058

18. Fattoruso, G., Agresta, A., Guarnieri, G., Toscanesi, M., De Vito, S., Fabbricino, M., Trifuoggi, M., Di Francia, G.: A software system for predicting trihalomethanes species in water distribution networks using online networked water sensors. In: Di Francia, G. (ed.) Sensors and Microsystems. LNEE, vol. 629, pp. 417–423. Springer, Cham (2020). https://doi.org/10.1007/978-3-030-37558-4_62

19. Behzadian, K., Kapelan, Z., Savic, D., Ardeshir, A.: Stochastic sampling design using a multi-objective genetic algorithm and adaptive neural networks. Environ. Model. Softw. 24(4), 530–541 (2009)

20. Fattoruso, G., et al.: Optimal sensors placement for flood forecasting modelling. Proc. Eng. 119, 927–936 (2015). ISSN 1877-7058

21. Gervasi, O. (ed.): Computational Science and Its Applications – ICCSA 2020. LNCS, vol. 12251. Springer, Cham (2020). https://doi.org/10.1007/978-3-030-58808-3

International Workshop on Scientific Computing Infrastructure (SCI 2021)

Textual Analysis of News for Stock Market Prediction

Alexander V. Bogdanov, Maxim Bogan, and Alexey Stankus[✉]

Saint Petersburg State University, 7-9 Universitetskaya emb., Saint Petersburg 199034, Russia
alexey@stankus.ru

Abstract. Stock market prediction constitutes an important factor in business. There are a large number of different mathematical models for predicting stock price movements. One of the alternative approaches is application of methods based on Natural Language Processing (NLP).

Though NLP tasks are getting popular, they remain complex and voluminous. In the digital age almost, all information has been transferred to digital records that is good achievement. That is a good achievement. But on the other side because of the ease in creating new information, information search in Internet becomes complicated. This problem becomes more relevant, and scientists continue to search ways to structure a huge amount of information.

There are many methods of traditional representations of words based on statistics. But these methods don't give representation about contexts and semantics of text document. In this paper, we will consider approaches that help to get semantics from news. To evaluate our methods, we will use them for predicting direction of S&P 500 Index. In other words, we will compare our approaches with a stock market prediction problem based on news.

Keywords: Recurrent neural network · Stock prediction · LSTM · Glove · Word2Vec · News · Word Embedding · Tf-idf · YAKE

1 Introduction

There are a number of works aimed at predicting the movement of stock prices based on news [1–5]. But in these works, news headlines used as input data. News contains full information about the event, and the information in the headline may not reflect the whole essence of the news. At the same time, these works do not cover in detail the issue of preliminary processing of texts as input data, but only the analysis of a neural network.

Our idea is to predict the direction of price movement based on the content of the entire text of the news. Taking the news texts themselves as an input parameter leads us to the task of a deeper analysis of the news texts themselves and determining the best way to prepare the data before using it in machine learning models.

News is a set of n sentences, consisting of m words, where n and m are different for each news item. Initially, we need to understand what data format we need to pass on

© Springer Nature Switzerland AG 2021
O. Gervasi et al. (Eds.): ICCSA 2021, LNCS 12956, pp. 313–323, 2021.
https://doi.org/10.1007/978-3-030-87010-2_22

to the machine learning algorithms in order to work correctly. Every machine learning algorithm must have a constant number of input variables in the processed data. Therefore, any preprocessing method must create a fixed vector of variable length of news texts.

One of the key questions is how to get a fixed number of functions from a different number of news objects. This issue will be discussed in this article. In this article, we will check several data preparation algorithms for both classifiers (Fig. 1) and neural networks (Fig. 2) and compare the work of each of them.

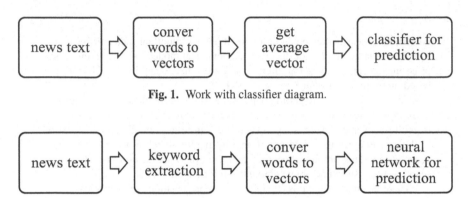

Fig. 1. Work with classifier diagram.

Fig. 2. Work with neural network diagram.

2   Work Vector Representation Model

In this section, we will first introduce methods for vector representation of words. After that, we will consider approaches to obtaining a news vector from vector words, which will correspond to some average meaning of the whole news.

2.1   Bag of Words Model and Word Embedding

There are two main models of vector representation of words - Bag of Words [6] and Word Embedding [7]:

The Bag of Words model creates a representation of a document as an unordered collection of words with no knowledge of the relationships between them. This algorithm creates a matrix, each row of which corresponds to a separate document or text, and each column corresponds to a specific word. Table 1 shows that the cell at the intersection of the row and column contains the number of occurrences of the word in the corresponding document. The main disadvantages of this approach are the lack of semantic meaning of words and entire documents, and does not consider the word order, which plays a big role. Therefore, this approach is not suitable for the task set in this work.

The Word Embedding model brings together a variety of natural language processing approaches. In this model, a corresponding fixed-length vector in an n-dimensional

Table 1. Word distribution in texts.

	I	love	dogs	hate	and	knitting	is	my	hobby	passion
Doc1	1	1	1							
Doc2	1		1	1	1	1				
Doc3				1	1		1	2	1	1

vector space is constructed for each word. But it is built in such a way as to maximize the semantic connection between words. One of the ways to express the semantic connection of words in a vector space is cosine similarity. It is calculated according to the following formula (1):

$$cos(\theta) = \frac{A \cdot B}{\|A\| \|B\|} = \frac{\sum_{i=1}^{n} A_i \times B_i}{\sqrt{\sum_{i=1}^{n} (A_i)^2} \times \sqrt{\sum_{i=1}^{n} (B_i)^2}},$$

$$\text{where } A_i \text{ and } B_i - \text{ is the } i - \text{th element of vectors } A \text{ and } B$$

(1)

Within the Word Embedding model, the following algorithms have been developed:

– Word2Vec [8]
– GloVe [9].

In the field of NLP, these models are the most modern and in demand today. Therefore, to create a vector representation of words that contains the semantic meaning of words, we will use the Word2Vec and Glove models.

2.2 Preparation of Texts

At this step, we have a vector representation of each word in the news corpus. A word represents a vector in n-dimensional vector space, that is, a word is a set of n - features, note that n is fixed. But in every news, the number of words is always different. Therefore, it is necessary to bring each news to a fixed number of signs.

Simple Averaging
The first way is simple - it is to take all the vector words belonging to the news and calculate the average vector, following formula (2):

$$\overrightarrow{\omega_{average}} = \frac{\sum_{i=1}^{m} \overrightarrow{\omega_i}}{m},$$

$$\text{where } \omega_i \text{ vector of the } i - \text{th word, } m - \text{the number of words in the news.}$$

(2)

Thus, we get a vector corresponding to the whole news. And if the vector of each word reflects the semantic meaning, then the vector of the whole news reflects some average meaning of the news. As a result, each news item is matched with a vector of dimension n, where n is fixed.

For example, the news: "Shanghai stocks opened lower, and the yuan was weaker against the dollar on Wednesday. Other Asian markets also declined. Hong Kong's benchmark declined 2% as the city faced heightened tensions". Converted to a single vector as follows:

$$\left.\begin{array}{r}\text{Shanghai} = \overrightarrow{(0.345, 0.101, \ldots, 0.640)} \\ \text{stocks} = \overrightarrow{(0.783, 0.089, \ldots, 0.554)} \\ \cdots = \cdots \\ \text{heightened} = \overrightarrow{(0.421, 0.484, \ldots, 0.054)} \\ \text{tensions} = \overrightarrow{(0.383, 0.211, \ldots, 0.954)}\end{array}\right\} \rightarrow \overrightarrow{\omega_{average}} = \overrightarrow{(0.497, 0.301, \ldots, 0.628)}$$

Term Frequency - Inverse Document Frequency (tf-idf)

Words in the news have different meanings or importance. Then it is worth not just counting the average, but constructing a linear combination, where each vector will be multiplied by a coefficient corresponding to the importance of the word. This idea is contained in the tf-idf (term frequency - inverse document frequency) formula [10]. It considers the frequency with which the word occurs in the text, a weighted average is taken.

tf - the ratio of the number of occurrences of a certain word to the total number of words of one text document.

$$tf(t, d) = \frac{n_t}{\sum_k n_k}, \tag{3}$$

где n_t– is the number of times the word t has been mentioned in the document, and the denominator is the total number of words in the document.

idf is the inverse of the frequency of occurrence of a word in all documents. Accounting for idf reduces the weight (weight) of commonly used words.

$$idf(t, D) = log\frac{|D|}{|\{d_i \in D | t \in d_i\}|}, \tag{4}$$

where $|D|$ – number of documents, $|\{d_i \in D | t \in d_i\}|$ – the number of documents in which we have t(when $n_t \neq 0$).

Hence, the tf-idf measure is the product of two factors:

$$tfi{-}df(t, d, D) = tf(t, d) \times idf(t, D) \tag{5}$$

Words with a high frequency within a particular document and with a low frequency of use in other documents will receive a lot of weight in tf-idf.

So, using the tf-idf measure, a linear combination of vectors is built and divided by the number of vectors. As a result, we get a vector of fixed length, which is also some mean sense of the news.

The example from "Simple averaging" the transformation looks like formula (6):

$$\left.\begin{array}{c} \overrightarrow{(0.345, 0.101, \ldots, 0.640)} \cdot 0.76 \\ \overrightarrow{(0.783, 0.089, \ldots, 0.554)} \cdot 0.34 \\ \cdots = \cdots \\ \overrightarrow{(0.421, 0.484, \ldots, 0.054)} \cdot 0.56 \\ \overrightarrow{(0.383, 0.211, \ldots, 0.954)} \cdot 0.48 \end{array}\right\} \rightarrow \overrightarrow{\omega_{average}} = \overrightarrow{(0.385, 0.094, \ldots, 0.670)} \quad (6)$$

Key Words

Certainly, when calculating the average meaning, the loss of information is possible since the meaning turns out to be very approximate and there are many words that do not carry meaning. Let's try to remove words that do not carry meaning.

We extract a fixed number of keywords from each news item. Further, to transfer several words to the algorithm sequentially, we will use a recurrent neural network LSTM (Long short-term memory). It is a recurrent neural network that can store values for both short and long periods of time.

The YAKE algorithm [11] developed by a team of French scientists [12] in 2018 was chosen to extract keywords. YAKE is an unsupervised automatic keyword extraction method that relies on the statistical characteristics of the text. Moreover, not only nominal and non-nominal entities are extracted in the form of words and noun phrases, but also predicates, adjectives and other parts of speech that carry key information of the news. In [12], the method is compared with ten modern unsupervised approaches such as tf-idf, KP-Miner, RAKE, TextRank, SingleRank, ExpandRank, TopicRank, TopicalPageRank, PositionRank and MultipartiteRank), and one supervised method (KEA). According to the results of the authors of the article, the YAKE method shows the best result.

In each news, using the YAKE algorithm, all keywords are marked in each sentence. Further, all unmarked words are deleted and as a result, only significant words remain. After that, using Word2Vec or Glove, all words are translated into the corresponding vectors, and news, consisting of a sequence of vectors, is fed into the LSTM network, where growth/fall markers (1/0) are at the output. Figure 3 depicts a network model with inner LSTM layers and a convolutional layer.

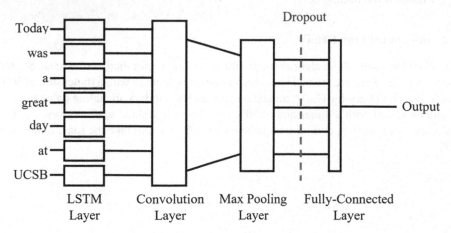

Fig. 3. Model with inner layers.

Let's give an example of processing news using keywords:

"Shanghai stocks opened lower and the yuan was weaker against the dollar on Wednesday. Other Asian markets also declined. Hong Kong's benchmark declined 2% as the city faced heightened tensions".

Therefore, we get:

"Shanghai stocks opened lower yuan weaker dollar Wednesday. Asian markets declined. Hong Kong's benchmark declined city faced heightened tensions".

3 Experiments

3.1 Data

The experiments were conducted on the basis of a set of news collected from BBC News, Breitbart News, CNN, The New York Times, Reuters, Washington Post, Bloomberg and Yahoo News for the period from November 2018 to August 2019 (Table 2). Next, data were taken with prices S&P500 Index. We use the closing price as the price.

Table 2. Time intervals and amount of news.

S&P 500 Index prediction data			
Data set	Training	Development	Testing
Time interval	25/11/2018– 21/07/2019	21/07/2019– 20/08/2019	20/08/2019– 19/09/2019
News	182,250	22,782	22,782

We use the news content published over the course of an hour to predict the S&P 500 movement up or down, comparing the closing price at t + 1 with the closing price at t, where t is the trading hour.

3.2 Implementation Details

For Word2Vec and GloVe algorithms, pre-trained word-vector dictionaries exist. So, for Word2Vec there are pre-trained word-vectors on Google news with a dimension of 300. There is a dictionary for GloVe trained on various textual data, including on news with Common Crawl with a dimension of 300. Based on pre-trained word vectors, we will train our word vectors, and for comparison of results we will take the same dimension 300.

To evaluate news processing approaches, we will use classifiers as machine learning algorithms:

- Extra trees
- Support Vector Classifier (SVC) with rbf
- Random Forest
- Logistic regression
- Linear SVC
- Naive Bayes
- Multilayer perceptron.

And also, for keywords - the recurrent neural network LSTM.

As an estimate, we will use the accuracy of the coincidence of the growth and fall of the true and predicted values.

3.3 Prediction Algorithms

Both Word2Vec and GloVe have two subsamples of experiments - these are eigenvectors of words and pre-trained word vectors. Word2Vec and GloVe methods are used in all experiments.

Next, the Averaging and tf-idf methods form a fixed vector. This vector is fed into classifiers and one standard deep learning model:

- Extra trees
- SVC with rbf
- Random Forest
- Logistic regression
- Linear SVC
- Naive Bayes.
- Multilayer perceptron.

But for the keywords method, only the LSTM recurrent neural network is suitable. Because the above classifiers and the standard deep learning model do not have such properties as LSTM - to accept as input a sequence of the same type of feature vectors and extract new features from them. In each model, the best hyperparameters are selected and cross-validation is carried out.

3.4 Results

The results of comparing news preparation approaches to machine learning algorithms in Tables 3 and 4 show that pre-trained vectors give a more accurate vector representation of words. This is due to the fact that the amount of news is probably not enough to determine the exact context of words in a vector representation. A comparison between the approaches of simple averaging and weighted averaging with tf-idf shows that simple averaging gives an idea of a certain mean sense worse than weighted averaging with the tf-idf measure. The vector representation algorithms for Word2Vec and GloVe work similarly, but GloVe in the end gives a 0.5% better result.

Table 3. Prediction results with Word2Vec preprocessing.

Word2Vec						
Embedding	Own trained word vectors			Pretrained word vectors		
Preprocess methods	Average	tf-idf	Key words	Average	tf-idf	Key words
ExtraTrees	54.53%	54.98%	–	56.44%	57.12%	–
SVC with rbf	55.45%	55.58%	–	56.90%	**57.20%**	–
Random forest	55.58%	55.61%	–	55.74%	55.90%	–
Logistic regression	53.02%	54.27%	–	53.23%	54.79%	–
Linear SVC	53.01%	53.98%	–	54.97%	53.56%	–
Naïve Bayes	49.87%	48.79%	–	50.43%	51.86%	–
Multilayer perceptron	53.11%	53.20%	–	53.22%	53.63%	–
LSTM	–	–	56,32%	–	–	**57,63%**

Table 4. Prediction results with GloVe preprocessing.

GloVe						
Embedding	Own trained word vectors			Pretrained word vectors		
Preprocess methods	Average	tf-idf	Key words	Average	tf-idf	Key words
ExtraTrees	55.21%	55.70%	–	57.44%	57.89%	–
SVC with rbf	56.11%	56.23%	–	57.56%	**58.00%**	–
Random forest	56.08%	56.07%	–	56.08%	56.23%	–
Logistic regression	53.32%	54.76%	–	53.61%	55.22%	–
Linear SVC	53.23%	54.31%	–	55.33%	53.97%	–
Naïve Bayes	49.87%	48.79%	–	50.43%	51.86%	–
Multilayer perceptron	53.31%	53.45%	–	53.52%	53.69%	–
LSTM	–	–	57,42%	–	–	**58,97%**

During the experiments in the method based on keywords, the optimal number of keywords was chosen equal to 1900. The experimental data are presented in Fig. 4. But it is worth noting that on average there are 2700 words in the news, which indicates that the selected number is approximately 2/3 of all words. As a result, the accuracy slightly exceeded the maximum value of averaging methods.

Further, a series of experiments was carried out with the dimension parameter of vectors in the case of training our vectors, since the maximum dimension of pre-trained vectors proposed by the authors of the algorithms does not exceed 300. Figures 5 and 6 show schedules of changes in prediction accuracy with respect to the dimension of word vectors.

It can be noted that in both cases, when the dimension reaches 1900, the accuracy of the prediction ceases to grow, and in the future it even worsens. As a result, by increasing the dimension of the vectors, it was possible to increase the accuracy by 0.5–1%.

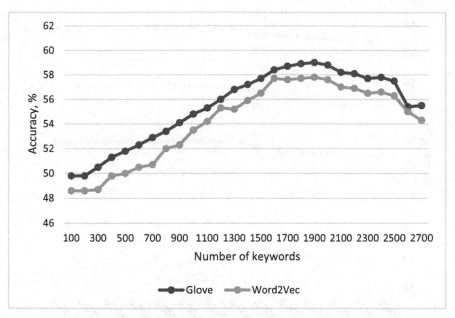

Fig. 4. Optimal number of keywords.

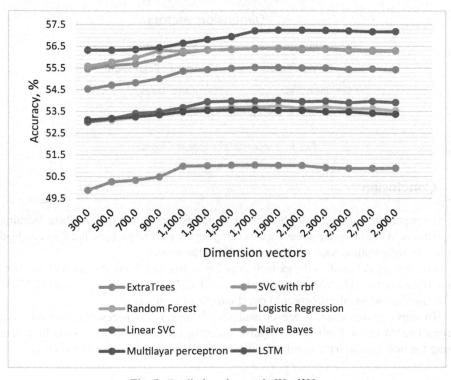

Fig. 5. Prediction changes in Word2Vec

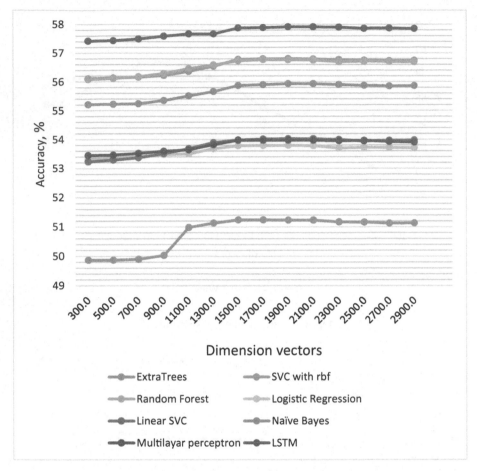

Fig. 6. Prediction changes in Glove.

4   Conclusion

In this paper, we consider news processing methods for feeding into machine learning algorithms. Algorithms based on vector averaging are easy to process, but they can lead to loss of information, such as the word order in the news.

The algorithm based on the extraction of keywords, that is combination of the most important words and LSTM showed the best result (57.63% with Word2Vec and 58.97% with GloVe) and has the prospect of development in such tasks.

To improve the result, a deeper analysis of the texts is necessary, including the determination of the positive or negative meaning of the news. We also believe that using the new Hierarchal Attention Network model can improve news prediction.

References

1. Liu, H.: Leveraging financial news for stock trend prediction with attention-based recurrent neural network (2018)
2. Liu, J., Chao, F., Lin, Y., Lin, C.: Stock prices prediction using deep learning models (2015)
3. Alam, F., Kumar, A., Vela, A.: Using news articles to predict stock movements based on different forecasting techniques statistical, Regression and Text Mining (2018)
4. Zhu, X., Nahar, S.: Predicting stock price trends using news headlines (2016)
5. Velay, M, Daniel, F.: Using NLP on news headlines to predict index trends (2018)
6. Zhang, Y., Jin, R., Zhou, Z.H.: Understanding bag-of-words model: a statistical framework. Int. J. Mach. Learn. Cybern. (2010)
7. Mikolov, T., Sutskever, I., Chen, K., Corrado, G.S., Dean, J.: Distributed representations of words and phrases and their compositionality. In: NIPS (2013)
8. Mikolov, T., Chen, K., Corrado, G., Dean, J.: Efficient estimation of word representations in vector space. ICLR (2013)
9. Pennington, J., Socher, R., Manning. C.D.: GloVe: global vectors for word representation (2014)
10. Jones, K.S.: A statistical interpretation of term specificity and its application in retrieval. MCB University (2006)
11. Campos R., Mangaravite V., Pasquali A., Jorge A.M., Nunes C., Jatowt A.: YAKE! collection-independent automatic keyword extractor. In: Pasi G., Piwowarski B., Azzopardi L., Hanbury A. (eds.) Advances in Information Retrieval. ECIR 2018. Lecture Notes in Computer Science, vol 10772. Springer, Cham (2018)
12. Campos R., Mangaravite V., Pasquali A., Jorge A.M., Nunes C., Jatowt A.: A text feature based automatic keyword extraction method for single documents. In: Pasi G., Piwowarski B., Azzopardi L., Hanbury A. (eds.) Advances in Information Retrieval. ECIR 2018. Lecture Notes in Computer Science, vol 10772. Springer, Cham (2018)
13. "Finam". https://www.finam.ru/
14. Pre-trained vocabulary Word2Vec. https://code.google.com/archive/p/word2vec/
15. Pre-trained vocabulary GloVe. https://nlp.stanford.edu/projects/glove/

Investigation of CW-Tree for Parallel Execution of Queries to Database

Vladislav S. Shevskiy(iD) and Yulia A. Shichkina(✉)(iD)

Saint Petersburg Electrotechnical University "LETI", Professor Popov Street, 5,
St. Petersburg 197022, Russia

Abstract. The efficiency of using the developed CW-tree data structure in comparison with the B+-tree were analyzed in this article. B+-tree is used in the popular MySQL relational database management system. It has been experimentally proven that B+-tree is not efficient for parallel data retrieval. The study of parallelizing queries with different numbers of threads showed that with an increase in the number of threads, the search speed becomes higher. However, when the number of threads is ≥ 4, the speed stopped changing. That means that, after four threads, there was no point in increasing the number of threads. For testing the CW-tree a separate physical drive connected via PCI-Express interface were used. The drive is INTEL MEMPEK1W016GA, it has volume of 13.41 gigabytes, its logical sector size is 512 bytes and physical sector size is 512 bytes. A database was created, filled in according to the data structure CW-tree on this intel drive. For the analysis of the CW-tree, 6 search queries were developed with different amounts of returned data. The experiment showed that executing these queries in parallel mode is faster for CW-tree than in B+-tree executing the same queries in MySQL, where B+-tree is used to index data.

Keywords: CW-tree · Database indexing algorithms · Parallel computing · Database management system

1 Introduction

1.1 Relevance of Research

In the modern world, the amount of stored data is growing very rapidly. This is happening against the background of digitalization in all areas of human life, from the financial sector to medicine. The number of mobile applications and electronic services is growing, which, based on the analysis of large amounts of data, make fore-casts and recommendations. In such analysis, fast data retrieval is especially important. Data retrieval makes a significant contribution to the efficiency of the entire system.

Physical storage systems adapt to the fast processing of big data, but this happens extremely slowly, so hardware remains a natural limiter of the acceleration of working with data. On the other hand, software in the form of a DBMS is programmatic and algorithmic support and can be improved much faster, especially when using parallel computations.

© Springer Nature Switzerland AG 2021
O. Gervasi et al. (Eds.): ICCSA 2021, LNCS 12956, pp. 324–335, 2021.
https://doi.org/10.1007/978-3-030-87010-2_23

However, not all modern DBMSs can be effectively parallelized. A study of the literature has shown that such a feature of the DBMS takes place due to the data structures used, which cannot be parallelized.

In early works [2, 3], the authors of this article proposed a new data structure CW-tree (Constantly Wide tree), developed by the authors in such a way that allows efficient use of parallelization.

This study compares the CW-tree and the most widespread in the DBMS B+-tree.

1.2 What is the CW-Tree

In [2] and [3], a description of the CW-tree algorithm is presented. CW-tree is a data structure that allows performing asynchronous tree traversal using not only the root, but also additional starting vertices. The main purpose of using the CW-tree algorithm is to speed up the search for data in the CW tree by using additional threads of the operating system that perform searches asynchronously starting from additional starting vertices.

1.3 What is the B+-Tree

B+-tree is a data structure containing nodes that store indexes as well as edges that define links between nodes. The traverse in B+-tree starts from the root vertex and continues through the nodes until the vertex with the target index is found.

Originally, the B+-tree structure was intended to store data for efficient retrieval in a block-oriented storage environment in particular for file systems; the application is due to the fact that, unlike binary search trees, B+-trees have a very high branching ratio (the number of pointers from the parent node to the children, usually of the order of 100 or more), which reduces the number of I/O operations that require searching for an element in the tree.

2 Analysis of CW-Tree

2.1 Disadvantages of B+-Tree in Parallel Mode

An important problem with the widely used B+-tree data indexing algorithm is the difficulty of using operating system threads while traversing a tree to find data.

The disadvantage of the search process in B+ is shown in Fig. 1 below, where B+-tree is displayed as an approximate one, each node of which has one index.

If it is necessary to find the vertices J, K, L and H in the tree that shown in Fig. 1, then all the paths composed of transitions between the vertices in the process of walking through the tree will intersect at the vertices A and B. And if we compare the tree passes in searches for the vertices K and L, then you can see that both paths inter-sect at the vertices A, B, E, K. It follows that if you construct an asynchronous search for the vertices J, K, L and H, that is, construct the traversal process in this way, so that the search for each of the given vertices occurs independently, then at the intersection of the vertices the threads will do unnecessary work, especially when comparing the threads searching for the vertices K and L.

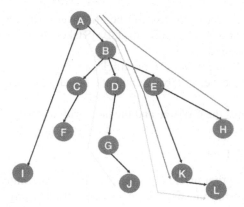

Fig. 1. An example of tree traversal when searching for different vertices

If it is necessary to find one vertex F in the tree shown in Fig. 1 and if you try to build an asynchronous search with four executing threads, then each of the four threads will do extra work due to the fact that each of the threads will perform the same path which contains passes A → B, B → C and C → F. This path follows from the property of B+-tree. Also, the root of the problem of forming a single path to find the required vertex in the tree is that in the tree there is only one starting point for searching for any vertex that is the root vertex.

In [1], an investigation of the execution time of various queries in the MySQL database, which uses indexing according to the rule of the B+-tree structure, was performed. Among the queries used for testing, various data read queries using the SELECT statement were designed. As well as subqueries of the original queries using the SELECT statement, which are called parallelized queries and divided according to the principles of data separation and task separation. As shown by the results of work [1], parallelized queries were executed faster than the original queries.

The database, which was used in testing in [1], was also used to identify the dependence of the query execution time on the amount of data read and the number of threads used within one task. For this, the following steps were performed:

1. A set of distributed queries has been formed in such a way that each one returns 1000000, 500000, 250000, 125000 first records from a table and uses 1, 2, ... 10 threads;
2. Separate query executed;
3. Stored the result into a LinkedList object in the Java programming language implementation;
4. The total time of execution and saving of the result has been calculated. The result is presented in Table 1.

It is necessary to compare the execution time of queries using 1 thread with queries using more than one thread to see if there is an advantage to using parallelized queries in MySql.

Table 1. Dependence of execution time on the number of threads and the amount of data in the database table

№	Number of threads	Number of records in the table	Total thread execution time
1	1	1000000	1478
2	1	500000	507
3	1	250000	252
4	1	125000	140
5	2	1000000	1155
6	2	500000	345
7	2	250000	176
8	2	125000	90
9	3	1000000	1075
10	3	500000	313
11	3	250000	156
12	3	125000	81
13	4	1000000	1040
14	4	500000	299
15	4	250000	163
16	4	125000	84
17	5	1000000	1021
18	5	500000	295
19	5	250000	146
20	5	125000	74
21	6	1000000	995
22	6	500000	278
23	6	250000	145
24	6	125000	85
25	7	1000000	1017
26	7	500000	287
27	7	250000	145
28	7	125000	67
29	8	1000000	1024
30	8	500000	307
31	8	250000	145
32	8	125000	109

(*continued*)

Table 1. (*continued*)

№	Number of threads	Number of records in the table	Total thread execution time
33	9	1000000	1003
34	9	500000	264
35	9	250000	150
36	9	125000	79
37	10	1000000	1020
38	10	500000	295
39	10	250000	187
40	10	125000	73

The comparison was made by calculating the difference in execution time using the formula:

$$\Delta t = t\_oneThread - t\_nThreads \tag{1}$$

where Δt is acceleration of query processing when using n threads; $t\_oneThread$ is the execution time of a query that returns the specified number of data records and uses one thread; $t\_nThreads$ is the execution time of a query that returns the specified amount of data and uses the specified number of threads. The result is presented in Table 2.

Table 2. Taking into account the difference in execution time of a parallelized query with different data volumes compared to single-threaded queries

№	Number of threads	Number of records in the table	Time when using n threads	Time when using 1 thread	Δt
1	1	1000000	1478	1478	0
2	1	500000	507	507	0
3	1	250000	252	252	0
4	1	125000	140	140	0
5	2	1000000	1155	1478	323
6	2	500000	345	507	162
7	2	250000	176	252	76
8	2	125000	90	140	50
9	3	1000000	1075	1478	403
10	3	500000	313	507	194
11	3	250000	156	252	96

(*continued*)

Table 2. (*continued*)

№	Number of threads	Number of records in the table	Time when using n threads	Time when using 1 thread	Δt
12	3	125000	81	140	59
13	4	1000000	1040	1478	438
14	4	500000	299	507	208
15	4	250000	163	252	89
16	4	125000	84	140	56
17	5	1000000	1021	1478	457
18	5	500000	295	507	212
19	5	250000	146	252	106
20	5	125000	74	140	66
21	6	1000000	995	1478	483
22	6	500000	278	507	229
23	6	250000	145	252	107
24	6	125000	85	140	55
25	7	1000000	1017	1478	461
26	7	500000	287	507	220
27	7	250000	145	252	107
28	7	125000	67	140	73
29	8	1000000	1024	1478	454
30	8	500000	307	507	200
31	8	250000	145	252	107
32	8	125000	109	140	31
33	9	1000000	1003	1478	475
34	9	500000	264	507	243
35	9	250000	150	252	102
36	9	125000	79	140	61
37	10	1000000	1020	1478	458
38	10	500000	295	507	212
39	10	250000	187	252	65
40	10	125000	73	140	67

The result of comparing the difference in execution time Δt between queries by the criterion of the amount of data returned is shown in the diagrams below (see Figs. 2, 3, 4, and 5).

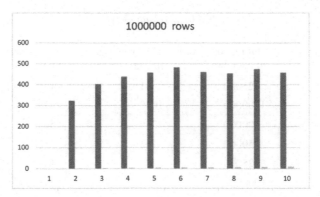

Fig. 2. Comparison of the execution time of a read query for 1000000 records based on the number of threads used during the execution of the query

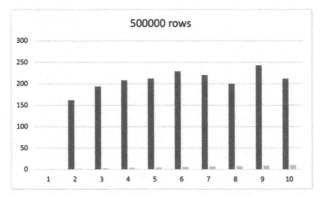

Fig. 3. Comparison of the execution time of a query to read 500000 records based on the number of threads used during the execution of the query

In the pictures (see Figs. 2, 3, 4, and 5) the time scale of queries execution in milliseconds vertically, and the number of threads used during the execution of queries horizontally shown.

The result of the experiment shown in the figures (see Figs. 2, 3, 4, and 5) shows that a parallelized query with more than 1 thread is executed faster than with 1 thread, however, as the number of threads used increases, there is no tendency to decrease the query execution time.

2.2 CW-Tree Data Structure

The CW-tree structure is designed to traverse the tree asynchronously using additional starting vertices from which the traversal will start. For such a passage to be possible, it is necessary that the CW-tree structure meets the following criteria:

– the structure should consist of two levels: the branch level, which stores the vertex indices, as well as the leaf level, which stores the data;

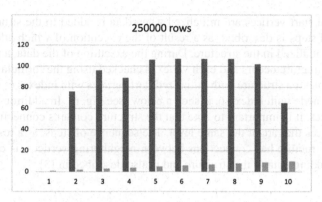

Fig. 4. Comparison of the execution time of a read query for 250000 records based on the number of threads used during the execution of the query

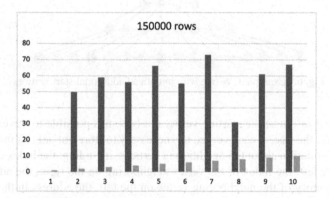

Fig. 5. Comparison of the execution time of a query to read 150000 records by the criterion of the number of threads used during the execution of the query

- adjacent vertices, which are at the same level, must be connected with each other by an edge in order to enable transition between them in the process of walking through the tree;
- in addition to the root vertex, the structure must contain additional starting vertices, from which the search for the vertex will be started.

Also, in order to carry out a parallel traversal through the CW-tree, it is necessary to determine the algorithms:

- initialization of starting vertices;
- bypassing the CW-tree.

In [3], detailed description of the mentioned algorithms, as well as a description of the features of the CW-tree data structure is presented.

Additional start vertices are initialized when data is added to the structure. In [3], a sequence of steps is described, as a result of the execution of which additional start vertices are initialized in the structure. During the execution of the data, a pass through the CW-tree structure occurs and each vertex is checked using the formula described in [3]. An example of a structure with initialized start vertices with indexes 6, 18 and 29, as well as a root node with index 16, is shown below (see Fig. 6). In addition to additional starting vertices, it is important to note that the structure contains connections between adjacent vertices that are at the same level. The sequence of steps, as a result of which the CW-tree structure has connections between neighboring vertices, is carried out at the stage of adding data to the structure and is also described in [3].

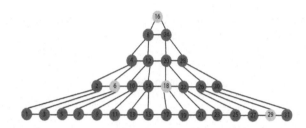

Fig. 6. Example CW-tree with initialized additional start vertices

After initialization of the starting vertices, it becomes possible to traverse the CW-tree. To traverse the tree, at each vertex, it is necessary to store not only its index, but also additional information about the neighboring vertices, including: the index of the vertex adjacent to the left, the index of the vertex neighboring on the right, the address in the permanent memory of the neighboring vertex on the left, the address in the permanent memory of the vertex adjacent to the right, etc. In [3], a complete list of information stored in each vertex is described. Thus, in the process of traversing the structure, at each step of the transition from one vertex to another, a choice is made - which vertex to go to due to the information that is known in the current vertex about neighboring vertices. The function of determining the next vertex to which the passage will be carried out within one iteration is called move. Its definition is given in [3].

An example of finding the vertex with index 1 in the CW-tree (see Fig. 6) is presented below (see Fig. 7).

vertex 16	16	8	4	2	1										
vertex 6	6	2	1												
vertex 18	18	14	10	6	2	1									
vertex 29	29	27	25	23	21	19	17	15	13	11	9	7	5	3	1

Fig. 7. Example of finding the vertex with index 1 in a CW-tree using additional start vertices

In the example of finding a vertex with index 1 (see Fig. 7), the first column shows the vertices from which the search was started, and the remaining columns, in order from left to right, show the vertices to which the transition was made during the search for the vertex with index 1. Thus, the search for vertex 1 from the additional starting vertex with index 6 was performed in fewer disk operations compared to the search for vertex 1 from the root vertex with index 16. As a result, the search for vertex 1 from vertex 6 will be faster than finding vertex 1 from vertex 16.

2.3 CW-Tree Application

To determine the effectiveness of the algorithm, we conducted comparative testing of query execution in the CW-tree and in the database created using the MySQL DBMS. During testing, we used two databases with the same database schema as in [1].

The number of data records in each database was equal to 500,000. The INTEL MEMPEK1W016GA device was used as a separate physical drive (volume is 13.41 gigabytes, logical sector size is 512 bytes, physical sector size is 512 bytes). The device was connected via built-in PCI-Express interface. In a database that used CW-tree index-ing, 3 additional start nodes were used, so one query was executed by 4 threads of execu-tion, one of which started searching from the root node, and the other 3 from additional start nodes. Query groups were developed, where a special parameter X was introduced which is the amount of data returned as a result. With this parameter, you can adjust the total amount of data returned. The groups of queries used in the testing process are presented in Table 3 below.

Table 3. Description of queries for testing

№	Content of the query
Query #1	select * from Table1 where A1 < X
Query #2	select * from Table1 inner join Table2 on A1 = A2 and A1 < X and A2 < X
Query #3	select * from Table1 inner join Table2 inner join Table3 on A1 = A2 and A2 = A3 and A1 < X and A2 < X and A3 < X
Query #4	select * from Table1 inner Table2 inner join Table3 inner join Table4 on A1 = A2 and A2 = A3 and A3 = D4 and A1 < X and A2 < X and A3 < X and D4 < X
Query #5	select * from Table1 where A1 < X and A1 in (select A2 from Table2 where A2 < X)
Query #6	select A1 from Table1 where A1 < X union all select A2 from Table2 where A2 < X

In Table 3, the parameter X, which indicates the amount of data returned, can be determined by the recursive formula:

$$X = \{x_i = x_{i-1} + \Delta, i = \{1, ..., 10\}, x_0 = 0, \Delta = 50000, x_{10} = 500000\}.$$

The results of testing the execution time of the queries shown in Table 3 are presented in Figs. 2, 3, 4, 5, and 6 below.

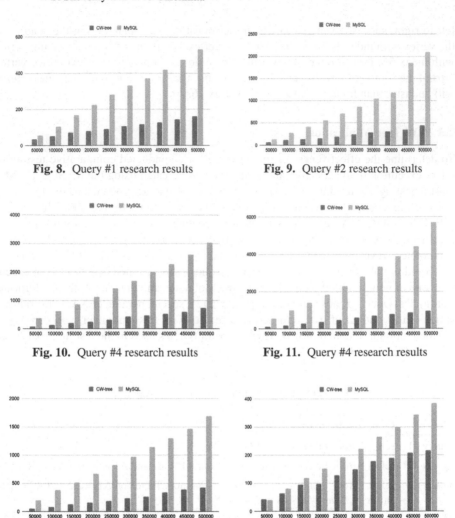

Fig. 8. Query #1 research results

Fig. 9. Query #2 research results

Fig. 10. Query #4 research results

Fig. 11. Query #4 research results

Fig. 12. Query #5 research results

Fig. 13. Query #6 research results

In the figures (see Figs. 8, 9, 10, 11, 12, and 13), the vertical scale of the query execution time in milliseconds is displayed, the horizontal is the X parameter, described above and indicating the amount of data returned as a result of queries.

As the results in Figs. 8, 9, 10, 11, 12, and 13 show, that the execution time of queries in the CW-tree is significantly less than the execution time of the corresponding queries in MySQL, which confirms the effectiveness of using the CW-tree when performing parallel data retrieval.

3   Conclusion

The results of investigation show that one query is executed simultaneously against the MySQL databases and the CW-tree, and all six are executed faster in the CW-tree database. The fact that all queries run faster in the CW-tree proves the effectiveness of the CW-tree method when processing various SQL queries, especially those that can be divided into independent parts. Thus, CW-tree with parallel search capability is much faster than analogs.

Acknowledgements. The reported study was funded by RFBR according to the research project № 19-07-00784.

References

1. Shichkina, Y., Kupriyanov, M., Shevsky, V.: The application of graph theory and adjacency lists to create parallel queries to relational databases. In: Galinina, O., Andreev, S., Balandin, S., Koucheryavy, Y. (eds.) NEW2AN/ruSMART -2018. LNCS, vol. 11118, pp. 138–149. Springer, Cham (2018). https://doi.org/10.1007/978-3-030-01168-0_13
2. Shevskiy, V.: Constantly wide tree for parallel processing. In: Conference 2019, ISTMC, Yalta, Crimea, pp. 285–292 (2019). http://ceur-ws.org/Vol-2522/paper28.pdf. Accessed 13 Jan 2021
3. Shevskiy, V.: Indexing data based on the CW-tree algorithm using parallel data reading. In: Conference 2020, MECO, pp. 1–6 (2020). https://doi.org/10.1109/MECO49872.2020.9134263
4. Graefe, G., Kuno, H.: Modern B-tree techniques. In: 2011, IEEE 27th International Conference on Data Engineering, pp. 1370–1373 (2011)
5. Bayer, R., McCreight, E.: Organization and maintenance of large ordered indexes. In: Broy, M., Denert, E. (eds.) Software Pioneers, pp. 245–262. Springer, Heidelberg (2002). https://doi.org/10.1007/978-3-642-59412-0_15
6. Comer, D.: Ubiquitous B-tree. ACM Comput. Surveys **11**(2), 121–137 (1979)

Harnessing Cloud Computing to Power Up HPC Applications: The BRICS CloudHPC Project

Jonatas A. Marques[1], Zhongke Wu[2], Xingce Wang[2], Ruslan Kuchumov[3],
Vladimir Korkhov[3,4], Weverton L. C. Cordeiro[1], Philippe O. A. Navaux[1],
and Luciano P. Gaspary[1(✉)]

[1] Federal University of Rio Grande do Sul, Porto Alegre, Brazil
{jamarques,weverton,navaux,paschoal}@inf.ufrgs.br
[2] Beijing Normal University, Beijing, China
{wangxingce,zwu}@bnu.edu.cn
[3] Saint Petersburg State University, St. Petersburg, Russia
v.korkhov@spbu.ru
[4] Plekhanov Russian University of Economics, Moscow, Russia

Abstract. In this paper, we report the main accomplishments obtained in the context of the CloudHPC project. Accepted in response to the BRICS Pilot Call 2016, the project gathered researchers from the Federal University of Rio Grande do Sul (UFRGS), the St. Petersburg State University (SPbSU), and Beijing Normal University (BNU). Its main objective was to identify cloud computing aspects that can be explored to provide a far-reaching, flexible, and efficient environment for running HPC applications. In addition to the main results, we also discuss the lessons learned and perspectives for future research in the area.

Keywords: HPC applications · Cloud · Virtualization · Containers · Network · Medical applications

1 Introduction

Handling massive amounts of data is commonplace for most modern scientific, engineering, and business applications. As these applications need to target several big data-related challenges while delivering expected results in a timely manner, they frequently pose large computing power requirements. In this context, High-Performance Computing (HPC) becomes a key factor for speeding up data processing while also enabling faster time to market, lower capital expenditures, and higher valued innovation. To this end, HPC solutions have traditionally taken advantage of cluster and datacenter infrastructures for running applications having those computing power requirements [3]. In addition, practitioners have also been leveraging cloud computing resources for meeting HPC demands when available resources do not suffice. In fact, the pay-per-use cost model and resource elasticity make cloud computing an exciting environment for HPC, which can be provided with instant availability and flexible scaling of resources, among other benefits.

© Springer Nature Switzerland AG 2021
O. Gervasi et al. (Eds.): ICCSA 2021, LNCS 12956, pp. 336–349, 2021.
https://doi.org/10.1007/978-3-030-87010-2_24

Despite the benefits of using cloud computing for HPC, a current approach has been the allocation of physical infrastructures in a dedicated mode for fast HPC provisioning. Although convenient, it frequently leads to underutilized resources, e.g., an application may not fully utilize provided CPU and/or network resources. It also prevents dealing adequately with those applications whose resource demands grow beyond available capacity. Traditional virtualization technologies can help to solve the problem. Still, the overhead of both bootstrapping a virtual infrastructure for each application and sharing physical resources among several virtual instances might be significant. Boosting available physical resources by using cloud computing, in turn, has been hampered because of limited support for shifting HPC applications to the cloud. These issues hinder the wide adoption of cloud computing by the HPC community, thus becoming paramount to understand how one can perform smooth and effective migration of (parts of) HPC applications to the cloud.

In the BRICS CloudHPC project, our primary goal was to identify cloud computing aspects that can be explored to provide a far-reaching, flexible (e.g., in terms of adaptation to fluctuating demands) and efficient environment for running HPC applications. In this paper, we report the main accomplishments during this three-year-long effort. We focus on (i) models, algorithms, and mechanisms to help users access a suitable cloud execution platform for running their HPC applications and (ii) science-related applications that can capitalize on these software artifacts to accelerate their execution.

The remainder of the paper is organized as follows. In Sect. 2, we characterize how existing public clouds perform when used to execute HPC applications. In Sect. 3, we summarize novel computing and networking techniques for HPC efficiency in cloud environments proposed in the context of the project. In Sect. 4, we describe a medical image processing use case used in CloudHPC. Research challenges and opportunities are then briefly discussed in Sect. 5. Finally, in Sect. 6 we close the paper with final remarks.

2 Tuning Public Cloud Instance Allocation for the Execution of HPC Applications

As mentioned earlier, executing HPC applications in cloud environments has become an important research topic in recent years. In contrast to traditional clusters, which consist of primarily homogeneous machines, running HPC applications in the cloud allows them to use heterogeneous resources offered by the cloud provider. Cloud instances can be adapted to match the imbalanced behavior of an HPC application, reducing the price of executing it in the cloud.

In the work [14], the authors performed a comprehensive set of experiments evaluating the potential of using heterogeneous instance types on three public cloud providers, Microsoft Azure, Amazon AWS, and Google Cloud. The difference in demands was explored by selecting multiple instance types adapted to the application's needs.

The experiments configured a cluster of 32 cores, consisting of four instances with eight cores each. All instances ran Ubuntu 18.04 LTS. To provide a fair comparison between the providers and their instances, the authors chose data-center locations as close as possible. They used ImbBench [15] as the workload to perform the tests of the cloud configurations. ImbBench is a proto-benchmark system that implements several load patterns for MPI processes [13]. To measure the cost of the configuration, the authors used the Cost Efficiency methodology [13]. Briefly, this methodology helps the user determine which provider and configuration offer the higher performance for the price paid.

Microsoft Azure has the largest number of instances, with eight cores, among the three providers of this study. The authors selected ten instance types for the evaluation, covering the whole spectrum of available configurations. To evaluate the CPU performance of Microsoft Azure, they performed tests with different instance types. To identify if the combination of varying instance types could reduce the execution cost, they built several combinations of instances.

To reduce the overall idle time, the authors proposed the execution of the application using a combination of different instances. They could achieve this by using instances with less performance and price. Figure 1 shows the execution of the application in a heterogeneous cluster. In this case, they configured a cluster with one A8v2 instance, two F8 instances, and one H8 instance. The execution time remains the same as the homogeneous cluster. However, the idle time was reduced by using the cheaper instances.

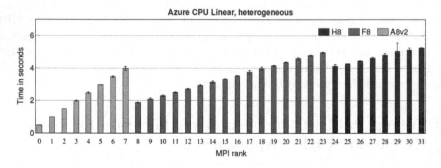

Fig. 1. CPU performance of the Azure heterogeneous cluster to run the Linear pattern.

The results showed that heterogeneous execution is most beneficial on Azure, improving cost efficiency by up to 50% compared to execution on homogeneous instances while maintaining the same performance. The other two providers are less suitable since the cheapest instance type either is the fastest as well (AWS) or the provider offers only instances that vary in memory size but not in performance (Google).

3   Novel Computing and Networking Techniques for HPC Efficiency in Cloud Environments

Our experience with cloud computing infrastructures showed that, although they allow for the execution of HPC applications, it is very hard (if possible) to achieve results comparable to those observed in dedicated infrastructures. Essential metrics such as execution time struggle to achieve acceptable levels. This is due to different issues such as the shared nature of cloud resources, the difficulty in enforcing VM allocation strategies that could potentially favor HPC, and well-known bottlenecks (e.g., virtualization and communication links).

In the project context, we focused on devising novel mechanisms to tailor the cloud towards a more convenient platform to execute HPC applications. Our work encompassed the proposal of solutions within two central axes, namely computing and networking. Next, we briefly review four primary outcomes of the CloudHPC project to make these components more efficient and, at the same time, resource usage judicious.

3.1   Collecting HPC Applications Processing Characteristics to Facilitate Co-scheduling

One of the goals of this project activity [6] was to reduce queue waiting times in cluster schedulers by applying co-scheduling using various strategies. This is especially important in virtualized and cloud environments that might share resources between multiple applications. Co-scheduling enables assigning various applications with different resource requirements to a single computing node with enough resources to run them simultaneously and without interference. For example, some applications that only require disk I/O may be running simultaneously with applications that only use the network intensively since they use entirely different resources. This strategy improves the use of cluster resources and reduces the waiting time for tasks in the queue compared to the commonly used scheduling strategies, where a node can run one application at a time. The scientific community is currently dedicating much attention to studies that assess the feasibility of this strategy and its practical aspects.

Since co-scheduling requires more information about the job resource requirements that the shared scheduler will ultimately use (e.g., the number of cores and the computation time), it is crucial to figure out these parameters and metrics of the job. They will be fed into a mathematical model that can then be used to schedule the solution.

Scheduling theory originated long before the field of high-performance computing. Its primary focus is on formalizing scheduling problems and applying various mathematical methods to create schedules that are subject to certain constraints and optimize a particular objective function. Nevertheless, when it comes to the classical theory, there are essential assumptions that may limit its applicability to the problem of joint planning. First, each job can be processed by no more than one machine, and each machine can process no more than one job (operation). Second, the task execution time does not change in time. Third, the task completion time is known in advance. In the latest development of scheduling theory, at least one of these assumptions is updated.

In the co-scheduling problem, all the provisions of the classical schedule theory are dynamic, which makes the problem of determining the model quite challenging. Moreover, from a practical point of view, there are also a number of open questions. For example, sharing a resource with multiple applications without provoking any disagreement is not always possible. Additional information about the resource consumption of the task should be collected and taken into account when planning. What is even worse is that the required information is not easily accessible. The user cannot provide it at the stage of submitting the task as well as it is not easy to get it by tracking the behavior of the task during its execution. The scientific community has already done a great job collecting such information by interpreting available metrics, such as hardware counters or operating system events.

In [6], the authors considered ways to define cluster environments using scheduling theory models and described how job processing characteristics from the scheduling theory can be applied to describe HPC applications. They detailed how to track and monitor various resource requirements, such as the number of computing nodes, CPU cores, memory bandwidth, and network bandwidth while the application is running. Using this approach, it is possible to estimate the application execution time as a function of resource constraints. This also enables decisions about the limit of constraining individual applications when they are scheduled together with a co-scheduling strategy.

3.2 Resource Allocation for Running HPC Workloads Simultaneously

An effective resource management system is the key to high-quality solutions for HPC and distributed computing. One of the major problems is to map applications to available computing resources so that optimal application performance is delivered and resources are used efficiently. The traditional solution is to adapt applications to the resources, which is not always easy or effective. There is an alternative way that implies configuring the infrastructure to the application needs. This leads to the necessity of abstracting resources, which can be done with virtualization technologies.

In [4], the authors consider the execution of parallel and distributed applications in virtual clusters that are explicitly configured to match application resource requirements. The authors analyze experimental usage of configurable virtual clusters on different workloads in different resource sharing scenarios: parallel applications (NAS Parallel Benchmarks) and distributed data processing frameworks (Apache Hadoop benchmarks: MRBench, TestDFSIO, and TeraSort) and demonstrate that efficiency of using distributed resources can be increased – even in case of utilizing cloud resources – by the simultaneous execution of lightweight virtual clusters on a single set of resources.

In high-performance computing, schedulers are widely used to maintain queues of jobs created by various users and assign compute nodes to run these jobs. Usually, at any moment, one computational node is assigned to perform one task. Sometimes nodes are divided into slots (for example, one slot per processor core), and a slot is assigned to one job. The latter approach leads to better utilization of compute nodes and increased cluster throughput, as multiple jobs can be running simultaneously. Nevertheless, with this approach, some computational nodes or slots may not be used completely. For example, a slot might not be fully utilized when its assigned tasks require I/O or network. Unused slots cannot be scheduled. The scheduler cannot reclaim them, and the resources allocated to them become idle for some portion of the job's execution time. There may exist an overused slot right next to an underutilized one that can benefit from these unoccupied resources.

Wasted node or slot resources, in some cases, can be significant and expensive. For example, when running HPC in the public cloud, this will increase the cost of job computation as users will also pay for these idle resources. Thus, using a single-slot assignment strategy is not ideal. By assigning one compute node to perform several tasks, it would be possible to reduce the number of unoccupied resources compared to the above strategy with slots. In addition, more jobs could run concurrently as the node resources would be used more efficiently. All this would lead to a reduction in the waiting time for jobs in the queue and an increase in the throughput of the infrastructure.

To achieve the aforementioned goal, it would not be enough to carry out several tasks simultaneously since it is necessary to ensure an equitable distribution of resources between tasks. For example, one job can spawn more processes than another, so on average, it will get more CPU time because the operating system scheduler distributes it evenly. In [5], the authors propose resource allocation strategies that can be applied to HPC workloads to guarantee equal shares of each resource (e.g., CPU time, memory, and network bandwidth) for the jobs and also allow jobs to exceed their shares at the expense of underutilized shares of other jobs. By grouping resource consumers into separate control groups, it is possible to provide fair resource shares between groups regardless of the number of resource consumers in each group.

3.3 Minimizing Communication Overheads in Container-Based Clouds for HPC Applications

Although the cloud computing model has been well adopted in the industry, there are still relevant challenges to be addressed concerning the quality of cloud services. Network-intensive applications may not scale in the cloud due to the sharing of the network infrastructure. Therefore, in another work carried out within the CloudHPC context [10], the authors proposed the aggregation of Network Interface Cards (NICs) in a ready-to-use integration with the OpenNebula cloud manager using Linux containers.

In the literature, we find that Vogel et al. [19] conducted a network performance evaluation using CloudStack IaaS manager, deploying KVM and

LXC-based clouds. They measured throughput and latency between the nodes with different configurations. The study of Wang et al. [20] proposed the applicability of the Multi-Path TCP (MPTCP) protocol for improving the performance of a distributed Hadoop/MapReduce architecture.

The motivation for using NIC aggregation is the need to achieve higher network performance without additional financial costs, ultimately leading to application execution speedups. The authors started the NIC aggregation configuration in the native environment by setting up the network bonding (Fig. 2). This configuration was done manually in Netplan (Network Configuration Abstraction Renderer) by selecting up to four interfaces to be slaves from bond0 interface.

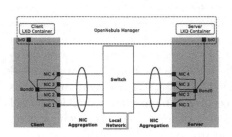

Fig. 2. High-level representation of the NIC aggregation environment.

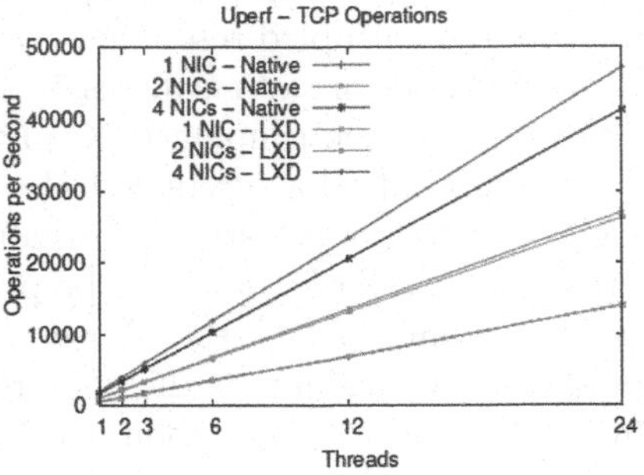

Fig. 3. TCP operations with NIC aggregation.

Figure 3 shows the Operations per second (Op/s) as provided by Uperf with the duration set to 90 s. Uperf uses threads in its evaluation, and the authors configured it to use up to 24 threads, twelve running on each machine. They used one NIC in each scenario to present a baseline where there is no aggregation. The linearity and difference between the scenarios are perceptible and highlight the gains of using link aggregation.

3.4 Boosting HPC Applications in the Cloud Through Dynamic Traffic-Aware Path Provisioning

As previously described, the pay-per-use cost model and resource allocation elasticity that cloud computing brings with it has the potential to improve HPC application performance while decreasing costs, as compared to clusters, grids, and data centers. Several studies [3, 11, 13] have sought to assess the feasibility of using cloud infrastructures to run HPC applications. The overall consensus is that clouds were not designed to run such applications. More specifically, clouds present poor network performance due to a combination of commodity interconnection technologies, processor sharing, and I/O virtualization overheads.

Additional studies [2,8] have identified the main reason for poor network performance as being the use of simplistic routing schemes (e.g., shortest path), which can lead to degradation in communication performance between compute nodes. In that context, they proposed routing approaches that avoid congested paths. Nevertheless, those approaches compute paths before the execution of an application, limiting their capability to handle fluctuations in network traffic and changes in the communication patterns of applications.

In our work [12], we proposed a novel mechanism for dynamic, just-in-time path provisioning in cloud infrastructures. Our mechanism takes advantage of new advances in programmable networks to dynamically compute and program the best paths between HPC application processes according to their current communication needs. Furthermore, we designed an algorithmic Link Usage-Aware Routing (LUAR) strategy to minimize end-to-end communication delays. Figure 4 illustrates an overview of our proposed mechanism, presenting its components and their interactions. Within the mechanism, LUAR represents a possible instantiation of the Forwarding Strategist component.

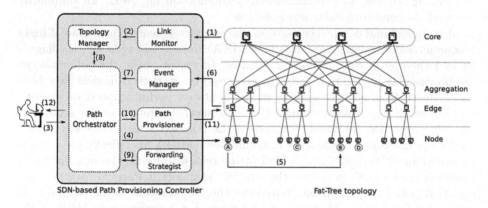

Fig. 4. Overview of the proposed path provisioning approach.

The experiments carried out considered a 32-host fat-tree topology emulated cloud infrastructure based on Mininet [7], Open vSwitch 2.0.2, and the Ryu SDN controller [16]. To generate the workload, the authors employed the NAS Parallel Benchmarks (NPB) version 3.3 [1]. Six representative benchmarks were selected for the evaluation: BT, EP, CG, LU, MG, and SP. Additional traffic was generated to simulate competing background traffic (at about 75% concurrency) in the infrastructure. Three different approaches to traffic routing were considered (*i*) Link Usage-Aware Routing (LUAR), (*ii*) Shortest path, and (*iii*) Random. The comparison metric was application runtime. Figure 5 shows the main results of this experiment.

The results show that LUAR outperforms Shortest Path by 31.35%, on average, among applications. EP, the shortest application, has obtained an improvement to its runtime of about 8% with LUAR as compared to Shortest Path. In turn, SP, the largest application, experimented a gain of 44.24% with LUAR.

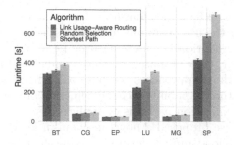

Fig. 5. Performance observed for the different NPB benchmark applications.

4 HPC Application Use Case: Medical Image Processing

In the context of the CloudHPC project, we used as use cases two medical imaging processing applications, namely registration with 3D medical models and efficient algorithms for cerebrovascular segmentation [9]. Next, we summarize the work on cerebrovascular segmentation.

A complete and detailed cerebrovascular image segmented from time-of-flight magnetic resonance angiography (TOF-MRA) data is essential for the diagnosis and therapy of cerebrovascular diseases. In recent years, three-dimensional cerebrovascular segmentation algorithms based on statistical models have been widely used. However, the existing methods always perform poorly on stenotic vessels and are not robust enough. Hence, a parallel cerebrovascular segmentation algorithm was proposed [9] based on the Focused Multi-Gaussians (FMG) model and heterogeneous Markov Random Field (MRF). Specifically, the authors proposed an FMG model with a local fitting region to model the vascular tissue more accurately and introduce the Chaotic Oscillation Particle Swarm Optimization (CO-PSO) algorithm to improve the global optimization capability in parameter estimation. Moreover, they designed a heterogeneous MRF in the three-dimensional neighborhood system to incorporate the precise local character of an image. Finally, the algorithm has been modeled to be parallelizable, as illustrated in Figs. 6, 7, and 8.

Experiments have been carried out using a test dataset to show the advantages of the proposed statistical cerebrovascular segmentation algorithm. The dataset of 3D TOF-MRA consisted of both the public CASILab dataset [17] and the dataset provided by the Peking Union Medical College Hospital. The MRA images consisted of $448 \cdot 448 \cdot 128$ axial slices with a resolution of $0.5 \cdot 0.5 \cdot 0.8 \, \text{mm}^3$. All tests were executed on the same Tianhe2A-2A supercomputer. Their execution on GPUs resulted in an approximate 60-time speed up (compared to a serial setup). The experiments showed that the proposed algorithm produces more detailed segmentation results (and quickly) and performs robustly on stenotic vessel segmentation (Table 1).

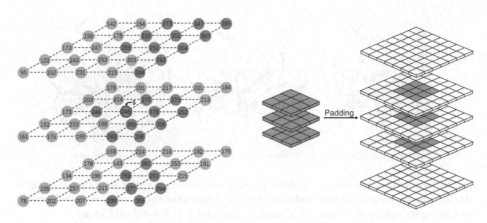

Fig. 6. Three-dimensional neighborhood system with a cuboid of size $5 \times 5 \times 3$ in the proposed heterogeneous MRF model.

Fig. 7. Padding preprocesses the TOF-MRA data. It extends the dimension of the raw data from $m \cdot n \cdot k$ to $(m+4) \cdot (n+4) \cdot (k+2)$ and sets the intensity value of the new extended voxels to zero.

Table 1. Results of the cerebrovascular parallel segmentation method on Tianhe.

CO-PSO + ICM	CPU	GPU (V100)	Speed-up ratio
200 + 10	493.782 s	8.271 s	59.711
200 + 20	967.123 s	15.358 s	62.975

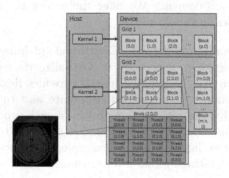

Fig. 8. Parallel programming model for the CO-PSO and ICM algorithms on CUDA.

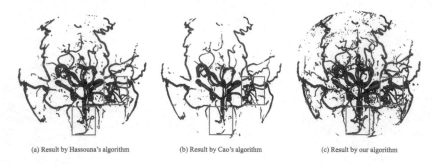

(a) Result by Hassouna's algorithm   (b) Result by Cao's algorithm   (c) Result by our algorithm

Fig. 9. Segmentation results by different statistical cerebrovascular segmentation algorithms. The segmentation result obtained by our algorithm shows more detailed vessels with stronger continuity than other models, especially in the colored areas.

5   Research Challenges and Opportunities

The work carried out demonstrated promising results and, more importantly, allowed us to reason about how to promote consistent advances in the area. Next, we elaborate on a few research challenges and opportunities.

Dealing with Varying Bottlenecks. HPC applications can be very different from one another regarding required resources. On the other extreme, they are time-stringent, requiring low execution times. The existing "knobs" for calibrating a cloud infrastructure are insufficient for HPC. While we proposed mechanisms for making the cloud less susceptible to well-known bottlenecks, we advocate more granularity is needed, e.g., from host/virtual machine to disaggregated resource allocation, on a per-job demand. We refer the reader to [18] for an insightful presentation corroborating this vision.

Getting Rid of Virtualization Layers. Existing cloud infrastructures resort to several software layers, e.g., especially to virtualize its resources. While traditional virtualization (i.e., hypervisor-based) provides flexibility in building a variety of environments, e.g., allowing to simulate and run completely different architectures and operating systems on top of each other, its overheads are high. Our work on this topic (e.g., [5], [6], and [10]) points towards the necessity to make the cloud more lightweight, for example, exploring techniques such as container-based or operating-system-level virtualization.

Modeling HPC Applications for the Cloud. Modeling applications for the cloud is paramount for fully harnessing the power of cloud computing to boost HPC applications. Design and algorithmic choices and abstractions that used to work well when executed on dedicated setups might underperform in shared infrastructures (e.g., due to the reasons outlined in Sects. 3.1, 3.2, 3.3, and 3.4). We advocate the need for new guidelines based on characterization studies and real experiences that can help application developers make more informed and correct design choices.

Operating Simultaneously with Private Cluster and Public Cloud. HPC solutions have traditionally taken advantage of powerful cluster and datacenter infrastructures. Given the increasingly complex and resource-demanding applications, we observe practitioners leveraging cloud computing resources for meeting HPC demands when available resources do not suffice. A significant challenge that arises in these scenarios is how to deploy applications properly in such hybrid setups. More research is needed to harmonize such distinct infrastructures "to get the best of both worlds" concerning *transparent* computing performance, scalability, and resilience (to mention a few non-functional requirements).

Hiding Complexity from the End-User. All efforts to enable the migration of HPC applications to the cloud result in more complexity to the end-user. The complexity reveals itself in multiple stages of the process of executing an application, ranging from the need to properly model the application for it to benefit, performance-wise, from the cloud all the way to the infrastructure provisioning and deployment phases. Hence, last but not least important, the advocated advances need to be accompanied by strategies that hide the complexity from the end-user. It is essential to work on adequate abstractions and interfaces that the user can interact with; otherwise, this big push towards the cloud might not be sustainable.

6   Conclusion

In this paper, we reported the main accomplishments obtained in the context of the CloudHPC project. To accomplish the project's objectives, researchers at UFRGS, SPbSU, and BNU worked synergistically towards an integrated, coherent result, taking advantage of each group's expertise. Solid contributions were made to understand the possibility of using existing public clouds as platforms for the execution of HPC applications (Sect. 2). Moreover, we proposed novel computing and networking techniques for HPC efficiency in cloud environments (Sect. 3). Finally, we worked on application modeling, focusing on medical image processing use cases (Sect. 4).

Despite the progress made, several challenges and opportunities remain, as briefly summarized in Sect. 5. It is our belief that solid advances in the area do require multi-party collaborations such as those promoted by the BRICS Calls. They allow researchers who work under quite different realities and have complementary expertise to build robust "bridges" and solutions to overcome big societal problems of our time, where HPC and cloud will together play a vital role.

Acknowledgements. This work was carried out in the context of the project CloudHPC – Harnessing Cloud Computing to Power Up HPC Applications, BRICS Pilot Call 2016. It was partially supported by the Brazilian National Council for Scientific and Technological Development (CNPq), Project Number 441892/2016-7, Call CNPq/MCTIC/BRICS-STI No 18/2016, the Coordination for the Improvement of Higher Education Personnel (CAPES), as well as the National Key Cooperation between the BRICS Program of China (No. 2017YE0100500) and the Beijing Natural Science Foundation of China (No. 4172033).

References

1. Bailey, D.H.: NAS parallel benchmarks. In: Encyclopedia of Parallel Computing, pp. 1254–1259 (2011). https://doi.org/10.1007/978-0-387-09766-4_133
2. Faizian, P., Mollah, M.A., Tong, Z., Yuan, X., Lang, M.: A comparative study of SDN and adaptive routing on dragonfly networks. In: Proceedings of the International Conference for High Performance Computing, Networking, Storage and Analysis, p. 51. ACM (2017)
3. Gupta, A., et al.: Evaluating and improving the performance and scheduling of HPC applications in cloud. IEEE Trans. Cloud Comput. **4**(3), 307–321 (2016). https://doi.org/10.1109/TCC.2014.2339858
4. Korkhov, V., et al.: Distributed virtual cluster management system. In: CEUR Workshop Proceedings, Selected Papers of the 8th International Conference on Distributed Computing and Grid-Technologies in Science and Education - GRID 2018, Cham, vol. 2267, pp. 383–387 (2018)
5. Kuchumov, R., Korkhov, V.: Fair resource allocation for running HPC workloads simultaneously. In: Misra, S., et al. (eds.) ICCSA 2019. LNCS, vol. 11622, pp. 740–751. Springer, Cham (2019). https://doi.org/10.1007/978-3-030-24305-0_55
6. Kuchumov, R., Korkhov, V.: Collecting HPC applications processing characteristics to facilitate co-scheduling. In: Gervasi, O., et al. (eds.) ICCSA 2020. LNCS, vol. 12254, pp. 168–182. Springer, Cham (2020). https://doi.org/10.1007/978-3-030-58817-5_14
7. Lantz, B., Heller, B., McKeown, N.: A network in a laptop: rapid prototyping for software-defined networks. In: Proceedings of the 9th ACM SIGCOMM Workshop on Hot Topics in Networks, p. 19. ACM (2010)
8. Lee, J., Tong, Z., Achalkar, K., Yuan, X., Lang, M.: Enhancing InfiniBand with OpenFlow-style SDN capability. In: Proceedings of the International Conference for High Performance Computing, Networking, Storage and Analysis, SC 2016, pp. 36:1–36:12. IEEE Press, Piscataway (2016). http://dl.acm.org/citation.cfm?id=3014904.3014953
9. Lv, Z., et al.: Cerebrovascular segmentation algorithm based on focused multi-Gaussians model and weighted 3D Markov random field. In: 2019 IEEE International Conference on Bioinformatics and Biomedicine (BIBM), pp. 846–851 (2019). https://doi.org/10.1109/BIBM47256.2019.8983106
10. Maliszewski, A.M., Vogel, A., Griebler, D., Roloff, E., Fernandes, L.G., Philippe O. A.N.: Minimizing communication overheads in container-based clouds for HPC applications. In: 2019 IEEE Symposium on Computers and Communications (ISCC), pp. 1–6 (2019). https://doi.org/10.1109/ISCC47284.2019.8969716
11. Netto, M.A.S., Calheiros, R.N., Rodrigues, E.R., Cunha, R.L.F., Buyya, R.: HPC cloud for scientific and business applications: taxonomy, vision, and research challenges. ACM Comput. Surv. **51**(1), 81–829 (2018). https://doi.org/10.1145/3150224
12. Pretto, G.R., et al.: Boosting HPC applications in the cloud through JIT traffic-aware path provisioning. In: Misra, S., et al. (eds.) ICCSA 2019. LNCS, vol. 11622, pp. 702–716. Springer, Cham (2019). https://doi.org/10.1007/978-3-030-24305-0_52

13. Roloff, E., Diener, M., Diaz Carreño, E., Gaspary, L.P., Navaux, P.O.A.: Leveraging cloud heterogeneity for cost-efficient execution of parallel applications. In: Rivera, F.F., Pena, T.F., Cabaleiro, J.C. (eds.) Euro-Par 2017. LNCS, vol. 10417, pp. 399–411. Springer, Cham (2017). https://doi.org/10.1007/978-3-319-64203-1_29
14. Roloff., E., Diener., M., Gaspary., L., Navaux., P.: Exploring instance heterogeneity in public cloud providers for HPC applications. In: Proceedings of the 9th International Conference on Cloud Computing and Services Science - CLOSER, pp. 210–222. INSTICC, SciTePress (2019). https://doi.org/10.5220/0007799302100222
15. Roloff, E., Diener, M., Gaspary, L.P., Navaux, P.O.: Exploiting load imbalance patterns for heterogeneous cloud computing platforms. In: CLOSER, pp. 248–259 (2018)
16. Ryu, A.: Component-based software defined networking framework (2021). https://ryu-sdn.org
17. TubeTK: TubeTK/Data - KitwarePublic (2021). http://public.kitware.com/Wiki/TubeTK/Data
18. Vahdat, A.: Coming of age in the fifth epoch of distributed computing: the power of sustained exponential growth (2020). https://tinyurl.com/8frtbpfs
19. Vogel, A., Griebler, D., Schepke, C., Fernandes, L.G.: An intra-cloud networking performance evaluation on cloudstack environment. In: 2017 25th Euromicro International Conference on Parallel, Distributed and Network-based Processing (PDP), pp. 468–472 (2017). https://doi.org/10.1109/PDP.2017.40
20. Wang, C.H., Yang, C.K., Liao, W.C., Chang, R.I., Wei, T.T.: Coupling GPU and MPTCP to improve Hadoop/MapReduce performance. In: 2016 2nd International Conference on Intelligent Green Building and Smart Grid (IGBSG), pp. 1–6 (2016). https://doi.org/10.1109/IGBSG.2016.7539430

On the Possibility of Using Neural Networks for the Thunderstorm Forecasting

Elena Stankova[1]([⊠]) [iD], Irina O. Tokareva[2], and Natalia V. Dyachenko[3] [iD]

[1] Saint-Petersburg State University, 7-9, Universitetskaya nab., St.Petersburg 199034, Russia
e.stankova@spbu.ru
[2] IBS AppLine, St. Skladochnaya, 3, Building 1, 127018 Moscow, Russia
[3] Russian State Hydrometeorological University, 98, Malookhtinsky pr., St.Petersburg 195196, Russia

Abstract. The paper explores the possibility of forecasting such dangerous meteorological phenomena as a thunderstorm by applying five types of neural network to the output data of a hydrodynamic model that simulates dynamic and microphysical processes in convective clouds. The ideas and the result delivered in [1] are developed and supplemented by the classification error calculations and by consideration of radial basic and probabilistic neural networks. The results show that forecast accuracy of all five networks reaches values of 90%. However, the radial basis function has the advantages of the highest accuracy along with the smallest classification error. Its simple structure and short training time make this type of neuralnetwork the best one in view of accuracy versus productivity relation.

Keywords: Machine learning · Neural networks · Perceptron complex · Radial basic neural network · Probabilistic neural network · Numerical model of convective cloud · Weather forecasting · Thunderstorm forecasting

1 Introduction

Throughout human history, meteorological processes prediction has always been a complex task mainly because the Earth's atmosphere system is very complex and dynamic.

Weather forecasts are calculated based on meteorological data collected by a network of weather stations, radiosondes, radars and satellites around the world. Data is sent to meteorological centres, where it is entered into forecast models for atmospheric conditions calculation. Such models are based on physical laws and work according to extremely complex algorithms.

Precipitation is determined by the physical processes occurring in the cloud, namely the physics of the interaction of water droplets, ice particles and water vapor. Convective clouds are very variable due to the large vertical speeds within the cloud and its environs. It is also difficult to conduct control experiments involving them. All this leads to the fact that the development of the cloud is usually analyzed using computer simulation, which allows us to do this without resorting to expensive field experiments.

© Springer Nature Switzerland AG 2021
O. Gervasi et al. (Eds.): ICCSA 2021, LNCS 12956, pp. 350–359, 2021.
https://doi.org/10.1007/978-3-030-87010-2_25

As a result of computer simulation of the cloud we get a data set that can be further used for forecasting various dangerous convective phenomena such as thunderstorm, hail and heavy rain.

In recent decades mathematicians and programmers are working hard to improve existing numerical weather forecasting models. Nowadays machine learning methods, especially neural networks are considered to be one of the most promising tool of such improvement [2, 3]. Authors in [2] state that advantages of neural networks are the intrinsic absence of model bias and possible savings of computational resources due to ability of neural network very efficiently calculate forecasts with new data after corresponding training.

The use of machine learning methods allows us to automate the forecasting process, which greatly facilitates data analysis. These methods conduct a series of computational experiments with the aim of analyzing, interpreting and comparing the simulation results with the given behavior of the object under study and, if necessary, subsequently refining their input parameters.

The idea to use neural networks to process output from numerical weather prediction models had been explored in far 1998 year in [4] in order to give more accurate and localized rainfall predictions already.

Prediction of rainfall amounts is very popular application for neural networks usage [5–7]. Thus in [5] researchers in Thailand tried to predict possible flooding dangers by estimating rainfall amounts using feed-forward neural networks. Authors in [6] tried to accurately predict heavy precipitation events (>25 mm h^{-1}) over Germany using also neural networks.

Tao et al. [8, 9] use deep neural networks for forecasting precipitation amount among meteorological factors and obtained promising results.

Authors in [10] used neural networks for predicting probabilities and quantitative values of precipitation with the help of the Eta atmospheric model and upper air soundings.

Researcher in [11] has investigated how effectively neural networks can perform classification prediction of freezing and gusty events as well as minimum temperature and maximum gust values. Paper [11] contains also the detailed review of neural networks application for solution of meteorological problems.

Neural networks have also been used to predict various weather phenomena (wind speed, barometric pressure, fog [12]) including extreme events, such as tornadoes [13] and typhoons [14, 15].

In [14] a multilayer perceptron is used to predict changes in tropical cyclone intensity in the northwestern Pacific Ocean. The paper [15] uses a generative adversarial network to predict typhoon trajectories. The neural network generates an image showing the future location of the typhoon center and cloud structure using satellite images as an input.

In this paper we continue the studies described in [1, 16–18] and analyze the possibility of the use of neural networks for dangerous convective phenomena forecasting by processing the output data of numerical model of convective cloud [19–22]. The idea is to retrieve the possibility of thunderstorm forecasting from the data of the model, able to simulate only dynamical and microphysical characteristics of convective clouds, but not electrical characteristics. The ideas and the result delivered in [1] are developed and supplemented by the classification error calculations and by consideration of radial basic and probabilistic neural networks.

2 Initial Data

Research using machine learning methods is based on data, therefore, in order to obtain the best results, it is necessary to use reliable sources of information to obtain data and form their correct structure.

In this work, the data was obtained using the following algorithm:

1. We receive data on the date and place of meteorological phenomena occurrence;
2. We select the data corresponding to the presence of a thunderstorm or the absence of any meteorological phenomena;
3. We obtain data from atmosphere radio sounding for the certain date and place;
4. We convert the radio sounding data to the model input data format;
5. Using the hydrodynamic model, we obtain the integral and spectral characteristics of the cloud;
6. We determine the height and time corresponding to the maximum development and maximum water content of the cloud. The cloud parameters corresponding to these height and time will be used for the thunderstorm forecasting.

Formed data set contains 416 records, where 220 samples correspond to the presence of a thunderstorm and 196 samples to its absence. This data was divided into training and test data sets. The training one contains 333 samples and the test one contains 83. Due to the small amount of data we decided to use test data set for validation.

We also created labels for each sample in the data set. Since there are only two cases, the presence and absence of phenomenon, we could have created one label per sample. But we decided to use two labels per sample, one for each case, mainly because we will need to divide the output variables of the neural network at some point.

3 Data Preprocessing

Solution of machine learning problems require to find an unknown relationship between a known set of objects and a set of answers. In our case the fact of dangerous phenomenon occurrence can be considered as an answer, and the results of numerical modeling, can be considered as an object. Radiosonde sounding data are used as the model input.

Neural networks, like all machine learning algorithms, depend significantly on the quality of the source data. Therefore, before proceeding to the construction of a neural network, we will need prepare the data.

First, we normalize the data using the Standard Scaler method from the Python scikit-learn library, which converts the data to the standard normal distribution.

Then we select the most significant features. To do this, we use the Recursive Feature Elimination method from the scikit-learn library with Random Forest algorithm as an estimator. The method is as follows. The estimator is firstly trained on the initial set of features, then the least important feature is pruned and the procedure is recursively repeated with smaller and smaller set. Figure 1 shows the resulting graph of the prediction accuracy versus the number of features used. As can be seen from the figure, maximum accuracy is achieved when using 8 features. Their names and their importance are shown in the Fig. 2. Thus, we will use the following features: vapor, aerosol, relative humidity, density, temperature excess (inside cloud), pressure, velocity, temperature (in the environment).

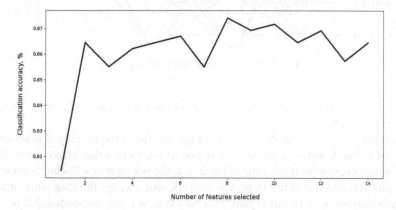

Fig. 1. Graph of prediction accuracy versus the number of features involved

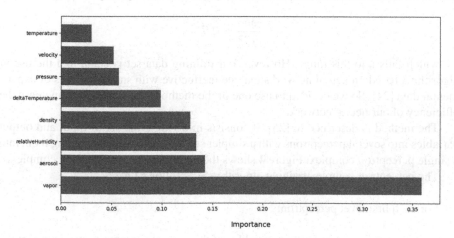

Fig. 2. Selected features and their importance.

4   Classical Multi-layer Perceptron and Perceptron Complexes

The main ideas and results achieved while using classical multilayer perceptron structure (Fig. 3) and perceptron complexes were described in [1]. Some additional explanations

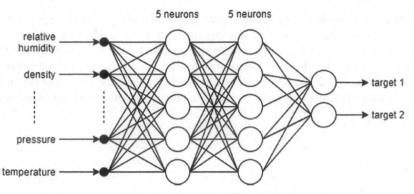

Fig. 3. Classical multi-layer perceptron

for using perceptron complexes and the values of the classification errors can be added to what is said there.

The article [23] mentions that the ratio of the volume of the training data set and the number of trainable network parameters is one of the factors that affect the modeling ability of the perceptron. If this ratio is close to 1, the perceptron will simply remember the training set, and if it is too large, the network will average the data without taking the details into account. In this regard, in most cases, it is recommended that this ratio falls in the range from 2 to 5. In our case, this ratio is.

$$\frac{333}{123} = 2.7$$

which falls into this range. However, our training data set is small and the use of algorithms based on neural networks may be ineffective with small amounts of experimental data [24]. So we decided to use one of the methods that can help to increase the efficiency of our neural network.

The method is described in [23]. It consists in dividing the set of input and output variables into several perceptrons with a simpler structure and then combining them into a single perceptron complex. Figure 4 shows the general structure of such a complex.

The perceptron complex training algorithm is as follows [24]:

1. For each first level perceptron:

   a. Given the input and output variables of the current perceptron, we construct the training and test data sets for it based on the initial data;
   b. Perceptron training is executed;
   c. For all samples of training and test data sets, the values of the perceptron outputs are calculated and stored.

2. For the resulting perceptron:

   a. Given the input and output variables of the perceptron, we construct the training
      and test data sets for it based on the initial data and the calculated output values
      of the first level perceptrons;
   b. Perceptron training is executed.

Two variants of the perceptron complexes were described in our previous work [1].
Here we can only add that classification errors are equal to 0.081 and 0.078 for the first
and the second perceptron complexes consequently.

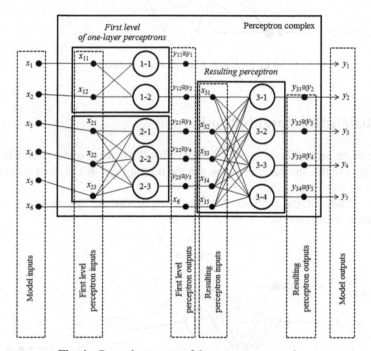

Fig. 4. General structure of the perceptron complex.

5   Radial Basis Function Network

Two types of networks that belong to radial basic networks are considered as they
show good results in problems of binary classification. Also, their advantage is a simple
structure where there is only one hidden layer.

In the process of training this network, three sets of parameters are determined. We
considered several ways to set their initial values and established how many neurons
there should be in the hidden layer to get the highest prediction accuracy.

The resulting neural network is shown on Fig. 5. Its accuracy is 91.6%, classification
error is 0.069.

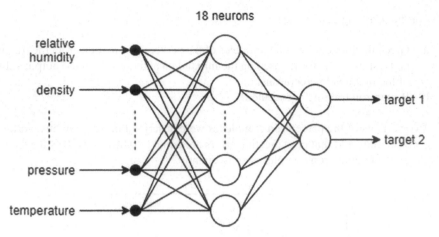

Fig. 5. Radial basis function network

6 Probabilistic Neural Network

A feature of the probabilistic neural network is that the number of neurons in the hidden layer is equal to the number of examples in the training set, that is, the network simply stores the entire training set.

The structure of the network is shown on the Fig. 6. The accuracy is 90.4%, classification error is 0.096.

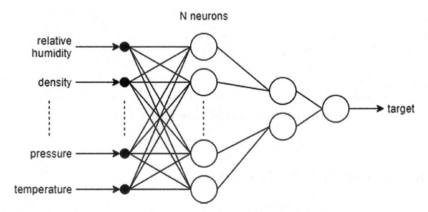

Fig. 6. Probabilistic neural network

7 Classification Accuracies and Classification Errors of the Neural Networks of Different Types

Table 1 presents the values of classification accuracy and classification error of the five types of neural networks considered by the authors. As can be seen from the table the best accuracy is achieved using the second perceptron complex and the radial basis function network.

Table 1. Maximum forecast accuracy and classification error of the five types of neural networks

Neural network	Classification accuracy, %	Classification error
Multi-layer perceptron	89,1	0,082
First perceptron complex	90,4	0,081
Second perceptron complex	91,6	0,078
Radial basis function network	91,6	0,069
Probabilistic neural network	90,4	0,096

8 Conclusions

The work analyzed the possibility of using neural networks to build forecasts of dangerous convective phenomena by the example of a thunderstorm.

The initial data set was obtained using numerical modeling of a convective cloud.

Using machine learning methods at the stage of data analysis and processing of features, the most significant features were identified.

Five networks were considered. The best accuracy was achieved using the second perceptron complex and the radial basis function network. However, the radial basis function network gave the smallest classification error. Also, its advantages over the perceptron complex are simple structure and short training time.

In future we will further explore the possibility of using neural networks for forecasting thunderstorm and other dangerous convective phenomena and specifically our research should be focused on obtaining sufficient number of radiosonde soundings with the corresponding model simulations for training data sets formation.

References

1. Stankova, E.N., Tokareva, I.O., Dyachenko, N.V.: On the effectiveness of using various machine learning methods for forecasting dangerous convective phenomena. In: Gervasi, O., et al. (eds.) ICCSA 2020. LNCS, vol. 12254, pp. 82–93. Springer, Cham (2020). https://doi.org/10.1007/978-3-030-58817-5_7
2. Schultz, M.G., et al.: Can deep learning beat numerical weather prediction? Phil. Trans. R. Soc. A **379**, 20200097 (2021). https://doi.org/10.1098/rsta.2020.0097

3. Scher, S., Messori, G.: Weather and climate forecasting with neural networks: using general circulation models (GCMs) with different complexity as a study ground. Geosci. Model Dev. **12**, 2797–2809 (2019). https://doi.org/10.5194/gmd-12-2797-2019

4. Kugliowski, R.J., Barros, A.P.: Localized precipitation forecasts from a numerical weather prediction model using artificial neural networks. Weather Forecast. **13**(4), 1194–1204 (1998)

5. Hung, N.Q., Babel, M.S., Weesakul, S., Tripathi, N.K.: An artificial neural network model for forecasting in Bangkok, Thailand. Hydrol. Earth Syst. Sci. **13**(8), 1413–1425 (2009)

6. Unwetterklimatologie: Starkregen. https://www.dwd.de/DE/leistungen/unwetterklima/starkr egen/starkregen.html. Accessed 30 April 2020

7. Luk, K.C., Ball, J.E., Sharma, A.: An application of artificial neural networks for rainfall forecasting. Math. Comput. Model. **33**(6–7), 683–693 (2001). https://doi.org/10.1016/S0895-7177(00)00272-7

8. Tao, Y., Gao, X., Ihler, A., Sorooshian, S.: Deep neural networks for precipitation estimation from remotely sensed information. In: Proceedings IEEE Congress on Evolutionary Computation, Vancouver, BC, Canada, pp. 1349–1355. IEEE (2016)

9. Tao, Y., Gao, X., Ihler, A., Sorooshian, S., Hsu, K.: Precipitation identification with bispectral satellite information using deep learning approaches. J. Hydrometeor. **18**, 1271–1283 (2017)

10. Hall, T., Brooks, H.E., Doswell, C.A., III.: Precipitation forecasting using a neural network. Weather Forecast. **14**(3), 338–345 (1999)

11. Culclasure, Andrew, Using Neural Networks to Provide Local Weather Forecasts" (2013). Electronic Theses and Dissertations. 32. https://digitalcommons.georgiasouthern.edu/etd/32

12. Santhanam, T., Subhajini, A.C.: An efficient weather forecasting system using radial basis function neural network. J. Comput. Sci. **7**(7), 962–966 (2011)

13. Marzban, C., Stumpf, G.J.: A neural network for tornado prediction based on Doppler radar-derived attributes. J. Appl. Meteorol. **35**(5), 617–626 (1996)

14. Baik, J.-J., Paek, J.-S.: A Neural Network Model for predicting typhoon intensity. J. Meteor. Soc. Japan. (2000). https://doi.org/10.2151/jmsj1965.78.6857

15. Ruettgers, M., Lee, S., Jeon, S., You, D.: Prediction of a typhoon track using a generative adversarial network and satellite images. Sci. Rep. **9**, 6057 (2019). https://doi.org/10.1038/s41598-019-42339-y

16. Stankova, E.N., Grechko, I.A., Kachalkina, Y.N., Khvatkov, E.V.: Hybrid approach combining model-based method with the technology of machine learning for forecasting of dangerous weather phenomena. In: Gervasi, O., et al. (eds.) ICCSA 2017. LNCS, vol. 10408, pp. 495–504. Springer, Cham (2017). https://doi.org/10.1007/978-3-319-62404-4_37

17. Stankova, E.N., Balakshiy, A.V., Petrov, D.A., Korkhov, V.V., Shorov, A.V.: OLAP technology and machine learning as the tools for validation of the numerical models of convective clouds. Int. J. Bus. Intell. Data Min. **14**(1/2), 254 (2019). https://doi.org/10.1504/IJBIDM.2019.096793

18. Stankova, E.N., Khvatkov, E.V.: Using boosted k-nearest neighbour algorithm for numerical forecasting of dangerous convective phenomena. In: Misra, S., et al. (eds.) ICCSA 2019. LNCS, vol. 11622, pp. 802–811. Springer, Cham (2019). https://doi.org/10.1007/978-3-030-24305-0_61

19. Raba, N.O., Stankova, E.N.: Research of influence of compensating descending flow on cloud's life cycle by means of 1.5-dimensional model with 2 cylinders. In: Proceedings of MGO, vol. 559, pp. 192–209 (2009). (in Russian)

20. Raba, N., Stankova, E.: On the possibilities of multi-core processor use for real-time forecast of dangerous convective phenomena. In: Taniar, D., Gervasi, O., Murgante, B., Pardede, E., Apduhan, B.O. (eds.) ICCSA 2010. LNCS, vol. 6017, pp. 130–138. Springer, Heidelberg (2010). https://doi.org/10.1007/978-3-642-12165-4_11

21. Raba, N.O., Stankova, E.N.: On the problem of numerical modeling of dangerous convective phenomena: possibilities of real-time forecast with the help of multi-core processors. In: Murgante, B., Gervasi, O., Iglesias, A., Taniar, D., Apduhan, B.O. (eds.) ICCSA 2011. LNCS, vol. 6786, pp. 633–642. Springer, Heidelberg (2011). https://doi.org/10.1007/978-3-642-21934-4_51

22. Raba, N.O., Stankova, E.N.: On the effectiveness of using the GPU for numerical solution of stochastic collection equation. In: Murgante, B., et al. (eds.) ICCSA 2013. LNCS, vol. 7975, pp. 248–258. Springer, Heidelberg (2013). https://doi.org/10.1007/978-3-642-39640-3_18

23. Dudarov, S.P., Diev, A.N.: Neural network modeling based on perceptron complexes withsmall training data sets. Math. Meth. Eng. Technol. **26**, 114–116 (2013). (in Russian)

24. Dudarov, S.P., Diev, A.N., Fedosova, N.A., Koltsova, E.M.: Simulation of properties of composite materials reinforced by carbon nanotubes using perceptron complexes. Comput. Res. Model. **7**(2), 253–262 (2015). https://doi.org/10.20537/2076-7633-2015-7-2-253-262

Reconstruction and Identification
of Dynamical Systems Based
on Taylor Maps

Anna Golovkina⬚, Vladimir Kozynchenko⬚, and Nataliia Kulabukhova$^{(\boxtimes)}$⬚

Saint Petersburg State University, St. Petersburg, Russia
{a.golovkina,v.kozynchenko,n.kulabukhova}@spbu.ru

Abstract. In the process of conducting various physical experiments, a certain set of data is accumulated. Processing and interpreting the simulation results is a fundamental task for analyzing the behaviour of the model, predicting its future actions, and managing the entire system. This paper provides an overview of the currently existing approaches to identification of dynamic systems models: white, gray and black boxes. Special attention is paid to methods based on neural networks. The article suggests a combined approach that allows both preserving a physical consistency of the model and using modern methods for learning from data. A polynomial neural network of a special architecture, approximating the general solution of the system of ordinary differential equations (ODEs) in the form of Taylor map is considered. This model can work in the case of a small amount of initial data, which is a problem when exploiting traditional machine learning methods, and neural networks in particular. The paper presents a new learning approach for PNN based on two steps: reconstructing an ODEs system based on a single trajectory, and identifying a general solution to initialize the weights of a neural network. Neural network representation allows using traditional learning algorithms for additional fine-turning the weights in line with new measured data. A toy example of a nonlinear deflector demonstrates the power and generalization ability of the proposed algorithm.

Keywords: Polynomial neural networks · Taylor mapping · System identification · Lie transformation · Dynamic systems

1 Introduction

Dynamical system reconstruction and identification from time series data is crucial for many applied problems, industries and experimental research. This is explained by the necessity to interpreter the data, to understand the underlying process and predict its behaviour in future. Identification and reconstruction belong to the class of inverse problems that are usually ill-posed, meaning that many standard numerical methods cannot achieve high accuracy when solving

Supported by Saint Petersburg State University, project ID: 75206008.

them. The approaches described in literature dedicated to dynamical system identification usually keep in line with one of these directions: white-box, grey-box and black-box models learning.

White-box models are based on first principles that are often expressed as systems of differential equations containing unknown parameters describing the concrete physical situation. These parameters are usually defined though optimization of least square error between the measured and the modelled data. Regularisation or other modification of optimization algorithms can improve the convergence. However, in many cases such models are overly complex and hard to obtain because of the nature of many systems and processes. In the same time their simplification can lead to a limited understanding of the underlying physical or technical setting.

Another very important approach in dynamical system identification are gray box models. They use both insights into the system e.g. in the form of conservation laws and black box models to infer hidden parameters. Usually, this group of methods requires both statistical data and numerical solvers to build the model and estimate its parameters.

On the other hand, applying black-box models usually based on machine learning (ML) methods allows avoiding numerical solvers completely and extracting the complex behaviour of the systems. Also, a strong motivation to use neural networks as a representation of system model comes from the universal approximation theorem, which states that a feed-forward network with a single hidden layer containing a finite number of neurons can approximate any continuous function on compact subsets of R^n, under mild assumptions on the activation function.

The idea of using neural networks (NNs) for physical systems learning is not new and elaborated in existing studies [6,13,15,16,21]. However, the approaches followed by the authors usually require large measured or simulated data sets for NN training. Otherwise, the prediction results are likely too far from the real physical behavior. Ordinary, the basic idea is either to build surrogate models that can replace physics-based models or incorporate NNs into the differential equation to approximate unknown terms (gray-box models). For example, [4] proposes dynamical systems learning from partial observations with ordinary differential equations (ODEs), while the [19] adds NNs to identify unknown coefficients in partial differential equations. Authors of [7] use a back-propagation technique through an ODE solver but this still requires traditional numerical solvers to simulate the dynamics.

Summarizing the generally adopted in the literature approaches, usually by the term physics-inspired NNs [11], authors mean either incorporating domain knowledge in the traditional NN architectures or providing additional loss functions for the physical inconsistency of the predictions [14]. Model-free systems learning and control considered in the papers [8,17] imply using various NN architectures. However, the generalisation ability of the constructed models for the inputs not presented in the training data range is not investigated.

Traditional and state-of-the-art ML/NN models are suitable for either forecasting or building surrogate models. Time series forecasting means that the information in the past values can alone be used to predict the future values. While a surrogate model extrapolates dynamics to new inputs that stem from the same training data range.

The paper aims to combine the strengths of the mentioned techniques to build an approach suitable for identification of wide variety of dynamical process with small training data. Moreover, the recovered model is requested to predict the dynamics for new inputs beyond the training samples.

To solve this problem, we consider a polynomial neural network (PNN) of a special architecture, approximating the general solution of system of ODEs in the form of Taylor map [12]. This means that the physical description of the provided data is preserved, but it becomes possible to use modern methods of training neural networks to adjust the coefficients in accordance with the collected data. The paper proposes PNN learning algorithm consisting in two steps.

The rest of the paper is organized as follows. Section 2 presents a brief description of the Taylor mapping approach and its connection with PNN. Section 3 introduces a PNN learning algorithm having two successive steps. The first one is reconstruction of system of ODE with a polynomial right side with only one sample. Then, Taylor mapping representation of the general solution is used to find an initial approximation of PNN weights. Step two utilizes the other available training data to fine tune the weights for a better correspondence of the model to the real process. Section 4 describes simple example of nonlinear cylindrical deflector to demonstrate the achieved results.

2   PNN Architecture

The transformation $\mathcal{M} : \mathbf{X}_0 = \mathbf{X}(t_0) \rightarrow \mathbf{X}(t_1)$ defines a Taylor map in form of

$$\mathbf{X}(t_1) = W_0 + W_1 \mathbf{X}_0 + W_2 \mathbf{X}_0^{[2]} + \ldots + W_k \mathbf{X}_0^{[k]}, \tag{1}$$

where $\mathbf{X}, \mathbf{X}_0 \in R^n$, matrices W_i are weights, and $\mathbf{X}^{[k]}$ means the k-th Kronecker power of vector $\mathbf{X}$ with the same terms reduction. For example, if $\mathbf{X} = (x_1, x_2)$, then $\mathbf{X}^{[2]} = (x_1^2, x_1 x_2, x_2^2)$ and $\mathbf{X}^{[3]} = (x_1^3, x_1^2 x_2, x_1 x_2^2, x_2^3)$. The transformation (1) is linear in weights W_i and nonlinear with respect to the $\mathbf{X}_0$. The transformation (1) sometimes may be named Taylor maps or models [5], tensor decomposition [9], matrix Lie transform [1], exponential machines [18], and others. In fact, transformation (1) is a polynomial regression with respect to the components of $\mathbf{X}$ that directly defines the polynomial neuron (see Fig. 1).   The Taylor map (1) approximates the general solution of the system of differential equations [2,10]. If the systems of ODE is known, the weights in (1) can be calculated directly. The initialized from ODEs Taylor map accurately represents the dynamics of the system without the necessity of using numerical solver [12].

This property of PNN based on Taylor map allows using it as a representation of dynamical system. The following section describes the procedure of PNN learning from time-series data.

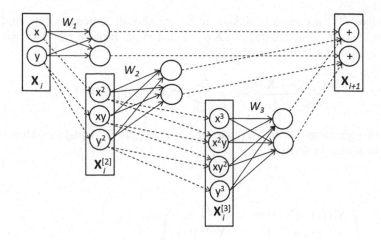

Fig. 1. Polynomial neuron of third order nonlinearity.

3 PNN Learning

PNN learning consists of two successive steps. Initialization of weights and their fine-tuning based on the measured data. According to the described in Sect.2 properties and structure of PPN, initialization of weights requires the presence of the system of ordinary differential equations. Then Taylor map approach is used to approximate the general solution of the system that correspond to the PNN. The following subsections contain the description of reconstruction approach of a system of ODEs from the data and Taylor mapping technique to identify its general solution.

3.1 Reconstruction of the Right Side of the System of Differential Equations

Let us denote the set of the parameters describing the process as vector $\mathbf{X}$ with changing in time components $X_j(t)$, $j = \overline{1,n}$. And we suppose to know the values of the vector function $\mathbf{X}(t)$ measured in M discrete times $t_0, \ldots, t_{M+1}$: $\mathbf{X}(t_0), \ldots \mathbf{X}(t_{M+1})$.

The main our assumption about the collected time-series data describing the multi parametric dynamical process is that it approximately follows autonomous ODE system with polynomial right-hand side

$$\frac{d\mathbf{X}}{dt} = \sum_{k=0}^{N} \mathrm{P}^{1k} \mathbf{X}^{[k]} \tag{2}$$

where t is an independent variable, $\mathbf{X} \in R^n$ is a state vector corresponding to the parameters of the dynamical process, and $\mathbf{X}^{[k]}$ means k-th Kronecker power of vector $\mathbf{X}$. For example, for $\mathbf{X} = (x_1, x_2)$ we have $\mathbf{X}^{[2]} = (x_1^2, x_1 x_2, x_2^2)$, $\mathbf{X}^{[3]} = (x_1^3, x_1^2 x_2, x_1 x_2^2, x_2^3)$ after reduction of the same terms.

Matrices P^{1k} are usually unknown, so we should approximately find them from the measurements $\mathbf{X}(t_0), \ldots \mathbf{X}(t_{M+1})$. Let us replace the derivatives $\frac{d\mathbf{X}}{dt}$ in the left side of (2) with finite differences:

$$\frac{\mathbf{X}(t_{i+1}) - \mathbf{X}(t_{i-1})}{t_{i+1} - t_{i-1}} = \sum_{k=0}^{N} P^{1k} \mathbf{X}^{[k]}(t_i), \quad i = \overline{1, M}. \tag{3}$$

System of equations (3) is a system of linear algebraic equations that can be written in a matrix form

$$AP = B, \tag{4}$$

where:

$$A = \begin{pmatrix} \mathbf{Y}(t_1) & \mathbf{Y}^{[2]}(t_1) & \ldots & \mathbf{Y}^{[N]}(t_1) \\ \mathbf{Y}(t_2) & \mathbf{Y}^{[2]}(t_2) & \ldots & \mathbf{Y}^{[N]}(t_2) \\ \vdots & \vdots & \ddots & \vdots \\ \mathbf{Y}(t_M) & \mathbf{Y}^{[2]}(t_M) & \ldots & \mathbf{Y}^{[N]}(t_M) \end{pmatrix}, \quad \mathbf{Y}^{[j]}(t_i) = \left(\mathbf{X}^{[j]}(t_i)\right)^T,$$

$$P = \left(P^{11}, \ldots, P^{1N}\right)^T,$$

$$B = \left((\mathbf{X}(t_2) - \mathbf{X}(t_0))/(t_2 - t_0), \ldots, (\mathbf{X}(t_{M+1}) - \mathbf{X}(t_{M-1}))/(t_{M+1} - t_{M-1})\right)^T.$$

The system (4) contains $n * (n + n_2 + \ldots + n_N)$ unknowns and $n * M$ equations. In these formulas, n is the dimension of the vector $\mathbf{X}$, and $n_i, i \geq 2$ is the dimension of its Kronecker degree $\mathbf{X}^{[i]}$. Hence it follows that in order to obtain a system with an equal number of equations and unknowns, the following condition must be met for the number of measurements $3 * M$:

$$M = n + n_2 + \ldots + n_N. \tag{5}$$

Condition (5) defines the connection between the system dimension which is related to the number of process parameters and the quantity of measurements. If (5) is violated, its impossible to unambiguously reconstruct the polynomial right side of (2) for the requested order of non linearity.

3.2   Identification of the General Solution of the System of Differential Equations

We consider autonomous system of ODEs with polynomial right-hand side approximately reconstructed from data in the previous subsection

$$\frac{d\mathbf{X}}{dt} = \sum_{k=0}^{N} P^{1k} \mathbf{X}^{[k]}$$

An iterative algorithm for constructing an approximate solution to nonlinear equation (1) is based on the technique introduced in [3]. Starting from the linear term in the right side of (1), we successively increase the order of polynomials to the required degree of non linearity. At the first step we consider the linear equation

$$\frac{d\mathbf{X}}{dt} = P^{11}\mathbf{X} \tag{6}$$

The solution to this equation can be found analytically or numerically (for example $R^{11}(t, t_0) = \exp\left((t - t_0) P^{11}\right)$) in the form

$$\mathbf{X}(t) = R^{11}(t, t_0) \mathbf{X_0}, \qquad \mathbf{X_0} = \mathbf{X}(t_0) \tag{7}$$

Then, let us consider the nonlinear equation with the second order polynomials in the right side

$$\frac{d\mathbf{X}}{dt} = P^{11}\mathbf{X} + P^{12}\mathbf{X}^{[2]}. \tag{8}$$

To find the solution of (8), we substitute the solution (7) of the linear equation (6) found at the previous step to the second term on the right side of nonlinear equation (8):

$$\frac{d\mathbf{X}}{dt} = P^{11}\mathbf{X} + P^{11}R^{22}(t, t_0) \mathbf{X_0}^{[2]}, \qquad R^{22}(t, t_0) = \left(R^{11}(t, t_0)\right)^{[2]} \tag{9}$$

The solution to the linear inhomogeneous equation (9) can be written in the form:

$$\mathbf{X}(t) = R^{11}(t, t_0) \mathbf{X_0} + R^{12}(t, t_0) \mathbf{X_0}^{[2]}, \tag{10}$$

where

$$R^{12}(t, t_0) = \int_{t_0}^{t} R^{11}(t, \tau) P^{12} R^{22}(\tau, t_0) \, d\tau \tag{11}$$

To obtain an approximate solution of the form

$$\mathbf{X}(t) = R^{11}(t, t_0) \mathbf{X_0} + R^{12}(t, t_0) \mathbf{X_0}^{[2]} + R^{13}(t, t_0) \mathbf{X_0}^{[3]}, \tag{12}$$

we substitute solution (10) in the nonlinear terms of the truncated equation

$$\frac{d\mathbf{X}}{dt} = P^{11}\mathbf{X} + P^{12}\mathbf{X}^{[2]} + P^{13}\mathbf{X}^{[3]}. \tag{13}$$

After substitution, we obtain the linear equation

$$\begin{aligned}
\frac{d\mathbf{X}}{dt} &= P^{11}\mathbf{X} + P^{12}\left(R^{11}(t, t_0) \mathbf{X_0} + R^{12}(t, t_0) \mathbf{X_0}^{[2]}\right)^{[2]} \\
&+ P^{13}\left(R^{11}(t, t_0) \mathbf{X_0} + R^{12}(t, t_0) \mathbf{X_0}^{[2]}\right)^{[3]} = P^{11}\mathbf{X} + P^{12}R^{22}(t, t_0) \mathbf{X_0}^{[2]} \\
&+ P^{12}\left(\left(R^{11}(t, t_0) \mathbf{X_0}\right) \otimes \left(R^{12}(t, t_0) \mathbf{X_0}^{[2]}\right)\right. \\
&+ \left.\left(R^{12}(t, t_0) \mathbf{X_0}^{[2]}\right) \otimes \left(R^{11}(t, t_0) \mathbf{X_0}\right)\right) + P^{13}R^{33}(t, t_0) \mathbf{X_0}^{[3]} + \dots
\end{aligned} \tag{14}$$

where

$$R^{33}(t) = \left(R^{11}(t)\right)^{[3]}. \tag{15}$$

Let us introduce the notation

$$\left(R^{11}(t,t_0)\mathbf{Y}\right) \otimes \left(R^{12}(t,t_0)\mathbf{Y}^{[2]}\right) + \left(R^{12}(t,t_0)\mathbf{Y}^{[2]}\right) \otimes \left(R^{11}(t,t_0)\mathbf{Y}\right) = f(t,t_0,\mathbf{Y}) \tag{16}$$

Let us solve the matrix system of linear algebraic equations with the matrix of unknowns R^{23}:

$$R^{23}M_Y = M_f \tag{17}$$

In the matrix system (17): $M_Y = \left(\mathbf{Y_1}^{[3]}, \ldots, \mathbf{Y_p}^{[3]}\right)$, $\mathbf{Y_1}, \ldots, \mathbf{Y_p}$ – arbitrary linearly independent system of vectors, $M_f = (f(t,t_0,\mathbf{Y_1}), \ldots, f(t,t_0,\mathbf{Y_p}))$.

The solution to system (17) is the matrix $R^{23} = R^{23}(t,t_0)$, which can also be obtained analytically by transforming the left-hand side of equality (16). As a result, we have

$$\left(R^{11}(t,t_0)\mathbf{X_0}\right) \otimes \left(R^{12}(t,t_0)\mathbf{X_0}^{[2]}\right)$$
$$+ \left(R^{12}(t,t_0)\mathbf{X_0}^{[2]}\right) \otimes \left(R^{11}(t,t_0)\mathbf{X_0}\right) = R^{23}(t,t_0)\mathbf{X_0}^{[3]} \tag{18}$$

Substituting equation (18) into equation (14) and taking into account the terms up to the third order, we obtain the linear equation

$$\frac{d\mathbf{X}}{dt} = P^{11}\mathbf{X} + P^{12}R^{22}(t,t_0)\mathbf{X_0}^{[2]} + \left(P^{12}R^{23}(t,t_0) + P^{13}R^{33}(t,t_0)\right)\mathbf{X_0}^{[3]}, \tag{19}$$

The solution to this system has the form

$$\mathbf{X}(t) = R^{11}(t,t_0)\mathbf{X_0} + R^{12}(t,t_0)\mathbf{X_0}^{[2]} + R^{13}(t,t_0)\mathbf{X_0}^{[3]},$$

$$R^{13}(t) = \int_{t_0}^{t} R^{11}(t,\tau)P^{12}R^{23}(\tau,t_0)\,d\tau + \int_{t_0}^{t} R^{11}(t,\tau)P^{13}R^{33}(\tau,t_0)\,d\tau$$

Continuing iterations up to order N, we get:

$$\mathbf{X}(t) = R^{11}(t,t_0)\mathbf{X_0} + \sum_{k=2}^{N} R^{1k}(t)\mathbf{X_0}^{[k]},$$

$$R^{1k}(t) = \sum_{j=2}^{k} \int_{t_0}^{t} R^{11}(t,\tau)P^{1j}R^{jk}(\tau,t_0)\,d\tau, \quad R^{ii}(t,t_0) = \left(R^{11}(t,t_0)\right)^{[i]}, \tag{20}$$

$$R^{11}(t,t_0) = \exp\left((t-t_0)P^{11}\right)$$

The matrices $R^{jk}(t,t_0)$ are calculated using an algorithm similar to the algorithm for calculating the matrices $R^{23}(t,t_0)$. The matrix $R^{jk}(t,t_0)$ can also be obtained analytically by transforming the left-hand side of equality

$$\sum_{\sum_{i=1}^{j} k_i = k} \left(R^{1k_1}(t,t_0)\mathbf{X_0}^{[k_i]}\right) \otimes \ldots \otimes \left(R^{1k_j}(t,t_0)\mathbf{X_0}^{[k_j]}\right) = R^{jk}(t,t_0)\mathbf{X_0}^{[k]}$$

3.3 Example

Let us consider an approximation [20] of particle motion in cylindrical deflector written in the form:

$$x' = y$$
$$y' = -2x + x^2/R \tag{21}$$

We generate a training data as a particular solution of the system (21) with the initial condition $\mathbf{X_0} = (-2, 4)$ (Fig. 2, green points). The training set includes 27 points ($R = 10$). After this solution was generated, the equation is not used further.

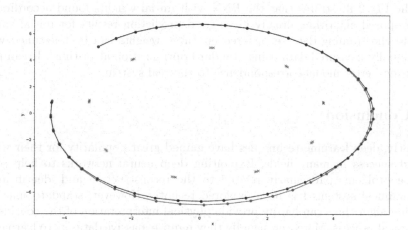

Fig. 2. Training data used for ODEs reconstruction (greed dots), system trajectory generated by PNN for another initial condition (red line), real system trajectory (blue line) (Color figure online)

Then, this generated trajectory is used to reconstruct the system of ordinary differential equations till the third order of non linearity according to the algorithm described in Sect. 3.1:

$$\frac{d\mathbf{X}}{dt} = \begin{pmatrix} 4.06732625 \cdot 10^{-6} & 0.999964923 \\ -1.99993049 & -4.38301027 \cdot 10^{-6} \end{pmatrix} \mathbf{X}$$

$$+ \begin{pmatrix} 1.24062940e \cdot 10^{-7} & 3.28166404 \cdot 10^{-6} & 2.00339676 \cdot 10^{-9} \\ 0.0999900634 & -9.71187750 \cdot 10^{-8} & 3.33946651 \cdot 10^{-6} \end{pmatrix} \mathbf{X}^{[2]}$$

$$+ 10^{-7} \begin{pmatrix} -3.26578011 & 1.48318573 & -1.79415514 & 0.72283912 \\ 1.07008208 & 3.66009614 & -1.31485102 & 1.79102455 \end{pmatrix} \mathbf{X}^{[3]} \tag{22}$$

Then, using the approximate system (22), we find the matrices of weights $\mathbf{R}^{11}(t, t_0)$ and $\mathbf{R}^{12}(t, t_0)$ for different values of t ($t_0 = 0$) according to the algorithm introduced in Sect. 3.2.

For example, for $t = 1.1$, the approximate solution to Eq. (21) for any initial values of $\mathbf{X_0}$ constructed up to the second order non linearity has the form:

$$\mathbf{X}\,(t = 1.1) = \begin{pmatrix} 0.0152181223886654 & 0.707024692103253 \\ -1.41404983954638 & 0.0152121475825109 \end{pmatrix} \mathbf{X_0}$$

$$+ \begin{pmatrix} 0.0330738670919230 & 0.0232052217767992 & 0.00808282751349695 \\ 0.0242876681630190 & 0.0338195709561698 & 0.0232073819255883 \end{pmatrix} \mathbf{X_0^{[2]}}(23)$$

An example of comparing the numerical solution of Eq. (21) with the Runge-Kutta method (blue line) and the solution we obtained for the initial conditions $\mathbf{X_0} = (-3, 5)$ (red line) is shown in Fig. 2.

The Fig. 2 illustrates that the PNN with initial weights found according to the proposed algorithm already gives good prediction results for initial values beyond the training data set. Moreover, these weights can be fine-tuned with additionally measured data using standard optimization algorithms. It can provide even better model correspondence to the real system.

4   Conclusion

Recently, deep learning techniques have gained great popularity for their widespread success in many fields. Exploiting deep neural networks to help solve inverse problems particularly related to the reconstruction and identification of dynamical systems has been explored recently. However, standard machine learning algorithms can hardly provide physical interpretation of the considered dynamical process. Moreover, usually they require massive datasets to learn end-to-end mappings from the measurement domain to the target system domain. This paper proposes an architecture and learning algorithm for polynomial neural networks based on Taylor maps for dynamical system learning with small datasets. The Taylor mapping technique provides transformation of the dynamic system represented in the form of ODEs to the initial weights of the polynomial neural network. Thus, as a first step the algorithm requires reconstructing the right side of ODEs, that we propose to do in the polynomial form. We shown in a toy example of nonlinear deflector that the PNN with the initial weights found according to the proposed algorithms allows PNN to achieve great generalisation ability. However, the results can be improved even more by fine-tuning the initial weights from additional data using the standard optimization algorithms.

Acknowledgements. The authors would like to thank Saint Petersburg State University for the research grant ID: 75206008.

References

1. Andrianov, S.: A matrix representation of the lie transformation. In: Proceedings of the Abstracts of the International Congress on Computer Systems and Applied Mathematics, vol. 14 (1993)

2. Andrianov, S.: Symbolic computation of approximate symmetries for ordinary differential equations. Math. Comput. Simul. **57**(3–5), 147–154 (2001)
3. Andrianov, S.: Dynamical modeling of control systems for particle beams. Saint Petersburg State University, SPb (2004)
4. Ayed, I., Bezenac, E., Pajot, A., Brajard, J., Gallinari, P.: Learning dynamical systems from partial observations. arxiv:1902.11136 (2019)
5. Berz, M.: From Taylor series to Taylor models (1997). https://bt.pa.msu.edu/pub/papers/taylorsb/taylorsb.pdf
6. Bieker, K., Peitz, S., Brunton, S., Kutz, J., Dellnitz, M.: Deep model predictive control with online learning for complex physical systems. arxiv:1905.10094 (2019)
7. Chen, T.Q., Rubanova, Y., Bettencourt, J., Duvenaud, D.K.: Neural ordinary differential equations. In: Advances in Neural Information Processing Systems, pp. 6571–6583 (2018)
8. Chen, Y., Shi, Y., Zhang, B.: Optimal control via neural networks: a convex approach (2019). https://arxiv.org/pdf/1805.11835.pdf
9. Dolgov, S.: A tensor decomposition algorithm for large odes with conservation laws. Comput. Meth. Appl. Math. **19**(1), 23–38 (2019)
10. Dragt, A.: Lie methods for nonlinear dynamics with applications to accelerator physics (2011). https://inspirehep.net/record/955313/files/TOC28Nov2011.pdf
11. Group, T.: Physics-based deep learning (2019). https://github.com/thunil/Physics-Based-Deep-Learning
12. Ivanov, A., Golovkina, A., Iben, U.: Polynomial neural networks and Taylor maps for dynamical systems simulation and learning. ECAI2020 Accepted, not published yet. arxiv:1912.09986 (2019)
13. Jia, X., et al.: Physics guided RNNs for modeling dynamical systems: a case study in simulating lake temperature profiles. In: Proceedings of the 2019 SIAM International Conference on Data Mining, pp. 558–566. SIAM (2019)
14. Karpatne, A., Watkins, W., Read, J., Kumar, V.: Physics-guided neural networks (PGNN): an application in lake temperature modeling (2018). https://arxiv.org/pdf/1710.11431.pdf
15. Koppe, G., Toutounji, H., Kirsch, P., Lis, S., Durstewitz, D.: Identifying nonlinear dynamical systems via generative recurrent neural networks with applications to fMRI. arxiv:1902.07186 (2019)
16. Mohajerin, N., Waslander, S.L.: Multistep prediction of dynamic systems with recurrent neural networks. IEEE Trans. Neural Netw. Learn. Syst. **30**(11), 3370–3383 (2019)
17. Nagabandi, A., Kahn, G., Fearing, R., Levine, S.: Neural network dynamics for model-based deep reinforcement learning with model-free fine-tuning (2017). https://arxiv.org/pdf/1708.02596.pdf
18. Novikov, A., Trofimov, M., Oseledets, I.: Exponential machines. arxiv:1605.03795 (2017)
19. Raissi, M., Perdikaris, P., Karniadakis, G.E.: Physics informed deep learning (part II): data-driven discovery of nonlinear partial differential equations (2017)
20. Senichev, Y., Møller, S.: Beam dynamics in electrostatic rings (2000). http://accelconf.web.cern.ch/AccelConf/e00/PAPERS/MOP1B04.pdf
21. Yu, R., Zheng, S., Anandkumar, A., Yue, Y.: Long-term forecasting using higher order tensor RNNs. arxiv:1711.00073 (2019)

Isolation and Comparison of Company Names in the News Text with Tickers of Companies Traded on Stock Exchanges

Stanislav Bachinsky[1] and Alexey Stankus[2(✉)]

[1] Dubna State University, 19 Universitetskaya street, Dubna 141980, Russia
[2] Saint Petersburg State University, 7-9 Universitetskaya Emb., Saint Petersburg 199034, Russia
alexey@stankus.ru

Abstract. Determining the names of companies in the news text is an important task in predicting changes in the prices of companies' shares. There is a large number of works devoted to this problem, a large number of algorithms have been created. On the other hand, in order to understand which stocks of which company may be affected by this or that news, it is necessary to understand exactly which ticker corresponds to the name of the company extracted from the text of the news.

Behind the seeming simplicity of the question, there is the difficulty of comparing the descriptions of tickers that exchanges provide with incomplete company names that are indicated in ordinary, non-financial news. Often in the news, companies are written in abbreviated form or abbreviations. At the same time, the description of tickers contains deliberately redundant information, which also needs to be isolated and removed to improve the results of matching names.

In this article, we will analyze several possible approaches to solving this problem and present an algorithm developed by us for comparing company names found in news texts with stock tickers.

Keywords: Company names · News · Tickers · Matching · Neural networks · Gestalt pattern matching · NASDAQ · NYSE · Sequential elimination method

1 Introduction

News is a change and reflection of some fragment of reality, timely covered in the media, which is of interest and value to a large number of audiences.

Thousands of news are published daily, containing information about everything that happens around us. News analysis is the cornerstone for predicting price changes and volatility in stocks traded on the stock exchange. Identifying the company that is being talked about in the news is the first step towards predicting the stock price using the news.

There are number of works aimed to extract company names from news [1–4]. But in this article discusses approaches that allow us to select the names of companies from the text of general news, as well as a method we have developed that allows us to compare the resulting name with a possible ticker (a short name in the exchange information of quoted instruments) of a company.

2   The Essence of the Problem

Unlike financial news text, company names mentioned in general news text may not contain the full company name or designator words such as Inc, Corp, Limited, Common Stock. Such words allow you to distinguish the company name from other proper names, or ordinary words. For example, the sentence "Apple is the healthiest fruit" is about apples, but "Apple is an American corporation" refers to the name of the company. The method of extracting company names from text should be applied universally to general and financial news.

Unfortunately, company names in general news and their official names often differ. Differences can be in punctuation marks, casing, references to subsidiaries, and inaccuracies in the selection methods.

1)   …. expect to see Nvidia's new pro-grade desktop GPUs in…
2)   … in a McDonalds parking lot in the…
3)   …. and Walmart Inc's Flipkart benefit only…

Such differences lead to the omission of company names in news texts, which later gives an error when trying to create a predictive model for a particular company or have grown.

This brings us to one requirement - False Negative minimization. At the same time, the presence of a large number of False Positives suits us, since all unnecessary words or phrases that would be mistaken for company names will be discarded at the stage of comparison with stock tickers.

On the other hand, the description of a ticker on the exchange contains redundant information and is broader than just the name of the company to which the ticker refers. For example - "International Business Machines Corporation Common Stock or Summit Hotel Properties, Inc. 9.25% Series A Cumulative Redeemable Preferred Stock". This feature of the ticker descriptions leads us to the need to process the ticker descriptions in order to increase the likelihood of subsequent matches and reduce the False Negative results of the matches.

Such disagreements in spelling lead to the fact that solving the problem of matching the names of companies mentioned in news texts and tickers of these companies traded on exchanges requires the solution of 3 subtasks:

a.   Highlight the names of companies mentioned in the news;
b.   Remove unnecessary text from tickers, leaving only the core.
c.   Compare highlighted company names in news texts and optimized ticker descriptions.

3   Extraction of Company Names from News Text

In this section, we will consider several existing methods for solving the problem of highlighting company names in the text.

3.1 Linguistic Analysis Method

This method is based on an article in Proceedings The Seventh IEEE Conference on Artificial Intelligence Application [5]. The solution to the problem of highlighting company names in the text, described in this article, is a heuristic: testing and improving the method on the texts of real news.

The method is based on sequential iteration over the words of the news text. The main components of the method are shown in Fig. 1. The condition for stopping the search is the detection of a word from the list of trigger words, such as: Inc, Corp, Co, Plc, Ltd, etc. In case of a stop, the previous word will be read and checked:

a) mixed case;
b) whether the word is a union;
c) whether the word is a sentence/phrase boundary.

Based on the results of the checks, the following outcomes are possible:

a) The current phrase (the trigger word and the previous words that passed the test) is recognized as the name of the company.
b) The current phrase is not recognized by the name of the company.

The disadvantage of this approach lies in its essence: the method is heuristic. To effectively identify titles, a large list of trigger words is required, which can be generated by manually marking news texts. However, the main disadvantage is that the company name must contain a trigger word in order to be identified. The phrase Amazon Inc, the considered method, would successfully define the name of the company, but the words Amazon or Amazon.Com would be omitted. This method is effective for highlighting company names in the text of financial news, in which full company names are indicated, containing suffixes and other indicators. This method is not suitable for general news that uses partial company names (for example, without the Inc: Amazon.Com or Amazon suffix).

3.2 Method Using Neural Networks

Another approach to solving the problem of extracting company names from the text is the use of neural networks called NER (Named Entity Recognition). This article discusses a pipeline developed by Explosion [6]. With the help of the pipeline (Fig. 2), we will carry out lexical analysis of the text. The pipeline consists of blocks [7]:

1. word2vec [8] - a component for converting words into a vector;
2. tagger - a component that predicts the likelihood of tags based on vectors of tokens;
3. parser - a component intended for a dependency parser;
4. attributer_ruller - a component that allows you to set attributes;
5. lemmatizer - a component for assigning basic forms to tokens using rules based on part-of-speech tags;
6. ner - named object recognition component.

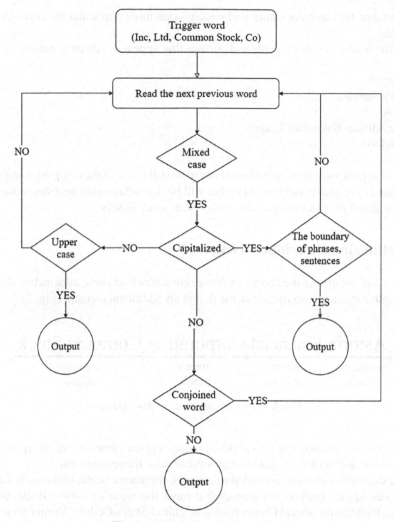

Fig. 1. Linguistic analysis method.

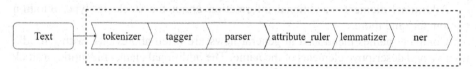

Fig. 2. NER data flow.

This method allows you to extract company names from the text of the news. Unlike the previously described method, the pipeline identifies companies regardless of the completeness of their name. However, it gives a high percentage of false positive errors, which suits us at this stage, due to the fact that in the future, the list of words and phrases that are taken for company names will undergo one more check and the excess will be discarded.

Below is an example of words and phrases that appear in company names:

a. Footfall
b. Cesar basanta
c. USA
d. The African Basketball League
e. Bluetooth

However, for us, it is more important not to miss the loss of the company name in the news than to get unnecessary meaning that will be discarded in the next step - matching the highlighted prospective company names with stock tickers.

4 Optimizing Description Tickers

The names of companies used on the exchange consist of four parts: a distinctive element, a descriptive element, a corporate element, and an additional element (Fig. 3).

Astoria	Financial	Corporation	Common Stock
distinctive element	descriptive element	corporate element	additional element

Fig. 3. Ticker company name description.

A distinctive element can be a personal name, a place name, or a made-up word. Its purpose is to distinguish companies with similar descriptive elements.

The descriptive element is needed to describe the nature of the business and allows you to distinguish between companies that have the same or similar distinguishing element: United States Steel Corporation and United States Cellular Corporation.

The corporate element is a suffix that carries information about the type of company: private limited company, public limited company, group of companies, and others.

Additional element - additional information about the stock: its type, duration, percentage, and more.

Company names mentioned in general news are often abbreviated with only distinctive and descriptive elements of the name. The additional element identifies a stock, not a company, therefore, to correctly match company names from the news text and company names from the stock exchange, the additional element should be removed.

To remove an additional element, you need to find the border between the additional and the descriptive element, that is, the corporate element. There is a limited number of words used as a corporate element, so we extract the 50 most frequently mentioned words in the entire list of companies from the stock exchange. Most of the words on the list are corporate words:

{Inc, Corporation, Shares, Class, Fund, Corp, Holdings, Trust, Depositary, Group, Ordinary, Limited,…}.

The list also contains words denoting the type of stock {Shares, Common Stock}, as well as popular words in the descriptive element {Energy, Oil}, therefore, words that are not related to the corporate element have also been removed.

5 Matching the Highlighted Company Name to the Ticker

5.1 Comparison Method for Hashed Sequences

The sequence comparison algorithm was published back in the late 1980s by John W. Ratcliff and John A. Obershelp under the hyperbolic title "Gestalt pattern matching". [9] The idea is to find the longest contiguous matching subsequence that does not contain "unnecessary" items. These "unnecessary" elements are in some sense uninteresting, for example, blank lines or spaces. (Garbage handling is an extension of Ratcliff and Obershelp's algorithm.) The same idea is then applied recursively to the portions of sequences to the left and right of the corresponding subsequence. This does not result in minimal edit sequences, but tends to produce matches that "look right" to humans.

The similarity of two strings S_1 and S_2 is determined by the formula, calculating twice the number of matching characters K_m divided by the total number of characters of both strings. The matching characters are defined as the longest common substring (LCS) plus recursively the number of matching characters in the non-matching regions on both sides of the LCS:

$$D_{ro} = \frac{2K_m}{|S_1| + |S_2|}$$

where the similarity metric can take a value between zero and one:

$$0 \leq D_{ro} \leq 1$$

The algorithm is effective for comparing slightly different words or sequences, but it is not suitable for comparing the results of methods for identifying potential companies with stock tickers, since the phrase representing a potential company found by the neural network method often contains words that are not included in the name of the company. For example, "Morgan Stanley Tactical Value Investing" extracted from news and its corresponding "Morgan Stanley have" a weak similarity ratio, and the phrase "Root Blocks in has" a strong similarity to "Riot Blockchain".

5.2 Sequential Elimination Method

The developed algorithm allows us to remove restrictions on the presence of unnecessary words in the studied phrase. Figure 4 shows a diagram of the algorithm for matching the selected, from news, word or phrase, and the name of the company from the stock exchange. The algorithm uses processed company names from the stock exchange, stock tickers, and words and phrases extracted from news, presumably being company names.

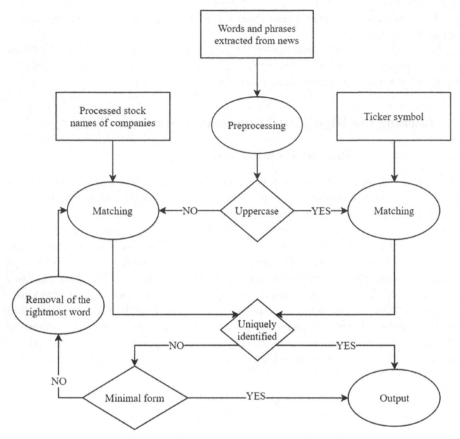

Fig. 4. Sequential elimination method.

Processing of Company Names Extracted from News Text

At the preprocessing stage, the problems associated with the operation of methods for highlighting words and phrases that are potentially company names in the text are minimized: the addition of insignificant spaces at the beginning or end of words and phrases, an error in the encoding of individual characters, incorrect addition of punctuation and quotation marks: "Mc Donadls", 'McDonald^{TM}s', 'McDonald's'. The solution is to use regular expressions and two-way encoding.

Processing Companies in Upper Case

The identified word or phrase, potentially a company name, in uppercase, may be a stock ticker (IBM, Bio), and may also be a stylistic feature of the news (APPLE instead of Apple). First, the word/phrase is compared with the stock ticker. If the comparison did not give any results, the entire word/phrase, except for the first letter, is converted to lower case.

Handling the Incorrect Selection of Potential Companies

There are situations when words that are not related to it are added after the actual name of the company in the identified phrase, which is potentially the name of the company, for example:

a. Fiat Chrysler Automobiles FCAU.N.Nissan replacing Fiat Chrysler Automobiles.
b. Morgan Stanley Tactical Value Investing instead of Morgan Stanley.

To process such cases, the rightmost word is removed from the phrase one by one, in the event that the part remaining after the deletion is minimally sufficient to unambiguously identify the company, after which it is compared with the exchange names. The minimum sufficient for an unambiguous definition is a phrase consisting of two words, one of which is not in common use (Astoria from Astoria Financial Corporation), or a phrase of 3 words.

Determination Results

As a result of the method of successive exclusions, the identified phrase is marked as unambiguously defined or as undefined. The resulting value is entered into the database with the ticker of the corresponding company.

6 Experiments

6.1 Initial Data

The experiments were based on news collected from BBC News, Business Wire, Breitbart News, CNN, The New York Times, Reuters, Washington Post, Trustnodes and Yahoo News from January 2018 to October 2020.

In total, 988 102 texts of various news were collected. To test the methods of allocation and comparison with the stock ticker of company names, 100 news were selected from the general list, 62 unique company names were manually marked in them, and 28 unique names of companies with shares on the NASDAQ or NYSE stock exchange were manually assigned the corresponding stock tickers.

To test the algorithm for matching phrases with a stock ticker, a list of companies trading on the NASDAQ and NYSE stock exchanges was used [10].

6.2 Testing Methods for Highlighting Company Names

Methods for extracting company names (linguistic and neural network) were tested on a test dataset of 100 news. Manual analysis showed that in these 100 news items, there are references to 62 companies. The experimental results are shown in Table 1.

It should be noted that the method using neural networks gives good results in terms of the number of correctly identified companies but produces a very large amount of unnecessary information that will have to be processed in the future.

Table 1. Highlighting company names.

Method	Total found	Detected	Not a company
Actual values	62	62	-
Linguistic analysis	32	8 (12.9%)	24
Neural networks	514	58 (93.5%)	456

6.3 Testing the Method of Matching Company Names and Stock Tickers

The method of comparing companies and stock tickers was tested on data obtained from the following initial processing:

- Checking the operation of the method of sequential elimination and the Gestalt Pattern method on the names of companies marked up manually;
- Checking the method of successive elimination and Gestalt Pattern method on the results of the linguistic method;
- Checking the method of successive elimination and the Gestalt Pattern method on the results of the neural network algorithm for extracting company names from the news text.

During manual checking, we received 62 unique company names, of which 28 names correspond to a specific ticker, 34 corresponds to an empty ticker (that is, the company's shares are not traded on NASDAQ and NYSE). The experimental results are presented in Table 2. All percentages are calculated from the correct number of tickers.

6.4 Experimental Results

The results of the experiments showed that the linguistic method is not suitable for solving the problem of separating the names of companies from the texts of ordinary, non-financial news, the result is less than 13% of the total number of companies mentioned.

The method using neural networks showed a significantly better result - 93.5%, but it is worth noting a very large number of unnecessary phrases that are perceived as company names and interfere with further processing.

To solve the matching of the ticker to the company name, we have the following result:

The Gestalt Pattern method shows an average result when you manually isolate company names (82.1%), but when you add random (obviously unnecessary) words that fall into phrases, the accuracy of the method drops significantly (57.1%). With a large amount of garbage data, the method gives a large number of errors.

The Sequential elimination method shows an excellent result (100%) with a good isolation of the company name from the news (manual method) and a good result with the presence of unnecessary words and phrases (89.2%).

Table 2. Matching company names and stock tickers.

Method	Number of companies	Correct ticker	Wrong ticker	Ambiguous tickers	No ticker
Actual values	62	28	0	0	34
Gestalt Pattern method (based on actual values)	62	23(82.1%)	7(25%)	3	29
Sequential elimination method (based on actual values)	62	28(100%)	3(10.7%)	0	31
Gestalt Pattern method (based on linguistic analysis values)	32	8(28.5%)	6(21.4%)	1	17
Sequential elimination method (based on linguistic analysis values)	32	8(28.5%)	4(14.2%)	0	20
Gestalt Pattern method (based on neural networks values)	514	16(57.1%)	27(96.4%)	66	405
Sequential elimination method (based on neural networks values)	514	25(89.2%)	5(17.8%)	56	428

7 Conclusion

The article examined and conducted tests of methods for separating company names from the texts of ordinary, non-financial news, as well as methods for comparing the selected company names to stock tickers.

The experimental results show that methods based on neural networks show good results in identifying company names, but they carry a large amount of garbage that contaminates the data obtained, which ultimately leads to a slight but increase in errors in the best of the algorithms for matching the company name to the exchange tickers.

To improve the results, it is necessary to concentrate on training neural networks for a more correct selection of company names, with a decrease in the amount of unnecessary information.

References

1. Loster, M., Zuo, Z., Naumann, F., Maspfuhl, O.: Improving company recognition from unstructured text by using dictionaries, March 2017
2. Oliya, A.: News to company linking with Bert, November 2019
3. Campos, R., Mangaravite, V., Pasquali, A., Jorge, A.M., Nunes, C., Jatowt, A.: YAKE! collection-independent automatic keyword extractor. In: Pasi, G., Piwowarski, B., Azzopardi, L., Hanbury, A. (eds.) ECIR 2018. LNCS, vol. 10772, pp. 806–810. Springer, Cham (2018). https://doi.org/10.1007/978-3-319-76941-7_80
4. https://www.analyticsinsight.net/company-names-standardization-using-a-fuzzy-nlp-app roach/, 28 March 2020
5. Rau, L.F.: Extracting company names from text. In: Proceedings the Seventh IEEE Conference on Artificial Intelligence Application (1991)
6. Introducing spaCy. explosion.ai. Accessed 18 Dec 2016
7. Models & Languages. spaCy Usage Documentation. spacy.io. Accessed 08 Feb 2021
8. Mikolov, T., Sutskever, I., Chen, K., Corrado, G.S., Dean, J.: Distributed representations of words and phrases and their compositionality. In: NIPS (2013)
9. Ratcliff, J.W., John, A.: Obershelp Gestalt pattern matching. https://en.wikipedia.org/wiki/Gestalt_Pattern_Matching
10. Tickers list. http://www.nasdaqtrader.com/trader.aspx?id=symboldirdefs

An Analytical Bound for Choosing Trivial Strategies in Co-scheduling

Ruslan Kuchumov$^{(\boxtimes)}$ (iD) and Vladimir Korkhov$^{(\boxtimes)}$ (iD)

Saint Petersburg State University, 7/9 Universitetskaya nab.,
St. Petersburg 199034, Russia
st058444@student.spbu.ru, v.korkhov@spbu.ru

Abstract. Efficient usage of shared high-performance computing (HPC) resources raises the problem of HPC applications co-scheduling, i.e. the problem of execution of multiple applications simultaneously on the same shared computing nodes. Each application may have different requirements for shared resources (e.g. network bandwidth or memory bus bandwidth). When these resources are used concurrently, their resource throughputs may decrease, which leads to performance degradation.

In this paper we define application behavior model in co-scheduling environment and formalize a scheduling problem. Within the model we evaluate trivial strategies and compare them with an optimal strategy. The comparison provides a simple analytical criteria for choosing between a naive strategy of running all applications in parallel or any sophisticated strategies that account for applications performance degradation.

Keywords: High performance computing · Co-scheduling · Scheduling theory · Linear programming

1 Introduction

Commonly used job schedulers in HPC do not allow to oversubscribe the same computational resources with multiple jobs. The main reason for that is job performance degradation due to simultaneous access to shared resources, such as CPU cores, shared cache levels, memory bus. Requirements for such resources may depend on job input parameters, on external factors and may change over time, so it is difficult to provide them at jobs start time.

Applications may have different requirements for resources, and some resources may not be fully utilized by one application, but for others they would be a bottleneck. As schedulers in HPC do not allow over-subscription and allocate a whole cluster node to a single job, underutilized resources will be wasted even if there are jobs waiting in the queue for them.

The scheduling strategy of assigning multiple jobs to the same computational resources so that their interference with each other and the degradation of performance is minimal, in the literature is usually referred to as co-scheduling. It

© Springer Nature Switzerland AG 2021
O. Gervasi et al. (Eds.): ICCSA 2021, LNCS 12956, pp. 381–395, 2021.
https://doi.org/10.1007/978-3-030-87010-2_28

has started to gain interest recently, due to advances in hardware and operating systems support [13].

In this research we are mostly focused on modelling part of co-scheduling. In our previous work [8] we have shown which metrics can be used to estimate application processing speed in co-scheduling environment. We have shown how they can be measured and how they relate to total processing time of the application.

In this paper we focus on the problem of scheduling applications on shared resources. In particular, we have defined application behavior model in co-scheduling environment and formalized a scheduling problem. An optimal strategy for this problem can be found by solving corresponding linear programming problem. Using the optimal solution as a reference we have evaluated two trivial strategies – a round-robin (RR) strategy and naive parallel (NP) strategy. The comparison allowed us to obtain boundaries on application processing speed that can be used for choosing between these strategies.

2   Related Work

Problem of co-scheduling started to gain interest in the scientific community recently in the context of HPC work scheduling. For example, there is a series of workshop proceedings papers [13,14] dedicated to co-scheduling problem of HPC applications. Overall, these publications are mostly focused on the practical aspects, such as feasibility of this approach in general.

There is also a few publications on modelling HPC applications for co-scheduling. For example, in [1–3] author focuses on solving static scheduling problem with cache partitioning. Models in these papers are based on application speedup profile (that must be known in advance) as function of cache size.

Dynamic co-scheduling strategies in the context of HPC schedulers are not covered abundantly in scientific literature. Among few publications, there is [15], where authors provide supervised machine learning approach for estimating applications slowdown based on performance counters. Nevertheless, authors used this model for solving static scheduling problem. Another machine learning approach (with reinforcement learning) was used in [9] for dynamic collocation of services and HPC workloads.

Dynamic co-scheduling problem, on the other hand, is covered vastly in the context of thread scheduling in simultaneous multithreading (SMT) CPUs. There are [7,10–12] to name a few. The general theme of approaches in these papers is to measure threads instruction-per-second (IPC) values when they were running alone on a core and when they were running in parallel with other threads. Then the ratio of these two values was used for making scheduling decisions.

In the paper [6] authors showed that optimal co-scheduling algorithm does not produce more than 3% gain in throughput (on Spec benchmarks) when compared to a naive strategy of running all threads in parallel in FCFS order. This was shown by gathering slowdown values for all threads combinations and solving linear programming problem for finding an optimal schedule that was later compared to a naive strategy.

In this paper we have done the similar work but in the context of HPC applications. Additionally, we have also provided theoretical boundaries for slowdown values when naive parallel strategy can not be applied and showed the form of deviation from the optimal strategy. These results were evaluated on numerical experiments.

3 Benchmarks

In the experiments below we have used benchmarks from NAS Parallel Benchmark (NPB) [4], Parsec [5], and a few of our own benchmarks. This set of benchmarks cover different examples of HPC applications as it includes CPU-, memory- and filesystem-intensive benchmarks, different parallelism granularities, data exchange patterns and workflow models. Datasets for all benchmarks were tuned to have approximately the same processing times.

Among these benchmarks we have selected only those that have constant or periodic processing speed profiles. This requirement comes from the model assumption that we will introduce later. The resulting list of benchmarks is shown in Table 1

Table 1. List of benchmarks used in experiments.

Name	Suite	Description
bt	NPB	Block Tri-diagonal solver
ft	NPB	Discrete 3D fast Fourier Transform
lu	NPB	Lower-Upper Gauss-Seidel solver
ua	NPB	Unstructured Adaptive mesh
sp	NPB	Scalar Penta-diagonal solver
freqmine	Parsec	Frequent Pattern Growth algorithm
swaptions	Parsec	HJM algorithm for pricing swap options
vips	Parsec	Image processing pipeline
streamcluster	Parsec	Online clustering problem in data mining
ffmpeg		Decoding of video file
raytracing		Ray tracing algorithm on CPU

We've run our benchmarks on a single Intel Xeon E5-2630 processor with 10 cores and 2 threads per core. Each benchmark was limited to any of 4 threads, and threads were assigned by Linux scheduler (they were not pinned manually). In some experiments we used only a half of all available cores by pinning threads to same 5 CPU cores (but within those cores threads were assigned by the Linux scheduler as well). In all of the experiments, each application had enough memory and swap was never used.

4   Application Processing Speed Metric

Degradation of application performance due to co-scheduling can be explained by concurrent use of shared resources, such as last level cache, memory bus, cpu time, network card etc. During application execution instructions that access shared resources may take more cycles to complete when underlying resources are preforming operations for other applications. For example, instructions that require memory access may take more cycles, if required addresses are not in the cache as CPU would access memory bus. In turns, if memory bus is busy, that instruction would take ever more cycles to complete.

To define metric of application performance, we used amount of work per unit of time. We used CPU instructions as a unit of work as its rate is affected by all of the resources simultaneously, unlike resource-specific metrics (e.g. bus access rate or transmitted bytes to network card). As for the time unit, we have to take into account that CPU frequency is not constant and that application may be preempted from CPU core and suspended by OS scheduler.

CPU performance counters allow to measure cumulative values of the executed instructions ($inst(t)$) and completed cycles ($cycl(t)$) when application was running in the user space (as opposed to system space). Also, OS scheduler provides values for amount of time the processes was using CPU core ($cpu(t)$). Dividing instructions by cycles during time period Δt would give processing speed during application active time ($cpu(t) - cpu(t - \Delta t)$), commonly denoted in the literature as IPC (instructions per second). To be able to scale this value to the whole period we would assume that CPU cycles rate did not change when the application was not running. This gives us the formula for estimating application performance:

$$\nu(t) = \frac{inst(t) - inst(t - \Delta t)}{cycl(t) - cycl(t - \Delta t)} \frac{cpu(t) - cpu(t - \Delta t)}{\Delta t}$$

For our purposes we do not need absolute values of $\nu(t)$, but rather we need its change due to scheduling decisions that we make (between t_1 and t_2 time points):

$$f(t_1, t_2) = \frac{\nu(t_2)}{\nu(t_1)}$$

Assuming Δt is the same for all measurements, and that the number threads in the application do not change between measurements, this value can be computed as a ratio of product of IPC and cpu-time before and after scheduling decision. We will call this ratio as performance speedup value. When this value is less than 1, then it measures performance slowdown.

4.1   Evaluation on Experimental Data

To evaluate the defined metric we have compared it with change of application processing time in ideal and co-scheduling conditions. To do that we measured application processing time when it was running alone in the server and when it was running simultaneously with different combinations of other applications. In the second case, we made sure that the application that is being measured was the first one to finish, otherwise its conditions would change before completion and comparison would not be fair. For the same reason we had to select benchmark applications with constant or periodic (with a small period) speed profiles.

To collect the data we run all possible combinations with different number of applications in parallel. Each application required 4 threads, we run up to 5 applications on 10 CPU cores, so each CPU core was oversubscribed with up to 2 applications. Application threads were not pinned to the core and the OS scheduler could migrate them between cores dynamically.

Results for some benchmarks are shown in the scatter plots in the Fig. 1 and the Table 2 contains linear regression model for all benchmarks. Good fit of the linear model with coefficients close to 1, shows that changes in processing speed (measured as described above) matches exactly with changes in total processing time.

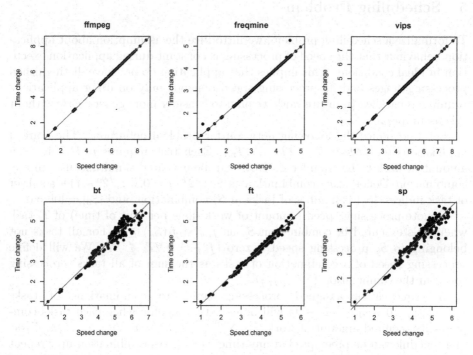

Fig. 1. Total time change vs processing speed change for different combinations of parallel tasks relative to ideal conditions

Table 2. Linear regression model parameters for processing time change as function of processing speed change (relative to ideal conditions)

	Coefficient	Intercept	R squared
ffmpeg	0.9791	0.0234	0.9999
freqmine	0.9976	0.0141	0.9947
vips	0.9491	0.0514	0.9999
bt	0.8217	0.1551	0.9199
ft	0.9387	−0.0627	0.9844
sp	0.8335	0.0187	0.9232
raytracing	1.0240	−0.0994	0.9999
streamcluster	0.6914	1.1861	0.7651
ua	1.7214	0.2477	0.6991
swaptions	1.0700	−0.1288	0.9928

5   Scheduling Problem

To formalize a scheduling problem, we introduce the assumption about application behaviour that the speed of processing is constant during application execution in ideal conditions. This implies that application do not have distinguished processing stages and its processing speed depends only on other applications running in parallel. In future work we plan to consider more general case without this assumption.

Let's introduce the following notation for problem definitions. There are n applications (or tasks): $T = \{T_1, \ldots, T_n\}$. Each task requires $p_i, i = 1, \ldots, n$ amount of work to be completed. Tasks can be executed simultaneously in any combination. Denote each combination as $S_j \in 2^T, j = 0, \ldots, (2^n - 1)$ – a subset of task indices. $|S_j|$ is number of tasks in S_j combination, and $|S_0| = |\emptyset| = 0$.

Denote processing speed (amount of work done per unit of time) of T_i task when it is executed in combination S_j as $f_{i,j} = f_i(S_j) \geq 0$. For all tasks not belonging to S_j processing speed is zero ($f_{i,j} = 0 \; \forall T_i \notin S_j$). We will define processing speed of a combination of tasks as the sum of all tasks' processing speed in the combination ($\sum_{i=1}^{n} f_{i,j}$).

A sequence of assigned processing times to combinations of tasks $x_{j_1}, \ldots, x_{j_m}, 0 \leq j_k \leq (2^n - 1)$ will be called a schedule when each tasks completes its required amount of work, i.e. $\sum_{k=1}^{m} f_{i,j_k} x_{j_k} = p_i \; \forall i = 1, \ldots, n$. Tasks in a schedule can be preempted at any time, i.e. a tasks combination may repeat in a schedule.

The scheduling problem is to find a schedule that has a minimal makespan value (C_{max}). Makespan is a completion time of the last task in a schedule.

5.1   Optimal Strategy

Makespan of a schedule can be written as a sum of assigned processing times to each tasks combination: $C_{max} = \sum_{k=1}^{m} x_{j_k}$. Since in the we can reorder terms in makespan sum and work amount sum without affecting their values, it allows us to consider only the schedules with non-recurring tasks combinations.

The problem then reduces to finding distribution of processing time among non-empty tasks combinations. Instead of a sequence of task combinations we will consider $x_j \geq 0, j = 1, \ldots, (2^n - 1)$ – a total processing time of combination S_j. This allows us to solve scheduling problem as linear programming problem:

$$\begin{array}{ll} \text{minimize} & \sum_{j=1}^{2^n-1} x_j \\ \text{subject to} & \sum_{j=1}^{2^n-1} f_{i,j} x_j = p, \ i = 1, \ldots, n \\ & x_j \geq 0, \qquad\qquad j = 1, \ldots, 2^n - 1 \end{array}$$

By solving this problem, we will find values $x_1^*, \ldots x_{2^n-1}^*$ that produce a minimum makespan. A schedule can be reconstructed from these values simply by running each task combination S_j for x_j^* time (if $x_j^* \neq 0$) in any order without interruptions. We will denote an optimal makespan value as C_{max}^{LP}.

This approach produces optimal solution but it can not be used in schedulers as it requires all a priory information about each application. Instead it can be used as a reference for evaluation of other scheduling strategies.

5.2   Heuristic Strategies

We will consider two heuristics strategies (naive parallel and round-robin) and compare their solutions with the optimal strategy.

Naive parallel (NP) strategy disregards all information about applications and runs all available applications in parallel. This strategy does not require any a priory information about applications and thus its implementation is the simplest.

Another heuristic strategy that we consider is round robin (RR). It works by finding subsets of active tasks with the maximum speed and running each subset one after another in a loop until one of the tasks finishes. Each subset is run continuously for at most one unit of time (denoted as T). Time unit may be smaller only when a task in a subset finishes earlier. We will call a sequence of subsets with the same speed executed in a single loop in RR strategy as a round. Round, in turn, consists of individual units of subset execution.

Unlike NP, RR strategy requires slowdown values for each subset of application. But, unlike the optimal strategy, it does not require amounts of works (p_i) of each application.

6   Strategies Comparison

In this section we will compare RR and NP heuristics strategies with the optimal strategy and provide bounds on slowdown function parameters when NP performs not worse than RR strategy.

6.1   Additional Assumptions on the Application Behaviour

There we will introduce additional assumptions about application behaviour in order to obtain analytical solutions. The first assumption is that the processing speed decreases linearly with an increase of the number applications running in parallel. We have seen this dependency in our experiments (as shown in Fig. 2 and Table 3). This assumption is introduced as linear dependency is the simplest non-trivial form of speedup function. The results that are obtained below will also hold for convex functions as well.

Another assumption is that each application has the same slowdown function. This is equivalent to claiming that each application is the same. This is very restrictive assumption, but by choosing slowdown functions with minimum or maximum slope value, we can obtain lower or upper limits for the slope value for switching strategies.

With these two assumptions we can write speedup function as $f_k = 1 - \alpha(k - 1)$ which only depends on $k = 1, \ldots, n$ – a number of tasks in the combination. α is a slope of slowdown function such that $0 < \alpha < \frac{1}{n-1}$ (since f_k should be $0 < f_k \leq 1, k = 1, \ldots, n$).

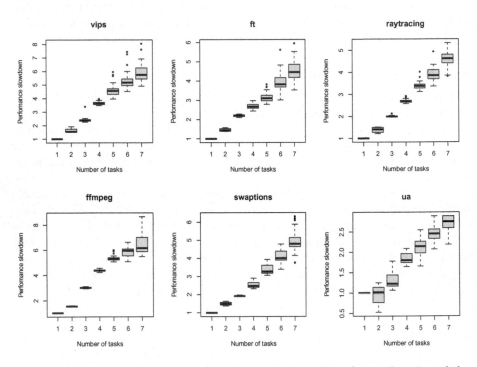

Fig. 2. Processing speed slowdown (relative to ideal conditions) as a function of the number of parallel applications

Table 3. Parameters of linear model of processing speed acceleration (relative to ideal conditions) vs. the number of parallel applications.

	Intercept	Coefficient	R squared
vips	0.7902	0.4483	0.8008
ft	0.6141	0.2133	0.7942
raytracing	0.6356	0.1496	0.9046
ffmpeg	0.8028	0.9821	0.7892
swaptions	0.7464	−0.3225	0.8771
ua	0.3239	0.4755	0.8215
bt	0.7315	0.5002	0.7941
freqmine	0.7315	0.5002	0.7941
sp	0.7315	0.5002	0.7941
streamcluster	0.7315	0.5002	0.7941

6.2 Comparison of Round-Robin and the Optimal Strategy

Since there's no analytical solution for linear programming problem, we ran numerical experiments to compare RR strategy with optimal strategy. We performed parameter sweeps on the number of tasks (n) and slowdown slope values ($alpha$). For each set of number of tasks and slope values we have generated 100 cases of differential amounts of works ($q_i = p_{i+1} - p_i$) that were drawn from uniform distribution (from 0 to 80 units bounds). For each case we solved linear programming problem (using lpsolve library) to find an optimal solution and found solution with RR strategy (with time unit $T = 2$).

Figure 3 shows boxes and whiskers plots with competitive rations of RR strategy for each slope value ($alpha$) containing results for 100 sets of random q_i values. Competitive ratio is computed as ratio of RR makespan value to optimal makepsan value. It can be seen that RR produces less than 15% deviation from the optimal strategy for 10 tasks.

6.3 Comparison of Round-Robin and Naive Parallel Strategy

Since RR makespan value is close to the optimal and we can derive analytical formula for it, we will use it as a reference for evaluation of NP strategy.

Lets consider that applications are sorted in increasing order of p_i, i.e. $p_i \leq p_{i+1}, i = 1, \ldots, n - 1$. Denote q_i as:

$$q_1 = p_1$$
$$q_k = p_k - p_{k-1}, k = 2, \ldots, n$$

NP strategy runs all tasks in parallel, as they finish in the increasing order of p_i, the first task, will finish after q_1 of work is completed, the second one after q_2 of work is completed and so on. The processing speed would also increase as tasks complete from f_n to f_{n-1} and so on until f_1. Using this, we can write makespan value for this strategy:

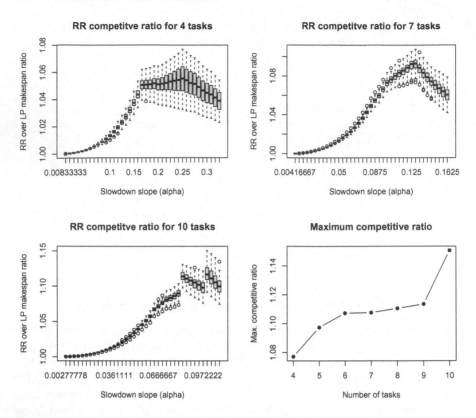

Fig. 3. Ratio of RR makespan to LP makespan as a function of slowdown slope value (alpha) for 4, 7 and 10 tasks. Bottom right plot shows max ratio value (across all alphas) for different number of tasks

$$C_{max}^{NP} = \sum_{k=1}^{n} \frac{q_k}{f_{n-k+1}}$$

Now, let's derive an estimate for makespan of RR strategy. We will do that by finding the sequence of tasks completion and number of rounds required to complete each task. This will allow us to derive exact makespan value, but it would contain rounding and modulo operations. To get rid of them, we will provide an upper bound instead. The deviation of the upper bound from the exact value would depend only on the time unit parameter (T), so after limit transition $(T \to 0)$ we will get a close approximation for RR makespan value.

Denote s as the size of tasks combination with the maximum speed, i.e. $s = \arg \max_{1 \le k \le n} \{k f_k\}$. RR strategy at first will choose combinations with s tasks and will ran each combination consequently for a single time unit (T). These combinations will be executed until the task with smallest amount of work $(q_1 = p_1)$ will finish.

There are $\binom{n}{s}$ combinations with s tasks, so until the first task finishes, each round would contain the same amount of time units. In a single round, each task would run $\binom{n-1}{s-1}$ times. Since the first task requires q_1 amount of work and Tf_s of work is completed per unit (processing speed of s tasks is f_s). This gives us an upper bound of processing time until the first task finishes as:

$$g_1 \leq \left\lceil \frac{q_1}{\binom{n-1}{s-1}Tf_s} \right\rceil \binom{n}{s} T$$

After the first task finishes, we would be left with $s - 1$ tasks and the next smallest task would require $q_2 = p_2 - p_1$ amount of work before completion. If s was less than n, reaming tasks would still run in combinations of s tasks, or if $s = n$, then remaining tasks would run in combinations of $s - 1$.

Let's consider the first case ($s < n$) when RR still chooses combinations with s tasks. Since one task is finished, there are now $\binom{n-1}{s}$ available combinations and each task would run $\binom{n-2}{s-1}$ times per round. This gives us the following upper bound for the second task:

$$g_2 \leq \left\lceil \frac{q_2}{\binom{n-2}{s-1}Tf_s} \right\rceil \binom{n-1}{s} T$$

The second case ($s = n$) or case when there are no combinations left with s tasks are similar, because in both cases RR chooses combinations with less than s tasks. Since RR chooses combinations with the fastest speed to run next, it would always run the same (fastest) combination until the next task finishes. There's only such combination as there is only one way of choosing $s - 1$ tasks from the subset of $s - 1$ tasks. If this case occurs for the third task, the upper bound would be:

$$g_3 \leq \left\lceil \frac{q_3}{Tf_{n-s}} \right\rceil T$$

We can now write general formulae for all tasks:

$$g_k \leq \left\lceil \frac{q_k}{\binom{n-k}{s-1}Tf_s} \right\rceil \binom{n-k+1}{s} T, \, k = 1, \ldots, (s-2)$$

$$g_k \leq \left\lceil \frac{q_k}{Tf_{n-k+1}} \right\rceil T, \qquad k = (s-1), \ldots, n$$

Using the fact that $\lceil \frac{a}{b} \rceil b < a + b$ for $a, b > 0$ and that $\binom{n-k+1}{s} = \frac{n-k+1}{s}\binom{n-k}{s-1}$ we can simplify the bounds as

$$g_k < \frac{n-k+1}{s}\left(T\binom{n-k}{s-1} + \frac{q_k}{f_s}\right), \, k = 1, \ldots, (s-2)$$
$$g_k < T + \frac{q_k}{f_{n-k+1}}, \qquad k = (s-1), \ldots, n$$

Which gives us the upper bound of makespan value:

$$C_{max}^{RR} < \sum_{k=1}^{n-s+1} \frac{n-k+1}{s}\left(T\binom{n-k}{s-1} + \frac{q_k}{f_s}\right) + \sum_{k=n-s+2}^{n}\left(T + \frac{q_k}{f_{n-k+1}}\right)$$

As the difference between each g_k and its upper bound is $O(T)$ by using very small time unit, we will get an approximation ($C_{max}^{RR^*}$) of an exact value. After limit transition $T \to 0$ we'll get:

$$C_{max}^{RR} \approx C_{max}^{RR^*} = \sum_{k=1}^{n-s+1} \frac{n-k+1}{s}\left(\frac{q_k}{f_s}\right) + \sum_{k=n-s+2}^{n} \frac{q_k}{f_{n-k+1}}$$

We can notice that the last sum in $C_{max}^{RR^*}$ upper bound matches exactly with the one in C_{max}^{NP} for $k > n-s+1$ and when $s = n$ these two value are the same. Because of that, we can claim that when the largest subset is the fastest, then round-robin strategy performs the same as naive parallel strategy.

Assuming that slowdown function is linear ($f_k = 1 - \alpha(k-1), k = 1, \ldots, n$) we can find the slope threshold (α^*) after which round-robin produces smaller makespan:

$$n = s = \arg\max_{0 \le k \le n}\{kf_k\} = \left\lceil \frac{\alpha^*+1}{2\alpha^*}\right\rceil = \left\lfloor \frac{\alpha^*+1}{2\alpha^*} + \frac{1}{2}\right\rfloor$$

Which gives the following bounds to α^*:

$$\frac{1}{2n} < \alpha^* \le \frac{1}{2(n-1)}$$

So, when f_k slope is greater than $\alpha^* = \frac{1}{2(n-1)}$ the difference between C_{max}^{NP} and $C_{max}^{RR^*}$ is non-zero. We can estimate the first term in makespan difference:

$$C_{max}^{NP} - C_{max}^{RR^*} = \frac{q_1}{f_n} - \frac{nq_1}{sf_s} = \cdots = -q_1\frac{(2n-1)^2\alpha^2 + (2-4n)\alpha + 1}{(n-1)\alpha^3 + (2n-3)\alpha^2 + (n-3)\alpha - 1}$$

Other non-zero terms will be similar, with the only difference in the first coefficient (q_k). Each term is a ratio of two polynomials with α variable and the polynomial in denominator has a larger degree and the one in numerator. Because of that, with increase of α value the difference in makespan values has hyperbolic growth.

The results obtained here can be seen on numerical to simulations. In the Fig. 4 there are plots corresponding to $C_{max}^{NP} - C_{max}^{RR}$ (brown line), $C_{max}^{RR^*} - C_{max}^{RR}$ (blue line) and $C_{max}^{LP} - C_{max}^{RR}$ (black line). Red line show threshold value α^*. As it can be seen, blue line is almost zero for all slopes values, which shows that approximate formulae match with exact value. NP makespan value also matches with RR strategy exactly until for $\alpha < \alpha^*$ and after threshold value (red line) it starts to increase significantly. Deviation of RR from the optimal strategy (black line) is negligible, when compared to NP strategy.

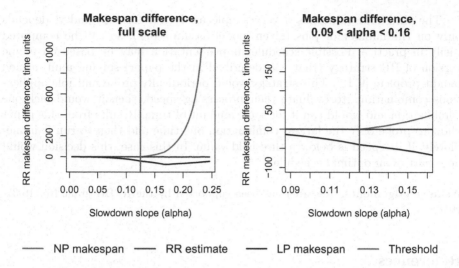

Fig. 4. Difference of makespan values of NP, LP, RR estimation with RR makespan for different slowdown slopes value (alpha). Vertical line shows threshold valued computed from derived formula. Both plots show the same data, but in different scales

7   Conclusion

In this paper we have defined application behavior model in co-scheduling environment, when applications can be executed simultaneously on shared resources. We have proposed to use application processing speed (measured based on IPC and cpu time) as a metric of performance degradation and have validated it on HPC benchmarks applications.

Based on that we have formalized a scheduling problem and found an optimal solution by reducing it to a linear programming problem. Optimal solution can not be implemented in schedulers as it requires a priory information about application performance slowdown values for all possible combinations of parallel applications. Besides that, linear programming problem does not have an analytical solution, it can only be solved iteratively.

To obtain more practical solution, we have considered two heuristic strategies, round-robin (RR) and naive parallel (NP). The first one (RR), takes into account application slowdown values and iterates over combinations of applications with the lowest slowdown in RR fashion. The second one (NP) simply runs all available applications in parallel disregarding slowdown completely. We have showed using numerical experiments that RR produces results very close to the optimal strategy and NP strategies matches with RR until some point.

We have derived an analytical bound for applications performance degradation value until which NP strategy matches exactly with RR strategy, and thus it is very close to the optimal strategy. When this threshold values is reached, the difference between an NP and RR starts to increase significantly (with hyperbolic growth).

The threshold value has a very simple analytical formula and ti depends only on the number of jobs (given model assumptions), so can be computed easily in practice. Possible scheduler implementation may be based on online version of RR strategy (that was described in the paper) solving multi-armed bandit problem [9,12]. This strategy would periodically probe multiple applications combinations to evaluate their processing speed, then it would pick one combination and would run it for some amount of time. Results from this paper allow to probe only the largest combination one time and then to run it immediately, if its speed is below a threshold value. In this case, this decision would be a part of an optimal schedule.

Acknowledgements. Research has been supported by the RFBR grant No. 19-37-90138.

References

1. Aupy, G., et al.: Co-scheduling Amdahl applications on cache-partitioned systems. Int. J. High Perform. Comput. Appl. **32**(1), 123–138 (2018)
2. Aupy, G., Benoit, A., Goglin, B., Pottier, L., Robert, Y.: Co-scheduling HPC workloads on cache-partitioned CMP platforms. Int. J. High Perform. Comput. Appl. **33**(6), 1221–1239 (2019)
3. Aupy, G., Benoit, A., Pottier, L., Raghavan, P., Robert, Y., Shantharam, M.: Co-scheduling high-performance computing applications. In: Big Data: Management, Architecture, and Processing, May 2017. https://hal.inria.fr/hal-02082818
4. Bailey, D., Harris, T., Saphir, W., Van Der Wijngaart, R., Woo, A., Yarrow, M.: The NAS parallel benchmarks 2.0. Technical report, Technical Report NAS-95-020, NASA Ames Research Center (1995)
5. Bienia, C.: Benchmarking Modern Multiprocessors. Ph.D. thesis, Princeton University, January 2011
6. Eyerman, S., Michaud, P., Rogiest, W.: Revisiting symbiotic job scheduling. In: 2015 IEEE International Symposium on Performance Analysis of Systems and Software (ISPASS), pp. 124–134. IEEE (2015)
7. Jain, R., Hughes, C.J., Adve, S.V.: Soft real-time scheduling on simultaneous multithreaded processors. In: 23rd IEEE Real-Time Systems Symposium, RTSS 2002, pp. 134–145. IEEE (2002)
8. Kuchumov, R., Korkhov, V.: Collecting HPC applications processing characteristics to facilitate co-scheduling. In: Gervasi, O., et al. (eds.) ICCSA 2020. LNCS, vol. 12254, pp. 168–182. Springer, Cham (2020). https://doi.org/10.1007/978-3-030-58817-5_14
9. Li, Y., Sun, D., Lee, B.C.: Dynamic colocation policies with reinforcement learning. ACM Trans. Architect. Code Optim. (TACO) **17**(1), 1–25 (2020)
10. Parekh, S., Eggers, S., Levy, H., Lo, J.: Thread-sensitive scheduling for SMT processors (2000)
11. Snavely, A., Mitchell, N., Carter, L., Ferrante, J., Tullsen, D.: Explorations in symbiosis on two multithreaded architectures. In: Workshop on Multi-Threaded Execution, Architecture, and Compilers (1999)

12. Snavely, A., Tullsen, D.M.: Symbiotic jobscheduling for a simultaneous multi-threaded processor. In: Proceedings of the Ninth International Conference on Architectural Support for Programming Languages and Operating Systems, pp. 234–244 (2000)
13. Trinitis, C., Weidendorfer, J.: Co-scheduling of HPC Applications, vol. 28. IOS Press (2017)
14. Trinits, C., Weidendorfer, J.: First workshop on co-scheduling of HPC Applications (COSH 2016)
15. Zacarias, F.V., Petrucci, V., Nishtala, R., Carpenter, P., Mossé, D.: Intelligent colocation of workloads for enhanced server efficiency. In: 2019 31st International Symposium on Computer Architecture and High Performance Computing (SBAC-PAD), pp. 120–127. IEEE (2019)

Translation of Query for the Distributed Document Database

Muon Ha and Yulia A. Shichkina(✉)

St. Petersburg State Electrotechnical University, St. Petersburg, Russia

Abstract. This article presents the results of the automatic process of building queries to the distributed document database based on SQL queries. Queries are submitted in the form of a graph. Next, taking into account the structure of the distributed database and information about sharding and replications, a graph is modified. Based on the database elements information to which queries are referred, sets are built. By operating on these sets, the optimal structure of document databases is determined, which is further optimized by the query graph. At the end of the article, the results of testing the proposed approach to the synthetic database generated by a special program are presented. Testing showed the correctness and efficiency of the application described in the approach article.

Keywords: NoSQL · Database query · Collection · Document · Data conversion · Data format · Database structure optimization

1 Introduction

Today there are many types of NoSQL database with various features which are divided into four categories: Key-value; Document, Column (or column families) and Graph.

Since the early 90s, the relational databases are most popular. However, with the increasing volume of data, there is a growing trend towards switching relational databases to NoSQL databases. At the same time, switching from relational databases to NoSQL results to a number of problems, such as the creation of the optimal structure of the NoSQL document or database columnar family, transferring data from the relational database format to the NoSQL database format, the translation of queries, taking into account the schema of the computing system used for storage of a distributed database.

This article presents the results of research on automation of the database translating from a relational format to the format of a distributed document database, in particular MongoDB and the automatic constructing of MongoDB databases based on existing SQL queries. Formalized approaches to solve the task of designing the effective structure of a distributed document database, taking into account the specifics of data and the planned database query, do not exist. In the literature, there are many results of studies on optimizing MongoDB database and queries in separate application areas or optimization for individual parameters.

© Springer Nature Switzerland AG 2021
O. Gervasi et al. (Eds.): ICCSA 2021, LNCS 12956, pp. 396–405, 2021.
https://doi.org/10.1007/978-3-030-87010-2_29

2 Related Works

Due to the popularity of document databases over the past 10 years, various researchers have been conducted by a large number of tasks which have worked on optimizing work with databases and on developing recommendations for efficient data to work in these databases.

So, in [1], the method of translation of data from SQL to NoSQL based on "Log-Base" is given. The essence of the method is to extract the modified data from the database based on log files and copy them to NoSQL. The disadvantage of this method is that the extraction of operations from the journal is heterogeneous. This approach is possible only if the source DBMS supports the work with log files and provides API to developers.

Some ETL - tools (Extract-Transform-Load) [2] allow to transfer data from the relational database in NoSQL. For example, Mongify [3] is a new tool for translating data from relational tables to document repository. This tool helps to migrate, without worrying about primary and external keys. The disadvantage of this method is that subsequent records will not be processed until the translation process of previous records is completed. Kettle in [4] provides powerful ETL capabilities using a new metadata-based approach that allows developers to determine the method of data migration and their conversion on one node, as well as in the cloud/cluster. The Apache Sqoop tool [5] is designed to effectively move the large data between structured data warehouses, such as relational databases and NoSQL databases. Many studies [6, 7] are aimed at working a hybrid database system using SQOOP as a data converter. The problem occurs in converting a database in these systems is synchronizing database objects.

Optimization of the structure of a distributed database is a big problem for all researchers in the sciences of data. It is known that sharding and replication are popular and powerful techniques for scaling distributed systems for data. The process of organizing sharding in NoSQL was investigated in [8–11]. But global reconfiguration operations focused on the data described in these works are really ineffective. This is due to the fact that their implementation depends on special mechanisms, and not from solving the main problems of algorithmic and systemic design. Another common solution is formed through 2 steps: the first is storing the tables or the entire database, and the second is the import of all data into a new configuration [12]. This approach leads to a significant period of unavailability of the database. Another option may be the creation of a new server cluster with a new database configuration, and then filling it with data from the old cluster [13–15].

In [16], the authors describe the system called Morphus. This system provides the support for the reconfiguration of the NOSQL repository online. Morphus allows to perform reading and writing operations simultaneously with data transfer between servers. Morphus works for NOSQL storage, which includes Master-Slave replication, range partitioning and flexible data placement. In [17], the authors represent the principles and mechanisms for implementing auto-sharding in the MongoDB database. They offer an improved algorithm based on the frequency of working with data, to solve the problem of uneven distribution of data in auto-sharding. Improved balancing strategy can effectively balance data between segments and improve the performance of the simultaneous reading and writing cluster. In [18], the authors solve the problem of choosing a key for sharding in MongoDB. The authors modeled the environment and measured reading/writing performance of various keys and found that shard key with random and good locality can give decent performance during writing and reading.

The analysis shows that at present, the problems of translation data and queries of the database from one format to another are very relevant. In this case, no good solution to these issues was found. There are private solutions for individual areas, for direct translation of tables in the collection, to transfer relational database to document databases, taking into account link types, to extract data from document databases using SQL queries, query optimization methods.

This article proposes a formalized approach, which takes into account the schemes of relational database, schemes of SQL-query and schemes of sharding and replication to build a distributed document database and automatically construct query to the distributed MongoDB database.

3 Application of an Information Graph to Build a Distributed Database

In the series works [21, 22], we have given two methods for optimizing the structure of a document database without and with Embedded Documents. These methods are in the solutions for the problem of consolidating databases of various types with a translation database from one to another. And we also developed a method and tool to translate queries from MySQL in MongoDB [20]. But these methods are only for centralized databases. The purpose of the current study is to develop an approach to translate queries to a distributed document database.

In our study, an approach based on information graphs was applied to study the dependencies of subqueries from the location and availability of data in accordance with the specified scheme of the distributed database and information about shards and replicas.

Based on the information graph, we will further mean an oriented acyclic multigraph, the vertices of which correspond to the sub-queries within the main query, and the arc - data transmission between them.

In the method of constructing an information graph of query for a distributed relational database, taking into account the information about the fragmentation of the tables, three types of links between the query elements are considered. We illustrate these three options in the examples.

Example. Suppose that the T1 tables are performed consistently queries Q1 and Q2. Both of T1 and T2 tables participate in Q1 query, two tables are involved in the Q2 query: a table with Q1 query results and T3 table. The source graph of query is shown in Fig. 1a. It is possible to occur the following options for performing queries, taking into account two fragments of T1 table.

Option 1. Q1 query is performed for each fragment of T1 table and the entire T2 table. The results are aggregated on each of the shards after the query Q1 is executed. The Q2 is then satisfied to T3 and the above-mentioned table with the results of aggregated data after executing the Q1 query over the T1 table fragments and T2 table. This graph is illustrated in Fig. 1b.

Option 2. Q1 query is divided into two parts. First, it is performed for each fragment of T1 table and does not affect T2 table. After the first part of the query Q1, the results are carried out on each of the shards. The second part of the query Q1 is then running to T2 table and the results of aggregated data after the first part of the Q1 query over the fragments of T1 tables. After that, the Q2 query is satisfied with T3 table and the table with the results of the Q1 query. This graph is illustrated in Fig. 1c.

Option 3. Q1 query is divided into two parts. First, it is performed for each fragment of T1 table and does not affect T2 table. After executing the first part of the Q1 query, the aggregation of the results on each of the shards is not carried out. The second part of the Q1 query is immediately performed to T2 table and the data results after the first part of the Q1 query over the T1 table fragments. The Q2 query is also divided into two parts. First, the first part of the query Q2 is performed to T3 table and the table with the results of the Q1 query. After the first part of the query Q2, the results are aggregated on one of the shards. After execution, an aggregation of results on each of the shards is carried out. This graph is illustrated in Fig. 2c. The Q2 is then executed to T3 table and the table with the results of aggregated data after the first part of the Q2 query is performed. This graph is illustrated in Fig. 1d.

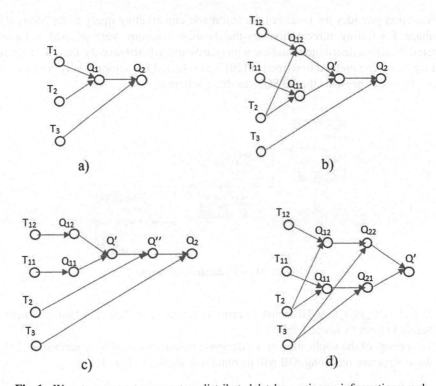

Fig. 1. Ways to represent a query to a distributed database using an information graph

4   Method for Constructing a Document Database Schema, Taking into Account the Structure of a Distributed Relational Database

1. Build an information graph without scarring and replication.
2. Create an information graph to a parallel form that minimizes data transmission from shard to shard using the method of optimizing parallel algorithms by the number of communications [19].
3. Perform an action 1–2 for all requests whose structure must be taken into account during optimizing the document database schema in order to accelerate the execution of these queries.
4. Based on the metadata on tables, fields, requests and links using the methods of optimizing a document database schema with nested or without nested documents, form the structure of the collections of documents.
5. Improve the structure of documents taking into account the graphs of information dependences of requests, minimizing the number of data combining operations.

5   Translation of Query from MySQL into a Distributed MongoDB Database

This section provides the results of the automatic constructing query to the MongoDB database. For testing, three options for the database structure were selected: not a distributed database, distributed database with shards and a distributed database with shards and replicas. The method described in [20] was selected for automatically constructing query. Figure 2. presents the MySQL database schema:

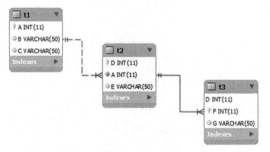

Fig. 2. MySQL database diagram

Select SQL_NO_CACHE count(*) From t1 where A in (Select A from t2 where D in (Select D from t3 where F%5=0));

As a result of the application of the database translating method described in [21], a database structure on MongoDB will be obtained, shown in Fig. 3:

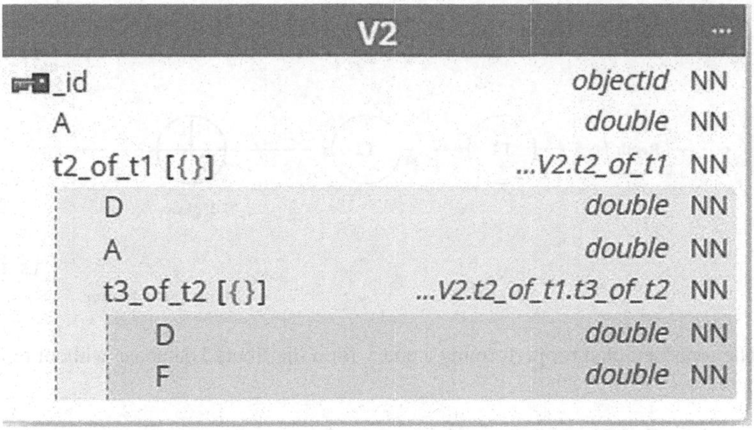

Fig. 3. MongoDB database collection structure

For the case of a non-distributed database using automatic translation query, a MongoDB format will be received, presented in Table 1.

Table 1. Source SQL query and automatically constructed MongoDB query.

MySQL	MongoDB
`Select          SQL_NO_CACHE count(*) From t1 where A in (Select A from t2 where D in (Select D from t3 where F%5=0));`	`db.V2.aggregate([` `{"$unwind": "$t2_of_t1"},` `{"$unwind": "$t2_of_t1.t3_of_t2"},` `{` `    "$match": {"t2_of_t1.t3_of_t2.F": {"$mod": [5, 0] }}` `},` `{` `    "$project":    {    "A": "$A","_id":0}` `},` `{` `    "$group": {"_id":"$A"}` `},` `{` `    "$count" :"Count"` `}` `])`

The proposed query execution plan for the case of a distributed database without replication is shown in Fig. 4.

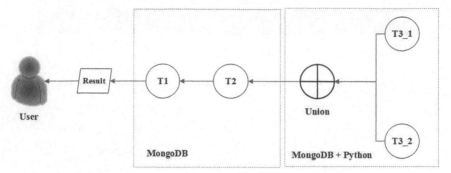

Fig. 4. The proposed plan for performing a query for a distributed database without replications

A query to a distributed database without replications, but with sharding was divided into subqueries that were parallel to shards. Since MongoDB does not support the parallel execution of subqueries, the method of translation query was applied to individual subqueries. To perform a general query, programs written in the Python programming language.

The proposed query execution plan for the case of a distributed database with replications is shown in Fig. 5.

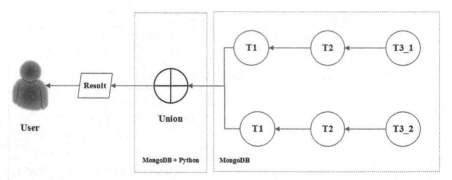

Fig. 5. The proposed plan for performing a query for a distributed database with replications

In contrast to the previous case, the query was divided into two subqueries, each of them chose all records in accordance with some conditions. The calculation of the number of records was made directly in the program written in the Python programming language.

6 Query Testing

Another test task was to determine which option parallel execution of the query time will be the smallest. To carry out this testing, synthetic databases with different volumes are generated, which are shown in Table 2.

Table 2. Databases for testing

	Option 1		Option 2		Option 3	
	Node 1	Node 2	Node 1	Node 2	Node 1	Node 2
Volume 1	1000	0	1000	849	997	849
Volume 2	10000	0	10000	8682	10000	8682
Volume 3	10000	0	10000	87461	10000	87461
Volume 4	1000000	0	1000000	874525	1000000	874525

Table 3. The execution time of the query.

	Option 1	Option 2	Option 3
Volume 1	0.0464	0.0189	0.0109
Volume 2	0.1423	0.112	0.0708
Volume 3	1.297	1.089	0.6801
Volume 4	13.445	11.531	6.884

Table 3 shows the execution time (in seconds) using the developed program:

The schedules of the query execution time for different variants of the database and data volume scheme are shown in Fig. 6

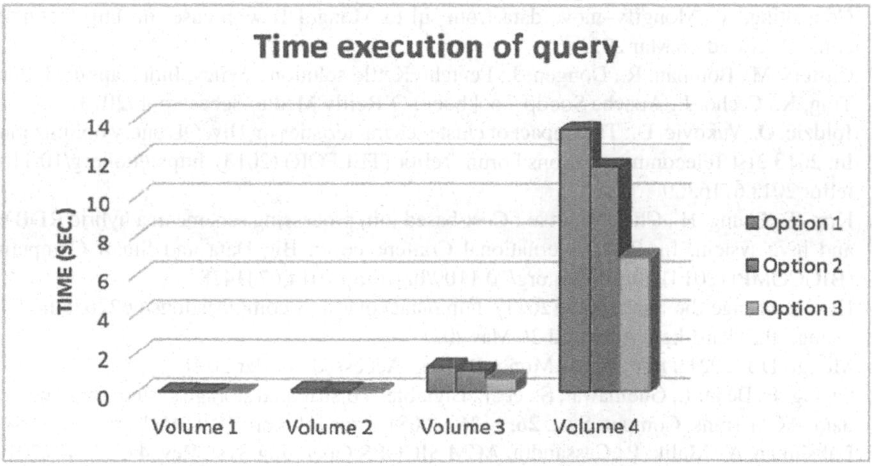

Fig. 6. The execution time of the query for the different volumes of databases

From the diagram in Fig. 6. It can be seen that the maximum parallelization of the database query with the maximum deferred operation of the program's result is faster.

7   Conclusion

Automatic translation of query from MySQL in MongoDB is a challenge, especially in the case of distributed data. In this article, we presented a method of automatically constructing queries to the MongoDB distributed database based on the MySQL query metadata of the distributed database architecture as well as using methods for optimizing the MongoDB database collections. The automatic query construct is based on the method which based on information graphs.

We have shown that various options for building an information graph of a query, taking into account the specifics of the query operations and the architecture of a distributed database.

Our test results showed the correctness and efficiency of the application to automatically build query to the distributed MongoDB database.

To build a more efficient query for the time database or other parameters, it is possible to use the query to the information graph of the pre-optimization method for optimizing parallel algorithms for various parameters based on information graphs.

In the future, we plan to conduct research on the classification of requests for the type of operations and the variants of their parallelization.

References

1. Shahra, G., Yap, J.: Cache augmented database management systems. In: Proceedings of the ACM SIGMOD Workshop on Databases and Social Networks, pp. 31–36. ACM, New York (2013)
2. Vassiliadis, P.: A survey of extract–transform–load technology. Int. J. Data Warehouse. Min. **5**, 1–27 (2009). https://doi.org/10.4018/jdwm.2009070101
3. Consulting, A.: Mongify–move data from sql to MongoDB with ease. In: http://mongify.com/. Accessed 26 Mar 2021
4. Casters, M., Bouman, R., Dongen, J.: Pentaho Kettle solutions. Wiley, Indianapolis, Indiana
5. Ting, K., Cecho, J.: Apache Sqoop Cookbook. O'Reilly Media, Sebastopol (2013)
6. Joldzic, O., Vukovic, D.: The impact of cluster characteristics on HiveQL query optimization. In: 2013 21st Telecommunications Forum Telfor (TELFOR) (2013). https://doi.org/10.1109/telfor.2013.6716360
7. Kim, T., Chung, H., Choi, W., et al.: Cost-based join processing scheme in a hybrid RDBMS and hive system. In: 2014 International Conference on Big Data and Smart Computing (BIGCOMP) (2014). https://doi.org/10.1109/bigcomp.2014.6741428
8. How to change the Shard Key (2021). http://stackoverflow.com/questions/6622635/how-to-change-the-shard-key. Accessed 26 Mar 2021
9. Mongo DB (2021). http://www.MongoDB.org. Accessed 26 Mar 2021
10. Chang, F., Dean, J., Ghemawat, S., et al.: Bigtable: a distributed storage system for structured data. ACM Trans. Comput. Syst. **26**, 1–26 (2008). https://doi.org/10.1145/1365815.1365816
11. Lakshman, A., Malik, P.: Cassandra. ACM SIGOPS Operating Syst. Rev. **44**, 35–40 (2010). https://doi.org/10.1145/1773912.1773922
12. Change shard key MongoDB faq (2021). http://docs.MongoDB.org/manual/faq/sharding/#can-i-change-the-shard-key-after-sharding-a-collection. Accessed 29 Mar 2021
13. Barker, S.K., et al.: Shuttledb: database-aware elasticity in the cloud. In: 11th International Conference on Autonomic Computing, ICAC 2014, Philadelphia, PA, USA, 18–20 June, pp. 33–43 (2014)

14. Das, S., Nishimura, S., Agrawal, D., El Abbadi, A.: Albatross: lightweight elasticity in shared storage databases for the cloud using live data migration. Proc. VLDB Endowment **4**, 494–505 (2011). https://doi.org/10.14778/2002974.2002977
15. Elmore, A., Das, S., Agrawal, D., El Abbadi, A.: Zephyr: live migration in shared nothing databases for elastic cloud platforms. In: Proceedings of the 2011 International Conference on Management of Data-SIGMOD 2011 (2011). https://doi.org/10.1145/1989323.1989356
16. Ghosh, M., Wang, W., Holla, G., Gupta, I.: Morphus: supporting online reconfigurations in sharded NoSQL systems. In: 2015 IEEE International Conference on Autonomic Computing (2015). https://doi.org/10.1109/icac.2015.42
17. Liu, Y., Wang, Y., Jin, Y.: Research on the improvement of MongoDB auto-sharding in cloud environment. In: 2012 7th International Conference on Computer Science and Education (ICCSE) (2012). https://doi.org/10.1109/iccse.2012.6295203
18. Kookarinrat, P., Temtanapat, Y.: Analysis of range-based key properties for sharded cluster of MongoDB. In: 2015 2nd International Conference on Information Science and Security (ICISS) (2015). https://doi.org/10.1109/icissec.2015.7370983
19. Shichkina, Y., Kupriyanov, M., Al-Mardi, M.: Optimization algorithm for an information graph for an amount of communications. Lecture Notes in Computer Science, pp. 50-62 (2016). https://doi.org/10.1007/978-3-319-46301-8_5
20. Ha, M., Shichkina, Y.: The query translation from MySQL to MongoDB taking into account the structure of the database. In: 2021 IEEE Conference of Russian Young Researchers in Electrical and Electronic Engineering (ElConRus). St. Petersburg and Moscow, Russia, pp. 383–386 (2021). https://doi.org/10.1109/ElConRus51938.2021.939659
21. Shichkina, Y., Ha, M.: Creating collections with embedded documents for document databases taking into account the queries. Computation **8**(2), 45 (2020). https://doi.org/10.3390/comput ation8020045
22. Ha, V.M., Shichkina, Y.A., Kostichev, S.V.: Determining the composition of collections for key-document databases based on a given set of object properties and database querie. Comput. Tools Educ. (3), 15–28 (2019). https://doi.org/10.32603/2071-2340-2019-3-15-28

Creation of Specialized Datasets for Satellite Monitoring of the State of Agricultural Lands

Grishkin Valery[⊠][iD], Zhivulin Evgeniy, and Khokhriakova Anastasiia

Saint-Petersburg State University, St.Petersburg 199034, Russia
v.grishkin@spbu.ru

Abstract. Currently, there is significant progress in the interpretation of remote images of the earth's surface using various recognition systems. To train these systems, large labeled datasets are required. The creation of such datasets is carried out by experts and is quite a time-consuming task. This paper proposes a method for creating specialized datasets for their use in monitoring the state of agricultural lands undergoing degradation. The method allows you to automate the process of creating such datasets The datasets are generated from freely available data obtained by the Sentinel satellites as part of the European Copernicus space program. The method is based on the processing of the results of the preliminary classification of images of the earth's cover, previously produced by the Sentinel Hub service.

Keywords: Remote sensing · Satellite image segmentation · Multispectral images · Scene classification · Training dataset

1 Introduction

Currently, remote sensing technologies allow for monitoring the state of the earth's surface. Such monitoring makes it possible to assess the state of the environment, explore natural resources, and carry out development planning.

The most successful recognition systems are based on the supervised learning method, which requires a large enough labeled dataset. Currently existing datasets for recognition of remote images are not universal and, as a rule, are focused on use in specialized applications. Therefore, to solve specific monitoring tasks, one has to either try to use existing data sets, or form specialized data sets intended for one or another type of monitoring.

There are two main approaches to solving the problems of identification and segmentation of satellite images. The first one is a method based on a pixel analysis of the intensity of spectral characteristics and corresponding derivative features. The second approach is based on the spatial characteristics of spectral images and is implemented using convolutional neural networks. To implement both approaches, a tagged set of multispectral images is required, taken with a certain periodicity. This is necessary to derive the various characteristics of the

© Springer Nature Switzerland AG 2021
O. Gervasi et al. (Eds.): ICCSA 2021, LNCS 12956, pp. 406–416, 2021.
https://doi.org/10.1007/978-3-030-87010-2_30

images specific to certain seasons. Currently, there are a number of datasets [1, 2] that contain satellite images of selected regions and are designed to meet the challenges of urban and road planning. There are also datasets [3–6] used for assessing and monitoring agricultural, forestry and water resources. They contain satellite images obtained in the visible and near infrared ranges, and some sets also contain multispectral images. Among these sets, the universal dataset SEN12MS [7] deserves special consideration, as it contains a large number of triplets of data types for various regions of the earth's surface. Each triplet of data obtained during all meteorological seasons includes polarimetric images, multispectral images and maps of land cover areas associated with them. These sites are fully georeferenced and are located on all inhabited continents. The information about these areas also contains their markup into land surface classes in accordance with such classification schemes as the International Geosphere-Biosphere Program (IGBP) and the Land cover classification system (LCCS).

Universal data sets are primarily designed to test and compare the performance of different algorithms for the identification of areas of the earth's surface. In the case of monitoring a specific region with its own specific land cover, universal datasets cannot provide sufficient characteristics of the quality of identification of areas in a given region, because this particular region may not be represented in these datasets. Therefore, to solve these problems, it is advisable to use specialized datasets generated for a specific region.

In this paper, we consider the creation of specialized datasets for their use in monitoring the state of agricultural land in certain areas undergoing sand degradation. Within the framework of this monitoring, it is necessary to identify zones of sands (deserts), considering that these zones are completely degraded and cannot be used in agriculture. It is also necessary to identify both transition zones in these areas, subject to varying degrees of degradation, and zones fully suitable for use in agriculture.

2 Data Acquisition and Preprocessing

2.1 Input Data

As input data, on the basis of which a specialized set is built, the data of multispectral imagery from the Sentinel-2 [8] satellites and the results of their preliminary processing are used. These data are freely available on the Copernicus Open Access Hub [9]. Images of the Earth's surface are taken at intervals of 5 days. Surface imagery from satellites is carried out in different spectral ranges with a resolution not better than 10×10 m in one pixel of the image. Table 1 provides a list of spectral channels used to construct the dataset. In addition, it contains channels that reflect the results of preliminary processing of images taken in the Sentinel data center. It should be noted that for the formation of specialized data sets, we use only 11 channels out of 23 channels available.

The first three channels represent reflected light in the optical range. The next three channels are infrared radiation. Then there are two near-infrared channels. The next spectral range is associated with reflection from water vapor.

Table 1. Wave range and maximum resolution of the channels used.

Channel	Description	Wavelength	Resolution
B02	Blue	492.4 nm	10 m
B03	Green	559.8 nm	10 m
B04	Red	664.6 nm	10 m
B05	Vegetation red edge	704.1 nm	20 m
B06	Vegetation red edge	740.5 nm	20 m
B07	Vegetation red edge	782.8 nm	20 m
B08	NIR	832.8 nm	20 m
B08A	Narrow NIR	864.7 nm	20 m
B09	Water vapour	945.1 nm	20 m
B11	SWIR	1613.7 nm	20 m
SNW	Snow probability	–	20 m
CLD	Cloud probability	–	20 m
SCL	Scene classification data	–	20 m

The last spectral channel is shortwave infrared data. Then three channels follow, reflecting the results of data processing by the Sentinel-hub service itself. The first one is the probability that a given pixel in the image is part of a snow-covered area, and the second one is the probability that it belongs to a cloud cover. The last of these channels is an image mask describing the belonging of each pixel to one of the 12 classes. Among these classes are the following: vegetation, bare soil, water, clouds, cloud shadows, snow.

2.2 Loading Input Data

Interaction with the Copernicus Open Access Hub website is carried out using requests that are supported by the corresponding Sentinel-hub service. The request itself is a Javascript code, which indicates: a date range (the service provides the latest snapshot from the specified range), coordinates of the area of interest (coordinates of the lower left and upper right corners of the rectangular area of interest), the height and width of the resulting image in pixels, a list of channels from which data is requested and the format in which they will be loaded.

The coordinates of the requested area are indicated in the UTM system. It is a coordinate system that divides the northern and southern hemispheres into 60 zones. The accuracy of this system is higher than the usual latitude and longitude. The size of the requested area is chosen equal to 10×10 km, which corresponds to the dimensions of the resulting image equaling to 512×512 pixels when using a channel resolution of 20 m.

Before loading data, it is possible to pre-process it directly on the site by performing arithmetic operations on it. These operations allow for normalizing the values in different channels. Data from channels is requested in the form of standard PNG images. Each image includes 3 channels of data displayed as red, green and blue. Since 13 channels are used, 5 images are loaded for any given area and date. The first image represents the visible part of the spectrum in natural colors. The next three images represent the data from the remaining channels, displayed on these images in pseudo colors. The last image is the grayscale displayed classification mask.

Downloading the data required for exploring large areas also requires a large number of downloads. Therefore, a specially developed script is used to load data. This script generates a request for satellite data for a specified location within a specified date period.

To automate loading, an array with coordinates saved in the configuration file is passed to the script, indicating areas on the map from which images are to be loaded. These coordinates are created by another script that splits the specified area into a set of squares. The division of the area of interest into sections is carried out after translating the boundary coordinates of the entire area in the form of latitude and longitude into the UTM system. This improves the precision of the split. Otherwise, when translating each section into UTM separately, there may be errors in neighboring sections, and the points that should coincide will differ slightly, which will be noticeable in the final images.

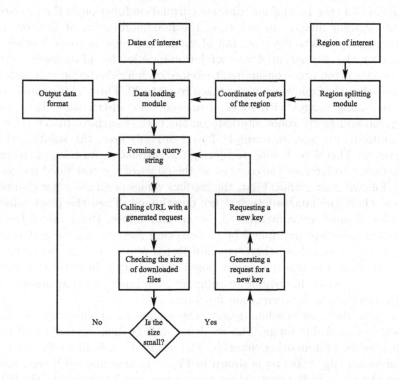

Fig. 1. The algorithm for downloading data from the Sentinel-hub service.

When requesting data from the service, the access key is transmitted which has been obtained earlier. This key is updated hourly and can be obtained as a result of another request to the service. Therefore, when exchanging with the hub, the size of uploaded images is checked, and if it is too small, this indicates that the service did not provide data, therefore, you need to request a new key is to be requested, and the script takes care of that.

For interaction with the site, the standard cURL utility [10] is used, which is part of almost all operating systems. After the request is generated, the script is passed to this utility as a parameter. The algorithm for downloading data from the Sentinel-hub service is shown in Fig. 1

2.3   Preliminary Processing

For various reasons, the resulting images of adjacent parts of the region may be slightly displaced relative to each other. Therefore, they are loaded with a small partial intersection of neighboring images. This is done in order to have a safety margin in case the images are displaced in different directions relative to each other, so as not to lose some of the information. In addition, such an intersection allows for use of the reference point method for the alignment of adjacent images. The essence of this method is to combine a set of points on both images so that all points coincide pairwise. The image displacement is determined based on the calculation of a two-dimensional discrete correlation function of the intersecting parts of adjacent images. In this case, the maximum value of the correlation function corresponds to the true shift of the images relative to each other.

However, the calculation of the correlation function for all intersecting points of the images is too time-consuming, therefore such a calculation was performed only for each n-th pixel, where n was taken equal to 20. This yields reliable results when combining images with edges of uneven color distribution, for example, when green and sandy zones alternate on the earth's surface. In case of a relatively uniform coverage, for example, for a sand only area, this solution yields a wrong result. Therefore, before calculating the correlation function of the image, it is necessary to increase the contrast at the edges of the combined images. We use the following algorithm. First, the median values of all the color channels in the area where the images intersect are determined. Then the pixel values for each color channel are compared to the median values. Pixel values less than the median value are multiplied by a correction factor k less than 1 ($k < 1$). For all other pixel values, the correction factor k is chosen to be larger than 1 ($k > 1$). Such processing made it possible to sharply increase the contrast, which, in turn, made it possible to compare even fairly uniform images at low costs for calculating the correlation function.

The procedure for combining adjacent images is applied only to images obtained in the visible range. The resulting shift is then applied to all images that display data for all other channels. The result of combining adjacent images with increased edge contrast is shown in Fig. 2. In this merged image, one can see that the roads in the contrasting area merge well into roads to the left and to the right from the contrasting area.

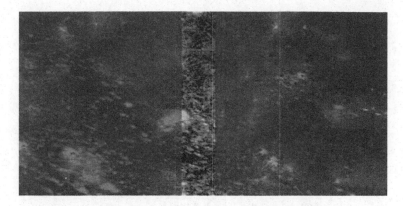

Fig. 2. The result of the algorithm for combining two adjacent images with a demonstration of increasing the contrast of the edges.

3   Creating a Specialized Dataset

To form a dataset suitable for the monitoring purposes, we use satellite data from the spring-summer and late autumn periods. The first period was chosen because it is in this period that the vegetation cover is the strongest and is well determined from satellite images using standard methods. The second period is characterized by the completed development of vegetation, and in these images, the surface that was covered with vegetation looks like soil. Thus, by comparing these images, it is possible to draw conclusions about the location and presence of productive soils in the area under observation, since the soil on which nothing grows is either degraded or unsuitable for agricultural purposes.

The requested data contains, among other things, the results of the preliminary classification of images obtained during data processing by the Sentinel Hub [7] service. This classification result is tied to each requested area of the earth's surface and is represented as a pixel mask M_{scl} of the image of this area. The values of each pixel in this mask correspond to specific types of ground surface or types of clouds. Mapping of mask pixel values to recognized types of objects is shown in Table 2.

This mask is used to segment areas containing agricultural soils. These areas are covered with vegetation in the spring and summer. Therefore, by segmenting such areas on images from the late autumn period, we will obtain data on the distribution of fertile soils. Thus, it is necessary to form two new masks out of the original summer classification mask. The M_{summer_veg} mask represents the vegetation cover only, while the M_{summer_soil} mask represents the soil. Two similar masks are also formed out of the autumn classification mask. The first M_{autumn_soil} mask represents the soil cover, and the second M_{autumn_veg} mask represents the vegetation cover. The first mask is directly used for the generation of a dataset for recognizing fertile soil cover. The $M_{goodsoil}$ fertile soil mask is calculated by applying a bitwise AND to the summer vegetation mask and the autumn soil distribution mask.

Table 2. Scene classification data.

Value	Recognized type	Mask color
0	No data	■
1	Saturated/Defective	■
2	Dark Area Pixels	■
3	Cloud Shadows	■
4	Vegetation	■
5	Bare Soils	
6	Water	■
7	Clouds low probability/Unclassified	■
8	Clouds medium probability	■
9	Clouds high probability	■
10	Cirrus	■
11	Snow/Ice	☐

$$M_{\text{goodsoil}} = M_{\text{summer\_veg}} \ \& \ M_{\text{autumn\_soil}}$$

The second mask contains additional information about the location of the fertile soil hidden under the vegetation. This mask can be used to obtain a complete mask of fertile soil $M_{\text{f\_goodsoil}}$.

$$M_{\text{f\_goodsoil}} = M_{\text{goodsoil}} \Big| \left(M_{\text{summer\_soil}} \ \& \ M_{\text{autumn\_veg}} \right)$$

Figure 3 shows satellite images of the same region in the visible range in the spring-summer and autumn periods, the corresponding classification masks and the resulting masks of fertile soils. Figure 3c shows a snapshot of an area whose surface is partially covered by clouds. Therefore, the masks shown in Fig. 3e and Fig. 3f do not fully describe the distribution of fertile soils. It is impractical to use such masks and images for monitoring purposes without filtering cloud images. However, if clouds and their shadows from them do not take up too much of the total area of the image, then these images and masks can be used to create a specialized dataset for fertile soil recognition systems. This is possible because the resulting mask shows the distribution of fertile soils in an area not covered by clouds, and thus it can be used as a markup for training the recognition system. The algorithm for creating a specialized dataset for training recognition systems that can be used when monitoring fertile soils is shown in Fig. 4.

Data for a selected area of the earth's surface is requested for both the period of greatest vegetation development and the period when plant development stops and harvest is completed. Typically, data for the first period is for late July and early August, and data for the second period is requested for the end of October. Since the selected area is divided into subareas with a slight overlap, preprocessing of the data is performed, as a result of which the boundaries of neighboring

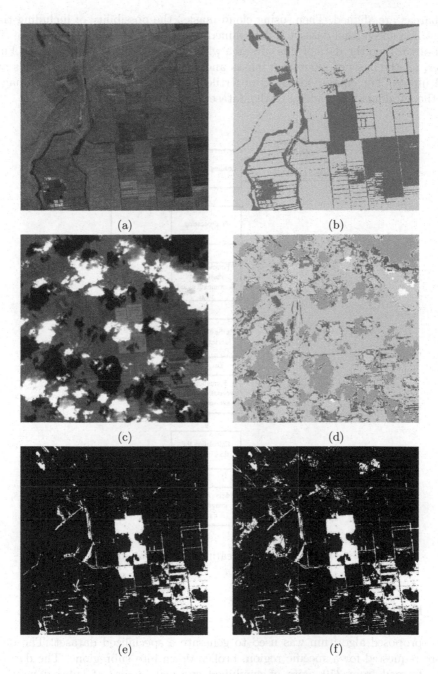

Fig. 3. Images of the region and corresponding masks: (a) image of the region—August; (b) classification mask—August; (c) image of the region—October; (d) classification mask—October; (e) the fertile soil mask without autumn vegetation; (f) the complete fertile soil mask vegetation.

subareas are aligned. Then, using cloud masks, the possibility of including this data in a specialized dataset is determined. If clouds cover more than half of the sub-area, then the data of this sub-area will not be included in the dataset. Further, on the basis of vegetation masks and soil masks, masks of fertile soils are calculated. The computed masks of fertile soils along with the spectral images of the subdomain are added to the dataset.

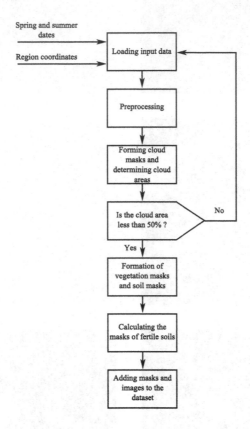

Fig. 4. Algorithm for creating a specialized dataset.

4   Experimental Results

The proposed algorithm was used to generate a specialized dataset. The data were requested for a specific region, broken down into subregions. The dataset was formed from 379 pairs of combined spectral images of subregions. The dataset was formed from 379 pairs of sets of combined spectral images of subregions. Each pair of sets for the same subregion consists of four combined images taken in August and four combined ones taken at the end of October. As a result of filtering out images with sufficiently large clouds, 159 such pairs of sets were included in the dataset itself. For these pairs of images, masks of fertile soils were calculated, which were also included in the dataset.

The created dataset is intended for a monitoring system for the state of agricultural land. It was used to train land cover type recognition systems. Two recognition systems were investigated. Both recognition systems are based on the support vector machine (SVM) [11]. As a markup of the input images, the corresponding masks of fertile soils were used. The training was carried out on 93 pairs of image sets. The rest of the pairs from the dataset were used for testing.

In the first system, the normalized values of 10 spectral channels B02–B11 were used as the feature vector. In the second system, normalized differential indices V_{ij} were used as features, calculated for combinations of different spectral channels. The calculation of the corresponding index V_{ij} was carried out similarly to the procedure for calculating the known vegetation index NDVI.

$$V_{ij} = \frac{B_i - B_j}{B_i + B_j}.$$

The recognition accuracy of the soil type for the first system was 82%. In an experimental study of the second system, it turned out that the best soil type recognition accuracy was 94%. This accuracy was achieved using a feature vector of 8 indices. In this case, the following indices were used: $V_{47}, V_{46}, V_{89}, V_{38}, V_{92}, V_{01}, V_{48}, V_{57}$. These indices are calculated using the following channel pairs: (B06 B8A), (B06 B08), (B09 B11), (B05 B09), (B8A B04), (B02 B03), (B06 B09), (B07 B8A).

5 Conclusion

The paper proposes a method for the automated creation of specialized datasets of satellite images for their use in monitoring the state of agricultural lands undergoing degradation. The datasets are generated from freely available data obtained by the Sentinel satellites as part of the European Copernicus space program. This data includes multispectral imagery and preliminary classification of land surface types in the region of interest. Based on the preliminary classification masks of the summer and autumn periods, the mask of fertile soils is calculated, which, together with the spectral images of the subregion, is added to the generated dataset.

To test the generated dataset, a soil type recognition system was built and investigated. The system works on the basis of a support vector machine. The results of an experimental study of the system showed a sufficiently high accuracy of recognition of fertile and infertile soils. This allows us to speak about the adequacy of the generated dataset, which can be used to develop and test soil type recognition systems based on other principles. Thus, the proposed method made it possible to automatically create specialized datasets for monitoring agricultural lands.

References

1. Ji, S., Wei, S., Lu, M.: Fully convolutional networks for multisource building extraction from an open aerial and satellite imagery data set. IEEE Trans. Geosci. Remote Sens. **57**(1), 574–586 (2018)
2. Volpi, M., Ferrari, V.: Semantic segmentation of urban scenes by learning local class interactions. In: Proceedings IEEE Conference Computer Vision and Pattern Recognition Workshop, pp. 1–9, June 2015
3. Xia, G.-S., et al.: AID: a benchmark data set for performance evaluation of aerial scene classification. IEEE Trans. Geosci. Remote Sens. **55**(7), 3965–3981 (2017)
4. Helber, P., Bischke, B., Dengel, A., Borth, D.: EuroSAT: a novel dataset and deep learning benchmark for land use and land cover classification. IEEE J. Sel. Top. Appl. Earth Obs. Remote Sens. **12**(7), 2217–2226 (2019)
5. Cheng, G., Han, J., Lu, X.: Remote sensing image scene classification: benchmark and state of the art. Proc. IEEE **105**(10), 1865–1883 (2017)
6. Tong, X.-Y., et al.: Land-cover classification with high-resolution remote sensing images using transferable deep models. Remote Sens. Environ. **237**, 111322 (2020)
7. Schmitt, M., Hughes, L.H., Qiu, C., Zhu, X.X.: SEN12MS- a curated dataset of georeferenced multi-spectral sentinel-1/2 imagery for deep learning and data fusion. arXiv preprint arXiv:1906.07789 (2019)
8. ESA Earth Observation Portal. https://directory.eoportal.org/web/eoportal/satel lite-missions/c-missions/copernicus-sentinel-2. Accessed 20 Apr 2021
9. Copernicus Open Access Hub. https://scihub.copernicus.eu/dhus/. Accessed 8 Apr 2021
10. Command line tool and library for transferring data with URLs. https://curl.se/. Accessed 15 Apr 2021
11. Cristianini, N., Shawe, T.J.: An Introduction to Support Vector Machines and other Kernel-based Learning Methods. Cambridge University Press, Cambridge (2000)

Ontology-Based Data Mining Workflow Construction

Man Tianxing[1]([✉]) [iD], Sergey Lebedev[3] [iD], Alexander Vodyaho[3] [iD],
Nataly Zhukova[2,3] [iD], and Yulia A. Shichkina[3] [iD]

[1] ITMO University, St. Petersburg, Russia
[2] St. Petersburg Federal Research Center of the Russian Academy of Sciences, St. Petersburg, Russia
[3] St. Petersburg State Electrotechnical University "LETI", St. Petersburg, Russia

Abstract. Currently, Data mining is applied in various domains. Many data science researchers are confused on which algorithms are suitable for the context. Hundreds of the operators/algorithms are combined within complex data mining workflows. A data mining assistant can significantly improve the efficiency of workflow construction. In our previous work, we constructed data mining ontologies based on "semantic meta mining" to support the selection of algorithms and operators for solving data mining tasks. But the use of such ontologies is still unfriendly. Strict query syntax still plagues many users. This paper proposes an interactive interface based on the reasoning mechanism to help users generate queries and build suitable data mining workflows.

Keywords: Meta-learning · Data mining · Semantic meta mining · Ontology

1 Introduction

Data mining (DM) technology allows extracting knowledge from real data in various domains. However, the raw data in real life is always complicated and messy. Researchers don't know which method can be used in context and often resort to trial and error. The task to construct the DM workflow for data processing in various domains is a complex one due to the complexity of data and the diversity of analysis methods.

To solve the DM algorithm selection task, some DM assistants were developed to support the DM workflow generation. As one type of such technique, semantic meta-mining (SMM) [1] is proposed for DM optimization through algorithm/model selection. It provides a suitable description framework to clarify the complex relationships between tasks, data, and algorithms at different stages in the DM process. SMM mines DM metadata through using knowledge bases that contain expertise on DM domain. This expertise should be stored in a machine-interpretable format, so it can be automatically extracted and applied for solving new tasks.

Most existing SMM systems support solving general DM problems. Panov et al. proposed a data mining ontology OntoDM, which includes formal definitions of basic DM entities [2]. Then, Panov et al. developed a separate ontology module, named OntoDT,

O. Gervasi et al. (Eds.): ICCSA 2021, LNCS 12956, pp. 417–431, 2021.
https://doi.org/10.1007/978-3-030-87010-2_31

for representing the knowledge about data types [3]. Hilario et al. present the data mining optimization ontology (DMOP), which provides a unified conceptual framework for analyzing data mining tasks, algorithms, models, datasets, workflows, and performance metrics, as well as their relationships [4]. There are several other data mining ontologies currently existing, such as the Knowledge Discovery (KD) Ontology [5], the OntoDTA ontology [6], the KDDONTO Ontology [7], which are based on similar ideas. These ontologies present the description of DM knowledge in a general situation, rather than in a specific domain.

In our previous work, we proposed a meta mining framework for data processing [8]. A DM core ontology was constructed by integrating the existing DM ontologies. The users can search the suitable algorithms according to the task requirements and the data characteristics and execute them in the corresponding applications.

Three DM ontologies are constructed to describe the knowledge about DM workflow:

- The DM core ontology describes the general DM workflow, including the algorithms, process, characteristics, goals, etc.
- The DM process ontology supports the management of DM processes, which assumes defining steps of the processes and selecting algorithms taking into account the input and the output data.
- The DM dataset characterization ontology describe the data characteristics and the corresponding definitions.

The application of the ontologies is based on building queries using OWL syntax. However, in actual use, the framework often loses its effect due to strict query syntax. Researchers who are non-computer professionals do not know how to construct the corresponding queries according to their needs.

In this article, we propose a rule-based interactive interface to support the ontology-based DM workflow building. We use DL query to search for answers in the DM ontologies [9]. The interactive interface is developed based on Drools engine [10]. It converts the user's request into the corresponding DL queries and uses the query results to plan DM workflow.

2   Related Work

2.1   CRISP-DM

To build DM workflows effectively and correctly, it is important to have a structured framework to follow. Today some frameworks are more frequently used than others. CRISP-DM [11] is a DM framework that defines six different phases: business understanding, data understanding, data preprocessing, modeling, evaluation, and deployment. KDD [12] is a DM framework that contains detailed descriptions of CRISP-DM phases. In KDD, more detailed phases are provided: developing and understanding of the application, creating a target dataset, data cleaning and preprocessing, data transformation, choosing a suitable data mining task, choosing a suitable data mining algorithm, employing data mining algorithm, interpreting mined patterns, and using discovered knowledge. Unlike CRISP-DM and KDD, SEMMA [13] focuses mostly on data management. The model of data mining consists of five phases: sample, explore, modify, model, and access. It doesn't consider the problem of understanding and the deployment of the generated models. At present, all the DM process frameworks are used manually to support the DM tasks solving. The premise of automatic workflow generation is to query for the suitable process from a DM knowledge base. By now the CRISP-DM framework is the most suitable framework for building DM processes, as it is more complete and has a more concise description compared to the others.

2.2 Meta Mining Framework for DM Workflow Construction

In our previous work [8], we proposed a meta mining framework for DM workflow construction based on CRISP-DM, which is shown in Fig. 1.

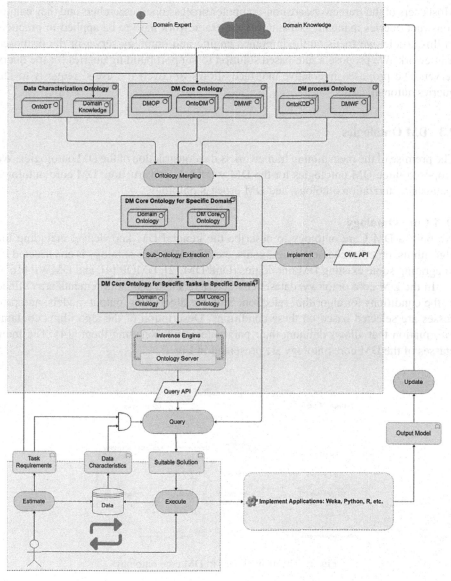

Fig. 1. The meta mining framework for DM workflow construction.

The data characterization ontology and DM core ontology describe the datasets and DM domain knowledge. The DM process ontology describes the hierarchy of DM processes, at the top of which are abstract processes that are detailed at lower levels. In the proposed framework, the ontologies are merged and extracted via an ontology merging method and sub-ontology extraction method [14]. The inference engine and ontology server provide the query API for the algorithm selection server. The users can search the suitable algorithms according to the task requirements and the data characteristics and execute them in the corresponding applications. The result can be used to update the domain knowledge.

The query server requires construction of queries using description logic (DL). The DL queries have to be formatted according to strict Manchester OWL syntax [15]. Most users of the framework are non-computer professional researchers and they cannot construct queries manually. This makes the framework hard to be applied in practice. In this article, we focus on the inference engine and ontology server of the proposed framework. We propose a rule-based solution to support building queries for the query server. The proposed interactive interface allows to covert the users' requests to DL queries automatically.

2.3 DM Ontologies

The premise of the meta mining framework is the construction of the DM ontologies. We proposed three DM ontologies for the DM workflow construction: DM core ontology, Data characterization ontology, and DM process ontology.

DM Core Ontology

We built a DM Core ontology to describe the general DM knowledge, including the algorithms, process, characteristics, goals, etc. The DM core ontology is constructed by integrating some existing DM ontologies (OntoDM [2], DMOP [4], and DMWF [16]).

In the DM core ontology, dataset characteristics and task requirements are defined as the conditions for algorithm selection. Suitable algorithms, output models, and processes are selected based on these conditions. Description of the algorithms contains information that allows defining their parameters and executing them [14]. The main classes of the DM core ontology are presented in Fig. 2.

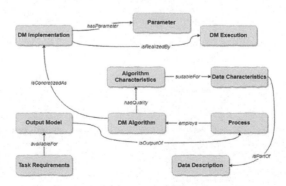

Fig. 2. The main classes in DM core ontology.

DM Data Characterization Ontology

We proposed a DM data characterization ontology to characterize the DM datasets with three categories of the characteristics:

- standard measures
- statistics measures
- information-theoretic measures

The ontology is built by integrating the existing DM ontologies (OntoDT and IAO [23]) and representing the abstract description of the dataset characteristics, which is shown in Fig. 3.

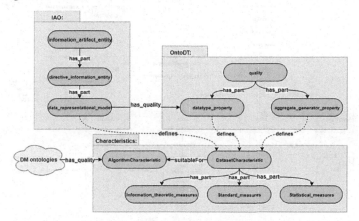

Fig. 3. The Data Characterization ontology.

The notions of domain data characteristics are described both in DM Core ontology and data characterization ontology as ontology classes. The definitions of the notions in the form of the axioms are given only in the data characterization ontology. when dealing with specific domain tasks these two ontologies are merged.

DM Process Ontology

The proposed DM process ontology has a hierarchical structure, which is shown in Fig. 4. Four layers are defined:

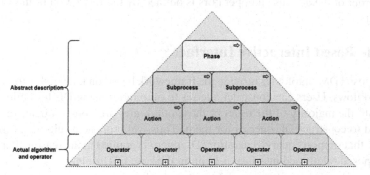

Fig. 4. The hierarchical structure of the DM process ontology.

- Phase
- Subprocess
- Action
- Operator

The first three layers describe the abstract processes and the last one presents the concrete implemented operators/algorithms [17].

The proposed ontology is constructed with a hierarchical structure and integrating OntoKDD [18], which provides the entities of DM process, ad DMWF [5], which provides the concrete operators, input and output objects.

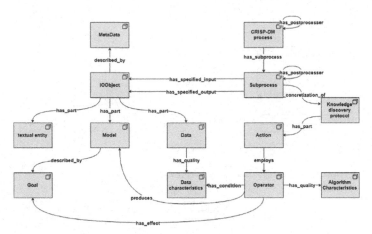

Fig. 5. The hierarchical DM process ontology

The DM hierarchical process ontology is presented in Fig. 5.

- At "Phases" layer, the general phases of DM process according to CRISP-DM framework are defined.
- At "Subprocesses" layer, the subprocesses are described as the decompotion of the "Phases." And the input and output of the process are also presented at this layer.
- At "Actions" layer, the specific activities in DM process are defined.
- At "Operators" layer, the concrete implemented operators/algorithms are described. The order of the actions and operators is defined by the restriction of their input and output.

3   Rule-Based Interactive Interface

The proposed DM ontologies provide the framework based on knowledge for support of DM workflows. Users can construct queries to ontologies using DL for building workflows. But the majority of the users of these ontologies are non-computer researchers. It is hard to construct DL queries for them. Thus, we propose a rule-based interactive interface that supports query generation. DL query is applied to the reasoned ontologies. The proposed rule-based interface is built on the base of Drools.

3.1 DL Query

For the application of the ontologies, many querying tools were developed for querying on a classified ontology [25] easily. In protégé [19], a DL query tab was developed as a plugin. DL query uses Manchester syntax, which is a user-friendly language.

The DL queries are expressed using constructs ("and," "some," "exactly" and so on). The subclasses, which match the conditions, are obtained. An example of DL query is as followings:

> *Q: Who is Matthew?*
> *DL query: hasGivenName value "Matthew"*
> *or*
> *Person and hasGivenName value "Matthew"*

Due to the ease of understanding of DL query, we choose it as the way to query the ontology. But in our previous work, we found that even though a DL query is simple to understand when it has been written, it is tricky to write the one.. This still makes some users give up ontologies.

3.2 Drools

A production system is based on using if-else rules: it executes those rules whose conditions are matched by some facts. So when the task is changed, the rules need to be modified, which can be difficult. In addition, it may cause errors due to neglecting the semantic relationship of context when modifying the rules, so the risk of modification is very high. So there is a need for a rule management system.

Drools, which is JBoss rules, is an open-source rule engine written in Java language. It is a hybrid reasoning system - it supports forward as well as backward reasoning [link on the official documentation]. Rules are stored in the production memory, while facts are maintained in the working memory. The production memory remains unchanged during an analysis session, i.e. no rules are added or removed, or changed. The contents of the working memory can change. Facts may be modified, removed or added, by executing rules or received from external sources. After a change in the working memory, the inference engine is triggered and it determines which rules become "true" for the given facts. If there are multiple selected rules, their execution order will be managed via the Agenda, using a conflict resolution strategy [21].

With the advantage of the Rete algorithm [20], the rules engine Drools is very convenient to manage the rules, it can also meet the demand of higher frequency of rule change. Drools is also more efficient than traditional logical inference for the application scenario with huge rule variables. In our case, as the DM ontologies are extended with new algorithms, the DL queries should be updated correspondingly. Thus, we choose Drools as the rule engine to develop the interactive interface to generate the needed DL queries for users.

3.3 Framework of the Rule-Based Interactive Interface

In this article, we propose a rule-based interactive interface developed using Drools. It receives the users' request and generates the needed DL queries for querying DM ontologies. The framework is shown in Fig. 6.

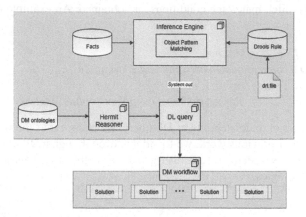

Fig. 6. The framework of the rule-based interactive interface.

The core of the Drools suite is an advanced Inference Engine that uses an improved Rete algorithm for object pattern matching. Rules are stored in the production memory, while facts are maintained in the working memory. The production memory remains unchanged during an analysis session, i.e. no rules are added or removed, or changed. The contents of the working memory can change. Facts may be modified, removed or added, by executing rules or received from external sources. After a change in the working memory, the inference engine is triggered and it determines which rules become "true" for the given facts. If there are multiple selected rules, their execution order will be managed via the Agenda, using a conflict resolution strategy.

In our case, the users' requests define the input facts and the needed DL queries are output. The queries are generated using preset rules. The output DL queries are formatted as the rules with two parts: 1. The fixed contents is presented in the form "String"; 2. The variables are presented as the name of the property of the class. An example is given in Fig. 7:

```
rule "query for actions which are suitable for the specific data characteristics"
when
    $a : Action(state == true)
    $dc : DataCharacteristics()
then
    System.out.println("query for actions which are suitable for "
        + $dc.getName()
        + " with the following query:"
        + " Action and suitableFor "
        + $dc.getName());
end
```

Fig. 7. An example of the Drools rules

The proposed DM ontologies are served as part of the knowledge base. After inferenced by the reasoner (we employ the reasoner "Hermit" [24]), DL queries on these ontologies are generated according to the users' requests. By triggering a preset Drools rule "starter()", the query for basic phases of DM workflow is generated. Users can query for suitable algorithms/operators/solutions according to the task requirements and the data characteristics and execute them in the corresponding operating environment at each phase of data processing. The corresponding DM workflow is generated as the sequence of the suitable algorithms/operators/solutions.

4   Rule-Based DM Workflow Construction

With the help of the Drools, the interactive interface supports the DM workflow construction.

The implementation of the DM workflow construction is based on defining specific queries on each layer of the DM process ontology. The queries are generated based on the designed Drools rules.

The functions of the layers are defined as following:

- "Phase" layer is used to define the general sequence of the DM process. It follows the CRISP-DM framework and defines six phases. The sequence of the phases, which is shown in Fig. 8, is specified by the property "hasPostprocess".

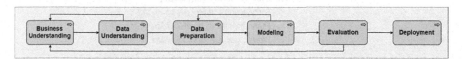

Fig. 8. The general sequence of the DM workflow defined in the DM process ontology

- "Subprocess" layer is used to decide whether the process is necessary for solvingspecific tasks. Each subprocess has specific input and output which are described in the class "IOObject", for example a precondition of a subprocess "handling_missing_attribute_values" is "has_specific_input some attributeWithMissingValues". "attributeWithMissingValues" is a type of dataset which is described in "IOObject". First, data properties (such as number of samples, number of attributes, number of missing values for each attribute, etc.) are queried. Then, the corresponding data characteristics/defects are obtained from the data characterization ontology according to the data properties.
- "Action" layer is used to decide which actions defined at the 'subprocess' layer are suitable for the data with characteristics/defects. The relations between the entities action and data characteristics are defined by the property "suitableFor".
- "Operator" layer is similar to the "Action" layer. But it decides which algorithms are suitable for the data with the defined characteristics/defects. The former determines

the abstract conceptual process, and the latter determines the specific algorithm or operator, for example: process "Imputation" and algorithm "KNN_Imputation_ED (K Nearest Neighbor algorithm with Euclidean distance)".

Algorithm Pseudocode of the DM workflow planning

//Notion

The query module is the process: users input the requests in Drools and get DL query, then run the DL query on the DM ontologies. The results are a list of ontology entities or an entity.

//init

Map<entity, entity> workflow = new HashMap();

//Task starts

List<entity> phase = query.starter();

//Get the subprocesses for each phase

For *(entity p : phase){*

    List<entity> subprocess = query.getSubprocess(p);

//Get the considered data property and corresponding data characteristics for each subprocess

    For *(entity sp : subprocess){*

        List<entity> dataProperty = query.getDataproperty(sp);

        For *(entity dp : dataProperty){*

            List<entity>   dataCharacteristics   = query.getDataCharacteristics(dp);

            For *(entity dc : dataCharacteristics){*

                While *(query.availableFor(dc, sp)){*

                    Entity Action = query.getAction(dc);

                    Entity Operater = query.GetAction(dc);

                    Workflow.add((Action, Operator));

                }

              }

            }

        }

    }

Return *workflow;*

Fig. 9. The pseudocode of the DM workflow construction process.

The pseudocode of the DM workflow construction process is presented in Fig. 9. The query module supports the following process: users input the requests in Drools program and get DL query, then run the DL query on the DM ontologies. The query results are a list of ontology entities or an entity. An example of such process is presented in Fig. 10.

At the beginning, the starter() function is called, the basic phases of the DM workflow are returned. Each phase has a list of the subprocesses. By querying data characterization ontology with the data basic properties, the data characteristics are obtained as the base for algorithm selection. If the subprocesses are available for the defined data characteristics, the suitable actions and operators/algorithms are obtained by querying on the ontology and added to the workflow. They are stored in the Map data structure with two

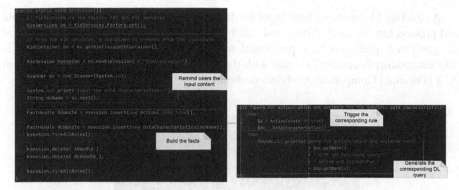

Fig. 10. An example of generating the DL query for defining suitable actions.

variables: key - process and value - operator. The former is the abstract description of the process, and the latter is the concrete employed algorithm or operator.

5 Case Study

As a case study, we consider the Labeled Faces in the Wild (LFW) people dataset [22], which is a database of face photographs designed for studying the problem of unconstrained face recognition. The data set contains more than 13,000 images of faces collected from the web. Each face has been labeled with the name of the person pictured. 1680 of the people pictured have two or more distinct photos in the data set.

We have extracted the data of the persons that have at least 70 photos and used them as our dataset and built a data mining workflow using the proposed framework. The extracted dataset has 1288 images and 1850 attributes (50*37 pixels) for 7 persons. We have considered the task to train the classification model for face recognition.

In the beginning, we start up by inputting a task name and triggering the Drools engine, the general sequence of the DM workflow which is shown in Fig. 8 has been returned. Then it has become possible to query on each phase. Following the guide of the interactive interface, we have obtained knowledge about the required input and the queries that should be performed.

The processes at some phases are subjectively determined, such as "Determine Business Objectives", "Verify Data Quality", etc. However, we need to consider the data characteristics to decide the suitable algorithms. In our case, according to the rules for phase "Data Preparation", we have considered the following data properties: number of samples and number of attributes. The corresponding data characteristics are queried based on the data properties. Since the number of attributes that equals 1850 is more than the number of samples that equals 1288, we have got the data characteristic "HighDimensionality".

As the Fig. 11 shows, we have input the data characteristics (1), the query for suitable DM process has returned "Action and suitableFor some HighDimensionality" (2). And the generated query has been performed on the DM ontology, the queried result is "DimensionalityReduction" (3) and with the similar process, the employed algorithm PCA (Principal Component Analysis) is obtained.

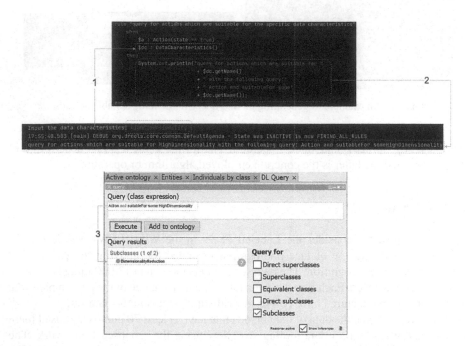

Fig. 11. The process of query for the suitable action for characteristics "HighDimensionality"

The similar procedure has been performed at the "modeling" phase. We have obtained the suitable classification algorithm for "HighDimensionality" that is SVC (Support Vector Classification algorithm).

Thus, we have followed the guide of the interactive interface step by step. The corresponding DM workflow for the LFW dataset that is shown in Fig. 12 has been built. The subprocesses and the actions are the abstract description of the DM workflow, and the algorithms (SVC and PCA) are the concrete implementation of the DM workflow.

In order to verify the effectiveness of the obtained workflow, we have constructed workflows using alternative algorithms and compared the results. The result of comparison is presented in Fig. 13. Three metrics are considered: precision, recall, and F1-score. Other workflows include: SVC, MLP (MutiLayer Perception), MLP + PCA, NB (Naive Bayes), NB + PCA, DT (Decision Tree), DT + PCA. The workflow SVC + PCA that was constructed using Drools has the best performance: 0.87, 0.86, 0.85. Usage of PCA in combination with SVC allowed reduce the dimension of the dataset attributes, and thus archive higher performance.

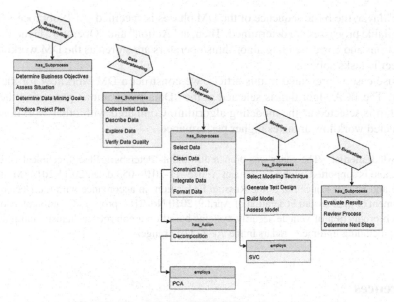

Fig. 12. The workflow for LFW dataset processing

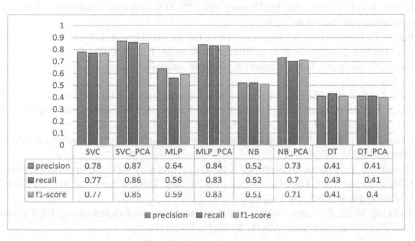

	SVC	SVC_PCA	MLP	MLP_PCA	NB	NB_PCA	DT	DT_PCA
■ precision	0.78	0.87	0.64	0.84	0.52	0.73	0.41	0.41
■ recall	0.77	0.86	0.56	0.83	0.52	0.7	0.43	0.41
■ f1-score	0.77	0.85	0.59	0.83	0.51	0.71	0.41	0.4

■ precision   ■ recall   ■ f1-score

Fig. 13. The comparison results of obtained workflow with alternative workflows

6 Conclusions

Addressing data mining workflow construction, we have built an ontology-based meta mining framework. In previous work, we found that the strict syntax makes users confused on using the framework. In this article, we propose a rule-based interactive interface based on Drools, which converts the users' requests to DL queries automatically.

The DM workflow construction is based on the DM process ontology that has hierarchical structure. It assumes that the workflows are constructed at different layers. At

"Phase" layer, the basic sequence of the DM phases is specified. At "Subprocess" layer, the available processes are determined. Then, at "Action" and "Operator" layer, the suitable actions and corresponding algorithms/operators are stored as the DM workflow for the specific tasks solving.

A use case is presented in this article, we construct a DM workflow for the LFW dataset. The PCA algorithm is selected at the "Data preparation" phase and the SVC algorithm is selected as the modeling algorithm. Compared with other workflows, the constructed workflow archives higher performance.

Acknowledgments. «The paper was prepared in Saint- Petersburg Electrotechnical University (LETI), and is supported by the Agreement № 075–11-2019–053 dated 20.11.2019 (Ministry of Science and Higher Education of the Russian Federation, in accordance with the Decree of the Government of the Russian Federation of April 9, 2010 No. 218), project «Creation of a domestic high-tech production of vehicle security systems based on a control mechanism and intelligent sensors, including millimeter radars in the 76–77 GHz range»

References

1. Hilario, M., et al.: Ontology-based meta-mining of knowledge discovery workflows. In: Meta-Learning in Computational Intelligence, pp. 273–315. Springer, Heidelberg (2011). https://doi.org/10.1007/978-3-642-20980-2_9
2. Panov, P., Džeroski, S., Soldatova, L.: OntoDM: an ontology of data mining. In: 2008 IEEE International Conference on Data Mining Workshops. IEEE (2008)
3. Panov, P., Soldatova, L.N., Džeroski, S.: Generic ontology of datatypes. Inf. Sci. **329**, 900–920 (2016)
4. Keet, C.M., et al.: The data mining optimization ontology. J. Web Semant. **32**, 43–53 (2015)
5. Žáková, M., et al.: Automating knowledge discovery workflow composition through ontology-based planning. IEEE Trans. Autom. Sci. Eng. **8**(2), 253–264 (2010)
6. Benali, K., Rahal, S.A.: OntoDTA: ontology-guided decision tree assistance. J. Inf. Knowl. Manag. **16**(03), 1750031 (2017)
7. Diamantini, C., Potena, D., Storti, E.: Kddonto: an ontology for discovery and composition of KDD algorithms. In: Third Generation Data Mining: Towards Service-Oriented Knowledge Discovery (SoKD'09), pp. 13–24 (2009)
8. Tianxing, M., et al.: A meta-mining ontology framework for data processing. Int. J. Embedded Real-Time Commun. Syst. (IJERTCS) **12**(2), 37–56 (2021)
9. Pan, J.Z., Thomas, E., Zhao, Y.: Completeness guaranteed approximations for OWL-DL query answering. Description Logics **477** (2009)
10. Proctor, M.: Drools: a rule engine for complex event processing. In: Schürr, A., Varró, D., Varró, G. (eds.) AGTIVE 2011. LNCS, vol. 7233, pp. 2–2. Springer, Heidelberg (2012). https://doi.org/10.1007/978-3-642-34176-2_2
11. Wirth, R., Hipp, J.: CRISP-DM: towards a standard process model for data mining. In: Proceedings of the 4th International Conference on the Practical Applications of Knowledge Discovery and Data Mining, vol. 1. Springer, London (2000)
12. Brachman, R.J., Anand, T.: The process of knowledge discovery in databases: a first sketch. In: KDD Workshop, vol. 3 (1994)
13. Shafique, U., Qaiser, H.: A comparative study of data mining process models (KDD, CRISP-DM and SEMMA). Int. J. Innov. Sci. Res. **12**(1), 217–222 (2014)

14. Tianxing, M., Stankova, E., Vodyaho, A., Zhukova, N., Shichkina, Y.: Domain-Oriented Multilevel Ontology for Adaptive Data Processing. In: Gervasi, O., et al. (eds.) ICCSA 2020. LNCS, vol. 12249, pp. 634–649. Springer, Cham (2020). https://doi.org/10.1007/978-3-030-58799-4_46
15. Horridge, M., et al.: The Manchester OWL Syntax. OWLed, vol. 216 (2006)
16. Doukas, C., Chatziioannou, A., Maglogiannis, I.: Intelligent planning of biomedical image mining workflows. In: Proceedings of the 10th IEEE International Conference on Information Technology and Applications in Biomedicine. IEEE (2010)
17. Tianxing, M., et al.: A hierarchical data mining process ontology. In: 2021 28th Conference of Open Innovations Association (FRUCT). IEEE (2021)
18. Panov, P., Soldatova, L., Džeroski, S.: OntoDM-KDD: ontology for representing the knowledge discovery process. In: Fürnkranz, J., Hüllermeier, E., Higuchi, T. (eds.) DS 2013. LNCS (LNAI), vol. 8140, pp. 126–140. Springer, Heidelberg (2013). https://doi.org/10.1007/978-3-642-40897-7_9
19. Noy, N.F., et al.: Protégé-2000: an open-source ontology-development and knowledge-acquisition environment. In: AMIA... Annual Symposium proceedings. AMIA Symposium, vol. 2003. American Medical Informatics Association (2003)
20. Liu, D., Gu, T., Xue, J.-P.: Rule engine based on improvement rete algorithm. In: The 2010 International Conference on Apperceiving Computing and Intelligence Analysis Proceeding. IEEE (2010)
21. Yang, P., et al.: An intelligent tumors coding method based on drools. J. New Media 2(3), 111 (2020)
22. Huang, G.B., et al.: Labeled faces in the wild: a database for studying face recognition in unconstrained environments. In: Workshop on Faces in'Real-Life'Images: Detection, Alignment, and Recognition (2008)
23. Information Artifact Ontology (IAO) web page. http://www.obofoundry.org/ontology/iao.html
24. Glimm, B., et al.: HermiT: an OWL 2 reasoner. J. Autom. Reasoning 53(3), 245–269 (2014)
25. DL Query tab. https://protegewiki.stanford.edu/wiki/DLQueryTab

Ontology for Knowledge Graphs of Telecommunication Network Monitoring Systems

Igor Kulikov[1]($\boxtimes$) iD, Alexander Vodyaho[1] iD, Elena Stankova[2] iD,
and Nataly Zhukova[3] iD

[1] Saint-Petersburg Electrotechnical University "LETI", Saint-Petersburg, Russia
[2] Saint Petersburg State University, Saint-Petersburg, Russia
[3] St. Petersburg Federal Research Centre of the Russian
Academy of Sciences (SPCRAS), Saint Petersburg, Russia

Abstract. When Knowledge Graphs (KG) are used in practice, in particular for complex objects modeling, Semantic web recommends building KGs using existing common and domain ontologies as the base ontologies for modeling and extend them when developing new applications. In this work, detailed ontology for telecommunication networks (TN) monitoring system based on KG is discussed. The proposed ontology uses common ontologies and TN domain ontologies like Telecommunication Services Domain Ontology (TSDO) and TOUCAN Ontology (ToCo) as basic ontologies. To build the required ontology TSDO is extended on application level, in particular, new sub-ontologies for subdomains tasks solving are added. The case study of creation an ontology for TN monitoring system of a Cable TV operator is introduced. The developed ontology is described using Web Ontology Language (OWL).

Keywords: Knowledge graph · Dynamic network · Monitoring system · Domain ontology · Semantic web

1 Introduction

Typically, telecommunication network monitoring systems are designed to solve the following tasks [1]:

a) network performance monitoring;
b) emergency monitoring;
c) user account monitoring.

There are a considerable number of different available open source and commercial monitoring tools [2]. However modern TN have dynamic structure and used monitoring systems must be reconfigured when TN structure changes. Also, there are monitoring tasks that need usage of several TN models, i.e. topology model and billing model for

© Springer Nature Switzerland AG 2021
O. Gervasi et al. (Eds.): ICCSA 2021, LNCS 12956, pp. 432–446, 2021.
https://doi.org/10.1007/978-3-030-87010-2_32

solving them. Traditional monitoring systems cannot deal with these tasks without their re-design. For solving the tasks TN monitoring systems based on knowledge graphs were proposed [3]. This new approach allows efficiently solve monitoring tasks in practice. The article [5] presented the architecture of a monitoring system based on a knowledge graph, however, the issues of developing ontologies for KG building require additional study. This article explores the following aspects of ontology building:

a) definition of the problem and requirements to ontologies used for KG building;
b) design of the proposed ontology and its representation in OWL;
c) methods for the ontology integration and enrichment;

Also in the article an example for Cable TV operator sub-domain ontology for TN monitoring system is given.

2 Problem Definition

Based on the scope of the tasks solved by monitoring systems based on KG, the following requirements to the developed ontology are defined:

- TNs have complex dynamic structure, the main source of information about them is operational data received from the networks. Ontology must provide possibility of describing heterogeneous static and dynamic data about TN, including the network structure and state that are changing in time.
- TN operators business processes have high complexity, their execution require close interconnections between multiple information systems, including 3rd party systems. It is necessary to assure integration of the developed ontology with other ontologies that are used by TN operators.
- The majority of TN networks have peculiar features defined by target groups of subscribers, technical resources, etc. These features are essential for solving monitoring tasks. A possibility for ontology extension with specific data about TN must be provided.
- The developed ontology should allow use standard Symantec web toolset for building and executing SPARQL [4] requests and for logical inference. It must be possible to use existing methods for ontologies integration and enrichment.

The following standard ontology metrics are used for developed ontology evaluation: Axioms count, Logical axioms count, Declaration axioms count, Class/Data Property/Data Property/Individual count, DL Expressivity [33].

The proposed ontology is designed as a layered ontology that consists of the following levels: core ontologies level, domain ontologies level and application ontologies level [11, 19–22]. It is based on already existing ontologies. Ontologies integration is supported on the level of core and domain ontologies, ontology extension is assumed on application ontology level.

3 Related Works Analysis

Ontology is used as the vocabulary, where a set of classes and relations between these classes in a domain are represented. This representation has a formally defined and universally agreed structure [15–18]. The main purpose of developing ontology for KGs is knowledge sharing and reusing [12]. Ontology and its instances can be represented as a domain knowledge base. For TN domain, the ontology describes a set of network nodes, such as switches, routers, storage devices, and links between them.

3.1 Telecommunication Network Ontologies

There is a number of existing ontologies developed for TN domain, which can be considered:

- **Network Description Language.** Network Description Language (NDL) is used to describe sub-ontologies. There are a topology sub-ontology - describes interconnections between network devices; a layer sub-ontology - describes technologies; a capability sub-ontology - describes network capabilities; a domain sub-ontology - creates abstracted views of TN; a physical sub-ontology - describes the physical views of TN elements [7].
- **Telecommunications Service Domain Ontology (TSDO)** defines concepts, relationships to describe knowledge about telecom service domains and supports functional/non-functional property descriptions. TSDO is based on the semantic description approach (TelecomOWL-S) to telecommunication network services building which assumes extension of OWL-S [8]. This enables accurate description and matching of telecom network services with the annotated semantic information in an open and integrated network [9].
- **Ontology for 3G Wireless Network** [10]. This ontology is developed for wireless network transport configuration. The ontology includes two sub-ontologies: domain ontology and task ontology.
- **Mobile ontology** [11]: The mobile Ontology provides a possibility to restructure ontologies. It is a scalable solution with several pluggable sub-ontologies: services, profile, content, presence, context, communication resources sub-ontology [12].
- **Ontology for Optical Transport Networks (OOTN)** [13]: There is a low-level ontology for optical transport networks based on ITU-T G.805 and G.872 recommendations.
- **Ontology adopted in "OpenMobileNetwork"** [14]: There is a linked Open Dataset of Mobile Networks and Devices. This dataset is developed on an open-source platform that provides semantically enriched mobile network and WiFi topology resource description in Resource Description Framework (RDF). The ontology is published online.
- **TOUCAN Ontology (ToCo)** [26]. One of the modern structured TN domain ontologies.

3.2 Ontology Structures and Examples

Based on [11, 19–22] the ontologies can be allocated into three levels, the upper-level ontologies (or core ontologies), the lower-level ontologies (or domain ontologies), and the application ontologies. The upper-level ontology should be quite compact, as domain ontologies inherit its classes and properties [13, 25]. The most general classes of the particular domain ontology are placed in upper-level ontology. The upper-level ontology bridges the gap between different domains. The lower-level ontology can be considered as a domain-specific part of the vocabulary. In general, the lower-level ontologies are not exposed because they contain detailed information about the domain. Additional details about the domain are placed in application level ontology. In fact, an application ontology is not really an ontology, due to this type of ontologies is not shared and just represents a vocabulary for a specific application or system [23, 24].

There are two TN domain ontologies that are most interesting for designing the proposed ontology: TSDO and ToCo.

TSDO ontology is proposed in [9]. In this ontology semantics for Parlay-based services to describe telecommunication networks and the Internet is applied. An OWL-S-based semantic description approach for telecommunication network services description is presented, which is enabled by the telecommunication service domain ontologies to address the semantic interoperability between services. In the article [6] Xiuquan Qiao et al. introduce detailed description of Telecommunications Service Domain Ontology (TSDO) and methods of its modelling.

TOUCAN (ToCo) ontology is presented by Qianru Zhou et al. in [26] as ontology for telecommunication networks. The Device-Interface-Link (DIL) ontology design pattern is also described by authors in the same article. This development is a part of an on-going project which is addressing the convergence of telecommunication networks across multiple technology domains. Build around the DIL pattern, the ToCo ontology describes the physical infrastructure, users and quality of channels, services in heterogeneous telecommunication networks.

Reviewed approaches and domain ontologies provide the base for development of an ontology for TN monitoring systems based on knowledge graphs.

3.3 Ontologies for Knowledge Graphs

H. Paulheim [34] introduces the following KG definition: "A knowledge graph (i) mainly describes real world entities and their interrelations, organized in a graph, (ii) defines possible classes and relations of entities in a schema, (iii) allows for potentially interrelating arbitrary entities with each other and (iv) covers various topical domains".

KGs provides flexible mechanism for building TN models which can be used for solving analytical, management and prediction tasks [3]. TN models based on KGs can be built and re-built using algorithms with low computational complexity that allow use them for TN monitoring.

Ontologies define the vocabulary for knowledge graphs. Usage of ontologies for KGs allows describe heterogeneous static and dynamic data about TN using ontology classes, relations and attributes. Usage of ontologies also allows integrate information systems based on KG. Ontologies can be extended quite easy by adding new classes, relations and attribute. In addition, ontology-based KG design allows use standard semantic web toolset including SPARQL for data retrieving.

4 Proposed Ontology

4.1 Core Ontologies and Domain Ontologies Extension

The layered structure of the proposed ontology is shown in Fig. 1.

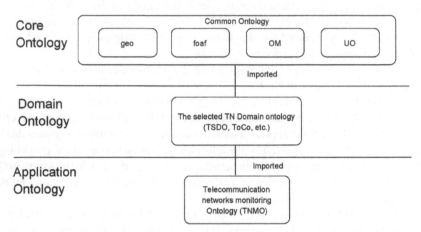

Fig. 1. The layered ontology for TN monitoring systems based on knowledge graphs.

There following core and domain ontologies are used for building the suggested ontology:

- Geo – Basic Geo (WGS84 lat/long) Vocabulary [27].
- FOAF - Friend of a Friend ontology [28].
- OM - Ontology of units of Measure (OM) [29].
- UO - Units of measurement ontology (UO) [30].
- TN Domain Ontology – any of the already developed TN domain ontologies, e.g. TSDO or ToCo.

The structure of the suggested ontology is multilevel and consists of core ontology level, domain ontology level and application ontology level. The set of common core ontologies are represented in the Fig. 1. On the domain level it is suggested to use TSDO or ToCo ontology. Domain ontologies are used as is. The core level ontologies are imported to the domain ontology. For the application level the new Telecommunication Network Monitoring Ontology (TNMO) is proposed.

For purpose of linking domain layer and application layer, the set of domain ontology entities are chosen for further linking with application ontology entities using object preferences mechanism. The following TN domain ontology entities are chosen as points for linking to TNMO:

- Device –any TN device;
- Link – wired or wireless TN link;
- Interface – any TN interface;
- Service – any TN service;
- Data – any data unit in TN (can be described by core ontology).

In TNMO the set of entities and links depend on the tasks solved by TN monitoring systems. Among the main subjects for monitoring in TN are:

- User actions;
- TN events;
- TN devices parameters.

TMNO oriented on solving the enumerated tasks is shown in Fig. 2.

To solve various monitoring tasks TNMO assumes import of different domain ontologies, thus, TNMO requires minimum redesign for adaptation to any domain task.

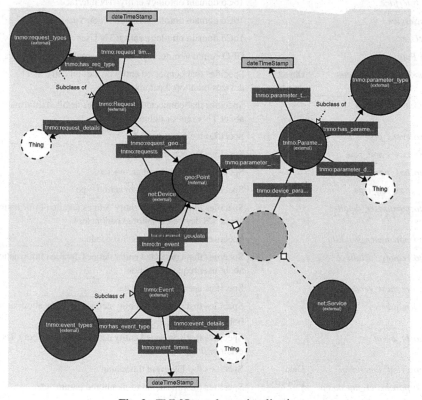

Fig. 2. TNMO ontology visualization

The description of the TMNO entities is given in Table 1.

Table 1. TNMO ontology description

Ontology entries	Entry type	Description
tnmo:Request	Class	Entity which contains detailed information about user request or actions
tnmo:Event		Entity which contains detailed information about TN event or failure
tnmo:Parameter_M		Entity which contains detailed information about TN devices monitoring parameters
tnmo:event_types		Defines the type of TN event or failure
tnmo:parameter_type		Defines the particular monitored parameter
tnmo:request_types		Defines the particular type of user request or monitored user action
net:Device		ToCo domain ontology entity: TN Device
net:Interface		ToCo domain ontology entity: TN Interface
net:Service		ToCo domain ontology entity: TN Service
net:User		ToCo domain ontology entity: TN User
geo:Point		GEO common ontology entity: geographical coordinates
tnmo:device_parameter	Object property	Specifies that connected entity defines an entry of TN devices monitored parameters
tnmo:event_details		Specifies that connected entity defines detailed information about TN event or failure
tnmo:event_geodata		Specifies the event geodata
tnmo:has_event_type		Specifies the event type
tnmo:has_parameter_type		Specifies the monitored parameter
tnmo:has_req_type		Specifies the user request or action type
tnmo:parameter_detailes		Specifies that connected entity defines detailed information about TN devices monitored parameters
tnmo:parameter_geodata		Specifies the monitored device geodata
tnmo:request_details		Specifies that connected entity defines detailed information about user request or action
tnmo:request_geodata		Specifies user device geodata
tnmo:requests		Specifies that connected entity defines an entry about user request or actions
tnmo:tn_event		Specifies that connected entity defines an entry about TN event or failure
tnmo:event_timestamp	Data property	Specifies the TN event timestamp
tnmo:parameter_tinestamp		Specifies the timestamp of monitored parameter
tnmo:request_timestamp		Specifies the user request or action timestamp

Application level ontology that was built for solving monitoring tasks is presented on Fig. 3, 4, and 5.

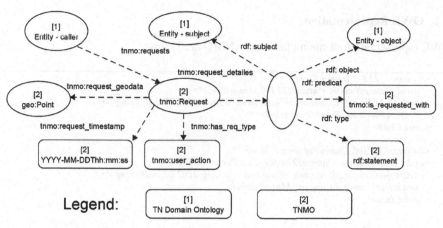

Fig. 3. Ontology for processing a user action in TN monitoring systems based on knowledge graph.

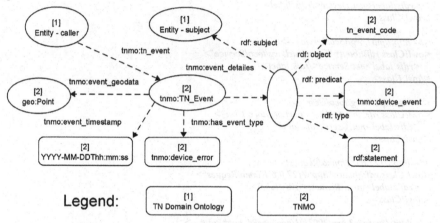

Fig. 4. Ontology for processing network events in TN monitoring systems based on knowledge graph.

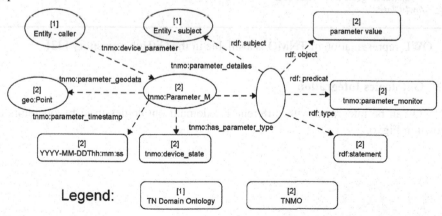

Fig. 5. Ontology for processing device parameters monitoring in TN monitoring systems based on knowledge graph.

4.2 OWL Representation

OWL representation of main classes of TNMO are below:

```
<!-- http://127.0.0.1/tnmo/Event -->
  <owl:Class rdf:about="http://127.0.0.1/tnmo/Event">
    <rdfs:subClassOf rdf:resource="http://www.w3.org/2002/07/owl#Thing"/>
    <rdfs:label>tnmo:Event</rdfs:label>
</owl:Class>

<!-- http://127.0.0.1/tnmo/Parameter_M -->
<owl:Class rdf:about="http://127.0.0.1/tnmo/Parameter_M">
    <rdfs:subClassOf rdf:resource="http://www.w3.org/2002/07/owl#Thing"/>
    <rdfs:label>tnmo:Parameter_M</rdfs:label>
</owl:Class>


<!-- http://purl.org/toco/Device -->
<owl:Class rdf:about="http://purl.org/toco/Device">
    <rdfs:label>net:Device</rdfs:label>
</owl:Class>

<!-- http://purl.org/toco/Service -->
<owl:Class rdf:about="http://purl.org/toco/Service">
    <rdfs:label>net:Service</rdfs:label>
</owl:Class>

<!-- http://purl.org/toco/User -->
<owl:Class rdf:about="http://purl.org/toco/User">
    <rdfs:label>net:User</rdfs:label>
</owl:Class>

<!-- http://127.0.0.1/tnmo/Request -->
<owl:Class rdf:about="http://127.0.0.1/tnmo/Reques">
    <rdfs:label>tnmo:Request</rdfs:label>
</owl:Class>

<!-- http://www.w3.org/2003/01/geo/wgs84_pos#Point -->
<owl:Class rdf:about="http://www.w3.org/2003/01/geo/wgs84_pos#Point">
    <rdfs:label>geo:Point</rdfs:label>
</owl:Class>
```

OWL representation of TNMO is available in the GitHub repository [32].

4.3 Ontologies Integration

TNMO can be integrated with different TN domain ontologies used by operators as shown in Fig. 6.

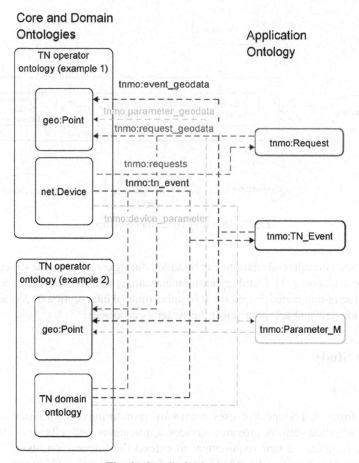

Fig. 6. Ontologies integration.

Integration of the developed TNMO application level ontology with other TN domain ontologies is based on using the similarity of the definitions of the subject area main entities (e.g. TN devises, users, services and interfaces). The ontologies integration methodologies are described in [35].

4.4 Methods of Ontology Enrichment

Ontology enrichment is the process of an ontology extending through adding new elements, relations and rules (Fig. 7). It is performed every time when the existing domain knowledge does not allow use data received from TN.

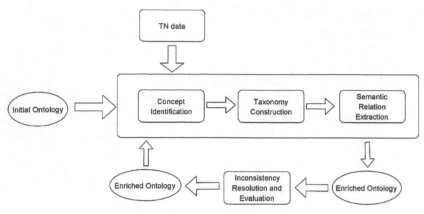

Fig. 7. Ontology enrichment method

Since new concepts and relations can be added during enrichment, the structure of the ontology can change [31]. Ontology enrichment cannot be full automated and remains typically a semi-automated procedure. It requires manual intervention of domain experts in order to review and accept or reject the system's proposals.

5   Case Study

5.1   Use-Case

Business Task: A TN operator uses a network monitoring system based on KG. A telecommunication network provides services, applications, and sells access to content. The operator defines a new requirement to extend the information about TN that is contained in the corporate knowledge graph (devices statistic, TN events and other monitoring data) with additional analytical data (geographical data, devices models, users tariff etc.). These parameters allow increase operativeness of TN issues and failures solving. To solve the task, the application-level TN monitoring ontology was developed and integrated with domain ontology.

Initial Data: The devices used are both stationary and mobile. The description of data used, data sources and data channels are presented in Table 2.

All this data must be collected, placed in the TN monitoring ontology and provided to the operator.

Task Detail: In the considered use case the following sub-tasks are resolved:

- Create TNMO based on domain ontology (ToCo [26]) for this case study;
- Check the developed ontology against requirements;
- Create knowledge representation of the monitoring data.

Table 2. The used data, sources and channels

Monitored parameter	Data source	Used data channel
Subscriber's service request	User action on subscriber device	Monitoring agent on subscriber device create and send to monitoring system the data pack with service request detail
Subscriber's device model	TN management system	This information is available in the KG as part of TN graph model
Subscriber's device geolocation	Subscriber's device geolocation service	Monitoring agent on subscriber device create and send to monitoring system the data pack with the device geolocation
TN device failure	TN device health checking system/TN monitoring system	Health checking system/Monitoring agent on TN device create and send to monitoring system the data pack with the failure detail

5.2 The TNMO Ontology

The suggested application level ontology is shown in Fig. 8.

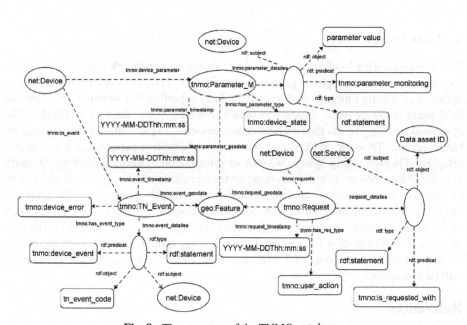

Fig. 8. The structure of the TNMO ontology.

This ontology is designed for solving the following TN monitoring tasks: collection data of user's actions and requests, TN events and failures and monitoring of TN devices parameters. The developed TNMO ontology is available on GitHub [32].

5.3 Ontology Metrics

The GEO core ontology, ToCo ontology and developed TNMO ontology metrics are shown in Table 3.

Table 3. Ontologies metrics

#	Ontology metrics	GEO	ToCo	TNMO
1	Axioms	28	725	128
2	Logical axiom count	2	303	57
3	Declaration axioms count	2	205	35
4	Class count	2	85	13
5	Object property count	1	41	13
6	Data property count		54	4
7	Individual count		1	6
8	Annotation property count	10	17	3

6   Conclusion

The new application level ontology for telecommunication network monitoring systems based on knowledge graphs is proposed in the paper. TNMO as application ontology is linked to domain ontology with specific object properties. For defining links, entities in domain ontology were chosen and object properties were defined in TNMO. The discussed ontology meets the formulated requirements, in particular, ability to describe heterogeneous TN static and dynamic data, ability of ontology enrichment. It also allows integrate TN monitoring system with other information systems, including 3rd party systems. The ontology is built according to the standards of Semantic web and can be extended or changed using standard methods and tools. The structure of the proposed ontology, method of integration with domain ontologies and method of the ontology enrichment are studied in the article. The main ontology metrics are provided. The case study of TNMO building for solving TN monitoring tasks is discussed. In the course of further research extending of TNMO and methods of its semi-automatic enrichment will be considered.

References

1. William Stallings. "SNMP, SNMPv2, and RMON Practical Network Management, Second Edition" Addison-Wesley Professional Computing and Engineering 1996. A Good General Reference in Basics of RMON

2. Stanford University. "Network Monitoring Tools" Stanford University. http://www.slac.sta nford.edu/xorg/nmtf/nmtf-tools.html. Accessed 20 Mar 2012
3. Kulikov, I., Wohlgenannt, G., Shichkina, Y., Zhukova, N.: An analytical computing infrastructure for monitoring dynamic networks based on knowledge graphs. In: Gervasi, O., et al. (eds.) ICCSA 2020. LNCS, vol. 12254, pp. 183–198. Springer, Cham (2020). https://doi.org/10.1007/978-3-030-58817-5_15
4. SPARQL Query Language for RDF. https://www.w3.org/TR/rdf-sparql-query/
5. Krinkin, K., Kulikov, I., Vodyaho, A., Zhukova, N.: Architecture of a telecommunications network monitoring system based on a knowledge graph. In: 2020 26th Conference of Open Innovations Association (FRUCT), Yaroslavl, Russia, pp. 231–239 (2020). https://doi.org/10.23919/FRUCT48808.2020.9087429
6. Qiao, X., Li, X., Chen, J.: Telecommunications service domain ontology: semantic interoperation foundation of intelligent integrated services, telecommunications networks - current status and future trends, Jesus Hamilton Ortiz, 30 March 2012. IntechOpen (2012). https://doi.org/10.5772/36794
7. van der Ham, J.J.: A Semantic model for complex computer networks: the network description language. Citeseer 3 (2010)
8. OWL-S. https://www.w3.org/Submission/OWL-S/
9. Qiao, X., Li, X., Fensel, A., Su, F.: Applying semantics to Parlay-based services for telecommunication and Internet networks. Open Comput. Sci. 1(4), 406–429 (2011). https://doi.org/10.2478/s13537-011-0029-6
10. Cleary, D., Danev, B., O'Donoghue, D.: Using ontologies to simplify wireless network configuration. In: FOMI (2005)
11. Villalonga, C., et al.: Mobile ontology: towards a standardized semantic model for the mobile domain. In: Di Nitto, E., Ripeanu, M. (eds.) ICSOC 2007. LNCS, vol. 4907, pp. 248–257. Springer, Heidelberg (2009). https://doi.org/10.1007/978-3-540-93851-4_25
12. Zhou, Q.: Ontology-driven knowledge based autonomic management for telecommunication networks: theory, implementation, and applications. Heriot-Watt University (2018)
13. Barcelos, P.P.F., Monteiro, M.E., Simoes, R.d.M., Garcia, A.S., Segatto, M.E.V.: OOTN-an ontology proposal for optical transport networks. In: IEEE ICUMT, pp. 1–7 (2009)
14. Uzun, A., Küpper, A.: OpenMobileNetwork: extending the web of data by a dataset for mobile networks and devices. In: ACM ICSS, pp. 17–24 (2012)
15. López de Vergara, J.E., Guerrero, A., Villagrá, V.A., Berrocal, J.: Ontology-based network management: study cases and lessons learned. J. Netw. Syst. Manag. 17(3), 234–254 (2009). https://doi.org/10.1007/s10922-009-9129-1
16. Buitelaar, P., Cimiano, P., Magnini, B.: Ontology Learning from Text: Methods, Evaluation and Applications, vol. 123. IOS Press (2005)
17. Noy, N.F., McGuinness, D.L.: Ontology development 101: a guide to creating your first ontology. Stanford Knowledge Systems Laboratory (2001)
18. Niskanen, I., Kantorovitch, J.: Ontology driven data mining and information visualization for the networked home. In: Research Challenges in Information Science (RCIS), 2010 Fourth International Conference on, pp. 147–156. IEEE (2010)
19. Fensel, D.: Ontology-based knowledge management. Computer 35(11), 56–59 (2002)
20. Guarino, N.: Formal ontology, conceptual analysis and knowledge representation. Int. J. Hum. Comput. Stud. 43(5–6), 625–640 (1995)
21. Sure, Y., Studer, R.: A methodology for ontology-based knowledge management. In: Towards the Semantic Web: Ontology-Driven Knowledge Management, pp. 33–46 (2003)
22. Noy, N.F., et al.: Protege-2000: an open-source ontology-development and knowledge-acquisition environment. In: AMIA Annual Symposium Proceedings, vol. 953, p. 953 (2003)

23. Berners-Lee, T., Hendler, J., Lassila, O.: The semantic web. Sci. Am. **284**(5), 28–37 (2001)
24. Bizer, C., Heath, T., Idehen, K., Berners-Lee, T.: Linked data on the web. In: ACM World Wide Web, pp. 1265–1266 (2008)
25. Niles, I., Pease, A.: Towards a standard upper ontology. In: ACM FOIS, pp. 2–9 (2001)
26. Zhou, Q., Gray, A.J.G., McLaughlin, S.: ToCo: an ontology for representing hybrid telecommunication networks. In: Hitzler, P., et al. (eds.) ESWC 2019. LNCS, vol. 11503, pp. 507–522. Springer, Cham (2019). https://doi.org/10.1007/978-3-030-21348-0_33
27. Basic Geo (WGS84 lat/long) Vocabulary. https://www.w3.org/2003/01/geo/
28. Friend of a Friend (FOAF) Ontology. http://xmlns.com/foaf/spec/
29. Ontology of Units of Measure (OM). http://purl.oclc.org/net/unis/ontology/sensordata.owl
30. Units of Measurement Ontology (UO). http://purl.obolibrary.org/obo/uo.owl
31. Petasis, G., Karkaletsis, V., Paliouras, G., Krithara, A., Zavitsanos, E.: Ontology population and enrichment: state of the art. In: Paliouras, G., Spyropoulos, C.D., Tsatsaronis, G. (eds.) Knowledge-Driven Multimedia Information Extraction and Ontology Evolution. LNCS (LNAI), vol. 6050, pp. 134–166. Springer, Heidelberg (2011). https://doi.org/10.1007/978-3-642-20795-2_6
32. GitHub Repository Link. https://github.com/kulikovia/ICCSA-2021
33. Ontology Metrics. http://protegeproject.github.io/protege/views/ontology-metrics/
34. Paulheim, H.: Knowledge graph renement: a survey of approaches and evaluation methods. Sem. Web J. 1–20 (2016)
35. Pinto, H.S., Martins, J.P.: A methodology for ontology integration. In: Proceedings of the 1st International Conference on Knowledge capture (K-CAP 2001), pp. 131–138. Association for Computing Machinery, New York (2001). https://doi.org/10.1145/500737.500759

Protection of Personal Data Using Anonymization

Alexander V. Bogdanov[1], Alexander Degtyarev[1,4], Nadezhda Shchegoleva[1(✉)], Vladimir Korkhov[1,4], Valery Khvatov[2], Nodir Zaynalov[3], Jasur Kiyamov[1], Aleksandr Dik[1], and Anar Faradzhov[1]

[1] Saint Petersburg State University, St. Petersburg, Russia
{a.v.bogdanov,a.degtyarev,n.shchegoleva,v.korkhov}@spbu.ru,
{st080634,st087383,st069744}@student.spbu.ru
[2] DGT Technologies AG., Toronto, Canada
[3] Samarkand branch Tashkent University of Information Technologies named after Muhammad al-Khwarizmi, Samarkand, Uzbekistan
[4] Plekhanov Russian University of Economics, Moscow, Russia

Abstract. Data quality and security issues are very closely related. To ensure a high level of reliability in distributed systems and resilience from external attacks, the process of consolidating distributed data is critical. For consolidated systems, the access process relies heavily on data preprocessing, which, in turn, allows them to be anonymized. The analysis of closely related processes of consolidation and anonymization allows us to offer a secure access platform for distributed data, which makes it possible to implement secure access systems that depend only on the type and format of the data. It turns out that in the program stack for working with data, optimization can be done only with the entire framework, but not with its components. In this paper we perform analysis of data security as a complex problem related to both data quality and system architectures used to protect personal data.

Keywords: Big Data · Data access · Data anonymization · Data consolidation · Data platforms

1 Introduction

Recently, Big Data is increasingly turning from a fashionable area of research into a tool for practical use for many areas of activity. However, the increase in the volume and decrease in the connectivity of data leads to serious problems, both in terms of the appearance of security problems and possible data leaks. The latter is especially relevant when working with personal data and the emergence of a serious problem of data anonymization. The amount of information plays a key role in the complexity of the anonymization process. The emergence of new sources of information makes it possible to compare them with those published (available) earlier and inevitably leads to the emergence of risks of re-identification of previously depersonalized data. This, in turn, forces us to abandon the concept of guaranteed anonymized data, introducing certain

© Springer Nature Switzerland AG 2021
O. Gervasi et al. (Eds.): ICCSA 2021, LNCS 12956, pp. 447–459, 2021.
https://doi.org/10.1007/978-3-030-87010-2_33

boundaries for dealing with risks and building a continuous threat assessment process. In doing so, it is important to consider two critical parameters that determine data security: data type and system connectivity [1].

To clarify this circumstance, we will consider three types of systems - a closed system, a private cloud, and a public cloud. For a closed system, these problems do not arise and there are a large number of products that solve this problem for both scientific and commercial structures. For private clouds, the situation becomes more complicated and a number of dangers appear. To ensure security, it is necessary to introduce a two-level access system, similar to the GRID system, and, in addition, it is necessary to consolidate data, and the consolidation is multi-level, not all stages of which are currently optimized [2].

For public clouds, these issues are on the rise, with data quality and criteria for selecting anonymization models being critical issues. The issue of data quality has been investigated in sufficient detail, and the conclusion from this study is very tough - before any work with data, the data quality must be checked and all possible adjustments must be implemented. If the data is well prepared, you can start data pre-processing.

The main stages of preparation are the following:

1. Anonymization:
   - Anonymization of personal data must be built into the overall data management system (Privacy By Design)
   - The results of anonymization should be measurable (benefits and risks)
   - Anonymization as a measure of information protection should include not only technical, but also organizational measures
   - Data should be categorized according to the degree of sensitivity, for different categories different methods should be used
2. Data quality check:
   - completeness (preservation of all information about specific subjects or groups of subjects that was available before depersonalization);
   - structuredness (preservation of structural links between the impersonal data of a specific subject or a group of subjects corresponding to the connections that existed before anonymization);
   - semantic integrity (preservation of the semantics of personal data during their depersonalization);
   - anonymity (impossibility of unambiguous identification of data subjects obtained as a result of anonymization);
3. Data Consolidation:
   - coordination of metamodels;
   - interpretation of data models;
   - comparison of classifiers, directories and domains;
   - combining information.

When implementing this process, a number of problems arise:

- conceptual differences between data models used in different sources within the same operating environment;

- interpretation of data models;
- comparison of classifiers, directories and domains;
- combining information.

The procedural approach implies hard coding of integration procedures based on specific data models. The advantages of this approach include the fact that there are practically no restrictions on the use of different structures and models in the database. The disadvantages are the following:

- for each interaction of data sources, you need to implement your own software integration module that uses the full cycle of operations;
- complexity of maintenance;
- hindered efficiency;
- instability of the software to change the data model.

There is no standard set of tools for solving these problems yet, so at this stage it is important to build a set of platform requirements and see on what basis such a solution can be built [3].

2 Ecosystems to Process and Store Super Large Amounts of Data

The architecture of the Big Data processing system uses complex systems in which several components or layers can be distinguished. Usually, there are four levels of components of such systems: reception, collection, analysis of data and presentation of results [2]. This division is largely arbitrary, since, on the one hand, each component can be divided into subcomponents, and on the other hand, some functions of the components can be redistributed depending on the problem being solved and the software used, for example, they allocate data storage in a separate layer.

To work with Big Data, system developers create data models that are related to the real world. Developing adequate data models is a complex analytical task performed by system architects and analysts. The data model allows you to create a mathematical model of interactions between objects in the real world and includes a description of the data structure, data manipulation methods and aspects of maintaining data integrity. Describing the development of data models is beyond the scope of this work. Distributed systems of various types are used to store data. These can be file systems, databases, journals, mechanisms for accessing shared virtual memory. Most storage systems focused exclusively on working with Big Data have an extremely limited number of functions due to the inherent complexity of creating highly efficient distributed systems.

In order to work with data faster, data storage and processing systems are parallelized in a computing cluster. However, according to Brewer's hypothesis, it is impossible to ensure the simultaneous data consistency, data availability and system resistance to the separation of individual nodes [7]. The hypothesis is proven for transactions of the ACID type (Atomic, Consistent. Isolated, Durable) and is known as the CAP theorem (Consistency, Availability, Partition tolerance).

2.1   Data Ingestion

Data sources have various parameters, such as the frequency of data receipt from the source, the size of the data portion, the data transfer rate, the type of data received and their reliability. To efficiently collect data, you need to establish data sources. These can be data warehouses, aggregated data providers, API of any sensors, system logs, human-generated content in social networks, in corporate information systems, geophysical information, scientific information, inherited data from other systems [4]. Data sources define the original data format. For example, we can independently conduct weather research on the territory of the airport, use data from aircraft taking off and landing, purchase data from satellites flying over airports from the local weather service, and also find it somewhere else on the network. In general, for each source, it is necessary to create its own collector (Data Crawler for collecting information on the network and Data Acquisition for making measurements). Receiving data consists in the initial preparation of data from sources in order to bring the data to a common data presentation format. This uniform format is chosen according to the accepted data model. Conversions of measurement systems, types (typification), verification are performed. Data processing does not meaningfully affect the information available in the data, but it can change its representation (for example, bring coordinates to a single coordinate system, and values to a single dimension).

2.2   Data Staging

The data collection phase is characterized by direct interaction with data storage systems. A collection point is established at which the collected data is supplied with local metadata and placed in a repository or transmitted for further processing. Data that for some reason did not pass the collection point is ignored.

For structured data, conversion from the original format is carried out according to predefined algorithms. This is the most efficient procedure when the data structure is known. However, if the data is presented in binary form, the structure and connections between the data are lost, then the development of algorithms and software based on them for data processing can be extremely difficult [2].

Semi-structured data requires the interpretation of the incoming data and the use of software that can work with the used data description language. A significant advantage of semi-structured data is that it often contains not only the data itself, but metadata in the form of information about the relationships between data and how to obtain it. The development of software for processing semi-structured data is a rather complex task. However, there are a significant number of ready-made converters that can, for example, extract data from XML format into a generated table view.

The largest amount of effort is required for processing unstructured data. To translate them into a given format may require the creation of special software, complex manual processing, recognition and selective manual control.

During the collection phase, data types are checked and basic data validation can be performed. For example, the coordinates of gas molecules contained in any region cannot lie outside this region, and the velocities cannot significantly exceed the speed of sound. In order to avoid typing errors, it is necessary to check if the units of measurement are specified correctly. For example, one dataset might measure elevation in kilometers and another in feet. In this case, it is necessary to convert the height to those units of measurement that are accepted in the used model.

When collected, data is systematized and provided with metadata stored in associated metadata. If you have a large number of data sources, you may need to manage the collection of data in order to balance the amount of information coming from different sources.

2.3   Analysis Layer

Data analysis, unlike data collection, uses the information contained in the data itself. The analysis can be carried out both in real time and in batch mode. Data analysis is the main task in terms of labor intensity when working with Big Data. There are many data processing techniques: predictive analysis, queries and reporting, mathematical model reconstruction, translation, analytical processing, and others. The techniques use specific algorithms depending on the goals set. For example, analytical processing can be image analysis, social media analysis, geographic location, feature recognition, text analysis, statistical processing, voice analysis, transcription. Data analysis algorithms, like data processing algorithms, rely on a data model. In this case, in the analysis, several models can be used that set the general data format, but simulate the meaningful processes in different ways, the data about which we process. When using artificial intelligence methods, in particular neural networks, in the analysis, the models are dynamically trained on various data sets.

When analyzing data, the entities described by the data are identified based on the information available in the data and the models used. The essence of analysis is an analytical mechanism that uses analytical algorithms, model management and entity identification to obtain new meaningful information that is the result of the analysis.

2.4   Consumption Layer

Data analysis results are provided at the consumption level. There are several mechanisms to use the results of Big Data analysis.

- Monitoring metadata.
  Subsystem for real-time display of essential parameters of the system, workload of computers, distribution of tasks in a cluster, distribution of information in storages, availability of free space in storages, data flow from sources, user activity, equipment failures, etc.

- Data monitoring.
  Subsystem for displaying in real time the processes of receiving, collecting and analyzing data, data navigation.
- Generation of reports, queries to data, presentation of data in the form of visualization on dashboards (Dashboard), in PDF format, infographics, pivot tables and quick references.
- Data transformation and export to other systems, interface with BI systems

3   Anonymizing the Data

In this paper, we consider the classical methods of anonymization, which are recommended in the standards, such as ISO 20889:2018 and NIST 8062. New modern methods are emerging, this is separate topic with some important methodological achievements available [7].

3.1   Approaches to Anonymization

Basic Methods of Anonymization

- Introduction of quasi-identifiers [8]. Methods of depersonalization based on the introduction of replacement identifiers - replacing part of the information attributes of personal data. The need to create conversion tables.
- Aggregation of data [8]. Aggregation - as part of the aggregation of data and thereby deletion of personal data.
- Data decomposition [8]. Separation of sets of personal data in order to protect personal identifiers. Organization of separate storage and processing of data. Boundary calculations.

Statistical Methods

- Sampling. Construction of approximate data, based on statistical data processing.
- Aggregation [11]. Formation of generalized data marts.

Cryptographic Methods

- Deterministic Encryption. Create unidirectional text data transformation using public keys - RSA Based.
- Encryption preserving the order of the attribute or format. Order-preserving encrypted, Format–preserving encryption - The order-preserving encryption scheme (OPES) allows you to directly apply comparison operations to encrypted data without decrypting the operands, so aggregated data can be applied directly to encrypted data.
- Homomorphic encryption [12]. Encryption of personal data while maintaining the ability to analyze and search for hidden data - RSA, El Gamal cryptosystem.
- Quantum resistance. The resistance of encryption to quantum computing.

Attribute Suppression Techniques

- Local suppression. Method of replacing several values of sensitive attributes with a missing value, can lead to data loss.
- Suppression of records. Record Suppression. Suppression of a number of records relating to one subject of personal data.

Pseudo-anonymization Methods

- Replacement of attributes. Selection Of Attributes - replacement of attributes from the number of substitution dictionaries.
- Use of aliases. Anonymization methods based on the introduction of the replacement of identifiers - replacement of part of the information attributes of personal data.

Summarizing Data

- Output of approximate values. Rounding – output of approximate values of attributes of personal data subjects.
- Method of limit values. Top and Bottom Coding - setting the upper and lower limits, exceeding or underestimation of which leads to the output of the limits themselves.
- Complex Attributes. Set Of Attributes-setting a combination of attributes instead of individual attributes.

Randomization

- Adding noise. Noise Addition, Blurring-Embedding of random data in a given set, distortion of sensitive attributes.
- Microaggregation [10]. Micro Aggregation is a special clustering task whose purpose is to group a set of points into groups of at least k points so that the groups are as homogeneous as possible.
- Shuffling of attributes [9]. Permutation, Swapping - entanglement of attributes between several subjects.

Privacy Models (Anonymization Metrics) – Protecting a dataset from re-identification by setting thresholds for the proportion of records. To do this, you must specify the basic information, based on this data, statistical models are used to evaluate the characteristics.

k-anonymity. The database is a table with n rows and m columns. Each row in a table is a record for a specific member of the population, and records in different rows do not have to be unique. The values in the various columns are the values of the attributes associated with the members of the population.

l-diversity. Given the existence of such attacks, in which sensitive attributes can be inferred for k-anonymity data, the l-diversity method was created to increase k-anonymity by further preserving the diversity of sensitive fields.

t-closeness. It is a further refinement of l-diversity group anonymization, which is used to preserve confidentiality in datasets by reducing the granularity of data

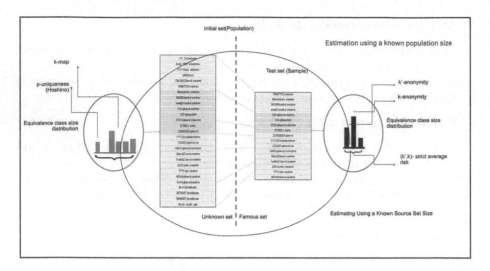

Fig. 1. k-anonymity illustration

presentation. This reduction is a tradeoff that results in some loss of efficiency in data management or data mining algorithms to achieve some privacy. The t-closeness model extends the l-diversity model by treating attribute values separately, taking into account the distribution of data values for that attribute (Fig. 1).

The Differential Privacy Model. [13] is a system for publicly exchanging information about a dataset by describing patterns of groups in the dataset without disclosing information about the individuals in the dataset. The idea behind differential privacy is that if the effect of doing an arbitrary single replacement on a database is small enough, the result of the query cannot be used to infer much about any particular person and therefore provides privacy. Another way of describing differential confidentiality is by limiting the algorithms used to publish aggregate information about the statistical database, which limits the disclosure of private information about the records that are in the database. For example, differentially private algorithms are used by some government agencies to publish demographic information or other statistical aggregates while maintaining the confidentiality of survey responses, and by companies to collect information about user behavior while monitoring what is visible even to internal analysts. Roughly speaking, an algorithm is differentially private if the observer, seeing its output, cannot say whether the information of a particular person was used in the calculations. Differential confidentiality is often discussed in the context of identifying individuals who may be in the database. While this does not directly apply to identification and re-identification attacks, differentially private algorithms are likely to resist such attacks (Table 1).

Table 1. Example of implementation and features of calculating risk

Anonymization method	Application	Risk calculation features
Permutation, Swapping	For the selected general group, the change of quasi-identifiers	Requires extensive attribute processing
Local Generalization	example: address →street → city →region	Based on anonymization metrics
Aggregation	Representation of generalized records	For big data and rare groups, the risk of pooled sets
Reduction	Used as a last resort as it destroys data	Significant degradation of data quality
Local Suppression	For example, to hide rare diseases, or the family status of young participants	Deterioration in utility. Risk - according to anonymization metrics
Masking	For example, credit cards are represented as XXXX XXXX XXXX6789	Loss of data quality, only suitable for certain data types
Pseudo-anonymization	For example, by splitting data or direct hashing	Vulnerable by preserving data uniqueness
Deterministic encryption	Create searchable ciphertexts	Limited to use on relatively small datasets
Homomorphic encryption	Creation of encrypted and searchable texts	Limited to use over relatively small datasets
Sampling	Small set statistical construction	Loss of quality due to safety

3.2 Privacy Models

Risk is a possible damage, that is, a combination (as a rule, a product), the likelihood of a threat being realized and damage from it.

Note that the threat and risk are determined not in general, but in relation to a specific protected resource. In the terminology of the theory of business process management, instead of a resource, a synonymous concept is used - an asset, which defines everything that has value for an organization, for example: databases, hardware and software, network infrastructure, specialists.

In the process of depersonalization, not only information about identifiers is lost, but also links between individual records, dependencies, information about average values, etc. It is difficult to estimate such losses on a sufficiently large data set, therefore, utility measures are applied:

1. Classification metric - loss of data value when performing a classification task;
2. Reuse metric - loss of granularity (on the number of unique attribute values within an equivalence class);

3. Shannon's measure is a measure based on the entropy of information, based on the assumption that the increase in information is equal to the lost uncertainty;

4. The measure of mutual utility is a measure based on the assessment of the granulation of information; it decreases with an increase in the size of the equivalence class (Fig. 2).

Graph Metrics	Pre-Analysis	Iteration-1	Iteration-2	Iteration-3
Nodes	36692	39521	40496	40983
Edges	183831	193726	205819	207883
Degree Distribution	5.01	4.9	5.08	5.07
Diameter	11	12	13	14
Clustering Coefficient	0.49	0.51	0.53	0.56
Data Utility		96.34	90.75	85.75

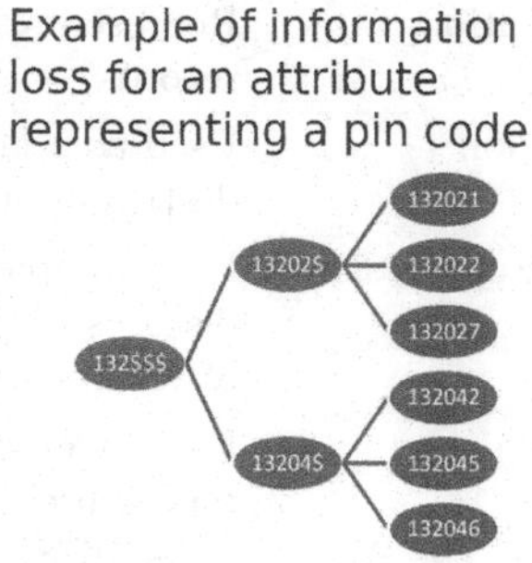

Example of information loss for an attribute representing a pin code

Fig. 2. Metrics of usefulness

Information security threats are classified according to a number of criteria:

- due to the occurrence (natural or man-made, including intentional or accidental);
- by source location (external or internal);
- by compromising subsystem or segment (network, cryptographic, etc.);
- by the stage of formation in the life cycle of the system (implementation and operational); by the resulting action (violate the level of confidentiality, integrity or availability).

3.3 Privacy Testing

Scripting Method. This method is the most natural in risk analysis, since it involves the formulation of those scenarios that can be realized in practice, and the assessment of financial results in each of these scenarios. In a particular case, when at each moment of time each of the recognized significant factors takes on a finite number of values (or the values are combined into a finite number of distinguishable groups), a scenario tree is drawn up. However, a direct analysis of all the possibilities is often impossible. Therefore, in most cases, some criteria are developed by which the scenarios are compared, and only a part of the scenarios called non-dominated is analyzed. In this formulation, the scenario method is somewhat modified - not those scenarios that are realized with different values of the uncertainty factors are considered, instead of them, the sets of our criteria are considered, depending on the decision we have already made, and the risk here can be taken into account as one of the criteria.

An obvious example of such criteria can be profitability (which must be maximized) and risk (it must be minimized). It is hardly possible to obtain a solution that is optimal for both criteria. It is clear, however, that a scenario in which both the risk is greater and the return is less always yields to the scenario with a higher return and less risk. Thus, among the scenarios, one can single out those for which there are, of course, the best (dominant) scenarios, and the remaining - non-dominant, which should be used as candidates for choosing a rational solution.

Decision-making on a large number of sometimes conflicting criteria from the point of view of a mathematician is one of the problems of multicriteria optimization. Another typical object arising in the formalization of the problem of financial risk management is the problem of stochastic optimization, which takes into account the presence of a random component. In this case, in the presence of randomness, the average value of some indicator is optimized. One of the numerical methods for solving the stochastic optimization problem is the Monte Carlo method (Fig. 3).

Monte Carlo Method. (one of the simulation methods) is applied when it is difficult to analytically calculate the mathematical expectation of a particular indicator. One way to calculate averages (as well as probabilities) is to run a large number of experiments. A series of random numbers generated by the corresponding sensor (more precisely, they should be called pseudo-random) are used as data for the assessment. Based on these data, a large number of scenarios are simulated, and to estimate the unknown mathematical expectation in accordance with the law of large numbers, the sample mean is used, which is the desired numerical estimate.

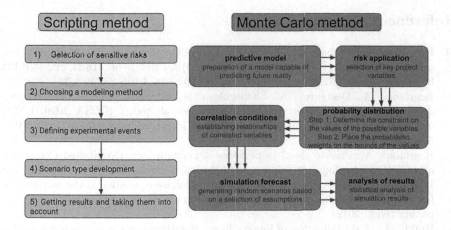

Fig. 3. Stress testing algorithm

In financial risk management, problems requiring the use of the Monte Carlo method arise quite often. It is important to understand that using this method involves a lot of computation. Therefore, if the system uses this method to help traders make decisions in real time, it requires serious computing power. Especially often the Monte Carlo method is used to solve the problem of pricing the so-called exotic options.

4   Conclusion

The issue of data security is a complex problem closely related to both the quality of data and the architecture of the systems used to process and store them. It becomes especially acute with the transition to Big Data. To build such systems, you have to apply completely new approaches to security, essentially determined by the type of data. As a result of the application of anonymization methods, data are obtained that have varying degrees of anonymization. The security of the dataset obtained cannot be judged solely on the basis of the data itself. External and internal connections have a significant impact: the availability of additional information, the attacker's motivation, the legal framework, the IT systems used, management practices, etc. This leads to the division of risk between the risks of the data itself (taking into account the applied methods of anonymization) and the risks of the environment (contextual risks). Most are based on the concept of an equivalence class - the ability to select identical records within a dataset in terms of quasi-identifiers. Therefore, the main parameters for evaluating the model depend on the type and quality of data, and not on a specific case, since for different types of attacks, attackers (such as a "marketer", "prosecutor", "journalist", which can be used in the scenario method) are based on the size of the equivalence class of the data itself.

References

1. Bogdanov, A., Uteshev, A., Khvatov, V.: Error detection in the decentralized voting protocol. In: Misra, S., et al. (eds.) ICCSA 2019. LNCS, vol. 11620, pp. 485–494. Springer, Cham (2019). https://doi.org/10.1007/978-3-030-24296-1_38
2. Bogdanov, A., Degtyarev, A., Shchegoleva, N., Khvatov, V.: Data quality in a decentralized environment. In: Gervasi, O., et al. (eds.) ICCSA 2020. LNCS, vol. 12251, pp. 58–71. Springer, Cham (2020). https://doi.org/10.1007/978-3-030-58808-3_6
3. Bogdanov, A.: Private cloud vs personal supercomputer. Distributed Computing and GRID Technologies in Science and Education, pp. 57–59. JINR, Dubna (2012)
4. Bogdanov, A, Shchegoleva, N., Ulitina, I.: Database ecosystem is the way to data lakes. In: Proceedings of the 27th Symposium on Nuclear Electronics and Computing (NEC 2019)
5. Rinku, N., et al.: Detection of forgery in art paintings using machine learning. Int, J. Innov. Res. Sci. Eng. Technol. 6(5), 8681–8692 (2017)
6. Di Pietro, R., Salleras, X., Signorini, M., Waisbard, E.: A blockchain-based distributed Trust System for the Internet of Things (2018)

7. The Trust Chain Consensus, COTI Whitepaper. https://coti.io/files/COTI-technical-whitepaper.pdf
8. Guidelines for the application of Roskomnadzor order of September 5, 2013 N 996 "On approval of requirements and methods for anonymization of personal data"
9. The Anonymization Decision-Making Framework, UKAN (2016)
10. El Emam, K., Arbuckle, L.: Anonymizing Health Data. O'Reilly, Sebastopol (2014)
11. Tomashchuk, O., Van Landuyt, D., Pletea, D., Wuyts, K., Joosen, W.: A data utility-driven benchmark for de-identification methods. In: Gritzalis, S., Weippl, E.R., Katsikas, S.K., Anderst-Kotsis, G., Tjoa, A.M., Khalil, I. (eds.) TrustBus 2019. LNCS, vol. 11711, pp. 63–77. Springer, Cham (2019). https://doi.org/10.1007/978-3-030-27813-7_5
12. Iyengar, V.S.: Transforming data to satisfy privacy constraints. In: Proceedings of the Eighth ACM SIGKDD International Conference on Knowledge Discovery and Data Mining - KDD 2002, p. 279 (2002)
13. NISTIR 8062. An Introduction to Privacy Engineering and Risk Management in Federal Systems
14. Ito, K., Kogure, J., Shimoyama, T., Tsuda, H.: De-identification and Encryption Technologies to Protect Personal Information (2016)
15. Gómez-Silva, M.J., Armingol, J.M., de la Escalera, A.: Triplet permutation method for deep learning of single-shot person re-identification. Fujitsu Sci. Tech. J. **52**(3), 28–36 (2020)
16. Lee, Y.J., Lee, K.H.: What are the optimum quasi-identifiers to reidentify medical records? In: ICACT Transactions on Advanced Communications Technology (TACT), vol. 6, no. 4, July 2017

Automated Marking of Underwater Animals Using a Cascade of Neural Networks

Oleg Iakushkin[1,3]([✉]), Ekaterina Pavlova[1,3], Evgeniy Pen[3], Anna Frikh-Khar[3,4], Yana Terekhina[2], Anna Bulanova[2], Nikolay Shabalin[2], and Olga Sedova[1]

[1] Saint-Petersburg University, Saint Petersburg, Russia
o.yakushkin@spbu.ru
[2] Lomonosov Moscow State University, Moscow, Russia
[3] BioGeoHab, Saint Petersburg, Russia
[4] Marine Research Center, Lomonosov Moscow State University, Moscow, Russia
https://www.biogeohab.com

Abstract. In this work, a multifactorial problem of analyzing the seabed state of plants and animals using photo and video materials is considered. Marine research to monitor benthic communities and automatic mapping of underwater landscapes make it possible to qualitatively assess the state of biomes. The task includes several components: preparation of a methodology for data analysis, their aggregation, analysis, presentation of results. In this work, we focused on methods for automating detection and data presentation.

For deep-sea research, which involves the detection, counting and segmentation of plants and animals, it is difficult to use traditional computer vision techniques. Thanks to modern automated monitoring technologies, the speed and quality of research can be increased several times while reducing the required human resources using machine learning and interactive visualization methods.

The proposed approach significantly improves the quality of the segmentation of objects underwater. The algorithm includes three main stages: correction of image distortions underwater, image segmentation, selection of individual objects. Combining neural networks that successfully solve each of the tasks separately into a cascade of neural networks is the optimal method for solving the problem of segmentation of aquaculture and animals.

Using the results obtained, it is possible to facilitate the control of the ecological state in the world, to automate the task of monitoring underwater populations.

Keywords: Few-shot learning · Neural networks · Video analysis · Segmentation

© Springer Nature Switzerland AG 2021
O. Gervasi et al. (Eds.): ICCSA 2021, LNCS 12956, pp. 460–470, 2021.
https://doi.org/10.1007/978-3-030-87010-2_34

1   Introduction

Today, marine research is relevant for monitoring benthic communities [22] and automatic mapping of underwater landscapes [9]. The tasks of segmentation and recognition underwater can be solved using machine learning methods [15]. Counting populations is necessary for analyzing the ecological state of the environment.

It is necessary to have labelled sets of various data to analyze data from photo and video observations. The existing databases describing the biological diversity of the deep seabed are scattered and contain little structured information. Also, the problem of creating extensive databases lies in the rarity of many benthic inhabitants, as a result of which the number of images of a certain species of animals can be very small. That is why it is advisable to solve the problem of segmentation of underwater communities with the help of neural networks solving the Few Shot Learning [11] class of problems. The peculiarity of FSL tasks is that with their help it is possible to segment an object having only a few images of each species of animals and plants. We prepared small datasets containing 60 species of marine life, and also analyzed the freely available datasets.

The study of benthic communities can also consist of determining the habitat on the map and calculating the volumes of the objects under study. 3D modelling of plant and animal surface coverage from the video can help localize the main biotopes on maps [24]. Localization coverage counts can be used for further environmental studies.

This paper will present a solution to the problem of counting deep-sea sedentary inhabitants using neural network technologies.

2   Problem Definition

The work aims to create a framework that solves the problem of marking, detecting and identifying sedentary underwater inhabitants on a map. To achieve this goal, it is necessary to solve several tasks, which in turn can be divided into 3 subsets presented in Fig. 1.

The tasks of the first stage are to form a dataset. After several iterations of finding objects, processing them and selecting object types, the main database will be formed. It will serve as a basis containing several photographs of the target objects, with the help of which the segmentation will be performed at the second stage of the work.

At the stage of preprocessing and segmentation, the video sequence undergoes preprocessing, which consists of splitting into frames and improving the image quality [17]. Finding and pre-training few-shot learning neural networks on underwater objects is one of the important tasks of the second stage. This task has the greatest impact on the quality of the result of the entire system.

After segmentation of objects, the third stage of mapping the bottom and localization of segmented objects begins on the 3D model built based on the video [21]. The constructed 3D model makes it possible to estimate the volume

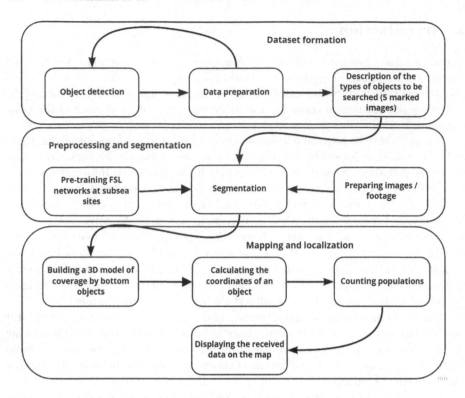

Fig. 1. Steps to complete the task of studying the seabed: dataset formation, preprocessing and segmentation, mapping and localization; and sequence of tasks.

of the object and its coordinates relative to the camera and the investigated point of the bottom [19].

3   Related Work

The article [10] described an approach for automatically detecting and segmenting underwater crabs for more accurate feeding. However, the significant disadvantages of this solution are the small depth of finding the animals, their close location to the camera. During deep-sea surveys, the terrain may not allow you to get so close to the objects of interest.

Our proposed solution is based on the creation of a cascade of neural networks, each of which is capable of solving one of the assigned tasks. The main tasks are: improving the quality of the image, segmentation and counting the coverage of surface individuals. By achieving the best result at every stage [12], it is possible to achieve the set goal. Neural networks must successfully cope with the tasks of unsupervised, semi-supervised or supervised segmentation on video or photos, as well as tasks of super-resolution for data preprocessing.

3.1   Architecture Components

One of the important criteria for choosing the algorithm components was the limitation on the size of the training dataset. Therefore, first of all, attention was paid to models capable of performing the segmentation without large-scale datasets (for example ImageNet and COCO). The model should perform the same task, but over several frames, that is, the number of training examples can be limited to five or less. An example of a model trained on FSS-1000 - a few-short segmentation database and described in the article [7,18]. The easy scalability of the FSS-1000 can also be attributed to the positive characteristics of this approach.

Convolutional neural networks efficiently handle the object segmentation task [20]. For a video stream, such problems are usually solved by separate processing of information about appearance and movement using standard 2D convolutional networks with the subsequent merging of two information sources. However, a new approach - DC-Seg, which is faster and more accurate than the masking described in the article [14], proposes to segment visible objects on video using 3D CNN. This approach has not previously been effectively used to solve computer vision problems.

Difficult terrain or objects that are too close to each other may make it difficult to segment them, and as a result, take them into account when counting. Therefore, the problem of segmentation of background or partially hidden object is also relevant for video monitoring of an underwater biotope. The semi-supervised model [25] aims to segment a specific object across the entire video sequence based on the object mask specified in the first frame. This technique can be useful for segmenting interactive objects.

Due to the nature of the underwater video, a hazy image is one of the most common obstacles to accurately masking an object. Therefore, a method was also tested, when the video sequence is divided into frames, to each of which SISR is applied [14] a generative super-resolution model for increasing the clarity of the frame.

To calculate the volume of coverage by bottom objects, it is necessary to compile a depth map for the landscape and segmented objects. Since we can only use one camera for underwater photography, we need to solve the Single-view reconstruction problem. The framework described in the article [23] solves this problem using a combination of 3 neural networks: DepthNet, PoseNet and FeatureNet for depth map prediction, egomotion prediction and feature learning respectively.

3.2 Data Preparation

Before solving the segmentation problem, it is necessary to create a set of classes of different species of animals and plants. In Fig. 1, after the object is detected, the data preparation stage begins, without which it is impossible to proceed to the segmentation stage. This is because the neural network needs small datasets with targets to be segmented in the image.

One of the most famous open databases - Fish Recognition Ground-Truth data [1], used in the Fish4Knowledge project to solve the problems of species detection and recognition [2]. However, it contains only 15 species of fish that live near the coral reef. Other datasets [3,4] contain about 500 views, but rectangles are used as object selection, in connection with which often the fins and parts of the body can be cut off.

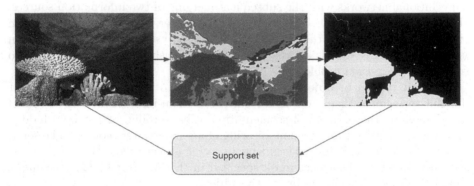

Fig. 2. Data preparation for support set: changing the resolution and size, semantic segmentation, highlighting the necessary masks.

SUIM Dataset for semantic segmentation of underwater imagery [13] could make it easier to create a dataset but contains 8 significantly larger than required classes, such as human divers or aquatic plants and sea-grass.

To solve the problem of segmentation of various marine life, a sample of 6 images for each species was created [16]. For this dataset, the resize the original image to 224 × 224 pixels and the creation of a black and white image mask of the same size was produced.

The first step in Fig. 1 is the automated creation of image masks and database preparation. With the help of a neural network that solves the semantic segmentation problem, different kinds of objects are segmented on each of the frames. After segmentation, the resulting masks belong to different classes of objects. The process of creating a dataset for its further use as a support set to generalize to unseen samples from a query set is shown in Fig. 2.

4   Implementation

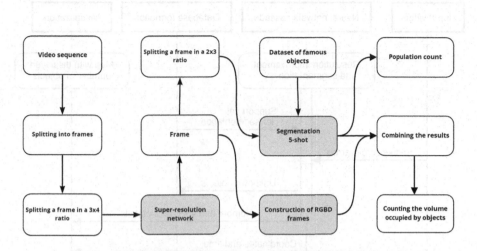

Fig. 3. Stages of video sequence processing.

Thus, at the first stage of dataset formation using the DC-Seg model, various kinds of objects are segmented on video materials, which will subsequently be marked up and formed into classes of 5 or more images (Fig. 4). At the second stage, video preprocessing takes place - splitting into frames and applying the super-resolution SISR model. With the help of a dataset prepared in advance at stage 1, the video sequence divided into frames is segmented using a 5-shot model pre-trained on the FSS-1000 dataset. The third stage begins by building a depth map for the incoming footage using the framework described above. The resulting RGBD frames are combined with previously segmented objects, which makes it possible not only to count the number of objects but also to calculate their occupied volume. The resulting solution is shown in Fig. 3.

The video sequence of underwater shooting is divided into frames, which, in turn, undergo preprocessing and, using a neural network, increase the image resolution. Segmentation of objects from the database performs on frames that have passed preprocessing. A more detailed description of the neural networks used is presented in the Table 1.

Unsupervised video segmentation task consists of segmentation of all pixels belonging to a "salient" object, while the categories of objects are not known a priori. The solution to this problem is necessary for the automatic collection of underwater databases. The 5-shot model uses elements of a previously created database as images of targets for segmentation. With SISR, each image frame is enlarged by 4 times.

Workflow

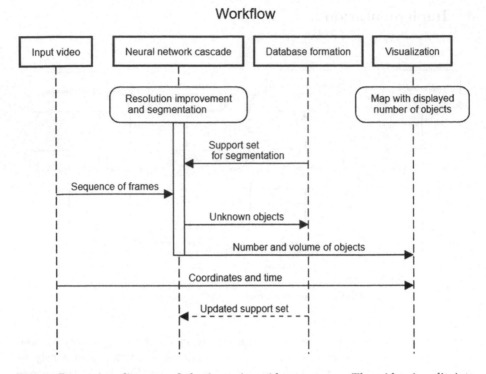

Fig. 4. Processing diagram of the incoming video sequence. The video is split into frames, each frame is processed by neural networks. Previously unknown objects are stored in the dataset. Coordinates, time and counting results are synchronized and visualized on the map.

Table 1. The main considered neural networks.

Model	Parameters	Pre-train model	Dataset	Applying segmentation
3DC-SEG	Total params: 103,244,936 Trainable params: 103,244,936	+	COCO, YouTubeVOS, DAVIS'17	Video segmentation (unsupervised task)
5-shot	Total params: 32,833,025 Trainable params: 32,833,025	+	FSS-1000	FSL segmentation
SISR	Total params: 1,944,579 Trainable params: 1,940,227	−	USR-248	Single Image Super-resolution

5   Visualization

The graphical display of results is generated using the open-source large-scale geolocation data sets [8] visualization application -Kepler.gl [5]. To build a relief on a world map you need to get high-rise models. We used global datasets [6] elaborated by NASA and NGA hosted on Amazon S3 and SRTM 90m Digital Elevation Database v4.1 elaborated by CGIAR-CSI. Using open libraries based on GDAL, the raster file is converted into a format suitable for Kepler.Gl.

Data derived from underwater survey videos, such as depth, latitude, longitude, surface area and timestamp, are built on top of global terrain digital models. Also, when rendered, the data is transformed from the dataset's own coordinate reference system to CRS84. The creation process is shown in Fig. 5.

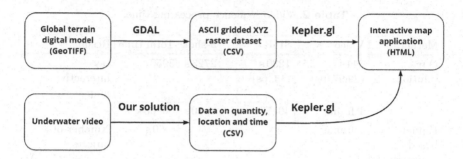

Fig. 5. The process of visualization of the depth map and the results obtained.

6   Results

One of the main problems we faced was the lack of underwater datasets for the segmentation of a large number of different objects. The solution to this problem has become part of the architecture of our system, with the help of which it is possible to form the necessary dataset from the original video sequence.

The lack of a large number of computational resources and the limited data contributed to the choice in favour of pre-trained models or models that do not require long training. However, the weights of the super-resolution model were obtained independently and published in the public domain.

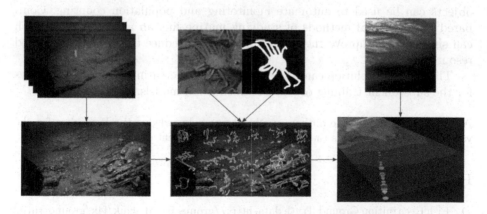

Fig. 6. Flowchart showing the results of each stage.

Today, there are a large number of solutions to the semantic segmentation problem, but underwater videos have a number of features, such as turbidity of the water, lack of light, partial visibility, etc. This imposes additional restrictions and makes it difficult to choose the architecture of the model.

Table 2. Video sequence processing time.

Method	Video	SISR	5-shot	Total time	Result
Our solution	144 s (29,97 fps)	1230 s (14 fps)	2723 s	3953 s	csv + interactive map
	1 frame	40–50 s	9–10 s	50–60 s	
Human based approach	1 frame			~60 s	Number of objects

The resulting solution is shown in Fig. 6. At each stage of the solution, the most modern methods and models are used. The neural networks and tools used are able to solve the assigned tasks quickly. The Table 2 shows the approximate operating time of the obtained automatic system in comparison with classical methods of bottom researches.

7   Conclusion

With the help of the presented architecture, it is possible to successfully solve the problem of marking and detecting sedentary underwater inhabitants.

New algorithms for image enhancement and segmentation of underwater objects can be used to automate monitoring and population counting. Compared to traditional methods of studying marine life, an automated approach can significantly improve the quality of data and reduce the number of wasted resources.

The resulting solution can be used as a basis for creating extensive databases for the subsequent training of static segmentation models.

Acknowledgments. The authors would like to acknowledge the Reviewers for the valuable recommendations that helped in the improvement of this paper.

References

1. Fish Recognition Ground-Truth data. http://groups.inf.ed.ac.uk/f4k/groundtruth/recog. Accessed 20 Mar 2021
2. Fish Species Recognition. http://www.perceivelab.com/datasets. Accessed 20 Mar 2021

3. Ozfish. https://aims.github.io/ozfish. Accessed 21 Mar 2021
4. Fish Dataset. https://wiki.qut.edu.au/display/raq/Fish+Dataset. Accessed 22 Mar 2021
5. Kepler.gl. https://github.com/keplergl/kepler.gl. Accessed 22 Mar 2021
6. LP DAAC - SRTMGL1. https://lpdaac.usgs.gov/products/srtmgl1v003. Accessed 22 May 2021
7. Azad, R., Fayjie, A.R., Kauffmann, C., Ben Ayed, I., Pedersoli, M., Dolz, J.: On the texture bias for few-shot CNN segmentation. In: Proceedings of the IEEE/CVF Winter Conference on Applications of Computer Vision, pp. 2674–2683 (2021)
8. Bakiev, M., Khasanov, K.: Comparison of digital elevation models for determining the area and volume of the water reservoir. Int. J. Geoinform. **17**(1), 37–45 (2021)
9. Benjamin, J., et al.: Aboriginal artefacts on the continental shelf reveal ancient drowned cultural landscapes in northwest Australia. PLoS ONE **15**(7), e0233912 (2020)
10. Cao, S., Zhao, D., Sun, Y., Liu, X., Ruan, C.: Automatic coarse-to-fine joint detection and segmentation of underwater non-structural live crabs for precise feeding. Comput. Electron. Agric. **180**, 105905 (2021)
11. Dong, N., Xing, E.P.: Few-shot semantic segmentation with prototype learning. In: BMVC, vol. 3 (2018)
12. Ghorbani, M.A., Deo, R.C., Kim, S., Hasanpour Kashani, M., Karimi, V., Izadkhah, M.: Development and evaluation of the cascade correlation neural network and the random forest models for river stage and river flow prediction in Australia. Soft Comput. **24**(16), 12079–12090 (2020). https://doi.org/10.1007/s00500-019-04648-2
13. Islam, M.J., et al.: Semantic segmentation of underwater imagery: dataset and benchmark. arXiv preprint arXiv:2004.01241 (2020)
14. Islam, M.J., Enan, S.S., Luo, P., Sattar, J.: Underwater image super-resolution using deep residual multipliers. In: 2020 IEEE International Conference on Robotics and Automation (ICRA), pp. 900–906. IEEE (2020)
15. Jian, M., Liu, X., Luo, H., Lu, X., Yu, H., Dong, J.: Underwater image processing and analysis: a review. Sig. Process. Image Commun., 116088 (2020)
16. Jung, A.B., et al.: imgaug (2020). https://github.com/aleju/imgaug. Accessed 1 Feb 2020
17. Li, C., Anwar, S., Porikli, F.: Underwater scene prior inspired deep underwater image and video enhancement. Pattern Recogn. **98**, 107038 (2020)
18. Li, X., Wei, T., Chen, Y.P., Tai, Y.W., Tang, C.K.: FSS-1000: a 1000-class dataset for few-shot segmentation. In: Proceedings of the IEEE/CVF Conference on Computer Vision and Pattern Recognition, pp. 2869–2878 (2020)
19. Liu, S., Yu, J., Ke, Z., Dai, F., Chen, Y.: Aerial-ground collaborative 3D reconstruction for fast pile volume estimation with unexplored surroundings. Int. J. Adv. Robot. Syst. **17**(2), 1729881420919948 (2020)
20. Miao, J., Wei, Y., Yang, Y.: Memory aggregation networks for efficient interactive video object segmentation. In: Proceedings of the IEEE/CVF Conference on Computer Vision and Pattern Recognition, pp. 10366–10375 (2020)
21. Nocerino, E., Menna, F., Chemisky, B., Drap, P.: 3D sequential image mosaicing for underwater navigation and mapping. Int. Arch. Photogramm. Remote Sens. Spat. Inf. Sci. **43**, 991–998 (2020)
22. Roach, T.N., et al.: A field primer for monitoring benthic ecosystems using structure-from-motion photogrammetry. JoVE (J. Vis. Exp.) **170**, e61815 (2021)

23. Shu, C., Yu, K., Duan, Z., Yang, K.: Feature-metric loss for self-supervised learning of depth and egomotion. In: Vedaldi, A., Bischof, H., Brox, T., Frahm, J.-M. (eds.) ECCV 2020. LNCS, vol. 12364, pp. 572–588. Springer, Cham (2020). https://doi.org/10.1007/978-3-030-58529-7_34

24. Urbina-Barreto, I., et al.: Quantifying the shelter capacity of coral reefs using photogrammetric 3D modeling: from colonies to reefscapes. Ecol. Ind. **121**, 107151 (2021)

25. Yang, Z., Wei, Y., Yang, Y.: Collaborative video object segmentation by foreground-background integration. In: Vedaldi, A., Bischof, H., Brox, T., Frahm, J.-M. (eds.) ECCV 2020. LNCS, vol. 12350, pp. 332–348. Springer, Cham (2020). https://doi.org/10.1007/978-3-030-58558-7_20

Wind Simulation Using High-Frequency Velocity Component Measurements

Anton Gavrikov[iD] and Ivan Gankevich[✉][iD]

Saint Petersburg State University, 7-9 Universitetskaya Emb.,
Saint Petersburg 199034, Russia
st047437@student.spbu.ru, i.gankevich@spbu.ru
https://spbu.ru/

Abstract. Wind simulation in the context of ships motions is used to estimate the effect of the wind on large containerships, sailboats and yachts. Wind models are typically based on a sum of harmonics with random phases and different amplitudes. In this paper we propose to use autoregressive model to simulate the wind. This model is based on autocovariance function that can be estimated from the real-world data collected by anemometers. We have found none of the data that meets our resolution requirements, and decided to produce the dataset ourselves using three-axis anemometer. We built our own anemometer based on load cells, collected the data with the required resolution, verified the data using well-established statistical distributions, estimated autocovariance functions from the data and simulated the wind using autoregressive model. We have found that the load cell anemometer is capable of recording wind speed for statistical studies, but autoregressive model needs further calibration to reproduce the wind with the same statistical properties.

Keywords: Load cell · Strain gauge · Anemometer ·
Three-dimensional ACF · Wind velocity PDF · Autoregressive model ·
Turbulence

1 Introduction

Wind simulation in the context of ship motion simulation is the topic where multiple mathematical models are possible, and the choice of the model depends on the purpose of the model. In the course of the research where we apply autoregressive model to ocean wave simulation, we decided to investigate whether the same model can be used to simulate wind flow around ship hull.

Wind simulation is studied at different scales and the closest scale for a ship in the ocean is wind turbine. One of the model that is used to describe air flow around wind turbines [12] is similar to Longuet—Higgins model which

---

Supported by Council for grants of the President of the Russian Federation (grant no. MK-383.2020.9).

O. Gervasi et al. (Eds.): ICCSA 2021, LNCS 12956, pp. 471–485, 2021.
https://doi.org/10.1007/978-3-030-87010-2_35

is typically used for ocean wave simulations. This model uses wind velocity frequency spectrum to determine coefficients and use them to generate wind velocity vector components.

Wind velocity distribution is described by Kaimal spectrum [10, 13]

$$S(f) = \frac{c_1 u_*^2 z / U(z)}{1 + c_2 \left(f z / U(z)\right)^{5/3}}, \quad u_* = \frac{kU(z)}{\ln\left(z/z_0\right)}, \quad c_1 = 105, \quad c_2 = 33.$$

Here u_* is shear velocity, $k = 0.4$ is von Karman constant, z_0 is surface roughness coefficient, f is frequency, z is height above ground, $U(z)$ is mean speed at height z.

This spectrum is used to simulate each wind velocity vector component at a specified point in space. For each component the same spectrum is used, but the coefficients are different [12]. The spectrum describes wind velocity vector in the plane that is perpendicular to the mean wind direction vector and travels in the same direction with mean wind speed. Time series is generated as Fourier series, coefficients of which are determined from the spectrum, and phases are random variables [12]:

$$V(t) = \overline{V} + \sum_{j=1}^{n} \left(A_j \sin \omega_j t + B_j \cos \omega_j t\right),$$

$$A_j = \sqrt{\frac{1}{2} S_j \Delta\omega} \sin \phi_j, \quad B_j = \sqrt{\frac{1}{2} S_j \Delta\omega} \cos \phi_j.$$

Here S_j is spectrum value at frequency ω_j, ϕ_j is random variable which is uniformly distributed in $[0, 2\pi]$. The result is one-dimensional vector-valued time series, each element of which is velocity vector at a specified point in time and space.

In order to simulate wind velocity vector at multiple points in space, the authors use the function of coherency — the amount of correlation between wind speed at two points in space. This function has a form of an exponent and depends on frequency [13]:

$$\mathrm{Coh}_{jk}(f) = \exp\left(-\frac{C \Delta r_{jk} f}{U(z)}\right),$$

where Δr_{jk} is the distance between i and j points and C is coherency decrement. Time series for each wind velocity vector component are generated independently and after that their spectra are modified in accordance with coherence function (the formulae are not presented here).

In order to simulate wind with autoregressive model it is easier to use autocovariance function instead of spectra and coherence function. We can obtain autocovariance function from spectra as inverse Fourier transform using Wiener—Khinchin theorem. The formula that we obtained this way using various computer algebra programmes is too complex, but can be approximated by a decaying exponent:

$$\gamma(t) = \sigma^2 \exp\left(-0.1 \frac{c_2^{3/5}}{c_1} t\right),$$

where σ^2 is process variance (area under the spectrum).

Unfortunately, this autocovariance function is one-dimensional and there is no easy way of obtaining three-dimensional analogue from the spectra. In order to solve this problem we looked into datasets of wind speed measurements available for the research. However, most of them contain either one or two wind velocity vector components (in a form of wind speed and direction), they are difficult to get and their resolution is very small (we found only one paper that deals with three components [15]). For our purposes we need resolution of at least one sample per second to simulate gusts and some form of turbulence. To summarise, our requirements for the dataset is to provide all three wind velocity vector components and has resolution of at least one sample per second.

We failed to find such datasets and continued our research into anemometers that can generate the required dataset. One of the anemometers that can record all three components is ultrasonic anemometer [1,6,14]. As commercial anemometers are too expensive for this research, we built our own version from the generally available electric components. However, this version failed to capture any meaningful data, and incidentally we decided to build an anemometer from load cells and strain gauges (which were originally intended for different research work). This anemometer is straightforward to construct, the electrical components are inexpensive, and it is easy to protect them from bad weather. This anemometer is able to record all three wind velocity vector components multiple times per second.

In this paper we describe how load cell anemometer is built, then we collect dataset of all three wind speed components with one-second resolution, verify this anemometer using commercial analogue, verify measurements from the dataset using well-established distributions for wind speed and direction, and estimate autocovariance functions for autoregressive model from our dataset. Finally, we present preliminary wind simulation results using autoregressive model.

2   Methods

2.1   Three-Axis Wind Velocity Measurements with Load Cell Anemometer

In order to generate wind velocity field using four-dimensional (one temporal and three spatial dimensions) autoregressive model, we need to use four-dimensional wind velocity autocovariance function. Using Wiener—Khinchin theorem it is easy to compute the function from the spectrum. Unfortunately, most of the existing wind velocity historical data contains only wind velocity magnitude and direction. We can use them to reconstruct x and y spectrum, but there is no way to get spectrum for z coordinate from this data. Also, resolution of historical data is too small for wind simulation for ship motions. To solve these problems, we decided to build our own three-axis anemometer that measures wind velocity for all three axes at one point in space multiple times per second.

To measure wind velocity we used resistive foil strain gauges mounted on the arms aligned perpendicular to the axes directions. Inside each arm we placed aluminium load cell with two strain gauges: one on the bending side and another one on the lateral side. Load cells use Wheatstone half-bridge to measure the resistance of the gauges and are connected to the circuit that measures the resistance and transmits it to the microcontroller in digital format. Microcontroller then records the value for each load cell and transmits all of them in textual form to the main computer. The main computer then adds a timestamp and saves it to the database. 3-D anemometer model is shown in Fig. 1.

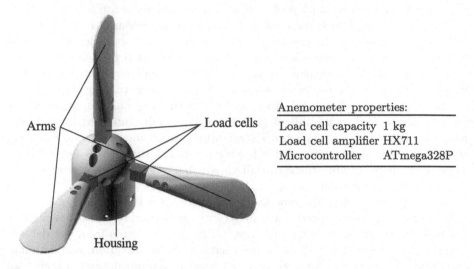

Anemometer properties:

Load cell capacity	1 kg
Load cell amplifier	HX711
Microcontroller	ATmega328P

Fig. 1. Three-axis anemometer. Arms are inserted into the housing and fixed using bolts that go through the circular holes. Red, green, blue colours denote load cells for x, y, z axes respectively (Color figure online).

Each load cell faces the direction that is perpendicular to the directions of other load cells. When the wind blows in the direction of particular load cell, only this cell bends. When the wind blows in an arbitrary direction which is not perpendicular to any load cell faces, then all load cells bend, but the pressure force is smaller. Pressures of all load cells are recorded simultaneously, and we can use Bernoulli's equation to compute wind velocity from them.

Bernoulli's equation is written as

$$\rho\frac{v^2}{2} + \rho g z = p_0 - p. \tag{1}$$

Here v is wind velocity magnitude, g is gravitational acceleration, z is vertical coordinate, ρ is air density, p is pressure on the load cell and p_0 is atmospheric pressure. Pressure force $\vec{F}$ acting on a load cell is written as

$$\vec{F} = pS\vec{n}, \tag{2}$$

where S is area of the side of the load cell on which the force is applied and $\vec{n}$ is normal vector. Arms in which load cells reside have front and back side with much larger areas than the left and right side, therefore we neglect forces on them. Additionally, on the ground $\rho g z$ term vanishes.

For all load cells we have a system of three equations

$$\begin{cases} v_x^2 \propto F_x \\ v_y^2 \propto F_y \\ v_z^2 \propto F_z \end{cases}. \tag{3}$$

Hence $v_x = \alpha_x \sqrt{F_x}$, $v_y = \alpha_y \sqrt{F_y}$, $v_z = \alpha_z \sqrt{F_z}$ where $\alpha_{x,y,z}$ are constants of proportionality. Therefore, to obtain wind velocity we take *square root* of the value measured by the load cell and multiply it by some coefficient determined empirically during anemometer calibration.

2.2 Per-Axis Probability Distribution Function for Wind Velocity

Scalar wind velocity is described by Weibull distribution [9]. Weibull probability distribution function is written as

$$f(v; b, c) = bc (bv)^{c-1} \exp\left(-(bv)^c\right). \tag{4}$$

Here $v > 0$ is scalar wind velocity, $b > 0$ is scale parameter and $c > 0$ is shape parameter. This function is defined for positive wind velocity, since scalar wind velocity is a length of wind velocity vector $v = \sqrt{v_x^2 + v_y^2 + v_z^2}$. However, projection of wind velocity vector on x, y or z axis may be negative. Our solution to this problem is to use two Weibull distributions: one for positive and one for negative projection — but with different parameters.

$$f(v_x; b_1, c_1, b_2, c_2) = \begin{cases} b_1 c_1 (b_1 |v_x|)^{c_1-1} \exp\left(-(b_1 |v_x|)^{c_1}\right). & \text{if } v_x < 0 \\ b_2 c_2 (b_2 |v_x|)^{c_2-1} \exp\left(-(b_2 |v_x|)^{c_2}\right). & \text{if } v_x \geq 0 \end{cases}. \tag{5}$$

Here $b_{1,2} > 0$ and $c_{1,2} > 0$ are parameters of the distribution that control the scale and the shape, v_x is the projection of the velocity vector on x axis. The same formula is used for y and z axis.

2.3 Three-Dimensional ACF of Wind Velocity

Usually, autocovariance is modelled using exponential functions [3]. In this paper we use one-dimensional autocovariance function written as

$$K(t) = a_3 \exp\left(-(b_3 t)^{c_3}\right). \tag{6}$$

Here $a_3 > 0$, $b_3 > 0$ and $c_3 > 0$ are parameters of the autocovariance function that control the shape of the exponent.

In order to construct three-dimensional autocovariance function we assume that one-dimensional autocovariance function is the same for each coordinate and multiply them.

$$K\left(t, x, y, z\right) = a \exp\left(-\left(b_t t\right)^{c_t} - \left(b_x x\right)^{c_x} - \left(b_y y\right)^{c_y} - \left(b_z z\right)^{c_z}\right). \tag{7}$$

Here $a > 0$, $b_{t,x,y,z} > 0$ and $c_{t,x,y,z} > 0$ are parameters of the autocovariance function. Parameter a and $\exp\left(b\right)$ are proportional to wind velocity projection on the corresponding axis. Parameter c controls the shape of the autocovariance function in the corresponding direction; it does not have simple relationship to the wind velocity statistical parameters.

2.4   Data Collection and Preprocessing

We installed anemometer on the tripod and placed it on the balcony. Then we connected load cells to the microcontroller via HX711 load cell amplifiers and programmed the microcontroller to record the output of each sensor every second and print it on the standard output. Then we connected the microcontroller to the computer via USB interface and wrote a script to collect the data coming from the USB and store it in the SQLite database. We decided to store raw sensor values in the range from 0 to 65535 to be able to calibrate anemometer later.

We calibrated three-axis anemometer using commercial anemometer HP-866A and a fan that rotates with constant speed. First, we measured the wind speed that the fan generates when attached to commercial anemometer. Then we successively placed the fan behind and in front of each arm of our anemometer and measured values that the corresponding load cell reported for each side of the arm with and without the fan. Then we were able to calculate two coefficients for each axis: one for negative and another one for positive wind velocities. The coefficient equals the raw sensor value that is equivalent to the wind speed of $1\,\mathrm{m/s}$ (Table 1).

Table 1. Calibration coefficients for each arm of three-axis anemometer: C_1 is for negative values and C_2 is for positive values.

Axis	C_1	C_2
X	11.19	12.31
Y	11.46	11.25
Z	13.55	13.90

Table 2. Dataset properties.

Time span	36 days
Size	122 Mb
No. of samples	3 157 234
No. of samples after filtering	2 775 387
Resolution	1 sample per second

We noticed that ambient temperature affects values reported by our load cells: when the load cell heats up (cools down), it reports values that increase (decrease) linearly in time due to thermal expansion of the material. We removed this linear trend from the measured values using linear regression. The code in R [11] that transforms raw sensor values into wind speed is presented in listing 1.1.

Listing 1.1. The code that transforms raw load cell sensor values into wind speed projections to the corresponding axis.

```
sampleToSpeed ← function(x, c1, c2) {
  t ← c(1:length(x))
  reg ← lm(x~t)
  x ← x - reg$fitted.values  # remove linear trend
  x ← sign(x)*sqrt(abs(x))   # convert from force to velocity
  x[x<0] = x[x<0] / c1        # scale sensor values to wind speed
  x[x>0] = x[x>0] / c2        # using calibration coefficients
  x
}
```

Over a period of one month we collected 3.1M samples and filtered out 12% of them because they had too large unnatural values. We attributed these values to measurement errors as they spread uniformly across all the time span and are surrounded by the values of regular magnitude. After that we divided each day into two-hour intervals over which we collected the statistics individually. The statistics for each interval is presented in Fig. 2, dataset properties are presented in Table 2.

Unique feature of three-axis anemometer is that it measures both velocity of incident air flow towards the arms and the turbulent flow that forms behind the arms. Turbulent flow velocity distribution peak is often smaller than the peak of incident flow. To exclude it from the measurements one can choose the side with the largest peak (either positive or negative part of (5)), but in this paper we left them as is for the purpose of the research.

3   Results

3.1   Anemometer Verification

In order to verify that our anemometer produces correct measurements we calculated wind speed and direction from the collected samples and fitted them into Weibull distribution and von Mises distribution respectively. These are typical models for wind speed and direction [4,5]. Then we found the intervals with the best and the worst fit for these models using normalised root-mean-square error (NRMSE) calculated as

$$\text{NRMSE} = \frac{\sqrt{\text{E}\left[(X_{\text{observed}} - X_{\text{estimated}})^2\right]}}{X_{\max} - X_{\min}}. \tag{8}$$

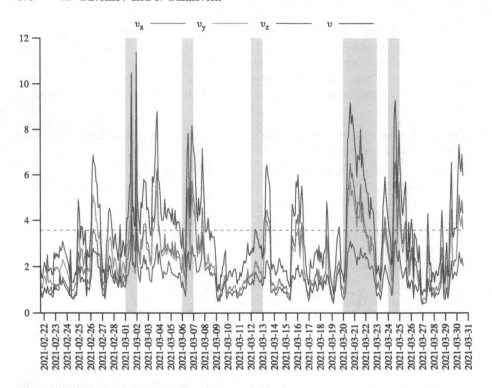

Fig. 2. The statistics for each interval of the collected data. Here v_x, v_y and v_z are mean speeds for each interval for the corresponding axes, v is mean scalar wind speed for each interval. The horizontal line shows overall average speed. Yellow rectangles denote days when EMERCOM of Russia (https://en.mchs.gov.ru/) reported wind speeds above average (Color figure online).

Here E is statistical mean, X_{observed} and $X_{\text{estimated}}$ are observed and estimated values respectively.

The wind speed data collected with three-axis anemometer was approximated by Weibull distribution using least-squares fitting. Negative and positive wind speed projections to each axis both have this distribution, but with different parameters. Most of the data intervals contain only one prevalent mean wind direction, which means that one of the distributions is for incident wind flow on the arm of the anemometer and another one is for the turbulent flow that forms behind the arm. For z axis both left and right distributions have similar shapes, for x and y axes the distribution for incident flow is taller than the distribution for turbulent flow. The best-fit and worst-fit distributions for each axis are presented in Fig. 3.

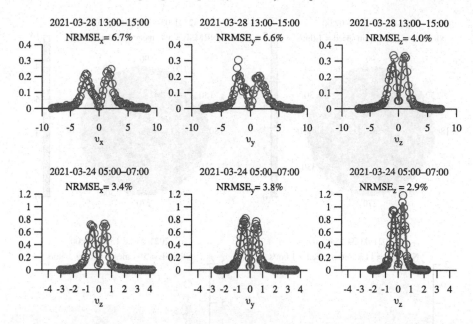

Fig. 3. Per-axis wind velocity distributions fitted into Weibull distribution. Data intervals with the largest error (the first row), data intervals with the smallest error (the second row). Red line shows estimated probability density of positive wind speed projections, blue line shows estimated probability density of negative wind speed projections and circles denote observed probability density of wind speed projections (Color figure online).

Wind direction was approximated by von Mises distribution using least-squares fitting. Following the common practice [7] we divided direction axis into sectors: from $-180°$ to $-90°$, from $-90°$ to $0°$, from 0 to $90°$ and from $90°$ to $180°$ — and fitted each sector independently. We chose four sectors to have one sector for each side of the anemometer. The best-fit and worst-fit distributions for each sector are presented in Fig. 4.

In order to verify that our anemometer produces correct time series we performed synchronous measurements with commercial anemometer HP-866A. Two anemometers were placed in the open field near the shore. The commercial anemometer was directed towards the mean wind direction as it measures the speed only. The data from the two anemometers was recorded synchronously. From the data we selected intervals with wind gusts and compared the

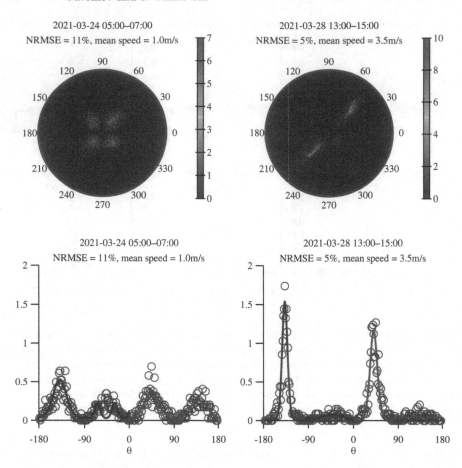

Fig. 4. Bivariate x and y velocity distribution in polar coordinates (first row), wind direction distributions fitted into von Mises distribution (second row). Data interval with the largest error (left column), data interval with the smallest error (right column). Red line shows estimated probability density of positive direction angles, blue line shows estimated probability density of negative direction angles and circles denote observed probability density of direction angles. 0° is north (Color figure online).

measurements of the two anemometers. To compare them we scaled load cell anemometer measurements to minimise NRMSE of the difference between the two time series to compensate for the errors in calibration coefficients. The results showed that there is some correspondence between the measurements of the two anemometers (Fig. 5).

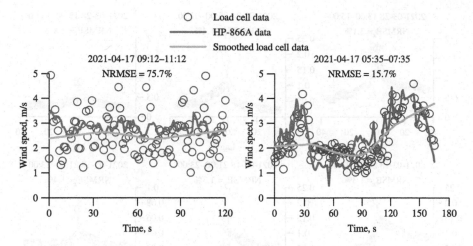

Fig. 5. Comparison of measurements obtained from three-axis and HP-866A anemometers.

Finally, we computed autocovariance for each axis as

$$K(\tau) = \mathrm{E}\left[\left(X_t - \bar{X}\right)\left(X_{t-\tau} - \bar{X}\right)\right] \tag{9}$$

and fitted it into (6). Per-axis ACFs have pronounced peak at nought lag and long tails. The largest NRMSE is 2.3%. Variances for x and y axes are comparable, but ACF for z axis has much lower variance. Parameters a and b from (6) are positively correlated with wind speed for the corresponding axis. The best-fit and worst-fit ACFs for each axis are presented in Fig. 6.

3.2   Turbulence Coefficient

Since our anemometer measures both incident and turbulent flow we took an opportunity to study the speed of the turbulent flow in relation to incident flow. We calculated the absolute mean values of positive and negative wind velocity projections for each time interval of the dataset. We considered the flow with the larger absolute mean value incident, and the other one is turbulent. Then we calculated turbulence coefficient as the ratio of absolute mean speed of turbulent flow to the absolute mean speed of incident flow. We found that the average ratio is close to 60%. It seems, that the ratio decreases as the wind speed increases for wind speeds of 1–5 m/s, but for higher wind speeds we do not have the data. Turbulence coefficient can be used in wind simulation models to control the magnitude of turbulent flow that forms behind the obstacle [8].

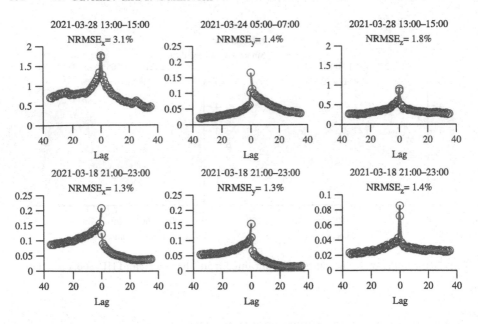

Fig. 6. Per-axis wind velocity ACF fitted into (6). Data intervals with the largest error (the first row), data intervals with the smallest error (the second row). Red line shows estimated ACF of positive wind speed projections, blue line shows estimated ACF of negative wind speed projections and circles denote observed ACF of wind speed projections. Note: graphs use mirrored axes (Color figure online).

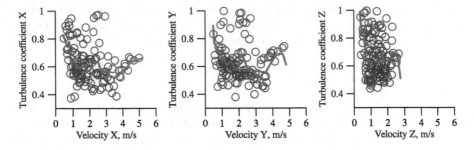

Fig. 7. The ratio of absolute mean speed of turbulent flow to the absolute mean speed of incident flow for each axis.

3.3   Wind Simulation Using Measured ACFs

We simulated three-dimensional wind velocity using autoregressive model implemented in Virtual Testbed [2] — a programme for workstations that simulates ship motions in extreme conditions and physical phenomena that causes them (ocean waves, wind, compartment flooding etc.). Using the data obtained with three-axis anemometer on March 28, 2021, 01:00–03:00 UTC we approximated four-dimensional autocovariance function using (7) by setting the corresponding parameters from one-dimensional autocovariance functions estimated from the data obtained with anemometer, all other parameters were set close to nought. Non-nought parameters are listed in Table 3. We found that velocity and direction distributions and ACFs of each axis of simulated wind and real wind are similar in shape, but are too far away from each other (see Fig. 8). We consider these results preliminary and will investigate them further in future work.

4 Discussion

NRMSE of wind speed distribution approximation has positive correlation with wind speed: the larger the wind speed, the larger the error and vice versa. Larger error for low wind speeds is caused by larger skewness and kurtosis (see the first row of Fig. 3). Similar approximation errors can be found in [5] where the authors improve approximation accuracy using joint wind speed and direction distributions. Such studies are outside of the scope of this paper, because here we verify anemometer measurements using well-established mathematical models, but the future work may include the study of these improvements.

NRMSE of wind direction distribution approximation has negative correlation with wind speed: the larger the wind speed, the smaller the error and vice

Table 3. Input parameters for AR model that were used to simulate wind velocity.

Axis	ACF a	ACF b	ACF c	Mean velocity, m/s
x	1.793	0.0214	0.2603	-2.439
y	1.423	0.01429	0.2852	-2.158
z	0.9075	0.06322	0.3349	-1.367

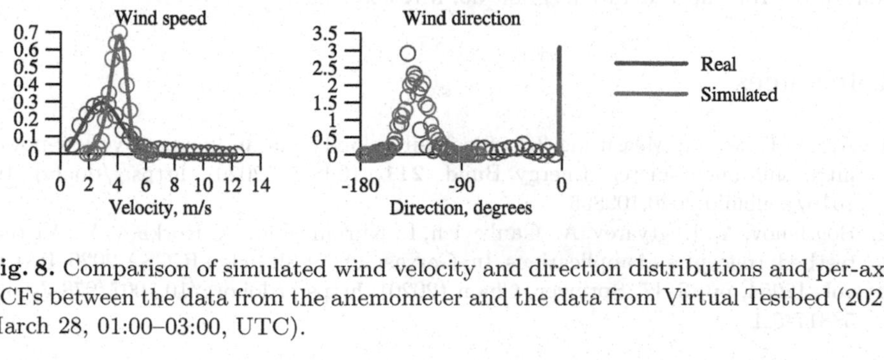

Fig. 8. Comparison of simulated wind velocity and direction distributions and per-axis ACFs between the data from the anemometer and the data from Virtual Testbed (2021, March 28, 01:00–03:00, UTC).

versa. This is in agreement with physical laws: the faster the flow is the more determinate its mean direction becomes, and the slower the flow is the more indeterminate its mean direction is.

Three-axis anemometer disadvantages are the following. The arm for the z axis is horizontal, and snow and rain put additional load on this cell distorting the measurements. Also, thermal expansion and contraction of the material changes the resistance of load cells and distorts the measurements. Pressure force on the arm is exerted by individual air particles and is represented by choppy time series, as opposed to real physical signal that is represented by smooth graph. The first two deficiencies can be compensated in software by removing linear trend from the corresponding interval. The last one makes anemometer useful only for offline studies, i.e. it is useful to gather statistics, but is unable to measure immediate wind speed and direction.

We used a balcony for long-term measurements and open field for verification and calibration. We found no clues that the balcony affected the distributions and ACFs of wind speed. The only visible effect is that the wind direction is always parallel to the wall which agrees with physical laws. Since we measure pressure force directly, the mean wind direction does not affect the form of the distributions, but only their parameters.

5   Conclusion

In this paper we proposed three-axis anemometer that measures wind speed for each axis independently. We analysed the data collected by this anemometer and verified that per-axis wind speeds fit into Weibull distribution with the largest NRMSE of 6.7% and wind directions fit into von Mises distribution with the largest NRMSE of 11%. We estimated autocovariance functions for wind speed for each axis of the anemometer and used this approximations to simulate wind flow in Virtual Testbed. The parameters of these functions allow to control both wind speed and mean direction. The future work is to construct an array of anemometers that is able to measure spatial autocovariance using the proposed anemometer as the base.

Acknowledgements. Research work is supported by Council for grants of the President of the Russian Federation (grant no. MK-383.2020.9).

References

1. Arens, E., et al.: Measuring 3D indoor air velocity via an inexpensive low-power ultrasonic anemometer. Energy Build. **211**, 109805 (2020). https://doi.org/10.1016/j.enbuild.2020.109805
2. Bogdanov, A., Degtyarev, A., Gankevich, I., Khramushin, V., Korkhov, V.: Virtual testbed: concept and applications. In: Gervasi, O., et al. (eds.) ICCSA 2020. LNCS, vol. 12254, pp. 3–17. Springer, Cham (2020). https://doi.org/10.1007/978-3-030-58817-5_1

3. Box, G.E.P., Jenkins, G.M.: Time Series Analysis: Forecasting and Control. Holden-Day, San Francisco (1976)
4. Carta, J.A., Bueno, C., Ramírez, P.: Statistical modelling of directional wind speeds using mixtures of von Mises distributions: case study. Energy Convers. Manage. **49**(5), 897–907 (2008). https://doi.org/10.1016/j.enconman.2007.10.017
5. Carta, J.A., Ramírez, P., Bueno, C.: A joint probability density function of wind speed and direction for wind energy analysis. Energy Convers. Manage. **49**(6), 1309–1320 (2008). https://doi.org/10.1016/j.enconman.2008.01.010
6. Cosgrove, M., Rhodes, B., Scott, J.B.: Ultra-low-cost logging anemometer for wind power generation feasibility surveys. In: Proceedings of the 14th New Zealand Electronics Conference, Wellington, New Zealand, pp. 153–158 (2007). https://hdl.handle.net/10289/1485
7. Feng, J., Shen, W.Z.: Modelling wind for wind farm layout optimization using joint distribution of wind speed and wind direction. Energies **8**(4), 3075–3092 (2015). https://doi.org/10.3390/en8043075
8. Gavrikov, A., et al.: Virtual testbed: simulation of air flow around ship hull and its effect on ship motions. In: Gervasi, O., et al. (eds.) ICCSA 2020. LNCS, vol. 12254, pp. 18–28. Springer, Cham (2020). https://doi.org/10.1007/978-3-030-58817-5_2
9. Justus, C.G., Hargraves, W.R., Yalcin, A.: Nationwide assessment of potential output from wind-powered generators. J. Appl. Meteorol. Climatol. **15**(7), 673–678 (1976). https://doi.org/10.1175/1520-0450(1976)015⟨0673:NAOPOF⟩2.0.CO;2
10. Kaimal, J., Wyngaard, J., Izumi, Y., Coté, O.: Spectral characteristics of surface-layer turbulence. Q. J. R. Meteorol. Soc. **98**(417), 563–589 (1972)
11. R Core Team: R: a Language and Environment for Statistical Computing. R Foundation for Statistical Computing, Vienna (2020). https://www.R-project.org/
12. Veers, P.: Modeling stochastic wind loads on vertical axis wind turbines. In: 25th Structures, Structural Dynamics and Materials Conference, p. 910 (1984)
13. Veers, P.S.: Three-dimensional wind simulation. Technical Report. Sandia National Labs, Albuquerque (1988)
14. Yakunin, A.G.: 3D ultrasonic anemometer with tetrahedral arrangement of sensors. In: Journal of Physics: Conference Series, vol. 881, pp. 12–30. IOP Publishing (2017)
15. Yim, J.Z., Chou, C.R., Huang, W.P.: A study on the distributions of the measured fluctuating wind velocity components. Atmos. Environ. **34**(10), 1583–1590 (2000). https://doi.org/10.1016/S1352-2310(99)00414-8

Testbed for the Extremal Waves Perturbations

Alexander V. Bogdanov[✉] and Vladimir V. Mareev[✉]

Faculty of Applied Mathematics and Control Processes, Saint-Petersburg State University,
Petergof, 198504 Saint-Petersburg, Russia
{bogdanov,map}@csa.ru

Abstract. The problem of forming mesoscale ocean waves is important for shipping, especially in connection with the increase in the size of supertankers and ferries. Although much research has been done on the formation and propagation of such waves, the question of the effect of background waves on wave behavior is unclear. We consider a model problem of soliton perturbation in the regime of extreme growth by various background wave fields. Due to the high complexity of this task, to solve it, it was necessary to use a specialized software and hardware complex (testbed) with software adapted for a hybrid architecture and special measures to suppress artifacts in complex nonlinear systems. Due to the essentially nonlinear nature of the propagation of extreme waves, a strong influence of background wave fields on the main wave was found.

Keywords: Mesoscale waves · Digital models · Numerical methods · Testbed · Extreme conditions

1 Introduction

The problem of the propagation of two-dimensional nonlinear waves has long been in the focus of researchers' attention due to its numerous applications in shipbuilding. Recently, special attention has been paid to mesoscopic-scale waves due to the specific extreme behavior and the special significance that it has for extra-large ships (supertankers and ferries). The wavelength of such a wave is comparable to the size of a supertanker, and its extreme growth can lead to severe maritime accidents. Although recently it has been possible to understand the features of the formation and growth of such waves, their stability and the effect of external wave disturbances on them has not yet been studied.

In this communication, we consider a model problem of perturbing an extreme wave by a wave field of various types. Several attempts [1–7] to deal with these problems have shown that it is not possible to achieve the result by simple approaches to calculations. Instabilities, artifacts, and distortion of the wave picture appear. Therefore, it was decided to create a specialized software and hardware complex (testbed) for this task, on which the approaches developed by the authors were tested.

© Springer Nature Switzerland AG 2021
O. Gervasi et al. (Eds.): ICCSA 2021, LNCS 12956, pp. 486–495, 2021.
https://doi.org/10.1007/978-3-030-87010-2_36

2 The Problem Statement

Consider the Kadomtsev – Petviashvili I equation:

$$\left[u_t + 0.5\left(u^2\right)_x + \beta u_{xxx} - G\right]_x = \eta u_{yy} \tag{1}$$

Equation (1) for the function $u(x, y, t)$ is specified in the domain $x, y \in (-\infty, \infty), t \geq 0$.

Numerical modeling was carried out for the transformed form of the Eq. (1):

$$u_t + \frac{1}{2}\left(u^2\right)_x + \beta u_{xxx} = S(x, y, t) + G(x, y, t), \beta \geq 0 \tag{2}$$

$$S(x, y, t) = \eta \frac{\partial^2}{\partial y^2} \int_{-\infty}^{x} u(x', y, t)\, dx', \eta \geq 0$$

where the source $G(x, y, t)$ in (2) is the specified perturbation.

The initial distribution is taken as a Gaussian distribution:

$$u(x, y, 0) = \sigma \exp\left[-d\left(x^2/a^2 + y^2/b^2\right)\right], \sigma > 0 \tag{3}$$

With the volume of the perturbation $V = \sigma \pi ab/d$ and a, b being the semiaxes.

Basic information on the construction of a numerical method for Eq. (2) can be found in our works [8–15].

Numerical modeling of Eq. (1) is carried out in a finite computational domain $[x_{\min}, x_{\max}] \times [y_{\min}, y_{\max}] \times [0, T]$. In the computational domain, a uniform space-time mesh is specified in coordinates x, y and time t:

$$x_j = j\Delta x, j \in [1, M], x_{\min} = x_1, x_{\max} = x_M$$

$$y_k = k\Delta y, k \in [1, L], y_{\min} = y_1, y_{\max} = y_L$$

$t^n = n\Delta t, n = 0, 1, 2, \ldots, T/\Delta t - 1$, with $\Delta x, \Delta y$ being the steps over the space coordinates, Δt being the time step.

Differential Eq. (2) is approximated on a given mesh and reduced to an implicit linearized finite-difference scheme. The resulting system of equations is solved using a five-point sweep.

The integral $S(x, y, t)$ is replaced by an approximate expression

$$\tilde{S}(x, y, t) = P(y) \cdot S(x, y, t),$$

with

$$P(y) = \begin{cases} 1, y \in [y_{\min} + \delta, y_{\max} - \delta] \\ h^-(y), y \in [y_{\min}, y_{\min} + \delta] \\ h^+(y), y \in [y_{\max} - \delta, y_{\max}] \end{cases} \tag{4}$$

The need to introduce such a procedure for smoothing the values of functions at the boundaries of the computational domain is discussed in detail in [13].

Finite smoothing on the segment δ is given in the form of a parabola

$$P(y) = ay^2 + by + c.$$

On the right side $h^-(y) = y^2$ with $y \in [y_{\min}, y_{\min} + \delta]$, and on the left side $h^+(y) = y^2 - 2y + 1$ with $y \in [y_{\max} - \delta, y_{\max}]$.

For the perturbation $G(x, y, t)$ at the edges of the region $x_{\min}$ and $x_{\max}$ similarly to expression (3) for the integral $\tilde{S}(x, y, t)$, the smoothing function is taken:

$$\tilde{G}(x, y, t) = P'(x) \cdot G(x, y, t),$$

где

$$P\prime(x) = \begin{cases} 1, & x \in [x_{\min} + \delta\prime, x_{\min} - \delta\prime] \\ h\prime^-(x), & x \in [x_{\min}, x_{\min} + \delta\prime] \\ h\prime^+(x), & x \in [x_{\max} - \delta\prime, x_{\max}] \end{cases} , \qquad (5)$$

Finite functions $P'(x)$, taking into account the direction of x, are similar to the case for the function $P(y)$ (4).

3   The Testbed

The performance of computation for such complex problem becomes crucial and due to matrix nature of internal loops it was decided to build a special testbed based on hybrid infrastructure.

The execution of a hybrid program consists of two parts: the host part of the program and the kernels that are executed on the GPU.

CPU AMD FX 8550   4 GHz

GPU AMD R9 380   970 Mhz

The host portion of the program defines the context in which the kernels are executed and controls their execution.

The main part of the execution model describes the execution of the kernels. When a kernel is queued for execution, an index space is defined. A copy of the kernel will be executed for each index from this space. A copy of the kernel running for a particular index is called a Work-Item or Thread and is identified by a point in the index space, that is, each "unit" is given a global identifier. Each unit executes the same code, but the specific path of execution (branches, etc.) and the data with which it operates may be different.

Work units are organized into groups (Work-Groups). Groups provide a larger partition in the index space. Each group is assigned a group ID with the same dimension that was used to address individual elements. Each element is associated with a unique, within the group, local identifier. In this way, work units can be addressed both by a global identifier and by a combination of a group and local identifier. There are slight differences between OpenCL and CUDA in how work units are organized and indexed, but these have no impact on the final functionality.

Units in a group are executed concurrently (in parallel) on the PE of one computing unit. The unified device model is clearly visible here: several PE $\Rightarrow$ CU, several CU $\Rightarrow$ device, several devices $\Rightarrow$ heterogeneous system.

The working unit executing the kernel can use four different types of memory:

- *Global memory.* This memory provides read and write access to members of all groups. Each unit can write to and read from any part of the memory object. Writing and reading of global memory can be cached depending on the capabilities of the device.
- *Constant memory.* A region of global memory that remains constant during kernel execution. The host allocates and initializes memory objects located in constant memory.
- *Local memory.* A memory area local to the group. This memory area can be used to create variables that are shared by the entire group. It can be implemented as a separate memory on the device. Alternatively, this memory can be mapped as an area in global memory.
- *Private memory.* The memory area owned by the unit. Variables defined in the private memory of one unit are not visible to others

The specification defines 4 types of memory, but does not impose any requirements on the implementation of memory in the device itself. All 4 types of memory can be located in global memory, and the separation of types can be carried out at the driver level, and on the contrary, there can be a strict separation of memory types dictated by the architecture of the device. The existence of these types of memory is quite logical: the processor core has its own cache, the processor has a shared cache, and the entire device has a certain amount of memory.

3.1 Programming Model

The OpenCL and CUDA execution model supports two programming models: Data Parallel and Task Parallel, and hybrid models are also supported. The main model that drives the design of both platforms is data parallelism.

3.2 Programming Model with Data Parallelism

This model defines computation as a sequence of instructions applied to multiple elements of a memory object. The index space associated with the execution model defines work units and how data is distributed among them. In a strict data parallelism model, there is a strict one-to-one correspondence between a unit and an element in a memory object with which the kernel can run in parallel. OpenCL and CUDA implement a softer data parallelism model where strict one-to-one correspondence is not required.

Both platforms provide a hierarchical data parallelism model. There are two ways to define hierarchical division. In an explicit model, the programmer defines the total number of items to be executed in parallel and how these items will be grouped. In the implicit model, the programmer only determines the total number of elements that should be executed in parallel, and the division into work groups is done automatically.

3.3 Programming Model with Job Parallelism

In this model, each copy of the kernel runs independently of any index space. Logically, this is equivalent to the execution of the kernel on a computational unit with a group consisting of one element. In such a model, users express concurrency in the following ways:

- use vector data types implemented in the device;
- queue up a lot of jobs;
- queue kernels that use a programming model orthogonal to the platform.

The existence of two programming models is also a tribute to versatility. The first model is well suited for modern GPUs and Cells. But not all algorithms can be effectively implemented within the framework of such a model, and there is also the possibility of a device whose architecture will be inconvenient for using the first model. In this case, the second model allows you to write applications specific to a different architecture.

3.4 Algorithm Migration Process

Before proceeding to the direct implementation of the hybrid version of the considered algorithm, it is necessary to investigate its acceleration potential and identify areas for optimization specific to hybrid platforms.

Optimization of Memory Transfer. The biggest obstacle to using GPUs in computing is the need to transfer data to and from the device. This gives us an obvious vector for optimization. Leaving these tasks on the device for several iterations can greatly increase overall performance.

Optimization of Device Memory Usage. 7The memory on a GPU device is not homogeneous and consists of several regions. They vary in size and speed by many orders of magnitude, and their correct use can bring tangible performance gains. We are interested in Global Memory, Shared Memory and Registers.

Load Optimization. Before starting the kernel, you need to set the "run configuration", which determines the size and number of thread blocks. Previous work has shown that choosing the optimal configuration can bring a fourfold increase in performance without changing the source code of the program.

4 The Test Problem

When choosing the sources $G(x, y, t)$, we focused on cases associated with perturbations of the form of a traveling wave moving with the speed $c > 0$. For all variants, the initial distribution was set at the following values: $V = 120, \sigma = 10, a = 2, b = 3, d = 1.570796$, the values of the parameters of the difference scheme being: number of nodes $M \times L = 800 \times 600, \Delta t = 5 \cdot 10^{-5}, \Delta x = \Delta y = 0.1, \varepsilon = 0.01$. The parameter ε is the amplitude for artificial convection in the smoothing procedure [13].

For the testing purposes, the model size was limited to 960 by 640 cells, with 200 iterations, which equates to 0.01 s of simulation time. The main attention was paid on the inter-column parallelization, which was found surprisingly straightforward, with little code changes required. Five-point tridiagonal matrix algorithm implementation required buffer arrays for each row, which were allocated using private memory which for datasets of this size is automatically projected onto the global device memory, and as such does not require additional synchronization. This resulted in an expected increase of performance.

The last step was to improve the five-point tridiagonal matrix algorithm parallelization. In this case local memory would not help as there is simply not enough of it to contain all the required data. The solution was to create a single buffer matrix and utilize the comparatively large 4 Gb global memory space. Big memory usage is unpleasant, but acceptable if it solves a much larger problem of slow global memory access.

Each matrix element is only dependent on the two previous ones, which allows us to store these two values in faster memory. This way, at the first stage of calculations, each iteration writes the data into global memory but does not read it, which allows the optimizer to perform a much faster asynchronous write. For subsequent iterations, the same data is stored in private memory, which is fast for both write and read. At the second stage of calculations, the intermediary data is only read from global memory, which avoid the need for additional synchronization. There was a risk that the intermediary data would not fit into the private memory, since it is very limited, but in practice, there were no problems with it, and it provided a significant boost to performance [10].

Next step was to implement the inter-row parallelism, at least in the trivial cases, such as calculation of U_{yy} and U_y matrices, which do not feature accumulation. This had significantly improved calculation times. This is most likely due to the memory block read optimization.

Some test results are given in the Table 1.

Table 1. Benchmark results

Version	Time (s)
CPU	28.683
GPU	1.355
GPU async	1.338
GPU 2d	0.304
GPU 2d async	0.302

Where CPU is the original implementation, GPU is simple column parallelization, GPU async is similar to GPU, but with asynchronous calling for cores, GPU 2d is parallelization in both rows and columns.

You can see that even simple parallelization by columns gave almost a 20-fold increase in performance, while parallelization by rows and columns increased it up to 90-fold.

4.1 Exponential Wave

Perturbation

$$G(x, y, t) = A \, \exp\left[-\theta(x - x_w + vt)^2\right].$$

is a wave. Two cases are considered when $\theta = 0.1$. For these cas, the maximum for the exponent is obviously equal to the amplitude A. Case a): wave moves fm left to right at $v = -4$. The initial position of the wave at the moment $t = 0$ is reached at $x_w = -5.6$. Case b): wave moves from right to left at $v = +3$. The initial position of the wave at the moment $t = 0$ is reached at $x_w = 15$.

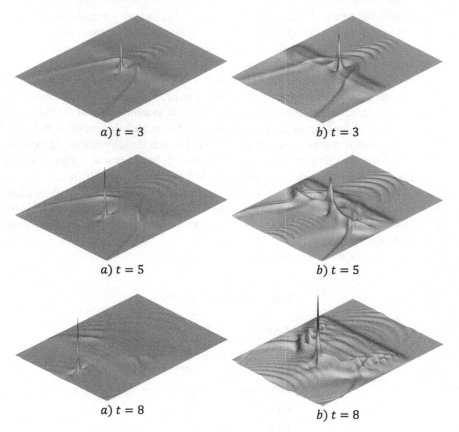

a) $t = 3$ b) $t = 3$

a) $t = 5$ b) $t = 5$

a) $t = 8$ b) $t = 8$

Fig. 1. Effect of an exponential wave formation of a soliton

To some extent, such a representation is like a single wave incident on a forming soliton.

Smoothing segments length δ from the system (4) and δ' from (5) is 10% of the length of $(x_{max} - x_{min})$ and $(y_{max} - y_{min})$, that is over x axis $\delta' = 8$, and over y axis $\delta = 6$, correspondingly. Let us present successive graphs of such an incident wave for $A = 1$ (Fig. 1).

4.2 Harmonic Wave

The perturbation form is represented as a harmonic:

$$G(x, y, t) = A \cos(\chi \cdot x - \omega \cdot t),$$

with A being the amplitude, $\varkappa$ being the wave number, $\omega = c \cdot \chi$, and c being the group speed.

Such a perturbation can be considered as a kind of ripple imposed on the forming soliton.

The length of the smoothing segments is 8% of the length of the sides of the computational domain, that is over x axis $\delta' = 6.4$, and over y axis $\delta = 4.8$, correspondingly.

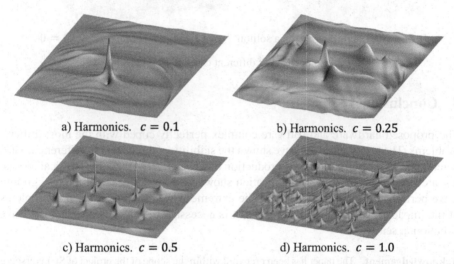

a) Harmonics. $c = 0.1$ b) Harmonics. $c = 0.25$

c) Harmonics. $c = 0.5$ d) Harmonics. $c = 1.0$

Fig. 2. Influence of harmonic perturbations on the destruction of a soliton

Let us present the results of calculations, fixing the amplitude $A = 1$ and changing the speed c. In this case, the wave number $\varkappa = \pi/10 = 0.3141592$. Figure 2 shows sequentially wave configurations for different velocities for the time moment $t = 8$.

It is interesting to compare the influence of perturbations at $t = 6$ on the soliton (Fig. 3b) for two extreme cases: without perturbations (Fig. 3a), that is $G(x, y, t) \equiv 0$, and only with perturbations without initial distribution (Fig. 3c), that is $u(x, y, 0) = 0$ (3).

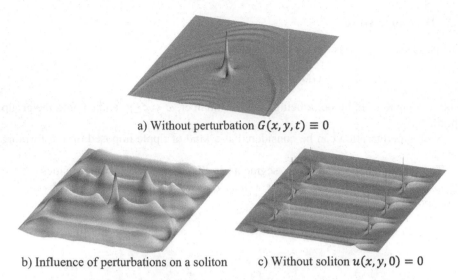

a) Without perturbation $G(x, y, t) \equiv 0$

b) Influence of perturbations on a soliton   c) Without soliton $u(x, y, 0) = 0$

Fig. 3. Comparison of different cases for $A = 1$, $c = 0.5$

5   Conclusion

The proposed hardware and software complex perfectly coped with the most difficult problems. The tests carried out have shown the stability of the system in different modes, reaching asymptotic and correct reproduction of wave effects. As for the physical results, research performed in this communication shows a strong influence of the background wave perturbation on the evolution of the extreme wave. Therefore, for real problems of the impact of extreme waves on ships, it is necessary to carefully consider the wave situation at sea.

Acknowledgement. The paper has been prepared within the scope of the project of St. Petersburg State University (id 51129503, 51129820).

References

1. Infeld, E., Rowlands, G.: Nonlinear Waves, Solitons and Chaos, 2nd edn., p. 406. Cambridge University Press, Cambridge (2000)
2. Rushchitsky, J.J.: Nonlinear ElasticWaves in Materials, p. 400. Springer International Publishing, Cham (2016)https://doi.org/10.1007/978-3-319-00464-8
3. Zeytounian, R.K.: Theory and Applications of Nonviscous Fluid Flows, p. 295.Springer Science & Business Media, Heidelberg (2012)https://doi.org/10.1007/978-3-642-56215-0
4. Kundu, A. (ed.) Tsunami and Nonlinear Wave, p. 316. Springer Science & Business Media, Heidelberg (2007). https://doi.org/10.1007/978-3-540-71256-5
5. Fujimoto, M.: Introduction to the Mathematical Physics of Nonlinear Waves, p. 156. Morgan & Claypool Publishers, San Rafael (2014)
6. Yang, J.: Nonlinear Waves in Integrable and Non-integrable Systems, p. 430. Society for Industrial and Applied Mathematics, Philadelphia (2010)

7. Todorov, M.D.: Nonlinear Waves: Theory, Computer Simulation, Experiment, p. 184. Morgan & Claypool Publishers, San Rafael (2018)
8. Bogdanov, A., Mareev, V.: Numerical simulation perturbed KdVB equation. In: EPJ Web of Conferences, vol. 108, p. 02014 (2016). MMCP 2015, Stará Lesná (2015)
9. Bogdanov, A.V., Mareev, V.V.: Numerical simulation KPI equation. In: Proceedings of the 15th International Ship Stability Workshop, 13–15 June 2016, Stockholm, Sweden, pp. 115–117.
10. Bogdanov, A.V., Mareev, V.V.: Hybrid approach for nonlinear wave equation. In: AIP Conference Proceedings, vol. 1863, p. 110005 (2017). Published by the American Institute of Physics (ICNAAM 2016), Rhodes, 9–25 September 2016
11. Bogdanov, A.V., Mareev, V.V., Kulabukhova, N.V., Degtyarev, A.B., Shchegoleva, N.L.: Influence of external source on KPI equation. In: Gervasi, O., et al. (eds.) ICCSA 2018. LNCS, vol. 10963, pp. 123–135. Springer, Cham (2018). https://doi.org/10.1007/978-3-319-95171-3_11
12. Bogdanov, A.V., Mareev, V.V., Storublevtcev, N.: Algorithms for the calculation of nonlinear processes on hybrid architecture clusters. In: Proceedings of the VIII International Conference "Distributed Computing and Grid-technologies in Science and Education" (GRID 2018), Dubna, Moscow region, Russia, 10–14 September, 2018, pp. 333–336
13. Bogdanov, A.V., Mareev, V.V.: On some problems of the numerical implementation of nonlinear systems on example of KPI equation. In: EPJ Web of Conferences, vol. 226, p. 01003 (2020). Mathematical Modeling and Computational Physics MMCP2019, Stara Lesha, 1–5 July 2019. https://doi.org/10.1051/epjconf/202022601003
14. Oran, E.S., Boris, J.P.: Numerical Simulation of Reactive Flow. Elsevier, Amsterdam (1987)
15. Feng, B.-F., Mitsui, T.: A finite difference method for the Korteweg-de Vries and the Kadomtsev-Petviashvili equations. J. Comput. Appl. Math. **90**(1), 95–116 (1998). https://doi.org/10.1016/S0377-0427(98)00006-5

Functional Programming Interface
for Parallel and Distributed Computing

Ivan Petriakov[iD] and Ivan Gankevich[✉][iD]

Saint Petersburg State University, 7-9 Universitetskaya Emb.,
St. Petersburg 199034, Russia
st049350@student.spbu.ru, i.gankevich@spbu.ru
https://spbu.ru/

Abstract. There are many programming frameworks and languages for
parallel and distributed computing which are successful both in industry and academia, however, all of them are isolated and self-contained.
We believe that the main reason that there is no common denominator
between them is that there is no intermediate representation for distributed computations. For sequential computations we have bytecode
that is used as an intermediate, portable and universal representation of
a programme written in any language, but bytecode lacks an ability to
describe process communication. If we add this feature, we get low-level
representation on top of which all the frameworks and languages for parallel and distributed computations can be built. In this paper we explore
how such intermediate representation can be made, how it can reduce
programming effort and how it may simplify internal structure of existing
frameworks. We also demonstrate how high-level interface can be build
for a functional language that completely hides all the difficulties that a
programmer encounters when he or she works with distributed systems.

Keywords: API · Intermediate representation · C++ · Guile

1 Introduction

There are many programming frameworks and languages for parallel and distributed computing [11,12,15–17] which are successful both in industry and
academia, however, all of them are isolated and self-contained. We believe that
the main reason that there is no common denominator between these frameworks
and languages is that there is no common protocol or low-level representation
for distributed computations. For sequential computations we have bytecode
(e.g. LLVM [9], Java bytecode, Guile bytecode) that is used as an intermediate,
portable and universal representation of a programme written in any language;
also we have assembler which is non-portable, but still popular intermediate
representation. One important feature, that bytecode and assembler lack, is an

---

Supported by Council for grants of the President of the Russian Federation (grant
no. MK-383.2020.9).

O. Gervasi et al. (Eds.): ICCSA 2021, LNCS 12956, pp. 496–510, 2021.
https://doi.org/10.1007/978-3-030-87010-2_37

ability to communicate between parallel processes. This communication is the common denominator on top of which all the frameworks and languages for parallel and distributed computations can be built, however, there is no universal low-level representation that describes communication.

Why common low-level representation exists for sequential computations, but does not exist for parallel and distributed ones? One of the reasons, which applies to both distributed and parallel computations, is the fact that people still think about programmes as sequences of steps — the same way as people themselves perform complex tasks. Imperative languages, in which programmes are written as series of steps, are still prevalent in industry and academia; this is in contrast to unpopular functional languages in which programmes are written as compositions of functions with no implied order of computation. Another reason which applies to distributed computations is the fact that these computations are inherently unreliable and there is no universal approach for handling cluster node failures. While imperative languages produce more efficient programmes, they do not provide safety from deadlocks and fault tolerance guarantees. Also, they are much more difficult to write, as a human have to work with mutable state (local and global variables, objects etc.) and it is difficult to keep this state in mind while writing the code. Functional languages minimise the usage of mutable state, provide partial safety from deadlocks (under the assumption that a programmer does not use locks manually) and can be modified to provide fault tolerance. From the authors' perspective people understand the potential of functional languages, but have not yet realised this potential to get all their advantages; people realised the full potential of imperative languages, but do not know how to get rid of their disadvantages.

In this paper we describe low-level representation based on *kernels* which is suitable for distributed and parallel computations. Kernels provide automatic fault tolerance and can be used to exchange the data between programmes written in different languages. We implement kernels in C++ and build a reference cluster scheduler that uses kernels as the protocol to run applications that span multiple cluster nodes. Then we use kernels as an intermediate representation for Guile programming language, run benchmarks using the scheduler and compare the performance of different implementations of the same programme.

To prevent ambiguity we use the term *parallel* to describe computations that use several processor cores of single cluster node, the term *distributed* to describe computations that use several cluster nodes and any number of cores on each node, and term *cluster* to describe anything that refers to local cluster (as opposed to geographically distributed clusters which are not studied in this paper). *Intermediate representation* in our paper is a particular form of abstract syntax tree, e.g. in functional languages *continuation passing style* is popular intermediate representation of the code.

2   Methods

2.1   Parallel and Distributed Computing Technologies as Components of Unified System

In order to write parallel and distributed programmes the same way as we write sequential programmes, we need the following components.

- Portable low-level representation of the code and the data and includes means of decomposition of the code and the data into parts that can be computed in parallel. The closest sequential counterpart is LLVM.
- Cluster scheduler that executes parallel and distributed applications and uses the low-level representation to implement communication between these applications running on different cluster nodes. The closest single-node counterpart is operating system kernel that executes user processes.
- High-level interface that wraps the low-level representation for existing popular programming languages in a form of a framework or a library. This interface uses cluster scheduler, if it is available and node parallelism is needed by the application, otherwise the code is executed on the local node and parallelism is limited to the parallelism of the node. The closest single-node counterpart is C library that provides an interface to system calls of the operating system kernel.

These three components are built on top of each other as in classical object-oriented programming approach, and all the complexity is pushed down to the lowest layer: low-level representation is responsible for providing parallelism and fault tolerance to the applications, cluster scheduler uses these facilities to provide transparent execution of the applications on multiple cluster nodes, and high-level interface maps the underlying system to the target language to simplify the work for application programmers.

High-performance computing technologies have the same three-component structure: message passing library (MPI) is widely considered a low-level language of parallel computing, batch job schedulers are used to allocate resources and high-level interface is some library that is built on top of MPI; however, the responsibilities of the components are not clearly separated and the hierarchical structure is not maintained. MPI provides means of communication between parallel processes, but does not provide data decomposition facilities and fault tolerance guarantees: data decomposition is done either in high-level language or manually, and fault tolerance is provided by batch job scheduler. Batch jobs schedulers provide means to allocate resources (cluster nodes, processor cores, memory etc.) and launch parallel MPI processes, but do not have control over messages that are sent between these processes and do not control the actual number of resources used by the programme (all resources are owned exclusively by the programme, and the programme decides how to use them), i.e. cluster schedulers and MPI programmes do not talk to each other after the parallel processes were launched. Consequently, high-level interface is also separated from the scheduler. Although, high-level interface is built on top of the low-level interface, batch job scheduler is fully integrated with neither of them: the cluster-wide counterpart of operating system kernel does not have control over communication of the applications that are run on the cluster, but is used as resource allocator instead.

The situation in newer big data technologies is different: there are the same three components with hierarchical structure, but the low-level representation is integrated in the scheduler. There is YARN cluster scheduler [14] with API that is used as a low-level representation for parallel and distributed computing, and there are many high-level libraries that are built on top of YARN [1,2,8,17]. The scheduler has more control over job execution as jobs are decomposed into tasks and execution of tasks is controlled by the scheduler. Unfortunately, the lack of common low-level representation made all high-level frameworks that are built on top of YARN API use their own custom protocol for communication, shift responsibility of providing fault tolerance to the scheduler and shift responsibility of data decomposition to higher level frameworks.

To summarise, the current state-of-the-art technologies for parallel and distributed computing can be divided into three classes: low-level representations, cluster schedulers and high-level interfaces; however, responsibilities of each class are not clearly separated by the developers of these technologies. Although, the structure of the components resembles the operating system kernel and its application interface, the components sometimes are not built on top of each other, but integrated horizontally, and as a result the complexity of the parallel and distributed computations is sometimes visible on the highest levels of abstraction.

Our proposal is to design a low-level representation that provides fault tolerance, means of data and code decomposition and means of communication for parallel and distributed applications. Having such a representation at your disposal makes it easy to build higher level components, because the complexity of cluster systems is hidden from the programmer, the duplicated effort of implementing the same facilities in higher level interfaces is reduced, and cluster scheduler has full control of the programme execution as it speaks the same protocol and uses the same low-level representation internally: the representation is general enough to describe any distributed programme including the scheduler itself.

2.2   Kernels as Objects that Control the Programme Flow

In order to create low-level representation for parallel and distributed computing we borrow familiar features from sequential low-level representations and augment them with asynchronous function calls and an ability to read and write call stack frames.

In assembler and LLVM the programme is written in imperative style as a series of processor instructions. The variables are stored either on the stack (a special area of the computer's main memory) or in processor registers. Logical parts of the programme are represented by functions. A call to a function places all function arguments on the stack and then jumps to the address of the function. When the function returns, the result of the computation is written to the processor register and control flow is returned to the calling function. When the main function returns, the programme terminates.

There are two problems with the assembler that need to be solved in order for it to be useful in parallel and distributed computing. First, the contents of the stack can not be copied between cluster nodes or saved to and read from the file, because they often contain pointers to memory blocks that may be invalid on another cluster node or in the process that reads the stack from the file. Second, there is no natural way to express parallelism in this language: all function calls are synchronous and all instructions are executed in the specified order. In order to solve these problems we use object-oriented techniques.

We represent each stack frame with an object: local variables become object fields, and each function call is decomposed into the code that goes before function call, the code that performs function call, and the code that goes after. The code that goes before the call is placed into **act** method of the object and after this code the new object is created to call the function asynchronously. The code that goes after the call is placed into **react** method of the object, and this code is called asynchronously when the function call returns (this method takes the corresponding object as an argument). The object also has **read** and **write** methods that are used to read and write its fields to and from file or to copy the object to another cluster node. In this model each object contains enough information to perform the corresponding function call, and we can make these calls in any order we like. Also, the object is self-contained, and we can ask another cluster node to perform the function call or save the object to disk to perform the call when the user wants to resume the computation (e.g. after the computer is upgraded and rebooted).

The function calls are made asynchronous with help of thread pool. Each thread pool consists of an object queue and an array of threads. When the object is placed in the queue, one of the threads extracts it and calls **act** or **react** method depending on the state of the object. There are two states that are controlled by the programmer: when the state is *upstream* **act** method is called, when the state is *downstream* **react** method of the parent object is called with the current object as the argument. When the state is *downstream* and there is no parent, the programme terminates.

We call these objects *control flow objects* or *kernels* for short. These objects contain the input data in object fields, the code that processes this data in object methods and the output data (the result of the computation) also in object fields. The programmer decides which data is input and output. To reduce network usage the programmer may delete input data when the kernel enters *downstream* state: that way only output data is copied back to the parent kernel over the network. The example programme written using kernels and using regular function call stack is shown in Table 1.

Table 1. The same programme written using regular function call stack (left) and kernels (right). Here `async_call` performs asynchronous function call by pushing the child kernel to the queue, `async_return` performs asynchronous return from the function call by pushing the current kernel to the queue.

```
int nested(int a) {            struct Nested: public Kernel {
  return 123 + a;                int result;
}                                int a;
                                 Nested(int a): a(a) {}
                                 void act() override {
                                   result = a + 123;
                                   async_return();
                                 }
                               };

void main() {                  struct Main: public Kernel {
  // code before                 void act() override {
  int result = nested();         // code before
  // code after                  async_call(new Nested);
  print(result);               }
}                                void react(Kernel* child) override {
                                   int result = ((Nested*)child)->result;
                                   // code after
                                   print(result);
                                   async_return();
                                 }
                               };

                               void main() {
                                 async_call(new Main);
                                 wait();
                               }
```

This low-level representation can be seen as an adaptation of classic function call stack, but with asynchronous function calls and an ability to read and write stack frames. These differences give kernels the following advantages.

- Kernels define dependencies between function calls, but do not define the order of the computation. This gives natural way of expressing parallel computations on the lowest possible level.
- Kernels can be written to and read from any medium: files, network connections, serial connections etc. This allows to implement fault tolerance efficiently using any existing methods: in order to implement checkpoints a programmer no longer need to save memory contents of each parallel process, only the fields of the main kernel are needed to restart the programme from the last sequential step. However, with kernels checkpoints can be replaced with simple restart: when the node to which the child kernel was sent fails, the copy of this kernel can be sent to another node without stopping the programme and no additional configuration from the programmer.

– Finally, kernels are simple enough to be used as an intermediate representation for high-level languages: either via a compiler modification, or via wrapper library that calls the low-level implementation directly. Kernels can not replace LLVM or assembler, because their level of abstraction is higher, therefore, compiler modification is possible only for languages that use high-level intermediate representation (e.g. LISP-like languages and purely functional languages that have natural way of expressing parallelism by computing arguments of functions in parallel).

2.3   Reference Cluster Scheduler Based on Kernels

Kernels are general enough to write any programme, and the first programme that we wrote using them was cluster scheduler that uses kernels to implement its internal logic and to run applications spanning multiple cluster nodes. Single-node version of the scheduler is as simple as thread pool attached to kernel queue described in Sect. 2.2. The programme starts with pushing the first (or *main*) kernel to the queue and ends when the main kernel changes its state to *downstream* and pushes itself to the queue. The number of threads in the pool equals the number of processor cores, but can be set manually to limit the amount of parallelism. Cluster version of the scheduler is more involved and uses kernels to implement its logic.

Cluster scheduler runs in a separate daemon process on each cluster node, and processes communicate with each other using kernels: process on node A writes some kernel to network connection with node B and process on node B reads the kernel and performs useful operation with it. Here kernels are used like messages rather than stack frames: kernel that always resides in node A creates child message kernel and sends it to the kernel that always resides in node B. In order to implement this logic we added *point-to-point* state and a field that specifies the identifier of the target kernel. In addition to that we added source and destination address fields to be able to route the kernel to the target cluster node and return it back to the source node: (parent-kernel, source-address) tuple uniquely identifies the location of the parent kernel, and (target-kernel, destination-address) tuple uniquely identifies the location of the target kernel. The first tuple is also used by *downstream* kernels that return back to their parents, but the second tuple is used only by *point-to-point* kernels.

There are several responsibilities of cluster scheduler:

– run applications in child processes,
– route kernels between application processes running on different cluster nodes,
– maintain a list of available cluster nodes.

In order to implement them we created a kernel queue and a thread pool for each concern that the scheduler has to deal with (see Fig. 1): we have

- timer queue for scheduled and periodic tasks,
- network queue for sending kernels to and receiving from other cluster nodes,
- process queue for creating child processes and sending kernels to and receiving from them, and
- the main processor queue for processing kernels in parallel using multiple processor cores.

This separation of concerns allows us to overlap data transfer and data processing: while the main queue processes kernels in parallel, process and network queues send and receive other kernels. This approach leads to small amount of oversubscription as separate threads are used to send and receive kernels, but benchmarks showed that this is not a big problem as most of the time these threads wait for the operating system kernel to transfer the data.

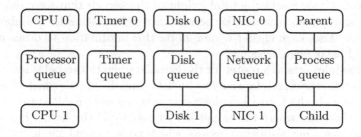

Fig. 1. Default kernel queues for each cluster scheduler concern.

Cluster scheduler runs applications in child processes; this approach is natural for UNIX-like operating systems as the parent process has full control of its children: the amount of resources can be limited (the number of processor cores, the amount of memory etc.) and the process can be terminated at any time. After introducing child processes into the scheduler we added cluster-wide source (target) application identifier field that uniquely identifies the source (the target) application from which the kernel originated (to which the kernel was sent). Also each kernel carries an application descriptor that specifies how to run the application (command line arguments, environment variables etc.) and if the corresponding process is not running, it is launched automatically by the scheduler. Child processes are needed only as means of controlling resources usage: a process is a scheduling unit for operating system kernel, but in cluster scheduler a child process performs something useful only when the kernel (which is a unit of scheduling in our scheduler) is sent to the corresponding application and launched automatically if there is no such application. Application spans multiple cluster nodes and may have any number of child processes (but no more than one process per node). These processes are launched on-demand and do nothing until the kernel is received. This behaviour allows us to implement dynamic parallelism: we do not need to specify the number of parallel processes on application launch, the scheduler will automatically create them. To reduce memory consumption stale processes, that have not received any kernel for a long period of time, may be terminated (new processes will be created automatically, when the kernel arrives anyway). Kernels can be sent from one application to another by specifying different application descriptor.

Child process communicates with its parent using optimised child process queue. If the parent process does not want to communicate, the child process continues execution on the local node: the applications written using cluster scheduler interface work correctly even when the scheduler is not available, but use local node instead of the cluster.

Since the node may have multiple child processes, we may have a situation when all of them try to use all processor cores, which will lead to oversubscription and suboptimal performance. In order to solve this problem, we introduce weight field which tells how many threads will be used by the kernel. The default is one thread for ordinary kernels and nought threads for cluster scheduler kernels. Process queue tracks the total weight of the kernels that were sent to child processes and queues incoming kernels if the weight reaches the number of processor cores. Also, each cluster node reports this information to other nodes for better load balancing decisions.

The scheduler acts as a router for the kernels: when the kernel is received from the application, the scheduler analyses its fields and decides to which cluster node it can be sent. If the kernel has *downstream* or *point-to-point* state, the kernel is sent to the node where the target kernel resides; if the kernel has *upstream* state, load balancing algorithm decides which node to send the kernel to. Load balancing algorithm tracks the total weight of the kernels that were sent to the specified node and also receives the same information from the node (in case other nodes also send there their kernels), then it chooses the node with the lowest weight and sends the kernel to this node. If all nodes are full, the kernel is retained in the queue until the enough processor cores become available. The algorithm is very conservative and does not use work-stealing for improved performance, however, the fault tolerance is easier to implement [4,5] when the target and the source node fields do not change during kernel lifetime which is not the case for work-stealing scenario.

The last but not the least responsibility of the scheduler is to discover and maintain a list of cluster nodes and establish persistent network connections to neighbours. Cluster scheduler does this automatically by scanning the network using efficient algorithm: the nodes in the network are organised in artificial tree topology with the specified fan-out value and each node tries to communicate with the nodes which are closer to the root of the tree. This approach significantly reduces the number of data that needs to be sent over the network to find all cluster nodes: in ideal case only one kernel is sent to and received from the parent node. The algorithm is described in [6]. After the connections are established, all the *upstream* kernels that are received from the applications' child processes are routed to neighbour nodes in the tree topology (both parent and child nodes). This creates a problem because the number of nodes "behind" the parent node is generally different than the number of nodes behind the child nodes. In order to solve this problem we track not only the total weight of all kernels of the neighbour node, but the total weight of each node in the cluster and sum the weight of all nodes that are behind the node A to compute the total weight of node A for load balancing. Also, we apply load balancing recursively: when the kernel arrives at the node, load balancing algorithm is executed once more to decide whether the kernel can be sent locally or to another cluster node (except the source node). This approach solves the problem, and now applications can be launched not only on the root node, but on any node without load balancing problems. This approach adds small overhead, as the kernel goes through intermediate node, but if the overhead is undesirable, the application can be launched on the root node. Node discovery and node state updates are implemented using *point-to-point* kernels.

To summarise, cluster scheduler uses kernels as unit of scheduling and as communication protocol between its daemon processes running on different cluster nodes. Daemon process acts as an intermediary between application processes running on different cluster nodes, and all application kernels are sent through this process to other cluster nodes. Kernels that are sent through the scheduler are heavy-weight: they have more fields than local kernels and the routing through the scheduler introduces multiple overheads compared to direct communication. However, using cluster scheduler hugely simplifies application development, as application developer does not need to worry about networking, fault tolerance, load balancing and "how many parallel processes are enough for my application": this is now handled by the scheduler. For maximum efficiency and embedded applications the application can be linked directly to the scheduler to be able to run in the same daemon process, that way application kernels are no longer sent though daemon process and the overhead of the scheduler is minimal.

2.4   Parallel and Distributed Evaluation of Guile Expressions Using Kernels

Kernels low-level interface and cluster scheduler are written in C++ language. From the authors' perspective C is too low-level and Java has too much overhead for cluster computing, whereas C++ is the middleground choice. The implementation is the direct mapping of the ideas discussed in previous sections on C++ abstractions: kernel is a base class (see listing 1.1) for all control flow objects with common fields (`parent`, `target` and all others) and `act`, `react`, `read`, `write` virtual functions that are overridden in subclasses. This direct mapping is natural for a mixed-paradigm language like C++, but functional languages may benefit from implementing the same ideas in the compiler or interpreter.

```
enum class states {upstream, downstream, point_to_point};

class kernel {
public:
  virtual void act();
  virtual void react(kernel* child);
  virtual void write(buffer& out) const;
  virtual void read(buffer& in);
  kernel* parent = nullptr;
  kernel* target = nullptr;
  states state = states::upstream;
};

class queue {
public:
  void push(kernel* k);
};
```

Listing 1.1. Public interface of the kernel and the queue classes in C++ (simplified for clarity).

We made a reference implementation of kernels for Guile language [3]. Guile is a dialect of Scheme [13] which in turn is a dialect of LISP [10]. The distinct feature of LISP-like languages is homoiconicity, i.e. the code and the data is represented by tree-like structure (lists that contain atoms or other lists as elements). This feature makes it possible to express parallelism directly in the language: every list element can be computed independently and it can be sent to other cluster nodes for parallel computation. To implement parallelism we created a Guile interpreter that evaluates every list element in parallel using kernels. In practice this means that every argument of a procedure call (a procedure call is also a list with the first element being the procedure name) is computed in parallel. This interpreter is able to run any existing Guile programme (provided that it does not use threads, locks and semaphores explicitly) and the output will be the same as with the original interpreter, the programme will automatically use cluster nodes for parallel computations, and fault tolerance will be automatically provided by our cluster scheduler. From the authors' perspective this approach is the most transparent and safe way of writing parallel and distributed programmes with clear separation of concerns: the programmer takes care of the application logic, and cluster scheduler takes care of the parallelism, load balancing and fault tolerance.

Our interpreter consists of standard *read-eval-print* loop out of which only *eval* step uses kernels for parallel and distributed computations. Inside *eval* we use hybrid approach for parallelism: we use kernels to evaluate arguments of procedure calls and arguments of cons primitive asynchronously only if these arguments contain other procedure calls. This means that all simple arguments (variables, symbols, other primitives etc.) are computed sequentially without creating child kernels.

Evaluating procedure calls and `cons` using kernels is enough to make `map` form parallel, but we had to rewrite `fold` form to make it parallel. Our parallelism is based on the fact that procedure arguments can be evaluated in parallel without affecting the correctness of the procedure, however, evaluating arguments in parallel in `fold` does not give speedup because of the nested `fold` and `proc` calls: the next recursive call to `fold` waits until the call to `proc` completes. Alternative procedure `fold-pairwise` does not have this deficiency, but is only correct for `proc` that does not care about the order of the arguments (`+`, `*` operators etc.). In this procedure we apply `proc` to successive pairs of elements from the initial list, after that we recursively call `fold-pairwise` for the resulting list. The iteration is continued until only one element is left in the list, then we return this element as the result of the procedure call. This new procedure is also iterative, but parallel inside each iteration. We choose `map` and `fold` forms to illustrate automatic parallelism because many other forms are based on them [7]. Our implementation is shown in listing 1.2.

```
(define (map proc lst) "Parallel map."
  (if (null? lst) lst
    (cons (proc (car lst)) (map proc (cdr lst)))))
(define (fold proc init lst) "Sequential fold."
  (if (null? lst) init
    (fold proc (proc (car lst) init) (cdr lst))))
(define (do-fold-pairwise proc lst)
  (if (null? lst) '()
    (if (null? (cdr lst)) lst
      (do-fold-pairwise proc
        (cons (proc (car lst) (car (cdr lst)))
          (do-fold-pairwise proc (cdr (cdr lst))))))))
(define (fold-pairwise proc lst) "Parallel pairwise fold."
  (car (do-fold-pairwise proc lst)))
```

Listing 1.2. Parallel `map` and `fold` forms in Guile.

3 Results

We tested performance of our interpreter using the forms in listing 1.2. For each form we applied synthetic procedure that sleeps 200 ms to the list with 96 elements. Then we ran the resulting script using native Guile interpreter and our interpreter and measured total running time for different number of threads. For native Guile interpreter the running time of all forms is the same for any number of threads. For our interpreter `map` and `fold-pairwise` forms run time decreases with the number of threads and for `fold` form run time stays the same (Fig. 2).

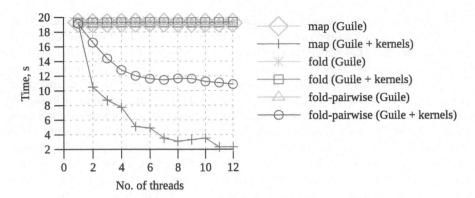

Fig. 2. The run time of the forms from listing 1.2 for different number of parallel threads and different interpreters.

4 Discussion

Computing procedure arguments in parallel is a natural way of expressing parallelism in functional language, and in our tests the performance of the programme is close to the one with manual parallelism. Lower performance is explained by the fact that we introduce more overhead by using asynchronous kernels to compute procedure arguments where this does not give large performance gains (even with ideal parallelism with no overhead). If we remove these overheads we will get the same time as the original programme with manual parallelism. This is explained by the fact that the main loop of the programme is written as an application of `map` form and our interpreter makes it parallel. Executing this loop in parallel gives the largest performance gains compared to other parts of the programme. We expect that the difference between automatic and manual parallelism to be more visible in larger and more complex programmes, and in future plan to benchmark more algorithms with known parallel implementations.

5 Conclusion

Using procedure arguments to define parallel programme parts gives new perspective on writing parallel programmes. In imperative languages programmers are used to rearranging loops to optimise memory access patterns and help the compiler vectorise the code, but with parallel-arguments approach in functional languages they can rearrange the forms to help the interpreter to extract more parallelism. This parallelism is automatic and does not affect the correctness of the programme (of course, you need to serialise access and modification of the global variables). With help of kernels these parallel computations are extended to distributed computations. Kernels provide standard way of expressing parallel and distributed programme parts, automatic fault tolerance for master and worker nodes and automatic load balancing via cluster scheduler. Together kernels and arguments-based parallelism provide low- and high-level programming interface for clusters and single nodes that conveniently hide the shortcomings of parallel and distributed computations allowing the programmer to focus on the actual problem being solved rather than fixing bugs in his or her parallel and distributed code.

Future work is to re-implement LISP language features that are relevant for parallelism in a form of C++ library and use this library for parallelism, but implement the actual computations in C++. This would allow to improve performance of purely functional programmes by using the functional language for parallelism and imperative language for performance-critical code.

Acknowledgements. Research work is supported by Council for grants of the President of the Russian Federation (grant no. MK-383.2020.9).

References

1. Apache Software Foundation: Hadoop. https://hadoop.apache.org
2. Apache Software Foundation: Storm. https://storm.apache.org
3. Galassi, M., Blandy, J., Houston, G., Pierce, T., Jerram, N., Grabmueller, M.: Guile Reference Manual (2002)
4. Gankevich, I., Tipikin, Y., Korkhov, V.: Subordination: providing resilience to simultaneous failure of multiple cluster nodes. In: Proceedings of International Conference on High Performance Computing Simulation (HPCS 2017), pp. 832–838. Institute of Electrical and Electronics Engineers (IEEE), NJ, USA, July 2017. https://doi.org/10.1109/HPCS.2017.126
5. Gankevich, I., Tipikin, Y., Korkhov, V., Gaiduchok, V.: Factory: non-stop batch jobs without checkpointing. In: International Conference on High Performance Computing Simulation (HPCS 2016), pp. 979–984, July 2016. https://doi.org/10.1109/HPCSim.2016.7568441
6. Gankevich, I., Tipikin, Y., Gaiduchok, V.: Subordination: cluster management without distributed consensus. In: International Conference on High Performance Computing Simulation (HPCS), pp. 639–642 (2015). https://doi.org/10.1109/HPCSim.2015.7237106
7. Hutton, G.: A tutorial on the universality and expressiveness of fold. J. Funct. Programm. **9**(4), 355–372 (1999). https://doi.org/10.1017/S0956796899003500
8. Islam, M., et al.: Oozie: towards a scalable workflow management system for Hadoop. In: Proceedings of the 1st ACM SIGMOD Workshop on Scalable Workflow Execution Engines and Technologies. SWEET 2012. Association for Computing Machinery, New York (2012). https://doi.org/10.1145/2443416.2443420
9. Lattner, C., Adve, V.: LLVM: a compilation framework for lifelong program analysis & transformation. In: Proceedings of the International Symposium on Code Generation and Optimization: Feedback-Directed and Runtime Optimization, CGO 2004, USA, p. 75. IEEE Computer Society (2004)
10. McCarthy, J.: Recursive functions of symbolic expressions and their computation by machine, part I. Commun. ACM **3**(4), 184–195 (1960). https://doi.org/10.1145/367177.367199

11. Pinho, E.G., de Carvalho, F.H.: An object-oriented parallel programming language for distributed-memory parallel computing platforms. Sci. Comput. Programm. **80**, 65–90 (2014). https://doi.org/10.1016/j.scico.2013.03.014. Special section on foundations of coordination languages and software architectures (selected papers from FOCLASA11)

12. Stewart, R., Maier, P., Trinder, P.: Transparent fault tolerance for scalable functional computation. J. Funct. Programm. **26**, e5 (2016). https://doi.org/10.1017/S095679681600006X

13. Sussman, G.J., Steele, G.L.: The first report on scheme revisited. High. Order Symb. Comput. **11**, 399–404 (1998). https://doi.org/10.1023/A:1010079421970

14. Vavilapalli, V.K., et al.: Apache Hadoop YARN: yet another resource negotiator. In: Proceedings of the 4th Annual Symposium on Cloud Computing, SOCC 2013, pp. 1–16. ACM, New York (2013). https://doi.org/10.1145/2523616.2523633

15. Wilde, M., Hategan, M., Wozniak, J.M., Clifford, B., Katz, D.S., Foster, I.: Swift: a language for distributed parallel scripting. Parallel Comput. **37**(9), 633–652 (2011)

16. Yu, Y., et al.: DryadLINQ: a system for general-purpose distributed data-parallel computing using a high-level language. Proc. LSDS-IR **8** (2009)

17. Zaharia, M., et al.: Apache Spark: a unified engine for big data processing. Commun. ACM **59**(11), 56–65 (2016). https://doi.org/10.1145/2934664

International Workshop on Smart Cities and User Data Management (SCIDAM 2021)

A Decision Tree for a Cost-Benefit Analysis on Flood Risk Management with Uncertain Funding

Massimo Di Francesco[1](✉) ⓘ, Jacopo Napolitano[2] ⓘ, and Giovanni Maria Sechi[2] ⓘ

[1] Department of Mathematics and Computer Science, University of Cagliari, Via Ospedale 72, 09124 Cagliari, Italy
mdifrance@unica.it

[2] Department of Civil and Environmental Engineering, University of Cagliari, Piazza d'Armi, 09123 Cagliari, Italy
{jacopo.napolitano,sechi}@unica.it

Abstract. River floods generated relevant disasters worldwide and motivated the need to set up Flood Risk Management plans. According to the European Directive 2007/60/CE, the flood-risk evaluation should include a cost–benefit analysis on a long-term planning horizon. However, the cost-benefit analysis is typically made under the deterministic assumption to know which uncertain events will be observed in the planning horizon and a priori establishes which actions will be taken throughout this long time interval. Clearly, this myopic policy is not adequate in the domain of Flood Risk Management, in which most of the data are uncertain when the cost-benefit analysis is made and decisions should dynamically respond to the observation of uncertain parameters. In order to face the former challenges, this paper shows how the cost-benefit analysis can be supported by a decision tree for structuring and analyzing decisions in the face of uncertainty on the available funding. Finally, the paper reports some outcomes in the experimentation on the Coghinas Basin (Sardinia, Italy).

Keywords: Flood mitigation · Cost-benefit analysis · Decision trees · Decision analysis

1 Introduction

Climate change and current urbanization trends increase the occurrences of flood events. Hence, Flood Risk Management plans are needed for preparation, mitigation and reconstruction when natural disasters occur [1]. The European Commission Flood Directive 2007/60 [2] requires a preliminary damage assessment to estimate flood impact and recommends policy-makers to decide upon flood mitigation strategies implementation via a Cost-Benefit approach.

The Directive draws attention to the assessment and management of flood mitigation measures. Flood damage and loss estimation analyses are essential for planning flood mitigation structural works, since decisions on scenarios mitigation achievements should

© Springer Nature Switzerland AG 2021
O. Gervasi et al. (Eds.): ICCSA 2021, LNCS 12956, pp. 513–525, 2021.
https://doi.org/10.1007/978-3-030-87010-2_38

be based on a Cost-Benefit Analysis (CBA). As a matter of fact, article 7 in Chapter IV of the Directive states that the "Flood Risk Management plans has to take into account relevant aspects such as costs and benefits". Benefits can be evaluated as the reduction in the expected damages, which are avoided by the realization of scenario mitigation works, the management of river systems and the consideration of flood flows resulting from hydrological analysis [3]. The expected flood flows frequently refer to a set of time return periods (expressed in years), which are denoted by T_r. Therefore, the expected damages are evaluated both in the current scenario and after the conclusions of works [4, 5].

Water flow depth and velocity in potential floodplain areas are, in addition, an essential information given from hydraulic simulation models of flood flows. Damage estimation functions (e.g., the European JRC "Flood Damages Functions") can be subsequently applied to express a relationship between the flood inundation and potential losses in flood scenarios [6]. Damages can be divided into two categories: tangible (i.e., physical damages due to contact with water and loss of production and income) and intangible damages (i.e., loss of life and trauma); the former damages are direct or indirect [7]. In this study, direct tangible and indirect tangible damages are considered to estimate benefits, which are evaluated as damages reduction avoided by the realization of mitigation works [8, 9].

Generally speaking, CBA is a systematic approach for estimating the strengths and weaknesses of several alternatives. It aims to select the best alternative for achieving benefits while preserving savings [10]. However, CBA typically concerns a long-term planning horizon under a deterministic setting. This means that one assumes to know the data observed and the decisions taken throughout the planning horizon. All in all, CBA is used by organizations to appraise the desirability of a given policy and the most important outcome is the year in which benefits start overcoming costs.

The former drawback does not match with the requirements of Flood Risk Management, which must be made in a highly uncertain climatic environment. Clearly, it is also impractical to make a CBA for all possible policies (i.e., all realizations of uncertain parameters and all possible decisions for each realization). Since CBA is based on a single objective criterion (the net benefit), it is of interest to build a decision tree with this criterion. Generally speaking, decision trees are logical and systematic ways to address a variety of problems involving decision making with a single criterion in an uncertain environment. To the best of our knowledge, they have never been adopted in the domain of Flood-Risk-Management.

In this paper we enhance the analysis of CBA for a flood-mitigation problem by a decision tree. We show which management insights can be obtained in the real case study of the Coghinas Basin in the Sardinia region (Italy). Three possible actions (or mitigation works configurations) are investigated to minimize the net benefit in the case of uncertain funding.

This paper is organized as follows. In Sect. 2, we briefly describe CBA with a focus on flood risk management. In Sect. 3, decision trees are briefly introduced. In Sect. 4, the case study of Coghinas river basin is presented and the outcomes are described. Conclusions are reported in Sect. 5.

2 The Cost-Benefit Analysis

The effectiveness (or suitability) of public structural works on flood risk mitigation could be evaluated through economic criteria, motivating the choice among different alternatives [3, 11]. In this research, the integration of cost-benefit analysis (CBA) and decision tree is introduced, to present an interesting decision-support system for the optimal planning on flood mitigation measures.

The CBA is widely used in economic and engineering fields to evaluate different projects or alternatives [12]. In CBA benefits and costs should be expressed in monetary terms and should be adjusted according to the time value of money.

Economic comparisons will be hereafter made by the Net Present Value (NPV). Alternative projects may be also evaluated using different indicators such as the Internal Rate of Return (IRR), the Benefit-Cost Ratio (BCR) and the payback period (PBP). In this study, all streams of benefits and costs over time must be expressed on a common basis in terms of their present values, regardless of whether they are incurred at different times. Therefore, one should evaluate the Present Value (PV) of future costs or benefit values, to perform a correct comparison between them. The PV represents the result of today's value of a future stream of payments. In a simple way, the PV can be evaluated as:

$$PV = \sum\nolimits_{t=1}^{T} \frac{R_t}{(1 + r)^t} \tag{1}$$

where:

R_t: net cash inflow/outflows during a period t;

r: discount rate;

T: number of time periods.

The PV in Eq. 1 allows to put all costs and benefits in a common temporal step, using time and money-values (cost/benefit) occurrence estimations. The expected Net Present Value (NPV) of Benefits can be obtained by the subtraction of the future expected streams of awaited benefits (B) and costs (C), as expressed in Eq. 2:

$$NPV = \sum\nolimits_{t=1}^{T} \frac{B_t - C_t}{(1 + r)^t} \tag{2}$$

In a CBA, the NPV should be maximized. This optimization allows the comparison for ranking alternative mitigation policies in terms of NPV.

2.1 CBA in Flood Risk Management Problem

In a flood risk management problem, a fixed time horizon should be considered to compute a correct and effective economical comparison between costs and benefits. Each alternative of infrastructures (or infrastructure configuration) can be considered as a flood mitigation solution [13]. These infrastructure configurations are characterized by different cost and benefit functions.

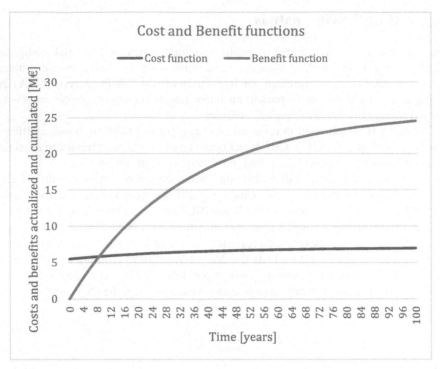

Fig. 1. Cost and benefit functions

Costs and Benefits values are actualized and cumulated along this fixed time horizon of analysis, as reported in Fig. 1. For this type of infrastructures, the cost function is usually made by two terms:

$$C_t = C_c + C_{OMR} \tag{3}$$

where:

C_T: Total costs;

C_C: Construction costs, usually stated in the first year of development of a built asset;

C_{OMR}: Operation, maintenance and replacement costs, usually referred to the entire infrastructure life. They start after the construction and are computed year by year.

The benefits are the revenues of a project along the "service life" of the infrastructure. In our problem they can be evaluated starting by the estimation of the expected annual mean value of flood damages. It can be estimated by Eq. 4:

$$E(D) = \int_0^1 D_s \, d(P_s) \tag{4}$$

Herein, D_S is the flood damage evaluated in economic terms which refers to a flood flow expected characterized by an estimated return period T_r and an occurrence probability P_S (where $P_S = \frac{1}{T_r}$).

The effectiveness of each alternative can be evaluated by comparing the mean annual value of flood damages in the configuration of no-intervention (Configuration 0) and the damages in the case of the i-th Configuration.

In Fig. 2 the area between these two functions represents the possible decrease in flood damages due to the adoption of this specific mitigation-works configuration. These damage functions are drawn by varying the occurrence probability P_S (i.e., changing the return periods T_r), modelling the water flood flow and considering damage estimation functions, as the European JRC "Flood Damages Functions", to evaluate D_S [15, 16].

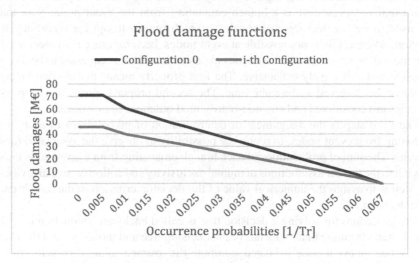

Fig. 2. Flood damage comparison: Configuration (0) - Configuration (i)

The horizontality of the curves for very exceptional floods has been adopted to depict the difficulties in these estimations for exceptional events. Expected benefits in each configuration can be evaluated by Eq. 5. It computes, in terms of annual mean value, the expected benefit for a specific configuration $(E(B)_{Conf(i)})$ as the difference between the expected damages in Configuration 0 (not-intervention) $(E(D)_{Conf(0)})$ and the expected damages in the i-th alternative $(E(D)_{Conf(i)})$.

$$E(B)_{Conf(i)} = E(D)_{Conf(0)} - E(D)_{Conf(i)} \tag{5}$$

After the evaluation of costs and benefits in each configuration, CBA procedure actualizes and cumulates their values along the fixed time-horizon. Finally, CBA should be synthesized in a performance index, to choose the configuration maximizing the net benefit among all flood mitigation configurations.

3 Building and Solving a Decision Tree

Decision trees are analytical models to systematically structure and analyze decision problems in an uncertain environment with a single criterion [14]. In what follows, we briefly list the steps to build a decision tree.

The first step in decision trees is the definition of the criterion. In this paper, we assume that the only criterion on which to differentiate between policies is the *NPV* of benefits and one obviously prefers a higher net benefit to a lower net benefit. This means that all other policies would offer a similar impact w.r.t. all parameters neglected in the criterion.

The second step is the construction of the decision tree from the list of possible decisions and the list of possible outcomes. Each decision is represented by a decision node and each possible choice is represented as a branch emanating from the decision node. Each uncertain event is represented by an event node and each possible outcome of an event is represented as a branch emanating from the event node. Note that in a decision node the decision-maker selects which branch to opt for according to the criterion, whereas this is not possible at event nodes, because one cannot decide which outcome will be observed. The outcomes in an event node are requested to be mutually exclusive and collectively exhaustive. The first property means that no two outcomes could ever be observed at the same time. The second property means that all possible outcomes are considered and any non-represented outcome cannot occur.

The third step is the assignment or determination of probabilities to each branch emanating from event nodes, to report the possibility to observe the associated random outcome. The sum of probabilities of each branch emanating from a given node must be 1, owing to the former assumptions of mutual exclusivity and collective exhaustivity. The next step is to assign the numerical value of the decision criterion to the final branches in the decision tree.

The procedure for solving a decision tree is called backwards induction or folding back. It starts from the final branches of the decision tree and moves toward the starting node. When an event node is visited, compute the average value of criterion from all possible outcomes. In a CBA analysis, this means to convert the distribution of possible net benefits to a single numerical value using the average, which weights all possible outcomes by their probability. When a decision node is visited, choose the branch emanating from this node with the best value of the criterion. In a CBA analysis, this means to cross off the branches emanating from a node with worse value of the *NPV* of benefits. The decision tree is solved after the evaluation of all nodes.

Finally, the sensitivity analysis must be performed to make a critical evaluation of the impact of key data on the optimal decision. This is particularly important when the decision-maker lacks confidence in some data. They are considered one at a time to test how the optimal decision strategy will change owing to a change in a data value.

4   Experimentation

4.1   The Coghinas Flood-Plain

The Coghinas river basin is located in the northern part of Sardinia region (Italy) and it is characterized by a drainage basin of 2551 km^2. It is the third longest river of the region and flows in the Mediterranean sea into the Asinara Gulf (Fig. 3).

In the lowland floodplain area urban settlements and some towns are located: Viddalba, Santa Maria Coghinas and Valledoria. Moreover, the Coghinas lowland valley has a strategic relevance for agricultural uses.

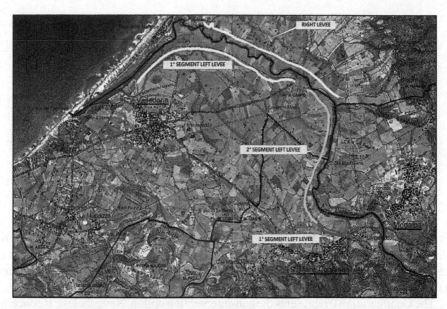

Fig. 3. Coghinas river with original levees configuration

Unfortunately, the valley has a long history of floods causing significant damages to civil properties, crops, infrastructures and environment. Therefore, to reduce the impact of flood damages, the Sardinia Region Administration defined some strategic solutions such as critical bridges demolition, levees and channel improvements and new constructions [15].

The possible flood damage reduction actions in the Coghinas floodplain area according to the Regional Plan for Flood Mitigation [15] are reported in Table 1 with the related construction costs.

Table 1. Flood-risk mitigation actions

Work code	Work description	$C_C[M€]$
A	New levee on the right bank to protect Viddalba town	2.38
B	Adjustment of the levee on the left bank	2.59
C	New levee to protect Santa Maria Coghinas town	1.81
D	Hydraulic arrangement of the hydrographic network upstream of the levee which protect Santa Maria Coghinas town	0.33
F	Demolition of the old bridge along the provincial road n° 146 over the Coghinas river near Viddalba town	0.09
G	Demolition of the bridge along the provincial road n° 90 over the Coghinas river near Valledoria town	0.32
O	Demolition of the bridge over the Badu Crabile river along the provincial road n° 35	0.19

The flood risk mitigation actions can be clustered into three main configurations.

Table 2. Cluster of works related to each project configuration

	Project configuration		
	Configuration 0	Configuration 1	Configuration 2
Work Code	F	A	B
	G	O	C
		F	D
		G	F
			G

As illustrated in Table 2 each configuration is made by clustering different works and aims to protect different areas from upstream to downstream along the Coghinas river [15]. Each configuration gathers different actions, which could be planned and financed in the Regional Plan for Flood Mitigation.

The Configuration 0 represents the non-intervention option. Nevertheless, it concerns the demolition of two existing bridges and these actions are also included in the other two possible configurations. The Configuration 1 and Configuration 2 aim to safeguard the two towns of Viddalba and Santa Maria Coghinas, respectively.

The benefits in each configuration are estimated from the expected damages referred to 12 categories of land use. Land uses are listed in Table 3 with their related values of maximum damage for surface unit [3]. As shown in the following table, economic maximum flood damage cannot be always defined in univocal way, such as for labels 9–12.

Table 3. Land-use classes and maximum damage values

Label	Land-use class	Max damage value [€/m^2]
1	Residential buildings	618
2	Commercial	511
3	Industry	440
4	Agriculture	0.63
5	Council roads	10
6	Provincial roads	20
7	Other roads	40
8	Infrastructural (areas with water supply network, electricity grid and similar systems)	40
9	Dams, rivers and similar areas	–
10	Environmental heritage areas	–
11	Historical and archeological heritage areas	–
12	Area subjected of other intangible damages	–

The definition of the damage function was made for each land-use according to the evaluation of water depths in the flood-plain area by hydraulic simulation models [3, 5]. To predict the expected damages, three flood peaks of flood return periods are considered: $T_r = 50$, 100 and 200 years.

As described in Sect. 2.1, the expected benefit of each alternative is evaluated using Eq. 5 by the comparison of each Configuration to the quantity of expected damages in Configuration 0.

All in all, Configuration 0 is cheap and leads to reduced benefits; Configuration 2 is the most expensive and leads to the largest benefits, whereas Configuration 1 is a trade-off between them in terms of costs and benefits.

4.2 Using a Decision Tree for the CBA on the Coghinas Floodplain

We investigate a CBA for mitigation measures in the Coghinas floodplain with a planning horizon of 100 years. The objective is to determine which of the three configurations should be selected and when this selection should be made. At the beginning of the planning horizon, there is a sufficient budget for Configuration 0 and Configuration 1, but it is uncertain in the future. More precisely, a budget change could be observed in the 10th and 20th year: in both cases it could increase with probability 0.5 and allow the realization of the most expensive configuration (i.e., Configuration 2) or it could be lower with probability 0.5 and allow to keep the current configuration only.

The criterion of the decision tree is the net benefit, which is computed as the difference between benefits and costs, which account for construction costs, operation, maintenance and replacement costs, as well as additional penalties. These penalties are paid if the budget for a more expensive configuration is available and the configuration is not made. More formally, if one denotes by I the number of configurations and T the number of years in the planning horizon, the criterion can be formalized as follows:

$$\sum_{i=1}^{I} \sum_{t=t_c+1}^{T} B_{i,t} - \sum_{i=1}^{I} C_{ci,t_c} - \sum_{i=1}^{I} \sum_{t=t_c+1}^{T} (C_{OMRi,t} - p_{NCi,t_{NC}}) \qquad (6)$$

where

- $B_{i,t}$ is the benefit of the construction of configuration $i \in I$ at year $t \in T$;
- C_{Ci,t_c} is the construction cost of configuration i actualized at the building year t_c;
- $C_{OMRi,t}$ are Operation, Maintenance and Replacement costs in configuration i at year t;
- $p_{NCi,t_{NC}}$ is the penalty for not constructing configuration i and actualized at year t_{NC}, when the choice has been done. More precisely, it is assumed to amount to 10% of construction costs.

At the beginning of the planning horizon, there is a sufficient budget only for Configuration 0 or Configuration 1 and only one of them can be selected. In Fig. 4 this choice is modeled by a decision node, which is represented by a small box with label A at year t = 0. Each possible choice is represented by a branch emanating from node A: the branch in red shows the selection of Configuration 0; the branch in green represents the choice of Configuration 1.

If Configuration 0 is selected, one must face the uncertainty of whether the budget will increase or decrease at year t = 10. Since it may decrease with probability 0.5 or increase with probability 0.5, in Fig. 4 this uncertain event is modeled by an event node, which is represented by a small cycle with label B at year t = 10. Each possible outcome of this event is represented by a branch emanating from B. More precisely, if the budget decreases, one joins node E from node B; if the budget increases, one joins node D from B.

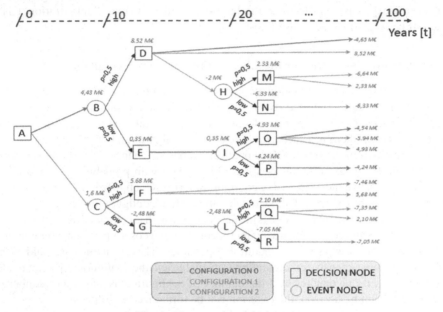

Fig. 4. The completed decision tree.

If a lower budget is observed at node B, the only possible decision at year t = 10 is to keep Configuration 0. In Fig. 4 this choice is represented by a red arc emanating from decision node E and joining node I. However, the budget could also change 10 years later (i.e., 20 years after the beginning of the planning horizon). It may be lower with probability 0.5 or higher with probability 0.5. In the first case, one joins node P from event node I and can only decide at this (decision) node to go on with Configuration 0. The value of the criterion at year 100 in path A, B, E, I, P is −4.24 M€. If a budget increase is observed after node I, one moves to decision node O. Here, one can opt for all the three possible configurations: if Configuration 0 is selected, the final value of the criterion at year 100 is −4.24 M€; if Configuration 1 is selected, the final value of the criterion at year 100 is −5.94 M€; if Configuration 2 is selected, the final value of the criterion at year 100 is 4.93 M€.

If a higher budget is observed at node B at year t = 10, one moves to decision node D, where one can choose all the three possible configurations. More precisely, one can go on with Configuration 0 or switch to Configuration 2 up to the end of the planning horizon. In the first case, the final value of the criterion is −4.65 M€; in the second case it amounts to 8.52 M€. Note that Configuration 1 cannot be selected up to the end of the planning horizon, but its choice is possible between year t = 10 and year t = 20, when the budget may change at year t = 20: it may become lower with probability 0.5 or higher with probability 0.5. This uncertainty is represented by event node H. If the budget is lower, one moves to decision node N, where it is possible to go on with Configuration 1 only and the final value of the criterion becomes −6.33 M€. If the budget is higher, one moves to decision node M, where two decisions are possible: go on with Configuration 1 or switch to Configuration 2. In the first case, the final value of the criterion is −6.64 M€; in the second case is 2.33 M€.

Consider again decision node A at year t = 0, assume to opt for Configuration 1. At year t = 10 one will observe if the budget is higher or lower. Therefore, one joins an event node from A. In Fig. 4 the event node is denoted by C and has two emanating branches: higher budget with probability 0.5 and lower budget with probability 0.5. If it is higher, one moves to decision node F, where one must decide to go on with Configuration 1 or switch to Configuration 2 up to the end of the planning horizon. In the first case, the final value of the criterion is −7.46 M€; in the second case it is 5.68 M€. Note that the selection of Configuration 0 is neglected at this stage, as the actions in this configuration are also included in configurations 1 and 2. If the budget is lower, one moves to decision node G, where one can only decide to go on with Configuration 1. Ten years later (i.e., 20 years after the beginning of the planning horizon) one will again face the uncertainty of whether the budget is higher with probability 0.5 or lower with probability 0.5. In Fig. 4 this uncertainty is described by event node L. If the budget is higher, one moves to decision node Q, which concerns whether to switch to Configuration 2 or keep Configuration 1. In the first case, the final value of the criterion is 2.10 M€; in the second case it is −7.35 M€. If the budget is lower, one moves to decision node R to decide to go on with Configuration 1 up to the end of the planning horizon. In this case, the final value of the criterion is −7.05 M€.

The solution of this problem is determined by folding back the decision tree. One must start from the final branches, choose that branch emanating from the decision node with the best value of the criterion, write this value above the node and cross off the branches with lower values of the criterion. For example, in Fig. 4 at decision node M we select Configuration 2 and disregard Configuration 1. For each event node, compute the weighted average of the criterion over each branch weighted by its probability and write this number above the event node. For example, in Fig. 4 at decision node H we compute the average between 2.33 M€ and −6.33 M€: −2.33 * 0.5 + 6.33 * 0.5 = − 2 M€. This algorithm is iterated until all nodes of the decision tree are visited.

The completed solution of the decision tree is reported in Fig. 5. We now examine the optimal decision strategy under uncertainty. According to the solution, one should select Configuration 0 at the beginning of the planning horizon (move along the branch from A to B). Then, if a higher budget is available after 10 years (move along the branch from B to D), select Configuration 2 up to the end of the planning horizon (this is shown at decision node D). If the budget is lower (move along the branch from B to E), keep Configuration 0 for 10 more years (move along the branch from E to I). If the budget becomes higher (move along the branch from I to O), select Configuration 2, else (move along the branch from I to P) and keep Configuration 0. The overall value of this decision strategy is the value of the criterion computed in the initial node A.

Finally, it is wise to adopt a sensitivity analysis on the optimal decision strategy. For example, the probability p of a high budget may increase at year 10 and may lead to the selection of Configuration 1 instead of Configuration 0. In this case, the average at node C becomes $5.68p - 2.48(1 - p)$ and, if it is larger than 4.43 M€, one should move to node C instead of node B. The change in the decision occurs when p is larger than the value satisfying equation $5.68p - 2.48(1 - p) = 4.43$ M€, i.e., when p is larger than 0.85. This is reassuring if one is confident that the probability of high budget after the selection of Configuration 1 is not high.

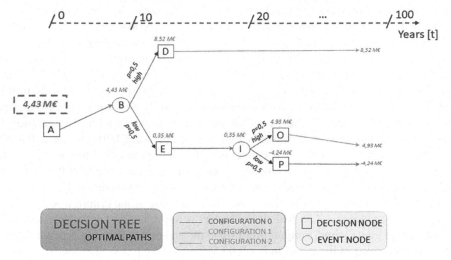

Fig. 5. The solution of the decision tree.

5   Conclusion

This paper has investigated the introduction of a decision tree in the cost-benefit analysis for planning flood risk mitigation works construction. The analysis starts from the classical CBA for optimizing the net value of expected benefits. Next, a decision tree is developed to make optimal decisions despite data uncertainty. More precisely, we have investigated the possibility to introduce uncertainty on budget availability during the considered life-time by the probability of funding each configuration. The optimization criterion of the decision tree is still the maximization of net benefit weighted by the former probabilities and accounts for construction costs, operation, maintenance and replacement costs. Moreover, additional penalties are considered when constructions are not made, even if the budget is available. Finally, a sensitivity analysis on the optimal decision strategy has been performed.

This approach can be considered suitable in future analysis to evaluate more complex systems even considering different kinds of costs, benefits and penalties. For example, in the river Coghinas basin, we will investigate the management rules of the higher stream dam of Muzzone by increasing the lamination potentiality in flood-risk evaluations. This extension should include a cost–benefit analysis and an integrated decision-making procedure to optimize operating rules for this multipurpose reservoir, while taking into account the mitigation of flood risks and the priority in water demand supplies.

Acknowledgements. This study has been supported by the Italian Ministry of the Environment and Protection of the Territory and the Sea, Project RIDES-IDRO.

References

1. Price, R.K., Vojinovic, Z.: Urban flood disaster management. Urban Water J. **5**(3), 259–276 (2008)
2. European Commission. EU Directive 2007/60 on the assessment and management of flood risks. Official Journal of the European Union (2007)
3. Sulis, A., Frongia, S., Liberatore, S., Zucca, R., Sechi, G.M.: Combining water supply and flood control purposes in the Coghinas Basin (Sardinia, Italy). Int. J. River Basin Manage. **18**(1), 13–22 (2020)
4. Pistrika, A., Tsakiris, G., Nalbantis, I.: Flood depth-damage functions for built environment. Environ. Process. **1**(4), 553–572 (2014)
5. Frongia, S., Liberatore, S., Sechi, G.M.: Flood damage risk assessment optimizing a flood mitigation system. In: Proceedings of 9th EWRA Conference, Istanbul (2015)
6. Dutta, D., Herath, S., Musiake, K.: A mathematical model for flood loss estimation. J. Hydrol. **277**, 24–49 (2003)
7. Jongman, B., et al.: Comparative flood damage model assessment: towards a European approach. Nat. Hazard. Earth Syst. Sci. **12**, 3733–3752 (2012)
8. Ramirez, J., et al.: Ex post analysis of flood control: benefit–cost analysis and the value of information. Water Resour. Res. **24**(8), 1397–1405 (1988)
9. Gissing, A., Blong, R.: Accounting for variability in commercial flood damage estimation. Austr. Geograph. **35**(2), 209–222 (2004)
10. Nas, T.F.: Cost-Benefit Analysis: Theory and Application. Sage, Thousand Oaks (1996)
11. Woodward, M., Gouldby, B., Kapelan, Z., Hames, D.: Multiobjective optimization for improved management of flood risk. J. Water Resour. Plann. Manage. **140**(2), 201–215 (2014)
12. Loucks, D.P., van Beek, E.: Water Resource Systems Planning and Management. Springer International Publishing, Cham (2017). https://doi.org/10.1007/978-3-319-44234-1
13. Haddad, O.B., Ashofteh, P.-S., Mariño, M.A.: Retracted: levee layouts and design optimization in protection of flood areas. J. Irrigat. Drainage Eng. **141**(8), 04015004 (2015)
14. Bertsimas, D., Freund, R.M.: Data, Models and Decisions. Dynamic Ideas (2004)
15. ARDIS. Piano di Gestione del rischio alluvioni, Hydrographic District - Regional Board of Sardinia, Cagliari (2014). http://www.regione.sardegna.it/autoritadibacino/pianificazione
16. Huizinga, J., de Moel, H., Szewczyk, W.: Global flood depth-damage functions: Methodology and the database with guidelines (No. JRC105688). Joint Research Centre (Seville site) (2017)

An Effective Method for Ensuring the Reliability of a Critical Infrastructure Monitoring Network

Vladimir V. Shakhov[1,2]($\boxtimes$) and Denis Migov[2]

[1] Novosibirsk State Technical University, Novosibirsk 630073, Russia
shaxov@corp.nstu.ru
[2] Institute of Computational Mathematics and Mathematical Geophysics,
Novosibirsk 630090, Russia
mdinka@rav.sscc.ru
http://www.nstu.ru, https://icmmg.nsc.ru

Abstract. One of the most valuable and compelling IoT applications are mission-critical infrastructure monitoring systems. Nowadays, research centers, commercial companies, and government agencies are actively researching and developing sensor-based long pipeline monitoring systems. In a wireless sensor network used to monitor pipelines, power grids, bridges, highways, all network nodes equipped with sensors form a special elongated topology. The harsh environment may cause wireless links to malfunction. Thus, maintaining network connectivity is a major issue. To improve network connectivity, i.e. to improve the reliability of monitoring, a number of approaches are used: networks are often supplemented with auxiliary relay nodes, the transmitter power is increased, resource-intensive protocols of error-correcting coding are used, etc. All this leads to unnecessary costs, which in many cases can be avoided. This paper proposes an effective method for assessing network connectivity that allows you to optimize and dose the costs of ensuring the reliability of a critical infrastructure monitoring systems.

Keywords: IoT · Wireless sensor network · Long pipeline monitoring

1 Introduction

The management and control of vital systems requires real-time monitoring, and the corresponding monitoring networks must be sufficiently reliable. Very often in the literature, network reliability is considered as the probability that any two nodes are connected (directly or through a set of intermediate nodes), taking into account unreliable links. A number of analytical approaches have been proposed to solve this problem. Researchers model the topology of a network using a random graph where any edge exists with some probability, and develop various

Funding: The reported study was funded by RFBR and NSFC, project number 21-57-53001.

O. Gervasi et al. (Eds.): ICCSA 2021, LNCS 12956, pp. 526–535, 2021.
https://doi.org/10.1007/978-3-030-87010-2_39

techniques to calculate the probability of the connectedness of the graph. This probability is also known as the reliability polynomial. Calculating the reliability polynomial is a complex computational task. Brute-force and branch-and-bound methods are not suitable for huge networks. However, as we show in this work, the features of the topology of some networks, such as pipeline monitoring systems, make it possible to obtain efficient methods for calculating the reliability polynomial.

To utilize the specificity of long pipeline monitoring network topology we use properties of a two-vertex cut. It allows to perform the structural decomposition of a network. Also, for networks of an extensional spatial structure with many such cuts, arranged in series, we describe a method for identifying such cuts and a method for their subsequent traversal. As a result, it becomes possible to calculate the reliability of the network with a united calculation of the reliability of its components, as well as components merged by the cutting nodes. This way can be used to significantly improve the calculation of the reliability of the networks under consideration.

One of the most valuable and compelling IoT applications are mission-critical infrastructure monitoring systems. There are several projects on, and standardization initiatives for, sensor networks, which may eventually converge with the Internet of Things (IoT), for example European Union projects of Internet of Things Architecture (IoT-A) have been addressing the challenges of IoT solutions development from the wireless sensor networks (WSNs) perspective. Therefore, it is reasonable to apply WSNs for pipeline monitoring. Moreover, nowadays, research centers, commercial companies, and government agencies are actively researching and developing sensor-based long pipeline monitoring systems. According to an analytical report from GlobeNewswire published in 2020, even for such a particular task as monitoring water pipes to detect leaks, the solution market reaches a billion dollars and is growing at 5% per year.

A WSNs based monitoring system reduces the damage of natural and man-made disasters, the effects of infrastructure wear, and environmental and economic risks. However, radio channels in WSNs are usually quite unreliable. In order to fully utilize the potential of such systems, it needs to solve the problem of the system reliability.

In a wireless sensor network used to monitor pipelines, power grids, bridges, highways, all network nodes equipped with sensors form a special elongated topology. The harsh environment may cause wireless links to malfunction. Thus, maintaining network connectivity is a major issue. To improve network connectivity, i.e. to improve the reliability of monitoring, a number of approaches are used: networks are often supplemented with auxiliary relay nodes, the transmitter power is increased, resource-intensive protocols of error-correcting coding are used, etc. All this leads to unnecessary costs, which in many cases can be avoided. This paper proposes an effective method for assessing network connectivity that allows you to optimize and dose the costs of ensuring the reliability of a long pipeline monitoring systems.

The article is structured on 4 sections: after this introduction, Sect. 2 demonstrates state of the arts. Subsequently, Sect. 3 presents computational method for reliability of network topology. Finally, Sect. 4 summaries the paper and discloses future research.

2 Preliminaries

Research into the use of WSNs for pipeline monitoring was carried out as part of joint research projects between Stanford University, the University of Southern California and Chevron Corporation [1]. As an application, pipelines for steam heating and water supply were indicated, but the research results can be extended to other types of pipelines. The authors concluded that the SCADA system is a low-efficiency digital telemetry system for real-time data collection and analysis, on the basis of which Cisco offers commercial solutions for pipeline monitoring. The disadvantages of SCADA are the lack of flexibility, scalability, as well as the very high cost of its deployment and maintenance. Also, American researchers noted a general drawback of existing pipeline monitoring systems (including modifications and improvements to SCADA) compared to a system based on the low-power wide-area network: they do not use the advantages of a distributed system, are limited to data collection, or are specially designed to solve one narrow class of problems. At the same time, the results of the study noted the importance of the problem of ensuring the reliability of the system, the need to take into account the specifics of the topology, but there are no solutions for this. In addition, the monitoring system proposed by the authors is based on the outdated WSNs concept, which does not provide for the expansion of the functionality of critical network nodes due to mobility, the use of the ability to recharge sensors (energy harvesting), etc.

In the present literature a number of the following works, only individual problems of using WSNs for monitoring pipelines or problems of WSNs deployed on extended objects with similar properties (linear sensor networks) are considered. For example, an approach is proposed to increase the lifetime of a wireless connection between a pair of stationary transmitters and receivers using mobile relays, which are initially placed arbitrarily on the line between the transmitter and the receiver [2]. An analytical model has been developed to assess the impact of damaged nodes on linear sensor networks coverage [3].

The lack of reliable, low-cost pipeline monitoring solutions is reported by the US Federal Government Agency (Bureau of Reclamation), which organized a competition to find the specified solution on the INNOCENTIVE crowdsourcing platform.

When analyzing the reliability of networks for various purposes, including wireless sensor networks, the apparatus of random graphs is used, as a rule. The most common index of network reliability is the probability of connectivity of a subset of vertices of a random graph with unreliable edges [4], which describes the reliability of the network in terms of the possibility of establishing a connection between each pair of network nodes from the selected subset K of the network nodes, which are called terminals. This index is called K-terminal network reliability. If this subset coincides with the set of all network nodes, we arrive to the network probabilistic connectivity (all-terminal network reliability).

This indicator is the major one, it allows us to describe the ability of proper functioning of networks for various purposes in conditions of independent failures of elements. We also note that various other reliability indices are considered and actively studied, including those for wireless sensor networks description [5–8].

However, the problem of calculating the reliability of the network is NP-hard [9], therefore, the exact calculation requires exponential complexity. In this regard, the probabilistic connectivity compares favorably with other reliability indices, since by now it has been developed an extensive mathematical and algorithmic apparatus for its calculation and estimation. So, for networks of a suitable structure of hundreds of elements, it is often possible to carry out an exact calculation of their probabilistic connectivity.

Thus, in next Section we focus on the problem of all-terminal connectivity and use the mentioned facility to offer an efficient method for the choice of optimal topology manning the required monitoring network reliability.

3 Computational Method for Reliability of Network Topology

Assume, a set of network architectures can be dynamically used to maintain a monitoring system: $A_1, A_2, \ldots A_k, \ldots$. These architectures are ordered by resource consumption (e.g. in terms of system cost). Each architecture A_i generates topology that is described by a graph G_i in which nodes correspond to sensors and edges to wireless channels. Due to harsh conditions channels are unreliable.

Let p be the channel reliability (the existence probability). Therefore, G_i is a random graph. Let $R(G_i)$ be the reliability polynomial of this graph (the probability of all-terminal connectivity). In fact, our task is as follows:

$$i^* = \arg\min\{R(G_i) \geq e\}$$

where e is the desired level of reliability. This approach was given further details in the paper [10].

In general, the problem of calculation $R(G_i)$ is NP-hard. Thus, our problem statement boils down to finding an efficient way to calculate $R(G_i)$ using their specific properties.

The reduction and decomposition methods [11] have become universal methods for speeding up the calculation; a more detailed overview of the calculation methods is given in [12]. One of corresponding approaches is the decomposition of the network via a vertex cut and reduction to the calculation of reliability in smaller subgraphs. This approach was firstly proposed by R.K. Wood for two-vertex cuts (2-cuts) [13]. This approach was developed, including for cuts of an arbitrary size, in our papers [14–16] and, later, by J.M. Burgos [17]. So, for a graph G with a 2-cut dividing it into G_1, G_2 (Fig. 1), we have got a formula that was presented in this form in [15, 16] later, as well as by J.M. Burgos in 2016 [17]:

$$R(G) = R(G_1)\big(R(G_2') - R(G_2)\big) + R(G_2)\big(R(G_1') - R(G_1)\big) + R(G_1)R(G_2). \quad (1)$$

Here, G_i' denotes the graph obtained from G_i by merging vertices x and y, $i = 1, 2$.

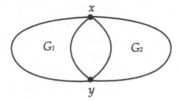

Fig. 1. Graph with two-vertex cut

Wireless sensor networks designed for monitoring the spatial extended objects, such as pipelines, themselves have an extensional structure. This class of networks is distinguished as linear wireless sensor networks. Despite their linear physical structure, a graph of such a network is not necessarily be linear topologically, since wireless communication channels are possible not only between the nearest neighboring nodes. The structure of such an extensional wireless sensor network is described by a graph with many cross-cuts. Let us consider the case when a network contains two-vertex cuts; the corresponding graph we call longitudinal (Fig. 2). The formal definition is given below.

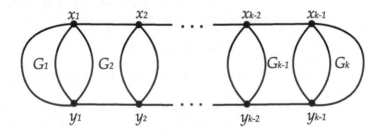

Fig. 2. Longitudinal graph

Note that if a network is decomposed into small-size biconnected components, then the calculation of its reliability is not a complicated task, since we may multiply the reliabilities of all biconnected components. It is also possible that a graph of such a longitudinal structure can be completely reduced by a serial-parallel transformation [11] within polynomial complexity. For example, any lattice of width 2. These cases are trivial. Thus, we assume that the graph of a wireless sensor network is already decomposed into biconnected components and reduced, and the components reliability calculation problem arises.

Let us generalize the calculation method based on the application of formula (1) to longitudinal graphs. The recursive application of this formula to such a graph leads to repeated recalculation of reliability the graph components. To avoid this, we propose a method for finding all cross-cuts and a method for their subsequent traversal using (1) formula, which significantly speeds up the calculation of the reliability of extensional WSNs.

Below we introduce the necessary definitions and notations.

Let $G_1, \ldots, G_k$ $(k > 1)$ be a sequence of biconnected graphs such that:

1) G_i and G_{i+1} have exactly two common vertices x_i, y_i and do not have common edges;
2) G_i and G_j such that $|i - j| > 1$, have no common elements.

Then graph

$$G = \bigcup_{i=1}^{k} G_i$$

is called *longitudinal graph* (Fig. 2). Subgraphs G_i $(1 \leq i \leq k)$ are the *components* of longitudinal graph G.

Obviously, each pair of vertices

$$\{x_i, y_i \mid 1 \leq i \leq k - 1\}$$

is a cut in graph G. We define *longitudinal cut* in G as set

$$\bigcup_{i=1}^{k-1} \{\{x_i, y_i\}\}.$$

Let $\{x_i, y_i\}$ be a *component* of longitudinal cut, which is also called *cross-cut* of longitudinal graph G. A longitudinal cut of G is *maximum* if no any 2-vertex cut of G can be added to it so that it remains longitudinal. Two cross-cuts $\{x_i, y_i\}$, $\{x_j, y_j\}$ are *adjacent* if $|i - j| = 1$.

For a component G_i, we denote by S_i the set of partitions of the set of longitudinal cut vertices that are in G_i. We use the following notation for a partition:

$$v_1 \ldots v_l | \ldots | u_1 \ldots u_t = \{\{v_1, \ldots, v_l\}, \ldots, \{u_1, \ldots, u_t\}\}. \tag{2}$$

By G_i^{Φ} $(\Phi \in S_i)$ we denote graph G_i contracted by each element of Φ. Thus, if vertices u and v are in the same element Φ, then they are contracted into one vertex in G_i^{Φ}.

During recursively application of formula (1) for longitudinal graph G, we obtain graphs, in addition to G_i, of the following types (Fig. 3, 4):

$$G_i' = \begin{cases} G_i^{x_{i-1}y_{i-1}|x_i|y_i} & ,1 < i < k, \\ G_k^{x_{k-1}y_{k-1}} & ,i = k; \end{cases} \tag{3}$$

$$G_i'' = \begin{cases} G_i^{x_{i-1}|y_{i-1}|x_iy_i} & ,1 < i < k, \\ G_1^{x_1y_1} & ,i = 1; \end{cases}$$

$$G_i''' = G_i^{x_{i-1}y_{i-1}|x_iy_i}, 1 < i < k; \tag{4}$$

$$G_{ik} = \bigcup_{i \le j \le k} G_j, 1 \le i \le k; \tag{5}$$

$$G_{ik}' = G_i' \bigcup_{i+1 \le j \le k} G_j, 1 < i \le k. \tag{6}$$

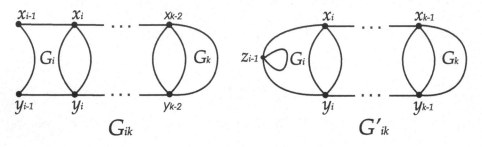

Fig. 3. Intermediate graphs

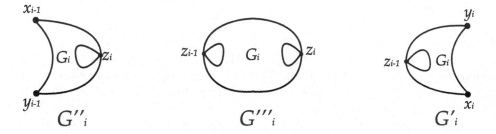

Fig. 4. Intermediate graphs

Let us remark that $R(G_{ik})$, $R(G_{ik}')$ can be calculated recursively:

$$R(G_{ik}) = R(G_i)R(G_{i+1k}') + R(G_i'')R(G_{i+1k}) - R(G_i)R(G_{i+1k}), \tag{7}$$

$$R(G_{ik}') = R(G_i')R(G_{i+1k}') + R(G_i''')R(G_{i+1k}) - R(G_i')R(G_{i+1k}). \tag{8}$$

From the definition of G_{ik} it follows that $G_{1k} = G$, therefore:

$$R(G) = R(G_{1k}). \tag{9}$$

Thus, having previously calculated the values of $R(G_i)$, $R(G'_i)$, $R(G''_i)$, $R(G'''_i)$, we can calculate $R(G)$ using recursive formulas. This results can essentially improve performance of reliability computing.

Finding the maximum longitudinal cut is a separate task. A natural way to construct it is a recursive search for 2-cuts in the components, into which the graph is decomposed by already found 2-cuts. The main problem is that obtained by such procedure a 2-cuts set remains a longitudinal cut. This problem can be easy solved for components G_1, G_k, because any of their 2-cuts can be chosen to complement an already formed longitudinal cut. The only condition for check is the difference between each vertex from new 2-cut in G_1 or G_k and the nodes $\{x_1, y_1\}$ or $\{x_{i-1}, y_{i-1}\}$, respectively.

For an internal component G_i $((2 \leq i \leq k - 1))$, not any its 2-cut can be added to a current longitudinal cut

$$\bigcup_{i=1}^{k-1} \{x_i, y_i\}.$$

Let there be a cut $\{x, y\}$ in the component G_i, dividing it into subgraphs H_1, H_2. Obviously, the longitudinal cut remains longitudinal due to location of vertices from neighboring cross-cuts with numbers $i, i-1$ to different subgraphs: H_1, H_2. That is,

$$\bigcup_{i=1}^{k-1} \{x_i, y_i\} \bigcup \{x, y\}$$

is also a longitudinal cut if nodes $\{x_{i-1}, y_{i-1}\}$ are in one subgraph H_i, and the nodes $\{x_i, y_i\}$ are in another. Thus, having a longitudinal cut C in the graph and wanting to complete it to the maximum longitudinal cut, we find an arbitrary two-vertex cut $\{x, y\}$, check where the nodes from neighboring cross-cuts are, and determine whether the cut is longitudinal.

By using formula 2-Cuts algorithm with a sequential enumeration of the components of the longitudinal cut, we have to calculate reliability of

$$2 + 2^{k-1} + 4 \sum_{i=0}^{k-3} 2^i$$

such graphs, with the middle cut choice—about 2^k graphs. Thus, the proposed method is significantly faster than the calculation by the traditional way.

Comparison of the calculation time is given below, including for calculating without cut decomposition, i.e. for calculating by factoring method *Factoring* [18] improved by series-parallel transformation at each step [11] and termination of recursive calls when reaching 5-vertex graphs [15]. The decomposition method uses this way to calculate the reliability of components. Finding the maximum longitudinal cut by the procedure above requires the enumeration of all pairs of nodes with checking the connectivity of graph obtained by removing each pair of nodes, that is, $O(MN^2)$ operations.

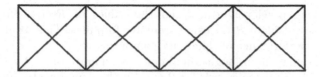

Fig. 5. Graph K_4^5

Numerical experiments were conducted on graphs obtained by the recursive procedure of joining to an already formed longitudinal graph of a complete graph on 4 vertices K_4, provided that two vertices of these graphs coincide. K_4 is also taken as an initial graph. The longitudinal graph obtained by this procedure of union of $k - 1$ graphs K_4 we denote by K_4^k (Fig. 5). For each edge of such a graph, we set its reliability value equal to 0.9.

Table 1 shows the execution time of algorithms for calculating the reliability of three graphs K_4^k and the calculated network reliability value with an accuracy of 6 decimal places. 4-core CPU (2.4 GHz) was used. It can be seen that as k grows, it is no longer possible to calculate network reliability by factorization. The decomposition approach makes such a calculation quite fast, while the use of longitudinal cuts additionally speeds up the calculation.

Table 1. Running time of algorithms for calculating the reliability of graphs K_4^k

Graph	Factoring	2-Cuts	Reliability value
K_4^{20}	4.3 s	1 s	0.993445
K_4^{25}	2 m 7 s	1 s	0.992753
K_4^{100}	24 h	2 s	0.982438

4   Discussion and Conclusion

In this paper we provide preliminary results of ongoing research in the area of reliability improvement for critical infrastructure monitoring network. We consider long pipeline monitoring networks to detect events of interest (leaks, unauthorized access, special states of the system and transported product, etc.). We are focused on developing a tool for jointly optimizing the structural reliability of WSNs used for pipeline monitoring and optimizing the functional reliability of WSNs for this purpose. To achieve this goal, we use sub-models that characterize the reliability of the channels during their operation, and then, we obtain the reliability of the entire network, taking into account its topology. The results obtained can be used to solve a number of the following practical problems: finding a compromise between minimizing the costs of a critical infrastructure monitoring system and improving the functional and structural reliability of this system. In future works, we will use the properties of the longitudinal cut to implement an algorithm outperforming 2-Cuts. Also, we will develop technique to maintain quality of service and quality of experience (QoS, QoE), that increases the profitability of IoT technologies.

References

1. Sunhee, Y., Wei, Y., Heidemann, J., Littlefield, B., Shahabi, C.: SWATS: wireless sensor networks for steamflood and waterflood pipeline monitoring. IEEE Netw. **25**(1), 50–56 (2011)
2. Phelan, B., et al.: Should I stay or should I go? Maximizing lifetime with relays. In: Proceedings of the IEEE DCOSS 2012, pp. 1–8 (2012)
3. Mohamed, N., et al.: Failure impact on coverage in linear wireless sensor networks. In: Proceedings of the SPECTS 2013, pp. 188–195 (2013)
4. Colbourn, C.J.: The Combinatorics of Network Reliability. Oxford University Press, New York (1987)
5. Petingi, L.: Introduction of a new network reliability model to evaluate the performance of sensor networks. Int. J. Math. Models Meth. Appl. Sci. **5**(3), 577–585 (2011)
6. Migov, D.A., Shakhov, V.: Reliability of ad hoc networks with imperfect nodes. In: Jonsson, M., Vinel, A., Bellalta, B., Belyaev, E. (eds.) MACOM 2014. LNCS, vol. 8715, pp. 49–58. Springer, Cham (2014). https://doi.org/10.1007/978-3-319-10262-7_5
7. Sun, F., Shayman, M.A.: On pairwise connectivity of wireless multihop networks. Int. J. Secur. Netw. **2**(1/2), 37–49 (2007)
8. Shazly, M., et al.: On area coverage reliability of wireless sensor networks. In: Proceedings of IEEE Conference on Local Computer Networks (LCN 2011), Bonn, Germany, pp. 580–588 (2011)
9. Ball, M.O.: Computational complexity of network reliability analysis: an overview. IEEE Trans. Reliab. **35**(3), 230–239 (1986)
10. Shakhov, V., Koo, I.: Graph-based technique for survivability assessment and optimization of IoT applications. Int. J. Softw. Tools Technol. Transf. **23**(1), 105–114 (2020). https://doi.org/10.1007/s10009-020-00594-9
11. Shooman, A.M., Kershenbaum, A.: Exact graph-reduction algorithms for network reliability analysis. In: IEEE Global Telecommunications Conference GLOBECOM, vol. 91, pp. 1412–1420 (1991)
12. Pérez-Rosés, H.: Sixty years of network reliability. Math. Comput. Sci. **12**(3), 275–293 (2018). https://doi.org/10.1007/s11786-018-0345-5
13. Wood, R.K.: Triconnected decomposition for computing K-terminal network reliability. Networks **19**, 203–220 (1989)
14. Migov, D.: Methods of network reliability calculation based on the use of vertex cuts. Comput. Technol. **13**, 425–431 (2008)
15. Rodionov, A.S., Migov, D.A., Rodionova, O.K.: Improvements in the efficiency of cumulative updating of all-terminal network reliability. IEEE Trans. Reliab. **61**(2), 460–465 (2012)
16. Migov, D.A., Rodionova, O.K., Rodionov, A.S., Choo, H.: Network probabilistic connectivity: using node cuts. In: Zhou, X., et al. (eds.) EUC 2006. LNCS, vol. 4097, pp. 702–709. Springer, Heidelberg (2006). https://doi.org/10.1007/11807964_71
17. Burgos, J., Amoza, F.: Factorization of network reliability with perfect nodes I: introduction and statements. Discr. Appl. Math. **198**, 82–90 (2016)
18. Page, L.B., Perry, J.E.: A practical implementation of the factoring theorem for network reliability. IEEE Trans. Reliab. **37**(3), 259–267 (1998)

RES-Q an Ongoing Project on Municipal Solid Waste Management Program for the Protection of the Saniq River Basin in Southern Lebanon

Aiman Rashid[1] , Kassem Aleik[2], Zeinab Alloush[2], Nathalie Awada[3],
Mohammad Baraki[2], Marco Bardus[3], Rabih Chaar[4], Bilal Chehade[2], Batoul Fakih[4],
Laura Maria Foddis[1], Chiara Garau[1], Rana Hajjar[4], Reem Khattar[4], May Massoud[3],
Michel Mockbel[3], Ali Mohammad[2], and Augusto Montisci[1(✉)]

[1] University of Cagliari, Cagliari, Italy
{aiman.rashid,augusto.montisci}@unica.it
[2] Union of Municipalities of Iqlim al-Tuffah, Beirut, Lebanon
[3] American University of Beirut, Beirut, Lebanon
[4] MONEERA, Non-profit Organization, Beirut, Lebanon

Abstract. Lebanon is currently facing an unprecedented mix of social, economic, and political crises, which exacerbate many public health and environmental health problems. Among these, solid waste management (SWM) is considered one of the biggest challenges that Lebanon has been facing for the past two decades. In the absence of national guidelines and ministerial action, SWM is a responsibility of local municipalities. In this paper, we describe the development of a technology-based Waste Management System (WMS) in an area of 43 villages in southern Lebanon. The project is inspired to the paradigms of circular economy and smart cities, and it aims to define affordable and efficient strategies to address SWM. The driving factor in defining the strategies is economic and environmental sustainability, as Lebanon imports most of its resources in hard currency, which is becoming less and less available. The lessons learned from this project can be transposed in other areas and countries with limited financial resources, representing an important paradigm for the WMSs in many areas of the world.

Keywords: Waste management · Circular economy · Sustainability · Smart governance · IoT · ICT · Lebanon

1 Introduction

The paper describes the EU-funded project RES-Q (EuropeAid/155108/DD/ACT/LB), whose objective is to implement a waste management system in the Sainiq River basin (Lebanon) according to a logic of circular economy. Since 1997 Lebanon had to face a challenging waste crisis, which led to task Municipalities and Unions with collection, treatment, and disposal often with limited and variable budgets each year, which in some instances forced municipalities to adopt quick solutions with harmful environmental consequences such as open dumps [1–3]. As the waste crisis in Lebanon continues to

© Springer Nature Switzerland AG 2021
O. Gervasi et al. (Eds.): ICCSA 2021, LNCS 12956, pp. 536–550, 2021.
https://doi.org/10.1007/978-3-030-87010-2_40

unfold, efforts to find sustainable and scalable solutions to solid waste management are being sought by various governmental and non-governmental entities, as well as by international organizations as European Commission, which realized that solving the waste crisis in Lebanon is of strategic importance for the entire area [4].

Municipalities are the local administrations charged with the day-to-day management of all public works located within their boundaries, that is why they are taking all responsibilities related to landscaping and beautification works, maintenance of water and wastewater networks, street lighting, waste disposal, internal roads, recreational facilities, as well as the urban planning in coordination with the Directorate General of Urban Planning [5].

Municipalities are considered as key players and actors in the management of municipal solid waste. In this respect, the decree no. 8735 of 1974 [6] on the maintenance of public cleanliness sets the responsibility of municipalities in the collection and disposal of household wastes, and emphasizes that the health council of the governorate should approve the location of waste disposal sites. Moreover, the municipal law no. 118 of 1977 [7] entitles the municipal councils to build solid waste disposal facilities.

The target area of the project represents the higher part of Jabal Amel in south Lebanon, where the open dumps scatter randomly, threatening the safety and integrity of surface water and ground water, as well as causing air and soil pollution. All these effects reflect negatively on the health and life of local citizens. The municipalities involved in the project fall within the scope of two governorates: Nabatieh governorate and South Lebanon governorate [8].

The main goal of the paper is to present a model of an Integrated Solid Waste Management (ISWM) which utilizes the concepts of ICT, IoT, smart city and circular economy. The paper addresses the problem by showing how an ICT platform, sensor-installed bins and algorithm-based scheduling and collection can optimize overall processes of ISWM. This paper is organized into five sections including Sect. 1, introduction. Section 2 is Lebanese context which discusses the project RES-Q, target area, problem of open dumps, and forecast the waste generation in the target area. Section 3 is current situation in the target area and shed some light on the climate conditions, human capital, waste sources, amounts of waste, waste composition, organized or unorganized method of SWM, CAPEX and OPEX. Section 4 presents the proposed WMS by the implementation of ICT, details of an ICT platform developed to address the problem and smart waste collecting system. Finally, Sect. 5 wraps up the paper with discussion, conclusion, and future advancements in the different dimensions of ISWM.

2   Lebanese Context

The EU programme ProMARE (EuropeAid/155108/DD/ACT/LB) [9], which finances the RES-Q project, comes under the umbrella of abovementioned actions. The RES-Q project is aimed at developing a model of Integrated Solid Waste Management (ISWM) system, which would preserve the environment surrounding the Sainiq River basin in the southern of Lebanon (Fig. 1). The target area covers three Unions of municipalities: Iqleem at-Tuffah (IET), Jezzine (JEZ) & Jabal Al Rihan (RIH) - encompassing a total of 44 municipalities. In the RES-Q project the unions of municipalities of IET and RIH are involved. The union of IET includes 10 municipalities (11 villages), for 96 km², and RIH (6 municipalities, 43 km²), in addition to Kfar Melki, a municipality that is out of any union. IET is the most populated region whether in winter or in summer, while RIH is the least populated one. The Rural target area witnesses a significant rural exodus given the significant variances in population between summer (108,269 inhabitants) and winter (63,845 inhabitants).

In the targeted area, the ISWM practices suffer a gap with the technologies available in the market, due in part to limited finances, but even without additional costs there is margin to reduce the footprint of waste caused by the consumers. The involved Municipalities and Unions of Municipalities continued to assume responsibilities, with some of them handling collection on their own and then dumping the waste randomly, and with others outsourcing the collection and disposal services (to seven private contractors). Therefore, there is no coordinated innovative efforts at the strategic level to address SWM and reduce waste going to landfills/open dumps.

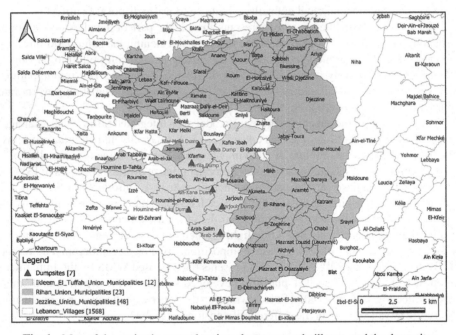

Fig. 1. Map of the project's covered region, the concerned villages, and the dumpsites

Many open dumps are spread throughout the target area (Fig. 1). Such dumps have immediate impact on residents' health and environment. Continuous burning of waste at open dump sites is also presumed to be a major cause of diseases/disorders. Several of these dumps are located directly onto the Sainiq riverbanks (Fig. 2). Leachates from these dumps directly pollute aquifers, the Sainiq River, and eventually the Mediterranean Sea. This is the central environmental concern that the project aims to address.

The region is therefore in deep need for an ISWM plan that provides a coherent approach to waste management while mitigating the negative environmental and social impacts. In order to mitigate the threats and effects and to meet the main objective of the solution, we aspire to build a 'Circular Economy' model by redesigning resource flows in the target area to maximize prevention and recycling of waste while preventing waste disposal from occurring in harmful ways, in addition to remediating existing open dumps.

It is estimated that by 2050, 66% of the global population will be residing in cities, compared to ~54% residing now [10]. This implies that 2.4 billion people will be potentially added to the global urban population. Consequently, this will inevitably result in a significant expansion of existing urban environments and lead to the need to create new ones. Cities use <2% of the earth's surface yet consume more than 75% of the natural resources available globally. The United Nations Environment Programme [10] estimates that the material consumption related to cities will augment to ~90 billion tons by 2050 compared to 40 billion tons in 2010. Some of these resources are primary energy, raw materials, fossil fuel, water, and food [11].

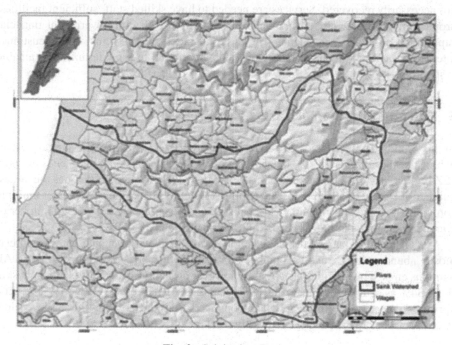

Fig. 2. Sainiq river Basin

As a result, cities are expected to experience challenges related to growth, performance, competitiveness and residents' livelihood [12]. Deterioration of liveability challenges related to waste management, scarce resources, air pollution and traffic congestion that cause human health concerns, as well as aging public infrastructure, are some of the problems generated by rapid urbanization [13]. In order to address these issues, the smart city concept has emerged as one of the possible solutions.

ISWM (Integrated Sustainable Waste Management) [14] concept is a technique that facilitates comprehensive study of dynamic and multi-dimensional processes. The concept was established by waste urban environment and planning consultants and associates or organizations operating in developing countries and further developed by the Collaborative Working Group (CWG) on solid waste management [15]. The model recognizes the importance of three dimensions when the waste management system is analysed, developed, or changed. The dimensions are: stakeholders interested in the management of solid waste, the elements or stages of movement or flow of materials from generation points to treatment and final disposal, and the aspects or 'lenses' through which the system is analysed [16]. Reliable data should be generated, and proper information networks should be established within and between municipalities. Decision makers, responsible for planning and policy making, need to be well educated about the city's situation to make positive changes, designing innovative waste management solutions geared to residents' desires, considering their ability to pay for the facilities.

Solid waste facilities, like any other programs, have an expense, but the investment is not necessarily recovered. Services are needed to have skilled staff, sufficient facilities, proper infrastructure, proper maintenance, and service. Central government financial support, local leaders' engagement in waste management problems, utility customer interaction, and proper management of funds are crucial to a modernized sustainable system.

3   Current Situation of Target Area

In this section the baseline of the target area is described which include sanitary establishments, and commercial and industrial entities. Only one hospital of 28 beds exists in JEZ region. Few dispensaries and clinics exist in IET, JEZ and RIH. JEZ has the largest number of commercial and industrial entities, while RIH lacks the existence of multiple commercial entities (slaughterhouses, patisseries, industries, etc.). The total number of commercial entities in IET are 285 while 442 in JEZ and 39 in RIH.

A considerable part of the three unions is covered with vegetation, with forests mostly abundant in JEZ and RIH unions (cover more than 50% of the surface area). All 3 unions engage in agricultural activities, however agricultural land use is the highest in IET - 34% as compared to 13% and 18% for JEZ and RIH, respectively. The "Artificial Territory" are areas of urbanization and populated areas, the cover of these areas is low in our project's area since they are mostly rural areas.

3.1   Climate Conditions

The study area is mainly influenced by the Mediterranean climate. It is an eclectic climate between the moderate cold temperate zones, and desert sub-tropical regions [17, 18]. The study area is exposed to several types of wind because of its rugged topography, and the south western winds prevail most of the year [19, 20]. The annual average is between 12 °C and 20 °C. The relative humidity in the study area ranges from 50% to 85% most of the days of the year [19]. Wind speed reaches up to nearly 14 m/s in the study area, and the annual average is 6 m/s. Moreover, the study area receives precipitation in several forms (water, hail, snow). The snow covers the mountains for around three months (Komat Jezzin). The average yearly mean precipitation ranges between 700 mm/year and 1500 mm/year.

IET is mostly dominated by red soil (Terra Rossa). JEZ is mostly dominated by red soil (Terra Rossa), white greyish soil and sandy soil. As to RIH, there is also a large part of it covered by red soil (Terra Rossa discontinued), but there is a wider mix of various soil types in the region [21].

In general, the region benefits from an ecological diversity which has relatively been maintained over the years. The pine and oaks forests are still widespread, and the flora is relatively stable. However, some of the springs have been exposed to pollution, which is affecting the diversity of living organisms [22]. There are currently five types of problems faced by the municipalities in land use and ecosystem managements, which are, random construction, ploughing the land which destroys large areas of pine trees especially in RIH, mismanagement of forest leading to a decreased forest surface area, forests fires during Israeli occupation and wars have also been a critical factor to the ecology and the negative effects of open waste dumps which has a major effect on both fauna and flora.

3.2 Human Capital

The unemployment rate in IET is 13.9% while 11.1% in JEZ and RIH. The percentage of families under the poverty line is about 40%, 44% of employees are paid monthly and same percentage of employees working in the production sectors. The health insurance coverage goes to 40% in IET and 49% in JEZ & RIH according to study conducted in 2014.

The level of education among the people of the target area is 66.7% and 70% up to elementary and middle school level, 9.4% and 13.1% up to secondary school level, 11.5% and 6.4% university and higher education while 12.4% and 10.5% vocational sector in IET and JEZ-RIH respectively.

3.3 Waste Sources, Amounts of Waste and Waste Composition

Municipal authorities do not possess any records concerning the composition of the general waste stream or the number of special wastes being generated within their respective towns. Therefore, the study team had to rely solely on the data provided by the waste characterization studies. Three sampling and sorting campaigns were conducted throughout year 2020, one during the season of winter (March 16th–26th), one during the season of summer (July 9th–16th), and one during the month of Ramadan (May 17th–21st).

The data recorded across the sorted samples was compiled to calculate the mean percentage estimates for each waste category. The sectors investigated during the winter and summer studies were the residential and the mixed residential and commercial (R&C) waste streams, with samples being collected from the unions of JEZ, RIH, and IET. The residential waste stream was broken down into four different sub-classifications based on housing density and income. The data derived from the summer and winter studies were compared with one another to determine if any notable alterations in the composition of the disposed stream had occurred as a result of temporal changes. Meanwhile, the characterization study conducted during the season of Ramadan was constricted to exploring the residential waste stream within the union of IET and the village of Kfar Melki. The objective of that exercise was directed towards determining if the season of Ramadan would bring about any pronounced alterations in the consumption and waste generation patterns of the residents.

The total production of mixed solid waste from the target area is 65 tons/day, distributed as follows: 35 tons/day in IET, 20 tons/day in JEZ & 10 tons/day in RIH. mixed SW production is higher in summer in all municipalities. Bodies providing mixed SWM services are the municipality or the union itself or private contractors. SWM operations are limited to collection, transfer, and disposal, unless for JEZ where SW treatment is applied. Frequency of collection depends on the produced quantity of waste and the population in each village and varies between winter and summer.

In IET, each municipality undertakes the SWM operations (collection and disposal) within its borders and disposes the waste in the seven open dumps located within its borders (Fig. 1). Only 4 municipalities, "Roumine, Azza, Houmine Tahta and Sarba", assigned private contractors for the SWM operations (collection and transfer) within their borders. In JEZ, the union undertakes the SWM operations for all the municipalities within its borders, by assigning private companies for the collection, transfer, and treatment of waste. In RIH, each municipality assigns a private company for the SWM operations (collection and disposal) within its borders. Only the municipality of Aychieh is responsible of the SWM operations within its borders. Currently, this municipality is disposing waste in an open dump located within its borders, but it is going in the nearest to subcontract a private company for the collection and treatment of produced waste.

Quantities of excavation, construction and demolition waste are not determined. Bodies providing construction waste management services are the municipalities or construction contractors when no specific municipal management is applied. SWM applied by some municipalities in IET, and JEZ are collecting and disposing construction waste in small holes dedicated for that and reusing construction waste in special construction works. In RIH, only reusing construction waste in special construction works or to cover ground cracks.

Bodies providing farms waste management are the owners of farms themselves or the farms workers with no specific municipal management. Waste produced from farms are compost, manure, or dried residues and all of them are being sold to the farmers in the bigger farms in IET, JEZ and RIH.

Quantities of waste produced from the slaughterhouse in JEZ are equal to 10 tons/month. Bodies providing slaughterhouses waste management are the slaughterhouses themselves while no specific municipal management is applied. The slaughterhouses in IET collect and landfill in rented land or dispose in the dumpsites while in JEZ, collect and landfill in a hole near to the slaughterhouse whereas there is no slaughterhouse in RIH.

Small amounts of clinical waste are produced in the target area. Bodies providing clinical waste management are the clinics themselves in cooperation with private companies, Arc en Ciel [23] and Mirage company, with no specific municipal management. SWM applied to one dispensary in IET by a private company which collects the clinical waste only from the bigger clinic, Islamic Health Society, Jbaa located in IET (quantity: 3 kg/month and payments: 55–60 cent/kg). All clinics send their waste to Jezzine Governmental Hospital, and then the hospital treats it with an incinerator existing in the hospital (quantity: 2.5 kg/day). The small clinics in IET, JEZ & RIH dispose their hazards waste with the mixed municipal waste.

Only JEZ union applies a specific management for the carton/cardboard. The quantity of cartons produced and managed in JEZ goes to 62 tons/year. The municipalities collect the cartons and sends them to a Factory Located in Beqaa (Sicomo SAL) with payments $ 50/ton.

Currently, the capital expenditure (CAPEX) of the target area for performing SWM is $ 256,950 in total out of which 80.4% ($ 206,500) is shared by IET while JEZ and RIH share 11.7% ($ 30,000) and 7.9% ($ 20,450). But the operational expenditure (OPEX) of the target area for performing SWM is $ 3,054,173 in total out of which 31.1% ($ 1,780,000) is shared by IET while JEZ and RIH share 58.3% ($ 288,000) and 10.1% ($ 325,343).

4 Proposed Waste Management System

Projects are most often series of processes where various levels of participation play a role in achieving a satisfactory outcome.

This project focuses on the four distinct target groups (TG) that are segments of the general public (Fig. 3): waste generators (TG1): individual citizens who generate MSW; organizations that generate MSW (food related entities, hotels, shops, markets and schools), and special waste (health units, industries and slaughterhouses); waste managers (TG2): technical staff operating at the municipalities (technical committee), dealing with MSW, NGOs and SMEs working in the collection sector, environmental health professionals and specialists, at the local, national and international level; policy makers (TG3): local (heads of municipalities and/or representatives responsible for waste management), national (Ministries of Environment, Industry, Municipalities, Public Health, Social Affairs, Agriculture, Administrative Reforms, Supreme Planning Council) and international (EU network working on similar issues), public authorities dealing with SWM strategies; and other influencers (TG4): journalist and news media agencies covering especially those covering environmental issues, civil society organizations (scouts, women's groups, activist groups, cultural and service associations) and local public figures (religious leaders, educational and social actors).

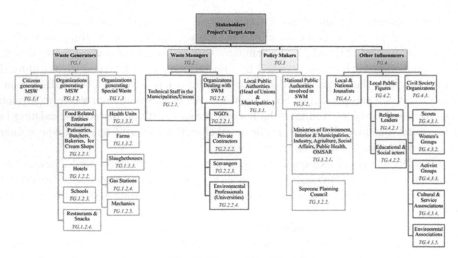

Fig. 3. Key stakeholders

4.1 ICT Platform

The concept of using information and communication technology (ICT) has influenced every sector of conventional workplace and solid waste management (SWM) is no different. Advanced technologies, such as big cloud, computing data, internet of things, cyber-physical systems, virtual and augmented reality, can play an essential part in the implementation of sustainable smart cities and green circular economy ideologies and the even out such initiatives by governments, organizations, and society all together [24]. The solution provided here has two dimensions, one is the introduction of technology like communication, computing, data analysis and another is the implementation of green economy such as reduce, reuse, recycle and restore. Both solutions help each other to resolve the issue of SWM [25].

Many researchers have presented the concept of green economy with different "R" models which include 3R, 4R, 6R, or even 9R [26]. The first three R's are related to "reduce", "reuse", and "recycle" of the model which are interlocked to achieve green economy [27]. Spatial technologies have been dominating the areas of environmental modelling and to manage complex spatial information for ICT platforms to integrate a variety of models, sub-systems and interfaces. These technologies can be categorized as geographic information systems (GIS), global positioning system (GPS) and remote sensing (RS). The main purpose of the technology is to capture, store, analyse and map spatial data. Most of such datasets may consist of attribute data, raster, features, spatial topology and networks of highways, roads, streets, and lanes [28].

GIS is one of the advanced computer-based spatial technology which has ability to collect, store, manage, integrate, manipulate, analyse and display of spatial data known as geospatial or geographically referenced data. Such data is present in the form of layers and GIS can separate theses layers for further manipulation [29].

In recent decades, organizations involved in ISWM have implemented different kinds of technologies to improve the effectiveness of waste management and automate the collection of bins [30]. To solve the problems in manual data collection, many researchers have studied the possibility of implementing advanced ISWM systems that are based on identification technologies. The proliferation of identification technologies, such as barcode and RFID technologies, brought a new strength to ISWM systems.

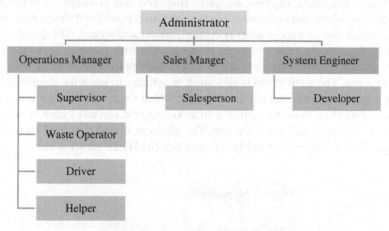

Fig. 4. Hierarchy of users with privileges

The platform discussed in this paper consists of user creation portal which is controlled by the administrator of the platform (Fig. 4). The administrator decides the role of the user and as with the role, the user can exercise the privileges of that role. For any specific user, administrator of the platform has right to award any particular privilege for a certain period of time. The administrator has also right to edit or delete any user. Currently, the platform holds the roles of administrator (ADM), operation manager (OM), sales manager (SM), system engineer (SE), supervisor (SU), waste operator (WO), driver (DR), helper (HLP), salesperson (SP) and developer (DLP) but not limited to these only and further roles can also be created upon requirement.

The OM has privileges to create tasks and user accounts for supervisors, drivers, and helpers, as well as OM creates, edits or removes scheduled tasks or daily tasks. He assigns tasks to the DRs and monitors the status of those tasks. He also manages the database of the tracks fleet. The SM has privilege to make quotations for the commercial customers and creating their task reports with his team which include SPs. The SE along with DLPs has responsibility of smooth functioning of the platform and troubleshoot any error that could hinder the operation of the platform. The SE is responsible for creation database of sources (bins/collection points) and destination (deposit locations: recycle plants, composting sites, and dumpsites). This data is generated with Google Maps location fetching tool (geolocation) and maintained/stored in the database. Similarly, the list type of waste and addition or removal of any specific type of waste is also performed by the SE/DLPs. The DRs input the data of point of collection, type, and quantity of waste as the job is completed. SUs assigns the WOs to crosscheck segregation and registering of the type of waste and the quantity against each completed task when DRs reaches the destination.

4.2 Implementation of ICT

The platform is organised into different groups and each group has its own tasks (Fig. 5). The first group is the roles which creates, edits, delete and manages the types of roles available in the platform and their privileges. The second group is users which include user creation, amending, deletion, assigning roles and user privileges. The third group is geolocation where data of source (waste collection point) and destination (recycle plant, compost site or export area) is created, edited and stored. The fourth group is waste which keeps the record of types of waste. The fifth group is fleet management which manages, creates, edits, and delete data pertaining to vehicles and trucks used to transport waste. The sixth group is allocation of vehicles to users for identification and keeping track of task and the last group is task which creates, schedules, edits, deletes the task of collection to dispose-off as well as keeping the record of users to whom task assigned to, quantity and type of waste. The platform is coded in PHP programming language, the database is kept in MySQL and Apache HTTP server is used.

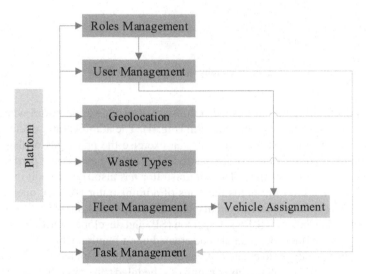

Fig. 5. Structure of platform

The bins are installed with IR sensors which senses how much the bin is filled. As soon as the bins are reached at 90% capacity, it sends a notification to the platform through the GSM module for the pickup of the bin. Each bin has an identification RFID on it, when the waste is collected, the quantity and type of waste is entered through the App which can be verified with the previously automatically sent data.

The routes of collection vehicles are optimized according to the real time traffic flow. Similarly, the placement of bins at the locations are also scheduled and optimized according to the daily/weekly waste collection of each type. This data is uploaded in the cloud and further used to perform statistical analysis to achieve breakeven and to maximize the benefit in terms of environment. This will not only increase the productivity, efficiency and effectiveness of the platform as well as reduce the OPEX of the whole process.

4.3 Waste Collecting System

The most crucial aspect of any ICT platform is the data flow and the technologies used. Figure 6 shows how the traffic and data flows among the data centre, waste bins and deposit sites. The waste collection follows two-way procedure, one with the scheduling and another upon notification that can be generated by any passer-by near the open waste. As of scheduling, all the types of waste are scheduled on the days of the week. This scheduling process is automated and is optimized by analysing the amount of specific type of waste collected from certain bin location (Fig. 7). The scheduled tasks are notified to the SRs and HLPs through a mobile application, SMS, and email. The other way of identification of waste can be notified by the any citizen through sending a picture along with the geographical coordinates and/or bar code present on the waste bin. This notification alerts the OM who analyses the state of the operation and in case of failure, he creates an appropriate remediation task.

Once the tasks are created, whether through scheduling or by OM and notifications are sent to the relevant operators (DRs and HLPs), they start the job and notify it back through the mobile application. The OM monitors the location of each truck in real time as well as the status of the task. As soon as the task is finished, the DRs feed the data through the mobile application against the completed task. The collected waste is sent to three main locations (Fig. 6), (1) recycle plants, in case of segregated inorganic waste like glass, plastic, aluminium, paper etc., (2) composting sites, in case of segregated organic waste like vegetables or meat and (3) export, in case of undifferentiated and such waste which is uneconomical to segregate. The type and quantity of each type of waste in entered in the database as it is collected from its source by the WOs.

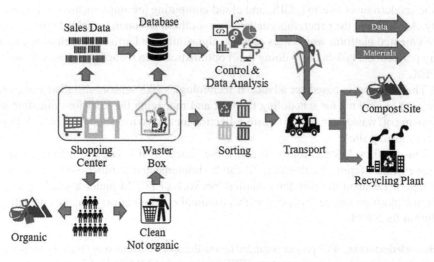

Fig. 6. Flowchart of data and materials

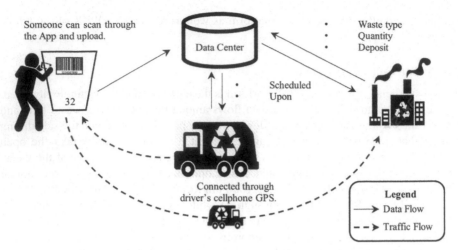

Fig. 7. Schematic of data and traffic flow among data centre, waste bins and deposit locations

5 Discussion and Conclusions

The intent of this paper was not only to summarize the existing problems and lack of organized management in Lebanon and the administrative, and public health challenges faced by the dwellers due to this scenario, but also to provide a smart solution to address these issues. The model presented in this paper provides a self-sustainable, economical, and data-driven solution. The concept of "how to implement circular economy and smart cities in developing countries" is discussed and feasible solution is provided in the form of a platform.

The problem of SW can be managed and resolved very efficiently and effectively if the modern tools like IoT, GIS, and cloud computing are implemented in a sensible way. As shown in the paper, this challenge in southern Lebanon is tackled with a newly implemented platform which uses sensors, algorithms, and artificial intelligence to not only perform the task but also doing them optimistically to reduce manpower as well as OPEX.

The platform is based on advanced technologies like sensors-installed bins, optimization algorithms for scheduling the task and managing the fleet for collection and disposing off waste from source (waste collection locations) to destination (recycle plants or composting site).

The platform has the ability to add more functions if needed to match a specific requirement in future. Furthermore, it can be implemented to other areas and municipalities of Lebanon to bring the complete network of ISWM under a single grid. For this, the platform can be expanded with a minimal cost and effort to make one national solution for SWM.

Acknowledgements. This project is funded by the European Commission under the umbrella of the European Neighbourhood Instrument (ENI) for the period 2014–2020 ("Complementary support to the development of waste management schemes" Ref. EuropeAid/155108/DD/ACT/LB).

References

1. Boutros, J.: Garbage Crisis in Lebanon - 1997: Same Policy, Repeated History (2015). https://english.legal-agenda.com/garbage-crisis-in-lebanon-1997-same-policy-repeated-history/
2. Human Rights Watch: Lebanon Needs a Long-Term Waste-Management Strategy, New York (2017)
3. Bassam, K.: Lebanon needs to clean up its act. (2017) https://www.executive-magazine.com/opinion/lebanon-needs-to-clean-up-its-act.
4. European Commission: European Neighbourhood Policy and Enlargement Negotiations: Lebanon. https://ec.europa.eu/neighbourhood-enlargement/neighbourhood/countries/lebanon_en
5. UN-Habitat: Reforming Urban Planning System in Lebanon: Findings of the Research/Assessment. , Nairobi (2013)
6. Official Gazette: Decree No. 8735: Maintaining public cleanliness (dated 23/08/1974). Office of the Prime Minister, Ministry of Public Works and Transport, Ministry of Interior, Ministry of Tourism, Ministry of Public Health (1974)
7. Ministry of Interior and Municipalities: Decree - Law No. 118: Municipal Act (dated 30/06/1977). Directorate General of Municipalities (1977)
8. Tohmé, J., Aouad, M.: Territorial administration of Lebanon, http://www.localiban.org/territorial-administration-of-lebanon, last accessed 2021/06/17.
9. European Commission: Complementary support to the development of waste management schemes (relaunch). https://webgate.ec.europa.eu/europeaid/online-services/index.cfm?do=publi.welcome&nbPubliList=15&orderby=upd&orderbyad=Desc&searchtype=RS&aofr=155108
10. Swilling, M., et al.: The Weight of Cities: Resource Requirements of Future Urbanization, Nairobi, Kenya (2014)
11. Swilling, M., et al.: The weight of cities: resource requirements of future urbanization, nairobi, kenya (2014)
12. Bouton, S., et al.: How to make a city great, Chicago (2013)
13. Washburn, D., Sindhu, U., Balaouras, S., Dines, R.A., Hayes, N.: Helping CIOs Understand "Smart City" Initiatives. , Cambridge (2010)
14. Shams, S., Juani, R.H.M., Guo, Z.: Integrated and sustainable solid waste management for Brunei Darussalam. In: 5th Brunei International Conference on Engineering and Technology (BICET 2014). pp. 1–6. Institution of Engineering and Technology, Bandar Seri Begawan, Brunei Darussalam (2014). https://doi.org/10.1049/cp.2014.1066.
15. Collaborative Working Group: Origins and development. http://www.cwgnet.net/about/origins-and-development/
16. Kumar, S., Singh, S., Banerjee, S.: Solid waste management in developing countries. J. Crit. Rev. 7, 1282–1285 (2020). https://doi.org/10.31838/jcr.07.10.252
17. Sanlaville, P.: Etude géomorphologique de la région littorale du Liban (1977)
18. Kabakian, V., Kai, L., Naddaf, Y., Sheikh, R.: Lebanon's Second National Communication to the United Nations Framework Convention on Climate Change. Beirut, Lebanon (2011)
19. Shaban, A.: Water Resources of Lebanon. Springer, Cham (2020). https://doi.org/10.1007/978-3-030-48717-1
20. Ministère des travaux publics et des transports Liban: Atlas climatique du Liban (Climatic Atlas of Lebanon). Service Météorologique du Liban, Beirut, Lebanon (1977)
21. Agriculture Department of Hunan Province: Soil Report of Hunan Province, Wageningen (1989)
22. Convention on Biological Diversity: Lebanon - Main Details: Biodiversity Facts. https://www.cbd.int/countries/profile/?country=lb

23. Arc en Ciel: Arc en Ciel. https://www.arc-en-ciel.it/. Accessed 24 May 2021
24. Esmaeilian, B., Wang, B., Lewis, K., Duarte, F., Ratti, C., Behdad, S.: The future of waste management in smart and sustainable cities: a review and concept paper (2018).https://doi.org/10.1016/j.wasman.2018.09.047
25. Demestichas, K., Daskalakis, E.: Information and communication technology solutions for the circular economy. Sustainability. **12**, 1–19 (2020). https://doi.org/10.3390/su12187272
26. Maťová, H., Kaputa, V., Triznová, M.: Responsible consumer in the context of circular economy. In: Chobanova, R. (ed.) 12th Woodema Annual International Scientific Conference - Digitisation and Circular Economy: Forestry and Forestry Based Industry Implications, pp. 69–74. Union of Scientists of Bulgaria, Varna (2019)
27. Das, S., Lee, S.H., Kumar, P., Kim, K.H., Lee, S.S., Bhattacharya, S.S.: Solid waste management: scope and the challenge of sustainability. J. Clean. Prod. **228**, 658–678 (2019). https://doi.org/10.1016/j.jclepro.2019.04.323
28. Milla, K.A., Lorenzo, A., Brown, C.: GIS, GPS, and Remote Sensing Technologies in Extension Services: Where to Start, What to Know. J. Ext. 43, 3FEA6 (2005).
29. Hameed, A.A.: Smart city planning and sustainable development. In: IOP Conference Series: Materials Science and Engineering. p. 022042. Institute of Physics Publishing (2019). https://doi.org/10.1088/1757-899X/518/2/022042
30. Gnoni, M.G., Lettera, G., Rollo, A.: A feasibility study of a RFID traceability system in municipal solid waste management. Int. J. Inf. Technol. Manag. **12**, 27–38 (2013). https://doi.org/10.1504/IJITM.2013.051632

Smart Governance Models to Optimise Urban Planning Under Uncertainty by Decision Trees

Chiara Garau[1]([⊠]) (iD), Giulia Desogus[1] (iD), Alfonso Annunziata[1]([⊠]) (iD), Mauro Coni[1] (iD), Claudio Crobu[2] (iD), and Massimo Di Francesco[2] (iD)

[1] Department of Civil and Environmental Engineering and Architecture, University of Cagliari,
09129 Cagliari, Italy
cgarau@unica.it
[2] Department of Mathematics and Computer Science, University of Cagliari, Via Ospedale 72,
09124 Cagliari, Italy

Abstract. In recent years, the applicative approach to smart governance in urban planning field has increasingly involved the decision-making processes of public administrations and has helped to solve economic, social and environmental challenges of cities. This approach has in fact allowed administrations to understand how changes are taking place in the territory and in real time, through big data, e-governance and city dashboards. However, the literature underlines the lack of decision-making models on which an agreement had been recognized for the organization and management of new projects on an urban scale. This need involves (1) understanding clearly the needs of all actors involved in a project (public or private financiers, public administration, control offices and stakeholders), (2) making optimal decisions w.r.t. the selected criteria, (3) providing a hedge against unexpected data changes. The main applicative goal is to have a full awareness of how much every single change means in economic, logistical and time lag terms. To this end, the authors investigate the viability of Decision Trees to support decision-making processes for urban planning.

Keywords: Replicability · Smart governance · Decision-making processes · Project sustainability · Project scalability

1 Introduction

The growing demand for transparency in decision-making processes and the plurality of contrasting interests involved in place-shaping actions calls for the development of

---

This paper is the result of the joint work of the authors. 'Abstract', 'A decision tree for the case of "via Roma"' and 'Discussion and Conclusion' were written jointly by all authors. Giulia Desogus wrote 'Introduction'. Alfonso Annunziata wrote 'Decision Tree Models applied to Urban Governance: Problem Identification and Construction'. Claudio Crobu wrote 'Guidelines on the construction of decision trees'. Chiara Garau, Mauro Coni, and Massimo Di Francesco coordinated and supervised the paper.

O. Gervasi et al. (Eds.): ICCSA 2021, LNCS 12956, pp. 551–564, 2021.
https://doi.org/10.1007/978-3-030-87010-2_41

techniques for supporting informed decisions within the context of urban planning and governance [1, 2].

Indeed, the always current problems of transparency/accountability and conflict (with its resolution) are central to the implementation of the smart city paradigm [3]. The smart city paradigm, in fact, focuses on the idea of using information and communication technologies to improve wellbeing, living conditions and democracy. Democracy implies participation and transparency; the conflict with different form of solutions is a frequent condition of cities, arising from different motivations, particularly in the case of competition for scarce resources.

This study investigates the usefulness of applying the decision tree model as a simple method to assist in decision-making processes on the identification of strategies for the transformation of the public space. In its simplest form a decision tree can be defined as a tree diagram, which is used for making decisions in business or computer programming by branches representing decisions or uncertain situations with associated risks, costs, results, or probabilities. Namely, it represents a model providing the identification of optimal solutions based on a hierarchical sequence of interdependent sub-decisions, probable results and postulated circumstances.

For these reasons, the decision tree model is a beneficial method for enhancing the judgement of decision-makers, solving possible conflicts and making understandable and transparent the rationale of decision-making processes. The proposed study presents the application of the decision tree model to the assessment of different strategies for the redevelopment of "via Roma", one of the main streets in Cagliari, Italy. The latter is a critical space, within the system of the Cagliari Metropolitan area, characterised by the concentration of different flows, practices, metropolitan and regional scale amenities, and by its ineliminable pre-eminent function as a corridor of mobility and accessibility.

The analysis aims to demonstrate the feasibility of utilizing the tree decision model as a technique for supporting the knowledge-based identification of urban planning strategies, while increasing transparency of the decision-making process and facilitating meaningful participation.

The article is structured on five sections: after this introduction, Sect. 2 analyses decision tree models applied to smart urban governance by identifying some shortcomings in the current literature. Subsequently, Sect. 3 presents the case study and Sect. 4 introduces some guidelines on the construction of decision trees. Section 5 illustrates the decision tree built for the case study at hand. Finally, Sect. 6 summarises the findings of the study and illustrates hypotheses for the future development of the research.

2 Decision Tree Models Applied to Urban Governance: Problem Identification and Construction

Chichernea (2014) argues that "the rapid evolution of Information and Communication Technologies (ICT), Cloud Computing Services, the Internet-of-Things, Everything-as-a-Service (XaaS), as well as the development of new mathematical models, artificial intelligence and data storage capabilities, position DSS at a unique advantage as a continuously improving tool in the process of planning and completing complex projects" [4, p. 1]. In literature, the DDS applied to the city are interpreted as a decision support in the planning process [3, 5] linked to various aspects including the size of the city [6], urban distribution [7], ecology and sustainability [8].

Among all DSSs, decision trees are analytical models useful for representing and solving optimization problems with single criterion in an uncertain environment. The construction of a decision tree is based on a logical and systematic way, and makes the decision maker in the position of addressing a variety of problems. Once a criterion is selected, the tree reports the optimal decision as a path, which is obtained by decomposing the problem into smaller and more manageable parts.

In a nutshell, they are constructed through (1) the definition of a criterion, (2) the construction of the decision tree with the list of possible decisions and possible outcomes and (3) the assignment of probabilities. This process allows to monitor changes, manage risks during construction and make changes. Decision trees are widely used in operations research (e.g., statistics, data mining, machine learning) to support different disciplines (e.g., medicine, statistics, psychology, engineering and management) [9].

Regarding the urban planning field, several studies use decision trees as predictive models rather than prescriptive models for optimization [3, 10]. These mainly concern the field of transport where it is used for the choice analysis of the modality and of the pedestrian's satisfaction in the transport planning process [11–15], to improve travel time prediction [16], to prevent accidents, and to investigate driver behaviour [17, 18]. In the specific domain of urban planning, predictive decision trees focus on specific interventions without taking into account two critical components of urban governance within the paradigm of the smart city: transparency and resolution of the conflict.

The smart city paradigm, in fact, investigates the opportunities for creating efficient, equitable, sustainable urban environments, determined by the integration of information and communication technologies (ICT) in urban economic, social, political processes. Within the perspective of implementing the smart city and governing urban transformations, several issues emerge, involving spatial, social, economic aspects, entangled in an ethical dimension [19, 20]. These issues include propinquity, inequality, precarity, conflict, fear, environmental problems, demographic issues, health emergencies, political representation. In particular, this study focuses on the issues of participation and transparency. Participation and transparency are considered, in fact, as central and interrelated aspects of improving democracy and creating efficient urban environments. The effective engagement of the broad ecosystem of city actors and urban populations, engendered by transparent and participatory governance processes, emerges as a central aspect of successful smart city models. It facilitates the mobilization of individuals' perception and experience of the urban realm, providing councils and public administrations with useful information on competing needs, perspective and concerns of different social groups. More precisely, the relevance of participation in assisting planning processes intersects the centrality of participation as a central aspect of democracy and the demand for participation and transparency determined by the availability of ICT. Transparency can be defined as the guarantee of access to information related to governance processes relevant to the interests of all population groups. In this respect, the notion of transparency is strictly related to that of accountability: the extent to which public agencies are responsible for their policies and able to give a satisfactory reason for them. The relevance of transparency is increased by the emergence of conflict as an ineradicable component of urban planning. Conflict can be defined as a condition of political antagonism revolving around the competition for limited resources. Three aspects of spatial planning determine the onset of conflict: first, decisions on land use are competitive and, often, mutually exclusive: space is a limited resource whose allocation for different land uses, each one respondent to the instances of a specific social group, constitutes the essential aspect of spatial planning. Moreover, decisions on land use are influenced by the system of relations of compatibility and incompatibility among different functions, determining the mutually exclusive relations among interests and instances of different groups.

Second, spatial planning determines the re-distribution of spatial capital. More precisely, planning defines, recognizes, amplifies symbolic and economic values and citizenship rights, by determining the conditions of access of different social and political groups to basic amenities and services. The ineliminable differences in the distribution of benefits, implies that distributive asymmetry is a peculiar component of spatial planning.

Lastly, a different form of asymmetry lies in the differences in the distribution of benefits and externalities of land use decisions, which reflects, in turn, the different dimensions of site involved in place shaping processes. Spatial planning, in fact, produces local transformations, engendering concentrated benefits and externalities that impact population groups at a non-local and trans-boundary scale.

Therefore, the definition of a decision tree model for clarifying criteria, objectives, circumstances and results of decisions, addresses two aspects of the realization of the smart city paradigm: first, by offering a rationale for decision making processes and for managing conflict and competition for space engendered by spatial planning and, second, by increasing the understandability of governance processes.

3 The Case Study

This article focuses on the decision problem related to the urban regeneration of the area of "via Roma", one of the main streets in Cagliari, Italy (Figs. 1 and 2). Opened in 1883, "via Roma" comprises two carriageways – "Lato Portici" delimiting the compact structure of the historic centre and "Lato Porto" delimiting the area of the port – separated by a central tree-lined promenade. "via Roma" is a primary distributor, connecting portions of the urban area separated by the compact structure of the compact city. Moreover, several major buildings related to the political and commercial activity, such as the Civic Palace and the Regional Council, are aligned along its margins. After the Second World War, "via Roma" assumed the role of fundamental urban distributor, intensely frequented by pedestrians and engaged by large flows of private vehicles, trolleybuses and buses. The redevelopment of "via Roma" is an optimal case study because it involves the issues of conflict and transparency, determined by its centrality in the metropolitan area. This condition of centrality results from two factors: i) the concentration of metropolitan-scale services (educational, cultural, social ones) and of administrative functions in the compact city; ii) its topological centrality in the road system of the metropolitan area reinforcing its function as a distributor serving the metropolitan area, (Fig. 2). The relevance of this function is magnified by the reliance of mobility in the metropolitan area on private car-based travel, determining a strong pressure on arterial distributors and on the system of urban primary and secondary distributors. Recent surveys measure

164.637 cars entering the urban area of Cagliari in an average week day and 130.336 cars leaving the urban centre (Comune di Cagliari, 2012), on a population of 156.538 residents (Comune di Cagliari, 2017; iii) the strong commitment of local authorities in policies able to foster sustainable modes of transport [21]; iv) the diversity and density of primary and secondary uses, determining the character of "via Roma" as a multi-modal and multi-functional space, and, thus, engendering a strong competition for space among different practices and social groups [22].

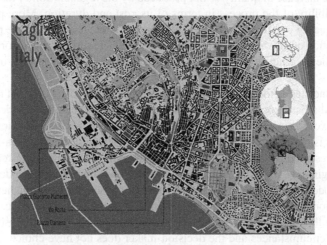

Fig. 1. The area of study: "via Roma" in Cagliari, Italy.

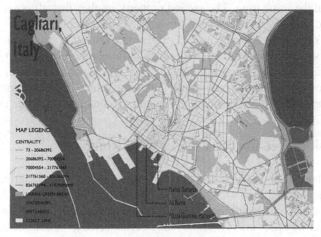

Fig. 2. Centrality, conceptualized as the potential as transit spaces, of streets in the central districts of Cagliari, Italy.

4   Guidelines on the Construction of Decision Trees

The construction of the decision tree model to structure the decision problem related to the regeneration of "via Roma" is a process articulated on three stages. The first step in decision trees is the definition of the criterion for evaluating the impact of alternative policies.

A possible criterion is the quality of the process. The quality of the process incorporates both the increase in quality of life produced by the regeneration of the urban space and the feasibility of the process in terms of its cost and duration. More precisely, the increase in quality of life encompasses the increase in the usability of the public space, the reconnection of the sea-front with the compact urban fabric of the historic centre, the increase in the accessibility of primary and secondary uses concentrated in the historic districts.

The second step is the construction of the decision tree based on a list of alternative decisions and a list of possible outcomes. Decisions are represented by decision nodes and alternative actions on a specific decision are represented by branches originating from the decision node. Uncertain circumstances affecting the decision-making process are represented by event nodes. Possible outcomes of an event are represented by branches originating from the event node. A central distinction between decision nodes and event nodes concerns the nature of respective consequences: branches originating from a decision node represent strategies selected by the decision-maker according to the criterion. On the other hand, branches emanating from event nodes represent outcomes of uncertain circumstances and the decision-maker does not have choice to opt for one of these branches. The outcomes in an event node are requested to be mutually exclusive and collectively exhaustive. The first property means that alternative outcomes could not be observed at the same time. The second property implies that all possible outcomes are considered, and any non-represented outcome cannot be observed.

The third step is the determination of probability values for each branch emanating from event nodes. The probability of a branch indicates the possibility to observe the random outcome associated to each branch. The sum of probabilities of the branches originating from a specific node must be 1, in order to satisfy the requirements of mutual exclusivity and collective exhaustivity of random outcomes of uncertain events.

5   A Decision Tree for the Case of "Via Roma"

This section shows the construction of the decision tree model for structuring the decision problem for the regeneration of "via Roma". The tree is reported in Fig. 3, 3a and 3b.

The root decision is the projected expansion of the light rail system, and its connection with the railway network. This intervention is expected to be completed in 2023 and reintroduces the question of the comprehensive regeneration of Via Roma. The alternative strategies of regeneration of the road space depend on the uncertain amount of available financial resources and include a large infrastructural intervention, a moderate re-configuration of the urban space and of the road network, and the management of the present situation, via regulation of practices and of mobility, and via interventions on the composition of the road space. The large infrastructural intervention includes the

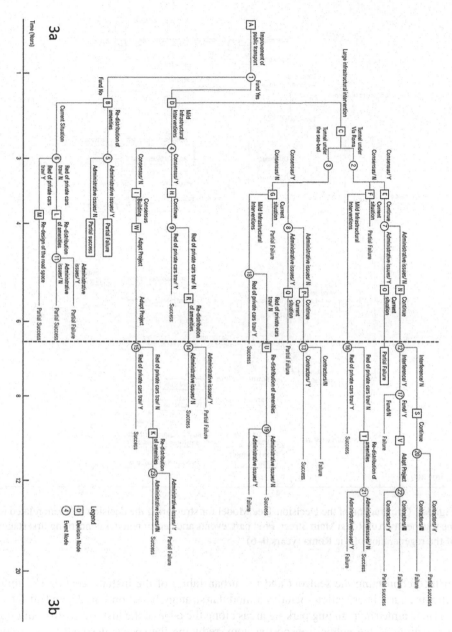

Fig. 3. Construction of the Decision Tree Model for structuring the decision problem related to the regeneration of Roma Main Street. The Decision Tree Model is divided in two parts (3a and 3b), presented separately in the sub-sequent pages.

alternative options of the construction of a road tunnel under the road space and of the construction of a road tunnel under the seabed. This strategy is based on the distinction and separation of spaces of mobility aimed at the realization of a large pedestrian

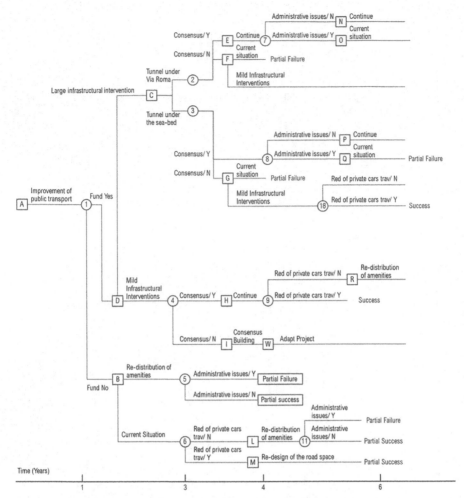

Fig. 3a. Construction of the Decision Tree Model for structuring the decision problem related to the regeneration of Roma Main Street. First part, events and decision nodes concerning first stages of the regeneration of Via Roma (years 0–6).

surface connecting the seafront and the urban fabric of the historic centre. The mild infrastructural intervention includes a modular strategy based on interdependent interventions aimed at: realizing parking areas along the edge of the historic centre, building connections to the public transport system, reducing the spaces destined to mobility, expanding and redesigning pedestrian surfaces, redesigning intersections among "via Roma" and adjacent primary streets. The layout of the decision tree model underlines three significant aspects.

The first is the uncertainty of strategies of regeneration based on large infrastructural interventions. This uncertainty is determined by the plurality of circumstances increasing the impedance of the process. Unfavourable circumstances include the complexity of

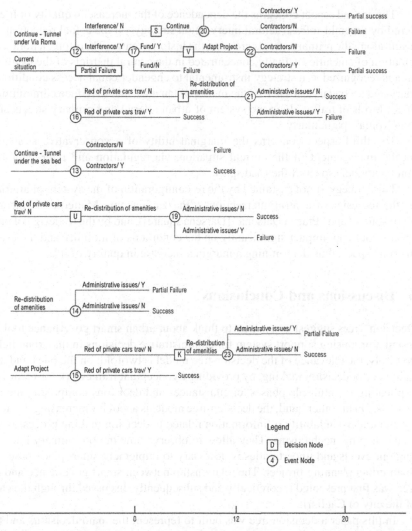

Fig. 3b. Construction of the Decision Tree Model for structuring the decision problem related to the regeneration of Roma Main Street. Second part, probable circumstances and relevant decisions after year 6.

the administrative process, and the duration of the process, increased by the involvement of several agencies, the probability of social protest, determined by the concentration of high financial resources on a single intervention, thus engendering conditions of inequality, and the probability of interferences of the construction site with archaeological remains and with the drainage basin. More precisely, a significant circumstance is represented by the event node consensus; consensus refers to the probability that radical infrastructural interventions in a vulnerable environment meets with the opposition of groups of residents and users directly involved in the transformation of a space.

The second aspect concerns the dependence of the increase in quality of life, engendered by the mild-infrastructural intervention strategy, on the actual reduction of traffic levels along the primary streets crossing the historic centre. Therefore, a policy of redistribution of amenities actually concentrated in the central districts of the Cagliari urban area is recognized as a strategy instrumental to engender equal access conditions to primary and secondary uses across the metropolitan area, and to reduce commuting, which affect levels of traffic along the system of urban arterial and primary streets and along "via Roma", particularly.

The third aspect concerns the marginal utility of a conservative strategy, based on the management of the current situation, via regulation and interventions on the compositional aspect of the road space.

This strategy, if not sustained by the re-configuration of the system of arterial roads, by the re-design of central intersections ("Piazza Giacomo Matteotti" [Giacomo Matteotti square] and "Piazza Darsena" [Darsena square]), and by the re-design of pedestrian spaces could not impact significantly on the conditions of mobility and the usability of the road space, thus determining a marginal increase in quality of life.

6 Discussions and Conclusions

Decision Trees suggest a new way to think about urban smart governance tool and represent a promising support system for administrative decisions in the urban field. More precisely, the relevance of the decision tree model is twofold: on the one hand it offers a rationale for decision making, by providing a conceptual framework for identifying and explicating the multiple phases, circumstances and decisions comprising the planning process. On the other hand, the decision-tree model is a tool for increasing the accessibility and understandability of information related to decision making processes affecting place-shaping mechanisms. They allow to observe how the preliminary knowledge of random events and uncertainties is necessary to implement smart place-based policies in an urban planning project. The relationship between smart governance and decision tree was first presented theoretically and subsequently discussed through the case study of the city of Cagliari.

In this paper a decision tree was built to represent the main decisions and the most relevant sources of uncertainty for evaluating several possible policies on the regeneration of "via Roma". The possible criterion could be the quality of life of the residents, of people who come from other parts of Sardinia and tourists. In fact, "via Roma" is a central node that connects the historic city to the waterfront, where the most important railway hub in Sardinia and the largest cruise terminal on the entire island are located.

In addition to the project itself, the theoretical process has allowed to understand how this decision-making tool can help evaluate the two most critical components of a policy based on smart governance (transparency and conflict) from the beginning of the project. In fact, as analysed in Sect. 2, transparency and conflict are increasingly critical issues between political choice in the urban planning field.

The (political and administrative) criterion of choice looks often unclear and undefined at the beginning of public works, and, particularly in Italy, the project is often modified or blocked upon the change of political mandate. The characteristics of the tree's construction, given a criterion (improving the quality of life), allow to determine an optimal solution from the city's viewpoint, while accounting for several sources of uncertainty (e.g., urban changes).

This, in the first instance, allows to make two distinct considerations on the use of the decision tree to define optimal political choices in the urban field:

1. The constructive logic of the decision tree favours the transparency of the administration through a synthetic representation of i) the political choice; ii) the goal intended to achieve; and especially iii) the interplay between decisions and uncertain situations. This allows to constantly monitor the works that are realised, as well as it is possible to monitor actions in progress or to ascertain renunciations in progress by the administration. Namely, if events external to the project modify the intervention (e.g., example the change of administration), through the decision tree the population can understand not only the logic used for the modification or interruption of the project, but also the criteria of the new administration and its choices.
2. The decision tree allows administrations to follow the logic of improving the quality of life of citizens, through a project management that allows to monitor and modify the process at every stage. In addition, at the time of the decision, the trees allow to measure variables and uncertainties to identify the optimal process that leads to the defined goal, even if this is a long process, such as urbanization works.

These two characteristics of the decision tree show that it can make possible a better planning. This is not only because it allows, a priori, to understand which is the best solution for a given context w.r.t. the objective to be pursued, but also because, once the work has begun, it can evaluate any changes to the project by expecting in advance what events may occur. The latter is fundamental in the field of urban governance. In fact, the interventions in the urban planning field, at the starting point, have a high rate of uncertainty that depends on different (physical, economic, administrative and social) dynamics, which make the entire project vary during construction. Generally speaking, it is essential for good planning to have a method determining the best decisions right from the start and understand what must be done when changes to the initial project occur.

Furthermore, these analyses highlight the importance of using the decision tree in a smart governance perspective that focuses on dual use of technology/social aspect, for two reasons:

1) the digital data produced in the last 20 years based on static and dynamic indicators provided in real time, make possible to automate these models, turning them into urban e-governance tools through, for example, city dashboards;
2) the use of the decision tree offers the population greater involvement by allowing not only the dissemination of information relating to the results of the decision-making process, but above all access to information relating to the structure of the process, its criteria and purposes.

However, some weaknesses in the use of the decision tree in urban planning need to be investigated. In fact, an extension of the method to a larger area than the single project (e.g., insertion of the subway in "Via Roma") could complicate the tree design process. Furthermore, planning requires a multidisciplinarity that would make the predictions of variables and uncertainties extremely challenging at the moment of the decision, while compromising the choice of the optimal process. Another critical point in the use of this methodology could be the risk of using a synthetic support system for urban planning that could not allow a total visualization of the process phases and may be affected by the specific choices on the distributions of probability.

Despite this, the decision tree still appears to be an excellent planning support system and, for further research, this study makes possible to have a methodological approach as a starting point for developing a set of indicators that identify a common criterion for a decision tree for urban policies in a smart governance context. With this in mind, future research will go in three different but complementary directions: (i) the theoretical approach proposed will be implemented with indicators and probability values that will objectively define the decision-making process; (ii) the proposed methodological approach could also be tested in other contexts to underline the potential that the decision tree has for making decisions in the urban field; (ii) the study will focus on the impact that the decision can have on the spatial dimension, and (iii) the authors will analyse how public administrations can include such decision-making tools in their daily practice.

Acknowledgments. This study was supported by the agreement with the Municipality of Cagliari – Strategic and Territorial Planning Service (CUP code: G22C20000080006 - CIG ZEA2E99622) entitled "Innovative methods for participatory urban planning in the drafting of the MUP in adaptation to the RLP and the HSP. Preparation of the preliminary environmental report in the SEA process. Study of the infrastructural structure in the light of the new forms of mobility in line with the drafting SUMPS". This study was developed within the Interdepartmental Center of the University of Cagliari "Cagliari Accessibility Lab".

This study was also supported by the MIUR through the project "WEAKI TRANSIT": WEAK-demand areas Innovative TRANsport Shared services for Italian Towns (Project protocol: 20174ARRHT_004; CUP Code: F74I19001290001), financed with the PRIN 2017 (Research Projects of National Relevance) programme. We authorize the MIUR to reproduce and distribute reprints for Governmental purposes, notwithstanding any copyright notations thereon. Any opinions, findings and conclusions or recommendations expressed in this material are those of the authors, and do not necessarily reflect the views of the MIUR.

References

1. Garau, C., Desogus, G., Zamperlin, P.: Governing technology-based urbanism: degeneration to technocracy or development to progressive planning? In: Willis, K.S., Aurigi, A. (eds.) The Routledge Companion to Smart Cities, pp. 157–174. Routledge, New York (2020) ISBN: 9781138036673
2. Garau, C.: Processi di piano e partecipazione. Gangemi Editore Spa (2013)
3. David, N., Justice, J., McNutt, J.G.: Smart cities are transparent cities: the role of fiscal transparency in smart city governance. In: Rodríguez-Bolívar, M.P. (ed.) Transforming city governments for successful Smart cities. PAIT, vol. 8, pp. 69–86. Springer, Cham (2015). https://doi.org/10.1007/978-3-319-03167-5_5
4. Chichernea, V.: The use of decision support systems (DSS) in smart city planning and management. Roman. Econ. Bus. Rev. Roman.-Am. Univ. **8**(2), 238–251 (2014)

5. Bartolozzi, M., Bellini, P., Nesi, P., Pantaleo, G., Santi, L.: A smart decision support system for smart city. In: IEEE International Conference on Smart City/SocialCom/SustainCom (SmartCity), 19–21 December 2015 (2015). https://doi.org/10.1109/SmartCity.2015.57

6. Borsekova, K., Korónya, S., Vaňováb, A., Vitálišováb, K.: Functionality between the size and indicators of smart cities: a research challenge with policy implications. Cities **78**, 17–26 (2018). https://doi.org/10.1016/j.cities.2018.03.010

7. Pribadi, A., Kumiawan, F., Hariadi, M., Nugroho, S.M.S.: Urban distribution CCTV for smart city using decision tree methods. In: International Seminar on Intelligent Technology and its Applications (ISITIA), 28–29 August 2017 (2017). https://doi.org/10.1109/ISITIA.2017.8124048

8. Ciumasu, I.M.: Dynamic decision trees for building resilience into future eco-cities. Technol. Forecast. Soc. Chang. **80**(9), 1804–1814 (2013). https://doi.org/10.1016/j.techfore.2012.12.010

9. Bertsimas, D., Freund, R.M.: Data, Models and Decisions. Dynamic Ideas (2004).

10. Karimi, F., Sultana, S., Babakan, A.S., Suthaharan, S.: Urban expansion modeling using an enhanced decision tree algorithm. GeoInformatica (2019). https://doi.org/10.1007/s10707-019-00377-8

11. Dong, W., Cao, X., Wu, X., Dong, Y.: Examining pedestrian satisfaction in gated and open communities: an integration of gradient boosting decision trees and impact-asymmetry analysis. Landsc. Urban Plan. **185**, 246–257 (2019). https://doi.org/10.1016/j.landurbplan.2019.02.012

12. Rasouli, S., Timmermans, H.J.P.: Using ensembles of decision trees to predict transport mode choice decisions: effects on predictive success and uncertainty estimates. Eur. J. Transp. Infrast. Res. **14**(4) (2014). https://doi.org/10.18757/ejtir.2014.14.4.3045

13. Sekhara, C.R., Minal, Madhuc, E.: Mode choice analysis using random forest decision trees. Transp. Res. Procedia **17**, 644–652 (2016). https://doi.org/10.1016/j.trpro.2016.11.119

14. Ding, C., Wang, D., Ma, X., Li, H.: Predicting short-term subway ridership and prioritizing its influential factors using gradient boosting decision trees. Sustainability **8**(11), 1100 (2016). https://doi.org/10.3390/su8111100

15. Ding, C., Cao, X., Liu, C.: How does the station-area built environment influence metrorail ridership? Using gradient boosting decision trees to identify non-linear thresholds. J. Transp. Geogr. **77**, 70–78 (2019). https://doi.org/10.1016/j.jtrangeo.2019.04.011

16. Zhang, Y., Haghani, A.: A gradient boosting method to improve travel time prediction. Transp. Res. Part C Emerg. Technol. **58**, 308–324 (2015). https://doi.org/10.1016/j.trc.2015.02.019

17. Ma, X., Ding, C., Luan, S., Wang, Y., Wang, Y.: Prioritizing influential factors for freeway incident clearance time prediction using the gradient boosting decision trees method. IEEE Trans. Intell. Transp. Syst. **18**(9), 2303–2310 (2017). https://doi.org/10.1109/TITS.2016.2635719

18. Ding, C., Wu, X., Yu, G., Wang, Y.: A gradient boosting logit model to investigate driver's stop-or-run behavior at signalized intersections using high-resolution traffic data. Transp. Res. Part C Emerg. Technol. **72**, 225–238 (2016). https://doi.org/10.1016/j.trc.2016.09.016

19. Azzari, M., Garau, C., Nesi, P., Paolucci, M., Zamperlin, P.: Smart city governance strategies to better move towards a smart urbanism. In: Gervasi, O., et al. (eds.) Computational Science and Its Applications – ICCSA 2018, pp. 639–653. Springer International Publishing, Cham (2018). https://doi.org/10.1007/978-3-319-95168-3_43

20. Garau, C., Zamperlin, P., Balletto, G.: Reconsidering the Geddesian concepts of community and space through the paradigm of smart cities. Sustainability **8**(10), 985 (2016)

21. Tilocca, P., et al.: Managing data and rethinking applications in an innovative mid-sized bus fleet. Transp. Res. Procedia **25**, 1899–1919 (2017). https://doi.org/10.1016/j.trpro.2017.05.184
22. Coni, M., Garau, C., Pinna, F.: How has Cagliari changed its citizens in smart citizens? Exploring the influence of ITS technology on urban social interactions. In: Gervasi, O., et al. (eds.) Computational Science and Its Applications – ICCSA 2018, pp. 573–588. Springer International Publishing, Cham (2018). https://doi.org/10.1007/978-3-319-95168-3_39

Computing 15MinCityIndexes on the Basis of Open Data and Services

Claudio Badii, Pierfrancesco Bellini, Daniele Cenni, Simone Chiordi, Nicola Mitolo, Paolo Nesi$^{(\boxtimes)}$, and Michela Paolucci

DISIT Lab, DINFO Department, University of Florence, Firenze, Italy
paolo.nesi@unifi.it
https://www.disit.org, https://www.snap4city.org

Abstract. Despite of the large discussions in the area of city strategies, the effective compliance assessment of each city area with respect to 15-Minute City concepts are still not clear in terms of computation. A huge amount of aspects have to be taken into account, such as: Housing, Govern, Safety, Culture and Cults Services, Environment, Slow Mobility, Fast Mobility, Sport, Economy/sustainability, Food, Health, Education, Services, Entertainment. Each of them may be assessed by taking into account a large number of factors and features. In this paper, 15MinCityIndexes model and its computability approach have been proposed. The proposed model is based on 13 different functions and addressed several features. In addition, the model has been produced by using a method that can be exploited to add more factors and details to the model when other kind of data may be available instead of those we found in our case. It has been produced and validated on Florence metro area which includes multiple cities and rural areas. The model and tools are accessible on a public online dashboard. The 15MinCityIndex approach described in this paper conquered the first place award and grant of the international ENEL-X open data challenge 2020.

Keywords: 15Minute Index · Smart city · Sustainability · Computability · Decision making

1 Introduction

In the context of Smart Cities there is a strong push on shaping cities to be more livable and sustainable for the citizens. The trend has been reinforced with the arrival of COVID-19 pandemic which led to lockdown limiting mobility of city users constraining them in their neighborhood. Thus, the 15-Minute City concept of Carlos Moreno [15] has been revitalized. On that path, a similar trend of *"chrono-urbanism"* has been followed by others whose proposed models for improving quality of life in cities. For example, the 15-Minute walkable neighborhood of [17] and the 20-Minute City model of [10]. They were proposed as viable models for modern cities to address their underlying challenges. Some cities followed this kind of strategies according to their vocation, for example, becoming a pedestrian city, a bike city, saving energy, etc. Without to arrive at

© Springer Nature Switzerland AG 2021
O. Gervasi et al. (Eds.): ICCSA 2021, LNCS 12956, pp. 565–579, 2021.
https://doi.org/10.1007/978-3-030-87010-2_42

a drastic decision, many cities have invested more resources in sustainability, services decentralization/distribution, etc., in order to reduce the mandatory movements of city users among the different part of the city. One of the effects has been a strong increment on the usage of slow and more sustainable mobility and to local/proximity services (selling more bikes for moving, and pet for walking), also forced by a strong reduction of mobility, parking, etc. for the lockdown due to COVID-19 pandemic [1, 3].

In more details, the concept of Carlos Moreno in the first paper of 2016 aimed at providing to city users all their basic essential services at no more than 15 Minute by walk or biking from the point in which they live [15]. Presently Moreno et al. are supporting the concepts a higher quality of life, which can be fulfilled by means of six urban/social **Functions** namely: *living, working, commerce, healthcare, education and entertainment*. For each of them, there is the need to be compliant with **Features** such as *proximity, diversity, density* and *ubiquity*. For example, working at short distance from one live, and with the opportunity of getting in the area different services to satisfy your needs. From the technical point of view, a number of studies have tried to assess *pros* and *cons* of having a 15-Minute City. For example, assessing the global cost and time reduction for the city users due to the possibility of having all in the short range from where they live. The total amount of time and money spent in the whole city for these activities is huge: tens of hours waste on traffic per person per year in US [14]. In addition, the reduction of traffic also produces a relevant reduction of pollutant on NOX and $CO2$ [16].

In [15], Carlos Moreno proposed a "modified 15-Minute City" framework with different 4 features: *proximity, diversity, density* and *digitization*. In some measure the digitization dimension has been an indirect observation that the ubiquity has been overcome by the technological solutions put in place on the push of pandemic, thus creating a sort of "*new normal*" conditions of ubiquity. The digitization also copes with the level of exploitation of ICT solutions including open data, IOT, smart city technologies, last mile delivering, 5G, etc. [2]. The *density* has been related to the number of people per square kilometer. This means that in substance the six functions have to be proportioned to the number of users in the area. The *proximity* has to cope with the distance, so that 15-Minute City can be regarded as a measure of the "*distance by waking*", while biking the real distance in terms of meters would be higher. In addition, the covered distance may be related to the age of the person, and to the contextual conditions. A mom with a baby would not be fast in moving such as a teenager. In substance, the proximity has to cope with both space and time, and accessibility of services; and it could be very complex to be actually estimated since the cities may have infrastructures that may lead to the impossibility to reach a very close area for the lack of walkable paths (barriers, e.g., the highways, the rivers, the reserved roads). The *diversity* describes the needs of having an assortment of the services which should be accessible in the area. The diversity should be related somehow with the social needs and culture of the city users. They have to be satisfied of the diversity provided.

Despite of the large discussions about city strategies, the effective compliance assessment of each city area with respect to 15-Minute City concepts are still not clear in terms of computation. If their simple computation from data is possible. The huge amount of aspects to be taken into account for each Function and Feature is impressive, and the cardinality (combination) is large. Please note that, the assessment could range from the identification of services to big data analysis taking into account all services details: capability, hours of opening, age target, quality of service, cultural target, etc. In most cases, the proposed assessments have been based on questionnaires posed to city users in some local areas, and thus are far to be objective and computable in wide areas as provinces or regions.

In [17], the proximity problem has been addressed taking into account the diversity of city user profiles in terms of their capability to cover the "15-Minute" distance. In particular, also the travel time computation may hide complexity due to the presence of barriers and diversity in routing according to the travel means [5]. The study proposed by [17] put the evidence that significant social inequalities exist in the 15-Minute City walkable neighborhoods. Spatial regression shows that the 15-Minute walkable neighborhoods score is positively correlated to proportion of adults and seniors, and it is negatively correlated to proportion of children population and temporary city user (visitor, tourist, commuters, etc.). On the other hand, children may not need to have access to services for adults. The approach proposed by [17] and also those based on detailed computation of walkability [12, 18] resulted to be very complex to be scaled on large area, and may need a continuous update for changes of road structure of the city. In [6], a number of indexes have been defined to assess the reachability, attractiveness, and the permeability of each city area from the city. Also in this case, the large region scalability is not clear. In [9], the network analysis has been performed for assessing metrics such as network betweenness and centrality of the road network of the city. This allowed to identify critical points and nodes in the road network. In [13], the 15-Minute City concept has been adopted as life circle in which a number of indexes can be computed on the basis of the presence of services (identified as Point of Interest, POI). The Functions have been on: *gov, roads, commerce, dining, edu, medical, entertainment and pension*. The approach aimed at providing suggestions for city planning.

In this paper, we are proposing a computability approach for the assessment of cities/area compliance with respect to the 15-Minute concept. It can be used for the assessment, raking and planning/restructuring of city services. The proposed computational model allows to produce an index to assess 15-Minute concept compliance for each point of an area that has been called **15MinCityIndex**. The index is based on a number of subindexes, each of which models a **Function** and its computation is based on a set of **Features**, thus providing a computational semantic to the 15-Minute concept. Please note that with respect to the state of the art indexes reported above, it addresses more functions and domains, and produces a unified **15MinCityIndex**. The proposed model has been produced and validated on Florence metro area which includes multiple cities and rural areas. The **15MinCityIndex** described in this paper conquered the first place award and grant of the international ENEL-X open data challenge 2020 [11].

It can be computed in different areas and can be easily extended to take into account data and aspects according to the data availability of the region/province in which it is applied. The processes of data collection, spatial reasoning and computing have been performed thanks to the Snap4City infrastructure in Tuscany area and in Florence in particular (https://www.snap4city.org) [4]. Snap4City is providing 100% open source tools and free registration on several different organization smart city areas.

This paper is organized as follows. In Sect. 2, the Functions considered and the corresponding subindexes are discussed, performing a comparison with former proposals. Section 3 reports the computational model of the subindexes. Section 4 describes the tool for the usage and validation of results which can be freely accessed on-line. Conclusions are drawn on Sect. 5.

2 Functions' Subindexes

The 6 Functions identified by Moreno and listed above are in somehow not adequate to assess the complexity of an area. In particular, the living Function is too generic and includes a lot of other aspects that should be addressed separately to better understand the area/city ranking. For this reason, additional aspects have been addressed with separate views in the model proposed as clarified in Table 1. The first step has been the identification of features which can characterize the 15MinCityIndex. The first point has been the literature and the second the taxonomical experience we had in defining the Km4City ontology for smart city [7]. As a result 13 Functions have been defined as follows.

Table 1. Comparing 15MinCityIndex

Moreno functions	Li et al., 2019 [13]	15MinCityIndex subindexes
living		Housing viability
	Gov	Govern Services
		Safety Services
		Culture and Cults Services
		Environment Quality
	Roads	Slow Mobility Services
		Fast Mobility Services
	[Medical]	Sport Services
working		Economy/sustainability
	pension	
commerce	*commerce*	
	dining	Food Services
healthcare	*medical*	Health Services
education	*edu*	Education Services
entertainment	*entertainment*	Entertainment Services

In **15MinCityIndex**, the distribution of commercial activities has been exploited into Economy and thus we mapped on Moreno's commerce only on Food Services for sustainability. Please note that with the on demand delivery most of the issues related to commerce are losing their relevance. The sport could be mapped on living aspects as well as on healthcare or entertainment according to the concept of the index. For these reasons we kept the aspects separate. As a result, the proposed 15MinCityIndex is capable to describe the city/area livability and self-sustainability with respect to the inhabitants of the area with a higher level of details. The challenge remains the computability of the index as described in the rest of the paper.

In the following, the **13 Subindexes/Functions of the 15MinCityIndex** are described positing the attention to the aspects of their *data sources, density, diversity, normative/reference values or KPI, proximity*. Moreover, the issues regarding the *computability* of the indexes are addressed in a successive section of this paper.

1. **Environment Quality**. In this case, the aim is to assess the environmental quality of the area for living. To this end, good indicators can be: EAQI (European Air Quality Index), quality of water, presence of green areas/gardens (which can be recovered from municipality or from Copernicus Satellite data with some limitations), noise level, specific pollutants (NO_2, CO_2, O_3, PM10, PM2.5, etc.). For most of them, recommended values are provided at the EC level. Please note that, most of the pollutants are also taken into account by the EAQI which is based on PM2.5, PM10, NO_2, O_2 and SO_2, so that, the EAQI supersede them.

2. **Economy/Sustainability**. This subindex aims at assessing the economic sustainability of the area, which is a sort of demand-vs-offer index. In practice, the area is self-sustainable if the potential amount of working places (on commercial and industrial) compared to the workforce available in the area is satisfactory to ensure the economic well-being of the dwellers. To perform this estimation the knowledge of the number of people living in the area is fundamental, considering those that are in the age of working and retired. In addition, the offer has to be computed on the basis of the shops, services, industries, etc., of the area. This means that, census data and commercial/economic data of the area have to be accessible. Commercial/industrial services are in most cases accessible as POI. On the other hand, their capability in terms of personnel could allow to be more precise, and it may be available from the chambre of commerce. A secondary index could be considered assessing at the level of municipality if the total salary of the area (including retired people) could be enough for the sustainability of the whole population of the area.

3. **Housing Viability**. It should be an index to assess the quality of houses in the area. Another view could be obtained on the basis of the age of the building. A simple approach can be performed on the basis of the prices for square meters of the real estate market, which is also related to the demand of living there. The average price/m2 in the area can be taken as a sort of index of quality, and it should be normalized with respect to the number of city users living in the area. Diversity aspect on this topic could lead to have a range of different houses in terms of prices.

4. **Health Services**. In this case, the subindex is focused on assessing the availability of health services (*diversity* as: pharmacies, private and public hospitals, labs, studio of doctors, presence of defibrillators, etc.) in the area of interest with respect to the number of users of the area. On this regard, there are some *KPI* provided by the EC. For example, for the coverage of the pharmacies in terms of potential clients of the area. For instance, a pharmacy every 3000 people for Italian govern, 500

hospitals' beds every 100.000 inhabitants, 80 dentists per 100.000 inhabitants, 1.6 hospitals per 100.000 inhabitants, etc.

5. **Food Services.** This subindex is focused on assessing the presence of food distribution and services in the area of interest with respect to the number of users of the area. The food distribution can provide a large *diversity* as groceries, restaurants, small food shops, supermarkets, etc. Most of the data can be taken from Open Data, chambre of commerce and POI. The critical aspect could be to take into account of the capability of each food service. National or regional average could give the reference values.

6. **Education Services.** This subindex is focused on assessing the presence of education services in the area of interest with respect to the number of users of the area which should be in the age of school. The educational services are: schools of any level, universities, private schools, etc., different languages and cultures. Most of the data can be taken from Open Data, and POI. More complex could be to get the capability in terms of students of each educational infrastructure. National or regional average could give the reference values.

7. **Slow Mobility Services.** This subindex should represent the suitability of the area to facilitate the local mobility. It could take into account: walkability, presence of sidewalks, number of Km of roads (that can be used for walking and biking), presence and number of cycling paths, availability of bike/cart sharing, number of sharing station for short range travel, and may be as critical point the presence of barriers such as bridges, highways, etc., which can limit the walkability. Please note that good slow mobility services can facilitate the movements in the area, and this may reduce the needs of taking less sustainable travel means. On the other hand, having a good rank on most of the subindexes (taking into account of services in the area) it would reduce the needs of exiting from the local area by using a private or public travel means to access at the not accessible services. Road information can be recovered from Open Street Map, OSM, as well as from the local govern.

8. **Govern Services.** This subindex is focused on assessing the availability of local govern services in the area of interest with respect to the number of users of the area which are in the age of use/need them. These services are: municipality services, taxes office, etc. Most of the data can be taken from Open Data, and POI. National or regional average could give the reference values.

9. **Safety Services.** This subindex is focused on assessing the level of safety services in the area of interest with respect to the number of users of the area. These services may have a large *diversity* and are: local and national police office, security office, number and position of monitoring cameras, fire brigade, civil protection, level of light and presence of smart lights, availability of alarm buttons on the area, coverage of security services by phone and Apps, etc. Additional information could be taken into account for marking the area on the basis of other risk factors such as: flooding, landslide, terrorist attack, risk level for the buildings, criminality (distribution of incidents and of criminal actions), etc., and on resilience capability [8]. Most of these details can be obtained from civil protection and local govern offices, data can be taken from Open Data, and POI. National or regional average could give the reference values.

10. **Culture and Cults Services**. This subindex is focused on assessing the presence of cultural and cults services in the area of interest with respect to the number of users of the area. The *diversity* of services should take into account: museum, monuments, vista points, mausoleum, churches of any kind (may be of cults in proportion to the demand of the city users of the area), libraries, book shops, etc. Most of the data can be taken from Open Data, and POI. National or regional average could give the reference values.

11. **Entertainment Services**. This subindex is focused on assessing the availability of entertainment services in the area of interest with respect to the number of users of the area. These services are: theaters, auditoriums, cinemas, game rooms, etc. Most of the data can be taken from Open Data, and POI. National or regional average could give the reference values.

12. **Fast Mobility Services**. In this case, the subindex aims at assessing the presence in the area of services for moving out of the area for medium (city busses, area busses) and long distances (railways, airports, highway joint), with respect to the number of users of the authorized age to use them. For the diversity, in addition to the above info, services such as the presence of fuel stations, the size of bus stops and railways stations, long range recharging stations, etc., should be taken into account. Most of the data can be taken from Open Data, and POI. National or regional average could give the reference values. Public transportation data (bus stops, bus lines, train stops, etc.) can be recovered from GTFS and/or Transmodel files which are generated by the operators.

13. **Sport Services**. This subindex is focused on assessing the availability of sport services in the area of interest with respect to the number of users. These services are: sport facilities, gyms, training infrastructures, arenas, swimming pools, etc. Most of the data can be taken from Open Data, and POI. National or regional average could give the reference values.

3   Computing the 15MinCityIndex

The implementation of the general concept of the 15MinCityIndex should lead to provide a dense heatmap in which all the points of an area are assessed in terms of Function aspects and on which the city/area officer can click to pick the values of the indexes in all parts of the area under analysis. This approach allows them to perform the assessment and to decide in which area the investment have to be performed, and on which Function. The present version of the 15MinCityIndex is mainly focused on city area, while a similar approach can be adopted for the computation of the index also on rural and industrialized area.

According to the above performed description and analysis, the computability of subindexes has to pass from the collection of the above mentioned data. The first step is to make a decision on the spatial resolution since it cannot be realistically computed for each civic number. To this end, we have identified a grid of points with 700 m of distance northings and eastings (y × coordinates). The grid of points determined a grid of circles with 400 m of ray which are partially overlapped. Once the grid is estimated a number of normalization factors has to be computed. The normalization factors are used for the computation of the subindexes, and the subindexes are used for the computation of the 15MinCityIndex. In the next subsection the single steps are presented. The following schema describes the whole process which has been implemented on Snap4City platform to accelerate the production.

Computation of the grid 700 × 700 m and center points. The basic element of the grid is a circle with ray of 500 m in each grid point thus taking a diagonal close to 1000 m. This means that they may be partially overlapped on (y × coordinates) and adjacent on the center point into the area in which the corners are the grid points.

Data gathering/ingestion and geolocalization on knowledge base Km4City (a classic GIS may be used as well, may be with more complexity), for the whole area of interest: (a) collection of POI data from Open Data; (b) collection of economic aspects such as PIL per area or per region; (c) collection of the normalization factors such as: density of population per age, etc.; (d) computation of the normalization point per grid area.

Computing each subindex and **for each center of the list of points**: (a) computation of the data performing geo spatial queries on the Snap4City KB; (b) normalization of data of the subindex, to align the distribution (see later for details); (c) computation of the subindex on the basis of the identified data; (d) production of the Heatmap;

Computation of the 15MinCityIndex, for each grid area: (a) computation of the index by integrating subindexes; (b) production of the Heatmap for the 15MinCityIndex.

In the next subsections, the most relevant steps are presented.

3.1 Computing Normalization Factors

On the basis of the above presented subindexes the most relevant normalization factor is the number of people living in each area. This information can be recovered from census data. Moreover, the distribution of civic numbers of houses and the size of the building can help in this sense.

3.2 Computing Subindex

The computation of the subindexes is almost similar for most of them. In the following, we assume the availability of the data described in Sect. 2 for each subindex and their loading on Snap4City KB where is possible to perform geospatial queries in the proximity of the grid points as described above. The subindexes can be visually accessed on Snap4City Dashboards such as: https://www.snap4city.org/dashboardSmartCity/view/index.php?iddasboard=MjkzOA== and the original data on ServiceMap http://firenze.km4city.org/.

The subindexes can be grouped in 5 categories on the basis of the computational model adopted for their production. The main reasons to have different models is due to the data sources and to their aim. And in particular those categories are:

- **A)** environment quality: quality of the environment in which one is going to live.
- **B)** economy/sustainability: this is focused on assessing the sustainability of the area matching the offer vs the demand of work, in first approximation.

- **C)** housing viability: this is focused on assessing the affordability of having a house of reasonable quality.
- **D)** health services, food services, education services, govern services, safety services, culture and cults services, slow mobility services, fast mobility services, entertainment services, sport services. They are focused on assessing the availability of services.

Environment Subindex (A) is computed combining EAQI and the square meter of green per inhabitants in the area. The EAQI is typically provided in terms of Likert scale from good to very poor. We reported all in Likert scale from Good (5) to critical (1). There is a normative that requests to have at least 9 square meters for citizen, and on the basis of that we have scaled by K to get satisfactory when that threshold is reached (Fig. 1).

$$SubIndex(env) = (EAQI + K\ GreenAreasSM/\#Inhabitants)/2$$

Index
- Critical
- Insufficient
- Satisfactory
- Fairly good
- Good

Fig. 1. Likert scale heatmap color index adopted

A similar approach has been adopted for each subindex and for the general 15MinCityIndex. Thus reporting all values on Likert scale from 1 to 5. This scale is able to give an immediate information about the positioning of the area with respect to the other area of the region/territory at the expense of resolution. On the other hand, a full resolution values would not be needed to identify critical areas.

The **Economy subindex** (B) is focused on assessing the economic sustainability of the area matching the number of people able to work with the job offer of companies situated in the area. For this purpose, a simple counting of all commercial and industrial activities POI on Snap4City ServiceMap KB has been performed. The main concept is to assess the difference of the offer with respect to the demand of work. If the offer is higher than the 5% would be green, 10% blue, −5% yellow and −10% or less orange. The obtained distribution of values for the grid areas was out of the 1–5 Likert scale. This computation is performed as follows:

$$SubIndex\ (economy) = (Offer - Demand)/Demand\ \%$$

$$Offer = (\#industrialPOI + \#commercialPOI) * MeanNumberOfWokersPerCompanyInMunicipality$$

$$Demand = NumberofInhabitantsworkinginthearea$$

For each specific grid area also an estimate of the available workforce has been provided assessing the number of people able to work on the basis of the population age groups data for each municipality. The mean number of workers per company in the municipality is a data obtained from ISTAT for all municipalities in Italy.

The **housing viability** (C) is focused on assessing the affordability of having a house of reasonable quality and price in the area. To this end, in first approximation we have used the real estate quotation in each specific grid area in Euro normalized with P which is the mean affordable price for square meter. Other kind of computations based on the assessment of the building can be also valid and substantially correlated in mean value areas.

$$\text{SubIndex (housing)} = \#\text{Inhabitants/priceforsquaremeter}/P.$$

The result is a measure on inhabitants that are demanding to stay in the area. According to national average we classified each grid area in Likert scale by using the following table, assuming that a higher demand would lead to a lower viability of the area. The calibration of the table values has been performed on the basis of the actual conditions in the validation area as described in the following. Please note that the non-computable cases may occur, for example when the quotation is not present.

Table 2. Example of thresholds defined for tuning the distribution as in Fig. 2

From	To	Class	
2000	Infinite	Orange	1
1500	2000	Yellow	2
1000	1500	White	3
20	1000	Green	4
0,01	20	Blue	5

The subindexes of Services (D) are focused on assessing their availability in the area. For this reason, a simple counting of POI on the ServiceMap KB has been performed. In Snap4City ServiceMap POI are classified on more than 20 classes and more than 500 different subclasses [7], they are all geolocated and provide additional details and information which can be taken into account. In all subindexes of services, the distribution of classes on grid areas has been discovered to be Gaussian. For example, in the case of SubIndex(health)

$$\text{SubIndex (health)} = \#\text{inhabitants}/(\#\text{Pharmacies} + \#\text{Healthcare} + \#\text{Hospital J}).$$

The normalization has been performed on the basis of the national reference values, considering that the Hospitals are serving J times more people than Pharmacies. The obtained value of the SubIndex has been assigned to classes on the basis of a table structurally similar to that reported in Table 2, and centering the distribution on Green class as reported in the Fig. 2, **where all the distributions of the SubIndexes are reported.** Therefore, similar computations have been adopted for all the subindex of this class.

This approach makes possible the comparative assessment of the areas in different municipalities. On this regard, it could be better to perform the alignment of the distributions of the area on the basis of a large number of grid areas. For example, at least at level of province or region.

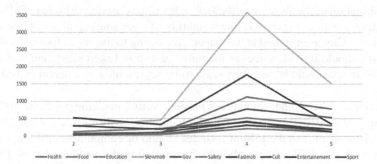

Fig. 2. Distributions of the areas in the Likert scale colors or the subindexes

Also in this cases, non-computable cases may occur, for example when the area does not report inhabitants or services. This happens in rural areas for which the 15MinCityIndex index has not been designed.

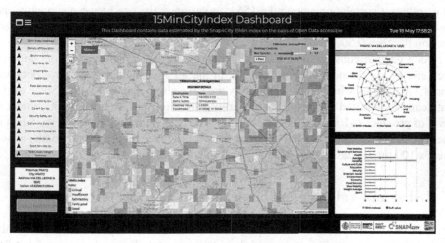

Fig. 3. 15MinCityIndex Dashboard on Florence area, https://www.snap4city.org/dashboardSmartCity/view/index.php?iddasboard=MjkzOA==

It should be noted that some of the subindexes may depend on complex data. For example, slow motion from the amount of Km in the grid area which has been estimated on Snap4City ServiceMap exploiting data coming from OSM (open street map), and the case of Bus Stops complexity (a bus stop may have multiple lines, and lines may have multiple rides per day, in the seasonal period in which the assessment is performed)

which has been estimated on the basis of GTFS data collected daily at regional level on
Snap4City infrastructure.

3.3 Computing the 15MinCityIndex

The combination of the above described subindexes may produce a global 15MinCityIn-
dex to express with a single value, the suitability of each single grid area to the concept
of 15-Minute City as proposed in this paper. According to the above formulation, all the
subindexes should provide values in the range of 1–5 in Likert scale, and thus also the
15MinCityIndex should be in Likert scale to be represented as a heatmap as the other
subindexes.

As a remark, the subindexes may not produce values in all the points since the value
may result not computable for the lack of inhabitants, or for the lack of data, or actual
services. This means that the 15MinCityIndex should be computable in absence of some
of the subindexes. Different possibilities for modeling the computation of 15MinCi-
tyIndex have been proposed such as the average of the subindex, the median, and the
weighted average/median. The weighted approaches may be focused on assessing in
different manner area which are city based with respect to those at prevalent industrial-
ization or vegetation. Most of the subindex can be considered orthogonal independent
aspects, while in reality some of them can be similar and thus one subindex could be
in some measure a partial surrogate of another. At the support of the independence of
the subindex we have performed a cross-correlation among them discovering that the
most relevant correlation among the 156 correlation is the one between economy and
fastmobility with 0.64%, the second one of SlowMobility and housing. All the others
are smaller than 0.50%

As a general consideration, the production of all the subindexes in large national
area can be very expensive. For example, in the area of validation we have obtained
about 1750 points while in the whole Italy we have about 150.000 points. Some of the
data can be collected at level of municipality which in Italy are about 8000, others at
level of province (110 in Italy) or region which are 20. On the other hand, if the target is
the 15Min grid areas at national level the grid would made up of 150000 points, which
means 100 times heavier than what we performed for Florence.

4   Using and Validating Subindexes and 15MinCityIndex

In order to validate the subindex proposed it has been computed in the Florence
area including city of Florence, several rural areas, and about a large set of smaller
cities/municipalities such as: Prato, Signa, Sesto Fiorentino, Scandicci, Empoli, Vinci,
Quarrata, etc. The whole area of observation and test presents about 1740 grid areas, for
about 800.000 inhabitants. In Fig. 3, the dashboard presenting the heatmaps is reported.
It has been the major tool for the validation of the solution during lockdown.

The dashboard allows to access at heatmaps of the density of inhabitants, of the
subindexes (different version for different dates) and of the 15MinCityIndex in different
versions. The heatmaps can be selected from the list on the left column. And then,
clicking on the heatmap, the tool estimates (in a few seconds, please wait) the profile

of the selected grid area in terms of all SubIndexes and 15MinCityIndex. The results are directly shown on the right side with: (i) full address recovered from georevers the selected GPS data on KB; (ii) a spidernet diagram comparing the value with min, max; (iii) barseries with the values of the subindex for a faster control, (iv) the specific value selected from the heatmap on the popup on the map. The indexes' values are shown with a range 1–5 according to the legenda visualized on left bottom corner, where 3 is considered satisfactory, 4 fairly good, 5 Good, 2 insufficient, and 1 critical.

These solutions have been tested in a number of verification points for a number of experts that validated them comparing several points for each subindex. The selected points for the comparison have been those related to areas in which they know the service level according to the legenda, ranging from good to critical. The validation allowed to calibrate some of the distributes described in Sect. 3.

For the general 15MinCityIndex, the experts preferred the map produced by the weighted average which count twice the Functions of: economy, housing, health, slow mobility, sport, education, which have been primary need in the period of lockdown for COVID-19. It should be noted that the general 15MinCityIndex is somehow arbitrary and thus it should not be considered as a driver for making decision, but only a general representation of the mode. Therefore, we suggest using the subindex and the spidernet diagram or bar series to understand the actual status of an area.

5 Conclusions

Despite of the extensive discussions regarding city strategies, the effective compliance assessment of each city area with respect to 15-Minute City concepts are still not clear in terms of computation. Several indexes have been proposed in the literature for specific aspects, and many others remained not addressed. In this paper, a larger amount of aspects have been taken into account, such as: Housing, Govern, Safety, Culture and Cults Services, Environment, Slow Mobility, Fast Mobility, Sport, Economy/sustainability, Food, Health, Education, Services, Entertainment. Each of them may be assessed by taking into account a large number of factors and features. In this paper, we have proposed a computability approach for the assessment of cities/area in compliance with the 15-Minute concept. It can be used for the assessment, ranking and planning/restructuring of city services. The proposed computational model allows to produce a set of 15Minute subIndexes for each point of an area. Each subindex is a **Function** and its computation is based on a set of **Features**, thus providing a computational semantic to the 15-Minute concept. Please note that with respect to the state of the art indexes, the proposed solution addressed more functions and domains, and produce a unified **15MinCityIndex**. The proposed model has been produced and validated on Florence metro area which includes multiple cities and rural areas. The **15MinCityIndex** described in this paper conquered the first place award and grant of the international ENEL-X open data challenge 2020 [11].

The solution proposed can be computed in different areas and can be easily extended to take into account data and aspects according to the data availability of the region/province in which it is applied. The processes of data collection, spatial reasoning, and computing have been performed thanks to the Snap4City infrastructure in

Tuscany area and in Florence in particular (https://www.snap4city.org) providing 100% open source tools and free registration on several different organization smart city areas.

As final consideration, we can state that the proposed 15MinCityIndex performs in a satisfactory manner in the city areas while in the rural areas, in most of the cases they are not computable and thus the global index fails in providing a correct assessment. On the other hand, its aim is to be an instrument to assess the compliance with 15MinCityIndex in the cities. A more precise evaluation of the index could be developed in the future when more open data will be made available, an updated version could also exploit territorial satellite data to evaluate the type of area, for instance whether it is rural, industrial or city in a way to customize the parameters and the subindexes of the 15MinCityIndex, this would allow to have a more consistent assessment also with the necessary services adequacy.

Acknowledgment. The authors would like to thank to the DISIT lab colleagues and to the many of them that contributed to the collection of data. The 15MinCityIndex approach described in this paper was submitted in this form and conquered the first place award and grant of the international ENEL-X open data challenge 2020 [11].

References

1. Aktay, A., et al.: Google COVID-19 community mobility reports: anonymization process description (version 1.0) (2020) https://arxiv.org/abs/2004.04145.
2. Allam, Z.: Cities and the Digital Revolution: Aligning Technology and Humanity. Springer International Publishing, Cham (2020). https://doi.org/10.1007/978-3-030-29800-5
3. Badii, C., et al.: How COVID-19 lockdown impacted on mobility and environmental data. Bollettino della Società Geografica Italiana, FuPress, June (2020)
4. Badii, C., Bellini, P., Difino, A., Nesi, P.: Smart city IoT platform respecting GDPR privacy and security aspects. IEEE Access (2020). https://doi.org/10.1109/ACCESS.2020.2968741
5. Badii, C., Difino, A., Nesi, P., Paoli, I., Paolucci, M.: Classification of users transportation modalities from mobiles in real operating conditions. Multimed. Tools Appl. (2021)
6. Balletto, G., et al.: A methodological approach on disused public properties in the 15-minute city perspective. Sustainability **13**(2), 593 (2021)
7. Bellini, P., Benigni, M., Billero, R., Nesi, P., Rauch, N.: Km4City ontology building vs data harvesting and cleaning for smart-city services. Int. J. Vis. Lang. Comput. (2014). https://doi.org/10.1016/j.jvlc.2014.10.023
8. Bellini, E., Coconea, L., Nesi, P.: A functional resonance analysis method driven resilience quantification for socio-technical system. IEEE Syst. J. 1–11 (2019). ISSN: 1932-8184, ISSN: 1937-9234
9. Bilotta, S., Nesi, P.: Traffic flow reconstruction by solving indeterminacy on traffic distribution at junctions. Future Gen. Comput. Syst. (2021). https://authors.elsevier.com/sd/article/S0167-739X(20)30835-9
10. Capasso Da Silva, D., King, D.A., Lemar, S.: Accessibility in practice: 20-minute city as a sustainability planning goal. Sustainability **12**, 129 (2020)
11. ENEL-X Openinnovability Website: New Smart City Solutions Enabled by Open Data. https://openinnovability.enel.com/projects/New-smart-city-solutions-enabled-by-open-data. Accessed 14 June 2021
12. Lee, S., Talen, E.: Measuring walkability: a note on auditing methods. J. Urban Des. **19**(3), 368–388 (2014)

13. Li, Z., Zheng, J., Zhang, Y.: Study on the layout of 15-minute community-life circle in third-tier cities based on POI: Baoding City of Hebei Province. Engineering **11**(9), 592–603 (2019)
14. Liu, J.: Commuters in This City Spend 119 Hours a Year Stuck in Traffic. https://www.cnbc.com/2019/09/04/commuters-in-this-city-spend-119-hours-a-year-stuck-in-traffic.html. Accessed 10 Nov 2020
15. Moreno, C., Allam, Z., Chabaud, D., Gall, C., Pratlong, F.: Introducing the "15-Minute City": sustainability, resilience and place identity in future post-pandemic cities. Smart Cities **4**, 93–111 (2021). https://doi.org/10.3390/smartcities4010006
16. Po, L., et al.: TRAFAIR: understanding traffic flow to improve air quality. In: The 1st IEEE African Workshop on Smart Sustainable Cities and Communities (IEEE ASC2 2019) In Conjunction with the 5th IEEE International Smart Cities Conference, ISC2 (2019)
17. Weng, M., et al.: The 15-minute walkable neighborhoods: measurement, social inequalities and implications for building healthy communities in urban China. J. Transp. Health **13**, 259–273 (2019)
18. Guo, Z., Loo, B.P.Y.: Pedestrian environment and route choice: evidence from New York City and Hong Kong. J. Transp. Geogr. **28**, 124–136 (2013)

Study on Vibrations Produced by New City Rail of Cagliari

Mauro Coni[1] (iD), Riccardo Murgia[2] (iD), Nicoletta Rassu[1](✉) (iD), and Francesca Maltinti[1](✉) (iD)

[1] Department of Civil and Environmental Engineering and Architecture (DICAAR), University of Cagliari, via Marengo 3, 09123 Cagliari, Italy
{nicoletta.rassu,maltinti}@unica.it
[2] Cagliari, Italy

Abstract. The vibrational impact of a city rail is a complex phenomenon, and an effective numerical prediction model has not been developed yet to describe the problem in a complete way. Vibrations induced by rail-way traffic depend significantly on mechanical characteristics of layers of soil underlying the track and type and conditions of rail superstructure. Finite Element Method (FEM) represent an interesting approach which can help to understand behavior and propagation of waves produced by vibration. This method gives trusted results; however, it must be calibrated correctly.

So, this paper presents a study aimed at estimating the forcing produced by light rail trains and the influence of the sediment soil in order to calibrate the FE model. The forcing was obtained by means of accelerometers that recorded accelerations on an active line.

Keywords: Sustainability · Vibration analysis · Finite Element Method · Forcing · Soil stratigraphy

1 Introduction

According to the UN World Urbanization Prospects 2018 dossier [1], today about 55% of the world population lives in urban areas. This percentage will reach 68% by 2050. The consequence of this phenomenon is that cities are, and will be even more in the future, centers of transport systems whose negative effects, such as congestion, air/noise pollution and road accidents are destined to grow.

The European Commission strongly recommends that European towns and cities of all sizes should adopt Sustainable Urban Mobility Plans (SUMPs) and developed guidelines in order to reduce externalities associated with transport sector [1]. Torrisi et al. [2] analyze these guidelines and the corresponding Italian one for the preparation of so-called "Piani Urbani della Mobilità Sostenibile" (PUMS) in order to provide essential elements for the critical assessment of best practices and the review of related SUMP.

R. Murgia—Independent Researcher.

© Springer Nature Switzerland AG 2021
O. Gervasi et al. (Eds.): ICCSA 2021, LNCS 12956, pp. 580–594, 2021.
https://doi.org/10.1007/978-3-030-87010-2_43

Today, the concept of sustainability is part of the broader concept of smart city and it is closely related to the concept of quality of life. Garau and Pavan [3] individuate a list of indicators to quantify the quality of life in Cagliari city. The indicators are grouped in sixth categories, one of them is "Use and Fruition", to this set is associated the quality and presence of services, accessibility, infrastructures, and mobility. So, public transport services play an important role in the sustainability of cities.

Quality of these services represents a fundamental aspect so that they can be perceived by citizens as a valid and functional tool for accessing the different areas of a city and for promoting a sustainable mobility. Passengers' viewpoint is a key tool in the monitoring of public transport quality. There are a lot of attributes to be measured (on-board and external), Barabino et al. [4] present criteria for the selection of attributes and the techniques of data collection based on the innovative concept of quality cycle. Another study focuses on the implementation of an Impact Score methodology which assesses the degree of perceived quality [5]. Perceived quality and expected quality by elderly users have been analyzed to highlight which are the most important attributes of a public transport service for over 65 years old passengers. Elderly represents that share of passengers who could benefit more from an efficient public transport system that meets their expectations [6]. Barabino develops an existing framework to automatically identify low quality vehicles and stops to help public transport managers to build systematically accurate monitoring plans and to increase passengers' satisfaction with the service [7]. Quality of travel experience can be also monitored by accelerations data detected on buses of a public transport system and related to the judgment of passengers [8, 9].

Accessibility is usually identified by people with the availability of an efficient transportation system because it provides the opportunity to access to several urban services to all categories of users [10]. It is no coincidence that general objective of UN's 2030 Agenda underlines the need to make cities smart [11], sustainable [12], inclusive and accessible by means, for instance, a suitable public transport system for all.

Numerous studies conducted in different cities have shown that accessibility can be improved by creating sustainable transport alternatives such as smart bike sharing systems, electric car sharing, public transport, and cycling mobility. This "Smart mobility" has several advantages including the reduction of city traffic congestion and therefore air/noise pollution, and the improvement of traffic safety [13]. An example of transition toward a smart, sustainable and green mobility is reported by Coni et al. [14]. From 2011, a new strategic plan was adopted by Cagliari city in cooperation with all its 17 municipalities which gradually led to sustainable and smart mobility. This plan provided using of Intelligent Transportation Systems (ITSs)'s technologies, improving routes and fleet buses, forbidding traffic cars in the historical center and promoting places and pedestrian areas, developing a network of cycle paths, supporting the use of car-sharing, car-pooling, bike sharing, electric mobility and completing and integrating tramway net-work. These actions have changed citizens' lifestyle: they started walking, running, cycling, using the public transport service, so discovering a different way to experience their city.

As far as a public transport system is a fundamental aspect in the context of smart mobility and therefore in a smart city, however, often, the construction of new lines for public transport meet difficulties to be accepted by citizens due to the negative environmental effects produced by the passage of the convoys. In urban areas, the impacts generated by the passage of convoys, whether they belong to subway lines or terminal sections of railway lines, are closely linked to four distinct aspects: noise, vibrations, visual impact and the fracture of the territory urbanized. Situations of conflict can occur with the residents of the areas adjacent to the routes and disputes with local authorities accompany the entry into operation of the lines.

Therefore, in order to prove if this kind of public work is effectively sustainable from every point of view, it is necessary to verify a priori if its presence leads to a reduction of quality of life of those who live nearby; and, if it occurs, providing systems to contain its impacts to guarantee a good quality of life for all citizens including those who live or work near the line.

A lot of studies present interesting contributes on noise/visual impact and the fracture of the territory urbanized produced by a city rail conversely the issue of vibrations has not been particularly explored.

Çaty et al. and Mottahed J. et al. [15, 16] tackle the problem of track degradation on transition zone from ordinary ballasted track to railway bridges due to sudden stiffness changes and ballast vibrations. They both propose solutions with the use of Under sleeper pads (USP) and find that they provide an important decrease in ballast acceleration.

Other Authors focus the attention on the vibration effects in adjacent buildings. Mertens et al. [17] propose numerical studies to find the critical points of building design as well as the optimization process of the building structure to limit discomfort to residents on higher floors due to passing trains on a nearby tracks. Coulier et al. [18] investigate the effect of neglecting source-receiver interaction in wave propagation in the soil on the accuracy of numerical predictions. They employ a coupled finite element boundary element methodology, and they demonstrate that the dynamic axle loads can be calculated with reasonable accuracy.

Slab tracks are often used to reduce train induced vibrations. Kece, et al. [19] analyse the behavior of typical concrete slab tracks using a 2D Finite Element Model. They compare concrete slab track with a typical ballasted track and find that slab track more effectively reduces train-induced vibrations and track level displacements. Zhu et al. [20] developed a new vibration attenuation track (VAT) to mitigate vibrations at low frequencies based on an integrated theoretical and experimental study. They build a full-scale VAT which incorporates a floating slab track (FST) and the attached dynamic vibration absorbers (DVAs) with key parameters determined by the fixed-point theory and modal analysis technique. Computational and experimental results both demonstrate that the attached DVAs adsorb vibrations and significantly reduce subgrade vibrations in low-frequency range.

Coni et al. [21] study acoustical and vibrational impact of the city rail of Cagliari by FE Method and analyzed different vertical alignment solution to reduce or restrict it.

All research presented above use numerical models to simulate and study the vibrations produced by trains, so Finite Element Method (FEM) represent an interesting approach which can help to understand behavior and propagation of waves produced by vibration. However, it must be calibrated correctly to give trusted results. This aspect is often overlooked in the literature.

This paper covers this gap and presents a study aimed at estimating the forcing produced by light rail trains and the influence of the sediment soil in order to calibrate the FE model. The forcing was obtained by means of accelerometers that recorded accelerations on an active line. The stratigraphy of the soil has been reconstructed by means of surveys which have allowed a precise evaluation of the mechanical characteristics of the soil. The calibration of the FE model was carried out through a series of iterations, combining the mechanical characteristics of the soil and further accelerometric measurements taken in correspondence with the road area that will accommodate the future metro line.

The remaining paper is organized as follows. Section 2 describes the second section of the light metro of Cagliari. Section 3 presents the methodology adopted to calibrate FE model and, finally, Sect. 4 draws conclusions and research perspectives.

2   The Second Section of the Light Metro of Cagliari (Italy)

The second section of the light metro line of Cagliari (Italy) will develop for about two and a half kilometers and will connect Piazza Matteotti to Piazza Repubblica. Its alignment will be completely at grade with double tracks and will cross a highly urbanized area (see Fig. 1). Horizontal alignment will follow existing city street: Roma and Bonaria streets, then it will turn with a curve and keep on Cimitero avenue and Dante street.

Seven stops are planned, including that called Repubblica which already exists:

1. Station stop/terminus;
2. City Hall stop (point km 0 + 414);
3. Darsena stop (point km 0 + 698);
4. Lussu stop (point km 1 + 076);
5. Bonaria stop (point km 1 + 429);
6. San Saturnino stop (point km 2 + 068);
7. Repubblica stop (point km 2 + 530)

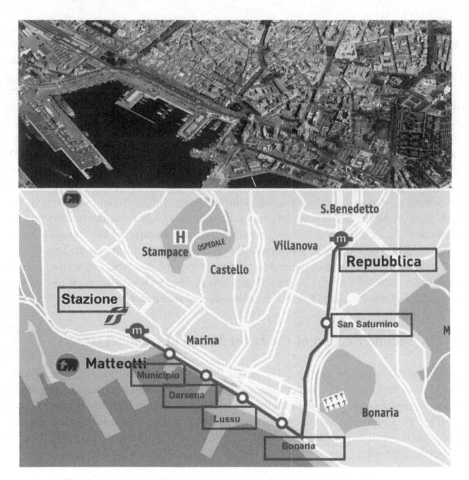

Fig. 1. Second section of the light metro of Cagliari (Italy) and its stops

3   Methodology

Design, construction and entry into operation of light metro lines requires a quantification of the negative effects due to the transit of convoys. The wheel-rail contact causes a dynamic stress on the railway structure which generates the oscillatory phenomenon of the vibrations that propagate in the adjacent ground. Therefore, the acceleration spectrum will be influenced by numerous factors such as the railway superstructure, the tracks and the mechanical characteristics of the soil crossed. In addition, small imperfections in the wheel and rail surfaces cause sudden changes of contact forces, which in turn cause the rail to vibrate. Vibrations propagate mainly vertically, but the interaction with the ground and buildings allows the development of significant movement components also horizontally.

The main difficulty is that vibrations evaluation must be analyzed ante operam, so it is necessary to estimate the forcing produced by light rail trains and soil characteristics. In Fig. 2, a simple framework for calibrating FE Model is presented. The study starts measuring accelerations produced by train on the active line Repubblica Square – Gottardo. Also, accelerations produced by buses that pass today in correspondence with the road part that will host the future rail area were collected. On this area, surveys and deflectometric tests were carried out for the geotechnical characterization of the soil. With these inputs, the finite element analysis was conducted with a series of iterations aimed, firstly, at calibrating the FE model and, secondly, at returning the distribution of vibrations consistent with that obtained by accelerometric measurements.

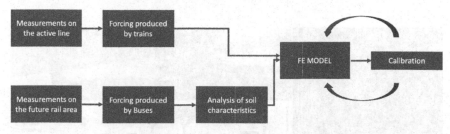

Fig. 2. Proposed framework for calibrating FE model

3.1 Measurements on the Active Line

Components x, y and z of accelerations produced by trains were collected along the active line Repubblica square-Gottardo; the accelerometer was placed between Cincinnato street and Attilio Regolo street, at a distance of 3.30 m from the rail. On visual analysis, rails appeared even and clean. Four passages were evaluated, two towards the Gotthard and two towards Repubblica. Component z assumed the highest values. In Fig. 3, the measurements relating to this axis are shown.

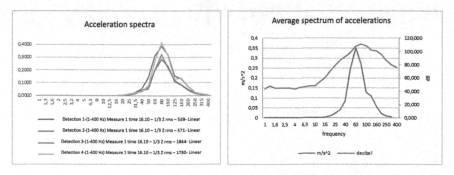

Fig. 3. Results of the surveys carried out on the Gottardo Repubblica line

Figure 3 shows that the phenomenon is dominated by the distance from the source, reducing exponentially with it and how different events have a similar response if evaluated to the same distance. For the above reason, the average spectrum is considered to reconstruct the forcing and calibrate FE models.

3.2 Measurements on the Future Rail Area

Measurements in Cimitero avenue were necessary to analyse the influence of the characteristics of the ground and how the vibrational phenomenon is attenuated with distance. In this case, forcings that determine the vibrations are those of the CTM and ARST buses that pass today in the road part that will host the future city rail.

Fig. 4. Seat area of the new metro stage and measuring point in Cimitero avenue

The accelerometer was positioned on the RAI field side, first at a distance of 1.70 m from the center of the bus lane, then at a distance of 5.1 m (see Fig. 4).

The most significant vibrations were those relating to the ARST buses, at the Z axis.

Four passes were recorded from the accelerometer at 1.70 m, and five from the one at 5.1 m.

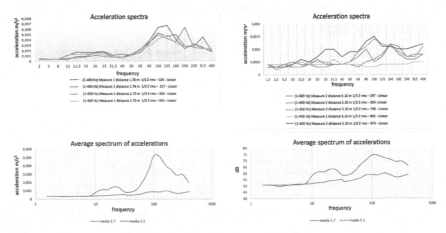

Fig. 5. Accelerations due to ARST buses

Figure 5 shows that the phenomenon is dominated by the distance from the source reducing exponentially with it and how different events have a similar response if evaluated at the same distance.

Also in this case, the average spectrum is considered for the reconstruction of forcings and the calibration of the FE models.

3.3 Stratigraphy of the Ground

The vibrations induced by railway traffic are a complex phenomenon and an effective general forecasting model, capable of describing this problem in a complete way, has not yet been developed.

Finite element calculation gives reliable results if FE models reproduce the different types of soils and materials and their mechanical characteristics. These are variable along the alignment, this affects the propagation of vibrations: rigid soils are linked to low damping values while low-stiff soils are highly damping and a lower transmissibility is connected to them.

A surveys campaign was carried out which provided stratigraphy of the ground for 10–20 m. Following parameters were collected for each layer:

- elastic modulus, longitudinal and transversal;
- poisson's ratio;
- internal friction angle;
- shear strength;
- cohesion.

Using these data, the stratigraphy shown in Fig. 6 was reconstructed:

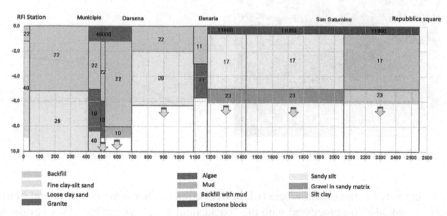

Fig. 6. Schematic representation of stratigraphy of the ground along the line Matteotti square – Repubblica square

It can be seen how the deep layers are made up of low-rigid and highly damping soils, while there are 2 sections, between the Municipio-Darsena and Bonaria-Repubblica stops, which have high stiffness values due respectively to the granite block paving and concrete slabs.

The geotechnical parameters reported refer to the value on a point scale, in particular the stiffness is assessed without taking into account the fracturing and segmentation of the granite paving that makes up the road pavement.

It was therefore necessary to reduce these values, this can be done arbitrarily or through deflectometric measurements.

For a correct evaluation, the second option was chosen, carrying out deflectometric measurements conducted with the Falling Weight Deflectometer (FWD) on the stone pavement of Roma street.

The FWD test is a non-destructive investigation method used to measure the structural properties of a pavement in situ. The test consists in measuring the vertical deflection of the pavement induced by an impulsive load generated by the fall of a mass on a plate placed on the surface layer of the superstructure. The applied load is measured through a load cell positioned at the circular plate. The deformations induced by the load are measured by means of a series of geophones positioned along different points lying on a horizontal alignment, so as to be able to identify the deflection basin produced at the moment of impact of the mass. The deflection values are subsequently obtained by integrating the acceleration signal recorded by each individual geophone with an accuracy of 0.5 ± 1 μm.

Coni et al. [22] propose an experimental approach to assess the vibration damping using the FWD. The instrumentation, well known in road pavement analysis, can reproduce the force impulse of train wheel and collect the oscillation value along 2.10 m (Fig. 7).

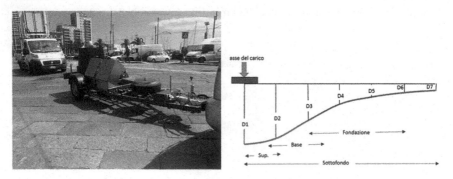

Fig. 7. The Falling Weight Deflectometer and the representation of the deflection basin

Data related to the measurements of the deflection basin and the measurement of the applied peak load are processed with the "backcalculation" system [23–25] to evaluate the stiffness modules of the individual layers of road pavement.

The module of granite paving found was much lower than that extracted from the geotechnical report.

Therefore, a new schematic stratigraphy was developed, as shown in the following image (see Fig. 8) to use in FE modeling.

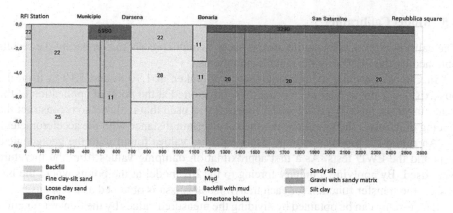

Fig. 8. Schematic stratigraphy used in Fe modeling

The schematization carried out led to the identification of 6 models:

- MODEL 1 from point 0.00 m to 36.50 m;
- MODEL 2 from point 36.50 m to 415.50 m;
- MODEL 3 from point 415.50 m to 693.50 m;
- MODEL 4 from point 693.50 m to 1088.50 m;
- MODEL 5 from point 1088.50 m to 1431.00 m;

for each of them a finite element model was created and processed with the Ansys software.

3.4 Finite Element Method

A two-dimensional model of the terrain was built with a dimension of 37.37 m × 10.0 m. The superstructure, the railway equipment, the base concrete plate and the reinforcement were modeled in detail by thickening the subdivision of the mesh in the vicinity of the forcing, constraints and geometric angularities (See Fig. 9).

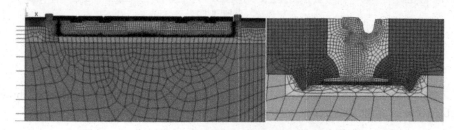

Fig. 9. Details of Model 6

Further FE modeling was carried out on the current situation of Cimitero avenue, and in a section of the Repubblica-Gottardo line for the estimation of forcings.

3.5 Model Calibrating

The calibration process is an iterative process, which consists in comparing the results obtained by the FEM with the real measurements.

In Cimitero avenue the measurements were taken at 1.70 m and 5.10 m from the bus axis, since the accelerometer cannot be positioned at the point of application of the load (under the bus wheel), a transfer function was used that it allows to reconstruct the forcing that causes the vibrations detected at a certain distance with the accelerometers.

An initial FE model was built, using stiffness values found with the geotechnical tests and the FWD tests. As a first approximation damping values from the literature were used. By applying a unitary forcing to the FE model at the points where the bus passes, the transfer function for each transverse abscissa is obtained as a response.

The forcing can be obtained by dividing the measured values by the transfer function and making a comparison.

At this point, the forcing was applied to the FE model and it was evaluated if there was a good correspondence between the average spectra and what was simulated. Otherwise, the damping values of the different materials are varied and the procedure is reapplied until a good result was found.

The result obtained after several iterations is the following (Fig. 10):

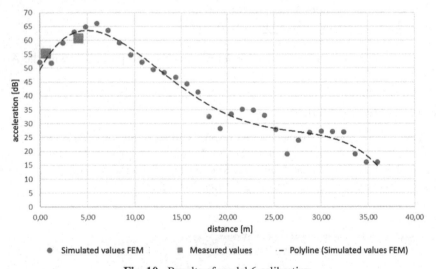

Fig. 10. Results of model 6 calibration.

The good correspondence between the measurements and what was simulated show effectiveness of the calibration method.

3.6 FE Simulation Results

The evaluation of the post-operam vibrational state was iterated for each different stratigraphic profile along the track, for each frequency component between 1 and 315 Hz, evaluating the vibrational levels in terms of accelerations. The load conditions were represented by simultaneous presence of 4 forcing at the 2 tracks, corresponding to the real forcing due to the passage of the light rail and obtained through measurements on the current line.

The following graph (see Fig. 11) shows the transverse distribution of the acceleration levels of each model, each of these lines represents a logarithmic sum of the levels relating to frequencies from 1 to 315 Hz in third-octave bands.

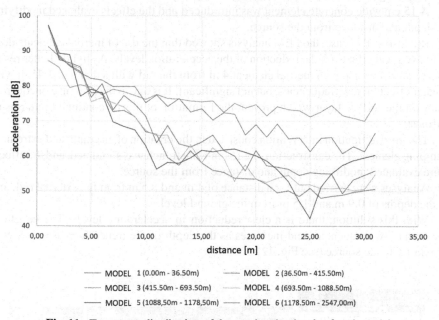

Fig. 11. Transverse distribution of the acceleration levels of each model

It can be seen how model 3 and model 6 have the highest acceleration values, this is linked to the presence of rigid stone paving in Roma street and concrete slab pavement in Dante Street a few meters from the line.

3.7 Mitigation Interventions

Three possible mitigation interventions were considered:

- insertion of anti-vibration mats;
- insertion of an inertial element;
- construction of a trench;

and they were applied to model 6 because the acceleration levels were greater than the limits set by Standard.

The presence of these mats is foreseen under the slab between the bedding mortar and the surface layer of the ground, furthermore they must be interposed in interference with manifolds and ducts and in any situation in which rigid elements are interfered under the armament and its support.

From the comparison between the results obtained with those of the model without mats, in a first approximation, there were not significant variations in acceleration levels. A more accurate analysis showed that the anti-vibration mats offer greater benefits for higher frequencies.

The second mitigation intervention concerned the insertion of an inertial element, extremely rigid with the aim of reflecting the waves towards the source.

A 15 cm wide concrete element was introduced and the effects evaluated modifying its depth and distance from the source.

But also in this case, the FEM analysis showed that the use of inertial elements does not have great effects on the reduction of the acceleration levels. A slightly better result was obtained by using an inertial element 4 m from the rail with a depth of 1.45 m with greater effects at low frequencies, but not significant. It is due to the presence of concrete slabs on the surface layer which prevent the formation of this discontinuity in terms of stiffness.

The third mitigation intervention consisted in the creation of an empty and extremely damping element. The construction of a 15 cm wide trench was simulated, and the effects were evaluated modifying depth and distance from the source.

Analyses were carried out for a distance of 4 m and 8.5 m from the external rail, and at the depths of 0.9 m and 1.5 m from the ground level.

With this solution, there is a clear reduction in acceleration levels. The benefit is greater at low frequencies and increases as the depth of the trench increases and with proximity to the source (see Fig. 12).

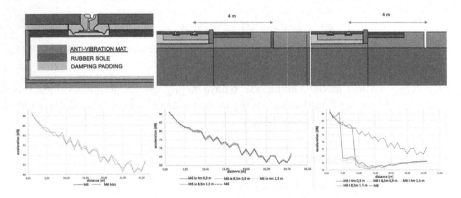

Fig. 12. Mitigation interventions and results

4   Conclusion

This paper presents a methodology aimed at estimating the forcing produced by light rail trains and the influence of the sediment soil in order to calibrate the FE model. The study overcomes the problem of the lack of a numerical model that can consider all the factors that influence phenomenon as the characteristics of the materials and the tramway superstructure, rail, railway equipment, and the inhomogeneity of soil. From FE analysis it was found that the behavior of vibrations is strongly influenced by the dissipative capacities of the surface layer, in which the Rayleigh waves are concentrated, but also by the damping capacities of the other layers, found starting from literature values and then modified during calibration.

Model 3 and 6 showed higher acceleration values due to the high stiffness of their surface layer, due respectively to the granite paving and the concrete slabs. Model 6 needed mitigation measures because accelerations values exceed the regulatory limits. The authors proposed three solutions: anti-vibration mats, inertial elements and trenches.

Trench is a more effective intervention with a much greater effect than the inertial element, which begins to have significant benefits with a thickness of 40–50 cm, thus increasing costs. The trench is the intervention that guarantees better attenuation, but it limits are surrounding conditions.

The anti-vibration mat has a greater effect at high frequencies which rises increasing thickness.

Future investigations comprise the monitoring of some trial sections on the Light Metro of Cagliari, where different anti-vibration materials will be employed. Their outcomes will be monitored through FWD and sensors embedded in the subgrade. Works are starting in June 2021 and will finish in 2024.

Author Contributions. Conceptualization, all; methodology and formal analysis, Mauro Coni and Riccardo Murgia; introduction and literary review Francesca Maltinti and Mauro Coni; writing-original draft preparation, Francesca Maltinti; writing-review and editing Francesca Maltinti, Mauro Coni and Nicoletta Rassu; visualization, all. All authors have read and agreed to the published version of the manuscript.

References

1. United Nations, Department of Economic and Social Affairs: World Urbanization Prospects. The 2018 Revision, United Nations (2019)
2. Torrisi, V., Garau, C., Ignaccolo, M., Inturri, G.: "Sustainable urban mobility plans": key concepts and a critical revision on SUMPs guidelines. In: Gervasi, O., et al. (eds.) ICCSA 2020. LNCS, vol. 12255, pp. 613–628. Springer, Cham (2020). https://doi.org/10.1007/978-3-030-58820-5_45
3. Garau, C., Pavan, V.M.: Evaluating urban quality indicators and assessment tools for smart sustainable cities. Sustainability 10(3), 575 (2018)
4. Barabino, B., Deiana, E., Mozzoni, S.: The quality of public transport service: the 13816 Standard and a methodological approach to an Italian case. Ingegneria Ferroviaria 68(5), 475–499. ISSN: 0020-0956 (2013)
5. Barabino B., Deiana, E., Tilocca, P.: Urban transport management and customer perceived quality: a case study in the Metropolitan area of Cagliari, Italy. Theor. Empirical Res. Urban Manage. 6(1), 19–32. ISSN: 2065-3913 (2011)
6. Maltinti, F., et al.: Vulnerable users and public transport service: analysis on expected and perceived quality data. In: Gervasi, O., et al. (eds.) ICCSA 2020. LNCS, vol. 12255, pp. 673–689. Springer, Cham (2020). https://doi.org/10.1007/978-3-030-58820-5_49
7. Barabino, B.: Automatic recognition of "low-quality" vehicles and bus stops in bus services. Public Transp. 10(2), 257–289 (2018). https://doi.org/10.1007/s12469-018-0180-8

8. Barabino, B., Coni, M., Olivo, A., Pungillo, G., Rassu, N.: Standing passenger comfort: a new scale for evaluating the real-time driving style of bus transit services. IEEE Trans. Intell. Transp. Syst. **20**(12), 4665–4678 (2019). https://doi.org/10.1109/TITS.2019.2921807

9. Coni, M., et al.: On-board comfort of different age passengers and bus-lane characteristics. In: Gervasi, O., et al. (eds.) ICCSA 2020. LNCS, vol. 12255, pp. 658–672. Springer, Cham (2020). https://doi.org/10.1007/978-3-030-58820-5_48

10. Höjer, M., Wangel, J.: Smart sustainable cities: definition and challenges. In: Hilty, L.M., Aebischer, B. (eds.) ICT Innovations for Sustainability. AISC, vol. 310, pp. 333–349. Springer, Cham (2015). https://doi.org/10.1007/978-3-319-09228-7_20

11. Dembski, F., Wössner, U., Letzgus, M., Ruddat, M., Yamu, C.: Urban digital twins for smart cities and citizens: the case study of Herrenberg Germany. Sustainability **12**(6), 2307 (2020). https://doi.org/10.3390/su12062307

12. Garau, C., Desogus, G., Zamperlin, P.: Governing technology-based urbanism: degeneration to technocracy or development to progressive planning? In: Aurigi, A.,Willis K.S. (eds.) The Routledge Companion to Smart Cities, Routledge, pp. 157–173 (2020). https://doi.org/10.4324/9781315178387

13. Pinna, F., Masala, F., Garau, C.: Urban policies and mobility trends in Italian smart cities. Sustainability (Switzerland) **9**(4), 494 (2017)

14. Coni, M., Garau, C., Pinna, F.: How has Cagliari changed its citizens in smart citizens? Exploring the influence of ITS technology on urban social interactions. In: Gervasi, O., et al. (eds.) ICCSA 2018. LNCS, vol. 10962, pp. 573–588. Springer, Cham (2018). https://doi.org/10.1007/978-3-319-95168-3_39

15. Çati, Y., Gökçeli, S., Anil, Ö., Korkmaz, C.S.: Experimental and numerical investigation of USP for optimization of transition zone of railway. Eng. Struct. **209**, 109971 (2020). https://doi.org/10.1016/j.engstruct.2019.109971

16. Mottahed, J., Zakeri, J.A., Mohammadzadeh, S.: A field investigation on the effects of using USPs in transition zone from ballasted track to bridges. Int. J. Civil Eng. **17**(9), 1421–1431 (2019). https://doi.org/10.1007/s40999-019-00440-3

17. Mertens, F., Jaquet, T.: Reducing vibrational impact lateral of a railway track on an urban development project. In: Proceedings of the International Conference on Structural Dynamic, EURODYN, vol. 2, pp. 2680–2687 (2020)

18. Coulier, P., Lombaert, G., Degrande, G.: The influence of source-receiver interaction on the numerical prediction of railway induced vibrations. J. Sound Vib. **333**(12), 2520–2538 (2014)

19. Kece, E., Reikalas, V., DeBold, R., Ho, C.L., Robertson, I., Forde, M.C.: Evaluating ground vibrations induced by high-speed trains. Transp. Geotech. **20**, 100236 (2019). https://doi.org/10.1016/j.trgeo.2019.03.004

20. Zhu, S., et al.: Development of a vibration attenuation track at low frequencies for urban rail transit. Comput. Aided Civil Infrastruct. Eng. **32**, 713–726 (2017)

21. Coni, M., Maltinti, F., Portas, S., Annunziata, F.: Criteri di progettazione di una metropolitana leggera in ambito urbano: un esempio applicativo sulla valutazione degli impatti ambientali. In: SIIV proceedings (1999)

22. Coni, M., Mistretta, F., Stochino, F., Rombi, J., Sassu, M., Puppio, M.L.: Fast falling weight deflectometer method for condition assessment of RC bridges. Appl. Sci. **11**, 1743 (2021). https://doi.org/10.3390/app11041743

23. Ji, Y., Wang, F., Luan, M., Zhongyin Guo, Z.: A simplified method for dynamic response of flexible pavement and applications in time domain backcalculation. J. Am. Sci. **2**(2) (2006)

24. Broutin, M., Theillout, J.N.: Towards a dynamical back-calculation procedure for HWD; a full-scale validation experiment. In: 2010 FAA Worldwide Airport Technology Transfer Conference: Next Generation of Airport Technology (2010)

25. Goktepe, A.B., Agarb, E., Lav, A.H.: Advances in backcalculating the mechanical properties of flexible pavements. Adv. Eng. Softw. **37**(7), 421–431 (2006)

Long Term Predictions of NO$_2$ Average Values via Deep Learning

Pierfrancesco Bellini, Stefano Bilotta, Daniele Cenni, Enrico Collini, Paolo Nesi$^{(\boxtimes)}$, Gianni Pantaleo, and Michela Paolucci

DISIT Lab, DINFO Dept, University of Florence, Florence, Italy
paolo.nesi@unifi.it
https://www.disit.org, https://www.snap4city.org

Abstract. Forecasting future values of air quality related metrics and specific pollutant concentration could be of pivotal importance in recent Smart City perspectives. A number of pollutants are dangerous for people's health and impact on environment and climate. In order to control and reduce the emissions, national and international organizations have defined guidelines and targeted limits to be respected currently, and to be progressively reduced along the year/months. On this regard, the European Union has set limits for the concentration of the yearly mean value of NO$_2$ which must not exceed 40 μg/m^3. To this end, in this paper, we propose a model and tool to compute long terms predictions, up to 180 days in advance, of the progressive mean value of NO$_2$ with a precision needed to enable decision makers to perform corrections. The solution proposed is based on machine learning approach taking into account measures of pollutant, traffic flow, weather and environmental variables coming from sensors on the field. A comparison of different techniques has been provided. The research activity has been developed in the context to TRAFAIR CEF project of EC which aimed to study the effect of traffic and of other human activities on NO and NO$_2$. The data and the solution have been developed by exploiting the Snap4City platform; the validation of the solution has been performed by using actual measured data from years 2014 to 2020 in the area of Florence, Italy. The results are accessible via a monitoring dashboard on Snap4City which reports real time values and predictions in real time.

1 Introduction

In the context of smart cities, tools for air quality monitoring are one of the main pillars. In recent years, the concentrations of air pollutants have reached critical values in the majority of industrialized cities over the world, and a large number of actions have been targeted by governs and international institutions to reduce them. Thanks to the development of Internet of Things (IoT) technologies, it has been possible to acquire useful data, for instance through air quality sensors, that can be used to develop real-time data analytics and predictive machine learning models. The search field of air quality predictions is experiencing an increasing interest due to its relevance. Despite this, the majority of related works are based on short-term predictions starting from hourly

© Springer Nature Switzerland AG 2021
O. Gervasi et al. (Eds.): ICCSA 2021, LNCS 12956, pp. 595–610, 2021.
https://doi.org/10.1007/978-3-030-87010-2_44

values up to a few days from the prediction time. The majority of state-of-the-art tools to forecast future air pollutant concentrations are machine learning techniques that need consistent historical data representing the features that determine or influence the specific air pollutant, in order to be trained to predict future concentrations. In [15], it has been shown that this problem can be solved using multivariate data. Recently, Deep learning based methods have been proposed for air quality prediction, such as [9, 14]. The Long Short-Term Network (LSTM) model has been used in [16], in which several air quality pollutant factors have been predicted such as CO, NO_2, O3, PM10 in short term. In [13], the importance of taking into account meteorological and temporal features for the development of predictive models for air pollutants has been highlighted. Therefore, data analytic enabled a number of applications that range from the development of territorial heatmaps [4] to alerting systems when the NO_2 concentration reaches dangerous values. In this context, the TRAFAIR project (in which this research has been developed) has been focused on the short and mid-term prediction of NOX (NO + NO_2) on the basis of traffic flow and on other factors [6, 17].

Among the air pollutants, nitrogen dioxide (NO_2) can cause serious problems not only for people's health but also for the environment [19]. Exposure to NO_2 has been linked to increased mortality of a relative risk factor of 1.04 every 10 $\mu g/m^3$ in the annual NO_2 concentration [8]. The European Union has created a legislative program [7] in which the limits of air pollutants concentrations, to preserve people's health are specified. For the nitrogen dioxide, the maximum yearly mean concentration value is set to 40 $\mu g/m^3$. Other limits have been imposed on other pollutants, while the overcome of the mean value over the year 1seems to be the most effective in pushing cities towards the control and thus it forces them to the improvement of air quality. In fact, the reduction of the mean NO_2 leads to the corresponding reduction of other pollutants and of GHG (greenhouse gas) also provoked by traffic and heating in general (https://en.wikipedia. org/wiki/Greenhouse_gas).

This paper aims to present a system to assess and produce long terms predictions of the yearly mean NO_2 concentration. The yearly mean nitrogen dioxide concentration is typically assessed by the European Commission in the most critical points of the city, that are the major roads, and since it is a long term average, it is particularly complex to correct it by imposing last minute traffic restrictions. Being the metrics, a long term average over the year, it is hard to revert the trend by closing roads for a few days; even a drastic total closure per a number of days risks to create a marginal reduction on progressive mean. Our work differentiates from the above-mentioned papers in the field of air quality prediction because it does not focus on predicting the hourly or daily concentration of NO_2. We focused on long term prediction of the yearly mean value of the NO_2 concentration. In the presented work, in order to develop a monitoring, predictive tool and a dashboard to study the trend of the yearly mean value of NO_2 concentration, we have developed six predictive LSTM deep neural networks to forecast the future progressive mean values of nitrogen dioxide for 30, 60, 90, 120, 150 and 180 days ahead of the current day. The LSTM solution has been selected among a number of solutions compared in the paper. The work presented in this paper has been developed in the context of TRAFAIR CEF Project of EC, on the basis of the data collected in the city of Florence. Indeed since 2014, the city of Florence has not respected the limit imposed by the EU for the mean value concentration of NO$_2$.

The paper is organized as follows. In Sect. 2, the description of data and selection of features are reported and discussed. Section 3 describes the production of the predictive models for mean progressive NO$_2$, and provides also the comparison with other machine learning techniques to demonstrate that the LSTM has been the better ranked. In Sect. 4, a description of the Real Time monitoring and prediction service set up on Snap4City are provided. Conclusions are drawn in Sect. 5.

2 Data Description and Feature Identification

Nitrogen dioxide, NO$_2$, is generated for the most part in the atmosphere for the oxidation of nitrogen monoxide (NO), which is produced by combustion processes, in particular by traffic of vehicles, heating houses, and industrial activities [1, 20]. However, other factors may influence NO$_2$ values. According to the introduction, this paper aimed to present a long term solution for predicting the yearly mean values of NO$_2$ concentration, in advance a much as possible with respect to the date in which the taxation to city may be produced. According to the European rules, the metrics is typically assessed at the end of the year, while the cities need to keep those metrics under control much in advance to take countermeasures on time. The progressive mean value in the specific year of study is calculated as the NO$_2$ mean concentration day after day, and dividing this by the number of passed days. The data for the problem as formulated, are structured as a time series. The city of Florence since 2014 have not respected the limit imposed by the EU for the mean value of NO$_2$, that has to be lower than 40 $\mu g/m^3$. The reference values have been estimated on the basis of the data acquired from sensor FI-GRAMSCI of regional agency of environment (Agenzia regionale per la protezione ambientale della Toscana, ARPAT) [1], recorded for year 2014 as yearly mean of 63.396 $\mu g/m^3$, for 2015: 65.173 $\mu g/m^3$, 2016 36.794 $\mu g/m^3$, for 2017: 63.396 $\mu g/m^3$, for 2018: 60.256 $\mu g/m^3$, for 2019: 56.111 $\mu g/m^3$, and for 2020 a value of 42.632 $\mu g/m^3$ (despite of the COVID-19). The data are accessible on the Snap4City infrastructure of DISIT lab https://www.snap4city.org [3, 5].

In order to build a long term predictive model, a number of features have been tested and relevant feature identified as described in the following. They refer to historical values of NO$_2$, traffic flow, weather conditions, heating conditions, etc. Therefore, a set of derived features have been computed according to the physical meaning of what we would like to predict, which is the progressive mean value of the measured variable in $\mu g/m^3$.

The most relevant predictor for the model is related to the traffic flow data. According to our analysis performed on ServiceMap (Snap4City) by DISIT lab, the position of the above mentioned ARPAT-Gramsci sensor for NO$_2$ has been analyzed. This sensor is positioned on "Viale Antonio Gramsci" in the city of Florence, and it detects the hourly mean value of NO$_2$ expressed in $\mu g/m^3$. The historical data cover the years starting from 2014. The time granularity is hourly. Using the same tool, the FI055ZTL00201 traffic sensor [18] has been considered. This sensor detects the number of vehicles that transit per hour in the same "Viale Antonio Gramsci" of Florence, in which the above mentioned

ARPAT-Gramsci sensor is also positioned. The prediction can only be performed on a single pollutant sensor since, that sensor is the sensor used by the EC to emit the taxation, and thus to take into account also other NO_2 sensors in other parts of the city has been demonstrated to be non relevant. As demonstrated in TRAFAIR, the pollutant are volatile and are moved by wind and thus a limit life 2on air. Figure 1 shows the position of the selected sensors.

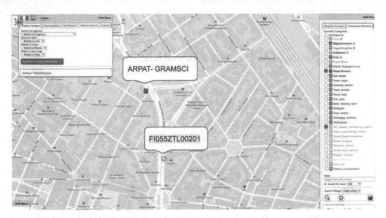

Fig. 1. Positions of FI055ZTL00201 traffic sensor and ARPATGRAMSCI air quality sensor shown on ServiceMap tool of https://www.snap4city.org portal and service.

The historical data of traffic covers the years starting from 2014 with a granularity of 5 min. It should be noted that, the traffic flow sensors provide data in terms of traffic density and/or in terms of number of vehicles passed in the unit of time (vechicleFlow), which in our case was an hour. On the other hand, we need to have values which take into account the total amount of pollutant produced over the whole day because the NO_2 taken into account is a cumulative data. Therefore, we estimated the following features:

$$numberOfVehicles_i = \sum_{l=1}^{24} vehicleFlow_{il} \tag{1}$$

$$numberOfVehiclesCumulated_i = \sum_{k=1}^{i} numberOfVehicles_i \tag{2}$$

Another relevant aspect, which influences the traffic and thus the pollutant, is represented by the environmental conditions. To this end, meteorological data have been acquired through Snap4City and IlMeteo.it [12] for the city of Florence. The data provided by these resources comprehend various parameters: minimum, mean, and maximum temperature of the day expressed in °C; Dew point also expressed in °C; mean and maximum wind speed expressed in km/h; humidity of the day expressed in percentage; the air pressure of the day expressed in millibar (mb). These data covers the historical period of interest starting from 2014 with daily values. The environmental conditions influence the NO_2 production with the usage of the house heating, and propagation with wind. The former factor has been taken into account exploiting a formula derived from TRAFAIR project [17]. Then, using the mean daily temperature, it is possible to determine, through a parametric formula, the domestic NOx produced in a day.

$$NO_x Domestic_i = \left(K + A * Tmedia_i + B * Tmedia_i^2 \right) * 1000 \tag{3}$$

where: $K = 2.22488$, $A = -0.14828$, $B = 0.00276$ computed and validated in TRAFAIR. Please note that they impact on pollutant only during the winter period and for about 1/10 of the NO$_2$ produced. So that, it is a corrective factor. The second aspects directly considering the wind as possible features. In order to forecast the progressive mean values of NO$_2$ it has been necessary to apply some pre-processing operations. Firstly, the conversion to the chosen time granularity, that is daily. The last operation consisted of deriving the cumulated progressive mean features starting from the NO$_2$, traffic values, and also for the domestic NOx and deriving some temporal features from the DateTime of the prediction day (Date, Year, Month, dayOfTheMonth, dayOfTheYear, dayOfThe-Week, weekEnd, festivity, workingDay, ferialDay). Considering the year j and the i-th day of this year as the day of the prediction, in the next lines the detailed formulas used to obtain the derived features are reported.

$$NO_2 Cumulated_i = \sum_{k=1}^{i} NO_{2_k} \tag{4}$$

$$NO_2 progressiveMean_i = \frac{NO_2 Cumulated_i}{i} \tag{5}$$

$$NO_X DomesticCumulated_i = \sum_{k=1}^{i} NO_X Domestic_k \tag{6}$$

$$NO_X DomesticCumulated_i = \frac{NO_X Domestic_k}{i} \tag{7}$$

The initial dataset taken into account is reported in Table 1 with the details of the features.

The aim was to create a set of long term predictive models to be used in a real-time process that every day of the current year may generate the prediction on the basis of collected data, and thus of the calculated features. The computed predictions shall be also be displayed in a monitoring dashboard on Snap4City, which can be used for the city control monitoring and forecast.

2.1 Feature Analysis

As above mentioned, the research aimed to identify a prediction model for the progressive mean values of nitrogen dioxide, NO$_2$. After having performed several testing, a machine learning technique has been chosen discharging the more classical ARIMA/SARIMA, ARIMAX approaches which are unsuitable for long term predictions. The process of feature analysis has been an important operation to reduce the dimension of the input space in terms of features, with the aim of selecting the most relevant features which can lead to generalize the model, reducing the eventual overfitting, and simplifying the computational architecture in real time. Moreover, this allows a significant reduction of

Table 1. Initial Data-set taken into account with details

Metric	Details
Date	UTC format of the day of prediction YYYY-MM-DD
Year	Of the observation {2014, ..., 2020}
Month	Of the observation {1, ...12}
dayOfTheYear	Day number in the year {1, ...365/366}
dayOfTheMonth	Day number in the month {1, ...31}
dayOfTheWeek	Day of the week {1, ..., 7}
weekend	Saturday or sunday 1, 0 otherwis
festivity	Festivity 1, 0 otherwise
workingDay	Not a saturday or sunday and it is not a festivity
ferialDay	1 if the day is not a sunday or a festivity
NO_2	The NO_2 hourly mean of the observation day in $\mu g/m^3$
Tmin	The min temperature of the day in °C
Tmean	The mean temperature of the day in °C
Tmax	The max temperature of the day in °C
dewpoint	The dew point temperature in °C
windMean	The mean value of the wind of the day in km/h
windMax	The max value of the wind of the day in km/h
Humidity	The humidity of the day in %
pressioneSLM	The air pressure in millibar (mb)
NOx	The NOx value of the day in kg
numberOfVehicles	The number of vehicles of the day
NO_2cumulated	The cumulated value of NO_2 up to the day
NO_2progressiveMean	The progressive mean value of NO_2 up to the day
numberOfVehiclesCumulated	The number of vehicles cumulated up to the day
NOxDomesticCumulated	The cumulated value of NOx up to the day
NOxDomesticProgressiveMean	The progressive mean value of NOx up to the day

the computational time which is performed every day. A first analysis was performed using Scatterplots and correlation matrices which did not shown useful information on the linear correlation of the target feature (the progressive mean value of the NO_2), and thus have not been reported in this paper. In order to select the most relevant features, Principal Component Analysis (PCA) has been applied. The PCA is used for multivariate problems, feature engineering and for machine learning [2]. The results of the PCA have been reported in Fig. 2. The trade-off for the explained variance has let us to selected the first 5 Principal Components, the figure reported the first 7.

The first component, which is largely the most relevant as shown in Table 2, includes the progressive mean features of NO$_2$ and NOxDomestic with also the min temperature, the dew point, and the cumulated number of vehicles. In the second component, the features cumulated are the most relevant, with the mean and max temperature and the humidity. The third component includes the wind features; the fourth the air pressure; and in the fifth the daily NO$_2$ with the number of vehicles.

According to the above reported analysis, we performed a number of tests with the aim of identifying a compromise between complexity (in terms of number of features) and precision. The identified compromise for the predictive features of the models has been to use: NO$_2$, Tmean, humidity, windMean, NOxDomestic, numberOfV ehicles, NO$_2$cumulated, NO$_2$progressiveMean, numberOfV ehiclesCumulated, with associated Month and dayOfT heY ear for their identification in the time series.

Scree Plot PCA

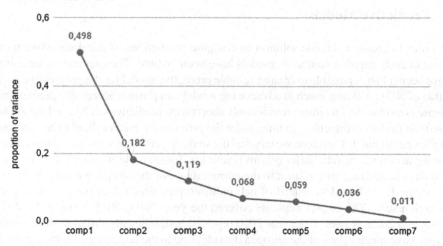

Fig. 2. Principal components with their corresponding explained variance.

Table 2. Principal components analysis (a part)

Parametro	comp1	comp2	comp3	comp4	comp5
NO$_2$	0.21492	0.03753	0.21523	0.12079	0.49583
NO$_2$cumulated	−0.29702	0.33402	−0.09504	−0.03905	0.03549
NO$_2$progressiveMean	0.31897	−0.25867	0.10213	0.05706	−0.04563
Tmin	−0.30745	−0.27795	0.06725	0.10825	0.08754
Tmean	−0.29595	−0.31203	0.16324	0.00393	0.13399
Tmax	−0.2687	−0.31676	0.24441	−0.06649	0.1375
dewPoint	−0.31326	−0.15871	0.17945	0.23102	0.04431
windMean.km.h	−0.00725	−0.28206	−0.6145	−0.14964	0.07701

(continued)

Table 2. (*continued*)

Parametro	comp1	comp2	comp3	comp4	comp5
windMax.km.h	−0.03454	−0.30142	−0.59137	−0.03938	0.09913
humidity	0.01218	0.43378	0.04680	−0.42877	−0.07932
pressioneSLM.mb	0.04822	−0.01663	0.18496	−0.91479	0.22794
numberOfVehicles	0.14502	0.16311	−0.12736	0.21015	0.78224
numberOfVehiclesCumulated	−0.29235	0.34455	−0.0991	−0.03161	0.03886
NOxDomestic	0.30408	0.27471	−0.06801	0.00842	−0.13415
NOxDomesticCumulated	−0.30356	0.30434	−0.11701	−0.04954	0.05715
NOxDomesticProgressiveMean	0.34165	−0.1894	0.07221	0.05133	−0.04398

3 Predictive Models

In order to create a reliable solution to compute predictions of the progressive mean value of NO_2 ahead, a number of models have been created. The questions to be solved have been: (1) it is possible to create a reliable predictive model for the progressive mean value of NO_2?, (2) how much in advance the model can provide acceptable predictions? Please note that, the literature provides only short terms predictions of NO_2 which are not useful to perform corrections in time, since the progressive mean is hard to be corrected as above explained. Therefore, we targeted the study to perform a set of predictive models aiming at computing reliable long terms prediction, for example 30, 60, 90, 120, 150, and 180 days in advance with respect to the current day. For this reason we have developed 6 specific LSTM models instead of one multi-output, which does not produced good enough results. The dataset available covered the years 2014, 2015, 2016, 2017, 2018, 2019, and 2020. However, the year 2020 reported a significantly different trend for the progressive mean values of the nitrogen dioxide (due to the restrictions for the Covid-19 pandemic), as it is shown in Fig. 3. For this reason, the data used for training have been those of the years 2014–2017. In addition, once the model has been obtained, it has been validated against the values of year 2018, and tested for precision assessment against data of 4year 2019, as reported in the following. We have also reported the results for year 2020 for completeness, but due to the COVID-19 they cannot be taken into account as a good example and validation of the model, as it can be observed in Fig. 3.

The LSTM model has been adopted [11] with its update [10]. Before selecting the LSTM we have tested a number of techniques as reported in Sect. 3.2. The architecture of the predictive models has been set to 3 layers with optimized hyperparameters for every temporal target through a Randomized Search CV:

- The first layer is made by 64 or 32 LSTM units
- The intermediate layer is a Dense layer with 64, 32 or 16 units with also a dropout rate of 0.1, 0.2, 0.5.
- The final layer has only one neuron to predict the selected time target.

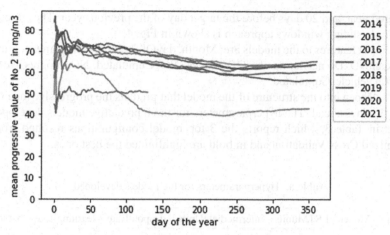

Fig. 3. Progressive mean trends for NO$_2$ in the years 2014, 2015, 2016, 2017, 2018, 2019, 2020, 2021 according to the ARPAT sensor adopted by the EC as a reference. Please note that NO$_2$ scale starts from 38 µg/m^3 on Y axis.

For each model, the Adam Optimizer has been chosen among learning rates 0.05, 0.005, 0.0005, or 0.00005. The considered loss has been assessed by using the Mean Squared Error (MSE). The batch size changed between 64 and 32; meanwhile the number of epochs has been set to a maximum value of 1000, while the training strategy used the Early Stopping method for determining the optimum epoch number which minimize the Medium Average Error (MAE) of the validation set, allowing also the restoring of the weights of the best model.

The input data for to the model have been organized through a multiple sliding window that contains the data of 20 days preceding the i-th day of prediction in the

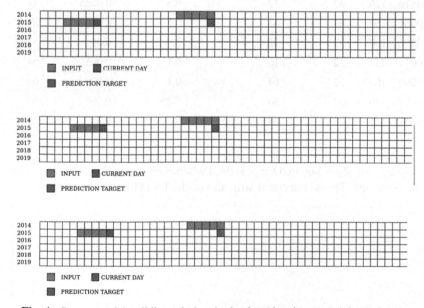

Fig. 4. Structure of the sliding window in the day (time instants): i, i + 1, i + 2.

considered year, and 20 days before the target day of the previous year. The structure of the multiple sliding windows approach is shown in Fig. 4.

The input features to the models are: Month, dayOfTheYear, NO_2, Tmean, humidity windMean,NOxDomestic, numberOfVehicles, NO_2Cumulated, NO_2progressiveMean, numberOfVehiclesCumulated.

Let's deepen into the structure of the model that predicts the progressive mean value of NO_2 30 days ahead. The hyperparameters for the 6 predictive models developed are reported in Table 3, which reports the 3 top model configurations resulted from the Randomized Cross Validation and in bold are highlighted the best ones.

Table 3. Hyperparameters for the models developed

negMSE	Model	LSTMunits	intermediateUnits	dropoutRate	learningRate	batchSize
−0.0017	30	64	64	0.1	0.00005	32
−0.0062	30	32	16	0.1	0.0005	64
−0.0077	30	64	16	0.5	0.05	32
−0.0031	60	32	64	0.1	0.0005	64
−0.0047	60	64	64	0.5	0.005	32
−0.0069	60	64	16	0.25	0.005	32
−0.0038	90	64	64	0.1	0.0005	32
−0.0049	90	64	64	0.1	0.0005	64
−0.0053	90	64	16	0.25	0.00005	32
−0.0059	120	64	64	0.25	0.005	64
−0.0092	120	32	16	0.1	0.005	64
−0.0116	120	32	32	0.5	0.0005	32
−0.0061	150	64	64	0.5	0.05	64
−0.0066	150	32	32	0.1	0.05	32
−0.0071	150	32	16	0.1	0.005	64
−0.0069	180	32	64	0.1	0.0005	64
−0.0124	180	64	64	0.25	0.005	64
−0.0158	180	32	64	0.5	0.05	64

The negative Mean Squared Error is used when minimizing the test score metrics of the combinations. The architectural structure of the LSTM neural network is visible in Fig. 5.

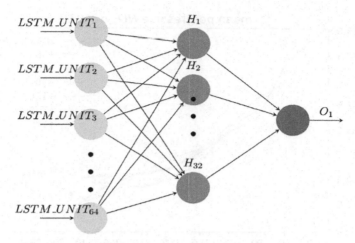

Fig. 5. Example of LSTM structure for the prediction model.

3.1 Experimental Results and Validation

The quantitative metrics used to evaluate the predictive models have been the Mean Absolute Error (MAE), the Root Mean Squared Error (RMSE), the Mean Absolute Percentage Error (MAPE), and the R-Squared (R2) which is the coefficient of determination. The results obtained by using the test set of year 2019 are reported in Table 4, and the outputs are visible in Fig. 6.

Table 4. Assessment of the predictive models with respect to the actual values of the 2019

Metric	model30	model60	model90	model120	model150	model180
MAE	1.21	1.31	1.52	2.04	2.31	2.37
RMSE	2.16	2.61	4.18	6.77	7.83	7.93
MAPE	1.99	2.20	2.65	3.57	4.07	4.18
R2	0.91	0.83	0.80	0.54	0.45	0.14

According to the results, larger errors in predictions are obtained by the models which try to provide longer terms predictions. They start from a MAE of 1.21 μg/m^3 for the prediction of 30 days ahead up to 2.37 μg/m^3 for the model of 180 days ahead. In percentage, these results correspond to the 1.99% for the 30 days predictions and to the 4.18% for 180 days predictions. Please note that the precision in prediction is acceptable even in the worst case, since the error is very low with respect of the 40 μg/m^3 of the reference value of the EC. We can state that obtaining a prediction 180 days in advance allows decision makers to put in place the needed measures to correct the NO$_2$ trend of the city.

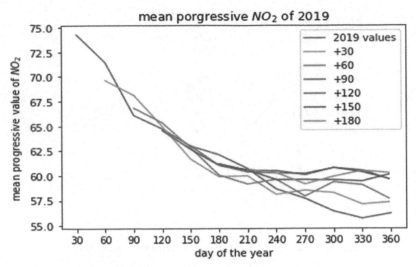

Fig. 6. Trend of the 6 predictive models with respect to the actual progressive mean NO_2 values of year 2019. Please note that NO_2 scale starts from 55 $\mu g/m^3$ on Y axis.

The results of the models for the year 2020 are visible in Fig. 7. Year 2020 has been a particular one due to the COVID-19 pandemic and the lockdowns that changed the volume of traffic vehicles, the amount of heating, and thus also the NO_2 concentration has been substantially changed, as it can be observed by its temporal trend with respect to the typical trends of the previous years. For this reason, the model puts in production

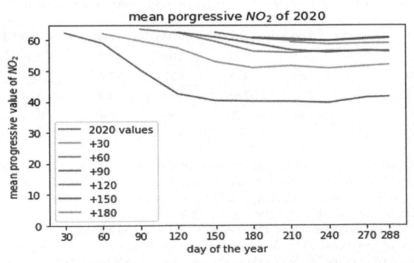

Fig. 7. Trends of the 6 predictive models with respect to the actual progressive mean NO_2 values of year 2020.

to generate the dashboard data for the year 2021 uses sliding windows with learning model based on 2019 and past data, instead of on those of the previous year.

3.2 Model Comparison

The sliding window approach proposed for past data has been tested with also other machine learning techniques.

The first comparison has been with a deep neural network, DNN, with the same number of layers as the LSTM architecture described in the previous section. Also, the hyperparameters tuning has been the same as the one described in Sect. 3.1 with the same values but of course, the units of the layers are not LSTM units but the ones used for the DNN.

Our approach has been tested with also ensemble learning techniques. In particular, the techniques chosen have been Random Forest (RF) and Extreme Gradient Boosting machines (XGBoost).

Regarding the implementation of the ensemble learning 6techniques the number of trees parameter for the RF has been set to 300, with min sample split set to 2, min number of samples allowed for a leaf equal to 1, without limits on the maximum number of features considered to split a node and the number of leafs and with the construction of bootstrapped datasets for creating the trees. The XGBoost regressor uses the least-squares loss function with learning rate optimized with values 0.1, 0.01, and 0.001 with max depth equal to 3 and min sample spilt, min sample leaf, max number of features equal to the ones chosen for the RF.

The results of these techniques vs LSTM have been compared in term of MAPE, Mean Absolute Percentage Error results for the prediction targets of 30, 60, 90, 120, 150, and 180 days. The results are reported in Table 5.

Table 5. MAPE for the prediction targets of 30, 60, 90, 120, 150 and 180 days resulted for the machine learning techniques LSTM, DNN, RF, and XGBoost

Target day	LSTM	DNN	XGBoost	RF
30	2.16	4.87	5,26	5,26
60	2.61	6.67	6,52	6,56
90	4.18	7.00	7,64	7,76
120	6.77	6.86	8,81	8,93
150	7.83	8.99	9,35	9,40
180	7.93	9.25	9,90	10

The results proved that the proposed LSTM approach outperforms the other techniques presented in terms of MAPE for every prediction target. For the 30 days prediction, the LSTM performs an error of about 2% compared to the 5% of the other techniques and performs better for the other targets up to the 180 days target with a MAPE of 7.93% where the others recorded MAPEs greater than 9%.

4   Dashboard for Real Time Monitoring and Prediction

As presented in previous section, substantially, we provided positive answers to the above reported two questions, regarding feasibility of the predictive model and the capability of providing predictions in advance enough to be exploitable by decision makers. On the other hand, a daily tool to visualize the results generated by the predictive models for the progressive mean NO_2 has been developed as a monitoring dashboard. It has been realized by exploiting the facilities of the DISIT Lab with its Snap4City Dashboard Builder of Snap4City https://www.snap4city.org [5]. The dashboards can easily exploit data collected in real time by the platform, as well as real-time rendering of results generated by Node-RED processes, which are called IOT Apps. The IOT App process, Node-Red/node.JS, exploiting Snap4City MicroServices, is executed daily and uses a Python script to generate the inputs for the predictive models and make the predictions for every temporal target. The dashboard developed is reported in Fig. 8 and it is made of three areas:

- The first contains the trends of the predictions made from the current day of the years for the temporal targets of 30, 60, 90, 120, 150 and 180 days ahead. These are reported through a bar series plot with a color scheme that darkens as the time target increases.
- The second contains a temporal multi series plot that shows the whole set of prevision models with respect to the trend of the actual values. In the plot, the horizontal green line is the EU limit value of 40 $\mu g/m^3$.
- The third on the right shows a heatmap of the NO_2 in Florence with the possibility to show the position of air quality and traffic sensors. It is also possible to monitor the trends of the traffic, NO_2, and of many other pollutants of the last weeks and months and years from the current day.

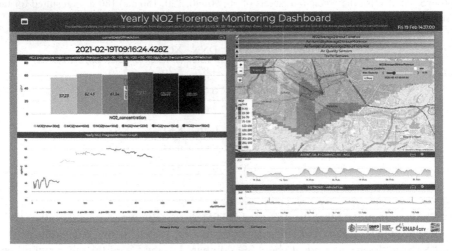

Fig. 8. Monitoring dashboard reporting real time value, prediction and actual cumulative values of NO_2 of the sensors considered for the official metrics.

The dashboard is accessible through any browser using the following link: https://www.snap4city.org/dashboardSmartCity/view/index.php?idasboard=MzA2OQ.

5   Conclusions and Future Developments

A number of pollutants are very critical for people's health, environment and climate. In order to reduce the emissions, national and international organizations have defined guidelines and targeted limits to be respected. On this regard, the European Union has set limits to the concentration for the yearly mean value of NO$_2$ which must not exceed 40 µg/m^3. In this paper, we described a model and tool to compute long terms predictions for 30, 60, 90, 120, 150, and 180 days ahead from the current day of estimation. The access to reliable long term predictions may allow decision 7makers to perform corrections. These models has produced results on a test set composed with the data of 2019, starting from a MAE of 1.21 µg/m^3 for the 30 days ahead prediction up to a 2.37 µg/m^3 for the 180 days prediction, that in percentage corresponds to 1.99% and 4.18%. The solution proposed is based on LSTM approach of deep learning taking into account measures of pollutant, traffic and environmental variables coming from sensors on the field. The LSTM solution has been demonstrated to be better ranked with respect to DNN, RF and XGBoost. The research activity has been developed in the context to TRAFAIR CEF project in which aimed to study the effect of traffic and other human activities on the NO and NO$_2$. The data and the solution have been developed exploiting the Snap4City platform, and the validation of the solution has been performed by using actual data from 2014 to 2020 in the area of Florence, Italy, from a large number of features and not only historical data. The results are accessible via a monitoring dashboard on Snap4City which report real time values and the predictions in real time. The approach presented in this paper can be further applied to the other air pollutants like PM2.5, PM10, CO, for which the EU has set yearly limits on their concentrations, and of course, this can be applied to other Smart Cities scenarios whenever the available data cover a sufficient historical range.

For citations of references, we prefer the use of square brackets and consecutive numbers. Citations using labels or the author/year convention are also acceptable.

The following bibliography provides a sample reference list with entries for journal articles [1], an LNCS chapter [2], a book [3], proceedings without editors [4], as well as a URL [5].

References

1. Agenzia regionale per la protezione ambientale della Toscana. Biossido di azoto (2021). http://www.arpat.toscana.it/temi-ambientali/aria/monitoraggio/inquinanti-monitorati/biossido-di-azoto
2. Azid, A., Juahir, H., Latif, M.T., Zain, S., Osman, R.: Feed-forward artificial neural network model for air pollutant index prediction in the southern region of peninsular Malaysia. J. Environ. Prot. **4**(1), 1–10 (2013)
3. Badii, C., Bellini, P., Difino, A., Nesi, P.: Smart city IoT platform respecting GDPR privacy and security aspects. IEEE Access **8**, 23601–23623 (2020)

4. Badii, C., et al.: High density real-time air quality derived services from IoT networks. Sensors **20**(18), 5435 (2020)
5. Bellini, P., Cenni, D., Marazzini, M., Mitolo, N., Nesi, P., Paolucci, M.: Smart city control room dashboards: big data infrastructure, from data to decision support. J. Vis. Lang. Comput. **4**, 75–82 (2018)
6. Bilotta, S., Nesi, P.: Traffic flow reconstruction by solving indeterminacy on traffic distribution at junctions. Future Gener. Comput. Syst. **114**, 649–660 (2021)
7. European Commission: European union commission air quality standards (2020). https://ec.europa.eu/environment/air/quality/standards.htm
8. Faustini, A., Rapp, R., Forastiere, F.: Nitrogen dioxide and mortality: review and meta-analysis of long-term studies. Eur. Respir. J. **44**(3), 744–753 (2014)
9. Freeman, B.S., Taylor, G., Gharabaghi, B., The, J.: Forecasting air quality time series using deep learning. J. Air Waste Manage. Assoc. **68**(8), 866–886 (2018)
10. Gers, F., Schmidhuber, J., Cummins, F.: Learning to forget: continual prediction with LSTM. Neural Comput. **12**, 2451–2471 (2000)
11. Hochreiter, S., Schmidhuber, J.: Long short-term memory. Neural Comput. **9**, 1735–1780 (1997)
12. IlMeteo.it: Dati meteorologici forniti da ilmeteo.it (2021). https://www.ilmeteo.it/meteo/firenze
13. Iskandaryan, D., Ramos, F., Trilles, S.: Air quality prediction in smart cities using machine learning technologies based on sensor data: a review. Appl. Sci. **10**(7), 2401 (2020)
14. Xing, J., et al.: Deep learning for prediction of the air quality response to emission changes. Environ. Sci. Technol. **54**, 8589–8600 (2020)
15. Masih, A.: Machine learning algorithms in air quality modeling. Glob. J. Environ. Sci. Manage. **5**(4), 515–534 (2019)
16. Navares, R., Aznarte, J.L.: Predicting air quality with deep learning LSTM: towards comprehensive models. Ecol. Inform. **55**, 101019 (2020)
17. Po, L., et al.: TRAFAIR: understanding traffic flow to improve air quality. In: 2019 IEEE International Smart Cities Conference (ISC2), pp. 36–43. IEEE (2019)
18. Regione Toscana: Regione toscana - osservatorio dei trasporti (2021). http://www501.regione.toscana.it/osservatoriotrasporti/
19. Sheng, Q., Zhu, Z.: Effects of nitrogen dioxide on biochemical responses in 41 garden plants. Plants **8**(2), 45 (2019)
20. Wikipedia Contributors: Nitrogen dioxide wikipedia the free encyclopedia (2020)

Author Index

Printed in the United States
by Baker & Taylor Publisher Services